with MyAccountingLab

- **Hallmark Features**—Personalized Learning Aids, like Help Me Solve This, Demo Docs, and instant feedback are available for further practice and mastery when students need the help most!

- **Learning Catalytics**—Generates classroom discussion, guides lecture, and promotes peer-to-peer learning with real-time analytics. Now, students can use any device to interact in the classroom.

- **Adaptive Study Plan**—Assists students in monitoring their own progress by offering them a customized study plan powered by Knewton, based on Homework, Quiz, and Test results. Includes regenerated exercises with unlimited practice and the opportunity to prove mastery through quizzes on recommended learning objectives.

- **Worked Solutions**—Provide step-by-step explanations on how to solve select problems using the exact numbers and data that were presented in the problem. Instructors will have access to the Worked Out Solutions in preview and review mode.

PEARSON

Prepare, Apply, and Confirm with MyAccountingLab®

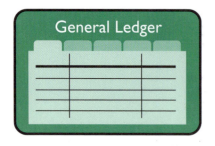

- **General Ledger**—Students can launch General Ledger software in MyAccountingLab, where they will be able to record transactions and adjusting entries, post to the ledger, close periods, and see the effects in the ledger accounts. Their work will be auto-graded, and grades will then automatically flow to the MyAccountingLab Gradebook.

- **Algorithmic Test Bank**—Instructors have the ability to create multiple versions of a test or extra practice for students.

- **Reporting Dashboard**—View, analyze, and report learning outcomes clearly and easily. Available via the Gradebook and fully mobile-ready, the Reporting Dashboard presents student performance data at the class, section, and program levels in an accessible, visual manner.

- **LMS Integration**—Link from any LMS platform to access assignments, rosters, and resources, and synchronize MyLab grades with your LMS gradebook. For students, new direct, single sign-on provides access to all the personalized learning MyLab resources that make studying more efficient and effective.

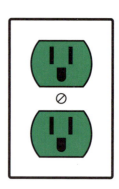

- **Mobile Ready**—Students and instructors can access multimedia resources and complete assessments right at their fingertips, on any mobile device.

ALWAYS LEARNING   PEARSON

HORNGREN'S
Accounting
THE MANAGERIAL CHAPTERS

ELEVENTH EDITION

Tracie Miller-Nobles
Austin Community College

Brenda Mattison
Tri-County Technical College

Ella Mae Matsumura
University of Wisconsin-Madison

PEARSON

Boston   Columbus   Indianapolis   New York   San Francisco   Hoboken
Amsterdam   Cape Town   Dubai   London   Madrid   Milan   Munich   Paris   Montréal   Toronto
Delhi   Mexico City   São Paulo   Sydney   Hong Kong   Seoul   Singapore   Taipei   Tokyo

Vice President, Business Publishing: Donna Battista
Senior Acquisitions Editor: Lacey Vitetta
Editorial Assistant: Christine Donovan
Vice President, Product Marketing: Maggie Moylan
Director of Marketing, Digital Services and Products: Jeanette Koskinas
Senior Product Marketing Manager: Alison Haskins
Executive Field Marketing Manager: Lori DeShazo
Senior Strategic Marketing Manager: Erin Gardner
Team Lead, Program Management: Ashley Santora
Program Manager: Mary Kate Murray
Team Lead, Project Management: Jeff Holcomb
Project Manager: Roberta Sherman
Supplements Project Manager: Andra Skaalrud
Operations Specialist: Carol Melville
Creative Director: Blair Brown
Art Director: Jon Boylan

Vice President, Director of Digital Strategy and Assessment: Paul Gentile
Manager of Learning Applications: Paul Deluca
Digital Editor: Sarah Peterson
Director, Digital Studio: Sacha Laustsen
Digital Studio Manager: Diane Lombardo
Product Manager: James Bateman
Digital Content Team Lead: Noel Lotz
Digital Content Project Lead: Martha LaChance
Full-Service Project Management and Composition: Integra Software Services Pvt. Ltd.
Interior Designer: Jon Boylan
Cover Designer: Jon Boylan
Cover Art: Determined/Fotolia
Printer/Binder: R. R. Donnelley
Cover Printer: Lehigh Phoenix Color/Hagerstown
Typeface: 11/13, Adobe Garamond Pro Regular

Library of Congress Cataloging-in-Publication is on file with the Library of Congress

10 9 8 7 6 5 4 3 2 1

ISBN-13: 978-0-13-385115-1
ISBN-10: 0-13-385115-X

About the Authors

Tracie L. Miller-Nobles, CPA, received her bachelor's and master's degrees in accounting from Texas A&M University and is currently pursuing her Ph.D. in adult learning also at Texas A&M University. She is an Associate Professor at Austin Community College, Austin, TX. Previously she served as a Senior Lecturer at Texas State University, San Marcos, TX, and has served as department chair of the Accounting, Business, Computer Information Systems, and Marketing/Management department at Aims Community College, Greeley, CO. In addition, Tracie has taught as an adjunct professor at University of Texas and has public accounting experience with Deloitte Tax LLP and Sample & Bailey, CPAs.

Tracie is a recipient of the Texas Society of CPAs Rising Star Award, TSCPAs Outstanding Accounting Educator Award, NISOD Teaching Excellence Award and the Aims Community College Excellence in Teaching Award. She is a member of the Teachers of Accounting at Two Year Colleges, the American Accounting Association, the American Institute of Certified Public Accountants, and the Texas State Society of Certified Public Accountants. She is currently serving on the Board of Directors as secretary/webmaster of Teachers of Accounting at Two Year Colleges, as a member of the American Institute of Certified Public Accountants nominations committee, and as chair of the Texas Society of CPAs Relations with Education Institutions committee. In addition, Tracie served on the Commission on Accounting Higher Education: Pathways to a Profession.

Tracie has spoken on such topics as using technology in the classroom, motivating non-business majors to learn accounting, and incorporating active learning in the classroom at numerous conferences. In her spare time she enjoys spending time with her friends and family and camping, kayaking, and quilting.

Brenda L. Mattison has a bachelor's degree in education and a master's degree in accounting, both from Clemson University. She is currently an Accounting Instructor at Tri-County Technical College in Pendleton, South Carolina. Brenda previously served as Accounting Program Coordinator at TCTC and has prior experience teaching accounting at Robeson Community College, Lumberton, North Carolina; University of South Carolina Upstate, Spartanburg, South Carolina; and Rasmussen Business College, Eagan, Minnesota. She also has accounting work experience in retail and manufacturing businesses.

Brenda is a member of Teachers of Accounting at Two Year Colleges and the American Accounting Association. She is currently serving on the board of directors as Vice President of Conference Administration of Teachers of Accounting at Two Year Colleges.

Brenda previously served as Faculty Fellow at Tri-County Technical College. She has presented at several conferences on topics including active learning, course development, and student engagement.

In her spare time, Brenda enjoys reading and spending time with her family. She is also an active volunteer in the community, serving her church and other organizations.

Ella Mae Matsumura, Ph.D. is a professor in the Department of Accounting and Information Systems in the School of Business at the University of Wisconsin–Madison, and is affiliated with the university's Center for Quick Response Manufacturing. She received an A.B. in mathematics from the University of California, Berkeley, and M.Sc. and Ph.D. degrees from the University of British Columbia. Ella Mae has won two teaching excellence awards at the University of Wisconsin–Madison and was elected as a lifetime fellow of the university's Teaching Academy, formed to promote effective teaching. She is a member of the university team awarded an IBM Total Quality Management Partnership grant to develop curriculum for total quality management education.

Ella Mae was a co-winner of the 2010 Notable Contributions to Management Accounting Literature Award. She has served in numerous leadership positions in the American Accounting Association (AAA). She was coeditor of *Accounting Horizons* and has chaired and served on numerous AAA committees. She has been secretary-treasurer and president of the AAA's Management Accounting Section. Her past and current research articles focus on decision making, performance evaluation, compensation, supply chain relationships, and sustainability. She coauthored a monograph on customer profitability analysis in credit unions.

Brief Contents

Contents

CHAPTER **22**

CHAPTER **25**

CHAPTER **26**

Changes to This Edition

Chapter 18
NEW! Added discussion of the Pathways Commission and incorporated the Pathways' Vision Model.
NEW! Included triple bottom line in Today's Business Environment section.
Expanded the cost flows exhibit to include T-accounts for manufacturing inventory accounts.

Chapter 19
Modified the exhibit on summary journal entries to include T-accounts for manufacturing inventory accounts and COGS.

Chapter 21
Clarified the explanation of the differences between target pricing and cost-based pricing.
NEW! Added comprehensive problem for Chapters 18–21.

Chapter 24
NEW! Added comprehensive problem for Chapters 22–24.

Chapter 26
NEW! Added comprehensive problem for Chapters 25 and 26.

http://www.pearsonhighered.com/Horngren

Horngren's Accounting...
Expanding on Proven Success

New to the Enhanced eText

The Enhanced eText keeps students engaged in learning on their own time, while helping them achieve greater conceptual understanding of course material. The worked examples bring learning to life, and algorithmic practice allows students to apply the very concepts they are reading about. Combining resources that illuminate content with accessible self-assessment, MyAccountingLab with Enhanced eText provides students with a complete digital learning experience—all in one place.

 Try It! Solution Videos— Author recorded solution videos accompany Try Its! Just click on the Try It! box and watch the author will walk students through the problem and the solution.

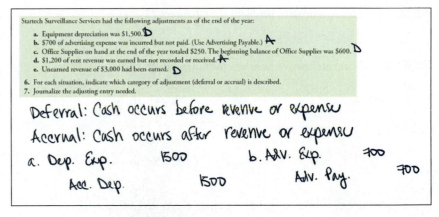

 Accounting Cycle Tutorial—MyAccountingLab's new interactive tutorial helps students master the Accounting Cycle for early and continued success in the introduction to Accounting course. The tutorial, accessed by computer, Smartphone, or tablet, provides students with brief explanations of each concept of the Accounting Cycle through engaging videos and/or animations. Students are immediately assessed on their understanding and their performance is recorded in the MyAccountingLab grade book. Whether the Accounting Cycle Tutorial is used as a remediation self-study tool or course assignment, students have yet another resource within MyAccountingLab to help them be successful with the accounting cycle.

Learning Catalytics—A "bring your own device" assessment and classroom activity system that expands the possibilities for student engagement. Using Learning Catalytics, you can deliver a wide range of auto-gradable or open-ended questions that test content knowledge and build critical thinking skills. Eighteen different answer types provide great flexibility, including graphical, numerical, textual input, and more.

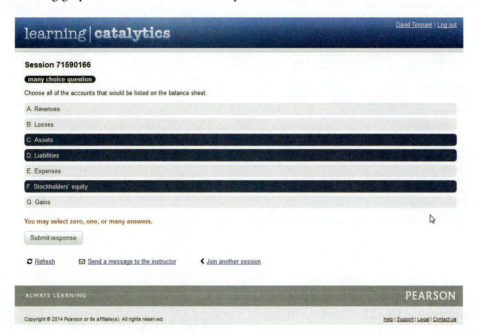

 Animated Lectures—These pre-class learning aids are available for every learning objective and are professor-narrated PowerPoint summaries that will help students prepare for class. These can be used in an online or flipped classroom experience or simply to get students ready for lecture.

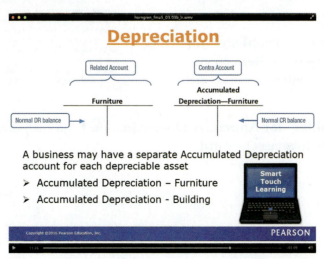

End-of-Chapter Continuing and Comprehensive Problems

> Continuing Problem

Problem P18-42 is the first problem in a sequence of problems for Daniels Consulting. This company was also used for the Continuing Problems in the financial accounting chapters as the business evolved from a service company to a merchandising company. However, it is not necessary to complete those problems prior to completing P18-42.

P18-42

Daniels Consulting is going to manufacture billing software. During its first month of manufacturing, Daniels incurred the following manufacturing costs:

Inventories:	Beginning	Ending
Raw Materials	$ 10,800	$ 9,600
Work-in-Process	0	23,000
Finished Goods	0	29,000
Other information:		
Raw materials purchases		$ 18,000
Plant janitorial services		200
Sales salaries expense		7,000
Delivery expense		1,100
Sales revenue		1,075,000
Utilities for plant		11,000
Rent on plant		12,000
Customer service hotline costs		12,000
Direct labor		200,000

Continuing Problem—Starts in Chapter 18 and runs through the entire book exposing students to recording entries for a service company and then moving into recording transactions for a merchandiser later in the text. The managerial chapters emphasize the relevant topics for that chapter using a continuous company.

NEW! **Comprehensive Problem for Chapters 18–21**—Covers fundamental managerial accounting concepts: job order costing, process costing, cost management systems, and cost-volume-profit analysis.

NEW! **Comprehensive Problem for Chapters 22–24**—Covers planning and control decisions for a manufacturing company, including a master budget, flexible budget, variance analysis, and performance evaluation.

NEW! **Comprehensive Problem for Chapters 25–26**—Covers decision making, both short-term business decisions and capital budgeting decisions.

Comprehensive Problem for Appendix D—Students use trend analysis and ratios to analyze a company for its investment potential.

COMPREHENSIVE PROBLEM

> **Comprehensive Problem for Chapters 18–21**

The Savannah Shirt Company makes two types of T-shirts: basic and custom. Basic shirts are plain shirts without any screen printing on them. Custom shirts are created using the basic shirts and then adding a custom screen printing design.

The company buys cloth in various colors and then makes the basic shirts in two departments, Cutting and Sewing. The company uses a process costing system (weighted-average method) to determine the production cost of the basic shirts. In the Cutting Department, direct materials (cloth) are added at the beginning of the process and conversion costs are added evenly through the process. In the Sewing Department, no direct materials are added. The only additional material, thread, is considered an indirect material because it cannot be easily traced to the finished product. Conversion costs are added evenly throughout the process in the Sewing Department. The finished basic shirts are sold to retail stores or are sent to the Custom Design Department for custom screen printing.

The Custom Design Department creates custom shirts by adding screen printing to the basic shirt. The department creates a design based on the customer's request and then prints the design using up to four colors. Because these shirts have the custom printing added, which is unique for each order, the additional cost incurred is determined using job order costing, with each custom order considered a separate job.

Chapter Openers

Chapter openers set up the concepts to be covered in the chapter using stories students can relate to. The implications of those concepts on a company's reporting and decision making processes are then discussed.

Effect on the Accounting Equation

Next to every journal entry, these illustrations help reinforce the connections between recording transactions and the effect those transactions have on the accounting equation.

Transaction 1—Raw Materials Purchased

During July, the company purchased materials on account for $175,000.

$$\left.\frac{A\uparrow}{RM\uparrow}\right\} = \left\{\frac{L\uparrow}{A/P\uparrow} + E\right.$$

Date	Accounts and Explanation	Debit	Credit
Trans. 1	Raw Materials Inventory	175,000	
	Accounts Payable		175,000
	Materials purchased, **accumulated** *in RM.*		

Instructor Tips & Tricks

Found throughout the text, these handwritten notes mimic the experience of having an experienced teacher walk a student through concepts on the "board." Many include mnemonic devices or examples to help students remember the rules of accounting.

Exhibit 25-5 | **Differential Analysis of Special Pricing Decision**

Expected increase in revenue	(250 tablets × $275)	$ 68,750
Expected increase in variable manufacturing costs	(250 tablets × $245)	(61,250)
Expected *increase* in operating income	(250 tablets × $ 30)	$ 7,500

In differential analysis, items are shown with their effect on profits. The increase in revenues will increase profits, so it is shown as a positive amount. The increase in costs will decrease profits, so it is shown as a negative amount.

Common Questions, Answered

Our authors have spent years in the classroom answering students' questions and have found patterns in the concepts or rules that consistently confuse students. These commonly asked questions are located in the margin of the text next to where the answer or clarification can be found highlighted in orange text.

Favorable variances are good, right? Why should they be investigated?

Both favorable and unfavorable variances should be investigated, if substantial, to determine their causes. **As an example, suppose a company avoided routine maintenance on machinery in order to have a favorable cost variance in the current period. In a later period, the company could have a major breakdown that could have been avoided if the machinery had been properly maintained. The breakdown could require not only a substantial repair bill, but also a halt in production that could lead to lost sales.** Therefore, managers should look at any variance that is significant.

Let's look at the flexible budget variances for direct materials and direct labor and separate them into their two components—cost and efficiency.

Try It! Boxes

Found after each learning objective, Try Its! give students the opportunity to apply the concept they just learned to an accounting problem. Deep linking in the eText will allow students to practice in MyAccountingLab without interrupting their interaction with the eText.

Identify the following characteristics as primarily related to financial accounting (FA) or managerial accounting (MA):

1. Helps creditors make lending decisions.
2. Helps in planning and controlling operations.
3. Is not required to follow GAAP.
4. Has a focus on the future.
5. Summary reports prepared quarterly or annually.

Check your answers online in MyAccountingLab or at http://www.pearsonhighered.com/Horngren.

For more practice, see Short Exercises S18-1 through S18-4. MyAccountingLab

Redesigned

The redesign includes clean and consistent art for T-accounts, journal entries, financial statements, and the accounting equation. New art types include clear explanations and connection arrows to help students follow the transaction process.

Date	Accounts and Explanation	Debit	Credit
Trans. 1	Raw Materials Inventory	175,000	
	Accounts Payable		175,000
	*Materials purchased, **accumulated** in RM.*		

Decision Boxes

This feature provides common questions and potential solutions business owners face. Students are asked to determine the course of action they would take based on concepts covered in the chapter and are then given potential solutions.

> Things You Should Know

1. **Why is managerial accounting important?**

   - Financial accounting prepares reports for external users, such as investors, creditors, and government agencies.
   - Managerial accounting provides information for managers to use in decision making.
   - Managers are accountable to many different stakeholders.
   - Today's business environment requires managers to use many tools to be successful.
   - The IMA Standards of Ethical Professional Practice include competence, confidentiality, integrity, and credibility.

2. **How do service, merchandising, and manufacturing companies differ?**

   - Service companies sell their time, skills, and knowledge. Examples include law firms, car washes, and banks.
   - Merchandising companies buy products from suppliers and resell them. Examples include grocery stores, drug stores, and clothing stores.
   - Merchandising companies have a Merchandise Inventory account.
   - Manufacturing companies convert raw materials into finished goods and then sell the finished goods. Examples include companies that make breakfast cereals, automobiles, and computers.
   - Manufacturing companies have three inventory accounts: Raw Materials Inventory, Work-in-Process Inventory, and Finished Goods Inventory.

Things You Should Know

Provides students with a brief review of each learning objective presented in a question and answer format.

Dear Colleague,

Thank you for taking time, out of what we know is a busy schedule, to review the newest edition of *Horngren's Accounting*. We are excited to share our innovations with you as we expand on the proven success of our significant revision to the Horngren franchise. Using what we have learned from focus groups, market feedback, and our colleagues, we've designed this edition to focus on several goals.

First, we made certain that our content was clear, consistent, and above all, accurate. As authors, we reviewed each chapter to ensure that students understand what they are reading and that there is consistency from chapter to chapter. In addition, our textbook goes through a multi-level accuracy check which includes the author team working every single accounting problem and having a team of accounting professors from across the nation review for accuracy. Next, through ongoing conversations with our colleagues and our time engaged at professional conferences, we confirmed that our pedagogy and content represents the leading methods used in the classroom and provides your students with the foundation they need to be successful in their future academic and professional careers. Lastly, we concentrated on student success and providing resources for professors to create an active and engaging classroom.

Student success. Using our experience as educators, our team carefully considered how students learn, what they learn, and where they struggle the most. We understand that sometimes there is a gap in students' understanding between the textbook content and what is done in the classroom or in an online environment, so we have included in the textbook and enhanced eText several great learning aids for students. *Instructor Tips and Tricks* and *Common Questions Answered* address areas that are typically challenging for students. These aids provide handy memory tools or address common student misconceptions or confusion. We also realized that students use our enhanced eText to study on their own time and we have built in many new features to bring learning to life and to allow students to apply the concepts they are reading about outside of the classroom. Available through MyAccountingLab, students have the opportunity to watch author recorded solution videos, practice the accounting cycle using an interactive tutorial, and watch in-depth author-driven animated lectures that cover every learning objective.

Professor expectations. As professors, we know it's critical to have excellent end-of-chapter material and instructor resources. With these expectations, all end-of-chapter problems have been revised and our author team, along with our trusted accuracy checkers, have checked every problem for accuracy and consistency. In addition to financial comprehensive problems, three NEW comprehensive problems have been added to the managerial content. These problems cover multiple chapters and encourage students to think reflectively about prior material learned and the connections between accounting concepts. We have also reviewed and updated ALL instructor resources to accompany this edition of the book. In addition, the PowerPoint presentations and Test Bank have had significant revisions based upon your feedback and needs.

Expanding on the proven success of our last edition, we believe that our enhancements to *Horngren's Accounting*, along with MyAccountingLab, will help your students achieve success in accounting. We welcome your feedback, suggestions, and comments. Please don't hesitate to contact us at *HorngrensAccounting@pearson.com.*

Tracie L. Miller-Nobles, CPA   *Brenda Mattison*   *Ella Mae Matsumura, PhD*

Instructor and Student Resources

Each supplement, including the resources in MyAccountingLab, has been reviewed by the author team to ensure accuracy and consistency with the text. Given their personal involvement, you can be assured of the high quality and accuracy of all supplements.

For Instructors

MyAccountingLab

Online Homework and Assessment Manager: http://www.myaccountinglab.com

Instructor Resource Center: http://www.pearsonhighered.com/Horngren

For the instructor's convenience, the instructor resources can be downloaded from the textbook's catalog page (http://www.pearsonhighered.com/Horngren) and MyAccountingLab. Available resources include the following:

Online Instructor's Resource Manual:

Course Content:
- Tips for Taking Your Course from Traditional to Hybrid, Blended, or Online
- Standard Syllabi for Financial Accounting (10-week & 16-week)
- Standard Syllabi for Managerial Accounting (10-week & 16-week)
- Sample Syllabi for 10- and 16-week courses
- "First Day of Class" student handouts include:
  - Student Walk-Through to Set-up MyAccountingLab
  - Tips on How to Get an A in This Class

Chapter Content:
- Chapter Overview
  - Contains a brief synopsis and overview of each chapter.
- Learning Objectives
- Teaching Outline with Lecture Notes
  - Revised to combine the Teaching Outline and the Lecture Outline Topics, so instructors only have one document to review.
  - Walks instructors through what material to cover and what examples to use when addressing certain items within the chapter.
- Handout for Student Notes
  - An outline to assist students in taking notes on the chapter.
- Student Chapter Summary
  - Aids students in their comprehension of the chapter.
- Assignment Grid
  - Indicates the corresponding Learning Objective for each exercise and problem.
- Answer Key to Chapter Quiz
- Ten-Minute Quiz
  - To quickly assess students' understanding of the chapter material.
- Extra Critical Thinking Problems and Solutions
  - Critical Thinking Problems removed from this edition of the text were moved to the IRM so instructors can continue to use their favorite problems.
- NEW Guide to Classroom Engagement Questions
  - Author-created element will offer tips and tricks to instructors in order to help them use the Learning Catalytic questions in class.

Online Instructor's Solutions Manual:
- Contains solutions to all end-of-chapter questions, short exercises, exercises, and problems.
- The Try It! Solutions, previously found at the end of each chapter, are now available for download with the ISM.
- All solutions were thoroughly reviewed by the author team and other professors.

Online Test Bank:
- Includes more than 3,900 questions.
- Both conceptual and computational problems are available in true/false, multiple choice, and open-ended formats.
- Algorithmic test bank is available in MyAccountingLab.

PowerPoint Presentations:

Instructor PowerPoint Presentations:
- Complete with lecture notes.
- Mirrors the organization of the text and includes key exhibits.

Student PowerPoint Presentations:
- Abridged versions of the Instructor PowerPoint Presentations.
- Can be used as a study tool or note-taking tool for students.

Demonstration Problem PowerPoint Presentations:
- Offers instructors the opportunity to review in class the exercises and problems from the chapter using different companies and numbers.

Clicker Response System (CRS) PowerPoint Presentations:
- 10 multiple-choice questions to use with a Clicker Response System.

Image Library:
- All image files from the text to assist instructors in modifying our supplied PowerPoint presentations or in creating their own PowerPoint presentations.

Working Papers and Solutions:
- Available in Excel format.
- Templates for students to use to complete exercises and problems in the text.

Data and Solutions Files:
- Select end-of-chapter problems have been set up in different software applications, including QuickBooks and General Ledger.
- Corresponding solution files are provided for QuickBooks.

For Students

MyAccountingLab

Online Homework and Assessment Manager: http://www.myaccountinglab.com

- Pearson Enhanced eText
- Data Files
- Animated Lectures
- Demo Docs
- Working Papers
- Student PowerPoint® Presentations
- Accounting Cycle Tutorial
- Flash Cards

Student Resource Web site: http://www.pearsonhighered.com/Horngren

The book's Web site contains the following:

- Data Files: Select end-of-chapter problems have been set up in QuickBooks software and the related files are available for download.
- Working Papers
- Try It! Solutions: The solutions to all in-chapter Try Its! are available for download.

http://www.pearsonhighered.com/Horngren

Acknowledgments

Acknowledgments for This Edition:

Tracie Miller–Nobles would like to thank her parents and sister: Kipp and Sylvia Miller and Michelle Miller. She would also like to express her gratitude to her many colleagues and friends who encourage and support her. In addition, she would like to thank Kevin Morris for always making her laugh and for being the best camping buddy she could ever ask for. Here's to many more trails.

Brenda Mattison has always had the loving support of her family and wishes to express her gratitude to them, especially her husband, Grant Mattison, who has been a constant and stable influence and inspiration for more than 25 years. Her family's faith in her, along with her faith in God, provided the solid foundation that allowed her to develop her gift of teaching and achieve her dreams while helping others to achieve theirs.

Ella Mae Matsumura thanks her family for their longstanding love and support in her endeavors: husband, Kam-Wah Tsui; son, David Tsui; sister and late parents, Linda, Lester, and Eda Matsumura. She would also like to express her appreciation to: the numerous colleagues and friends who have encouraged her and helped her grow as a scholar and a person; the many students who have provided constructive feedback that has shaped her teaching; and her faith community for its enduring love and affirmation.

The authors would like to sincerely thank Lacey Vitetta, Roberta Sherman, Mary Kate Murray, Andra Skaalrud, Alison Haskins, and Donna Battista for their unwavering support of this edition. They express their extreme pleasure in working with each of them and are appreciative of their guidance, patience, and belief in the success of this project.

Contributor:

Lori Hatchell, *Aims Community College*

Advisory Panels, Focus Group Participants, and Reviewers:

Samad Adams, *Bristol Community College*

Sharon Agee, *Rollins College*

Markus Ahrens, *St. Louis Community College*

Janice Akao, *Butler County Community College*

Anna Alexander, *Caldwell Community College and Technical Institute*

Sheila Ammons, *Austin Community College*

Sidney Askew, *Borough of Manhattan Community College*

Michael Barendse, *Grossmont College*

Vikki Bentz, *Yavapai College*

Jennifer Cainas, *University of South Florida*

Anne Cardozo, *Broward College*

Elizabeth Carlson, *University of South Florida Sarasota-Manatee*

Martha Cavalaris, *Miami Dade College*

Donna Chadwick, *Sinclair Community College*

Colleen Chung, *Miami Dade College*

Tom Clement, *University of North Dakota*

Geoffrey Danzig, *Miami Dade College–North*

Judy Daulton, *Piedmont Technical College*

Michelle Davidowitz, *Kingsborough Community College*

Annette Fisher Davis, *Glendale Community College*

Anthony Dellarte, *Luzerne County Community College*

Crystal Drum, *Guilford Technical Community College*

Mary Ewanechko, *Monroe Community College*

Elisa Fernandez, *Miami Dade College*

Lori Grady, *Bucks County Community College*

Marina Grau, *Houston Community College*

Gloria Grayless, *Sam Houston State University*

Dawn D. Hart, *Darton State College*

Lori Hatchell, *Aims Community College*

Shauna Hatfield, *Salt Lake Community College*

Patricia Holmes, *Des Moines Area Community College*

Cynthia Johnson, *University of Arkansas, Little Rock*

Jeffrey Jones, *The College of Southern Nevada*

Thomas K. Y. Kam, *Hawaii Pacific University*

Anne Kenner, *Brevard Community College*

Stephanie (Sam) King, *Edison State College*

Paul Koulakov, *Nashville State Community College*

Christy Land, *Catawba Valley Community College*

Wayne Lewis, *Hudson Valley Community College*

Mabel Machin, *Valencia College*

Mostafa Maksy, *Kutztown University*

Richard Mandau, *Piedmont Technical College*

Maria C. Mari, *Miami Dade College*

Cynthia J. Miller, *University of Kentucky*

Joanne Orabone, *Community College of Rhode Island*

Kimberly Perkins, *Austin Community College*

William Quilliam, *Florida Southern College*

Marcela Raphael, *Chippewa Valley Technical College*

Ryan Rees, *Salt Lake Community College*

Cecile Robert, *Community College of Rhode Island*

Shani Nicole Robinson, *Sam Houston State University*

Carol Rowey, *Community College of Rhode Island*

Amanda J. Salinas, *Palo Alto College*

Dennis Shea, *Southern New Hampshire University*
Jaye Simpson, *Tarrant County*
John Stancil, *Florida Southern*
Diana Sullivan, *Portland Community College*
Annette Taggart, *Texas A&M University–Commerce*
Linda Tarrago, *Hillsborough Community College*
Teresa Thompson, *Chaffey College*
Judy Toland, *Bucks County Community College*

Robin D. Turner, *Rowan-Cabarrus Community College*
William Van Glabek, *Edison State College*
Stanley Walker, *Georgia Northwestern Tech*
Deb Weber, *Hawkeye Community College*
Denise A. White, *Austin Community College*
Donald R. Wilke, *Northwest Florida State College*
Wanda Wong, *Chabot College*
Judy Zander, *Grossmont College*

Accuracy Checkers:

James L. Baker, *Harford Community College*
Nancy Emerson, *North Dakota State University*
Richard Mandau, *Piedmont Technical College*

Carolyn Streuly
Carol Hughes, *Asheville-Buncombe Technical Community College*

Supplements Authors and Reviewers:

David Dearman, *Piedmont Technical College*
Kelly Damron, *Glendale Community College*
Helen Brubeck, *Saint Mary-of-the-Woods College*
Brett Killion, *Lakeland College*
Sheila Ammons, *Austin Community College*

Dave Alldredge, *Salt Lake Community College*
Michelle Suminski, *Marygrove College*
Connie Belden, *Butler Community College*
Kate Demarest, *Carroll Community College*

The authors would like to express their gratitude for the diligent and exemplary work of all of our contributors, reviewers, accuracy checkers, and supplement authors. Each of you played a part in making this book successful! Thank you!

Introduction to Managerial Accounting 18

How Should I Decide?

Robert Bennett's first experience with the new entree was amazing! The presentation was pleasing to his eye, and the food texture was perfect. But most importantly, the taste was wonderful. Robert is sure that this latest creation from his chef is the item they have been looking for to add to the menu.

Robert is a restaurant manager. He knows that he cannot let the business stagnate and is constantly looking for ways to improve his customers' dining experience while also keeping a close eye on the bottom line. He realizes there is a balancing act between keeping customers happy and producing enough profits to keep investors and creditors satisfied. So now Robert is faced with a lot of decisions. When should the new entree be revealed? How will he promote it? How much should the restaurant charge? What if the price is too high and customers won't try it? What if it's so successful the kitchen can't keep up with orders or runs out of food? Will he need to hire more employees? What if the price is too low and the restaurant's profits decline?

Robert needs more information before making his decisions. Managers use accounting information to help with the decision-making process, but the information found in annual financial reports will be of limited value to Robert. He needs more detailed information. Managers use *managerial accounting* to help make these decisions. A good managerial accounting system will help Robert make plans for the restaurant and later determine whether those plans were successful.

Why Managerial Accounting?

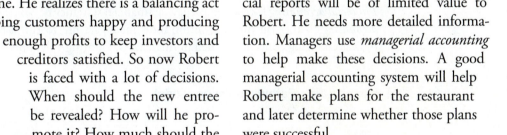

Have you ever wondered how companies like Red Lobster determine their menu prices? Or how their special offers affect their profits? How does changing the menu draw in new customers?

Red Lobster was founded by Bill Darden in 1968 in Lakeland, Florida. The company was acquired by General Mills in 1970 when there were five restaurants. By 2014, there were nearly 700 Red Lobster locations in the United States and Canada. In 1995, General Mills spun off its restaurant division by forming Darden Restaurants, Inc. naming the new company after the Red Lobster founder. Darden Restaurants also includes Olive Garden, Longhorn Steakhouse, The Capital Grille, Bahama Breeze, Seasons 52, Eddie V's, and Yard House.

Darden Restaurants' five-year average (2009–2013) net profit margin was 5.51%. When compared with the industry average of 0.27%, it is obvious the company is making profitable decisions. Let's begin our study of managerial accounting to see how successful companies use accounting information to make good internal business decisions.

Chapter 18 Learning Objectives

1 Define managerial accounting and understand how it is used

2 Describe the differences between service, merchandising, and manufacturing companies

3 Classify costs for service, merchandising, and manufacturing companies

4 Prepare an income statement and schedule of cost of goods manufactured for a manufacturing company and calculate cost per item

5 Calculate cost per service for a service company and cost per item for a merchandising company

WHY IS MANAGERIAL ACCOUNTING IMPORTANT?

Learning Objective 1

Define managerial accounting and understand how it is used

Recently, leaders from across the accounting community, called the Pathways Commission, came together to create a vision model (see Exhibit 18-1) to help students and the public understand what accounting is. The model is intended to explain in a visual way what accountants really do. Accounting starts with economic activities that accountants review and evaluate using critical thinking and judgment to create useful information that helps individuals make good decisions. The model emphasizes that good decisions have an impact on accounting judgments and economic activity, thus creating a circular flow of cause and effect. Accountants are more than boring, tedious number crunchers. Instead, accountants play a critical role in supporting a prosperous society.

In this chapter, we shift the focus from financial accounting to managerial accounting. *Financial accounting* focuses on preparing financial statements. *Managerial* (or *management*) *accounting* focuses on the accounting tools managers use to run a business. So while the basic accounting concepts learned in financial accounting still apply, you need to learn how

Exhibit 18-1 | **Pathways Vision Model**

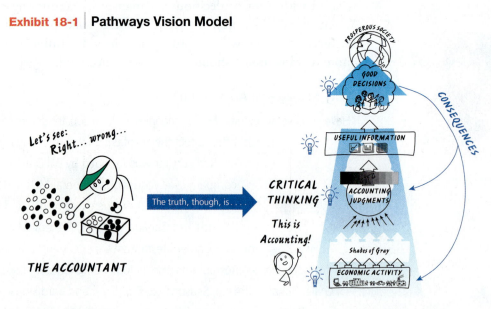

We tend to think of accountants as boring and dry.

Accountants are instrumental in helping to create a prosperous society.

This work is by The Pathways Commission and is licensed under a Creative Commons Attribution—NoDerivs 3.0 Unported License. To learn more, go to http://www.pathwayscommission.org.

to use these new tools. Anyone with an interest in owning or managing a business will find managerial accounting helpful in providing the information needed to make decisions. We'll explain these concepts using our fictitious company Smart Touch Learning. Smart Touch Learning began operations as a service company that specialized in providing online courses in accounting, economics, marketing, and management. The company later evolved into a merchandising company. Currently, Smart Touch Learning buys touch screen tablet computers, uploads its online courses, and then resells the tablets.

Financial Versus Managerial Accounting

The managers at Smart Touch Learning need information that will help them plan and control operations as they lead the business. This includes managing the company's plant, equipment, and human resources.

- **Planning** means choosing goals and deciding how to achieve them. For example, a common goal is to increase operating income. To achieve this goal, managers may raise selling prices to increase total revenues or advertise less to decrease costs. A managerial accounting tool called a **budget** is one example of a planning tool. The budget shows the expected financial impact of decisions, such as increasing prices or cutting costs. The budget also helps identify the resources needed to achieve goals. Budgeting is covered in detail in a later chapter.

- **Controlling** means implementing the plans and evaluating operations by comparing actual results to the budget. For example, managers can compare actual costs to budgeted costs to evaluate their performance. If actual costs fall below budgeted costs, that is usually good news. But if actual costs exceed the budget, managers may need to make changes.

Planning
Choosing goals and deciding how to achieve them.

Budget
A financial plan that managers use to coordinate a business's activities.

Controlling
Implementing plans and evaluating the results of business operations by comparing the actual results to the budget.

Financial accounting has a focus on the past, reporting on the results of previous accounting periods. Managers, however, need to make decisions about future operations, so managerial accounting often requires forward-looking information. Additionally, managerial accounting reports may contain proprietary information that is company specific and nonpublic. Financial reports prepared for investors and creditors do not contain this type of information. Exhibit 18-2 illustrates the major differences between financial and managerial accounting.

Managers tailor their managerial accounting system to help them make wise decisions. Managers weigh the *benefits* of the system, which include obtaining better information that

Exhibit 18-2 | **Financial Accounting Versus Managerial Accounting**

	Financial Accounting	Managerial Accounting
Primary users	External—investors, creditors, and government authorities	Internal—the company's managers and employees
Purpose of information	Help investors and creditors make investment and credit decisions	Help managers and employees plan and control operations
Focus and time dimension of the information	Relevant and faithfully representative information and focus on the past Example: 2017 actual performance reported in 2018	Relevant information and focus on the future Example: 2018 budget prepared in 2017
Rules and restrictions	Required to follow Generally Accepted Accounting Principles (GAAP); public companies required to be audited by an independent CPA	Not required to follow GAAP
Scope of information	Summary reports prepared primarily on the company as a whole, usually on a quarterly or annual basis	Detailed reports prepared on parts of the company (products, departments, territories), often on a daily or weekly basis
Behavioral	Concern about adequacy of disclosures; behavioral implications are secondary	Concern about how reports will affect employee behavior

Cost/Benefit Analysis
Weighing costs against benefits to help make decisions.

leads to more informed decisions, against the *costs* to develop and run the system. Weighing the costs against the benefits is called **cost/benefit analysis**.

Management Accountability

Management Accountability
The manager's responsibility to wisely manage the resources of an organization.

Stakeholder
An individual or group that has an interest in a business, including customers, creditors, suppliers, and investors.

Management accountability is the manager's *responsibility* to the various stakeholders of the company to wisely manage the resources of the organization. **Stakeholders** include customers, creditors, suppliers, and investors. We call these groups the stakeholders of the company because each group has an interest of some sort in the business. Exhibit 18-3 shows the links between management and the various stakeholders of a company. The exhibit is organized by the three main categories of cash-flow activities: operating, investing, and financing. It also includes actions that affect society as a whole. For each activity, we list the stakeholders and what they provide to the organization. The far-right column shows how managers are accountable to the stakeholders.

Exhibit 18-3 | **Management Accountability to Stakeholders**

Stakeholders	Provide	Management Accountability
Operating activities		
Suppliers	Products and services	Making timely payments to suppliers
Employees	Time and expertise	Providing a safe and productive work environment and paying wages and salaries
Customers	Cash	Providing products and services that are safe and defect free; backing up the products and services provided
Investing activities		
Asset vendors	Long-term assets	Making timely payments to vendors
Financing activities		
Investors	Cash and other assets	Providing a return on investment
Creditors	Cash	Repaying principal and interest
Actions that affect society		
Governments	Permission to operate	Obeying laws and paying taxes
Communities	Human and physical resources	Operating in an ethical manner to support the community; ensuring the company's environmental impact does not harm the community

To earn the stakeholders' trust, managers provide information about their decisions and the results of those decisions. *Financial accounting* provides financial statements that report results of operations, financial position, and cash flows both to managers and to external stakeholders. Financial accounting satisfies management's accountability to the following groups:

- Investors and creditors
- Regulatory agencies, such as the Securities Exchange Commission, the Federal Trade Commission, and the Internal Revenue Service
- Customers and society

Managerial accounting provides the information needed to plan and control operations. Managers are responsible to many stakeholders, so they must plan and control operations carefully. Making decisions that cause the company to decline affects many different groups, from investors to employees, and may have an economic impact on the entire community.

Today's Business Environment

In order to be successful, managers of both large corporations and small, privately owned businesses must consider recent business trends.

Shift Toward a Service Economy Service companies provide health care, communication, banking, and other important benefits to society. The Office of the United States Trade Representative reports that service industries account for 68% of the U.S. gross domestic product and four out of five U.S. jobs. The U.S. Census Bureau's 2012 Service Annual Survey reported that 10 out of 11 service sectors had increases in revenue from 2011 to 2012.

Global Competition To be competitive, many companies are moving operations to other countries to be closer to new markets. Other companies are partnering with foreign companies to meet local needs. For example, Toyota, a Japanese company, has 15 manufacturing plants located in North America.

Time-Based Competition The Internet, electronic commerce (e-commerce), and express delivery speed the pace of business. Customers who instant message around the world will not want to wait two weeks to receive merchandise they purchased online. Time is the new competitive turf for world-class business. To compete, companies have developed the following time-saving responses:

- **Advanced Information Systems** Many companies use **Enterprise Resource Planning (ERP)** systems to integrate all their worldwide functions, departments, and data. ERP systems help to streamline operations and enable companies to respond quickly to changes in the marketplace.

- **E-commerce** The Internet allows companies to sell to customers around the world by providing 24/7 access to company information and products.

- **Just-in-Time Management** Inventory held too long may become obsolete. Stored goods take space and must be insured, which increases costs. The just-in-time philosophy helps managers cut costs by speeding the transformation of raw materials into finished products. Using a **Just-in-Time (JIT) Management** system means producing products *just in time* to satisfy needs. Ideally, suppliers deliver materials for today's production in exactly the right quantities *just in time* to begin production, and finished units are completed *just in time* for delivery to customers.

Total Quality Management Companies must deliver high-quality goods and services in order to be successful. **Total Quality Management (TQM)** is a philosophy of continuous improvement of products and processes. Continuous improvement leads to fewer defects and higher customer satisfaction. TQM also emphasizes the importance of each person in the organization, creating a culture of cooperation across all business processes: research and development, design, production, marketing and sales, distribution, and customer service. Each step in the process adds value to the end product. Therefore, these steps are referred to as the **value chain**.

The Triple Bottom Line The **triple bottom line** refers to profits, people, and the planet—the economic, social, and environmental impact of doing business. Companies are recognizing that they have multiple responsibilities and that generating profits for owners

---

Enterprise Resource Planning (ERP)
Software system that can integrate all of a company's functions, departments, and data into a single system.

Just-in-Time (JIT) Management
A cost management system in which a company produces products just in time to satisfy needs. Suppliers deliver materials just in time to begin production, and finished units are completed just in time for delivery to the customer.

Total Quality Management (TQM)
A philosophy designed to integrate all organizational areas in order to provide customers with superior products and services, while meeting organizational goals throughout the value chain.

Value Chain
Includes all activities that add value to a company's products and services.

Triple Bottom Line
Evaluating a company's performance by its economic (profits), social (people), and environmental (planet) impact.

and investors is only one aspect of being a socially responsible organization. Increasingly, customers and stockholders are choosing to support companies based on their labor practices, community service, and sustainable environmental practices.

Ethical Standards

Managers often face ethical challenges. The Institute of Management Accountants (IMA) has developed standards that must be maintained as managerial accountants face ethical challenges. The IMA standards remind us that society expects professional accountants to exhibit the highest level of ethical behavior. An excerpt from the IMA's Statement of Ethical Professional Practice appears in Exhibit 18-4. These standards require managerial accountants to do the following:

- Maintain their professional competence.
- Preserve the confidentiality of the information they handle.
- Act with integrity and credibility.

To resolve ethical dilemmas, the IMA suggests following organizationally established policies. If additional steps are needed, discuss the ethical situation with: (1) an immediate supervisor; (2) an objective adviser; and, if necessary, (3) an attorney.

Exhibit 18-4 | **IMA Statement of Ethical Professional Practice (excerpt)**

Management accountants have a commitment to ethical professional practice which includes principles of Honesty, Fairness, Objectivity, and Responsibility. The standards of ethical practice include the following:

I. COMPETENCE
1. Maintain an appropriate level of professional expertise by continually developing knowledge and skills.
2. Perform professional duties in accordance with relevant laws, regulations, and technical standards.
3. Provide decision support information and recommendations that are accurate, clear, concise, and timely.
4. Recognize and communicate professional limitations or other constraints that would preclude responsible judgment or successful performance of an activity.

II. CONFIDENTIALITY
1. Keep information confidential except when disclosure is authorized or legally required.
2. Inform all relevant parties regarding appropriate use of confidential information. Monitor subordinates' activities to ensure compliance.
3. Refrain from using confidential information for unethical or illegal advantage.

III. INTEGRITY
1. Mitigate actual conflicts of interest, regularly communicate with business associates to avoid apparent conflicts of interest. Advise all parties of any potential conflicts.
2. Refrain from engaging in any conduct that would prejudice carrying out duties ethically.
3. Abstain from engaging in or supporting any activity that might discredit the profession.

IV. CREDIBILITY
1. Communicate information fairly and objectively.
2. Disclose all relevant information that could reasonably be expected to influence an intended user's understanding of the reports, analyses, or recommendations.
3. Disclose delays or deficiencies in information, timeliness, processing, or internal controls in conformance with organization policy and/or applicable law.

Excerpt from "IMA Statement of Ethical Professional Practices." Adapted with permission from IMA, Montvale, New Jersey. www.imanet.org.

ETHICS

Where do you draw the line?

As the staff accountant of Casey Computer Co., Sam Butler is aware of Casey's weak financial condition. Casey is close to signing a lucrative contract that should ensure its future. The controller, who is Sam's supervisor, states that the company *must* report a profit this year. He suggests: "Two customers have placed orders that are scheduled to be shipped on January 3, when production of those orders is completed. Let's record the goods as finished and bill the customer on December 31 so we can show the profit from those orders in the current year."

What should Sam do? What would you do?

Solution

Sam could consider working with the production manager to get the orders completed and shipped in December. The orders could then be recorded in December, and the profits would be reflected in the current year's financial statements. However, if that is not possible, Sam should convince the controller that the income manipulation is not ethical and violates the revenue recognition principle—and that the company should not record these transactions in December. If Sam is unable to convince the controller, he has an obligation to report the situation to the controller's supervisor.

Try It!

Identify the following characteristics as primarily related to financial accounting (FA) or managerial accounting (MA):

1. Helps creditors make lending decisions.
2. Helps in planning and controlling operations.
3. Is not required to follow GAAP.
4. Has a focus on the future.
5. Summary reports prepared quarterly or annually.

Check your answers online in MyAccountingLab or at http://www.pearsonhighered.com/Horngren.

For more practice, see Short Exercises S18-1 through S18-4.   MyAccountingLab

HOW DO SERVICE, MERCHANDISING, AND MANUFACTURING COMPANIES DIFFER?

Businesses are generally classified as service, merchandising, or manufacturing companies. This section examines the differences between the business types.

Service Companies

Service companies sell their time, skills, and knowledge. Examples include accounting firms, phone companies, and cleaning services. As with other types of businesses, service companies seek to provide services that are high quality with reasonable prices and timely delivery. We focused on the financial statements for service companies in the financial accounting chapters of this book.

From a financial accounting perspective, service companies have the simplest accounting because they carry no inventories of products for sale. All of their costs are **period costs**, those costs that are incurred and expensed in the same accounting period. Usually, the largest expense for service companies is the salaries and wages of personnel who work for the company.

Learning Objective 2

Describe the differences between service, merchandising, and manufacturing companies

Service Company

A company that sells services—time, skills, and/or knowledge—instead of products.

Period Cost

Operating cost that is expensed in the accounting period in which it is incurred.

Merchandising Companies

Merchandising Company
A company that resells products previously bought from suppliers.

Merchandising companies resell products they buy from suppliers. Merchandisers keep an inventory of products, and managers are accountable for the purchasing, storage, and sale of the products. You also learned about merchandising companies in the financial accounting chapters of this book.

In contrast with service companies, merchandisers' income statements usually report Cost of Goods Sold as the major expense. Cost of Goods Sold represents the business's cost of the merchandise inventory sold. The calculation of Cost of Goods Sold is generally not shown on the income statement in most external financial reports but is simply listed as one item, Cost of Goods Sold or Cost of Sales. This section is often detailed on internal management reports to show the flow of costs through Merchandise Inventory. These costs are *inventoriable product costs* because the cost of the products is held in Merchandise Inventory, an asset, until the product is sold. The term *inventoriable product costs* emphasizes the fact that the costs are first recorded in an inventory account. However, in practice, inventoriable product costs are more often referred to as **product costs**, so that is the term we will use. For *external reporting*, GAAP requires companies to treat product costs as an asset until the product is sold or consumed, at which time the costs are expensed.

Product Cost
The cost of purchasing or making a product. The cost is recorded as an asset and then expensed when the product is sold.

Merchandising companies' product costs include the cost to purchase the merchandise inventory plus incoming freight costs. In other words, product costs are the cost to purchase the inventory and get the inventory *in* the warehouse or store. Product costs are recorded as an asset (Merchandise Inventory) on the balance sheet until the asset is sold. The cost is then transferred to an expense account—Cost of Goods Sold. The change in the Merchandise Inventory account provides the information for determining the cost of goods sold section of the income statement as shown in the following formula:

> Beginning Merchandise Inventory
> + Purchases and Freight In
> _____
> Cost of Goods Available for Sale
> − Ending Merchandise Inventory
> _____
> Cost of Goods Sold

In managerial accounting, we distinguish product costs from period costs. As noted previously, *period costs* are operating costs that are expensed in the period in which they are incurred. Therefore, period costs are the expenses that are not part of the product costs. Examples include sales staff salaries, advertising, store utilities, and store rent. These are referred to as Selling and Administrative Expenses. On the income statement, Cost of Goods Sold (an expense representing the cost of the products sold) is subtracted from Sales Revenue to calculate gross profit. Then the period costs are subtracted to determine operating income.

> Don't confuse prices with costs. <u>Price</u> (or sales price) is the amount the company charges the customer for the goods or services provided. <u>Cost</u> is the amount the company incurs to acquire the goods or services. If a company purchases an item for $4 and sells it for $10, the cost is $4 and the price is $10.

Manufacturing Companies

Manufacturing companies use labor, equipment, supplies, and facilities to convert raw materials into finished products. Managers in manufacturing companies must use these resources to create a product that customers want at a price customers are willing to pay. Managers are responsible for generating profits and maintaining positive cash flows.

In contrast with service and merchandising companies, manufacturing companies have a broad range of production activities that require tracking costs on three kinds of inventory:

1. **Raw Materials Inventory (RM)** includes materials used to make a product. For example, a bakery's raw materials include flour, sugar, and eggs.
2. **Work-in-Process Inventory (WIP)** includes goods that are in the manufacturing process but are not yet complete. Some production activities have transformed the raw materials, but the product is not yet finished or ready for sale. A bakery's Work-in-Process Inventory could include bread dough ready for baking. The process has been started but not completed.
3. **Finished Goods Inventory (FG)** includes completed goods that have not yet been sold. Finished goods are the products that the manufacturer sells, such as a finished cake or loaf of bread.

In a manufacturing company, as in a merchandising company, Cost of Goods Sold is usually the largest expense. The activity in the Finished Goods Inventory account provides the information for the cost of goods sold section of the income statement as shown in the following formula:

> Beginning Finished Goods Inventory
> + Cost of Goods Manufactured
> _____
> Cost of Goods Available for Sale
> − Ending Finished Goods Inventory
> _____
> Cost of Goods Sold

The calculation of cost of goods manufactured is explained later in the chapter.

Exhibit 18-5 (on the next page) shows a comparison of balance sheets and income statements for service, merchandising, and manufacturing companies. Notice the accounts highlighted in blue, which illustrate the different kinds of inventory accounts used by various types of companies.

Sidebar Glossary

Manufacturing Company
A company that uses labor, equipment, supplies, and facilities to convert raw materials into finished products.

Raw Materials Inventory (RM)
Materials used to manufacture a product.

Work-in-Process Inventory (WIP)
Goods that have been started in the manufacturing process but are not yet complete.

Finished Goods Inventory (FG)
Completed goods that have not yet been sold.

Match the accounting terminology to the examples.

6. Service company	a. Salaries paid to lawyers
7. Merchandising company	b. Company that makes cast iron pans
8. Manufacturing company	c. Tires used in the manufacture of automobiles
9. Period cost	d. Department store
10. Product cost	e. Dentist office

Check your answers online in MyAccountingLab or at http://www.pearsonhighered.com/Horngren.

For more practice, see Short Exercises S18-5 and S18-6. **My**AccountingLab

Exhibit 18-5 | **Financial Statement Comparison**

Service Company Income Statement Month Ended December 31, 2017		
Revenues:		
Service Revenue		$ 7,600
Expenses:		
Salaries Expense	$ 3,800	
Rent Expense	1,000	
Utilities Expense	400	
Total Expenses		5,200
Operating Income		**$ 2,400**

Merchandising Company Income Statement Month Ended December 31, 2017		
Revenues:		
Sales Revenue		$ 7,600
Cost of Goods Sold:		
Beginning Merchandise Inventory	$ 2,000	
Purchases and Freight In	3,800	
Cost of Goods Available for Sale	5,800	
Ending Merchandise Inventory	(2,200)	
Cost of Goods Sold		3,600
Gross Profit		4,000
Selling and Administrative Expenses		1,600
Operating Income		**$ 2,400**

Manufacturing Company Income Statement Month Ended December 31, 2017		
Revenues:		
Sales Revenue		$ 7,600
Cost of Goods Sold:		
Beginning Finished Goods Inventory	$ 2,000	
Cost of Goods Manufactured	3,800	
Cost of Goods Available for Sale	5,800	
Ending Finished Goods Inventory	(2,200)	
Cost of Goods Sold		3,600
Gross Profit		4,000
Selling and Administrative Expenses		1,600
Operating Income		**$ 2,400**

Service Company Balance Sheet (Partial) December 31, 2017	
Assets	
Cash	$ 10,500
Accounts Receivable	8,750
Equipment	60,000
Total Assets	**$ 79,250**

Merchandising Company Balance Sheet (Partial) December 31, 2017	
Assets	
Cash	$ 10,500
Accounts Receivable	8,750
Merchandise Inventory	2,200
Equipment	60,000
Total Assets	**$ 81,450**

Manufacturing Company Balance Sheet (Partial) December 31, 2017	
Assets	
Cash	$ 10,500
Accounts Receivable	8,750
Raw Materials Inventory	1,500
Work-in-Process Inventory	800
Finished Goods Inventory	2,200
Equipment	60,000
Total Assets	**$ 83,750**

HOW ARE COSTS CLASSIFIED?

Learning Objective 3

Classify costs for service, merchandising, and manufacturing companies

In the previous section, we discussed the difference between period costs and product costs. Now we will spend some more time exploring these costs for a manufacturing company.

Direct and Indirect Costs

Direct Cost

Cost that can be easily and cost-effectively traced to a cost object.

Cost Object

Anything for which managers want a separate measurement of cost.

Indirect Cost

Cost that cannot be easily or cost-effectively traced to a cost object.

A **direct cost** is a cost that can be easily and cost-effectively traced to a cost object. A **cost object** is anything for which managers need a separate breakdown of its component costs. Managers may want to know the cost of a product, a department, a sales territory, or an activity. Costs that cannot be easily or cost-effectively traced directly to a cost object are **indirect costs**. In manufacturing, the cost objects are often units of product. Indirect product costs are required to make the finished product but are not as easy or cost effective to track to one specific finished product. One example is a production supervisor. The person in this position oversees the production of all products in a facility but does not directly work on any of them. Therefore, it is difficult to trace the cost of the production supervisor to any specific product. In manufacturing companies, product costs include both direct and indirect costs.

Product Costs

In a manufacturing company, product costs are classified into three categories.

1. **Direct materials (DM)** are the raw materials that are converted into the finished product and are considered direct costs. For example, for a furniture manufacturer, the wood used to build a table is a direct material.

2. **Direct labor (DL)** is the labor of employees who convert the raw materials into the finished product. Direct labor is also a direct cost that can be easily traced to the finished product. Using the furniture manufacturer as an example, direct labor would include the labor costs of the employees who cut the wood and assemble the tables.

3. **Manufacturing overhead (MOH)** refers to indirect manufacturing costs that cannot be easily traced to specific products. It includes all manufacturing costs other than direct materials and direct labor. These costs are created by all of the supporting production activities, including storing materials, setting up machines, and cleaning the work areas. Examples include costs of indirect materials, manufacturing plant managers' salaries and other indirect labor, repair and maintenance, and depreciation on manufacturing buildings and equipment. Other examples include the following costs for the factory: utilities, rent, insurance, and property taxes. Manufacturing overhead is also called *factory overhead* or *indirect manufacturing costs*.

Let's look at two of the components of manufacturing overhead more closely. It is important to be able to distinguish between direct and indirect materials and direct and indirect labor.

- **Indirect materials** are the raw materials used in production that are difficult or not cost-effective to trace. For a furniture manufacture, it may be the cost of wood glue used in assembling tables. The cost of tracing the drops of glue used on each table and then determining the cost of those drops exceeds the benefit of having this information.

- **Indirect labor** includes the cost of labor in the factory for persons not directly producing the product. Examples include production supervisors, factory janitors, and maintenance employees.

Let's assume Smart Touch Learning has decided to expand operations and manufacture its own brand of touch screen tablet computers that are preloaded with the company's e-learning software. Exhibit 18-6 (on the next page) shows examples of period and product costs for Smart Touch Learning.

Prime and Conversion Costs

The purpose of managerial accounting is to provide useful information to managers. To make cost information more useful, product costs for manufacturing companies are sometimes combined in different ways, depending on the managers' needs.

Prime costs combine the direct costs of direct materials and direct labor. In a manufacturing process that is labor-intensive, the direct costs are the *primary* costs. *Labor-intensive* means people do most of the work, not machines. In that type of environment, managers may want to concentrate on these direct, or prime, costs. To be profitable, it is vital for the company to control these costs.

Conversion costs combine direct labor with manufacturing overhead. These are the costs to *convert* the raw materials into the finished product. In a manufacturing process that is machine-intensive, the cost of direct labor is minimal because machines do most of the work. Employees primarily set up and oversee the machine production. Overhead costs, however, can be substantial, including the cost of utilities and depreciation on the machinery. In that type of environment, managers may want to focus on the total conversion cost rather than tracking direct labor and manufacturing overhead separately.

Direct Materials (DM)
Materials that become a physical part of a finished product and whose costs are easily traced to the finished product.

Direct Labor (DL)
The labor cost of employees who convert raw materials into finished products.

Manufacturing Overhead (MOH)
Manufacturing costs that cannot be easily and cost-effectively traced to a cost object. Includes all manufacturing costs except direct materials and direct labor.

Indirect Materials
Materials used in making a product but whose costs either cannot be conveniently traced directly to specific finished products or are not large enough to justify tracing to the specific product.

Indirect Labor
Labor costs for activities that support the production process but either cannot be conveniently traced directly to specific finished products or are not large enough to justify tracing to the specific product.

Prime Costs
Direct materials plus direct labor.

Conversion Costs
The cost to convert raw materials into finished goods: Direct labor plus manufacturing overhead.

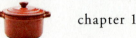

Exhibit 18-6 | **Period and Product Costs for Smart Touch Learning**

Cost Incurred	Period Costs	Product Costs		
	Selling and Administrative	Direct Materials	Direct Labor	Manufacturing Overhead
Depreciation on manufacturing equipment				X
Depreciation on office equipment	X			
Advertising	X			
Property taxes and insurance on office	X			
Property taxes and insurance on factory				X
Production supervisor's salary				X
CEO's salary	X			
Wages for assembly line workers			X	
Batteries, processors, and other materials used in making tablets		X		
Manufacturing supplies				X
Freight costs on purchase of materials		X		
Delivery expense	X			

> Overhead costs can be confusing. For example, for a service or merchandising company, the cost of rent is a period cost and is classified as a selling and administrative expense. For a manufacturing company, you must consider the reason for the cost. If the rent is for the corporate office, it is still a period cost. However, if the rent is for the factory, then it is a product cost because it is a cost incurred in the manufacturing process. Because the rent is neither direct materials nor direct labor, it is classified as manufacturing overhead.

Exhibit 18-7 illustrates the relationship between prime costs and conversion costs. Notice that direct labor is considered both a prime cost and a conversion cost.

Exhibit 18-7 | **Prime and Conversion Costs**

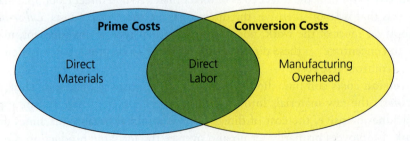

Identify each cost as a period cost or a product cost. If it is a product cost, further indicate if the cost is direct materials, direct labor, or manufacturing overhead. Then determine if the product cost is a prime cost and/or a conversion cost.

11. Wages of assembly line workers
12. Wages of the office receptionist
13. Property taxes on the factory
14. Sugar and flour used to make cookies
15. Salary of the factory maintenance supervisor
16. Salary of the sales manager

Check your answers online in MyAccountingLab or at http://www.pearsonhighered.com/Horngren.

For more practice, see Short Exercises S18-7 through S18-9.   **My**AccountingLab

HOW DO MANUFACTURING COMPANIES DETERMINE THE COST OF MANUFACTURED PRODUCTS?

Earlier in the chapter, we compared the financial statements of service, merchandising, and manufacturing companies. We noted that unlike service and merchandising companies, manufacturing companies have a range of production activities that require tracking in order to determine the cost of goods manufactured and cost of goods sold. Now that we have learned more about the types of costs manufacturing companies incur, we can look at the calculation for cost of goods manufactured.

Learning Objective 4

Prepare an income statement and schedule of cost of goods manufactured for a manufacturing company and calculate cost per item

Calculating Cost of Goods Sold

As we saw earlier in the chapter, the activity in the Finished Goods Inventory account provides the information for the cost of goods sold section of the income statement. The cost of goods sold is then subtracted from net sales revenue to determine gross profit. The next step is to subtract the period costs, the selling and administrative expenses, to determine the operating income. Exhibit 18-8 (on the next page) shows the income statement for the first year Smart Touch Learning became a manufacturing company, producing its own brand of touch screen tablet computers that are preloaded with the company's e-learning software. Take time to carefully study the income statement. Notice how the statement separates the product costs from the period costs, and be sure you understand the calculations before proceeding.

Calculating Cost of Goods Manufactured

Notice that the term **cost of goods manufactured** is in the past tense. It is the manufacturing cost of the goods that Smart Touch Learning *completed during 2018*. The cost of goods manufactured summarizes the activities and the costs that take place in a manufacturing plant during the accounting period.

Cost of Goods Manufactured

The manufacturing costs of the goods that finished the production process in a given accounting period.

Exhibit 18-8 | **Income Statement—Manufacturing Company**

SMART TOUCH LEARNING
Income Statement
Year Ended December 31, 2018

Sales Revenue		$ 1,200,000
Less: Sales Returns and Allowances	$ 120,000	
Sales Discounts	80,000	200,000
Net Sales Revenue		1,000,000
Cost of Goods Sold:		
Beginning Finished Goods Inventory	0	
Cost of Goods Manufactured	660,000	
Cost of Goods Available for Sale	660,000	
Ending Finished Goods Inventory	(60,000)	
Cost of Goods Sold		600,000
Gross Profit		400,000
Selling and Administrative Expenses:		
Wages Expense	120,000	
Rent Expense	100,000	
Insurance Expense	10,000	
Depreciation Expense	6,000	
Supplies Expense	5,000	
Total Selling and Administrative Expenses		241,000
Operating Income		159,000
Other Revenues and (Expenses):		
Interest Expense		(7,600)
Income Before Income Tax Expense		151,400
Income Tax Expense		53,000
Net Income		$ 98,400

> COGS is a product cost.

> S&A Expenses are period costs.

In order to understand how to calculate cost of goods manufactured, we need to understand the flow of product costs for a manufacturer. Exhibit 18-9 illustrates these relationships. Notice that the flow of product costs for a manufacturer begins with the purchase of raw materials. The manufacturer then uses direct labor and manufacturing overhead to convert these materials into Work-in-Process Inventory. When the manufacturing process is completed, the costs are transferred to Finished Goods Inventory. The direct materials, direct labor, and manufacturing overhead are all product costs because they are required for the production process.

Finished Goods Inventory is the only category of inventory that is ready to sell. The cost of the finished goods that the manufacturer sells becomes its Cost of Goods Sold on the income statement. Note that the product costs remain in inventory accounts on the balance sheet until the product is sold. At that point, the costs are expensed and moved to the income statement.

Costs the manufacturer incurs in nonmanufacturing activities, such as sales salaries, are period costs and are expensed in the period incurred. On the income statement, they are called selling and administrative expenses.

Exhibit 18-9 | Manufacturing Company: Product Costs and Period Costs

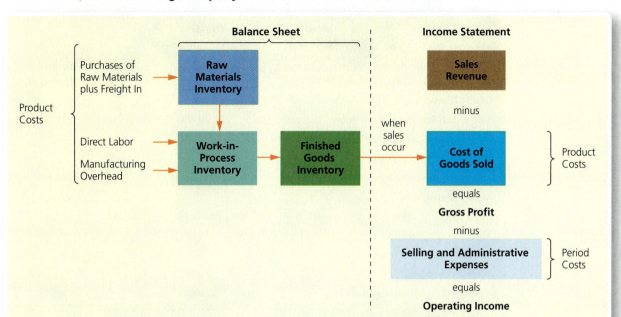

Armed with a clear understanding of the flow of activities and costs in the manufacturing plant, you are ready to calculate the cost of goods manufactured. Exhibit 18-10 (on the next page) shows a schedule of cost of goods manufactured for Smart Touch Learning. The company computed its cost of goods manufactured for 2018 to be $660,000. This is the cost of making 2,200 touch screen tablet computers that Smart Touch Learning *finished* during 2018.

Cost of goods manufactured summarizes the activities and related costs incurred to produce inventory during the year. As of December 31, 2017, Smart Touch Learning had just started manufacturing and had not yet completed the first tablet. However, the company had begun production and had spent a total of $80,000 to partially complete some tablets. This 2017 ending Work-in-Process Inventory became the beginning Work-in-Process Inventory for 2018.

Exhibit 18-10 (on the next page) shows that during the year, Smart Touch Learning used $355,000 of direct materials, $169,000 of direct labor, and $83,000 of manufacturing overhead. Therefore, the total manufacturing costs incurred during the year are the sum of these three amounts, $607,000. Adding total manufacturing cost for the year to the beginning Work-in-Process Inventory (WIP) of $80,000 gives the total manufacturing cost to account for, $687,000. At December 31, 2018, unfinished tablets costing only $27,000 remained in WIP Inventory. The company finished 2,200 tablets and sent them to Finished Goods Inventory (FG). Cost of goods manufactured for the year was $660,000. The following is the computation of the cost of goods manufactured (COGM):

Beginning WIP	+	Direct Materials Used	+	Direct Labor	+	Manufacturing Overhead	−	Ending WIP	=	COGM
$80,000	+	$355,000	+	$169,000	+	$83,000	−	$27,000	=	$660,000

If you refer back to Smart Touch Learning's December 2018 income statement, shown in Exhibit 18-8, you will find the $660,000 listed as the cost of goods manufactured.

Exhibit 18-10 | **Schedule of Cost of Goods Manufactured**

SMART TOUCH LEARNING Schedule of Cost of Goods Manufactured Year Ended December 31, 2018			
Beginning Work-in-Process Inventory			$ 80,000
Direct Materials Used:			
Beginning Raw Materials Inventory	$ 70,000		
Purchases of Raw Materials (including Freight In)	350,000		
Raw Materials Available for Use	420,000		
Ending Raw Materials Inventory	(65,000)		
Direct Materials Used		$ 355,000	
Direct Labor		169,000	
Manufacturing Overhead:			
Indirect Materials	17,000		
Indirect Labor	28,000		
Depreciation—Plant and Equipment	20,000		
Plant Utilities, Insurance, and Property Taxes	18,000		
Total Manufacturing Overhead		83,000	
Total Manufacturing Costs Incurred during the Year			607,000
Total Manufacturing Costs to Account For			687,000
Ending Work-in-Process Inventory			(27,000)
Cost of Goods Manufactured			$ 660,000

Flow of Costs Through the Inventory Accounts

Exhibit 18-11 diagrams the flow of costs through Smart Touch Learning's inventory accounts. Notice that the format is the same for all three inventory accounts:

> Beginning balance + Additions − Ending balance = Amount used, manufactured, or sold

The final amount at each stage is added at the beginning of the next stage. Take time to see how the schedule of cost of goods manufactured in Exhibit 18-10 uses the flows of the Raw Materials and Work-in-Process stages and the income statement in Exhibit 18-8 uses the flows of the Finished Goods stage. Understanding the flow of costs through a manufacturing company is very important and will be used in future chapters.

Exhibit 18-11 | **Flow of Costs Through Smart Touch Learning's Inventory Accounts**

Raw Materials Inventory		Work-in-Process Inventory		Finished Goods Inventory	
Beginning Inventory	$ 70,000	Beginning Inventory	$ 80,000	Beginning Inventory	$ 0
+ Purchases and Freight In	350,000	+ Direct Materials Used	355,000	+ Cost of Goods Manufactured	660,000
= Direct Materials Available for Use	420,000	+ Direct Labor	169,000	= Cost of Goods Available for Sale	660,000
− Ending Inventory	(65,000)	+ Manufacturing Overhead	83,000	− Ending Inventory	(60,000)
= Direct Materials Used	$ 355,000	= Total Manufacturing Costs to Account For	687,000	= Cost of Goods Sold	$ 600,000
		− Ending Inventory	(27,000)		
		= Cost of Goods Manufactured	$ 660,000		

Raw Materials Inventory			Work-in-Process Inventory			Finished Goods Inventory		
Beg. Bal.	70,000		Beg. Bal.	80,000		Beg. Bal.	0	
Purchased	350,000	355,000 DM Used	DM Used	355,000	660,000 COGM	COGM	660,000	600,000 COGS
End Bal.	65,000		DL	169,000		End. Bal.	60,000	
			MOH	83,000				
			End. Bal.	27,000				

Calculating Unit Product Cost

Knowing the unit product cost helps managers decide on the prices to charge for each product to ensure that each product is profitable. They can then measure operating income and determine the cost of Finished Goods Inventory. Smart Touch Learning produced 2,200 tablets during 2018. What did it cost to make each tablet?

Cost of goods manufactured	/	Total units produced	=	Unit product cost
$660,000	/	2,200 tablets	=	$300 per tablet

During 2018, Smart Touch Learning sold 2,000 tablets, and the company knows each tablet cost $300 to produce. With this information, Smart Touch Learning can compute its Cost of Goods Sold as follows:

Number of units sold	×	Unit product cost	=	Cost of Goods Sold
2,000 tablets	×	$300 per tablet	=	$600,000

Keep in mind that the manufacturer still has period costs in addition to the product costs. These selling and administrative expenses are reported on the company's income statement because they are necessary expenses in running the business but are reported separately from the product costs.

DECISIONS

Was expansion a good choice?

Refer to the information in Exhibits 18-8 and 18-10 for Smart Touch Learning. How would you rate management's performance for the accounting period? Was expanding into the manufacturing sector a good decision?

Solution

Smart Touch Learning manufactured 2,200 tablets and sold 2,000. That is a good indication that there is a market for its product. The unit product cost was $300 per tablet. The tablets sold for an average price of $500 (Net Sales Revenue / Units sold = $1,000,000 / 2,000 tablets = $500 per tablet), which is a gross profit of $200 per tablet, or 40% ($200 / $500). After subtracting Selling and Administrative Expenses of $241,000, the Operating Income was $159,000. Expressing the income on a per unit basis, the operating income was $79.50 per tablet, or 15.9% ($159,000 / 2,000 tablets = $79.50 per tablet; $79.50 / $500 = 15.9%). Based on these calculations, management made a good decision!

Try It!

17. ABC Manufacturing Company has the following data for 2017 (amounts in millions):

Raw Materials Inventory, January 1	$ 5
Raw Materials Inventory, December 31	7
Work-in-Process Inventory, January 1	12
Work-in-Process Inventory, December 31	16
Finished Goods Inventory, January 1	8
Finished Goods Inventory, December 31	6
Raw Materials Purchased, including Freight In	25
Direct Labor	36
Manufacturing Overhead	17

Prepare the schedule of cost of goods manufactured and the cost of goods sold section of the income statement for the year ended December 31, 2017.

Check your answer online in MyAccountingLab or at http://www.pearsonhighered.com/Horngren.

For more practice, see Short Exercises S18-10 through S18-12. MyAccountingLab

HOW IS MANAGERIAL ACCOUNTING USED IN SERVICE AND MERCHANDISING COMPANIES?

Learning Objective 5

Calculate cost per service for a service company and cost per item for a merchandising company

The previous two sections of this chapter focused on manufacturing companies, but managerial accounting is used in all types of businesses. We now know how to determine the cost of a manufactured product. Let's see how managerial accounting can be used to calculate costs for service and merchandising companies.

Calculating Cost per Service

Knowing the cost per service helps managers set the price of each service provided. Service companies do not have product costs, so they often consider *all* operating expenses as part of their cost of service. In larger, more advanced service companies, the period costs may be split between service costs and nonservice costs. Let's assume that in 2016, before Smart Touch Learning began buying or manufacturing tablets, the company incurred costs of $3,900 and provided 1,950 e-learning services. What is the cost per service? Use the following formula to calculate the unit cost per service:

Total costs	/	Total number of services provided	=	Unit cost per service
$3,900	/	1,950 services	=	$2 per service

Calculating Cost per Item

Merchandising companies need to know which products are most profitable. Knowing the unit cost per product helps managers set appropriate selling prices. Let's assume that in December 2017, Smart Touch Learning sold 260 tablets that cost $90,800 to purchase (this was before it expanded into manufacturing). What is the cost of each item sold? Use the following formula to calculate the average unit cost per item:

Total cost of goods sold	/	Total number of items sold	=	Unit cost per item
$90,800	/	260 tablets	=	$349.23 per tablet

Note that this further justifies Smart Touch Learning's decision to manufacture the tablets. The company was purchasing the tablets for $349.23 and was able to manufacture them for $300.

18. ABC Cleaning Company cleaned 45 offices and incurred costs of $2,340. What was the cost to clean each office?

Check your answer online in MyAccountingLab or at http://www.pearsonhighered.com/Horngren.

For more practice, see Short Exercise S18-13. MyAccountingLab

REVIEW

> Things You Should Know

1. **Why is managerial accounting important?**

   - Financial accounting prepares reports for external users, such as investors, creditors, and government agencies.

   - Managerial accounting provides information for managers to use in decision making.

   - Managers are accountable to many different stakeholders.

   - Today's business environment requires managers to use many tools to be successful.

   - The IMA Standards of Ethical Professional Practice include competence, confidentiality, integrity, and credibility.

2. **How do service, merchandising, and manufacturing companies differ?**

   - Service companies sell their time, skills, and knowledge. Examples include law firms, car washes, and banks.

   - Merchandising companies buy products from suppliers and resell them. Examples include grocery stores, drug stores, and clothing stores.

   - Merchandising companies have a Merchandise Inventory account.

   - Manufacturing companies convert raw materials into finished goods and then sell the finished goods. Examples include companies that make breakfast cereals, automobiles, and computers.

   - Manufacturing companies have three inventory accounts: Raw Materials Inventory, Work-in-Process Inventory, and Finished Goods Inventory.

3. **How are costs classified?**

   - Product costs are all costs incurred in the manufacture of final products.

   - The three categories of product costs are direct materials, direct labor, and manufacturing overhead.

   - Product costs are first recorded as inventory and are not expensed until the product is sold.

   - Period costs are all costs not considered product costs.

   - Period costs are expensed in the accounting period incurred.

   - Direct costs can be easily traced directly to a cost object, whereas indirect costs cannot.

   - Prime costs are direct materials and direct labor.

   - Conversion costs are direct labor and manufacturing overhead.

4. **How do manufacturing companies determine the cost of manufactured products?**

   - Direct Materials Used = Beginning Raw Materials Inventory + Purchases and Freight In − Ending Raw Materials Inventory.

   - Cost of Goods Manufactured = Beginning Work-in-Process Inventory + Direct Materials Used + Direct Labor + Manufacturing Overhead − Ending Work-in-Process Inventory.

- Cost of Goods Sold = Beginning Finished Goods Inventory + Cost of Goods Manufactured − Ending Finished Goods Inventory.
- Cost of Goods Sold = Number of units sold × Unit product cost.

5. How is managerial accounting used in service and merchandising companies?

- Managerial accounting isn't just for manufacturing companies. Service and merchandising companies also use managerial accounting.
- Unit cost per service = Total costs / Total number of services provided.
- Unit cost per item = Total cost of goods sold / Total number of items sold.

> Summary Problem 18-1

Requirements

1. For a manufacturing company, identify the following as either a product cost or a period cost:
   a. Depreciation on plant equipment
   b. Depreciation on salespersons' automobiles
   c. Insurance on plant building
   d. Marketing manager's salary
   e. Raw materials
   f. Manufacturing overhead
   g. Electricity bill for home office
   h. Production employee wages

2. Show how to compute cost of goods manufactured. Use the following amounts: direct materials used, $24,000; direct labor, $9,000; manufacturing overhead, $17,000; beginning Work-in-Process Inventory, $5,000; and ending Work-in-Process Inventory, $4,000.

3. Using the results from Requirement 2, calculate the cost per unit for goods manufactured assuming 1,000 units were manufactured.

4. Beginning Finished Goods Inventory had 100 units that had a unit cost of $50 each. Ending Finished Goods Inventory has 200 units left. Using the results from Requirement 3, calculate cost of goods sold assuming FIFO inventory costing is used.

> Solution

Requirement 1

Product cost: a, c, e, f, h

Period cost: b, d, g

Requirement 2

Cost of goods manufactured:

Beginning Work-in-Process Inventory		$ 5,000
Direct Materials Used	$ 24,000	
Direct Labor	9,000	
Manufacturing Overhead	17,000	
Total Manufacturing Costs Incurred during Period		50,000
Total Manufacturing Costs to Account For		55,000
Ending Work-in-Process Inventory		(4,000)
Cost of Goods Manufactured		$ 51,000

Requirement 3

Cost of Goods Manufactured	/	Total Units Produced	=	Unit Product Cost
$51,000	/	1,000 units	=	$51 per unit

Requirement 4

Beginning Finished Goods Inventory (100 units × $50 per unit)	$ 5,000
Cost of Goods Manufactured	51,000
Cost of Goods Available for Sale	56,000
Ending Finished Goods Inventory (200 units × $51 per unit)	(10,200)
Cost of Goods Sold [(100 units × $50 per unit) + (800 units × $51 per unit)]	$ 45,800

> Key Terms

Budget (p. 939)

Controlling (p. 939)

Conversion Costs (p. 947)

Cost/Benefit Analysis (p. 940)

Cost Object (p. 946)

Cost of Goods Manufactured (p. 949)

Direct Cost (p. 946)

Direct Labor (DL) (p. 947)

Direct Materials (DM) (p. 947)

Enterprise Resource Planning (ERP) (p. 941)

Finished Goods Inventory (FG) (p. 945)

Indirect Cost (p. 946)

Indirect Labor (p. 947)

Indirect Materials (p. 947)

Just-in-Time (JIT) Management (p. 941)

Management Accountability (p. 940)

Manufacturing Company (p. 945)

Manufacturing Overhead (MOH) (p. 947)

Merchandising Company (p. 944)

Period Cost (p. 943)

Planning (p. 939)

Prime Costs (p. 947)

Product Cost (p. 944)

Raw Materials Inventory (RM) (p. 945)

Service Company (p. 943)

Stakeholder (p. 940)

Total Quality Management (TQM) (p. 941)

Triple Bottom Line (p. 941)

Value Chain (p. 941)

Work-in-Process Inventory (WIP) (p. 945)

> Quick Check

1. Which is *not* a characteristic of managerial accounting information?   **Learning Objective 1**
   a. Emphasizes the external financial statements
   b. Provides detailed information about individual parts of the company
   c. Emphasizes relevance
   d. Focuses on the future

2. World-class businesses use which of these systems to integrate all of a company's   **Learning Objective 1**
   worldwide functions, departments, and data into a single system?
   a. Cost standards   c. Just-in-time management
   b. Enterprise resource planning   d. Items a, b, and c are correct.

3. Today's business environment is characterized by   **Learning Objective 1**
   a. global competition.   c. a shift toward a service economy.
   b. time-based competition.   d. Items a, b, and c are correct.

4. A management accountant who avoids conflicts of interest meets the ethical standard of   **Learning Objective 1**
   a. confidentiality.   c. credibility.
   b. competence.   d. integrity.

5. Which of the following accounts does a manufacturing company have that a service   **Learning Objective 2**
   company does not have?
   a. Advertising Expense   c. Cost of Goods Sold
   b. Salaries Payable   d. Retained Earnings

6. Dunaway Company reports the following costs for the year: **Learning Objective 3**

Direct Materials Used	$ 120,000
Direct Labor Incurred	150,000
Manufacturing Overhead Incurred	75,000
Selling and Administrative Expenses	175,000

   How much are Dunaway's period costs?
   a. $120,000   c. $345,000
   b. $270,000   d. $175,000

7. Which of the following is a direct cost of manufacturing a sport boat?   **Learning Objective 3**
   a. Salary of an engineer who rearranges plant layout
   b. Depreciation on plant and equipment
   c. Cost of the boat engine
   d. Cost of the customer service hotline

8. Which of the following is *not* part of manufacturing overhead for producing a computer?   **Learning Objective 3**
   a. Manufacturing plant property taxes
   b. Manufacturing plant utilities
   c. Depreciation on delivery trucks
   d. Insurance on plant and equipment

CHAPTER 18

Questions 9 and 10 use the data that follow.

Suppose a bakery reports the following information:

Beginning Raw Materials Inventory	$ 6,000
Ending Raw Materials Inventory	5,000
Beginning Work-in-Process Inventory	3,000
Ending Work-in-Process Inventory	2,000
Beginning Finished Goods Inventory	4,000
Ending Finished Goods Inventory	6,000
Direct Labor	29,000
Purchases of Raw Materials	102,000
Manufacturing Overhead	20,000

Learning Objective 4

9. What is the cost of direct materials used?

   a. $101,000   c. $114,000
   b. $103,000   d. $102,000

Learning Objective 4

10. What is the cost of goods manufactured?

    a. $151,000   c. $150,000
    b. $153,000   d. $177,000

Check your answers at the end of the chapter.

ASSESS YOUR PROGRESS

> Review Questions

1. What is the primary purpose of managerial accounting?

2. Explain the difference between planning and controlling.

3. List six differences between financial accounting and managerial accounting.

4. How does managerial accounting assist managers with their responsibilities to the company's stakeholders?

5. List the four IMA standards of ethical practice, and briefly describe each.

6. Describe a service company, and give an example.

7. Describe a merchandising company, and give an example.

8. What are product costs?

9. How do period costs differ from product costs?

10. How do manufacturing companies differ from merchandising companies?

11. List the three inventory accounts used by manufacturing companies, and describe each.

12. How does a manufacturing company calculate cost of goods sold? How is this different from a merchandising company?

13. Explain the difference between a direct cost and an indirect cost.

14. What are the three product costs for a manufacturing company? Describe each.

15. Give five examples of manufacturing overhead.

16. What are prime costs? Conversion costs?

17. How is cost of goods manufactured calculated?

18. How does a manufacturing company calculate unit product cost?

19. How does a service company calculate unit cost per service?

20. How does a merchandising company calculate unit cost per item?

> Short Exercises

S18-1 Comparing managerial accounting and financial accounting

Learning Objective 1

For each of the following, indicate whether the statement relates to managerial accounting (MA) or financial accounting (FA):

a. Helps investors make investment decisions.

b. Provides detailed reports on parts of the company.

c. Helps in planning and controlling operations.

d. Reports must follow Generally Accepted Accounting Principles (GAAP).

e. Reports audited annually by independent certified public accountants.

S18-2 Identifying management accountability and the stakeholders

Learning Objective 1

For each of the following management responsibilities, indicate the primary stakeholder group to whom management is responsible.

1. Providing high-quality, reliable products/services for a reasonable price in a timely manner.

2. Paying taxes in a timely manner.

3. Providing a safe, productive work environment.

4. Generating a profit.

5. Repaying principal plus interest in a timely manner.

a. Investors
b. Creditors
c. Suppliers
d. Employees
e. Customers
f. Government
g. Community

S18-3 Matching business trends terminology

Learning Objective 1

Match the term with the correct definition.

1. A philosophy designed to integrate all organizational areas in order to provide customers with superior products and services while meeting organizational objectives. Requires improving quality and eliminating defects and waste.

2. Use of the Internet for business functions such as sales and customer service. Enables companies to reach customers around the world.

3. Evaluating a company's performance by its economic, social, and environmental impact.

4. Software system that integrates all of a company's functions, departments, and data into a single system.

5. A system in which a company produces products just when they are needed to satisfy needs. Suppliers deliver materials when they are needed to begin production, and finished units are completed at the right time for delivery to customers.

a. ERP
b. JIT
c. E-commerce
d. TQM
e. Triple bottom line

CHAPTER 18

Learning Objective 1

S18-4 Identifying ethical standards

The Institute of Management Accountants' Statement of Ethical Professional Practice requires managerial accountants to meet standards regarding competence, confidentiality, integrity, and credibility. Consider the following situations. Which standard(s) are violated in each situation?

a. You tell your brother that your company will report earnings significantly above financial analysts' estimates.

b. You see others take home office supplies for personal use. As an intern, you do the same thing, assuming that this is a "perk."

c. At a company-paid conference on e-commerce, you skip the afternoon session and go sightseeing.

d. You failed to read the detailed specifications of a new accounting software package that you asked your company to purchase. After it is installed, you are surprised that it is incompatible with some of your company's older accounting software.

e. You do not provide top management with the detailed job descriptions they requested because you fear they may use this information to cut a position in your department.

Learning Objective 2

S18-5 Computing cost of goods sold, merchandising company

Use the following information for The Windshield Pro, a retail merchandiser of auto windshields, to compute the cost of goods sold:

Web Site Maintenance	$ 7,000
Delivery Expense	800
Freight In	2,700
Purchases	40,000
Ending Merchandise Inventory	5,100
Revenues	57,000
Marketing Expenses	10,100
Beginning Merchandise Inventory	8,200

Learning Objective 2

S18-6 Computing cost of goods sold and operating income, merchandising company

Consider the following partially completed income statements for merchandising companies and compute the missing amounts:

	Jones, Inc.	Corrigan, Inc.
Sales	$ 99,000	$ (d)
Cost of Goods Sold:		
Beginning Merchandise Inventory	(a)	29,000
Purchases and Freight In	50,000	(e)
Cost of Goods Available for Sale	(b)	92,000
Ending Merchandise Inventory	(2,100)	(2,100)
Cost of Goods Sold	63,000	(f)
Gross Profit	36,000	115,000
Selling and Administrative Expenses	(c)	86,000
Operating Income	$ 13,000	$ (g)

S18-7 Distinguishing between direct and indirect costs

Learning Objective 3

Granger Cards is a manufacturer of greeting cards. Classify its costs by matching the costs to the terms.

1. Direct materials	**a.** Artists' wages
2. Direct labor	**b.** Wages of materials warehouse workers
3. Indirect materials	**c.** Paper
4. Indirect labor	**d.** Depreciation on manufacturing equipment
5. Other manufacturing overhead	**e.** Manufacturing plant manager's salary
	f. Property taxes on manufacturing plant
	g. Glue for envelopes

S18-8 Computing manufacturing overhead

Learning Objective 3

Glass Doctor Company manufactures sunglasses. Following is a list of costs the company incurred during May. Use the list to calculate the total manufacturing overhead costs for the month.

Glue for frames	$ 200
Depreciation on company cars used by sales force	3,500
Plant depreciation	6,000
Interest Expense	1,500
Lenses	49,000
Company president's salary	26,000
Plant foreman's salary	3,000
Plant janitor's wages	1,100
Oil for manufacturing equipment	150

S18-9 Identifying product costs and period costs

Learning Objective 3

Classify each cost of a paper manufacturer as either product cost or period cost:

a. Salaries of scientists studying ways to speed forest growth.

b. Cost of computer software to track WIP Inventory.

c. Cost of electricity at the paper mill.

d. Salaries of the company's top executives.

e. Cost of chemicals to treat the paper.

f. Cost of TV ads.

g. Depreciation on the manufacturing plant.

h. Cost to purchase wood pulp.

i. Life insurance on the CEO.

CHAPTER 18

Learning Objective 4

S18-10 Computing direct materials used

Lazio, Inc. has compiled the following data:

Purchases of Raw Materials	$ 6,600
Freight In	500
Property Taxes	1,200
Ending Inventory of Raw Materials	1,300
Beginning Inventory of Raw Materials	3,700

Assume all materials used are direct materials (none are indirect). Compute the amount of direct materials used.

Learning Objective 4

S18-11 Computing cost of goods manufactured

Use the following inventory data for Slicing Golf Company to compute the cost of goods manufactured for the year:

Direct Materials Used	$ 12,000
Manufacturing Overhead	22,000
Work-in-Process Inventory:	
Beginning	7,000
Ending	5,000
Direct Labor	13,000
Finished Goods Inventory:	
Beginning	19,000
Ending	15,000

Learning Objective 4

S18-12 Computing cost of goods sold, manufacturing company

Use the following information to calculate the cost of goods sold for The Eaton Company for the month of June:

Finished Goods Inventory:	
Beginning Balance	$ 32,000
Ending Balance	17,000
Cost of Goods Manufactured	160,000

Learning Objective 5

S18-13 Calculating unit cost per service

Knots and Reynolds provides hair-cutting services in the local community. In February, the business cut the hair of 240 clients, earned $4,900 in revenues, and incurred the following operating costs:

Hair Supplies Expense	$ 375
Wages Expense	1,321
Utilities Expense	150
Depreciation Expense—Equipment	50

What was the cost of service to provide one haircut?

> Exercises

E18-14 Comparing managerial accounting and financial accounting

Learning Objective 1

Match the following terms to the appropriate statement. Some terms may be used more than once, and some terms may not be used at all.

Budget	Managerial
Creditors	Managers
Controlling	Planning
Financial	Stockholders

a. Accounting systems that must follow GAAP.

b. External parties for whom financial accounting reports are prepared.

c. The role managers play when they are comparing the company's actual results with the planned results.

d. Internal decision makers.

e. Accounting system that provides information on a company's past performance.

f. Accounting system not restricted by GAAP but chosen by comparing the costs versus the benefits of the system.

g. The management function that involves choosing goals and the means to achieve them.

E18-15 Understanding today's business environment

Learning Objective 1

Match the following terms to the appropriate statement. Some terms may be used more than once, and some terms may not be used at all.

E-commerce	Just-in-time management (JIT)
Enterprise resource planning (ERP)	Total quality management (TQM)

a. A management system that focuses on maintaining lean inventories while producing products as needed by the customer.

b. A philosophy designed to integrate all organizational areas in order to provide customers with superior products and services while meeting organizational objectives.

c. Integrates all of a company's functions, departments, and data into a single system.

d. Adopted by firms to conduct business on the Internet.

E18-16 Making ethical decisions

Learning Objective 1

Sue Peters is the controller at Vroom, a car dealership. Dale Miller recently has been hired as the bookkeeper. Dale wanted to attend a class in Excel spreadsheets, so Sue temporarily took over Dale's duties, including overseeing a fund used for gas purchases before test drives. Sue found a shortage in the fund and confronted Dale when he returned to work. Dale admitted that he occasionally uses the fund to pay for his own gas. Sue estimated the shortage at $450.

Requirements

1. What should Sue Peters do?
2. Would you change your answer if Sue Peters was the one recently hired as controller and Dale Miller was a well-liked, longtime employee who indicated he always eventually repaid the fund?

Use the following data for Exercises E18-17, E18-18, and E18-19.

Selected data for three companies are given below. All inventory amounts are ending balances and all amounts are in millions.

Company A		Company B		Company C	
Cash	$ 5	Wages Expense	$ 16	Administrative Expenses	$ 5
Sales Revenue	28	Equipment	35	Cash	27
Finished Goods Inventory	1	Accounts Receivable	6	Sales Revenue	28
Cost of Goods Sold	21	Service Revenue	54	Selling Expenses	2
Selling Expenses	2	Cash	14	Merchandise Inventory	8
Equipment	68	Rent Expense	9	Equipment	52
Work-in-Process Inventory	1			Accounts Receivable	16
Accounts Receivable	6			Cost of Goods Sold	16
Cost of Goods Manufactured	20				
Administrative Expenses	1				
Raw Materials Inventory	10				

Learning Objective 2

E18-17 Identifying differences between service, merchandising, and manufacturing companies

Using the above data, determine the company type. Identify each company as a service company, merchandising company, or manufacturing company.

Learning Objective 2

Company B: $29

E18-18 Identifying differences between service, merchandising, and manufacturing companies

Using the above data, calculate operating income for each company.

Learning Objective 2

Company C: $51

E18-19 Identifying differences between service, merchandising, and manufacturing companies

Using the above data, calculate total current assets for each company.

E18-20 Classifying costs

Learning Objective 3

Wheels, Inc. manufactures wheels for bicycles, tricycles, and scooters. For each cost given below, determine if the cost is a product cost or a period cost. If the cost is a product cost, further determine if the cost is direct materials (DM), direct labor (DL), or manufacturing overhead (MOH) and then determine if the product cost is a prime cost, conversion cost, or both. If the cost is a period cost, further determine if the cost is a selling expense or administrative expense (Admin). *Cost (a) is answered as a guide.*

Cost	Product					Period	
	DM	DL	MOH	Prime	Conversion	Selling	Admin.
a. *Metal used for rims*	X			X			
b. Sales salaries							
c. Rent on factory							
d. Wages of assembly workers							
e. Salary of production supervisor							
f. Depreciation on office equipment							
g. Salary of CEO							
h. Delivery expense							

E18-21 Computing cost of goods manufactured

Learning Objective 4

Consider the following partially completed schedules of cost of goods manufactured. Compute the missing amounts.

	Baker, Inc.	Lawson's Bakery	Outdoor Gear
Beginning Work-in-Process Inventory	$ (a)	$ 40,200	$ 2,600
Direct Materials Used	14,800	35,400	(g)
Direct Labor	10,100	20,000	1,800
Manufacturing Overhead	(b)	10,300	600
Total Manufacturing Costs Incurred during the Year	45,100	(d)	(h)
Total Manufacturing Costs to Account For	55,300	(e)	8,200
Ending Work-in-Process Inventory	(c)	(25,800)	(2,000)
Cost of Goods Manufactured	$ 50,800	$ (f)	$ (i)

CHAPTER 18

Learning Objective 4

1. COGM: $427,000

(Requirement 1 only)

E18-22 Preparing a schedule of cost of goods manufactured

Clarkson Corp., a lamp manufacturer, provided the following information for the year ended December 31, 2016:

Inventories:	Beginning	Ending
Raw Materials	$ 58,000	$ 22,000
Work-in-Process	100,000	63,000
Finished Goods	47,000	51,000

Other information:	
Depreciation, plant building and equipment	$ 13,000
Raw materials purchases	157,000
Insurance on plant	21,000
Sales salaries	46,000
Repairs and maintenance—plant	4,000
Indirect labor	30,000
Direct labor	129,000
Administrative expenses	56,000

Requirements

1. Use the information to prepare a schedule of cost of goods manufactured.
2. What is the unit product cost if Clarkson manufactured 2,135 lamps for the year?

Learning Objective 4

COGM: $204,000

E18-23 Computing cost of goods manufactured and cost of goods sold

Use the following information for a manufacturer to compute cost of goods manufactured and cost of goods sold:

Inventories:	Beginning	Ending
Raw Materials	$ 20,000	$ 26,000
Work-in-Process	38,000	34,000
Finished Goods	14,000	22,000

Other information:	
Purchases of materials	$ 75,000
Direct labor	89,000
Manufacturing overhead	42,000

E18-24 Calculating income and cost per service for a service company

One Stop Grooming provides grooming services for pets. In April, the company earned $16,000 in revenues and incurred the following operating costs to groom 600 dogs:

Wages Expense	$ 3,900
Grooming Supplies Expense	1,730
Building Rent Expense	1,000
Utilities Expense	285
Depreciation Expense—Equipment	105

Requirements

1. What is One Stop's net income for April?
2. What is the cost of service to groom one dog?

E18-25 Calculating income and cost per unit for a merchandising company

White Brush Company sells standard hair brushes. The following information summarizes White's operating activities for 2016:

Selling and Administrative Expenses	$ 34,020
Purchases	65,880
Sales Revenue	97,200
Merchandise Inventory, January 1, 2016	8,100
Merchandise Inventory, December 31, 2016	23,436

Requirements

1. Calculate the operating income for 2016.
2. White sold 5,400 brushes in 2016. Compute the unit cost for one brush.

> Problems Group A

P18-26A Applying ethical standards, management accountability

Natalia Wallace is the new controller for Smart Software, Inc. which develops and sells education software. Shortly before the December 31 fiscal year-end, James Cauvet, the company president, asks Wallace how things look for the year-end numbers. He is not happy to learn that earnings growth may be below 13% for the first time in the company's five-year history. Cauvet explains that financial analysts have again predicted a 13% earnings growth for the company and that he does not intend to disappoint them. He suggests that Wallace talk to the assistant controller, who can explain how the previous controller dealt with such situations. The assistant controller suggests the following strategies:

a. Persuade suppliers to postpone billing $13,000 in invoices until January 1.

b. Record as sales $115,000 in certain software awaiting sale that is held in a public warehouse.

c. Delay the year-end closing a few days into January of the next year so that some of the next year's sales are included in this year's sales.

d. Reduce the estimated Bad Debts Expense from 5% of Sales Revenue to 3%, given the company's continued strong performance.

e. Postpone routine monthly maintenance expenditures from December to January.

Requirements

1. Which of these suggested strategies are inconsistent with IMA standards?

2. How might these inconsistencies affect the company's stakeholders?

3. What should Wallace do if Cauvet insists that she follow all of these suggestions?

Learning Objective 3

P18-27A Classifying period costs and product costs

Lawlor, Inc. is the manufacturer of lawn care equipment. The company incurs the following costs while manufacturing weed trimmers:

- Shaft and handle of weed trimmer
- Motor of weed trimmer
- Factory labor for workers assembling weed trimmers
- Nylon thread used by the weed trimmer (not traced to the product)
- Glue to hold the housing together
- Plant janitorial wages
- Depreciation on factory equipment
- Rent on plant
- Sales commissions
- Administrative salaries
- Plant utilities
- Shipping costs to deliver finished weed trimmers to customers

Requirements

1. Describe the difference between period costs and product costs.

2. Classify Lawlor's costs as period costs or product costs. If the costs are product costs, further classify them as direct materials, direct labor, or manufacturing overhead.

Learning Objectives 2, 4, 5

3. Company B: $218,600

P18-28A Calculating cost of goods sold for merchandising and manufacturing companies

Below are data for two companies:

	Company A	Company B
Beginning balances:		
Merchandise Inventory	$ 10,400	
Finished Goods Inventory		$ 16,200
Ending balances:		
Merchandise Inventory	12,900	
Finished Goods Inventory		12,100
Net Purchases	158,000	
Cost of Goods Manufactured		214,500

Requirements

1. Define the three business types: service, merchandising, and manufacturing.

2. Based on the data given for the two companies, determine the business type of each one.

3. Calculate the cost of goods sold for each company.

P18-29A Preparing an income statement and calculating unit cost for a service company

Sandman repairs chips in car windshields. The company incurred the following operating costs for the month of February 2016:

Salaries and wages	$ 6,000
Windshield repair materials	4,500
Depreciation on truck	250
Depreciation on building and equipment	600
Supplies used	500
Utilities	2,180

Sandman earned $27,000 in revenues for the month of February by repairing 200 windshields. All costs shown are considered to be directly related to the repair service.

Requirements

1. Prepare an income statement for the month of February.

2. Compute the cost per unit of repairing one windshield.

3. The manager of Sandman must keep unit operating cost below $60 per windshield in order to get his bonus. Did he meet the goal?

P18-30A Preparing an income statement and calculating unit cost for a merchandising company

Cam Smith owns Cam's Pets, a small retail shop selling pet supplies. On December 31, 2016, the accounting records of Cam's Pets showed the following:

Inventory on December 31, 2016	$ 10,400
Inventory on January 1, 2016	15,100
Sales Revenue	58,000
Utilities Expense for the shop	3,700
Rent for the shop	4,900
Sales Commissions	2,950
Purchases of Merchandise Inventory	29,000

Requirements

1. Prepare an income statement for Cam's Pets for the year ended December 31, 2016.

2. Cam's Pets sold 5,450 units. Determine the unit cost of the merchandise sold, rounded to the nearest cent.

Learning Objectives 2, 5

2. $70.15

Learning Objectives 2, 5

1. Net income: $12,750

CHAPTER 18

Learning Objectives 2, 4

2. Net income: $34,900

P18-31A Preparing a schedule of cost of goods manufactured and an income statement for a manufacturing company

Yum Yum Treats manufactures its own brand of pet chew bones. At the end of December 2016, the accounting records showed the following:

Inventories:	Beginning	Ending
Raw Materials	$ 13,100	$ 8,500
Work-in-Process	0	2,500
Finished Goods	0	5,700

Other information:	
Raw materials purchases	$ 30,000
Plant janitorial services	800
Sales salaries	5,000
Delivery costs	1,800
Sales revenue	105,000
Utilities for plant	1,100
Rent on plant	16,000
Customer service hotline costs	1,000
Direct labor	18,000

Requirements

1. Prepare a schedule of cost of goods manufactured for Yum Yum Treats for the year ended December 31, 2016.

2. Prepare an income statement for Yum Yum Treats for the year ended December 31, 2016.

3. How does the format of the income statement for Yum Yum Treats differ from the income statement of a merchandiser?

4. Yum Yum Treats manufactured 17,600 units of its product in 2016. Compute the company's unit product cost for the year, rounded to the nearest cent.

P18-32A Preparing a schedule of cost of goods manufactured and an income statement for a manufacturing company

Certain item descriptions and amounts are missing from the monthly schedule of cost of goods manufactured and income statement of Chili Manufacturing Company. Fill in the blanks with the missing words, and replace the Xs with the correct amounts.

CHILI MANUFACTURING COMPANY		
_____ June 30, 2016		
Beginning _____		$ 21,000
Direct _____ :		
Beginning Raw Materials Inventory	$ X	
Purchases of Raw Materials	58,000	
_____	84,000	
Ending Raw Materials Inventory	(24,000)	
Direct _____	$ X	
Direct _____	X	
Manufacturing Overhead	40,000	
Total _____ Costs _____		171,000
Total _____ Costs _____		X
Ending _____		(23,000)
_____		$ X

CHILI MANUFACTURING COMPANY		
_____ June 30, 2016		
Sales Revenue		$ X
Cost of Goods Sold:		
Beginning _____	$ 112,000	
_____	X	
Cost of Goods _____	X	
Ending _____	X	
Cost of Goods Sold		212,000
Gross Profit		298,000
_____ Expenses:		
Selling Expenses	95,000	
Administrative Expenses	X	
Total _____		156,000
_____ Income		$ X

P18-33A Determining flow of costs through a manufacturer's inventory accounts

West Shoe Company makes loafers. During the most recent year, West incurred total manufacturing costs of $19,600,000. Of this amount, $2,700,000 was direct materials used and $12,800,000 was direct labor. Beginning balances for the year were Raw Materials

Inventory, $500,000; Work-in-Process Inventory, $800,000; and Finished Goods Inventory, $500,000. At the end of the year, balances were Raw Materials Inventory, $700,000; Work-in-Process Inventory, $1,600,000; and Finished Goods Inventory, $620,000.

Requirements

Analyze the inventory accounts to determine:

1. Cost of raw materials purchased during the year.
2. Cost of goods manufactured for the year.
3. Cost of goods sold for the year.

> Problems **Group B**

Learning Objective 1

P18-34B Applying ethical standards, management accountability

Ava Borzi is the new controller for Halo Software, Inc. which develops and sells education software. Shortly before the December 31 fiscal year-end, Jeremy Busch, the company president, asks Borzi how things look for the year-end numbers. He is not happy to learn that earnings growth may be below 9% for the first time in the company's five-year history. Busch explains that financial analysts have again predicted a 9% earnings growth for the company and that he does not intend to disappoint them. He suggests that Borzi talk to the assistant controller, who can explain how the previous controller dealt with such situations. The assistant controller suggests the following strategies:

a. Persuade suppliers to postpone billing $18,000 in invoices until January 1.

b. Record as sales $120,000 in certain software awaiting sale that is held in a public warehouse.

c. Delay the year-end closing a few days into January of the next year so that some of the next year's sales are included in this year's sales.

d. Reduce the estimated Bad Debts Expense from 3% of Sales Revenue to 2%, given the company's continued strong performance.

e. Postpone routine monthly maintenance expenditures from December to January.

Requirements

1. Which of these suggested strategies are inconsistent with IMA standards?
2. How might these inconsistencies affect the company's stakeholders?
3. What should Borzi do if Busch insists that she follow all of these suggestions?

Learning Objective 3

P18-35B Classifying period costs and product costs

Langley, Inc. is the manufacturer of lawn care equipment. The company incurs the following costs while manufacturing edgers:

- Handle and shaft of edger
- Motor of edger
- Factory labor for workers assembling edgers
- Lubricant used on bearings in the edger (not traced to the product)
- Glue to hold the housing together
- Plant janitorial wages
- Depreciation on factory equipment
- Rent on plant
- Sales commissions
- Administrative salaries
- Plant utilities
- Shipping costs to deliver finished edgers to customers

Requirements

1. Describe the difference between period costs and product costs.

2. Classify Langley's costs as period costs or product costs. If the costs are product costs, further classify them as direct materials, direct labor, or manufacturing overhead.

P18-36B Calculating cost of goods sold for merchandising and manufacturing companies

Learning Objectives 2, 4, 5

3. Company 2: $216,500

Below are data for two companies:

	Company 1	Company 2
Beginning balances:		
Merchandise Inventory	$ 10,800	
Finished Goods Inventory		$ 15,800
Ending balances:		
Merchandise Inventory	12,300	
Finished Goods Inventory		11,300
Net Purchases	153,500	
Cost of Goods Manufactured		212,000

Requirements

1. Define the three business types: service, merchandising, and manufacturing.

2. Based on the data given for the two companies, determine the business type of each one.

3. Calculate the cost of goods sold for each company.

P18-37B Preparing an income statement and calculating unit cost for a service company

Learning Objectives 2, 5

2. $166.40

The Windshield Doctors repair chips in car windshields. The company incurred the following operating costs for the month of July 2016:

Salaries and wages	$ 7,000
Windshield repair materials	4,200
Depreciation on truck	450
Depreciation on building and equipment	1,200
Supplies used	300
Utilities	3,490

The Windshield Doctors earned $26,000 in revenues for the month of July by repairing 100 windshields. All costs shown are considered to be directly related to the repair service.

Requirements

1. Prepare an income statement for the month of July.

2. Compute the cost per unit of repairing one windshield, rounded to the nearest cent.

3. The manager of The Windshield Doctors must keep unit operating cost below $150 per windshield in order to get his bonus. Did he meet the goal?

CHAPTER 18

Learning Objectives 2, 5

1. Net income: $13,300

P18-38B Preparing an income statement and calculating unit cost for a merchandising company

Clyde Synder owns Clyde's Pets, a small retail shop selling pet supplies. On December 31, 2016, the accounting records for Clyde's Pets showed the following:

Inventory on December 31, 2016	$ 10,250
Inventory on January 1, 2016	15,400
Sales Revenue	58,000
Utilities Expense for the shop	3,100
Rent for the shop	4,700
Sales Commissions	2,750
Purchases of Merchandise Inventory	29,000

Requirements

1. Prepare an income statement for Clyde's Pets for the year ended December 31, 2016.
2. Clyde's Pets sold 3,200 units. Determine the unit cost of the merchandise sold, rounded to the nearest cent.

Learning Objectives 2, 4

2. Net income: $43,000

P18-39B Preparing a schedule of cost of goods manufactured and an income statement for a manufacturing company

Organic Bones manufactures its own brand of pet chew bones. At the end of December 2016, the accounting records showed the following:

Inventories:	Beginning	Ending
Raw Materials	$ 13,100	$ 9,000
Work-in-Process	0	3,500
Finished Goods	0	5,800

Other information:	
Raw materials purchases	$ 30,000
Plant janitorial services	400
Sales salaries	5,200
Delivery costs	1,900
Sales revenue	114,000
Utilities for plant	1,700
Rent on plant	15,000
Customer service hotline costs	1,000
Direct labor	21,000

Requirements

1. Prepare a schedule of cost of goods manufactured for Organic Bones for the year ended December 31, 2016.
2. Prepare an income statement for Organic Bones for the year ended December 31, 2016.

3. How does the format of the income statement for Organic Bones differ from the income statement of a merchandiser?

4. Organic Bones manufactured 17,400 units of its product in 2016. Compute the company's unit product cost for the year, rounded to the nearest cent.

P18-40B Preparing a schedule of cost of goods manufactured and an income statement for a manufacturing company

Learning Objectives 2, 4

COGM: $191,000

Certain item descriptions and amounts are missing from the monthly schedule of cost of goods manufactured and income statement of Maria Manufacturing Company. Fill in the blanks with the missing words, and replace the Xs with the correct amounts.

MARIA MANUFACTURING COMPANY		
_____ June 30, 2016		
Beginning _____		$ 29,000
Direct _____ :		
Beginning Raw Materials Inventory	$ X	
Purchases of Raw Materials	56,000	
_____	81,000	
Ending Raw Materials Inventory	(21,000)	
Direct _____	$ X	
Direct _____	X	
Manufacturing Overhead	49,000	
Total _____ Costs _____		184,000
Total _____ Costs _____		X
Ending _____		(22,000)
_____		$ X

MARIA MANUFACTURING COMPANY		
_____ June 30, 2016		
Sales Revenue		$ X
Cost of Goods Sold:		
Beginning _____	$ 116,000	
_____	X	
Cost of Goods _____	X	
Ending _____	X	
Cost of Goods Sold		241,000
Gross Profit		229,000
_____ Expenses:		
Selling Expenses	98,000	
Administrative Expenses	X	
Total _____		165,000
_____ Income		$ X

Learning Objective 4

3. $23,670,000

P18-41B Determining the flow of costs through a manufacturer's inventory accounts

Best Shoe Company makes loafers. During the most recent year, Best incurred total manufacturing costs of $24,300,000. Of this amount, $2,200,000 was direct materials used and $17,800,000 was direct labor. Beginning balances for the year were Raw Materials Inventory, $700,000; Work-in-Process Inventory, $900,000; and Finished Goods Inventory, $900,000. At the end of the year, balances were Raw Materials Inventory, $900,000; Work-in-Process Inventory, $1,700,000; and Finished Goods Inventory, $730,000.

Requirements

Analyze the inventory accounts to determine:

1. Cost of raw materials purchased during the year.
2. Cost of goods manufactured for the year.
3. Cost of goods sold for the year.

> Continuing Problem

Problem P18-42 is the first problem in a sequence of problems for Daniels Consulting. This company was also used for the Continuing Problems in the financial accounting chapters as the business evolved from a service company to a merchandising company. However, it is not necessary to complete those problems prior to completing P18-42.

P18-42

Daniels Consulting is going to manufacture billing software. During its first month of manufacturing, Daniels incurred the following manufacturing costs:

Inventories:	Beginning	Ending
Raw Materials	$ 10,800	$ 9,600
Work-in-Process	0	23,000
Finished Goods	0	29,000
Other information:		
Raw materials purchases		$ 18,000
Plant janitorial services		200
Sales salaries expense		7,000
Delivery expense		1,100
Sales revenue		1,075,000
Utilities for plant		11,000
Rent on plant		12,000
Customer service hotline costs		12,000
Direct labor		200,000

Prepare a schedule of cost of goods manufactured for Daniels for the month ended January 31, 2018.

CRITICAL THINKING

> Decision Case 18-1

PowerSwitch, Inc. designs and manufactures switches used in telecommunications. Serious flooding throughout North Carolina affected Power Switch's facilities. Inventory was completely ruined, and the company's computer system, including all accounting records, was destroyed.

Before the disaster recovery specialists clean the buildings, Stephen Plum, the company controller, is anxious to salvage whatever records he can to support an insurance claim for the destroyed inventory. He is standing in what is left of the accounting department with Paul Lopez, the cost accountant.

"I didn't know mud could smell so bad," Paul says. "What should I be looking for?"

"Don't worry about beginning inventory numbers," responds Stephen, "we'll get them from last year's annual report. We need first-quarter cost data."

"I was working on the first-quarter results just before the storm hit," Paul says. "Look, my report is still in my desk drawer. All I can make out is that for the first quarter, material purchases were $476,000 and direct labor, manufacturing overhead, and total manufacturing costs to account for were $505,000, $245,000, and $1,425,000, respectively. Wait! Cost of goods available for sale was $1,340,000."

"Great," says Stephen. "I remember that sales for the period were approximately $1,700,000. Given our gross profit of 30%, that's all you should need."

Paul is not sure about that but decides to see what he can do with this information. The beginning inventory numbers were:

- Raw Materials, $113,000
- Work-in-Process, $229,000
- Finished Goods, $154,000

Requirements

1. Prepare a schedule showing each inventory account and the increases and decreases to each account. Use it to determine the ending inventories of Raw Materials, Work-in-Process, and Finished Goods.

2. Itemize a list of the cost of inventory lost.

> Ethical Issue 18-1

Becky Knauer recently resigned from her position as controller for Shamalay Automotive, a small, struggling foreign car dealer in Upper Saddle River, New Jersey. Becky has just started a new job as controller for Mueller Imports, a much larger dealer for the same car manufacturer. Demand for this particular make of car is exploding, and the manufacturer cannot produce enough to satisfy demand. The manufacturer's regional sales managers are each given a certain number of cars. Each sales manager then decides how to divide the cars among the independently owned dealerships in the region. Because of high demand for these cars, dealerships all want to receive as many cars as they can from the regional sales manager.

Becky's former employer, Shamalay Automotive, receives only about 25 cars each month. Consequently, Shamalay is not very profitable.

Becky is surprised to learn that her new employer, Mueller Imports, receives more than 200 cars each month. Becky soon gets another surprise. Every couple of months, a local jeweler bills the dealer $5,000 for "miscellaneous services." Franz Mueller, the owner of the dealership, personally approves payment of these invoices, noting that each invoice is a "selling expense." From casual conversations with a salesperson, Becky learns that Mueller frequently gives Rolex watches to the manufacturer's regional sales manager and other sales executives. Before talking to anyone about this, Becky decides to work through her ethical dilemma. Put yourself in Becky's place.

Requirements

1. What is the ethical issue?
2. What are your options?
3. What are the possible consequences?
4. What should you do?

> Communication Activity 18-1

In 100 words or fewer, explain the difference between product costs and period costs. In your explanation, explain the inventory accounts of a manufacturer.

MyAccountingLab   For a wealth of online resources, including exercises, problems, media, and immediate tutorial help, please visit http://www.myaccountinglab.com.

> Quick Check Answers

1. a   **2.** b   **3.** d   **4.** d   **5.** c   **6.** d   **7.** c   **8.** c   **9.** b   **10.** b

Job Order Costing 19

Why Are We Losing Clients?

Melinda Duncan is deep in thought. Melinda works for a regional accounting firm. A major part of the business is in the audit field, and Melinda really enjoys the work. She likes getting out of the office and going to the clients' locations. She thinks audits are like puzzles and finds it challenging to put the pieces together. Recently her firm has lost clients to a competitor that is charging lower audit fees. Melinda is considering the situation and has lots of questions. Does Melinda's company need to lower its fees to stay competitive? If the company drops its fees, will it remain profitable?

Melinda knows the amount charged for an audit has to cover the cost of providing the service. The largest cost associated with an audit is the accountants' salaries. But the company has other salaries that have to be covered, too—for example, the salaries of the support staff at the office. There are other costs involved in running the office as well, including utilities, supplies, and office equipment. Before the accounting firm can make a decision about lowering the fees charged to clients, it must first determine an accurate cost of providing the service. How can the firm determine the full cost of an audit job? Accounting firms can use a *job order costing system* to track the cost of providing each service to clients and then use the information to make pricing decisions.

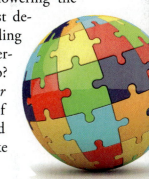

What Does It Really Cost?

All companies need to know the cost of their products and services. Major CPA firms such as KPMG LLP track the costs associated with providing services to each client. Some costs are easy to determine. The accountants can record hours worked on an audit to determine the direct labor cost. But other costs, such as support staff salaries, office rent, and office equipment depreciation, are indirect costs and cannot be easily traced to a job. This chapter shows how manufacturing and service companies determine the cost of their products and services.

Chapter 19 Learning Objectives

1   Distinguish between job order costing and process costing

2   Record materials and labor costs in a job order costing system

3   Calculate the predetermined overhead allocation rate and allocate overhead costs

4   Record the completion and sales of finished goods

5   Adjust for overallocated and underallocated overhead

6   Calculate job costs for a service company

HOW DO MANUFACTURING COMPANIES USE JOB ORDER AND PROCESS COSTING SYSTEMS?

Learning Objective 1

Distinguish between job order costing and process costing

Cost accounting systems are used to *accumulate* product cost information so that managers can measure how much it costs to produce each unit of product. Knowing these unit costs helps managers do the following:

- Set selling prices that will lead to profits.
- Compute cost of goods sold for the income statement.
- Compute the cost of inventory for the balance sheet.

Remember that a manager's primary duties include planning and controlling. If a manager knows the cost to produce each unit of product, then the manager can plan and control the cost of resources needed to create the product and deliver it to the customer. A cost accounting system is a tool that managers use to help make planning and controlling decisions. Exhibit 19-1 gives some examples of unit product and service costs managers may want to calculate.

As you can see from Exhibit 19-1, cost accounting systems are not just for manufacturing companies. All businesses need to know the cost of their products or services.

There are two main types of traditional cost accounting systems: job order costing and process costing. This chapter concentrates on job order costing; process costing is covered in the next chapter. But before we begin our study of job order costing, you need to understand the differences between the two systems.

Exhibit 19-1 | **Examples of Unit Costs**

Managers of a(n)	Need to know the cost to
Fast food restaurant	Make a cheeseburger
Freight service	Transport a pound of freight for a mile
Automobile manufacturer	Make a car
Construction firm	Build a house
Accounting firm	Prepare a tax return

Job Order Costing

Some companies manufacture batches of *unique products* or provide *specialized services*. A **job order costing system** accumulates costs for each unique batch, or **job**. Accounting firms, music studios, health care providers, building contractors, and custom furniture manufacturers are examples of companies that use job order costing systems. As we move to a more service-based economy and with the increased use of enterprise resource planning (ERP) systems, job order costing has become more prevalent because the software allows companies to track costs more efficiently. The benefit of knowing more detailed cost information outweighs the cost of obtaining the information through the ERP system.

Job Order Costing System
An accounting system that accumulates costs by job. Used by companies that manufacture unique products or provide specialized services.

Process Costing

Other companies produce *identical units* through a series of production steps or processes. A **process costing system** accumulates the costs of each *process* needed to complete the product. For example, a soft drink company's processes may include mixing, bottling, and packaging. A surfboard manufacturing company's processes may include sanding, painting, waxing, and packaging. A medical equipment manufacturer of a blood glucose meter may have processes that include soldering, assembling, and testing. Process costing is used primarily by companies that produce large quantities of similar products.

Both job order and process costing systems use a four-step method to track product costs: *accumulate, assign, allocate,* and *adjust.* Look for the four steps as we track the product costs through the inventory accounts on the balance sheet to Cost of Goods Sold on the income statement.

Job
The production of a unique product or specialized service. May be one unit or a batch of units.

Process Costing System
An accounting system that accumulates costs by process. Used by companies that manufacture identical units through a series of uniform production steps or processes.

Would the following companies most likely use a job order costing system or a process costing system?

1. Paint manufacturer
2. Print shop
3. Caterer
4. Soft drink bottler
5. Yacht builder

Check your answers online in MyAccountingLab or at http://www.pearsonhighered.com/Horngren.

For more practice, see Short Exercise S19-1. MyAccountingLab

HOW DO MATERIALS AND LABOR COSTS FLOW THROUGH THE JOB ORDER COSTING SYSTEM?

A job order costing system tracks costs as raw materials move from the storeroom to the production floor, where they are converted into finished products. Let's consider how a manufacturer uses job order costing. To illustrate the process, we will use our fictitious company, Smart Touch Learning. Remember that Smart Touch Learning manufactures touch screen tablet computers that are preloaded with its e-learning software programs. Most customers order a batch of customized tablets, and the company considers each customer order as a separate job (batch). Smart Touch Learning uses a **job cost record** to document the product costs for each job: direct materials, direct labor, and manufacturing overhead.

Learning Objective 2
Record materials and labor costs in a job order costing system

Job Cost Record
A document that shows the direct materials, direct labor, and manufacturing overhead costs for an individual job.

The company starts the job cost record when work begins on the job. As Smart Touch Learning incurs costs, the company adds costs to the job cost record, and the costs are added to the Work-in-Process Inventory (WIP). When Smart Touch Learning finishes a job, the company totals the costs and transfers the costs from Work-in-Process Inventory to Finished Goods Inventory (FG). The costs transferred to Finished Goods Inventory are called Cost of Goods Manufactured.

When the job's units are sold, the costing system moves the costs from Finished Goods Inventory, an asset, to Cost of Goods Sold (COGS), an expense. Exhibit 19-2 diagrams the flow of costs for three jobs at Smart Touch Learning.

Exhibit 19-2 indicates that Smart Touch Learning worked on three jobs during the accounting period: Job 27, Job 28, and Job 29. Jobs 27 and 28 were completed, and their costs were transferred from WIP to FG. Job 27 was delivered to the customer, so those costs were transferred from FG to COGS.

Exhibit 19-2 | **Flow of Product Costs in Job Order Costing**

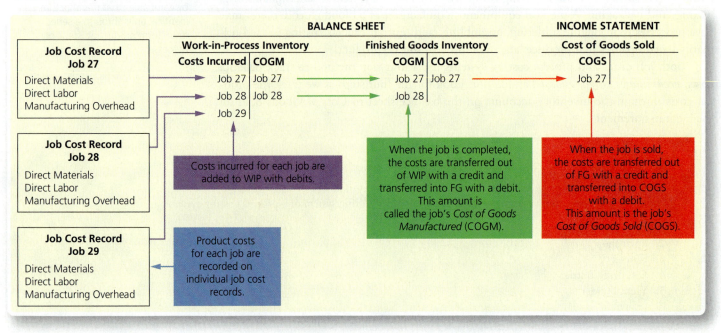

The ending balance in WIP is the cost of Job 29, the only job that is not complete and still in process at the end of the period. The ending balance in FG is the cost of Job 28, the only job that was completed but still not delivered to the customer. The ending balance in COGS is the cost of Job 27, the only job completed and sold during the period. These balances can be verified by comparing the balances in the general ledger accounts with the job cost records.

The next sections of the chapter show the cost flow in more detail. We will use Job 27 as an example. On December 31, 2017, Smart Touch Learning had the following inventory balances:

Raw Materials Inventory	Work-in-Process Inventory	Finished Goods Inventory
Bal. 70,000	Bal. 80,000	Bal. 0

Materials

There are two aspects to accounting for raw materials: purchasing materials and using materials in production. Because raw materials do not have to be used immediately when purchased and can be stored for later use, materials purchased and materials used in production are usually two different amounts. This is what creates an ending balance in the Raw Materials Inventory account. Let's look at the recording of both activities: purchasing and using materials.

Purchasing Materials

Transaction 1—Materials Purchased: During 2018, Smart Touch Learning purchased raw materials of $367,000 on account. This is a product cost that *accumulates* in the Raw Materials Inventory account. To simplify the recording process, we are recording the materials purchases as a summary journal entry for the year, rather than showing each individual purchase. The purchase is recorded as follows:

Date	Accounts and Explanation	Debit	Credit
Trans. 1	Raw Materials Inventory	367,000	
	Accounts Payable		367,000

$$\left.\begin{array}{r} \text{A}\uparrow \\ \text{RM}\uparrow \end{array}\right\} = \left\{\begin{array}{l} \text{L}\uparrow \quad + \quad \text{E} \\ \text{A/P}\uparrow \end{array}\right.$$

Raw Materials Inventory

Bal.	70,000
Trans. 1	367,000

Raw Materials Inventory is a general ledger account. Smart Touch Learning also uses a subsidiary ledger for raw materials. A subsidiary ledger contains the details of a general ledger account, and the sum of the subsidiary ledger records equals the balance in the general ledger account.

The raw materials subsidiary ledger includes a separate record for each type of material, so there is a separate page for the batteries, processors, cases, and other materials used in producing the tablets. The subsidiary ledger records show the raw materials purchased (received), used in production (issued), and balance on hand (balance) at all times. **The use of a subsidiary ledger allows for better control of inventory because it helps track each type of material used in production.** Exhibit 19-3 shows the subsidiary ledger of one type of battery that Smart Touch Learning uses. The balance of the Raw Materials Inventory account in the general ledger should always equal the sum of the balances in the raw materials subsidiary ledger.

Why would the company use a subsidiary ledger for raw materials?

Exhibit 19-3 | **Raw Materials Subsidiary Ledger**

RAW MATERIALS SUBSIDIARY LEDGER

STL SMART TOUCH LEARNING

Item No. B-103   Description: STL Batteries

	Received			Issued				Balance		
Date	Units	Unit Cost	Total Cost	Mat. Req. No	Units	Unit Cost	Total Cost	Units	Unit Cost	Total Cost
2017										
12–05	200	$55	$11,000					200	$55	$11,000
12–10				334	50	$55	$2,750	150	$55	$8,250
2018										
1–14				342	15	$55	$825	135	$55	$7,425

Exhibit 19-4 | **Materials Requisition**

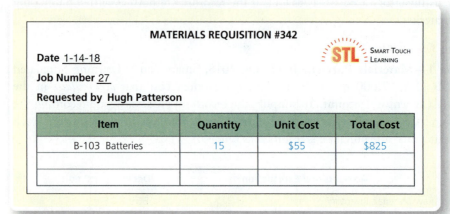

MATERIALS REQUISITION #342

Date 1-14-18

Job Number 27

Requested by Hugh Patterson

Item	Quantity	Unit Cost	Total Cost
B-103 Batteries	15	$55	$825

Using Materials

Materials Requisition

Request for the transfer of raw materials to the production floor.

Materials Used, Job 27: Smart Touch Learning started Job 27 in 2018. On January 14, the production team requested materials for the job. Exhibit 19-4 illustrates the **materials requisition** for batteries—the request to transfer raw materials to the production floor. Note that the subsidiary ledger in Exhibit 19-3 records the materials requisition number (342) along with the number of units requisitioned and their cost.

When the raw materials are issued to the production floor, the transfer is recorded in the raw materials subsidiary ledger, as shown in Exhibit 19-3. When they are received on the production floor, they are recorded on the job cost record. Exhibit 19-5 shows the job cost record for Job 27 after Materials Requisition 342 has been recorded.

The materials added to Job 27 from Materials Requisition 342 are considered *direct* materials because the batteries can be easily and cost-effectively traced directly to the

Exhibit 19-5 | **Job Cost Record—Direct Materials Recorded**

JOB COST RECORD

Job Number   27

Customer   Central College Bookstore

Job Description   15 tablets with accounting e-learning software

Direct Materials			Direct Labor			Manufacturing Overhead		
Date	Requisition Number	Amount	Date	Labor Time Record Number	Amount	Date	Rate	Amount
1/14	342	$825						

Cost Summary

    Direct Materials   _____

    Direct Labor   _____

    Manufacturing Overhead   _____

Total Cost   _____

Unit Cost   _____

finished product. The materials cost has been *assigned* to Job 27 and recorded as a decrease on the raw materials subsidiary ledger and as an increase on the job cost record. However, Smart Touch Learning will not complete a journal entry at this time but will wait and record a summary journal entry at the end of the period for all materials used.

Transaction 2—Materials Used: Smart Touch Learning worked on many jobs during the year in addition to Job 27. In 2018, the company used materials costing $355,000, including batteries, processors, and cases. This amount includes the materials used in Job 27 as well as all other jobs the company worked on during the year. These materials can be traced to specific jobs and are all *direct materials*. The cost of direct materials is transferred out of Raw Materials Inventory and is *assigned* to Work-in-Process Inventory. The individual job cost records would indicate the amount of direct materials cost *assigned* to each job.

By contrast, the company used materials costing $17,000 that are difficult to trace to a specific job. These costs are *indirect materials*. The cost of indirect materials is transferred out of the Raw Materials Inventory account and is *accumulated* in the Manufacturing Overhead account. The following summary journal entry records the issuance of the materials used in production during the year:

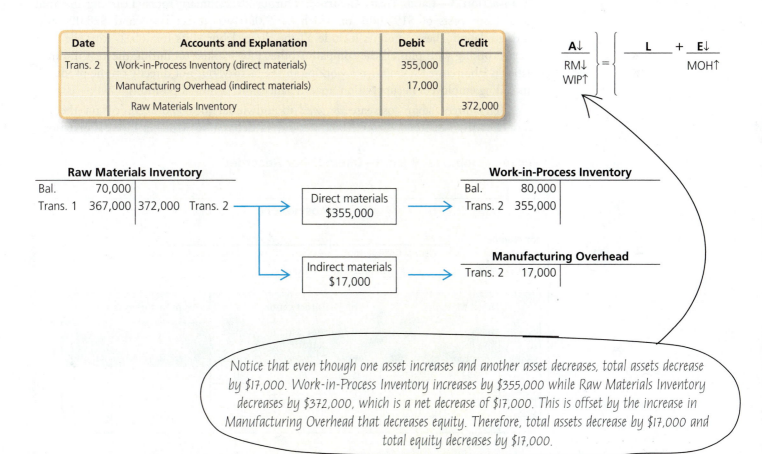

Date	Accounts and Explanation	Debit	Credit
Trans. 2	Work-in-Process Inventory (direct materials)	355,000	
	Manufacturing Overhead (indirect materials)	17,000	
	Raw Materials Inventory		372,000

$$\begin{array}{ccc} A\downarrow & L & + & E\downarrow \\ RM\downarrow & & & MOH\uparrow \\ WIP\uparrow & & & \end{array}$$

Raw Materials Inventory

Bal.	70,000		
Trans. 1	367,000	372,000	Trans. 2

Direct materials $355,000

Indirect materials $17,000

Work-in-Process Inventory

Bal.	80,000	
Trans. 2	355,000	

Manufacturing Overhead

Trans. 2	17,000	

Notice that even though one asset increases and another asset decreases, total assets decrease by $17,000. Work-in-Process Inventory increases by $355,000 while Raw Materials Inventory decreases by $372,000, which is a net decrease of $17,000. This is offset by the increase in Manufacturing Overhead that decreases equity. Therefore, total assets decrease by $17,000 and total equity decreases by $17,000.

Manufacturing Overhead is a temporary account used to *accumulate* indirect production costs during the accounting period. Because it is a temporary account, it is classified as an equity account. We will adjust Manufacturing Overhead later in the chapter.

For both direct materials and indirect materials, the production team completes materials requisitions to request the transfer of materials to the production floor. Because we showed a summary journal entry for these requisitions, we are not showing each document. Also, these requisitions are often in electronic form rather than on paper. Samples of these documents are shown for illustrative purposes only.

Labor

Direct Labor Incurred, Job 27: Most companies use electronic labor/time records to streamline the tracking of labor costs. Employees use ID cards to swipe and enter job information. The time is automatically added to the appropriate job cost record. If a manual system is used, each employee completes a **labor time record** that indicates the amount of time spent on each job. The labor time record shows that one employee spent 5 hours on Job 27. The employee earns $18 per hour. The system then charged $90 to the job (5 hours × $18 per hour).

Exhibit 19-6 shows how Smart Touch Learning adds the direct labor cost to the job cost record for Job 27.

The employee's labor is considered direct labor, so the cost is *assigned* to the job. The cost is added to the job cost record. Smart Touch Learning will make summary journal entries for the labor costs each pay period.

Transaction 3—Labor Costs Incurred: During 2018, Smart Touch Learning incurred total labor costs of $197,000, of which $169,000 was direct labor and $28,000 was indirect labor. These amounts include all the direct labor costs for Job 27 that we have been working with plus all the company's other jobs worked on during the year. Indirect labor is labor costs for employees working in the factory, but not directly on the products, including employees in supervision, maintenance, and janitorial positions.

The direct labor costs are *assigned* to individual jobs and recorded on the job cost records. The total direct labor amount is debited to Work-in-Process Inventory.

Exhibit 19-6 | **Job Cost Record—Direct Labor Recorded**

JOB COST RECORD

STL SMART TOUCH LEARNING

Job Number: 27
Customer: Central College Bookstore
Job Description: 15 tablets with accounting e-learning software

Direct Materials			Direct Labor			Manufacturing Overhead		
Date	Requisition Number	Amount	Date	Labor Time Record Number	Amount	Date	Rate	Amount
1/14	342	$825	1/15	236	$90			

Cost Summary
Direct Materials _____
Direct Labor _____
Manufacturing Overhead _____
Total Cost _____
Unit Cost _____

The indirect labor costs are *accumulated* in Manufacturing Overhead. This is the same treatment as the direct and indirect materials illustrated in Transaction 2.

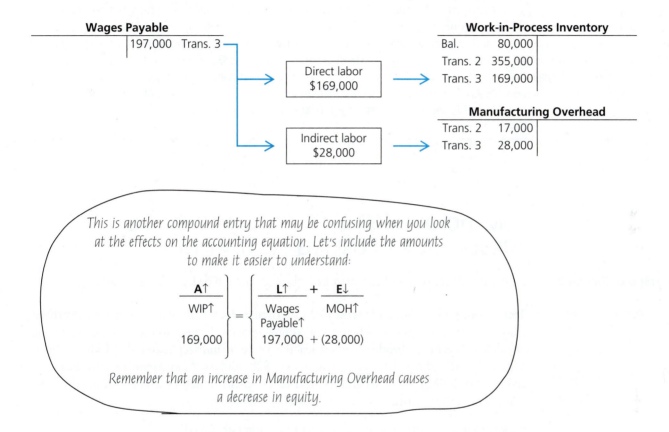

Date	Accounts and Explanation	Debit	Credit
Trans. 3	Work-in-Process Inventory (direct labor)	169,000	
	Manufacturing Overhead (indirect labor)	28,000	
	Wages Payable		197,000

$$\frac{A\uparrow}{WIP\uparrow} \Big\} = \Big\{ \frac{L\uparrow}{\substack{Wages \\ Payable\uparrow}} + \frac{E\downarrow}{MOH\uparrow}$$

Wages Payable

197,000   Trans. 3

Direct labor $169,000

Indirect labor $28,000

Work-in-Process Inventory

Bal.	80,000	
Trans. 2	355,000	
Trans. 3	169,000	

Manufacturing Overhead

| Trans. 2 | 17,000 | |
| Trans. 3 | 28,000 | |

This is another compound entry that may be confusing when you look at the effects on the accounting equation. Let's include the amounts to make it easier to understand:

$$\frac{A\uparrow}{WIP\uparrow} \Big\} = \Big\{ \frac{L\uparrow}{\substack{Wages \\ Payable\uparrow}} + \frac{E\downarrow}{MOH\uparrow}$$

$$169,000 \Big\} = \Big\{ 197,000 + (28,000)$$

Remember that an increase in Manufacturing Overhead causes a decrease in equity.

We have now accounted for the direct product costs and some of the indirect product costs; it is time to take a closer look at the indirect product costs.

Try It!

Record the following journal entries for Smith Company:

6. Purchased materials on account, $10,000.
7. Used $6,000 in direct materials and $500 in indirect materials in production.
8. Incurred $8,000 in labor costs, of which 80% was direct labor.

Check your answers online in MyAccountingLab or at http://www.pearsonhighered.com/Horngren.

For more practice, see Short Exercises S19-2 through S19-5. **MyAccountingLab**

ETHICS

Should I help my friends?

Cole Woods works for a contractor. The firm is currently building two houses. One house is for the McDonalds, whose house is 10,000 square feet and located on Park Place. The other house is for Cole's friends, the Tuckers, whose house is 2,500 square feet and located on Midway. Cole's job includes tracking job costs, where each house is a job. Customers are charged on a cost-plus basis. The customers pay for the actual *costs* incurred *plus* a markup of 15%. Cole is concerned that the Tuckers are getting in over their heads and will not be able to afford the new house. He decides to charge some of the materials and labor costs of their house to the McDonald's house. Cole feels it is a great solution because no one gets hurt. The company still receives the markup, his friends get a discount on their house, and the McDonalds can obviously afford to pay a little extra. Should Cole charge costs for the Tucker's house to the McDonald's house?

Solution

Cole's plan may initially help his friends financially, but he is wrong in thinking no one will be adversely affected. The McDonalds signed a contract with the firm and should not be overcharged. If Cole's scheme is discovered, the company's reputation will be tarnished, which could jeopardize future business. Additionally, Cole could lose his job. Cole's plan would violate the IMA ethical standards of competence, integrity, and credibility.

HOW DO OVERHEAD COSTS FLOW THROUGH THE JOB ORDER COSTING SYSTEM?

Learning Objective 3

Calculate the predetermined overhead allocation rate and allocate overhead costs

Next we look at how overhead costs flow through the job order costing system.

Transactions 4–7—Actual Overhead Costs Incurred: All actual manufacturing overhead costs are *accumulated* as debits to a single general ledger account—Manufacturing Overhead. We have already *accumulated* the costs of indirect materials (Transaction 2, $17,000) and indirect labor (Transaction 3, $28,000) to Manufacturing Overhead. In addition to indirect materials and indirect labor, Smart Touch Learning also incurred the following overhead costs:

- Depreciation on manufacturing plant and equipment, $20,000
- Plant utilities, $7,000
- Plant insurance, $6,000 (previously paid)
- Plant property taxes incurred but not yet paid, $5,000

Transactions 4 through 7 record these manufacturing overhead costs. The actual manufacturing overhead costs are debited to Manufacturing Overhead as they occur throughout the year. By the end of the year, the Manufacturing Overhead account has *accumulated* all the actual overhead costs as debits.

Date	Accounts and Explanation	Debit	Credit
Trans. 4	Manufacturing Overhead	20,000	
	Accumulated Depreciation		20,000
Trans. 5	Manufacturing Overhead	7,000	
	Cash		7,000
Trans. 6	Manufacturing Overhead	6,000	
	Prepaid Insurance		6,000
Trans. 7	Manufacturing Overhead	5,000	
	Property Taxes Payable		5,000

$$\frac{A\downarrow}{\text{Accumulated Depreciation}\uparrow} \Big\} = \Big\{ \frac{L}{} + \frac{E\downarrow}{\text{MOH}\uparrow}$$

$$\frac{A\downarrow}{\text{Cash}\downarrow} \Big\} = \Big\{ \frac{L}{} + \frac{E\downarrow}{\text{MOH}\uparrow}$$

$$\frac{A\downarrow}{\text{Prepaid Insurance}\downarrow} \Big\} = \Big\{ \frac{L}{} + \frac{E\downarrow}{\text{MOH}\uparrow}$$

$$\frac{A}{} \Big\} = \Big\{ \frac{L\uparrow}{\text{Property Taxes Payable}\uparrow} + \frac{E\downarrow}{\text{MOH}\uparrow}$$

Manufacturing Overhead

Trans. 2	17,000
Trans. 3	28,000
Trans. 4	20,000
Trans. 5	7,000
Trans. 6	6,000
Trans. 7	5,000
Bal.	83,000

As you can see, overhead includes a variety of costs that the company cannot trace to individual jobs. For example, it is impossible to say how much of the cost of plant utilities is related to Job 27. Yet manufacturing overhead costs are as essential as direct materials and direct labor, so Smart Touch Learning must find some way to *allocate* overhead costs to specific jobs. Otherwise, each job would not bear its fair share of the total cost. If Smart Touch Learning does not have accurate cost information, the company might make bad pricing decisions. If the sales price is set too low, the company could be selling below cost and operating at a net loss rather than a net profit.

The accounting for the *allocation* of overhead costs is a three-step process and occurs at three different points in the accounting cycle:

1. Calculating the predetermined overhead rate before the period
2. Allocating overhead during the period
3. Adjusting overhead at the end of the period

Before the Period—Calculating the Predetermined Overhead Allocation Rate

The most accurate allocation can be made only when total overhead cost is known—and that is not until the end of the period. But managers cannot wait that long for product cost information. So the **predetermined overhead allocation rate** is calculated before the period begins. Companies use this predetermined rate to allocate estimated overhead cost to individual jobs.

Predetermined Overhead Allocation Rate
Estimated overhead cost per unit of the allocation base, calculated at the beginning of the accounting period. Total estimated overhead costs / Total estimated quantity of the overhead allocation base.

$$\text{Predetermined overhead allocation rate} = \frac{\text{Total estimated overhead costs}}{\text{Total estimated quantity of the overhead allocation base}}$$

The predetermined overhead allocation rate is based on two factors:

- Total *estimated* overhead costs for the period (in Smart Touch Learning's case, one year)
- Total *estimated* quantity of the overhead allocation base

Allocation Base

A denominator that links indirect costs to cost objects. Ideally, the allocation base is the primary cost driver of the indirect costs.

The key to *allocating* indirect manufacturing costs to jobs is to identify a workable manufacturing overhead allocation base. The **allocation base** is a denominator that links overhead costs to the products. Ideally, the allocation base is the primary cost driver of manufacturing overhead. As the phrase implies, a **cost driver** is the primary factor that causes (drives) a cost. For example, the cost of electricity to operate machinery increases with increased machine use. Therefore, the cost driver for electricity is the amount of machine usage, and the allocation base would be machine hours (the number of hours the machine runs). There is a relationship between the overhead cost and the allocation base; that is, the higher the quantity of the allocation base, the higher the overhead costs, and vice versa.

Cost Driver

The primary factor that causes a cost to increase or decrease.

Traditionally, manufacturing companies have used the following as cost drivers:

- Direct labor hours (for labor-intensive production environments)
- Direct labor cost (for labor-intensive production environments)
- Machine hours (for machine-intensive production environments)

Smart Touch Learning uses only one allocation base, direct labor cost, to *allocate* manufacturing overhead to jobs. Later in the textbook, we will look at other ways to allocate overhead to jobs. At the end of 2017, Smart Touch Learning estimated that total overhead costs for 2018 would be $68,000 and direct labor cost would total $170,000. Using this information, we can compute the predetermined overhead allocation rate as follows:

$$\text{Predetermined overhead allocation rate} = \frac{\text{Total estimated overhead costs}}{\text{Total estimated quantity of the overhead allocation base}}$$

$$= \frac{\$68,000}{\$170,000} = 0.40 = 40\% \text{ of direct labor cost}$$

During the Period—Allocating Overhead

As we have seen, Smart Touch Learning assigns direct costs directly to each job. But how does the company *allocate* overhead cost to jobs? As jobs are completed in 2018, Smart Touch Learning will *allocate* overhead costs using the predetermined overhead allocation rate and assign 40% of each direct labor dollar incurred for the job as manufacturing overhead cost. Smart Touch Learning uses the same predetermined overhead rate to allocate manufacturing overhead to all jobs worked on throughout the year, including jobs still in process at the end of the accounting period. Let's use Job 27 as an example. The total direct labor cost for Job 27 is $1,250, and the predetermined overhead allocation rate is 40% of direct labor cost. Therefore, Smart Touch Learning *allocates* $500 ($1,250 × 0.40) of manufacturing overhead to Job 27. The $500 of overhead is recorded on the job cost record.

Allocated manufacturing overhead cost	=	Predetermined overhead allocation rate	×	Actual quantity of the allocation base used by each job	
	=	40%	×	$1,250	= $500

The completed job cost record for the Central College Bookstore order (Exhibit 19-7) shows that Job 27 cost Smart Touch Learning a total of $4,500, composed of $2,750 for direct materials, $1,250 for direct labor, and $500 of allocated manufacturing overhead. Job 27 produced 15 tablets, so Smart Touch Learning's cost per tablet is $300.

Exhibit 19-7 | **Job Cost Record, Job 27, Completed**

JOB COST RECORD

Job Number 27
Customer Central College Bookstore
Job Description 15 tablets with accounting e-learning software

STL SMART TOUCH LEARNING

Direct Materials			Direct Labor			Manufacturing Overhead		
Date	Requisition Number	Amount	Date	Labor Time Record Number	Amount	Date	Rate	Amount
1/14	342	$ 825	1/15	236	$ 90	1/31	40% of DL Cost	$500
1/16	345	650	1/15	237	450			
1/25	352	1,275	1/31	252	710			

Cost Summary

Direct Materials	$ 2,750
Direct Labor	1,250
Manufacturing Overhead	500
Total Cost	$ 4,500
Unit Cost	$ 300

Cost of goods manufactured	/	Total units produced	=	Unit product cost
$4,500	/	15 tablets	=	$300 per tablet

Transaction 8—Overhead Allocation: Smart Touch Learning worked on many jobs, including Job 27, during 2018. The company allocated manufacturing overhead to each of these jobs, including jobs still in process at the end of 2018. Smart Touch Learning's total direct labor cost for 2018 was $169,000, so total overhead allocated to all jobs is 40% of the $169,000 direct labor cost, or $67,600. The journal entry to allocate manufacturing overhead cost to Work-in-Process Inventory is as follows:

$$\left.\frac{A\uparrow}{WIP\uparrow}\right\} = \left\{\frac{L + E\uparrow}{MOH\downarrow}\right.$$

Date	Accounts and Explanation	Debit	Credit
Trans. 8	Work-in-Process Inventory	67,600	
	Manufacturing Overhead		67,600

Manufacturing Overhead

Trans. 2	17,000	67,600	Trans. 8
Trans. 3	28,000		
Trans. 4	20,000		
Trans. 5	7,000		
Trans. 6	6,000		
Trans. 7	5,000		
Bal.	15,400		

Overhead Allocated

Work-in-Process Inventory

Bal.	80,000	
Trans. 2	355,000	
Trans. 3	169,000	
Trans. 8	67,600	

At the End of the Period—Adjusting for Overallocated and Underallocated Overhead

After *allocating* manufacturing overhead to jobs for 2018, a $15,400 debit balance remains in the Manufacturing Overhead account. This means that Smart Touch Learning's actual overhead costs of $83,000 were greater than the overhead allocated to jobs in Work-in-Process Inventory of $67,600. We say that Smart Touch Learning's Manufacturing Overhead is *underallocated* because the company allocated less costs to jobs than actual costs incurred. Recall that Manufacturing Overhead is a temporary account used to *accumulate* indirect production costs during the accounting period. At the end of the accounting year, the Manufacturing Overhead account must have a zero balance. Therefore, an adjustment is required if overhead is underallocated or overallocated at the end of the period. We will show how to prepare this adjustment after we account for the completion and sale of the goods.

Try It!

Smith Company expected to incur $10,000 in manufacturing overhead costs and use 4,000 machine hours for the year. Actual manufacturing overhead was $9,700, and the company used 4,250 machine hours.

9. Calculate the predetermined overhead allocation rate using machine hours as the allocation base.
10. How much manufacturing overhead was allocated during the year?

Check your answers online in MyAccountingLab or at http://www.pearsonhighered.com/Horngren.

For more practice, see Short Exercises S19-6 through S19-10. **MyAccountingLab**

WHAT HAPPENS WHEN PRODUCTS ARE COMPLETED AND SOLD?

Now you know how to *accumulate*, *assign*, and *allocate* the cost of direct materials, direct labor, and overhead to jobs. To complete the process, we must do the following:

- Account for the completion of jobs.
- Account for the sale of jobs.
- Adjust Manufacturing Overhead at the end of the period.

Learning Objective 4

Record the completion and sales of finished goods

Transferring Costs to Finished Goods Inventory

Let's look at how Smart Touch Learning recorded the completion and sale of its jobs for 2018. The company reported the following inventory balances one year ago, on December 31, 2017:

Raw Materials Inventory	$ 70,000
Work-in-Process Inventory	80,000
Finished Goods Inventory	0

The following transactions occurred in 2018:

Cost of Goods Manufactured	$ 644,600
Sales on Account	1,200,000
Cost of Goods Sold	584,600

Transaction 9—Jobs Completed: The $644,600 Cost of Goods Manufactured is the cost of all jobs Smart Touch Learning completed during 2018. Normally, this entry would be made as each individual job is completed, but we are showing it as one summary journal entry. The Cost of Goods Manufactured is transferred from Work-in-Process Inventory to Finished Goods Inventory as jobs are completed and moved into the finished goods storage area. Smart Touch Learning records goods completed in 2018 as follows:

Date	Accounts and Explanation	Debit	Credit
Trans. 9	Finished Goods Inventory	644,600	
	Work-in-Process Inventory		644,600

$$\left.\begin{array}{c} A\uparrow\downarrow \\ FG\uparrow \\ WIP\downarrow \end{array}\right\} = \left\{\begin{array}{c} L \ + \ E \end{array}\right.$$

Transferring Costs to Cost of Goods Sold

Transaction 10—Jobs Sold: As the tablets are sold on account, Smart Touch Learning records Sales Revenue and Accounts Receivable as follows:

Date	Accounts and Explanation	Debit	Credit
Trans. 10	Accounts Receivable	1,200,000	
	Sales Revenue		1,200,000

$$\left.\begin{array}{c} A\uparrow \\ A/R\uparrow \end{array}\right\} = \left\{\begin{array}{c} L \ + \ E\uparrow \\ Sales \\ Revenue\uparrow \end{array}\right.$$

Transaction 11—Cost of Jobs Sold: The goods have been shipped to customers. Assuming Smart Touch Learning uses a perpetual inventory system, the company must decrease the Finished Goods Inventory account and increase Cost of Goods Sold with the following journal entry:

$$\frac{A\downarrow}{FG\downarrow}\Bigg\} = \Bigg\{ \ \underline{\ L\ } + \frac{E\downarrow}{COGS\uparrow}$$

Date	Accounts and Explanation	Debit	Credit
Trans. 11	Cost of Goods Sold	584,600	
	Finished Goods Inventory		584,600

The T-accounts for Smart Touch Learning's manufacturing costs now show:

BALANCE SHEET — **INCOME STATEMENT**

Work-in-Process Inventory

Costs Incurred		COGM	
Bal.	80,000	644,600	Trans. 9
Trans. 2	355,000		
Trans. 3	169,000		
Trans. 8	67,600		
Bal.	27,000		

Finished Goods Inventory

	COGM	COGS	
Bal.	0		
Trans. 9	644,600	584,600	Trans. 11
Bal.	60,000		

Cost of Goods Sold

COGS	
Trans. 11 584,600	

As jobs are completed, their costs are transferred to Finished Goods Inventory. We end the period with other jobs started but not finished, which are represented by the $27,000 ending balance of Work-in-Process Inventory. We also have jobs completed and not sold, which are represented by the $60,000 ending balance of Finished Goods Inventory.

> Remembering the journal entries is easier if you concentrate on the account you are transferring the costs into. The transfer is always to either an asset account or an expense account. Both account types are increased by debits, so the Transfer *To* account is Debited (TTD). Therefore, the Transfer *From* account is Credited (TFC). To help you remember this relationship, an easy memory tool is "The Talking Donkey" and "The Fuzzy Cat."

Try It!

The following information pertains to Smith Company, which you worked with previously in this chapter:

11. Smith Company completed jobs that cost $25,000 to manufacture. Record the journal entry.
12. Smith Company sold jobs to customers on account for $52,000 that cost $22,000 to manufacture. Record the journal entries.

Check your answers online in MyAccountingLab or at http://www.pearsonhighered.com/Horngren.

For more practice, see Short Exercise S19-11.   MyAccountingLab

HOW IS THE MANUFACTURING OVERHEAD ACCOUNT ADJUSTED?

The last step of recording costs in a job order costing system is to *adjust* the Manufacturing Overhead account for the amount of overallocated or underallocated overhead.

Transaction 12—Adjust Manufacturing Overhead: During the year, the Manufacturing Overhead account is debited for actual overhead costs incurred and credited for overhead costs allocated to jobs.

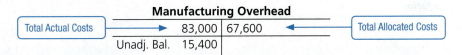

The total debits to the Manufacturing Overhead account rarely equal the total credits. Why? **Because Smart Touch Learning allocates overhead to jobs using a *predetermined overhead allocation rate* that is based on *estimates*.** The predetermined overhead allocation rate represents the *expected* relationship between overhead costs and the allocation base. In our example, the $15,400 debit balance of Manufacturing Overhead is called **underallocated overhead** because the manufacturing overhead allocated to Work-in-Process Inventory was *less* than the actual overhead cost. If it had been **overallocated overhead** instead, the Manufacturing Overhead account would have had a credit balance, which occurs when the actual manufacturing overhead costs are less than allocated manufacturing costs.

Accountants *adjust* underallocated and overallocated overhead at the end of the period when closing the Manufacturing Overhead account. Closing the account means zeroing it out. So, when overhead is underallocated, as in our example, a credit to Manufacturing Overhead of $15,400 is needed to bring the account balance to zero. What account should we debit? The underallocated overhead indicates that Smart Touch Learning *undercosted* jobs by $15,400 during the year. The costs flowed through Work-in-Process Inventory and Finished Goods Inventory and ultimately were transferred to Cost of Goods Sold. Therefore, the *adjustment* should increase Cost of Goods Sold. Cost of Goods Sold is an expense account, so it is increased with a debit:

Why does the Manufacturing Overhead account have a balance after allocating manufacturing overhead to jobs?

Underallocated Overhead
Occurs when the actual manufacturing overhead costs are more than allocated manufacturing overhead costs.

Overallocated Overhead
Occurs when the actual manufacturing overhead costs are less than allocated manufacturing overhead costs.

Date	Accounts and Explanation	Debit	Credit
Trans. 12	Cost of Goods Sold	15,400	
	Manufacturing Overhead		15,400

$$A \Bigg\} = \Bigg\{ \; L \; + \; \frac{E\uparrow\downarrow}{\substack{COGS\uparrow \\ MOH\downarrow}}$$

Manufacturing Overhead			
Trans. 2	17,000	67,600	Trans. 8
Trans. 3	28,000		
Trans. 4	20,000		
Trans. 5	7,000		
Trans. 6	6,000		
Trans. 7	5,000		
Unadj. Bal.	15,400		
		15,400	Trans. 12
Adj. Bal.	0		

Cost of Goods Sold		
Trans. 11	584,600	
Trans. 12	15,400	
Adj. Bal.	600,000	

The Manufacturing Overhead account balance is now zero, and the Cost of Goods Sold account is up to date.

Exhibit 19-8 summarizes the accounting for Manufacturing Overhead.

Exhibit 19-8 | Accounting for Manufacturing Overhead

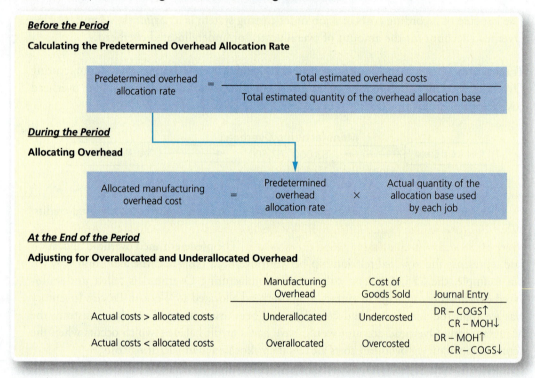

Summary

As costs flow through the job order costing system, we go through a four-step process to *accumulate, assign, allocate,* and *adjust.* Exhibit 19-9 is a list of all journal entries illustrated in the chapter with notations on the four steps.

Exhibit 19-9 | Summary of Journal Entries

$\dfrac{A\uparrow}{RM\uparrow} \Big\} = \Big\{ \dfrac{L\uparrow}{A/P\uparrow} + E$

$\dfrac{A\downarrow}{RM\downarrow} \atop WIP\uparrow \Big\} = \Big\{ L + \dfrac{E\downarrow}{MOH\uparrow}$

$\dfrac{A\uparrow}{WIP\uparrow} \Big\} = \Big\{ \dfrac{L\uparrow}{Wages \atop Payable\uparrow} + \dfrac{E\downarrow}{MOH\uparrow}$

Date	Accounts and Explanation	Debit	Credit
Trans. 1	Raw Materials Inventory	367,000	
	Accounts Payable		367,000
	*Materials purchased, **accumulated** in RM.*		
Trans. 2	Work-in-Process Inventory	355,000	
	Manufacturing Overhead	17,000	
	Raw Materials Inventory		372,000
	*Materials used, direct materials **assigned** to WIP, indirect*		
	*materials **accumulated** in MOH.*		
Trans. 3	Work-in-Process Inventory	169,000	
	Manufacturing Overhead	28,000	
	Wages Payable		197,000
	*Labor incurred, direct labor **assigned** to WIP, indirect*		
	*labor **accumulated** in MOH.*		

(Exhibit continued on next page.)

Exhibit 19-9 | **Continued**

Date	Accounts and Explanation	Debit	Credit
Trans. 4	Manufacturing Overhead	20,000	
	Accumulated Depreciation		20,000
	*Overhead incurred, costs **accumulated** in MOH.*		
Trans. 5	Manufacturing Overhead	7,000	
	Cash		7,000
	*Overhead incurred, costs **accumulated** in MOH.*		
Trans. 6	Manufacturing Overhead	6,000	
	Prepaid Insurance		6,000
	*Overhead incurred, costs **accumulated** in MOH.*		
Trans. 7	Manufacturing Overhead	5,000	
	Property Taxes Payable		5,000
	*Overhead incurred, costs **accumulated** in MOH.*		
Trans. 8	Work-in-Process Inventory	67,600	
	Manufacturing Overhead		67,600
	*Overhead **allocated** to WIP.*		
Trans. 9	Finished Goods Inventory	644,600	
	Work-in-Process Inventory		644,600
	*Jobs completed, costs **assigned** to FG.*		
Trans. 10	Accounts Receivable	1,200,000	
	Sales Revenue		1,200,000
	Jobs sold; entry reflects sales price, not costs.		
Trans. 11	Cost of Goods Sold	584,600	
	Finished Goods Inventory		584,600
	*Jobs sold, costs **assigned** to COGS.*		
Trans. 12	Cost of Goods Sold	15,400	
	Manufacturing Overhead		15,400
	*MOH **adjusted** for underallocated overhead.*		

Accounting equations (right margin):

$$A\downarrow \text{ Accumulated Depreciation}\uparrow = \{ L + E\downarrow \text{ MOH}\uparrow$$

$$A\downarrow \text{ Cash}\downarrow = \{ L + E\downarrow \text{ MOH}\uparrow$$

$$A\downarrow \text{ Prepaid Insurance}\downarrow = \{ L + E\downarrow \text{ MOH}\uparrow$$

$$A = \{ L\uparrow \text{ Property Taxes Payable}\uparrow + E\downarrow \text{ MOH}\uparrow$$

$$A\uparrow \text{ WIP}\uparrow = \{ L + E\uparrow \text{ MOH}\downarrow$$

$$A\uparrow\downarrow \text{ FG}\uparrow \text{ WIP}\downarrow = \{ L + E$$

$$A\uparrow \text{ A/R}\uparrow = \{ L + E\uparrow \text{ Sales Revenue}\uparrow$$

$$A\downarrow \text{ FG}\downarrow = \{ L + E\downarrow \text{ COGS}\uparrow$$

$$A = \{ L + E\uparrow\downarrow \text{ COGS}\uparrow \text{ MOH}\downarrow$$

(Exhibit continued on next page.)

Exhibit 19-9 | **Continued**

Raw Materials Inventory

Beg. Bal.	70,000		
Trans. 1	367,000	372,000	Trans. 2
End. Bal.	65,000		

Work-in-Process Inventory

Beg. Bal.	80,000		
Trans. 2	355,000	644,600	Trans. 9
Trans. 3	169,000		
Trans. 8	67,600		
End. Bal.	27,000		

Finished Goods Inventory

Beg. Bal.	0		
Trans. 9	644,600	584,600	Trans. 11
End. Bal.	60,000		

Manufacturing Overhead

Trans. 2	17,000	67,600	Trans. 8
Trans. 3	28,000		
Trans. 4	20,000		
Trans. 5	7,000		
Trans. 6	6,000		
Trans. 7	5,000		
Unadj. Bal.	15,400		
		15,400	Trans. 12
Adj. Bal.	0		

Cost of Goods Sold

Trans. 11	584,600		
Trans. 12	15,400		
Adj. Bal.	600,000		

Now that you've had the opportunity to closely follow the flow of product costs through the job order costing system, review them again. Exhibit 19-10 shows the schedule of cost of goods manufactured for Smart Touch Learning for 2018. Exhibit 19-11 shows the income statement for the same period. Notice on the income statement that the underallocated overhead is added in the cost of goods sold calculation so that the cost of goods sold on the income statement matches the amount in the T-account. If overhead had been overallocated, the adjustment amount would have been subtracted.

Exhibit 19-10 | **Schedule of Cost of Goods Manufactured**

SMART TOUCH LEARNING
Schedule of Cost of Goods Manufactured
Year Ended December 31, 2018

Beginning Work-in-Process Inventory		$ 80,000
Direct Materials Used:		
Beginning Raw Materials Inventory	$ 70,000	
Purchases of Raw Materials (including Freight In)	367,000	
Raw Materials Available for Use	437,000	
Ending Raw Materials Inventory	(65,000)	
Indirect Materials Used	(17,000)	
Direct Materials Used		$ 355,000
Direct Labor		169,000
Manufacturing Overhead Allocated		67,600
Total Manufacturing Costs Incurred during the Year		591,600
Total Manufacturing Costs to Account for		671,600
Ending Work-in-Process Inventory		(27,000)
Cost of Goods Manufactured		**$ 644,600**

Exhibit 19-11 | Income Statement

SMART TOUCH LEARNING Income Statement Year Ended December 31, 2018		
Sales Revenue		$ 1,200,000
Less: Sales Returns and Allowances	$ 120,000	
Sales Discounts	80,000	200,000
Net Sales Revenue		1,000,000
Cost of Goods Sold:		
Beginning Finished Goods Inventory	0	
Cost of Goods Manufactured	644,600	
Cost of Goods Available for Sale	644,600	
Ending Finished Goods Inventory	(60,000)	
Cost of Goods Sold Before Adjustment	584,600	
Adjustment for Underallocated Overhead	15,400	
Cost of Goods Sold		600,000
Gross Profit		400,000
Selling and Administrative Expenses:		
Wages Expense	120,000	
Rent Expense	100,000	
Insurance Expense	10,000	
Depreciation Expense	6,000	
Supplies Expense	5,000	
Total Selling and Administrative Expenses		241,000
Operating Income		159,000
Other Income (Expense):		
Interest Expense		(7,600)
Income Before Income Tax Expense		151,400
Income Tax Expense		53,000
Net Income		$ 98,400

The following information pertains to Smith Company for the year:

Estimated manufacturing overhead	$ 500,000	Actual manufacturing overhead	$ 550,000
Estimated direct labor hours	10,000 hours	Actual direct labor hours	10,500 hours

13. Calculate the predetermined overhead allocation rate using direct labor hours as the allocation base.
14. Determine the amount of overhead allocated during the year. Record the journal entry.
15. Determine the amount of underallocated or overallocated overhead. Record the journal entry to adjust Manufacturing Overhead.

Check your answers online in MyAccountingLab or at http://www.pearsonhighered.com/Horngren.

For more practice, see Short Exercise S19-12. MyAccountingLab

HOW DO SERVICE COMPANIES USE A JOB ORDER COSTING SYSTEM?

Learning Objective 6

Calculate job costs for a service company

As we have seen, service firms have no inventory. These firms incur only noninventoriable costs. But their managers still need to know the costs of different jobs in order to set prices for their services. We will use a law firm to illustrate how service firms *assign* and *allocate* costs to jobs.

The law firm of Walsh Associates considers each client a separate job. Walsh's most significant cost is direct labor—attorney time spent on clients' cases. How do service firms trace direct labor to individual jobs?

Walsh's employees can fill out a weekly electronic labor time record. Software totals the amount of time spent on each job. For example, attorney Lois Fox's electronic time record shows that she devoted 14 hours to Client 367 and 26 hours to other clients during the week of June 10, 2018.

Fox's salary and benefits total $100,000 per year. Assuming a 40-hour workweek and 50 workweeks in each year (which allows for a standard two-week vacation), Fox has 2,000 available work hours per year (50 weeks × 40 hours per week). Fox's hourly pay rate is as follows:

$$\text{Hourly rate to the employer} = \frac{\$100,000 \text{ per year}}{2,000 \text{ hours per year}} = \$50 \text{ per hour}$$

Fox worked 14 hours for Client 367, so the direct labor cost *assigned* to Client 367 is 14 hours × $50 per hour = $700. This direct labor cost would be recorded on the job cost record for Client 367.

Founding partner Jacob Walsh wants to know the total cost of serving each client, not just the direct labor cost. Walsh Associates also *allocates* indirect costs to individual jobs (clients). The law firm develops a predetermined overhead allocation rate, following the same approach that Smart Touch Learning used. In December 2017, Walsh estimates that the following indirect costs will be incurred in 2018:

Office rent	$ 200,000
Office support staff	70,000
Maintaining and updating law library for case research	25,000
Advertisements	3,000
Office supplies used	2,000
Total indirect costs	$ 300,000

Walsh uses direct labor hours as the allocation base because direct labor hours are the main driver of indirect costs. He estimates that Walsh attorneys will work 10,000 direct labor hours in 2018.

Step 1: Compute the predetermined overhead allocation rate.

$$\text{Predetermined overhead allocation rate} = \frac{\$300,000 \text{ expected indirect costs}}{10,000 \text{ expected direct labor hours}}$$
$$= \$30 \text{ per direct labor hour}$$

Step 2: Allocate indirect costs to jobs by multiplying the predetermined overhead allocation rate (Step 1) by the actual quantity of the allocation base used by each job. Client 367, for example, required 14 direct labor hours of Fox's time, so the indirect costs are allocated as follows:

$$14 \text{ direct labor hours} \times \$30/\text{hour} = \$420$$

To summarize, the total costs *assigned* and *allocated* to Client 367 are as follows:

Direct labor: 14 hours × $50/hour	$ 700
Indirect costs: 14 hours × $30/hour	420
Total costs	$ 1,120

As you can see from the above example, just like a manufacturing company, a service company can use a job order cost system to *assign* direct costs and *allocate* indirect costs to jobs.

Now that the service company has a good estimate for total job costs, it is better prepared to make pricing decisions. The total hourly rate for the company is $80, which is $50 per hour for direct labor plus $30 per hour for indirect costs. The firm can use cost-plus pricing to set the rate charged to clients. For example, if the firm desires a profit equal to 75% of the firm's cost, then the price would be calculated as follows:

> Markup = Total Cost × Markup Percentage
>
> = $80 per hour × 75% = $60 per hour
>
> Price = Total Cost + Markup
>
> = $80 per hour + $60 per hour = $140 per hour

Based on the above calculations, the firm should charge clients $140 per hour.

DECISIONS

What should the company charge?

Refer to the information for the service company example, Walsh Associates. Assume Jacob Walsh desires a profit equal to 50% of the firm's cost. Should Walsh consider only the direct costs when making pricing decisions? How much should the firm bill Client 367?

Solution

Walsh should consider more than just the direct labor costs when determining the amount to charge his clients. Client 367 incurred $700 in direct costs. At a 50% markup, Walsh would add $350 ($700 × 50%) and charge the client $1,050. That means Walsh would not cover the full cost of providing service to the client. The loss on the job would be $70 ($1,050 service revenue less $1,120 cost = $70 loss). He left out the indirect costs. The markup should be 50% of the total cost, $560 ($1,120 × 50%). The amount charged to the client would be $1,680, which would generate a profit of $560 ($1,680 service revenue less $1,120 cost = $560 profit).

Try It!

Wesson Company is a consulting firm. The firm expects to have $45,000 in indirect costs during the year and bill customers for 6,000 hours. The cost of direct labor is $75 per hour.

16. Calculate the predetermined overhead allocation rate for Wesson.
17. Wesson completed a consulting job for George Peterson and billed the customer for 15 hours. What was the total cost of the consulting job?
18. If Wesson wants to earn a profit equal to 60% of the cost of a job, how much should the company charge Mr. Peterson?

Check your answers online in MyAccountingLab or at http://www.pearsonhighered.com/Horngren.

For more practice, see Short Exercises S19-13 and S19-14. MyAccountingLab

REVIEW

> Things You Should Know

1. **How do manufacturing companies use job order and process costing systems?**

   - All businesses need to know the cost of their products or services.
   - Job order costing is used by companies that manufacture unique products or provide specialized services.
   - Process costing is used by companies that produce identical units through a series of uniform processes.
   - The four steps for tracking product costs are:
     - Accumulate
     - Assign
     - Allocate
     - Adjust

2. **How do materials and labor costs flow through the job order costing system?**

   - Purchases of materials on account increase Raw Materials Inventory.

Date	Accounts and Explanation	Debit	Credit
	Raw Materials Inventory	XXX	
	Accounts Payable		XXX

   - The use of materials decreases Raw Materials Inventory. The use of direct materials increases Work-in-Process Inventory; the use of indirect materials increases Manufacturing Overhead.

Date	Accounts and Explanation	Debit	Credit
	Work-in-Process Inventory	XXX	
	Manufacturing Overhead	XXX	
	Raw Materials Inventory		XXX

   - Labor incurred increases Wages Payable. Direct labor increases Work-in-Process Inventory; indirect labor increases Manufacturing Overhead.

Date	Accounts and Explanation	Debit	Credit
	Work-in-Process Inventory	XXX	
	Manufacturing Overhead	XXX	
	Wages Payable		XXX

3. **How do overhead costs flow through the job order costing system?**

   - Before the period: Calculate the predetermined overhead allocation rate.
     - Predetermined overhead allocation rate = Total estimated overhead costs / Total estimated quantity of the overhead allocation base

- During the period: Use the predetermined overhead allocation rate to allocate overhead to jobs.
  - Allocated manufacturing overhead cost = Predetermined overhead allocation rate × Actual quantity of the allocation base used for each job

4. What happens when products are completed and sold?

- The cost of completed jobs is transferred from Work-in-Process Inventory to Finished Goods Inventory.

Date	Accounts and Explanation	Debit	Credit
	Finished Goods Inventory	XXX	
	Work-in-Process Inventory		XXX

- Jobs are sold on account.

Date	Accounts and Explanation	Debit	Credit
	Accounts Receivable	XXX	
	Sales Revenue		XXX

- The cost of sold jobs is transferred from Finished Goods Inventory to Cost of Goods Sold.

Date	Accounts and Explanation	Debit	Credit
	Cost of Goods Sold	XXX	
	Finished Goods Inventory		XXX

- The transfer from Finished Goods Inventory to Cost of Goods Sold moves the product costs from the balance sheet to the income statement.

5. How is the manufacturing overhead account adjusted?

- At the end of the period: Adjust Manufacturing Overhead for any underallocated or overallocated overhead.
  - Actual costs > allocated costs, underallocated

Date	Accounts and Explanation	Debit	Credit
	Cost of Goods Sold	XXX	
	Manufacturing Overhead		XXX

  - Actual costs < allocated costs, overallocated

Date	Accounts and Explanation	Debit	Credit
	Manufacturing Overhead	XXX	
	Cost of Goods Sold		XXX

CHAPTER 19

6. **How do service companies use a job order costing system?**

  - Service companies also have direct and indirect costs.

  - Direct costs are assigned to jobs.

  - Indirect costs are allocated to jobs using the predetermined overhead allocation rate.

  - Knowing the full cost of the job allows for better pricing decisions.

> Summary Problem 19-1

Skippy Scooters manufactures motor scooters. The company has automated production, so it allocates manufacturing overhead based on machine hours. Skippy expects to incur $240,000 of manufacturing overhead costs and to use 4,000 machine hours during 2016. At the end of 2015, Skippy reported the following inventories:

Raw Materials Inventory	$ 20,000
Work-in-Process Inventory	17,000
Finished Goods Inventory	11,000

During January 2016, Skippy actually used 300 machine hours and recorded the following transactions:

a. Purchased materials on account, $31,000

b. Used direct materials, $39,000

c. Manufacturing wages incurred totaled $40,000, of which 90% was direct labor and 10% was indirect labor

d. Used indirect materials, $3,000

e. Incurred other manufacturing overhead on account, $13,000

f. Allocated manufacturing overhead for January 2016

g. Cost of completed motor scooters, $100,000

h. Sold scooters on account, $175,000; cost of scooters sold, $95,000

Requirements

1. Compute Skippy's predetermined overhead allocation rate for 2016.

2. Journalize the transactions in the general journal. Use the following accounts: Accounts Receivable, Raw Materials Inventory, Work-in-Process Inventory, Finished Goods Inventory, Accounts Payable, Wages Payable, Sales Revenue, Manufacturing Overhead, and Cost of Goods Sold.

3. Set up T-accounts for the accounts listed in Requirement 2. Enter the beginning balances for the inventory accounts and assume the remaining accounts have a beginning balance of $0. Post the transactions to the T-accounts and determine the ending balances.

4. Adjust Manufacturing Overhead for the overallocated or underallocated overhead. Post your entry to the T-accounts.

5. What are the ending balances in the three inventory accounts and in Cost of Goods Sold?

> Solution

Requirement 1

Compute Skippy's predetermined overhead allocation rate for 2016.

$$\text{Predetermined overhead allocation rate} = \frac{\text{Total estimated overhead costs}}{\text{Total estimated quantity of the overhead allocation base}}$$

$$= \frac{\$240,000}{4,000 \text{ machine hours}} = \$60 \text{ per machine hour}$$

Requirement 2

Journalize the transactions in the general journal.

Date	Accounts and Explanation	Debit	Credit
(a)	Raw Materials Inventory	31,000	
	Accounts Payable		31,000
(b)	Work-in-Process Inventory	39,000	
	Raw Materials Inventory		39,000
(c)	Work-in-Process Inventory ($40,000 × 0.90)	36,000	
	Manufacturing Overhead ($40,000 × 0.10)	4,000	
	Wages Payable		40,000
(d)	Manufacturing Overhead	3,000	
	Raw Materials Inventory		3,000
(e)	Manufacturing Overhead	13,000	
	Accounts Payable		13,000
(f)	Work-in-Process Inventory (300 machine hours × $60/hr.)	18,000	
	Manufacturing Overhead		18,000
(g)	Finished Goods Inventory	100,000	
	Work-in-Process Inventory		100,000
(h)	Accounts Receivable	175,000	
	Sales Revenue		175,000
	Cost of Goods Sold	95,000	
	Finished Goods Inventory		95,000

CHAPTER 19

Requirement 3

Post the transactions.

Accounts Receivable		
(h)	175,000	

Raw Materials Inventory			
Bal.	20,000	39,000	(b)
(a)	31,000	3,000	(d)
Bal.	9,000		

Work-in-Process Inventory			
Bal.	17,000	100,000	(g)
(b)	39,000		
(c)	36,000		
(f)	18,000		
Bal.	10,000		

Finished Goods Inventory			
Bal.	11,000	95,000	(h)
(g)	100,000		
Bal.	16,000		

Accounts Payable		
	31,000	(a)
	13,000	(e)
	44,000	Bal.

Wages Payable		
	40,000	(c)

Sales Revenue		
	175,000	(h)

Manufacturing Overhead			
(c)	4,000	18,000	(f)
(d)	3,000		
(e)	13,000		
Bal.	2,000		

Cost of Goods Sold		
(h)	95,000	

Requirement 4

Adjust Manufacturing Overhead.

Date	Accounts and Explanation	Debit	Credit
(i)	Cost of Goods Sold	2,000	
	Manufacturing Overhead		2,000

Manufacturing Overhead			
(c)	4,000	18,000	(f)
(d)	3,000	2,000	(i)
(e)	13,000		
Bal.	0		

Cost of Goods Sold		
(h)	95,000	
(i)	2,000	
Bal.	97,000	

Requirement 5

Ending balances:

Raw Materials Inventory (from Requirement 3)	$ 9,000
Work-in-Process Inventory (from Requirement 3)	10,000
Finished Goods Inventory (from Requirement 3)	16,000
Cost of Goods Sold (from Requirement 4)	97,000

> Key Terms

Allocation Base (p. 992)

Cost Driver (p. 992)

Job (p. 983)

Job Cost Record (p. 983)

Job Order Costing System (p. 983)

Labor Time Record (p. 988)

Materials Requisition (p. 986)

Overallocated Overhead (p. 997)

Predetermined Overhead Allocation Rate (p. 991)

Process Costing System (p. 983)

Underallocated Overhead (p. 997)

> Quick Check

1. Would an advertising agency use job order or process costing? What about a cell phone manufacturer?

   Learning Objective 1

   a. Advertising agency—process costing; Cell phone manufacturer—process costing

   b. Advertising agency—job order costing; Cell phone manufacturer—job order costing

   c. Advertising agency—process costing; Cell phone manufacturer—job order costing

   d. Advertising agency—job order costing; Cell phone manufacturer—process costing

2. When a manufacturing company *uses* direct materials, it *assigns* the cost by debiting

   Learning Objective 2

   a. Direct Materials.
   c. Manufacturing Overhead.

   b. Work-in-Process Inventory.
   d. Raw Materials Inventory.

3. When a manufacturing company *uses* indirect materials, it *accumulates* the cost by debiting

   Learning Objective 2

   a. Work-in-Process Inventory.
   c. Raw Materials Inventory.

   b. Indirect Materials.
   d. Manufacturing Overhead.

4. When a manufacturing company *uses* direct labor, it *assigns* the cost by debiting

   Learning Objective 2

   a. Work-in-Process Inventory.
   c. Direct Labor.

   b. Manufacturing Overhead.
   d. Wages Payable.

Questions 5, 6, 7, and 8 are based on the following information:

Gell Corporation manufactures computers. Assume that Gell:

- allocates manufacturing overhead based on machine hours
- estimated 12,000 machine hours and $93,000 of manufacturing overhead costs
- actually used 16,000 machine hours and incurred the following actual costs:

Indirect labor	$ 11,000
Depreciation on plant	48,000
Machinery repair	11,000
Direct labor	75,000
Plant supplies	6,000
Plant utilities	7,000
Advertising	35,000
Sales commissions	27,000

CHAPTER 19

Learning Objective 3

5. What is Gell's predetermined overhead allocation rate?

    a. $7.75/machine hour   c. $6.92/machine hour

    b. $5.81/machine hour   d. $5.19/machine hour

Learning Objective 3

6. What is Gell's actual manufacturing overhead cost?

    a. $158,000   c. $145,000

    b. $83,000   d. $220,000

Learning Objective 3

7. How much manufacturing overhead would Gell allocate?

    a. $83,000   c. $124,000

    b. $93,000   d. $220,000

Learning Objective 5

8. What entry would Gell make to adjust the manufacturing overhead account for overallocated or underallocated overhead?

Date	Accounts and Explanation	Debit	Credit
a.	Manufacturing Overhead	10,000	
	Cost of Goods Sold		10,000
b.	Manufacturing Overhead	41,000	
	Cost of Goods Sold		41,000
c.	Cost of Goods Sold	41,000	
	Manufacturing Overhead		41,000
d.	Cost of Goods Sold	10,000	
	Manufacturing Overhead		10,000

Learning Objective 4

9. A manufacturing company completed work on a job. The cost of the job is transferred into _____ with a _____.

    a. Work-in-Process Inventory; debit   c. Finished Goods Inventory; debit

    b. Finished Goods Inventory; credit   d. Cost of Goods Sold; credit

Learning Objective 6

10. For which of the following reasons would David Laugherty, owner of the Laugherty Associates law firm, want to know the total costs of a job (serving a particular client)?

    a. For inventory valuation   c. For external reporting

    b. To determine the fees to charge clients   d. a, b, and c are correct

Check your answers at the end of the chapter.

ASSESS YOUR PROGRESS

> Review Questions

1. Why do managers need to know the cost of their products?
2. What types of companies use job order costing systems?
3. What types of companies use process costing systems?
4. What is the purpose of a job cost record?
5. Explain the difference between cost of goods manufactured and cost of goods sold.

6. A job was started on May 15, completed on June 27, and delivered to the customer on July 6. In which accounts would the costs be recorded on the financial statements dated May 31, June 30, and July 31?

7. Give the journal entry for raw materials purchased on account. Explain how this transaction affects the accounting equation.

8. What is the purpose of the raw materials subsidiary ledger? How is it related to the general ledger?

9. How does the use of direct and indirect materials in production affect the accounts?

10. Give the journal entry for direct and indirect labor costs incurred. Explain how this transaction affects the accounting equation.

11. Give five examples of manufacturing overhead costs. Why are they considered indirect costs?

12. What is the predetermined overhead allocation rate?

13. What is an allocation base? Give some examples.

14. How is manufacturing overhead allocated to jobs?

15. A completed job cost record shows the unit cost of the products. How is this calculated?

16. Explain the journal entry for the allocation of overhead. What accounts are affected? Are they increased or decreased?

17. Give the journal entry for the completion of a job. How is the accounting equation affected?

18. Why does the sale of a completed job require two journal entries? What are they?

19. Explain the difference between underallocated overhead and overallocated overhead. What causes each situation?

20. If a company incurred $5,250 in actual overhead costs and allocated $5,575 to jobs, was the overhead overallocated or underallocated? By how much?

21. Refer to the previous question. Give the journal entry to adjust the Manufacturing Overhead account for overallocated or underallocated overhead.

22. Explain the terms *accumulate, assign, allocate,* and *adjust* as they apply to job order costing.

23. Why would the manager of a service company need to use job order costing?

24. How is the predetermined overhead allocation rate used by service companies?

> Short Exercises

S19-1 Distinguishing between job order costing and process costing

Would the following companies most likely use job order costing or process costing?

a. A manufacturer of refrigerators

b. A manufacturer of specialty wakeboards

c. A manufacturer of luxury yachts

d. A professional services firm

e. A landscape contractor

f. A custom home builder

g. A cell phone manufacturer

h. A manufacturer of frozen pizzas

i. A manufacturer of multivitamins

j. A manufacturer of tennis shoes

Learning Objective 1

Learning Objective 2

S19-2 Determining the flow of costs in job order costing

For the following accounts, indicate what causes the account to increase and decrease. The first account is completed as an example.

Account	Is increased by:	Is decreased by:
Raw Materials Inventory	Materials purchased	Materials used
Work-in-Process Inventory		
Finished Goods Inventory		
Cost of Goods Sold		

Learning Objective 2

S19-3 Accounting for materials

Pack Rite manufactures backpacks. Its plant records include the following materials-related data:

Raw Materials Inventory, beginning balance	$ 31,000
Purchases of canvas, on account	65,000
Purchases of sewing machine lubricating oil, on account	1,000
Materials requisitions:	
Canvas	63,000
Sewing machine lubricating oil	400

Journalize the entries to record the transactions, post to the Raw Materials Inventory account, and determine the ending balance in Raw Materials Inventory.

Learning Objective 2

S19-4 Accounting for materials

Analyze the following T-accounts to determine the amount of direct and indirect materials used.

Raw Materials Inventory

Bal.	15		
Purchased	245	???	Used
Bal.	30		

Work-in-Process Inventory

Bal.	30		
Direct Materials	???	540	Cost of Goods Manufactured
Direct Labor	310		
Manufacturing Overhead	130		
Bal.	40		

Learning Objective 2

S19-5 Accounting for labor

Journalize the following labor-related transactions for Portland Glass at its plant in Portland, Oregon. Assume that the labor has been incurred, but not yet paid.

Plant janitor's wages	$ 650
Plant furnace operator's wages	850
Glass blower's wages	71,000

S19-6 Accounting for overhead

Learning Objective 3

Sparrow Furniture manufactures wood patio furniture. If the company reports the following costs for June 2016, what is the balance in the Manufacturing Overhead account before overhead is allocated to jobs? Assume that the labor has been incurred, but not yet paid. Prepare journal entries for overhead costs incurred in June.

Wood	$ 180,000
Nails, glue, stain	17,000
Depreciation on saws	4,900
Indirect manufacturing labor	37,000
Depreciation on delivery truck	2,100
Assembly-line workers' wages	52,000

S19-7 Allocating overhead

Learning Objective 3

Job 303 includes direct materials costs of $500 and direct labor costs of $420. If the predetermined overhead allocation rate is 70% of direct labor cost, what is the total cost assigned to Job 303?

S19-8 Calculating predetermined overhead allocation rate, allocating overhead

Learning Objective 3

Milestone Company estimates the company will incur $96,900 in overhead costs and 5,100 direct labor hours during the year. Actual direct labor hours were 4,400. Calculate the predetermined overhead allocation rate, and prepare the journal entry for the allocation of overhead.

S19-9 Comparing actual to allocated overhead

Learning Objective 3

Columbia Enterprises reports the following information at December 31, 2016:

Manufacturing Overhead	
3,300	51,700
15,000	
37,000	

Requirements

1. What is the actual manufacturing overhead of Columbia Enterprises?
2. What is the allocated manufacturing overhead?
3. Is manufacturing overhead underallocated or overallocated? By how much?

S19-10 Calculating under/overallocated overhead

Learning Objective 3

The T-account showing the manufacturing overhead activity for Edith Corp. for 2016 is as follows:

Manufacturing Overhead	
205,000	209,000

Requirements

1. What is the actual manufacturing overhead?
2. What is the allocated manufacturing overhead?
3. Is manufacturing overhead underallocated or overallocated? By how much?

CHAPTER 19

Learning Objective 4

S19-11 Completing and selling products

Ford Company completed jobs that cost $37,000 to produce. In the same period, the company sold jobs for $86,000 that cost $45,000 to produce. Prepare the journal entries for the completion and sales of the jobs. All sales are on account.

Learning Objective 5

S19-12 Adjusting Manufacturing Overhead

Robertson Company's Manufacturing Overhead account is given below. Use this information to prepare the journal entry to adjust for overallocated or underallocated overhead.

Manufacturing Overhead

151,000	147,000

Learning Objective 6

S19-13 Using job order costing in a service company

Blake Accounting pays Jaclyn Sawyer $63,250 per year.

Requirements

1. What is the hourly cost to Blake Accounting of employing Sawyer? Assume a 25-hour week and a 46-week year.
2. What direct labor cost would be assigned to Client 507 if Sawyer works 16 hours to prepare Client 507's financial statements?

Learning Objective 6

S19-14 Using job order costing in a service company

Assume that Blake's accountants are expected to work a total of 12,000 direct labor hours in 2016. Blake's estimated total indirect costs are $192,000 and the allocation base used is direct labor hours.

Requirements

1. What is Blake's predetermined overhead allocation rate?
2. What indirect costs will be allocated to Client 507 if Sawyer works 11 hours to prepare the financial statements?

> Exercises

Learning Objective 1

E19-15 Distinguishing between job order costing and process costing

Following is a list of cost system characteristics and sample companies. Match each to either job order costing or process costing.

a. Companies that produce small quantities of many different products.
b. A company that pulverizes wood into pulp to manufacture cardboard.
c. A company that manufactures thousands of identical files.
d. Companies that produce large numbers of identical products.
e. A computer repair service that makes service calls to homes.
f. A company that assembles electronic parts and software to manufacture millions of portable media players.
g. A textbook publisher that produces copies of a particular book in batches.
h. A company that bottles milk into one-gallon containers.

i. A company that makes large quantities of one type of tankless hot water heaters.

j. A governmental agency that takes bids for specific items it utilizes where each item requires a separate bid.

E19-16 Defining terminology

Match the following terms to their definitions.

a. A record used to assign direct labor cost to specific jobs.

b. A request for the transfer of materials to the production floor.

c. A document that shows the direct materials, direct labor, and manufacturing overhead costs for an individual job.

d. An accounting system that accumulates costs by process.

e. The production of a unique product or specialized service

f. Used by companies that manufacture unique products or provide specialized services.

1. Job
2. Job Cost Record
3. Job Order Costing System
4. Labor Time Record
5. Materials Requisition
6. Process Costing System

E19-17 Accounting for job costs

Spring Trailers' job cost records yielded the following information:

Job No.	Date Started	Date Finished	Date Sold	Total Cost of Job at July 31
1	June 21	July 16	July 17	$ 3,000
2	June 29	July 21	July 26	13,800
3	July 3	August 11	August 13	6,700
4	July 7	July 29	August 1	4,800

Use the dates in the table to identify the status of each job. Compute the following balances for Spring:

a. Work-in-Process Inventory at July 31

b. Finished Goods Inventory at July 31

c. Cost of Goods Sold for July

E19-18 Recording materials and labor costs

Azalea Company makes artificial flowers and reports the following data for the month:

Purchases of materials, on account	$ 52,000
Materials requisitions:	
Direct materials	47,800
Indirect materials	600
Labor incurred (not yet paid):	
Direct labor	26,400
Indirect labor	1,830

Journalize the entries relating to materials and labor.

E19-19 Allocating and adjusting manufacturing overhead

Selected cost data for Antique Poster Co. are as follows:

Estimated manufacturing overhead cost for the year	$ 120,000
Estimated direct labor cost for the year	100,000
Actual manufacturing overhead cost for the year	90,000
Actual direct labor cost for the year	71,000

Requirements

1. Compute the predetermined overhead allocation rate per direct labor dollar.

2. Prepare the journal entry to allocate overhead costs for the year.

3. Use a T-account to determine the amount of underallocated or overallocated manufacturing overhead.

4. Prepare the journal entry to adjust for the underallocated or overallocated manufacturing overhead.

E19-20 Allocating and adjusting manufacturing overhead

Metal Foundry uses a predetermined overhead allocation rate to allocate overhead to individual jobs, based on the machine hours required. At the beginning of 2016, the company expected to incur the following:

Manufacturing overhead cost	$ 870,000
Direct labor costs	1,450,000
Machine hours	72,500 hours

At the end of 2016, the company had actually incurred:

Direct labor cost	$ 1,160,000
Depreciation on manufacturing plant and equipment	610,000
Property taxes on plant	40,000
Sales salaries	27,500
Delivery drivers' wages	24,000
Plant janitor's wages	18,000
Machine hours	65,000 hours

Requirements

1. Compute Metal's predetermined overhead allocation rate.

2. Prepare the journal entry to allocate manufacturing overhead.

3. Post the manufacturing overhead transactions to the Manufacturing Overhead T-account. Is manufacturing overhead underallocated or overallocated? By how much?

4. Prepare the journal entry to adjust for the underallocated or overallocated manufacturing overhead. Does your entry increase or decrease cost of goods sold?

E19-21 Allocating and adjusting manufacturing overhead

Learning Objectives 3, 5

2. Underallocated by $15,500

The manufacturing records for Bob's Boats at the end of the 2016 fiscal year show the following information about manufacturing overhead:

Overhead allocated to production	$ 409,500
Actual manufacturing overhead costs	425,000
Predetermined overhead allocation rate	45 per machine hour

Requirements

1. How many machine hours did Bob's Boats use in 2016?

2. Was manufacturing overhead overallocated or underallocated for the year, and by how much?

3. Prepare the journal entry to adjust for the underallocated or overallocated manufacturing overhead.

E19-22 Completing and selling jobs

Learning Objective 4

4. Gross profit $12,000

June production generated the following activity in Car Chassis Company's Work-in-Process Inventory account:

June 1 balance	$ 38,000
Direct materials used	43,000
Direct labor assigned to jobs	42,000
Manufacturing overhead allocated to jobs	29,400

Additionally, Car Chassis has completed Jobs 142 and 143, with total costs of $46,000 and $35,000, respectively.

Requirements

1. Prepare the journal entry for production completed in June.

2. Open a T-account for Work-in-Process Inventory. Post the journal entry made in Requirement 1. Compute the ending balance in the Work-in-Process Inventory account on June 30.

3. Prepare the journal entry to record the sale on account of Job 143 for $47,000. Also, prepare the journal entry to record Cost of Goods Sold for Job 143.

4. What is the gross profit on Job 143?

Learning Objective 5

N.I. $90

E19-23 Preparing a schedule of cost of goods manufactured and an income statement

Shaffer Company has the following information for the year ended December 31, 2016. Use the information to prepare a schedule of cost of goods manufactured and an income statement. Assume no indirect materials are used and all amounts are shown in millions.

Inventories:	Beginning	Ending
Raw Materials	$ 8	$ 9
Work-in-Process	14	19
Finished Goods	4	11
Other information:		
Sales Revenue		$ 228
Selling and Administrative Expenses		64
Direct Labor		46
Manufacturing Overhead; actual and allocated		16
Materials Purchases		25

Learning Objectives 2, 3, 4, 5

i. Underallocated by $9,200

E19-24 Preparing job order costing journal entries

Journalize the following transactions for Blanche's Benches:

a. Incurred and paid Web site expenses, $2,800.

b. Incurred manufacturing wages of $10,000, 70% of which was direct labor and 30% of which was indirect labor.

c. Purchased raw materials on account, $19,000.

d. Used in production: direct materials, $8,000; indirect materials, $3,500.

e. Recorded manufacturing overhead: depreciation on plant, $14,000; plant insurance (previously paid), $1,300; plant property tax, $3,500 (credit Property Tax Payable).

f. Allocated manufacturing overhead to jobs, 230% of direct labor costs.

g. Completed production on jobs with costs of $36,000.

h. Sold inventory on account, $26,000; cost of goods sold, $12,000.

i. Adjusted for overallocated or underallocated overhead.

Learning Objectives 2, 3, 4, 5

E19-25 Identifying job order costing journal entries

Analyze the following T-accounts, and describe each lettered transaction. Note that some transactions may be compound entries.

Raw Materials Inventory	Work-in-Process Inventory	Finished Goods Inventory	Prepaid Insurance
(a) | (b)	(b) | (f) (c) (e)	(f) | (g)	| (d)

Accounts Payable	Wages Payable	Manufacturing Overhead	Cost of Goods Sold
| (a)	| (c)	(b) | (e) (c) | (h) (d)	(g) | (h) |

E19-26 Determining missing amounts

Analyze the following T-accounts, and determine the missing amounts.

Raw Materials Inventory			Work-in-Process Inventory			Finished Goods Inventory			Accumulated Depreciation	
25,000	(a)		(b)	30,000		(c)	(d)			9,000
Bal. 3,000			4,000			Bal. 4,000				
			6,750							
			Bal. 750							

Accounts Payable			Wages Payable			Manufacturing Overhead			Cost of Goods Sold	
	25,000			(e)		2,000	6,750		(g)	
						500	(f)		4,750	
						9,000			Bal. 30,750	
						Bal. 0				

E19-27 Using job order costing in a service company

Martin Realtors, a real estate consulting firm, specializes in advising companies on potential new plant sites. The company uses a job order costing system with a predetermined overhead allocation rate, computed as a percentage of direct labor costs.

At the beginning of 2016, managing partner Jennifer Martin prepared the following budget for the year:

Direct labor hours (professionals)	22,000 hours
Direct labor costs (professionals)	$ 2,750,000
Office rent	390,000
Support staff salaries	1,685,000
Utilities	400,000

Root Manufacturing, Inc. is inviting several consultants to bid for work. Jennifer Martin wants to submit a bid. She estimates that this job will require about 240 direct labor hours.

Requirements

1. Compute Martin Realtors' (a) hourly direct labor cost rate and (b) predetermined overhead allocation rate.
2. Compute the predicted cost of the Root Manufacturing job.
3. If Martin wants to earn a profit that equals 55% of the job's cost, how much should she bid for the Root Manufacturing job?

> Problems Group A

Learning Objectives 1, 2, 4

5. Gross profit $1,000

P19-28A Analyzing cost data, recording completion and sales of jobs

Brandon Manufacturing makes carrying cases for portable electronic devices. Its costing records yield the following information:

| Job | Date | | | Total | Total |
| | | | | Cost of Job | Manufacturing Costs Added |
No.	Started	Finished	Sold	at October 31	in November
1	10/03	10/12	10/13	$ 1,000	
2	10/03	10/30	11/01	1,300	
3	10/17	11/24	11/27	600	$ 800
4	10/29	11/29	12/03	500	1,600
5	11/08	11/12	11/14		350
6	11/23	12/06	12/09		100

Requirements

1. Which type of costing system is Brandon using? What piece of data did you base your answer on?

2. Use the dates in the table to identify the status of each job at October 31 and November 30. Compute Brandon's account balances at October 31 for Work-in-Process Inventory, Finished Goods Inventory, and Cost of Goods Sold. Compute, by job, account balances at November 30 for Work-in-Process Inventory, Finished Goods Inventory, and Cost of Goods Sold.

3. Prepare journal entries to record the transfer of completed jobs from Work-in-Process Inventory to Finished Goods Inventory for October and November.

4. Record the sale of Job 3 for $2,400 on account.

5. What is the gross profit for Job 3?

Learning Objectives 2, 3, 4

1. Cost per DVD $0.37

P19-29A Preparing and using a job cost record to prepare journal entries

Yu Technology Co. manufactures CDs and DVDs for computer software and entertainment companies. Yu uses job order costing.

On April 2, Yu began production of 5,700 DVDs, Job 423, for Portrait Pictures for $1.40 sales price per DVD. Yu promised to deliver the DVDs to Portrait Pictures by April 5. Yu incurred the following costs:

Date	Labor Time Record No.	Description	Amount
4/02	655	10 hours @ $18 per hour	$ 180
4/03	656	20 hours @ $13 per hour	260

Date	Materials Requisition No.	Description	Amount
4/02	63	31 lbs. polycarbonate plastic @ $12 per lb.	$ 372
4/02	64	25 lbs. acrylic plastic @ $27 per lb.	675
4/03	74	3 lbs. refined aluminum @ $45 per lb.	135

Yu Technology allocates manufacturing overhead to jobs based on the relation between estimated overhead of $495,000 and estimated direct labor costs of $450,000. Job 423 was completed and shipped on April 3.

Requirements

1. Prepare a job cost record for Job 423. Calculate the predetermined overhead allocation rate; then allocate manufacturing overhead to the job.

2. Journalize in summary form the requisition of direct materials and the assignment of direct labor and the allocation of manufacturing overhead to Job 423. Wages are not yet paid.

3. Journalize completion of the job and the sale of the 5,700 DVDs on account.

P19-30A Accounting for transactions, construction company

Learning Objectives 2, 3, 4

3. WIP Bal. $284,000

Sunset Construction, Inc. is a home builder in Arizona. Sunset uses a job order costing system in which each house is a job. Because it constructs houses, the company uses an account titled Construction Overhead. The company applies overhead based on estimated direct labor costs. For the year, it estimated construction overhead of $1,250,000 and total direct labor cost of $2,500,000. The following events occurred during August:

a. Purchased materials on account, $440,000.

b. Requisitioned direct materials and used direct labor in construction. Recorded the materials requisitioned.

	Direct Materials	Direct Labor
House 402	$ 56,000	$ 41,000
House 403	65,000	35,000
House 404	62,000	57,000
House 405	84,000	55,000

c. The company incurred total wages of $210,000. Use the data from Item b to assign the wages. Wages are not yet paid.

d. Depreciation of construction equipment, $6,800.

e. Other overhead costs incurred: Equipment rentals paid in cash, $34,000; Worker liability insurance expired, $6,000.

f. Allocated overhead to jobs.

g. Houses completed: 402, 404.

h. House sold on account: 404 for $220,000.

Requirements

1. Calculate Sunset's predetermined overhead allocation rate for the year.

2. Prepare journal entries to record the events in the general journal.

3. Open T-accounts for Work-in-Process Inventory and Finished Goods Inventory. Post the appropriate entries to these accounts, identifying each entry by letter. Determine the ending account balances, assuming that the beginning balances were zero.

4. Add the costs of the unfinished houses, and show that this total amount equals the ending balance in the Work-in-Process Inventory account.

5. Add the cost of the completed house that has not yet been sold, and show that this equals the ending balance in Finished Goods Inventory.

6. Compute gross profit on the house that was sold. What costs must gross profit cover for Sunset Construction?

Learning Objectives 3, 5

1. $8.00 per machine hour

P19-31A Accounting for manufacturing overhead

Premium Woods manufactures jewelry boxes. The primary materials (wood, brass, and glass) and direct labor are assigned directly to the products. Manufacturing overhead costs are allocated based on machine hours. Data for 2016 follow:

	Estimated	Actual
Machine hours	26,500 hours	32,600 hours
Maintenance labor (repairs to equipment)	$ 12,000	$ 29,500
Plant supervisor's salary	43,000	49,000
Screws, nails, and glue	23,000	48,000
Plant utilities	49,000	90,850
Freight out	35,000	47,500
Depreciation on plant and equipment	85,000	84,000
Advertising expense	44,000	54,000

Requirements

1. Compute the predetermined overhead allocation rate.

2. Post actual and allocated manufacturing overhead to the Manufacturing Overhead T-account.

3. Prepare the journal entry to adjust for underallocated or overallocated overhead.

4. The predetermined overhead allocation rate usually turns out to be inaccurate. Why don't accountants just use the actual manufacturing overhead rate?

P19-32A **Preparing comprehensive accounting for manufacturing transactions**

Learning Stars produces stars for elementary teachers to reward their students. Learning Stars' trial balance on June 1 follows:

Learning Objectives 2, 3, 4, 5

4. COGM $47,275

5. NI $16,300

LEARNING STARS Trial Balance June 1, 2016		
	Balance	
Account Title	**Debit**	**Credit**
Cash	$ 18,000	
Accounts Receivable	180,000	
Inventories:		
Raw Materials	6,100	
Work-in-Process	41,100	
Finished Goods	21,100	
Plant Assets	210,000	
Accumulated Depreciation		$ 74,000
Accounts Payable		131,000
Wages Payable		1,800
Common Stock		145,000
Retained Earnings		124,500
Sales Revenue		
Cost of Goods Sold		
Manufacturing Overhead		
Selling and Administrative Expenses		
Totals	$ 476,300	$ 476,300

June 1 balances in the subsidiary ledgers were as follows:

- Raw Materials Inventory subsidiary ledger: Paper, $4,100; indirect materials, $2,000
- Work-in-Process Inventory subsidiary ledger: Job 120, $41,100; Job 121, $0
- Finished Goods Inventory subsidiary ledger: Large Stars, $9,400; Small Stars, $11,700

June transactions are summarized as follows:

a. Collections on account, $150,000.

b. Selling and administrative expenses incurred and paid, $33,000.

c. Payments on account, $40,000.

d. Materials purchases on account: Paper, $20,000; indirect materials, $5,000.

e. Materials requisitioned and used in production:

Job 120: Paper, $550

Job 121: Paper, $7,750

Indirect materials, $1,800

f. Wages incurred during June, $37,000. Labor time records for the month: Job 120, $3,750; Job 121, $18,500; indirect labor, $14,750.

g. Wages paid in June include the balance in Wages Payable at May 31 plus $35,000 of wages incurred during June.

h. Depreciation on plant and equipment, $3,000.

i. Manufacturing overhead allocated at the predetermined overhead allocation rate of 50% of direct labor cost.

j. Jobs completed during the month: Job 120 with 300,000 Large Stars at a total cost of $47,275.

k. Sales on account: all of Job 120 for $105,000.

l. Adjusted for overallocated or underallocated manufacturing overhead.

Requirements

1. Journalize the transactions for the company.

2. Open T-accounts for the general ledger, the Raw Materials Inventory subsidiary ledger, the Work-in-Process Inventory subsidiary ledger, and the Finished Goods Inventory subsidiary ledger. Insert each account balance as given, and use the reference *Bal.* Post the journal entries to the T-accounts using the transaction letters as a reference.

3. Prepare a trial balance at June 30, 2016.

4. Use the Work-in-Process Inventory T-account to prepare a schedule of cost of goods manufactured for the month of June.

5. Prepare an income statement for the month of June.

Learning Objective 6

2. Delicious Treats $313,400

(Requirements 1 and 2 only)

P19-33A Using job order costing in a service company

Hummingbird Design, Inc. is a Web site design and consulting firm. The firm uses a job order costing system in which each client is a different job. Hummingbird Design assigns direct labor, licensing costs, and travel costs directly to each job. It allocates indirect costs to jobs based on a predetermined overhead allocation rate, computed as a percentage of direct labor costs.

At the beginning of 2016, managing partner Sally Simone prepared the following budget estimates:

Direct labor hours (professionals)	6,250 hours
Direct labor costs (professionals)	$ 1,800,000
Support staff salaries	767,000
Computer leases	46,000
Office supplies	27,000
Office rent	60,000

In November 2016, Hummingbird Design served several clients. Records for two clients appear here:

	Delicious Treats	Mesilla Chocolates
Direct labor hours	700 hours	100 hours
Software licensing costs	$ 5,000	$ 300
Travel costs	6,000	0

Requirements

1. Compute Hummingbird Design's direct labor rate and its predetermined overhead allocation rate for 2016.

2. Compute the total cost of each job.

3. If Simone wants to earn profits equal to 20% of service revenue, what fee should she charge each of these two clients?

4. Why does Hummingbird Design assign costs to jobs?

> Problems **Group B**

P19-34B Analyzing cost data, recording completion and sales of jobs

Sloan Manufacturing makes carrying cases for portable electronic devices. Its costing records yield the following information:

Learning Objectives 1, 2, 4

5. Gross profit $400

Job No.	Date Started	Date Finished	Sold	Total Cost of Job at October 31	Total Manufacturing Costs Added in November
1	10/03	10/12	10/13	$ 1,100	
2	10/03	10/30	11/01	2,000	
3	10/17	11/24	11/27	1,000	$ 800
4	10/29	11/29	12/03	900	1,500
5	11/08	11/12	11/14		550
6	11/23	12/06	12/09		500

Requirements

1. Which type of costing system is Sloan using? What piece of data did you base your answer on?

2. Use the dates in the table to identify the status of each job at October 31 and November 30. Compute Sloan's account balances at October 31 for Work-in-Process Inventory, Finished Goods Inventory, and Cost of Goods Sold. Compute, by job, account balances at November 30 for Work-in-Process Inventory, Finished Goods Inventory, and Cost of Goods Sold.

3. Prepare journal entries to record the transfer of completed jobs from Work-in-Process Inventory to Finished Goods Inventory for October and November.

4. Record the sale of Job 3 for $2,200 on account.

5. What is the gross profit for Job 3?

Learning Objectives 2, 3, 4

1. Cost per DVD $0.39

P19-35B Preparing and using a job cost record to prepare journal entries

Tu Technology Co. manufactures CDs and DVDs for computer software and entertainment companies. Tu uses job order costing.

On November 2, Tu began production of 5,700 DVDs, Job 423, for Cyclorama Pictures for $1.50 sales price per DVD. Tu promised to deliver the DVDs to Cyclorama by November 5. Tu incurred the following costs:

Date	Labor Time Record No.	Description	Amount
11/02	655	10 hours @ $16 per hour	$ 160
11/03	656	20 hours @ $15 per hour	300

Date	Materials Requisition No.	Description	Amount
11/02	63	31 lbs. polycarbonate plastic @ $12 per lb.	$ 372
11/02	64	25 lbs. acrylic plastic @ $27 per lb.	675
11/03	74	3 lbs. refined aluminum @ $48 per lb.	144

Tu Technology allocates manufacturing overhead to jobs based on the relation between estimated overhead of $564,000 and estimated direct labor costs of $470,000. Job 423 was completed and shipped on November 3.

Requirements

1. Prepare a job cost record for Job 423. Calculate the predetermined overhead allocation rate; then allocate manufacturing overhead to the job.

2. Journalize in summary form the requisition of direct materials and the assignment of direct labor and the allocation of manufacturing overhead to Job 423. Wages are not yet paid.

3. Journalize completion of the job and the sale of the 5,700 DVDs on account.

Learning Objectives 2, 3, 4

3. WIP Bal. $272,200

P19-36B Accounting for transactions, construction company

Sunrise Construction, Inc. is a home builder in Arizona. Sunrise uses a job order costing system in which each house is a job. Because it constructs houses, the company uses an account titled Construction Overhead. The company applies overhead based on estimated direct labor costs. For the year, it estimated construction overhead of $1,300,000 and total direct labor cost of $3,250,000. The following events occurred during August:

a. Purchased materials on account, $450,000.

b. Requisitioned direct materials and used direct labor in construction. Recorded the materials requisitioned.

	Direct Materials	Direct Labor
House 402	$ 51,000	$ 43,000
House 403	66,000	36,000
House 404	63,000	57,000
House 405	83,000	52,000

c. The company incurred total wages of $250,000. Use the data from Item b to assign the wages. Wages are not yet paid.

d. Depreciation of construction equipment, $6,800.

e. Other overhead costs incurred: Equipment rentals paid in cash, $34,000; Worker liability insurance expired, $8,000.

f. Allocated overhead to jobs.

g. Houses completed: 402, 404.

h. House sold on account: 404 for $230,000.

Requirements

1. Calculate Sunrise's predetermined overhead allocation rate for the year.

2. Prepare journal entries to record the events in the general journal.

3. Open T-accounts for Work-in-Process Inventory and Finished Goods Inventory. Post the appropriate entries to these accounts, identifying each entry by letter. Determine the ending account balances, assuming that the beginning balances were zero.

4. Add the costs of the unfinished houses, and show that this total amount equals the ending balance in the Work-in-Process Inventory account.

5. Add the cost of the completed house that has not yet been sold, and show that this equals the ending balance in Finished Goods Inventory.

6. Compute gross profit on the house that was sold. What costs must gross profit cover for Sunrise Construction?

P19-37B Accounting for manufacturing overhead

Learning Objectives 3, 5

1. $7.50 per machine hour

Custom Woods manufactures jewelry boxes. The primary materials (wood, brass, and glass) and direct labor are assigned directly to the products. Manufacturing overhead costs are allocated based on machine hours. Data for 2016 follow:

	Estimated	Actual
Machine hours	28,960 hours	32,800 hours
Maintenance labor (repairs to equipment)	$ 14,000	$ 29,500
Plant supervisor's salary	45,000	48,000
Screws, nails, and glue	25,000	49,000
Plant utilities	46,000	93,850
Freight out	36,000	45,500
Depreciation on plant and equipment	87,200	86,000
Advertising expense	41,000	59,000

Requirements

1. Compute the predetermined overhead allocation rate.

2. Post actual and allocated manufacturing overhead to the Manufacturing Overhead T-account.

3. Prepare the journal entry to adjust for underallocated or overallocated overhead.

4. The predetermined overhead allocation rate usually turns out to be inaccurate. Why don't accountants just use the actual manufacturing overhead rate?

Learning Objectives 2, 3, 4, 5

4. COGM $46,750

5. NI $19,150

P19-38B Preparing comprehensive accounting for manufacturing transactions

Student Stars produces stars for elementary teachers to reward their students. Student Stars' trial balance on June 1 follows:

STUDENT STARS Trial Balance June 1, 2016		
	Balance	
Account Title	**Debit**	**Credit**
Cash	$ 24,000	
Accounts Receivable	175,000	
Inventories:		
Raw Materials	5,700	
Work-in-Process	41,000	
Finished Goods	21,300	
Plant Assets	220,000	
Accumulated Depreciation		$ 73,000
Accounts Payable		133,000
Wages Payable		2,000
Common Stock		143,000
Retained Earnings		136,000
Sales Revenue		
Cost of Goods Sold		
Manufacturing Overhead		
Selling and Administrative Expenses		
Totals	**$ 487,000**	**$ 487,000**

June 1 balances in the subsidiary ledgers were as follows:

- Raw Materials Inventory subsidiary ledger: Paper, $4,300; indirect materials, $1,400
- Work-in-Process Inventory subsidiary ledger: Job 120, $41,000; Job 121, $0
- Finished Goods Inventory subsidiary ledger: Large Stars, $9,100; Small Stars, $12,200

June transactions are summarized as follows:

a. Collections on account, $154,000.

b. Selling and administrative expenses incurred and paid, $30,000.

c. Payments on account, $41,000.

d. Materials purchases on account: Paper, $21,600; indirect materials, $4,000.

e. Materials requisitioned and used in production:

Job 120: Paper, $550

Job 121: Paper, $7,850

Indirect materials, $1,200

f. Wages incurred during June, $35,000. Labor time records for the month: Job 120, $3,250; Job 121, $18,500; indirect labor, $13,250.

g. Wages paid in June include the balance in Wages Payable at May 31 plus $33,000 of wages incurred during June.

h. Depreciation on plant and equipment, $2,700.

i. Manufacturing overhead allocated at the predetermined overhead allocation rate of 60% of direct labor cost.

j. Jobs completed during the month: Job 120 with 900,000 Large Stars at a total cost of $46,750.

k. Sales on account: all of Job 120 for $100,000.

l. Adjusted for overallocated or underallocated manufacturing overhead.

Requirements

1. Journalize the transactions for the company.

2. Open T-accounts for the general ledger, the Raw Materials Inventory subsidiary ledger, the Work-in-Process Inventory subsidiary ledger, and the Finished Goods Inventory subsidiary ledger. Insert each account balance as given, and use the reference *Bal*. Post the journal entries to the T-accounts using the transaction letters as a reference.

3. Prepare a trial balance at June 30, 2016.

4. Use the Work-in-Process Inventory T-account to prepare a schedule of cost of goods manufactured for the month of June.

5. Prepare an income statement for the month of June.

P19-39B Using job order costing in a service company

Learning Objective 6

2. Food Co-op $277,600

Robin Design, Inc. is a Web site design and consulting firm. The firm uses a job order costing system in which each client is a different job. Robin Design assigns direct labor, licensing costs, and travel costs directly to each job. It allocates indirect costs to jobs based on a predetermined overhead allocation rate, computed as a percentage of direct labor costs.

At the beginning of 2016, managing partner Judi Jacquin prepared the following budget estimates:

Direct labor hours (professionals)	10,000 hours
Direct labor costs (professionals)	$ 2,100,000
Support staff salaries	706,000
Computer leases	49,000
Office supplies	25,000
Office rent	60,000

CHAPTER 19

In November 2016, Robin Design served several clients. Records for two clients appear here:

	Food Co-op	Martin Chocolates
Direct labor hours	900 hours	100 hours
Software licensing costs	$ 3,000	$ 300
Travel costs	10,000	0

Requirements

1. Compute Robin Design's direct labor rate and its predetermined overhead allocation rate for 2016.

2. Compute the total cost of each job.

3. If Judi wants to earn profits equal to 20% of service revenue, what fee should she charge each of these two clients?

4. Why does Robin Design assign costs to jobs?

> Continuing Problem

P19-40 Accounting for manufacturing overhead

This problem continues the Daniels Consulting situation from Problem P18-42 of Chapter 18. Daniels Consulting uses a job order costing system in which each client is a different job. Daniels assigns direct labor, meal per diem, and travel costs directly to each job. It allocates indirect costs to jobs based on a predetermined overhead allocation rate, computed as a percentage of direct labor costs.

At the beginning of 2018, the controller prepared the following budget:

Direct labor hours (professionals)	6,250 hours
Direct labor costs (professionals)	$ 1,100,000
Support staff salaries	90,000
Computer leases	57,000
Office supplies	40,000
Office rent	55,000

In November 2018, Daniels served several clients. Records for two clients appear here:

	Tommy's Trains	Marcia's Cookies
Direct labor hours	720 hours	200 hours
Meal per diem	$ 2,700	$ 600
Travel costs	8,000	0

Requirements

1. Compute Daniels's predetermined overhead allocation rate for 2018.

2. Compute the total cost of each job.

3. If Daniels wants to earn profits equal to 25% of sales revenue, what fee should it charge each of these two clients?

4. Why does Daniels assign costs to jobs?

CRITICAL THINKING

> Decision Case 19-1

Hiebert Chocolate, Ltd. is located in Memphis. The company prepares gift boxes of chocolates for private parties and corporate promotions. Each order contains a selection of chocolates determined by the customer, and the box is designed to the customer's specifications. Accordingly, Hiebert uses a job order costing system and allocates manufacturing overhead based on direct labor cost.

One of Hiebert's largest customers is the Goforth and Leos law firm. This organization sends chocolates to its clients each Christmas and also provides them to employees at the firm's gatherings. The law firm's managing partner, Bob Goforth, placed the client gift order in September for 500 boxes of cream-filled dark chocolates. But Goforth and Leos did not place its December staff-party order until the last week of November. This order was for an additional 100 boxes of chocolates identical to the ones to be distributed to clients.

Hiebert budgeted the cost per box for the original 500-box order as follows:

Chocolate, filling, wrappers, box	$ 14.00
Employee time to fill and wrap the box (10 min.)	2.00
Manufacturing overhead	1.00
Total manufacturing cost	$ 17.00

Ben Hiebert, president of Hiebert Chocolate, Ltd., priced the order at $20 per box.

In the past few months, Hiebert has experienced price increases for both dark chocolate and direct labor. All other costs have remained the same. Hiebert budgeted the cost per box for the second order as follows:

Chocolate, filling, wrappers, box	$ 15.00
Employee time to fill and wrap the box (10 min.)	2.20
Manufacturing overhead	1.10
Total manufacturing cost	$ 18.30

Requirements

1. Do you agree with the cost analysis for the second order? Explain your answer.

2. Should the two orders be accounted for as one job or two in Hiebert's system?

3. What sale price per box should Ben Hiebert set for the second order? What are the advantages and disadvantages of this price?

> Fraud Case 19-1

Jerry never imagined he'd be sitting there in Washington being grilled mercilessly by a panel of congressmen. But a young government auditor picked up on his scheme last year. His company produced high-tech navigation devices that were sold to both military and civilian clients. The military contracts were "cost-plus," meaning that payments were calculated based on actual production costs plus a profit markup. The civilian contracts were bid out in a very competitive market, and every dollar counted. Jerry knew that because all the jobs were done in the same factory, he could manipulate the allocation of overhead costs in a way that would shift costs away from the civilian contracts and into the military "cost-plus" work. That way, the company would collect more from the government and be able to shave its bids down on civilian work. He never thought anyone would discover the alterations he had made in the factory workers' time sheets, but one of his accountants had noticed and tipped off the government auditor. Now, as the congressman from Michigan rakes him over the coals, Jerry is trying to figure out his chances of dodging jail time.

Requirements

1. Based on what you have read above, what was Jerry's company using as a cost driver to allocate overhead to the various jobs?

2. Why does the government consider Jerry's actions fraudulent?

3. Name two ways that reducing costs on the civilian contracts would benefit the company and motivate Jerry to commit fraud.

MyAccountingLab   **For a wealth of online resources, including exercises, problems, media, and immediate tutorial help, please visit http://www.myaccountinglab.com.**

> ## Quick Check Answers

1. d **2.** b **3.** d **4.** a **5.** a **6.** b **7.** c **8.** b **9.** c **10.** b

Process Costing

Soft Drink, Anyone?

Carl Marino watched the plastic bottles go by. His machine was running smoothly, and it looked like it was going to be a good shift. Carl works at the Drake Drink Company. The company runs two 10-hour shifts for full-time employees and a four-hour mini-shift for part-timers. The mini-shift is perfect for Carl, a college student. It gives Carl the opportunity to earn some money without cutting into his study time. But the best part of the job is the management. The managers at Drake are always willing to answer Carl's questions. And as a business student, Carl has lots of questions about managing a business.

Lately, Carl has been wondering about the cost of producing a bottle of Drake's soft drink. With the company producing a large quantity of soft drinks, how does the company know the cost of one bottle of a particular soft drink? Carl's managers have been explaining their costing system to him. Drake uses a process costing system, where the company determines the cost of each manufacturing process, such as mixing, bottling, and packaging. Then, at the end of the month, the company uses the costing system to determine the average cost of producing one bottle of soft drink. Knowing the cost per bottle allows the managers to make good pricing decisions and stay competitive in the market.

As Carl watches the bottles go by, he decides to find out more about the company's process costing system.

How Much Does That Soft Drink Cost?

You stop at a convenience store to buy a soft drink. As you pay for your purchase, you may wonder about the cost of producing such a product. PepsiCo, Inc. has 22 billion-dollar brands, which means it has 22 brands, such as Pepsi, Lay's, Mountain Dew, and Gatorade, that generate more than $1 billion in sales each year. With that volume of production and sales, how does the company track its production costs? Many food and beverage companies mass-produce their products. Production consists of a series of processes, and costs are associated with each process. By tracking costs by process, the company can determine the total product cost at the end of the accounting period.

Chapter 20 Learning Objectives

1 Describe the flow of costs through a process costing system

2 Calculate equivalent units of production for direct materials and conversion costs

3 Prepare a production cost report using the weighted-average method

4 Prepare journal entries for a process costing system

5 Use a production cost report to make decisions

6 Prepare a production cost report using the first-in, first-out method (Appendix 20A)

HOW DO COSTS FLOW THROUGH A PROCESS COSTING SYSTEM?

Learning Objective 1

Describe the flow of costs through a process costing system

In the previous chapter, you learned the importance of using a costing system to determine the cost of products and services. Managers use cost information in their primary duties of planning and controlling. The focus in the previous chapter was on job order costing systems. This chapter concentrates on process costing systems. Let's review the differences and similarities between the two systems.

Job Order Costing Versus Process Costing

In the previous chapter, you learned that companies like Smart Touch Learning, our fictitious company that manufactures touch screen tablet computers that are preloaded with its e-learning software programs, use a **job order costing system** to determine the cost of its custom goods and services. Job order costing is appropriate for companies that manufacture batches of unique products or provide specialized services. Other examples of companies that use job order costing systems include accounting firms, building contractors, and custom furniture manufacturers.

Job Order Costing System
An accounting system that accumulates costs by job. Used by companies that manufacture unique products or provide specialized services.

Process
One of a series of steps in manufacturing production; usually associated with making large quantities of similar items.

Process Costing System
An accounting system that accumulates costs by process. Used by companies that manufacture identical units through a series of uniform production steps or processes.

In contrast, other companies use a series of steps, which are called **processes**, to make large quantities of similar products. Examples of companies that manufacture homogenous products include soft drink bottlers, paint manufacturers, and gasoline refiners. These companies use a **process costing system**. There are two methods for handling process costing: weighted-average and first-in, first-out (FIFO). This chapter's focus is on the weighted-average method; however, you learn about the FIFO method in Appendix 20A at the end of the chapter.

Both job order and process costing systems track the product costs of direct materials, direct labor, and manufacturing overhead through the three inventory accounts on the balance sheet: Raw Materials Inventory, Work-in-Process Inventory, and Finished Goods Inventory. When the products are sold, both systems transfer the product costs to Cost of Goods Sold, an expense account on the income statement.

The primary differences between job order costing and process costing are *how* and *when* costs are recorded in Work-in-Process Inventory. Job order costing has one Work-in-Process Inventory account, with a subsidiary ledger containing individual job cost records for each job. Costs are transferred to Finished Goods Inventory when the jobs are completed. Process costing has a separate Work-in-Process Inventory account for each process or department. A production cost report is completed for each process or department, and costs are transferred at the end of each period. The cost transfer is from one Work-in-Process Inventory account to the next Work-in-Process Inventory account and eventually to Finished Goods Inventory.

Exhibit 20-1 summarizes the differences between job order costing systems and process costing systems.

Exhibit 20-1 | **Job Order Costing Versus Process Costing**

	Job Order Costing System	Process Costing System
Company Type	Manufactures batches of unique products or provides specialized services	Manufactures homogenous products through a series of uniform steps or processes
Cost Accumulation	By job	By process
Work-in-Process Inventory	One general ledger account with a subsidiary ledger containing individual job cost sheets	Separate Work-in-Process Inventory accounts for each process or department
Record Keeping	Job cost sheet for each job	Production cost report for each process or department
Timing of Cost Transfers	When each job is completed	At the end of the accounting period

Flow of Costs Through a Process Costing System

To gain an understanding of process costing, consider the crayon manufacturing process. Cheerful Colors, a fictitious crayon manufacturing company, divides its manufacturing operations into three processes: mixing, molding, and packaging. The Mixing Department combines direct materials such as paraffin wax and pigments. The heated mixture is pumped to the Molding Department, where it is poured into molds. After the molds cool, the crayons are removed from the molds and transferred to the Packaging Department, where paper wrappers are added to each crayon and the crayons are boxed. The crayons *accumulate* production costs during each process. The company then *assigns* these costs to the crayons passing through that process. At Cheerful Colors, each process is a separate department.

Suppose the company's production costs incurred to make 10,000 crayons and the costs per crayon are as follows:

	Total Costs	Cost per Crayon
Mixing	$ 200	$ 0.02
Molding	100	0.01
Packaging	300	0.03
Total Cost	$ 600	$ 0.06

The total cost to produce 10,000 crayons is the sum of the costs incurred for the three processes ($600). The cost per crayon is the total cost divided by the number of crayons, or

$600 / 10,000 crayons = $0.06 per crayon

Cheerful Colors uses the cost per unit of each process to do the following:

- **Control costs.** The company can look for ways to cut the costs when actual process costs are more than planned process costs.
- **Set selling prices.** The company wants the selling price to cover the costs of making the crayons, and it also wants to earn a profit.

- **Calculate account balances.** The company needs to know the ending balances in Work-in-Process Inventory and Finished Goods Inventory for the balance sheet and Cost of Goods Sold for the income statement.

At any moment, some crayons are in the mixing process, some are in the molding process, and others are in the packaging process. Computing the crayons' cost becomes more complicated when the units are at different places in the production cycle.

Exhibit 20-2 compares cost flows in a job order costing system for Smart Touch Learning and a process costing system for Cheerful Colors.

Exhibit 20-2 | **Comparison of Cost Flows: Job Order Costing and Process Costing**

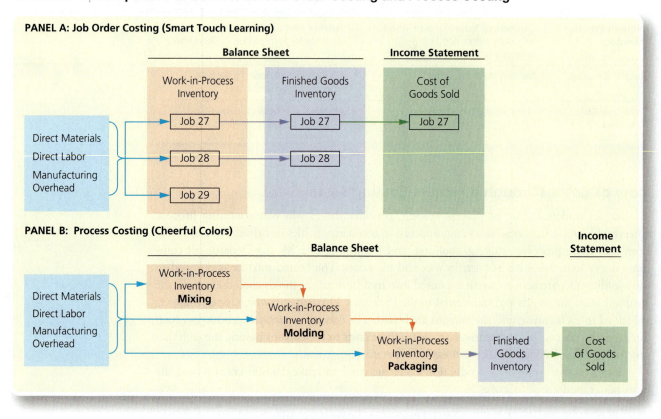

Panel A shows that a job order costing system has a single Work-in-Process Inventory control account. The Work-in-Process Inventory account in the general ledger is supported by an individual subsidiary cost record for each job. Panel B summarizes the flow of costs for a process costing system. Notice the following:

1. Each process (mixing, molding, and packaging) is a separate department, and each department has its own Work-in-Process Inventory account.
2. Direct materials, direct labor, and manufacturing overhead are assigned to Work-in-Process Inventory for each process that uses them.
3. When the Mixing Department's process is complete, the mixture moves out of the Mixing Department and into the Molding Department. The Mixing Department's costs are also transferred out of the Mixing Department's Work-in-Process Inventory into Work-in-Process Inventory—Molding.
4. When the Molding Department's process is complete, the crayons move from the Molding Department into the Packaging Department. The costs of the crayons are transferred out of the Molding Department's Work-in-Process Inventory into Work-in-Process Inventory—Packaging.

5. When production is complete, the boxes of crayons go into finished goods storage. The combined costs from all departments then flow into Finished Goods Inventory, but only from the Work-in-Process Inventory account of the *last* manufacturing process. For Cheerful Colors, Packaging is the last department.

6. The total cost of the crayons includes the costs of mixing, molding, and packaging. The costs incurred in the first process are transferred to the second process. The costs incurred in the first and second processes are then transferred to the third process. Then the entire cost is transferred to Finished Goods Inventory.

Match each costing system characteristic to job order costing, process costing, or both.

1. Used by companies that manufacture identical items through a series of uniform production steps or processes
2. Transfers costs from Work-in-Process Inventory to Finished Goods Inventory to Cost of Goods Sold
3. Used by companies that manufacture unique products or provide specialized services
4. Has multiple Work-in-Process Inventory accounts
5. Tracks direct materials, direct labor, and manufacturing overhead costs

Check your answers online in MyAccountingLab or at http://www.pearsonhighered.com/Horngren.

For more practice, see Short Exercises S20-1 and S20-2. **My**AccountingLab

WHAT ARE EQUIVALENT UNITS OF PRODUCTION, AND HOW ARE THEY CALCULATED?

The production process takes time, so companies may have products that are not completed and are still in process at the end of the accounting period. In process costing, production costs are *accumulated* by process. At the end of the period, the total production costs incurred in each process must be split between the following:

Learning Objective 2

Calculate equivalent units of production for direct materials and conversion costs

- The units that have been completed in that process and transferred to the next process (or to Finished Goods Inventory if it is the last process).

- The units not completed and remaining in Work-in-Process Inventory for that department.

Exhibit 20-3 illustrates the point that all costs must be accounted for. They must either remain in the department or be transferred to the next department.

Exhibit 20-3 | **Assignment of Department 1 Costs at the End of the Period**

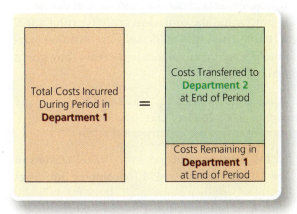

When the production costs have to be split between completed and uncompleted units, we cannot just divide the total cost by the number of units started to get a unit cost because some units are not complete and, therefore, have not incurred the same amount of costs. The unit cost of the completed units is more than the unit cost of the incomplete units. So how are the costs divided?

Equivalent Units of Production

Equivalent Units of Production (EUP)
Used to measure the amount of materials added to or work done on partially completed units and expressed in terms of fully completed units.

The concept of **equivalent units of production (EUP)** allows businesses to measure the amount of materials added to or work done on a partially finished group of units during a period and to express it in terms of fully complete units of output.

Let's apply the concept of equivalent units of production to a manufacturing setting. Assume Cheerful Color's production plant has 10,000 crayons in ending Work-in-Process Inventory—Packaging. Each of the 10,000 crayons has the paper wrapper attached, but they are not yet packaged in the box. Both the paper wrapper and the box are considered direct materials for the Packaging Department. If the cost of the wrappers is 40% of the total cost of direct materials in this process, then 10,000 crayons with 40% of the materials is the equivalent of 4,000 crayons with 100% of the materials.

> 10,000 crayons × 40% complete = 4,000 EUP for Direct Materials

Therefore, ending Work-in-Process Inventory—Packaging has 4,000 equivalent units of production for direct materials.

> Consider this example: A young boy is helping his father in the garden by carrying buckets of water for the plants. But the boy is small and the bucket is heavy, so the father only fills the bucket half full. At the end of the day, the boy tells his mother he carried 6 buckets of water. While he may have made 6 trips, he only carried the *equivalent* of 3 buckets of water because 6 buckets that are half full is the *equivalent* of 3 buckets that are completely full. In mathematical terms, 6 × 50% = 3 × 100%.

Conversion Costs

Conversion Costs
The cost to convert raw materials into finished goods: Direct labor plus manufacturing overhead.

Many manufacturing companies that use process costing are highly automated, so direct labor is a small part of total manufacturing costs. To simplify the accounting, direct labor is often combined with manufacturing overhead and called **conversion costs**. This term is used because it is the cost to *convert* raw materials into finished goods.

Suppose the 10,000 crayons in the Packaging Department are 80% complete for conversion. If conversion costs are incurred evenly throughout the process, then the cost of getting 10,000 crayons 80% through the process has the equivalent cost of getting 8,000 crayons completely through the process (10,000 crayons × 80% complete = 8,000 crayons × 100% complete). We use this formula when costs are incurred evenly throughout production. This is usually true for conversion costs.

> 10,000 crayons × 80% complete = 8,000 EUP for Conversion Costs

In summary, Cheerful Colors ended the accounting period with 10,000 crayons in process in the Packaging Department. The 10,000 crayons were 40% complete for direct materials and 80% complete for conversion. Expressed in terms of equivalent units of production, the 10,000 partially completed crayons are equal to 4,000 EUP for direct materials and 8,000 EUP for conversion costs.

> This example illustrates an important point: The equivalent
> units of production can be different for direct materials and conversion costs
> and therefore must be calculated separately.

Try It!

6. The Cutting Department has 6,500 units in process at the end of September that are 100% complete for direct materials and 85% complete for conversion costs. Calculate the equivalent units of production for direct materials and conversion costs.

Check your answer online in MyAccountingLab or at http://www.pearsonhighered.com/Horngren.

For more practice, see Short Exercises S20-3 through S20-6. **My**AccountingLab

HOW IS A PRODUCTION COST REPORT PREPARED?

For a comprehensive example of a process costing system, let's look at Puzzle Me, a fictitious company that manufactures jigsaw puzzles. Exhibit 20-4 illustrates the two major production processes:

- The Assembly Department applies glue to the cardboard and then presses a picture onto the cardboard.
- The Cutting Department cuts the board into puzzle pieces and packages the puzzles in a box. The box is then moved to finished goods storage.

Learning Objective 3

Prepare a production cost report using the weighted-average method

Exhibit 20-4 | **Flow of Costs in Producing Puzzles**

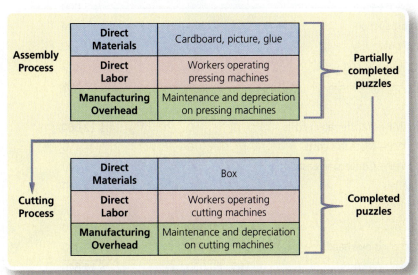

The production process uses materials, machines, and labor in both departments, and there are two Work-in-Process Inventory accounts: one for the Assembly Department and one for the Cutting Department.

> We are going to complete a lot of calculations in this chapter. As you work through the computations, keep the picture in Exhibit 20-4 in mind so you don't confuse inputs with outputs. The *inputs* are the materials, labor, and overhead. The *outputs* are the completed puzzles.

Production Cost Report
A report prepared by a processing department for equivalent units of production, production costs, and the assignment of those costs to the completed and in process units.

Puzzle Me must complete a **production cost report** for each department each month. The production cost reports show the calculations for the *physical flows* and the *cost flows* of the products. There are four steps to preparing a production cost report:

1. Summarize the flow of physical units.
2. Compute output in terms of equivalent units of production.
3. Compute the cost per equivalent unit of production.
4. Assign costs to units completed and units in process.

There are two unique terms used on a production cost report:

- *To account for* includes the amount in process at the beginning of the period plus the amount started or added during the period.

- *Accounted for* shows what happened to the amounts to account for. They are either still in process or completed and transferred out.

These terms are used for both units and costs. *To account for* and *accounted for* must always be equal. To illustrate the use of these terms, let's prepare production cost reports for Puzzle Me's two departments for the month of July.

Production Cost Report—First Process—Assembly Department

The production cost reports prepared in the chapter use the weighted-average method. The first-in, first-out (FIFO) method is illustrated in Appendix 20A at the end of the chapter.

Puzzle Me has the following data for July:

	Assembly Dept.	Cutting Dept.
Units		
Beginning WIP—units	0	5,000
Started in production	50,000	must calculate
Transferred out in July	40,000	38,000
Beginning WIP—% complete	N/A	60%
Ending WIP—% complete	25%	30%
Costs		
Beginning WIP—Transferred in costs	$ 0	$ 22,000
Beginning WIP—Materials costs	0	0
Beginning WIP—Conversion costs	0	1,200
Direct materials	140,000	19,000
Conversion costs:		
Direct labor	20,000	3,840
Manufacturing overhead	48,000	11,000
Total conversion costs	$ 68,000	$ 14,840

Step 1: Summarize the Flow of Physical Units The Assembly Department had no units in process on July 1 and started 50,000 units during the month. Therefore, *to account for* is 50,000 units.

To account for = Beginning balance + Amount started = 0 units + 50,000 units = 50,000 units

The Assembly Department completed the assembly process on 40,000 units and transferred those units to the Cutting Department. Therefore, 10,000 units must still be in process and we have *accounted for* all units.

Accounted for = Transferred out + In process = 40,000 units + 10,000 units = 50,000 units

To account for equals *accounted for,* so we are ready to record this information on the production cost report. Exhibit 20-5 shows units to account for and units accounted for. Notice that we are completing the UNITS section of the report. At this point, we are not yet assigning costs to units.

Exhibit 20-5 | Production Cost Report—Assembly Department—Whole Units

PUZZLE ME
Production Cost Report—ASSEMBLY DEPARTMENT
Month Ended July 31, 2016

UNITS	Whole Units	Transferred In	Direct Materials	Conversion Costs
		Equivalent Units		
Units to account for:				
Beginning work-in-process	0	Step 1: Physical flow of units		
Started in production	50,000			
Total units to account for	50,000			
Units accounted for:				
Completed and transferred out	40,000			
Ending work-in-process	10,000			
Total units accounted for	50,000			

Step 2: Compute Output in Terms of Equivalent Units of Production The Assembly Department adds all direct materials at the beginning of the process. In contrast, conversion costs are incurred evenly throughout the process. Thus, we must compute equivalent units of production separately for direct materials and conversion costs.

The Assembly Department worked on 50,000 puzzle boards during July. We have already determined that 40,000 puzzle boards are completed and have been transferred to the next department. If they are completed and transferred out, then they are 100% complete for both direct materials and conversion costs in this department. Another 10,000 puzzle boards are only 25% complete. How many equivalent units of production did the Assembly Department produce during July? Let's look at the calculation for each input.

Equivalent Units of Production for Direct Materials Equivalent units of production for direct materials total 50,000 because all the direct materials have been added to all 50,000

units worked on during July. Because the direct materials are added at the beginning of the process, if the units are started, then 100% of the materials have been added.

Completed units: 40,000 units × 100%	= 40,000 EUP for direct materials
In process units: 10,000 units × 100%	= 10,000 EUP for direct materials
Total EUP for direct materials	= 50,000 EUP for direct materials

Equivalent Units of Production for Conversion Costs Conversion costs are 100% complete for the 40,000 puzzle boards completed and transferred out to the Cutting Department, but only 25% of the conversion work has been done on the 10,000 puzzle boards in ending Work-in-Process Inventory. To calculate the equivalent units of production for conversion costs

Completed units: 40,000 units × 100%	= 40,000 EUP for conversion costs
In process units: 10,000 units × 25%	= 2,500 EUP for conversion costs
Total EUP for conversion costs	= 42,500 EUP for conversion costs

We can now add this information to the production cost report. Exhibit 20-6 shows the updated report. Notice that there are no entries in the Transferred In column. The Assembly Department is the first department in the manufacturing process, so there are no units transferred in from a previous department. We will use this column when we complete the production cost report for the Cutting Department.

Exhibit 20-6 | Production Cost Report—Assembly Department—EUP

PUZZLE ME
Production Cost Report—ASSEMBLY DEPARTMENT
Month Ended July 31, 2016

UNITS	Whole Units	Equivalent Units		
		Transferred In	Direct Materials	Conversion Costs
Units to account for:				
Beginning work-in-process	0			
Started in production	50,000			
Total units to account for	50,000			
			Step 2: EUP	
Units accounted for:				
Completed and transferred out	40,000	n/a	40,000	40,000
Ending work-in-process	10,000	n/a	10,000	2,500
Total units accounted for	50,000	n/a	50,000	42,500

Step 3: Compute the Cost per Equivalent Unit of Production Now that we have completed the UNITS section of the report, it is time to complete the COSTS section. The

cost per equivalent unit of production requires information about total costs and equivalent units of production. Computations are required for each input.

$$\text{Cost per EUP for direct materials} = \frac{\text{Total direct materials costs}}{\text{Equivalent units of production for direct materials}}$$

$$\text{Cost per EUP for conversion costs} = \frac{\text{Total conversion costs}}{\text{Equivalent units of production for conversion costs}}$$

The Assembly Department has $208,000 of costs to account for: $140,000 in direct materials costs and $68,000 in conversion costs. Our next task is to split these costs between the 40,000 puzzle boards transferred out to the Cutting Department and the 10,000 partially complete puzzle boards that remain in the Assembly Department's ending Work-in-Process Inventory.

In Step 2, we computed equivalent units of production for direct materials as 50,000 EUP and conversion costs as 42,500 EUP. Because the equivalent units of production differ, we must compute a separate cost per equivalent unit of production for direct materials and for conversion costs. The cost per equivalent unit of production for direct materials is $2.80, which is calculated as follows:

$$
\begin{aligned}
\textbf{Cost per EUP for direct materials} \;=\; & \frac{\textbf{Total direct materials costs}}{\textbf{Equivalent units of production for direct materials}} \\[6pt]
=\; & \frac{\$140{,}000}{50{,}000 \text{ EUP}} \\[6pt]
=\; & \$2.80 \text{ per EUP}
\end{aligned}
$$

The cost per equivalent unit of production for conversion costs is $1.60, which is calculated as follows:

$$
\begin{aligned}
\textbf{Cost per EUP for conversion costs} \;=\; & \frac{\textbf{Total conversion costs}}{\textbf{Equivalent units of production for conversion costs}} \\[6pt]
=\; & \frac{\$68{,}000}{42{,}500 \text{ EUP}} \\[6pt]
=\; & \$1.60 \text{ per EUP}
\end{aligned}
$$

Exhibit 20-7 (on the next page) shows these calculations added to the production cost report.

Exhibit 20-7 | **Cost Production Report—Assembly Department—Costs to Account For**

PUZZLE ME
Production Cost Report—ASSEMBLY DEPARTMENT
Month Ended July 31, 2016

		Equivalent Units		
UNITS	**Whole Units**	**Transferred In**	**Direct Materials**	**Conversion Costs**
Units to account for:				
Beginning work-in-process	0			
Started in production	50,000			
Total units to account for	50,000			
Units accounted for:				
Completed and transferred out	40,000	n/a	40,000	40,000
Ending work-in-process	10,000	n/a	10,000	2,500
Total units accounted for	50,000	n/a	50,000	42,500

COSTS		**Transferred In**	**Direct Materials**	**Conversion Costs**	**Total Costs**
Costs to account for:					
Beginning work-in-process	Step 3: Costs to account for	n/a	$ 0	$ 0	$ 0
Costs added during period		n/a	140,000	68,000	208,000
Total costs to account for		n/a	140,000	68,000	208,000
Divided by: Total EUP		n/a	÷ 50,000	÷ 42,500	
Cost per equivalent unit		n/a	$ 2.80	$ 1.60	$ 4.40
Costs accounted for:					
Completed and transferred out					
Ending work-in-process					
Total costs accounted for					

Step 4: Assign Costs to Units Completed and Units in Process The last step on the production cost report is to determine where the $208,000 total costs to be accounted for by the Assembly Department should be assigned. The costs must be divided between two categories:

- The 40,000 completed puzzle boards that have been transferred out to the Cutting Department.
- The 10,000 partially completed puzzle boards remaining in the Assembly Department's ending Work-in-Process Inventory.

This is accomplished by multiplying the cost per equivalent unit of production times the equivalent units of production. This step must be completed four times to assign direct materials cost to the completed units and the in process units and to assign the conversion costs to the completed units and the in process units. The cost of each input must be assigned to each output or partially completed output.

Direct Materials:

	Completed	40,000 EUP	×	$ 2.80 per EUP	=	$ 112,000
	In Process	10,000 EUP	×	$ 2.80 per EUP	=	28,000
Total						$ 140,000

Conversion Costs:

	Completed	40,000 EUP	×	$ 1.60 per EUP	=	$ 64,000
	In Process	2,500 EUP	×	$ 1.60 per EUP	=	4,000
Total						$ 68,000

We have accomplished our goal of splitting the $208,000 total cost between the completed units and the in process units and can record these costs on the production cost report. Exhibit 20-8 shows the completed production cost report for the Assembly Department.

Exhibit 20-8 | **Cost Production Report—Assembly Department—Costs Accounted For**

PUZZLE ME
Production Cost Report—ASSEMBLY DEPARTMENT
Month Ended July 31, 2016

UNITS	Whole Units	Transferred In	Direct Materials	Conversion Costs	
			Equivalent Units		
Units to account for:					
Beginning work-in-process	0				
Started in production	50,000				
Total units to account for	50,000				
Units accounted for:					
Completed and transferred out	40,000	n/a	40,000	40,000	
Ending work-in-process	10,000	n/a	10,000	2,500	
Total units accounted for	50,000	n/a	50,000	42,500	

COSTS	Transferred In	Direct Materials	Conversion Costs	Total Costs
Costs to account for:				
Beginning work-in-process	n/a	$ 0	$ 0	$ 0
Costs added during period	n/a	140,000	68,000	208,000
Total costs to account for	n/a	140,000	68,000	208,000
Divided by: Total EUP	n/a	÷ 50,000	÷42,500	
Cost per equivalent unit	n/a	$ 2.80	$ 1.60	$ 4.40
Costs accounted for:				
Completed and transferred out	n/a	$ 112,000	$ 64,000	$ 176,000
Ending work-in-process	n/a	28,000	4,000	32,000
Total costs accounted for	n/a	$ 140,000	$ 68,000	$ 208,000

Step 4: Costs accounted for

> *Review the completed production cost report on the previous page to make sure you understand the calculations. It is important to understand these steps before moving on to the next section of the chapter.*

We have now *accounted for* all units and costs for the Assembly Department, and it is time to complete the same process for the Cutting Department.

ETHICS

When do you stop production?

Douglas is just starting his shift at the cake mix factory, replacing Wade, who appears more than ready to go home. Douglas's job is to make sure the machines that measure ingredients are properly calibrated so the correct combination of ingredients goes into each mix. When Douglas checks one machine, he notices the amount of baking powder is too low. Douglas points out the problem to Wade, but Wade doesn't seem too concerned. "It doesn't really matter," says Wade. "You can't tell by looking at the mix, so they'll never know in the Packaging Department. Besides, do you know how much it costs to stop production?" Douglas is not convinced. He knows enough about baking to know the cakes won't bake properly without the correct amount of baking powder. But he doesn't want to get Wade into trouble, either. What should Douglas do? What would you do?

Solution

Wade is correct—stopping production can be costly. Idle machines and workers do not add to profits, and restarting machines after a shutdown can be expensive. Therefore, Douglas should first check the production standards to determine if the amount of baking powder is within the accepted limits. If the amount is not within the acceptable range, Douglas should stop production on the machine that is improperly calibrated and notify his supervisor. Douglas has an obligation to his employer to produce a quality product. Knowingly distributing an inferior product could have devastating consequences for the company. Consumers will not continue to buy cake mixes that do not bake properly, the company's reputation could be irreversibly harmed, and the company could lose significant market share. Failure to report the problem is a violation of the IMA's ethical standards of integrity and competence.

Production Cost Report—Second Process—Cutting Department

The Cutting Department receives the puzzle boards from the Assembly Department and cuts the boards into puzzle pieces before inserting the pieces into the box at the end of the process. Operations for this department include:

• Glued puzzle boards with pictures are transferred in from the Assembly Department at the beginning of the Cutting Department's process.

• The Cutting Department's conversion costs are added evenly throughout the process.

• The Cutting Department's direct materials (boxes) are added at the end of the process.

Transferred In Costs
Costs that were incurred in a previous process and brought into a later process as part of the product's cost.

Keep in mind that *direct materials* in the Cutting Department refers to the boxes added *in that department* and not to the materials (cardboard, pictures, and glue) added in the Assembly Department. The costs of the materials from the Assembly Department that are *transferred into* the Cutting Department are called **transferred in costs**. Likewise, *conversion costs* in the Cutting Department refers to the direct labor and manufacturing overhead costs incurred only in the Cutting Department. The conversion costs incurred in the Assembly Department are also transferred in costs for the Cutting Department.

Let's review the cost information presented earlier for Puzzle Me:

	Assembly Dept.	Cutting Dept.
Units		
Beginning WIP—units	0	5,000
Started in production	50,000	must calculate
Transferred out in July	40,000	38,000
Beginning WIP—% complete	N/A	60%
Ending WIP—% complete	25%	30%
Costs		
Beginning WIP—Transferred in costs	$ 0	$ 22,000
Beginning WIP—Materials costs	0	0
Beginning WIP—Conversion costs	0	1,200
Direct materials	140,000	19,000
Conversion costs:		
Direct labor	20,000	3,840
Manufacturing overhead	48,000	11,000
Total conversion costs	$ 68,000	$ 14,840

The data show that Puzzle Me's Cutting Department started the July period with 5,000 puzzle boards partially completed through work done in the Cutting Department in June. During July, the Cutting Department started work on 40,000 additional puzzle boards that were received from the Assembly Department.

> Remember: Units and costs that are transferred *out* for the Assembly Department become transferred *in* for the Cutting Department.

The Cutting Department has to account for costs associated with the following:

- Work done *last* month on the 5,000 partially completed units that are still in the Cutting Department at the end of June (and therefore at the beginning of July)
- Work done *this* month to complete the 5,000 partially completed units
- Work done *this* month on the 40,000 units that were transferred in during July

The **weighted-average method** combines these costs into one cost pool when calculating the cost per equivalent unit. Let's prepare a production cost report for the Cutting Department using the weighted-average method and the same four-step procedure we used for the Assembly Department.

Step 1: Summarize the Flow of Physical Units The Cutting Department had 5,000 units in process on July 1 and received 40,000 units during the month from the Assembly Department. Therefore, *to account for* is 45,000 units.

Weighted-Average Method (for Process Costing)
Determines the average cost of equivalent units of production by combining beginning inventory costs with current period costs.

> To account for = Beginning balance + Amount transferred in
> = 5,000 units + 40,000 units
> = 45,000 units

The Cutting Department completed the cutting and boxing process on 38,000 units and transferred those units to Finished Goods Inventory. Therefore, 7,000 units must still be in process and we have *accounted for* all units.

> **Accounted for = Transferred out + In process** = 38,000 units + 7,000 units = 45,000 units

To account for equals *accounted for,* so we are ready to record this information on the production cost report. Just as we did with the Assembly Department, we start with completing the UNITS section of the report. At this point, we are not yet assigning costs to units. Exhibit 20-9 shows the units to account for and units accounted for.

Exhibit 20-9 | **Production Cost Report—Cutting Department—Whole Units**

		Equivalent Units		
UNITS	**Whole Units**	**Transferred In**	**Direct Materials**	**Conversion Costs**
PUZZLE ME				
Production Cost Report—CUTTING DEPARTMENT				
Month Ended July 31, 2016				
Units to account for:				
Beginning work-in-process	5,000			
Transferred in	40,000	Step 1: Physical flow of units		
Total units to account for	45,000			
Units accounted for:				
Completed and transferred out	38,000			
Ending work-in-process	7,000			
Total units accounted for	45,000			

Step 2: Compute Output in Terms of Equivalent Units of Production The Cutting Department adds direct materials at the end of the process, and conversion costs are incurred evenly throughout the process. Thus, we must compute equivalent units of production separately for direct materials and conversion costs. Additionally, the units have costs that were transferred in with them that must be accounted for.

The Cutting Department worked on 45,000 puzzle boards during July. We have already determined that 38,000 puzzles are completed and have been transferred to Finished Goods Inventory. If they are completed and transferred out, then they are 100% complete for transferred in, direct materials, and conversion costs in this department. Another 7,000 puzzle boards are only 30% complete. How many equivalent units of production did the Cutting Department produce during July?

Why is EUP for transferred in always 100%?

Equivalent Units of Production for Transferred In The Cutting Department is the second department in the process system, so it receives units from the Assembly Department. These units are the *transferred in* units. **The equivalent units of production for transferred in are always 100%. Why? Because these units came in with costs assigned to them from the previous department, which was calculated on the production cost report for the Assembly Department. If they were not 100% complete with respect to the previous process, then they would not have been**

transferred in. They would still be in process in the previous department. Therefore, any costs associated with the work done in the Assembly Department stay with them at 100% EUP.

> Completed units: 38,000 units × 100% = 38,000 EUP for transferred in
> In process units: 7,000 units × 100% = 7,000 EUP for transferred in
> Total EUP for transferred in   = 45,000 EUP for transferred in

Equivalent Units of Production for Direct Materials Equivalent units of production for direct materials total 38,000 for the completed units because they are 100% complete. However, the units that are in process do not yet have any direct materials added in this department because the box is added at the end of the process. Because they are still in process, the box has not yet been added.

> Completed units: 38,000 units × 100% = 38,000 EUP for direct materials
> In process units: 7,000 units ×   0% =   0 EUP for direct materials
> Total EUP for direct materials   = 38,000 EUP for direct materials

Equivalent Units of Production for Conversion Costs Conversion costs are complete for the 38,000 puzzle boards completed and transferred out to Finished Goods Inventory, but only 30% of the conversion work has been done on the 7,000 puzzle boards in ending Work-in-Process Inventory. To calculate the equivalent units of production for conversion costs:

> Completed units: 38,000 units × 100% = 38,000 EUP for conversion costs
> In process units: 7,000 units ×   30% = 2,100 EUP for conversion costs
> Total EUP for conversion costs   = 40,100 EUP for conversion costs

We can now add this information to the production cost report as shown in Exhibit 20-10.

Exhibit 20-10 | Production Cost Report—Cutting Department—EUP

		Equivalent Units		
UNITS	**Whole Units**	**Transferred In**	**Direct Materials**	**Conversion Costs**
PUZZLE ME				
Units to account for:				
Beginning work-in-process	5,000			
Transferred in	40,000			
Total units to account for	45,000			
		Step 2: EUP		
Units accounted for:				
Completed and transferred out	38,000	38,000	38,000	38,000
Ending work-in-process	7,000	7,000	0	2,100
Total units accounted for	45,000	45,000	38,000	40,100

PUZZLE ME
Production Cost Report—CUTTING DEPARTMENT
Month Ended July 31, 2016

Step 3: Compute the Cost per Equivalent Unit of Production Now that we have completed the UNITS section of the report, it is time to complete the COSTS section. The formulas to compute the cost per equivalent unit of production are the same as used for the Assembly Department; we just need to add the calculation for the transferred in costs. The Cutting Department has three inputs and therefore must make three calculations for cost per equivalent unit of production.

$$\text{Cost per EUP for transferred in} = \frac{\text{Total transferred in costs}}{\text{Equivalent units of production for transferred in}}$$

$$\text{Cost per EUP for direct materials} = \frac{\text{Total direct materials costs}}{\text{Equivalent units of production for direct materials}}$$

$$\text{Cost per EUP for conversion costs} = \frac{\text{Total conversion costs}}{\text{Equivalent units of production for conversion costs}}$$

The Cutting Department has $233,040 of costs to account for, as illustrated in Exhibit 20-11.

Exhibit 20-11 | Cutting Department: Costs to Account For

	Transferred In	Direct Materials	Conversion Costs	Totals
Beginning balance in Work-in-Process Inventory—Cutting, July 1	$ 22,000	$ 0	$ 1,200	$ 23,200
Transferred in from Assembly Department during July	176,000			176,000
Additional added in Cutting Department during July		19,000	14,840	33,840
Totals	$ 198,000	$ 19,000	$ 16,040	$ 233,040

The beginning balances and the additional costs incurred were given in the original data. The amount transferred in from the Assembly Department, $176,000, is the amount calculated on the production cost report for the Assembly Department for July as the amount completed and transferred out in the costs accounted for section.

Our next task is to split these costs between the 38,000 completed puzzles transferred out to Finished Goods Inventory and the 7,000 partially complete puzzle boards that remain in the Cutting Department's ending Work-in-Process Inventory.

In Step 2, we computed equivalent units of production for transferred in as 45,000 EUP, direct materials as 38,000 EUP, and conversion costs as 40,100 EUP. Because the equivalent units of production differ, we must compute a separate cost per unit for each category.

The cost per equivalent unit of production for transferred in is $4.40, which is calculated as follows:

$$\text{Cost per EUP for transferred in} = \frac{\text{Total transferred in costs}}{\text{Equivalent units of production for transferred in}}$$

$$= \frac{\$198,000}{45,000 \text{ EUP}}$$

$$= \$4.40 \text{ per EUP}$$

> Look back at the completed production cost report for the Assembly Department in Exhibit 20-8. Notice in the Total Cost column that the total cost per equivalent unit is $4.40. The units were *transferred out* of the Assembly Department at $4.40 per unit, so they are *transferred in* to the Cutting Department at $4.40 per unit. However, the calculation above includes costs from beginning Work-in-Process, which were previously transferred in ($22,000 for 5,000 units = $4.40 per unit), and costs transferred in this month ($176,000 for 40,000 units = $4.40 per unit). In this case, the cost per unit is the same for both periods. If costs had varied from last month to this month, the weighted-average cost would not have been $4.40. Appendix 20A, which illustrates the FIFO method, illustrates how varied costs affect the cost per unit.

The cost per equivalent unit of materials is $0.50, which is calculated as follows:

$$\text{Cost per EUP for direct materials} = \frac{\text{Total direct materials costs}}{\text{Equivalent units of production for direct materials}}$$

$$= \frac{\$19,000}{38,000 \text{ EUP}}$$

$$= \$0.50 \text{ per EUP}$$

The cost per equivalent unit of production for conversion costs is $0.40, which is calculated as follows:

$$\text{Cost per EUP for conversion costs} = \frac{\text{Total conversion costs}}{\text{Equivalent units of production for conversion costs}}$$

$$= \frac{\$16,040}{40,100 \text{ EUP}}$$

$$= \$0.40 \text{ per EUP}$$

These calculations are added to the production cost report as shown in Exhibit 20-12 (on the next page).

Exhibit 20-12 | **Production Cost Report—Cutting Department—Costs to Account For**

PUZZLE ME
Production Cost Report—CUTTING DEPARTMENT
Month Ended July 31, 2016

		Equivalent Units			
UNITS	**Whole Units**	**Transferred In**	**Direct Materials**	**Conversion Costs**	
Units to account for:					
Beginning work-in-process	5,000				
Transferred in	40,000				
Total units to account for	45,000				
Units accounted for:					
Completed and transferred out	38,000	38,000	38,000	38,000	
Ending work-in-process	7,000	7,000	0	2,100	
Total units accounted for	45,000	45,000	38,000	40,100	

COSTS	**Transferred In**	**Direct Materials**	**Conversion Costs**	**Total Costs**
Costs to account for:				
Beginning work-in-process	$ 22,000	$ 0	$ 1,200	$ 23,200
Costs added during period	176,000	19,000	14,840	209,840
Total costs to account for	198,000	19,000	16,040	233,040
Divided by: Total EUP	÷ 45,000	÷ 38,000	÷ 40,100	
Cost per equivalent unit	$ 4.40	$ 0.50	$ 0.40	$ 5.30
Costs accounted for:				
Completed and transferred out				
Ending work-in-process				
Total costs accounted for				

Step 3: Costs to account for

Step 4: Assign Costs to Units Completed and Units in Process The last step on the production cost report is to determine how the $233,040 total costs accounted for by the Cutting Department should be assigned to the following:

- The 38,000 completed puzzles that have been transferred out to Finished Goods Inventory.
- The 7,000 partially completed puzzle boards remaining in the Cutting Department's ending Work-in-Process Inventory.

This is accomplished by multiplying the cost per equivalent unit of production times the equivalent units of production. To assign the costs of the three inputs to the two outputs, this step must be completed six times to assign:

- Transferred in costs to:
  - Completed units
  - In process units
- Direct materials cost to:
  - Completed units
  - In process units
- Conversion costs to:
  - Completed units
  - In process units

Transferred In

	Completed	38,000 EUP	×	$ 4.40 per EUP	=	$ 167,200
	In Process	7,000 EUP	×	$ 4.40 per EUP	=	30,800
Total						$ 198,000

Direct Materials

	Completed	38,000 EUP	×	$ 0.50 per EUP	=	$ 19,000
	In Process	0 EUP	×	$ 0.50 per EUP	=	0
Total						$ 19,000

Conversion Costs

	Completed	38,000 EUP	×	$ 0.40 per EUP	=	$ 15,200
	In Process	2,100 EUP	×	$ 0.40 per EUP	=	840
Total						$ 16,040

We have accomplished our goal of splitting the $233,040 total cost between the completed units and the in process units and can record these costs on the production cost report. The completed report is shown in Exhibit 20-13.

Exhibit 20-13 | Production Cost Report—Cutting Department—Costs Accounted For

PUZZLE ME
Production Cost Report—CUTTING DEPARTMENT
Month Ended July 31, 2016

UNITS	Whole Units	Equivalent Units Transferred In	Equivalent Units Direct Materials	Equivalent Units Conversion Costs
Units to account for:				
Beginning work-in-process	5,000			
Transferred in	40,000			
Total units to account for	45,000			
Units accounted for:				
Completed and transferred out	38,000	38,000	38,000	38,000
Ending work-in-process	7,000	7,000	0	2,100
Total units accounted for	45,000	45,000	38,000	40,100

COSTS	Transferred In	Direct Materials	Conversion Costs	Total Costs
Costs to account for:				
Beginning work-in-process	$ 22,000	$ 0	$ 1,200	$ 23,200
Costs added during period	176,000	19,000	14,840	209,840
Total costs to account for	198,000	19,000	16,040	233,040
Divided by: Total EUP	÷ 45,000	÷ 38,000	÷ 40,100	
Cost per equivalent unit	$ 4.40	$ 0.50	$ 0.40	$ 5.30
Costs accounted for:				
Completed and transferred out [Step 4: Costs accounted for]	$ 167,200	$ 19,000	$ 15,200	$ 201,400
Ending work-in-process	30,800	0	840	31,640
Total costs accounted for	$ 198,000	$ 19,000	$ 16,040	$ 233,040

Try It!

WHAT JOURNAL ENTRIES ARE REQUIRED IN A PROCESS COSTING SYSTEM?

Learning Objective 4

Prepare journal entries for a process costing system

As costs flow through the process costing system, we go through a four-step process to *accumulate, assign, allocate,* and *adjust.* This is the same process that was illustrated in the previous chapter for job order costing. Remember, the primary differences between the two costing systems are how costs are accumulated and when costs are assigned. In a process costing system, costs are accumulated in the following accounts: Raw Materials Inventory, the various Work-in-Process Inventory accounts, and Manufacturing Overhead. At the end of the month, when the production costs reports are prepared, the costs are assigned to units. The costs assigned to the units completed in each process are transferred from one Work-in-Process Inventory account to the next and eventually to Finished Goods Inventory and Cost of Goods Sold. Following is a description of the journal entries associated with Puzzle Me's process costing system for July.

Transaction 1—Raw Materials Purchased

During July, the company purchased materials on account for $175,000.

$$\left.\frac{A\uparrow}{RM\uparrow}\right\} = \left\{\frac{L\uparrow}{A/P\uparrow} + \underline{\quad E\quad}\right.$$

Date	Accounts and Explanation	Debit	Credit
Trans. 1	Raw Materials Inventory	175,000	
	Accounts Payable		175,000
	Materials purchased, **accumulated** *in RM.*		

Transaction 2—Raw Materials Used in Production

During July, direct materials were assigned to the two production departments: $140,000 to the Assembly Department and $19,000 to the Cutting Department; $2,000 in indirect materials was accumulated in Manufacturing Overhead.

Date	Accounts and Explanation	Debit	Credit
Trans. 2	Work-in-Process Inventory—Assembly	140,000	
	Work-in-Process Inventory—Cutting	19,000	
	Manufacturing Overhead	2,000	
	Raw Materials Inventory		161,000
	*Materials used, direct materials **assigned** to WIP, indirect*		
	*materials **accumulated** in MOH.*		

$$\frac{A\downarrow}{\substack{RM\downarrow \\ WIP—Assembly\uparrow \\ WIP—Cutting\uparrow}} \bigg\} = \bigg\{ \quad L \quad + \quad \frac{E\downarrow}{MOH\uparrow}$$

Transaction 3—Labor Costs Incurred

During the month, Puzzle Me incurred $20,000 in direct labor costs in the Assembly Department; $3,840 in direct labor costs in the Cutting Department; and $1,500 in indirect labor costs that were accumulated in Manufacturing Overhead.

Date	Accounts and Explanation	Debit	Credit
Trans. 3	Work-in-Process Inventory—Assembly	20,000	
	Work-in-Process Inventory—Cutting	3,840	
	Manufacturing Overhead	1,500	
	Wages Payable		25,340
	*Labor incurred, direct labor **assigned** to WIP, indirect*		
	*labor **accumulated** in MOH.*		

$$\frac{A\uparrow}{\substack{WIP—Assembly\uparrow \\ WIP—Cutting\uparrow}} \bigg\} = \bigg\{ \frac{L\uparrow}{\substack{Wages \\ Payable\uparrow}} + \frac{E\downarrow}{MOH\uparrow}$$

Transaction 4—Additional Manufacturing Costs Incurred

In addition to the indirect materials and indirect labor costs, Puzzle Me incurred $35,000 in machinery depreciation and $20,000 in indirect costs that were paid in cash, which included rent and utilities.

Date	Accounts and Explanation	Debit	Credit
Trans. 4	Manufacturing Overhead	35,000	
	Accumulated Depreciation		35,000
	*Overhead incurred, costs **accumulated** in MOH.*		
	Manufacturing Overhead	20,000	
	Cash		20,000
	*Overhead incurred, costs **accumulated** in MOH.*		

$$\frac{A\downarrow}{\substack{Accumulated \\ Depreciation\uparrow}} \bigg\} = \bigg\{ \quad L \quad + \quad \frac{E\downarrow}{MOH\uparrow}$$

$$\frac{A\downarrow}{Cash\downarrow} \bigg\} = \bigg\{ \quad L \quad + \quad \frac{E\downarrow}{MOH\uparrow}$$

Transaction 5—Allocation of Manufacturing Overhead

Puzzle Me used a predetermined overhead allocation rate to allocate indirect costs to the departments: $48,000 to the Assembly Department and $11,000 to the Cutting Department.

$$\dfrac{\mathbf{A}\uparrow}{\text{WIP—Assembly}\uparrow \quad \text{WIP—Cutting}\uparrow} \Bigg\} = \Bigg\{ \quad \mathbf{L} \quad + \quad \dfrac{\mathbf{E}\uparrow}{\text{MOH}\downarrow}$$

Date	Accounts and Explanation	Debit	Credit
Trans. 5	Work-in-Process Inventory—Assembly	48,000	
	Work-in-Process Inventory—Cutting	11,000	
	Manufacturing Overhead		59,000
	*Overhead **allocated** to WIP.*		

Transaction 6—Transfer from the Assembly Department to the Cutting Department

At the end of July, when the production cost report for the Assembly Department was prepared, Puzzle Me assigned $176,000 to the 40,000 units transferred from the Assembly Department to the Cutting Department.

$$\dfrac{\mathbf{A}\uparrow\downarrow}{\text{WIP—Assembly}\downarrow \quad \text{WIP—Cutting}\uparrow} \Bigg\} = \Bigg\{ \quad \mathbf{L} \quad + \quad \mathbf{E}$$

Date	Accounts and Explanation	Debit	Credit
Trans. 6	Work-in-Process Inventory—Cutting	176,000	
	Work-in-Process Inventory—Assembly		176,000
	*Transfer costs **assigned** to units transferred.*		

Transaction 7—Transfer from Cutting Department to Finished Goods Inventory

At the end of July, when the production cost report for the Cutting Department was prepared, Puzzle Me assigned $201,400 to the 38,000 units transferred from the Cutting Department to Finished Goods Inventory. This is the cost of goods manufactured.

$$\dfrac{\mathbf{A}\uparrow\downarrow}{\text{FG}\uparrow \quad \text{WIP—Cutting}\downarrow} \Bigg\} = \Bigg\{ \quad \mathbf{L} \quad + \quad \mathbf{E}$$

Date	Accounts and Explanation	Debit	Credit
Trans. 7	Finished Goods Inventory	201,400	
	Work-in-Process Inventory—Cutting		201,400
	*Units completed, costs **assigned** to FG.*		

Transaction 8—Puzzles Sold

During July, Puzzle Me sold 35,000 puzzles. We have already determined from the production cost report for the Cutting Department that the cost of goods manufactured is $5.30 per puzzle. Therefore, the cost of 35,000 puzzles is $185,500 (35,000 puzzles × $5.30 per puzzle). The puzzles were sold on account for $8.00 each, which is a total of $280,000 (35,000 puzzles × $8.00 per puzzle).

Date	Accounts and Explanation	Debit	Credit
Trans. 8	Accounts Receivable	280,000	
	Sales Revenue		280,000
	Units sold; entry reflects sales price, not costs.		
	Cost of Goods Sold	185,500	
	Finished Goods Inventory		185,500
	*Units sold, costs **assigned** to COGS.*		

$$\left.\frac{A\uparrow}{A/R\uparrow}\right\} = \left\{ \frac{L}{} + \frac{E\uparrow}{\text{Sales Revenue}\uparrow} \right.$$

$$\left.\frac{A\downarrow}{FG\downarrow}\right\} = \left\{ \frac{L}{} + \frac{E\downarrow}{\text{COGS}\uparrow} \right.$$

Transaction 9—Adjust Manufacturing Overhead

The actual manufacturing overhead costs incurred were $58,500, which includes the indirect materials in Transaction 2, the indirect labor in Transaction 3, and the accumulated depreciation and other indirect costs in Transaction 4. The amount of manufacturing overhead allocated to the two departments was $59,000, as shown in Transaction 5.

Manufacturing Overhead

Trans. 2	2,000	59,000	Trans. 5
Trans. 3	1,500		
Trans. 4	35,000		
Trans. 4	20,000		
		500	Unadj. Bal.

The T-account for Manufacturing Overhead shows that the amount of manufacturing overhead allocated was $500 more than the actual costs incurred. This means the overhead was overallocated. To adjust for the overallocation, Manufacturing Overhead must be debited to bring the account to zero. The credit is to Cost of Goods Sold to decrease the expense account for the amount the puzzles were overcosted.

Date	Accounts and Explanation	Debit	Credit
Trans. 9	Manufacturing Overhead	500	
	Cost of Goods Sold		500
	*MOH **adjusted** for overallocated overhead.*		

$$\left.\frac{A}{}\right\} = \left\{ \frac{L}{} + \frac{E\uparrow\downarrow}{\substack{\text{COGS}\downarrow \\ \text{MOH}\uparrow}} \right.$$

> The adjusting entry for overallocated or underallocated manufacturing overhead is usually prepared at the end of the year. We are showing it here at the end of the month so we can illustrate all journal entries for a process costing system.

After posting, the key accounts appear as follows:

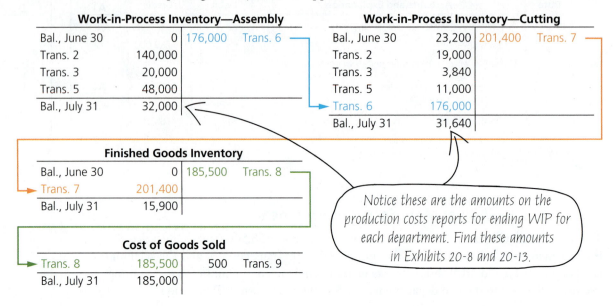

Work-in-Process Inventory—Assembly			
Bal., June 30	0	176,000	Trans. 6
Trans. 2	140,000		
Trans. 3	20,000		
Trans. 5	48,000		
Bal., July 31	32,000		

Work-in-Process Inventory—Cutting			
Bal., June 30	23,200	201,400	Trans. 7
Trans. 2	19,000		
Trans. 3	3,840		
Trans. 5	11,000		
Trans. 6	176,000		
Bal., July 31	31,640		

Finished Goods Inventory			
Bal., June 30	0	185,500	Trans. 8
Trans. 7	201,400		
Bal., July 31	15,900		

Notice these are the amounts on the production costs reports for ending WIP for each department. Find these amounts in Exhibits 20-8 and 20-13.

Cost of Goods Sold			
Trans. 8	185,500	500	Trans. 9
Bal., July 31	185,000		

Try It!

11. Castillo Company has three departments: Mixing, Bottling, and Packaging. At the end of the month, the production cost reports for the departments show the costs of the products completed and transferred were $75,000 from Mixing to Bottling, $50,000 from Bottling to Packaging, and $65,000 from Packaging to Finished Goods Inventory. Prepare the journal entries for the transfer of the costs.

Check your answer online in MyAccountingLab or at http://www.pearsonhighered.com/Horngren.

For more practice, see Short Exercise S20-11.   MyAccountingLab

HOW CAN THE PRODUCTION COST REPORT BE USED TO MAKE DECISIONS?

Learning Objective 5

Use a production cost report to make decisions

So far in the chapter, you have learned how to prepare the production cost report. Now let's consider how managers can use production cost reports to make decisions for their companies.

- **Controlling costs.** Puzzle Me uses product cost data to look for ways to reduce costs. A manager may decide that the company needs to change suppliers to reduce the cost of its raw materials. Or a manager may change a component in the production process to reduce direct materials costs. To reduce labor costs, a manager may need employees with different skill levels paid at different hourly rates. Perhaps more skilled employees would require a higher pay rate but be more efficient. The increase in cost per labor hour may be more than offset by the increased productivity of the workers. Managers may also evaluate the efficiency of the production equipment. Newer, more efficient equipment may reduce manufacturing overhead costs.

- **Evaluating performance.** Managers are often rewarded based on how well they meet the budget. Puzzle Me compares the actual direct materials and conversion costs with expected amounts. If actual costs are too high, managers look for ways to cut them. If actual costs are less than expected, the managers may receive a bonus.

DECISIONS

Can we cut these costs?

The management team of Puzzle Me is looking at the production cost reports for July, and discussing opportunities for improvement. The production manager thinks the production process is very efficient, and there is little room for cost savings in conversion costs. The purchasing manager tells the team that he was recently approached by a supplier with an excellent reputation for quality. This supplier submitted a bid for cardboard that was a little thinner but would allow the company to decrease direct materials costs by 5%. What should the team do?

Solution

The production cost reports for the Assembly and Cutting Departments show direct materials costs of $2.80 and $0.50 per puzzle, for total direct materials cost of $3.30 per puzzle. A decrease of 5% in direct materials costs would result in a savings

of $0.165 per puzzle ($3.30 × 5%) and decrease total costs from $5.30 to $5.135 per puzzle. Based on the completed production of 38,000 puzzles in July, the total cost savings would be $6,270 per month ($0.165 per puzzle × 38,000 puzzles). The purchasing manager recommends using the new supplier.

Alternate Solution

The marketing manager has a different perspective. He points out that most of the puzzles produced are for toddlers. Based on market research, the adults who purchase these puzzles like the sturdy construction. If Puzzle Me changes materials and the puzzles do not stand up well to the treatment they receive by young children, the company could rapidly lose market share. The marketing manager does not recommend using a thinner cardboard.

- **Pricing products.** Puzzle Me must set its selling price high enough to cover the manufacturing cost of each puzzle plus selling and administrative costs. The production cost report for the Cutting Department, Exhibit 20-12, shows that the total production cost of manufacturing a puzzle (direct materials, direct labor, and manufacturing overhead) is $5.30. Obviously, the puzzle must be priced more than this for the company to be profitable.

- **Identifying the most profitable products.** Selling price and cost data help managers figure out which products are most profitable. They can then promote these products to help increase profits.

- **Preparing the financial statements.** Finally, the production cost report aids financial reporting. It provides inventory data for the balance sheet and cost of goods sold for the income statement.

12. Describe some ways managers use production cost reports to make business decisions.

Check your answer online in MyAccountingLab or at http://www.pearsonhighered.com/Horngren.

For more practice, see Short Exercise S20-12. **My**Accounting**Lab**

APPENDIX 20A: Process Costing: First-In, First-Out Method

The chapter illustrated how to complete the production costs reports for Puzzle Me using the weighted-average method. In the weighted-average method, the costs from the beginning balance in Work-in-Process Inventory are combined with the current period costs when determining the costs per equivalent unit of production. In this appendix, you look

**First-In, First-Out Method
(for Process Costing)**
Determines the cost of equivalent
units of production by accounting
for beginning inventory costs
separately from current period costs.
It assumes the first units started in
the production process are the first
units completed and sold.

at another method for assigning production costs—the **first-in, first-out method**—in which the costs from the beginning balance in Work-in-Process Inventory that were incurred in the prior period are accounted for separately from the current period costs. The first-in, first-out method is also known as *FIFO*.

The Assembly Department of Puzzle Me did not have a beginning inventory in July. Therefore, all the costs to be accounted for in July were costs incurred that month. Because there was no intermingling of costs from a prior month, the calculations for the weighted-average method and FIFO method would be the same for the Assembly Department. The Cutting Department, however, did have costs brought forward from June as well as additional costs incurred in July. We will use the July data for the Cutting Department to illustrate the FIFO method.

HOW IS A PRODUCTION COST REPORT PREPARED USING THE FIFO METHOD?

Learning Objective 6

Prepare a production cost report using the first-in, first-out method

The initial data for July for Puzzle Me are repeated here with one difference: the costs in Beginning WIP—Conversion Costs have been changed from $1,200 to $700. This $500 difference will help illustrate how changes in costs incurred in different periods affect the cost per unit calculations in FIFO.

	Assembly Dept.	Cutting Dept.
Units		
Beginning WIP—units	0	5,000
Started in production	50,000	must calculate
Transferred out in July	40,000	38,000
Beginning WIP—% complete	N/A	60%
Ending WIP—% complete	25%	30%
Costs		
Beginning WIP—Transferred in costs	$ 0	$ 22,000
Beginning WIP—Materials costs	0	0
Beginning WIP—Conversion costs	0	700
Direct materials	140,000	19,000
Conversion costs:		
Direct labor	20,000	3,840
Manufacturing overhead	48,000	11,000
Total conversion costs	$ 68,000	$ 14,840

We will use the same four-step procedure to complete the production cost report for the Cutting Department for July:

1. Summarize the flow of physical units.
2. Compute output in terms of equivalent units of production.
3. Compute the cost per equivalent unit of production.
4. Assign costs to units completed and units in process.

Step 1: Summarize the Flow of Physical Units The Cutting Department had 5,000 units in process on July 1 and received 40,000 units during the month from the Assembly Department. Therefore, *to account for* is 45,000 units. This is the same as the weighted-average method.

> **To account for = Beginning balance + Amount transferred in**
> = 5,000 units + 40,000 units
> = 45,000 units

Using the FIFO method creates three groups of units to be accounted for:

- Units in beginning inventory that were started in June and completed in July
- Units started in July and completed in July
- Units started in July but not completed in July. These units are still in process at the end of July and will be completed in August.

The information for the Cutting Department shows 5,000 units in beginning inventory and 38,000 units transferred out. If 38,000 units were completed and transferred, this would include the 5,000 units in beginning inventory plus another 33,000 units that were started in July. Remember, FIFO stands for first-in, first-out. Therefore, it is assumed that the first units in (those in beginning inventory) are the first units out. We must account for 45,000 units. If 38,000 were transferred out, then that leaves 7,000 still in process at the end of July. We have now *accounted for* all units.

> **Accounted for = Beginning balance + Started and completed + In process**
> = 5,000 units + 33,000 units + 7,000 units
> = 45,000 units

Exhibit 20A-1 illustrates the three groups of units accounted for.

Exhibit 20A-1 | **July Units Accounted For**

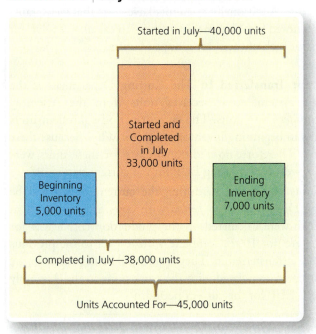

To account for equals *accounted for,* so we are ready to record this information on the production cost report. Just as we did with the weighted-average method, we start with completing the UNITS section of the report. At this point, we are not yet assigning costs to units. Exhibit 20A-2 (on the next page) shows the units to account for and units accounted for.

Exhibit 20A-2 | **Production Cost Report—Cutting Department—FIFO Method—Whole Units**

PUZZLE ME
Production Cost Report—CUTTING DEPARTMENT
Month Ended July 31, 2016

UNITS	Whole Units	Equivalent Units for Current Period		
		Transferred In	Direct Materials	Conversion Costs
Units to account for:				
Beginning work-in-process	5,000			
Started in production	40,000			
Total units to account for	45,000	Step 1: Physical flow of units		
Units accounted for:				
Beginning work-in-process	5,000			
Started and completed	33,000			
Transferred to Finished Goods	38,000			
Ending work-in-process	7,000			
Total units accounted for	45,000			

Step 2: Compute Output in Terms of Equivalent Units of Production In the FIFO method, costs from the previous period are not merged with the costs from the current period. Therefore, the EUP calculation is for *the current period*. The Cutting Department adds direct materials at the end of the process, and conversion costs are incurred evenly throughout the process. Thus, we must compute equivalent units of production separately for direct materials and conversion costs. Additionally, the units have costs that were transferred in with them that must be accounted for. That means we have to calculate equivalent units of production for three inputs for each of the three groups of units.

Equivalent Units of Production for Transferred In The Cutting Department is the second department in the process system, so it receives units from the Assembly Department. These units are the *transferred in* units. The current-period equivalent units of production for transferred in units in beginning inventory are zero. Why? Because these units were transferred in last period. Therefore, no additional costs for these units were transferred in *this period*. Remember, we are calculating EUP for the current period only.

However, the EUP for the units transferred in during the current period will be 100%. They came into the Cutting Department *this period* with costs assigned to them from the previous department, which were calculated on the production cost report for the Assembly Department. If they were not 100% complete with respect to the previous process, then they would not have been transferred in. They would still be in process in the previous department. Therefore, any costs associated with the work done in the Assembly Department stays with them at 100% EUP for the current period.

Beginning WIP units: 5,000 units × 0% =	0 EUP for transferred in
Started and completed units: 33,000 units × 100% =	33,000 EUP for transferred in
In process units: 7,000 units × 100% =	7,000 EUP for transferred in
Total EUP for transferred in	= 40,000 EUP for transferred in

Equivalent Units of Production for Direct Materials Current-period equivalent units of production for direct materials is 100% for the completed units, both beginning WIP units and units started and completed this period, because they are 100% complete and direct materials (boxes) are added at the end of the process. However, the units that are in process do not yet have any direct materials added *in this department* because the box has not yet been added.

Beginning WIP units:	5,000 units ×	100% =	5,000	EUP for direct materials
Started and completed units:	33,000 units ×	100% =	33,000	EUP for direct materials
In process units:	7,000 units ×	0% =	0	EUP for direct materials
Total EUP for direct materials			= 38,000	EUP for direct materials

Equivalent Units of Production for Conversion Costs This is the section where the difference between the weighted-average and FIFO methods is most obvious.

- **Beginning WIP.** The 5,000 units that were in process at the beginning of July were 60% complete. That means 60% of the work was done in June. We are concerned with the work completed in July. If 60% of the work was done in June and the units were completed in July, then 40% of the work was done in July (100% − 60% = 40%). Therefore, the EUP for these units is 5,000 units × 40% = 2,000 EUP.

- **Started and Completed.** All (100%) of the work done on the units started and completed was done in July, so the equivalent units of production are 33,000 units × 100% = 33,000 EUP.

- **In Process.** Only 30% of the conversion work has been done on the 7,000 puzzle boards in ending Work-in-Process Inventory. Equivalent units of production are 7,000 units × 30% = 2,100 EUP.

  To calculate the equivalent units of production for conversion costs:

Beginning WIP units:	5,000 units ×	40% =	2,000	EUP for conversion costs
Started and completed units:	33,000 units ×	100% =	33,000	EUP for conversion costs
In process units:	7,000 units ×	30% =	2,100	EUP for conversion costs
Total EUP for conversion costs			= 37,100	EUP for conversion costs

Exhibit 20A-3 illustrates the timing of the incurrence of conversion costs. Exhibit 20A-4 (on the next page) shows the production cost report with the EUP calculations added.

Exhibit 20A-3 | **Timing of Conversion Costs**

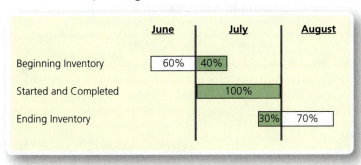

Exhibit 20A-4 | **Production Cost Report—Cutting Department—FIFO Method—EUP**

PUZZLE ME
Production Cost Report—CUTTING DEPARTMENT
Month Ended July 31, 2016

| | | Equivalent Units for Current Period | | |
	Whole Units	Transferred In	Direct Materials	Conversion Costs
UNITS				
Units to account for:				
Beginning work-in-process	5,000			
Started in production	40,000			
Total units to account for	45,000			
Units accounted for:				
Beginning work-in-process	5,000	0	5,000	2,000
Started and completed	33,000	33,000	33,000	33,000
Transferred to Finished Goods	38,000	33,000	38,000	35,000
Ending work-in-process	7,000	7,000	0	2,100
Total units accounted for	45,000	40,000	38,000	37,100

Step 2: EUP

Step 3: Compute the Cost per Equivalent Unit of Production Now that we have completed the UNITS section of the report, it is time to complete the COSTS section. The Cutting Department has three inputs and therefore must make three calculations for cost per equivalent unit of production.

$$\text{Current period cost per EUP for transferred in} = \frac{\text{Total transferred in costs}}{\text{Equivalent units of production for transferred in}}$$

$$\text{Current period cost per EUP for direct materials} = \frac{\text{Total direct materials costs}}{\text{Equivalent units of production for direct materials}}$$

$$\text{Current period cost per EUP for conversion costs} = \frac{\text{Total conversion costs}}{\text{Equivalent units of production for conversion costs}}$$

The Cutting Department has $232,540 of costs to account for, as illustrated in Exhibit 20A-5.

Exhibit 20A-5 | **Cutting Department: Costs to Account For**

	Transferred In	Direct Materials	Conversion Costs	Totals
Beginning balance in Work-in-Process Inventory—Cutting, July 1	$ 22,000	$ 0	$ 700	$ 22,700
Transferred in from Assembly Department during July	176,000			176,000
Additional added in Cutting Department during July		19,000	14,840	33,840
Totals	$ 198,000	$ 19,000	$ 15,540	$ 232,540

The beginning balances and the additional costs incurred were given in the original data. The amount transferred in from the Assembly Department, $176,000, is the amount calculated on the production cost report for the Assembly Department for July as the amount completed and transferred out in the costs accounted for section.

Our next task is to split these costs between the 38,000 completed puzzles transferred out to Finished Goods Inventory and the 7,000 partially complete puzzle boards that remain in the Cutting Department's ending Work-in-Process Inventory.

In Step 2, we computed equivalent units of production for transferred in as 40,000 EUP, direct materials as 38,000 EUP, and conversion costs as 37,100 EUP. Because the equivalent units of production differ, we must compute a separate cost per unit for each input. Also, the numerator for each calculation is the cost incurred in the current period, not total costs, because of the FIFO method. We need to calculate the *cost per EUP for the current period*.

The cost per equivalent unit for transferred in is $4.40, which is calculated as follows:

$$\text{Current period cost per EUP for transferred in} = \frac{\text{Total transferred in costs}}{\text{Equivalent units of production for transferred in}}$$

$$= \frac{\$176,000}{40,000 \text{ EUP}}$$

$$= \$4.40 \text{ per EUP}$$

The cost per equivalent unit of direct materials is $0.50, which is calculated as follows:

$$\text{Current period cost per EUP for direct materials} = \frac{\text{Total direct materials costs}}{\text{Equivalent units of production for direct materials}}$$

$$= \frac{\$19,000}{38,000 \text{ EUP}}$$

$$= \$0.50 \text{ per EUP}$$

The cost per equivalent unit of production for conversion costs is $0.40, which is calculated as follows:

$$\text{Current period cost per EUP for conversion costs} = \frac{\text{Total conversion costs}}{\text{Equivalent units of production for conversion costs}}$$

$$= \frac{\$14,840}{37,100 \text{ EUP}}$$

$$= \$0.40 \text{ per EUP}$$

The cost to account for calculations are added to the production cost report as shown in Exhibit 20A-6 (on the next page).

Exhibit 20A-6 | Production Cost Report—Cutting Department—FIFO Method—Costs to Account For

PUZZLE ME
Production Cost Report—CUTTING DEPARTMENT
Month Ended July 31, 2016

UNITS	Whole Units	Equivalent Units for Current Period		
		Transferred In	Direct Materials	Conversion Costs
Units to account for:				
Beginning work-in-process	5,000			
Started in production	40,000			
Total units to account for	45,000			
Units accounted for:				
Beginning work-in-process	5,000	0	5,000	2,000
Started and completed	33,000	33,000	33,000	33,000
Transferred to Finished Goods	38,000	33,000	38,000	35,000
Ending work-in-process	7,000	7,000	0	2,100
Total units accounted for	45,000	40,000	38,000	37,100

COSTS	Transferred In	Direct Materials	Conversion Costs	Total Costs	Cost per Unit
Costs to account for:					
Beginning work-in-process	$ 22,000	$ 0	$ 700	$ 22,700	
Costs added during period	176,000	19,000	14,840	209,840	
Total costs to account for	$ 198,000	$ 19,000	$ 15,540	$ 232,540	
Costs added during current period	$ 176,000	$ 19,000	$ 14,840		
Divided by: EUP this period	÷ 40,000	÷ 38,000	÷ 37,100		
Cost per equivalent unit this period	$ 4.40	$ 0.50	$ 0.40		
Costs accounted for:					
Beginning work-in-process					
Costs to complete beginning WIP					
Total costs for beginning WIP					
Started and completed					
Transferred to Finished Goods					
Ending work-in-process					
Total costs accounted for					

Step 3: Costs to account for

Step 4: Assign Costs to Units Completed and Units in Process The last step on the production cost report is to assign the $232,540 total costs to be accounted for by the Cutting Department to the following:

- The 5,000 puzzle boards from beginning inventory that have now been completed and transferred to Finished Goods Inventory.

- The 33,000 started and completed puzzles that have also been transferred to Finished Goods Inventory.

- The 7,000 partially completed puzzle boards remaining in the Cutting Department's ending Work-in-Process Inventory.

This is accomplished by multiplying the cost per equivalent unit of production times the equivalent units of production. To assign the costs of the three inputs to the three groups of outputs, this step must be completed nine times to assign:

- Transferred in costs to:
  - Beginning units
  - Started and completed units
  - In process units
- Direct materials cost to:
  - Beginning units
  - Started and completed units
  - In process units
- Conversion costs to:
  - Beginning units
  - Started and completed units
  - In process units

- In addition to the above calculations for costs incurred in the current period, the costs in beginning WIP must be added to those units.

Transferred In

Beginning WIP		$ 22,000
To complete beginning WIP	0 EUP × $4.40 per EUP =	0
Started and Completed	33,000 EUP × $4.40 per EUP =	145,200
Transferred to FG		167,200
In process	7,000 EUP × $4.40 per EUP =	30,800
Total		$ 198,000

Direct Materials

Beginning WIP		$ 0
To complete beginning WIP	5,000 EUP × $0.50 per EUP =	2,500
Started and Completed	33,000 EUP × $0.50 per EUP =	16,500
Transferred to FG		19,000
In process	0 EUP × $0.50 per EUP =	0
Total		$ 19,000

Conversion Costs

Beginning WIP		$ 700
To complete beginning WIP	2,000 EUP × $0.40 per EUP =	800
Started and Completed	33,000 EUP × $0.40 per EUP =	13,200
Transferred to FG		14,700
In process	2,100 EUP × $0.40 per EUP =	840
Total		$ 15,540

We have accomplished our goal of splitting the $232,540 total cost between the completed units and the in process units and can record these costs on the production cost report. The completed report is shown in Exhibit 20A-7 (on the next page).

Exhibit 20A-7 | **Production Cost Report—Cutting Department—FIFO Method—Costs Accounted For**

PUZZLE ME
Production Cost Report—CUTTING DEPARTMENT
Month Ended July 31, 2016

UNITS	Whole Units	Equivalent Units for Current Period		
		Transferred In	Direct Materials	Conversion Costs
Units to account for:				
Beginning work-in-process	5,000			
Started in production	40,000			
Total units to account for	45,000			
Units accounted for:				
Beginning work-in-process	5,000	0	5,000	2,000
Started and completed	33,000	33,000	33,000	33,000
Transferred to Finished Goods	38,000	33,000	38,000	35,000
Ending work-in-process	7,000	7,000	0	2,100
Total units accounted for	45,000	40,000	38,000	37,100

COSTS	Transferred In	Direct Materials	Conversion Costs	Total Costs	Cost per Unit
Costs to account for:					
Beginning work-in-process	$ 22,000	$ 0	$ 700	$ 22,700	
Costs added during period	176,000	19,000	14,840	209,840	
Total costs to account for	$ 198,000	$ 19,000	$ 15,540	$ 232,540	
Costs added during current period	$ 176,000	$ 19,000	$ 14,840		
Divided by: EUP this period	÷ 40,000	÷ 38,000	÷ 37,100		
Cost per equivalent unit this period	$ 4.40	$ 0.50	$ 0.40		
Costs accounted for:					
Beginning work-in-process	$ 22,000	$ 0	$ 700	$ 22,700	
Costs to complete beginning WIP	0	2,500	800	3,300	
Total costs for beginning WIP	22,000	2,500	1,500	26,000	$ 5.20[a]
Started and completed	145,200	16,500	13,200	174,900	5.30[b]
Transferred to Finished Goods	167,200	19,000	14,700	200,900	
Ending work-in-process	30,800	0	840	31,640	
Total costs accounted for	$ 198,000	$ 19,000	$ 15,540	$ 232,540	

Step 4: Costs accounted for

(a) Beginning WIP: $26,000 / 5,000 units = $5.20 per unit
(b) Started and completed: $174,900 / 33,000 units = $5.30 per unit

Notice the cost per unit for the units that were in beginning WIP is $5.20 ($26,000 / 5,000 units) and the cost per unit for the units started and completed in July is $5.30 ($174,900 / 33,000 units). This indicates that costs varied from June to July. Exhibit 20A-8 shows the completed production cost report for July for the Cutting Department using the weighted-average method. This is a duplicate of Exhibit 20-13 from the chapter. Take a moment to study the reports. Find the similarities and differences.

Exhibit 20A-8 | **Production Cost Report—Cutting Department—Weighted-Average Method**

PUZZLE ME
Production Cost Report—CUTTING DEPARTMENT—Weighted-Average Method
Month Ended July 31, 2016

UNITS	Whole Units	Equivalent Units Transferred In	Direct Materials	Conversion Costs
Units to account for:				
Beginning work-in-process	5,000			
Transferred in	40,000			
Total units to account for	45,000			
Units accounted for:				
Completed and transferred out	38,000	38,000	38,000	38,000
Ending work-in-process	7,000	7,000	0	2,100
Total units accounted for	45,000	45,000	38,000	40,100

COSTS	Transferred In	Direct Materials	Conversion Costs	Total Costs
Costs to account for:				
Beginning work-in-process	$ 22,000	$ 0	$ 1,200	$ 23,200
Costs added during period	176,000	19,000	14,840	209,840
Total costs to account for	198,000	19,000	16,040	233,040
Divided by: Total EUP	÷ 45,000	÷ 38,000	÷ 40,100	
Cost per equivalent unit	$ 4.40	$ 0.50	$ 0.40	$ 5.30
Costs accounted for:				
Completed and transferred out	$ 167,200	$ 19,000	$ 15,200	$ 201,400
Ending work-in-process	30,800	0	840	31,640
Total costs accounted for	$ 198,000	$ 19,000	$ 16,040	$ 233,040

Comparison of Weighted-Average and FIFO Methods

In our example, there were no significant differences between the two methods, only $0.10 per unit, which is less than 2% of the cost ([$5.30 − $5.20] / $5.20 = 1.9%). However, we have only considered one product produced by a small company. In a large company with many products, small fluctuations can have a significant impact.

If a business operates in an industry that experiences significant cost changes, it would be to its benefit to use the FIFO method. The weighted-average method merges costs from the prior period with the current period. This creates a smoothing effect, where cost changes are not as exposed. The FIFO method would create better month-to-month cost comparisons. This would be especially evident when there are substantial quantities of units in process at the end of the period. The more detailed cost information obtained from the FIFO method would allow managers to make better pricing and product mix decisions.

If a business operates in an industry that does not experience significant cost changes, the weighted-average method would be appropriate. This method is easier to use, and the additional benefit derived from more detailed calculations would not outweigh the cost of obtaining them.

Which method is better: weighted-average or first-in, first-out? Why?

Try It!

Bishop Company uses the FIFO method in its process costing system. The Finishing Department started the month with 500 units in process that were 20% complete, received 2,000 units from the Assembly Department, and transferred 2,100 units to the finished goods storage area. All materials are added at the beginning of the process and conversion costs occur evenly. The units in process at the end of the month are 45% complete with respect to conversion costs. The department incurred the following costs:

	Beginning WIP	Added this month	Total
Transferred In	$ 6,250	$ 25,000	$ 31,250
Direct Materials	500	2,000	2,500
Conversion Costs	1,250	5,450	6,700
Total	$ 8,000	$ 32,450	$ 40,450

13A. How many units are still in process at the end of the month?

14A. Compute the equivalent units of production for the Finishing Department for the current month.

15A. Determine the cost per equivalent unit for the current period for transferred in, direct materials, and conversion costs.

16A. Determine the cost to be transferred to Finished Goods Inventory.

Check your answers online in MyAccountingLab or at http://www.pearsonhighered.com/Horngren.

For more practice, see Short Exercises S20A-13 and S20A-14. **My**Accounting**Lab**

REVIEW

> Things You Should Know

1. How do costs flow through a process costing system?

- Process costing systems have multiple Work-in-Process Inventory accounts—one for each process or department.
- Costs flow from one Work-in-Process Inventory account to the next until production is complete.
- Costs flow from the last Work-in-Process Inventory account to Finished Goods Inventory.
- When the products are sold, costs flow from Finished Goods Inventory to Cost of Goods Sold.

2. What are equivalent units of production, and how are they calculated?

- Equivalent units of production are a way of expressing partially completed units in terms of completed units.
- For example, assuming conversion is uniform throughout the process, units that are halfway through a production process will have incurred half of the conversion costs. Therefore, 10 units that are one-half complete have the equivalent costs of 5 units that are complete: 10 × 50% = 5 × 100%.

3. **How is a production cost report prepared?**
   - Step 1: Summarize the flow of physical units.
   - Step 2: Compute output in terms of equivalent units of production.
   - Step 3: Compute the cost per equivalent unit of production.
   - Step 4: Assign costs to units completed and units in process.

4. **What journal entries are required in a process costing system?**
   - Costs incurred during the period are added to *each* Work-in-Process Inventory account

     DR—Work-in-Process—Department

     CR—Raw Materials Inventory (for amount of direct materials used)

     CR—Wages Payable (for amount of direct labor incurred)

     CR—Manufacturing Overhead (for amount of overhead allocated)
   - Costs transferred to the next department are deducted (credited) from the Work-in-Process Inventory account of the department transferred from and added (debited) to the Work-in-Process Inventory account of the department transferred to.
   - If costs are transferred from the last department, they are transferred using a debit to Finished Goods Inventory.
   - When goods are sold, the cost is credited to Finished Goods Inventory and debited to Cost of Goods Sold.

5. **How can the production cost report be used to make decisions?**
   - Controlling costs
   - Evaluating performance
   - Pricing products
   - Identifying most profitable products
   - Preparing financial statements

6. **How is a production cost report prepared using the FIFO method? (Appendix 20A)**
   - Prior period costs are not merged with current period costs.
   - Equivalent units of production must be calculated for
     - Units in beginning inventory completed in current period
     - Units started and completed during current period
     - Units started and still in process at end of current period

CHAPTER 20

> Summary Problem 1

Santa Fe Paints provides the following information for the Mixing Department for the month of September 2016:

	Units	Costs
Beginning Work-in-Process Inventory	0	$ 0
Started in Production in September	18,000	38,000*
Total to Account For	18,000	38,000
Completed and Transferred to Finishing Department during September	14,000	?
Ending Work-in-Process Inventory (25% complete for direct materials; 50% complete for conversion costs)	4,000	?
Total Accounted For	18,000	$ 38,000

*Includes $6,000 direct materials and $32,000 conversion costs

Complete a production cost report for the Mixing Department for the month of September 2016 to determine the cost of the units completed and transferred out and the cost of the ending Work-in-Process Inventory. Assume Santa Fe Paints uses the weighted-average method.

> Summary Problem 1 Solution

SANTA FE PAINTS
Production Cost Report—MIXING DEPARTMENT
Month Ended September 30, 2016

		Equivalent Units		
UNITS	**Whole Units**	**Transferred In**	**Direct Materials**	**Conversion Costs**
Units to account for:				
Beginning work-in-process	0			
Started in production	18,000			
Total units to account for	18,000			
Units accounted for:				
Completed and transferred out	14,000	n/a	14,000	14,000
Ending work-in-process	4,000	n/a	1,000[a]	2,000[b]
Total units accounted for	18,000	n/a	15,000	16,000

COSTS	**Transferred In**	**Direct Materials**	**Conversion Costs**	**Total Costs**
Costs to account for:				
Beginning work-in-process	n/a	$ 0	$ 0	$ 0
Costs added during period	n/a	6,000	32,000	38,000
Total costs to account for	n/a	6,000	32,000	38,000
Divided by: Total EUP	n/a	÷ 15,000	÷16,000	
Cost per equivalent unit	n/a	$ 0.40[c]	$ 2.00[d]	$ 2.40[e]
Costs accounted for:				
Completed and transferred out	n/a	$ 5,600[f]	$ 28,000[g]	$ 33,600[h]
Ending work-in-process	n/a	400[i]	4,000[j]	4,400[k]
Total costs accounted for	n/a	$ 6,000	$ 32,000	$ 38,000

Calculations:

(a)	4,000 units × 25% complete = 1,000 EUP
(b)	4,000 units × 50% complete = 2,000 EUP
(c)	$6,000 ÷ 15,000 EUP = $0.40 per EUP
(d)	$32,000 ÷ 16,000 EUP = $2.00 per EUP
(e)	$0.40 per EUP + $2.00 per EUP = $2.40 per EUP
(f)	14,000 EUP × $0.40 per EUP = $5,600
(g)	14,000 EUP × $2.00 per EUP = $28,000
(h)	$5,600 + $28,000 = $33,600
(i)	1,000 EUP × $0.40 per EUP = $400
(j)	2,000 EUP × $2.00 per EUP = $4,000
(k)	$400 + $4,000 = $4,400

The Mixing Department transferred 14,000 units with a cost of $33,600 to the Finishing Department in September. The ending balance in Work-in-Process Inventory—Mixing is $4,400.

> Summary Problem 2

This problem extends Summary Problem 1 into a second department, Finishing. During September, Santa Fe Paints reports the following in its Finishing Department:

UNITS

Beginning Work-in-Process Inventory (20% complete for direct materials; 70% complete for conversion costs)	4,000 units
Transferred in from Mixing Department during September	14,000 units
Completed and transferred out to Finished Goods Inventory during September	15,000 units
Ending Work-in-Process Inventory (30% complete for direct materials; 80% complete for conversion costs)	3,000 units

COSTS

Work-in-Process Inventory, August 31 (transferred in costs, $11,400; direct materials costs, $1,000; conversion costs, $1,800)	$ 14,200
Transferred in from Mixing Department (see Summary Problem 1)	33,600
Direct materials added during September	5,360
Conversion costs added during September	24,300

Complete a production cost report to assign the Finishing Department's September total costs to units completed and to units in process at the end of the month. Assume Santa Fe Paints uses the weighted-average method.

> Summary Problem 2 Solution

SANTA FE PAINTS
Production Cost Report—FINISHING DEPARTMENT
Month Ended September 30, 2016

UNITS	Whole Units	Equivalent Units — Transferred In	Direct Materials	Conversion Costs
Units to account for:				
Beginning work-in-process	4,000			
Started in production	14,000			
Total units to account for	18,000			
Units accounted for:				
Completed and transferred out	15,000	15,000	15,000	15,000
Ending work-in-process	3,000	3,000	900[a]	2,400[b]
Total units accounted for	18,000	18,000	15,900	17,400

COSTS	Transferred In	Direct Materials	Conversion Costs	Total Costs
Costs to account for:				
Beginning work-in-process	$ 11,400	$ 1,000	$ 1,800	$ 14,200
Costs added during period	33,600	5,360	24,300	63,260
Total costs to account for	45,000	6,360	26,100	77,460
Divided by: Total EUP	÷ 18,000	÷ 15,900	÷ 17,400	
Cost per equivalent unit	$ 2.50[c]	$ 0.40[d]	$ 1.50[e]	$ 4.40[f]
Costs accounted for:				
Completed and transferred out	$ 37,500[g]	$ 6,000[h]	$ 22,500[i]	$ 66,000[j]
Ending work-in-process	7,500[k]	360[l]	3,600[m]	11,460[n]
Total costs accounted for	$ 45,000	$ 6,360	$ 26,100	$ 77,460

Calculations:

(a)	3,000 units × 30% complete = 900 EUP
(b)	3,000 units × 80% complete = 2,400 EUP
(c)	$45,000 ÷ 18,000 EUP = $2.50 per EUP
(d)	$6,360 ÷ 15,900 EUP = $0.40 per EUP
(e)	$26,100 ÷ 17,400 EUP = $1.50 per EUP
(f)	$2.50 per EUP + $0.40 per EUP + $1.50 per EUP = $4.40 per EUP
(g)	15,000 EUP × $2.50 per EUP = $37,500
(h)	15,000 EUP × $0.40 per EUP = $6,000
(i)	15,000 EUP × $1.50 per EUP = $22,500
(j)	$37,500 + $6,000 + $22,500 = $66,000
(k)	3,000 EUP × $2.50 per EUP = $7,500
(l)	900 EUP × $0.40 per EUP = $360
(m)	2,400 EUP × $1.50 per EUP = $3,600
(n)	$7,500 + $360 + $3,600 = $11,460

The Finishing Department transferred 15,000 units with a cost of $66,000 to Finished Goods Inventory in September. The ending balance in Work-in-Process Inventory—Finishing is $11,460.

> Key Terms

Conversion Costs (p. 1038)

Equivalent Units of Production
(EUP) (p. 1038)

First-In, First-Out Method
(for Process Costing) (p. 1060)
(Appendix 20A)

Job Order Costing System (p. 1034)

Process (p. 1034)

Process Costing System (p. 1034)

Production Cost Report (p. 1040)

Transferred In Costs (p. 1046)

Weighted-Average Method
(for Process Costing) (p. 1047)

> Quick Check

1. Which company is least likely to use a process costing system?

   a. Paper manufacturer

   b. Soft drink bottler

   c. Accounting firm

   d. Petroleum processor

Learning Objective 1

2. Which characteristic is the same in both job order costing systems and process costing systems?

   a. Types of product costs

   b. Flow of costs through the accounts

   c. Number of Work-in-Process Inventory accounts

   d. Method of record keeping

Learning Objective 1

3. Conversion costs are

   a. direct materials plus direct labor.

   b. direct labor plus manufacturing overhead.

   c. direct materials plus manufacturing overhead.

   d. indirect materials plus indirect labor.

Learning Objective 2

Use the following information for Questions 4–7:

Burton Company uses the weighted-average method in its process costing system. The Packaging Department started the month with 200 units in process that were 70% complete, received 1,500 units from the Finishing Department, and had 150 units in process at the end of the period. All materials are added at the beginning of the process, and conversion costs are incurred uniformly. The units in process at the end of the month are 20% complete with respect to conversion costs. The department incurred the following costs:

	Beginning WIP	Added this month	Total
Transferred In	$ 700	$ 12,900	$ 13,600
Direct Materials	200	3,200	3,400
Conversion Costs	500	5,820	6,320
Total	$ 1,400	$ 21,920	$ 23,320

4. How many units were completed and transferred out?

   a. 150 units

   b. 1,500 units

   c. 1,350 units

   d. 1,550 units

Learning Objective 3

Learning Objective 3

5. For conversion costs, the equivalent units of production are
   a. 1,700 units.   b. 1,580 units.   c. 1,500 units.   d. 1,550 units.

Learning Objective 3

6. The cost per equivalent unit for direct materials is
   a. $2.00.   b. $4.00.   c. $8.00.   d. $14.00.

Learning Objective 3

7. Of the $3,400 total costs for direct materials, what amount will be transferred out?
   a. $3,400   b. $300   c. $1,200   d. $3,100

Learning Objective 4

8. The Mixing Department incurred the following costs during the month:

	Transferred In	Direct Materials	Direct Labor	Manufacturing Overhead Allocated
Beginning WIP	$ 250	$ 50	$ 25	$ 80
Added this month	1,000	225	150	500
Total	$ 1,250	$ 275	$ 175	$ 580

What is the journal entry to record the costs incurred during the month?

Date	Accounts and Explanation	Debit	Credit
a.	Work-in-Process Inventory—Mixing	1,030	
	Raw Materials Inventory		275
	Wages Payable		175
	Manufacturing Overhead		580
b.	Work-in-Process Inventory—Mixing	2,280	
	Transfer Costs		1,250
	Raw Materials Inventory		275
	Wages Payable		175
	Manufacturing Overhead		580
c.	Work-in-Process Inventory—Mixing	875	
	Raw Materials Inventory		225
	Wages Payable		150
	Manufacturing Overhead		500
d.	Work-in-Process Inventory—Mixing	875	
	Raw Materials Inventory		225
	Conversion Costs		650

Learning Objective 4

9. Department 1 completed work on 500 units and transferred them to Department 2. The cost of the units was $750. What is the journal entry to record the transfer?

Date	Accounts and Explanation	Debit	Credit
a.	Work-in-Process Inventory—Dept. 1	750	
	Work-in-Process Inventory—Dept. 2		750
b.	Work-in-Process Inventory—Dept. 2	750	
	Work-in-Process Inventory—Dept. 1		750
c.	Work-in-Process Inventory—Dept. 2	750	
	Cost of Goods Sold		750
d.	Cost of Goods Sold	750	
	Work-in-Process Inventory—Dept. 1		750

CHAPTER 20

10. The manager of Gilbert Company used the production cost report to compare budgeted costs to actual costs and then based bonuses on the results. This is an example of using the reports to

    a. prepare financial statements.

    b. control costs.

    c. evaluate performance.

    d. identify profitable products.

11A. Which statement is accurate concerning the FIFO method for assigning costs in a process costing system?

    a. FIFO method assumes the first costs incurred are transferred out.

    b. FIFO method merges costs from prior periods with costs from current periods.

    c. FIFO method assumes the first costs incurred are still in process.

    d. FIFO method treats units in process at the beginning of the period in the same manner as units in process at the end of the period.

**Learning Objective 6
Appendix 20A**

Check your answers at the end of the chapter.

ASSESS YOUR PROGRESS

> Review Questions

1. What types of companies use job order costing systems?

2. What types of companies use process costing systems?

3. What are the primary differences between job order costing systems and process costing systems?

4. List ways in which job order costing systems are similar to process costing systems.

5. Describe the flow of costs through a process costing system.

6. What are equivalent units of production?

7. Why is the calculation of equivalent units of production needed in a process costing system?

8. What are conversion costs? Why do some companies using process costing systems use conversion costs?

9. What is a production cost report?

10. What are the four steps in preparing a production cost report?

11. Explain the terms *to account for* and *accounted for*.

12. If a company began the month with 50 units in process, started another 600 units during the month, and ended the month with 75 units in process, how many units were completed?

13. Most companies using process costing systems have to calculate more than one EUP. Why? How many do they have to calculate?

14. How is the cost per equivalent unit of production calculated?

15. What is the purpose of the Costs Accounted For section of the production cost report?

16. What are transferred in costs? When do they occur?

17. What is the weighted-average method for process costing systems?

18. Explain the additional journal entries required by process costing systems that are not needed in job order costing systems.

19. Department 1 is transferring units that cost $40,000 to Department 2. Give the journal entry.

20. Department 4 has completed production on units that have a total cost of $15,000. The units are ready for sale. Give the journal entry.

21. Describe ways the production cost report can be used by management.

22A. Describe how the FIFO method is different from the weighted-average method.

23A. Describe the three groups of units that must be accounted for when using the FIFO method.

24A. When might it be beneficial for a company to use the FIFO method? When is the weighted-average method more practical?

> Short Exercises

For all Short Exercises, assume the weighted-average method is to be used unless you are told otherwise.

Learning Objective 1

S20-1 Comparing job order costing versus process costing

Identify each costing system characteristic as job order costing or process costing.

a. One Work-in-Process Inventory account

b. Production cost reports

c. Cost accumulated by process

d. Job cost sheets

e. Manufactures homogenous products through a series of uniform steps

f. Multiple Work-in-Process Inventory accounts

g. Costs transferred at end of period

h. Manufactures batches of unique products or provides specialized services

Learning Objective 1

S20-2 Tracking the flow of costs

The Jimenez Toy Company makes wooden toys. Arrange the company's accounts in the order the production costs are most likely to flow, using 1 for the first account, 2 for the second, and so on.

Order	Account
_____	Work-in-Process—Packaging
_____	Cost of Goods Sold
_____	Work-in-Process—Cutting
_____	Work-in-Process—Finishing
_____	Finished Goods Inventory

S20-3 Calculating conversion costs

Learning Objective 2

Hamlin Orange manufactures orange juice. Last month's total manufacturing costs for the Jacksonville operation included:

Direct materials	$ 600,000
Direct labor	32,000
Manufacturing overhead	155,000

What was the conversion cost for Hamlin Orange's Jacksonville operation last month?

S20-4 Calculating EUP

Learning Objective 2

Monga manufactures cell phones. The conversion costs to produce cell phones for November are added evenly throughout the process in the Assembly Department. For each of the following separate assumptions, calculate the equivalent units of production for conversion costs in the ending Work-in-Process Inventory for the Assembly Department:

1. 7,000 cell phones were 85% complete

2. 24,000 cell phones were 15% complete

S20-5 Calculating conversion costs and unit cost

Learning Objective 2

Russia Spring produces premium bottled water. Russia Spring purchases artesian water, stores the water in large tanks, and then runs the water through two processes: filtration and bottling.

During February, the filtration process incurred the following costs in processing 150,000 liters:

Wages of workers operating filtration equipment	$ 19,950
Manufacturing overhead allocated to filtration	22,050
Water	150,000

Russia Spring had no beginning Work-in-Process Inventory in the Filtration Department in February.

Requirements

1. Compute the February conversion costs in the Filtration Department.

2. The Filtration Department completely processed 150,000 liters in February. What was the filtration cost per liter?

Note: Short Exercise S20-5 must be completed before attempting Short Exercise S20-6.

S20-6 Computing EUP

Learning Objective 2

Refer to Short Exercise S20-5. At Russia Spring, water is added at the beginning of the filtration process. Conversion costs are added evenly throughout the process. Now assume that in February, 80,000 liters were completed and transferred out of the Filtration Department into the Bottling Department. The 70,000 liters remaining in Filtration's ending Work-in-Process Inventory were 80% of the way through the filtration process. Recall that Russia Spring has no beginning inventories.

Compute the equivalent units of production for direct materials and conversion costs for the Filtration Department.

Learning Objective 3

S20-7 Computing costs transferred

The Finishing Department of Carter and Nelson, Inc., the last department in the manufacturing process, incurred production costs of $310,000 during the month of June. If the June 1 balance in Work-in-Process—Finishing is $0 and the June 30 balance is $70,000, what amount was transferred to Finished Goods Inventory?

Learning Objectives 2, 3

S20-8 Computing EUP

The Mixing Department of Fresh Foods had 50,000 units to account for in October. Of the 50,000 units, 40,000 units were completed and transferred to the next department, and 10,000 units were 20% complete. All of the materials are added at the beginning of the process. Conversion costs are added evenly throughout the mixing process.

Compute the total equivalent units of production for direct materials and conversion costs for October.

Note: Short Exercise S20-8 must be completed before attempting Short Exercise S20-9.

Learning Objective 3

S20-9 Computing the cost per EUP

Refer to the data in Short Exercise S20-8 and your results for equivalent units of production. The Mixing Department of Fresh Foods has direct materials costs of $48,000 and conversion costs of $29,400 for October.

Compute the cost per equivalent unit of production for direct materials and for conversion costs.

Note: Short Exercises S20-8 and S20-9 must be completed before attempting Short Exercise S20-10.

Learning Objective 3

S20-10 Assigning costs

Refer to Short Exercises S20-8 and S20-9. Use Fresh Foods's costs per equivalent unit of production for direct materials and conversion costs that you calculated in Short Exercise S20-9.

Calculate the cost of the 40,000 units completed and transferred out and the 10,000 units, 20% complete, in the ending Work-in-Process Inventory.

Note: Short Exercises S20-8, S20-9, and S20-10 must be completed before attempting Short Exercise S20-11.

Learning Objective 4

S20-11 Preparing journal entry

Refer to Short Exercise S20-10. Prepare the journal entry to record the transfer of costs from the Mixing Department to the Packaging Department.

Learning Objective 5

S20-12 Making decisions

Miller Company sells several products. Sales reports show that the sales volume of its most popular product has increased the past three quarters while overall profits have decreased. How might production cost reports assist management in making decisions about this product?

Learning Objective 6
Appendix 20A

S20A-13 Calculating conversion costs and unit cost—FIFO method

Spring Rain produces premium bottled water. Spring Rain purchases artesian water, stores the water in large tanks, and then runs the water through two processes: filtration and bottling.

During February, the filtration process incurred the following costs in processing 100,000 liters:

Wages of workers operating filtration equipment	$ 20,950
Manufacturing overhead allocated to filtration	24,050
Water	170,000

Spring Rain had no beginning Work-in-Process Inventory in the Filtration Department in February.

Requirements

1. Use the FIFO method to compute the February conversion costs in the Filtration Department.

2. The Filtration Department completely processed 100,000 liters in February. Use the FIFO method to determine the filtration cost per liter.

Note: Short Exercise S20A-13 must be completed before attempting Short Exercise S20A-14.

S20A-14 Computing EUP—FIFO Method

Refer to Short Exercise S20A-13. At Spring Rain, water is added at the beginning of the filtration process. Conversion costs are added evenly throughout the process. Now assume that in February, 80,000 liters were completed and transferred out of the Filtration Department into the Bottling Department. The 20,000 liters remaining in Filtration's ending Work-in-Process Inventory were 70% of the way through the filtration process. Recall that Spring Rain has no beginning inventories.

Compute the equivalent units of production for direct materials and conversion costs for the Filtration Department using the FIFO method.

Learning Objective 6
Appendix 20A

> Exercises

For all Exercises, assume the weighted-average method is to be used unless you are told otherwise.

E20-15 Comparing job order costing versus process costing

For each of the following products or services, indicate if the cost would most likely be determined using a job order costing system or a process costing system.

a. Soft drinks

b. Automobile repairs

c. Customized furniture

d. Aluminum foil

e. Lawn chairs

f. Chocolate candy bars

g. Hospital surgery

h. Pencils

Learning Objective 1

CHAPTER 20

Learning Objectives 1, 2, 3

E20-16 Understanding terminology

Match the following terms to their definitions.

1. Direct labor plus manufacturing overhead
2. Prepared by department for EUP, production costs, and assignment of costs
3. Equivalent units of production
4. Process costing system
5. Transferred in costs
6. Weighted-average method

a. Expresses partially completed units in terms of fully completed units
b. Used by companies that manufacture homogenous products
c. Previous costs brought into later process
d. Conversion costs
e. Combines prior period costs with current period costs
f. Production cost report

Learning Objectives 1, 4

c. $9,000

E20-17 Tracking the flow of costs

Complete the missing amounts and labels in the T-accounts.

Work-in-Process Inventory—Cutting

Balance, May 1	0	(a)	Transfer out to _____
Direct Materials	48,000		
Direct Labor	14,000		
Manufacturing Overhead	30,000		
Balance, May 31	8,000		

Work-in-Process Inventory—Finishing

Balance, May 1	14,000	130,000	Transfer out to _____	
Transfer in from _____	(b)			
Direct Materials	22,000			
Direct Labor	(c)			
Manufacturing Overhead	23,000			
Balance, May 31	22,000			

Work-in-Process Inventory—Packaging

Balance, May 1	10,000	(d)	Transfer out to _____
Transfer in from _____	(e)		
Direct Materials	8,000		
Direct Labor	5,000		
Manufacturing Overhead	8,000		
Balance, May 31	11,000		

Finished Goods Inventory

Balance, May 1	0	(f)	Transfer out to _____
Transfer in from _____	(g)		
Balance, May 31	7,000		

Cost of Goods Sold

Balance, May 1	0	
Transfer in from _____	(h)	
Balance, May 31	(i)	

E20-18 Computing EUP

Learning Objective 2

3. EUP for DM 1,900

Collins Company has the following data for the Assembly Department for August:

Units in process at the beginning of August	300
Units started in August	1,800
Units completed and transferred	1,900
Units in process at end of August	200

Conversion costs are added evenly throughout the process. Compute the equivalent units of production for direct materials and conversion costs for each independent scenario:

1. Units in process at the beginning of August are 40% complete; units in process at the end of August are 30% complete; materials are added at the beginning of the process.

2. Units in process at the beginning of August are 60% complete; units in process at the end of August are 70% complete; materials are added at the beginning of the process.

3. Units in process at the beginning of August are 40% complete; units in process at the end of August are 30% complete; materials are added at the end of the process.

4. Units in process at the beginning of August are 60% complete; units in process at the end of August are 70% complete; materials are added at the halfway point.

E20-19 Computing EUP, assigning cost, no beginning WIP or cost transferred in

Learning Objectives 2, 3

1. Total EUP for CC 7,050

Ceramic Painting prepares and packages paint products. Ceramic Painting has two departments: Blending and Packaging. Direct materials are added at the beginning of the blending process (dyes) and at the end of the packaging process (cans). Conversion costs are added evenly throughout each process. Data from the month of May for the Blending Department are as follows:

Gallons	
Beginning Work-in-Process Inventory	0 gallons
Started in production	9,500 gallons
Completed and transferred out to Packaging in May	6,000 gallons
Ending Work-in-Process Inventory (30% of the way through the blending process)	3,500 gallons
Costs	
Beginning Work-in-Process Inventory	$ 0
Costs added during May:	
Direct materials	5,700
Direct labor	2,085
Manufacturing overhead allocated	2,004
Total costs added during May	$ 9,789

Requirements

1. Compute the Blending Department's equivalent units of production for direct materials and for conversion costs.

2. Compute the total costs of the units (gallons)

   a. completed and transferred out to the Packaging Department.
   b. in the Blending Department ending Work-in-Process Inventory.

Note: Exercise E20-19 must be completed before attempting Exercise E20-20.

Learning Objectives 4, 5

2. WIP Balance $2,709

E20-20 Preparing journal entries, posting to T-accounts, making decisions

Refer to your answers from Exercise E20-19.

Requirements

1. Prepare the journal entries to record the assignment of direct materials and direct labor and the allocation of manufacturing overhead to the Blending Department. Also, prepare the journal entry to record the costs of the gallons completed and transferred out to the Packaging Department.

2. Post the journal entries to the Work-in-Process Inventory—Blending T-account. What is the ending balance?

3. What is the average cost per gallon transferred out of the Blending Department into the Packaging Department? Why would the company managers want to know this cost?

Learning Objectives 2, 3

1. EUP for CC 7,200

E20-21 Computing EUP, assigning costs, no beginning WIP or cost transferred in

Anderson Winery in Pleasant Valley, New York, has two departments: Fermenting and Packaging. Direct materials are added at the beginning of the fermenting process (grapes) and at the end of the packaging process (bottles). Conversion costs are added evenly throughout each process. Data from the month of March for the Fermenting Department are as follows:

Gallons	
Beginning Work-in-Process Inventory	0 gallons
Started in production	7,900 gallons
Completed and transferred out to Packaging in March	4,400 gallons
Ending Work-in-Process Inventory (80% of the way through the fermenting process)	3,500 gallons
Costs	
Beginning Work-in-Process Inventory	$ 0
Costs added during March:	
Direct materials	8,611
Direct labor	2,196
Manufacturing overhead allocated	4,500
Total costs added during March	$ 15,307

CHAPTER 20

Requirements

1. Compute the Fermenting Department's equivalent units of production for direct materials and for conversion costs.

2. Compute the total costs of the units (gallons)
   a. completed and transferred out to the Packaging Department.
   b. in the Fermenting Department ending Work-in-Process Inventory.

Note: Exercise E20-21 must be completed before attempting Exercise E20-22.

E20-22 Preparing journal entries and posting to T-accounts

Refer to the data and your answers from Exercise E20-21.

Requirements

1. Prepare the journal entries to record the assignment of direct materials and direct labor and the allocation of manufacturing overhead to the Fermenting Department. Also prepare the journal entry to record the cost of the gallons completed and transferred out to the Packaging Department.

2. Post the journal entries to the Work-in-Process Inventory—Fermenting T-account. What is the ending balance?

3. What is the average cost per gallon transferred out of the Fermenting Department into the Packaging Department? Why would Anderson Winery's managers want to know this cost?

Learning Objectives 4, 5

2. WIP Balance $6,419

CHAPTER 20

E20-23 Preparing production cost report, missing amounts

Complete the missing amounts in the following production report. Materials are added at the beginning of the process; conversion costs are incurred evenly; the ending inventory is 60% complete.

BRYAN COMPANY
Production Cost Report—FINISHING DEPARTMENT
Month Ended September 30, 2016

UNITS	Whole Units	Equivalent Units Transferred In	Direct Materials	Conversion Costs
Units to account for:				
Beginning work-in-process	900			
Started in production	1,400			
Total units to account for	(a)			
Units accounted for:				
Completed and transferred out	(b)	n/a	(d)	(g)
Ending work-in-process	900	n/a	(e)	(h)
Total units accounted for	(c)	n/a	(f)	(i)

COSTS	Transferred In	Direct Materials	Conversion Costs	Total Costs
Costs to account for:				
Beginning work-in-process	n/a	$ 1,600	(j)	$ 3,050
Costs added during period	n/a	15,420	3,691	(k)
Total costs to account for	n/a	(l)	5,141	22,161
Divided by: Total EUP	n/a	(m)	(n)	
Cost per equivalent unit	n/a	(o)	(p)	(q)
Costs accounted for:				
Completed and transferred out	n/a	(r)	(s)	(t)
Ending work-in-process	n/a	(u)	(v)	(w)
Total costs accounted for	n/a	(x)	(y)	$ 22,161

E20-24 Computing EUP, first and second departments

Selected production and cost data of Sharon's Color Co. follow for May 2016:

	Mixing Department	Heating Department
Units to account for:		
Beginning work-in-process, April 30	40,000	8,000
Started in May	55,000	
Transferred in during May		80,000
Total units to account for	95,000	88,000
Units accounted for:		
Completed and transferred out during May	80,000	76,000
Ending work-in-process, May 31	15,000	12,000
Total units accounted for	95,000	88,000

On May 31, the Mixing Department ending Work-in-Process Inventory was 65% complete for materials and 25% complete for conversion costs. The Heating Department ending Work-in-Process Inventory was 75% complete for materials and 60% complete for conversion costs.

Requirements

1. Compute the equivalent units of production for direct materials and for conversion costs for the Mixing Department.

2. Compute the equivalent units of production for transferred in costs, direct materials, and conversion costs for the Heating Department.

E20-25 Preparing production cost report, journalizing, second department

Learning Objectives 2, 3, 4

3. WIP Balance $20,700

(Requirement 1 only)

Pure Spring Company produces premium bottled water. In the second department, the Bottling Department, conversion costs are incurred evenly throughout the bottling process, but packaging materials are not added until the end of the process. Costs in beginning Work-in-Process Inventory include transferred in costs of $1,500, direct labor of $500, and manufacturing overhead of $430. February data for the Bottling Department follow:

PURE SPRING COMPANY						
Work-in-Process Inventory—Bottling						
Month Ended February 29, 2016						
		Dollars				
	Units	**Transferred In**	**Direct Materials**	**Direct Labor**	**Manufacturing Overhead**	**Total Costs**
Beginning inventory, Feb. 1 (40% complete)	4,000	$ 1,500		$ 500	$ 430	$ 2,430
Production started	166,000	132,800	$ 33,000	33,200	23,270	222,270
Transferred out	150,000					
Ending inventory, Feb. 29 (70% complete)	20,000					

Requirements

1. Prepare a production cost report for the Bottling Department for the month of February.

2. Prepare the journal entry to record the cost of units completed and transferred out.

3. Post all transactions to the Work-in-Process Inventory—Bottling T-account. What is the ending balance?

CHAPTER 2

Learning Objective 4

E20-26 Preparing journal entries—inputs

Austin Company had the following transactions in October:

- Purchased raw materials on account, $50,000

- Used materials in production: $20,000 in the Mixing Department; $5,000 in the Packaging Department; $900 in indirect materials

- Incurred labor costs: $8,000 in the Mixing Department; $3,500 in the Packaging Department; $2,400 in indirect labor

- Incurred manufacturing overhead costs: $9,000 in machinery depreciation; paid $2,900 for rent and $1,730 for utilities

Prepare the journal entries for Austin Company.

Learning Objective 4

E20-27 Preparing journal entries—outputs

Galvan Company has a production process that involves three processes. Units move through the processes in this order: cutting, stamping, and then polishing. The company had the following transactions in November:

- Cost of units completed in the Cutting Department, $19,000

- Cost of units completed in the Stamping Department, $23,000

- Cost of units completed in the Polishing Department, $39,000

- Sales on account, $20,000

- Cost of goods sold is 40% of sales

Prepare the journal entries for Galvan Company.

Learning Objective 6
Appendix 20A

2. Mixing Dept. EUP for CC 70,850

E20A-28 Computing EUP—FIFO method

Paul's Frozen Pizzas uses FIFO process costing. Selected production and cost data follow for April 2016.

	Mixing Department	Cooking Department
Units to account for:		
Beginning work-in-process, March 31	22,000	10,000
Started in April	70,000	
Transferred in during April		47,000
Total units to account for	92,000	57,000
Units accounted for:		
Completed and transferred out during April		
From beginning work-in-process inventory	22,000	10,000
Started and completed during April	25,000	40,000
Ending work-in-process, April 30	45,000	7,000
Total units accounted for	92,000	57,000

Requirements

1. Calculate the following:

   a. On March 31, the Mixing Department beginning Work-in-Process Inventory was 30% complete for materials and 45% complete for conversion costs. This means that for the beginning inventory _____ % of the materials and _____ % of the conversion costs were added during April.

   b. On April 30, the Mixing Department ending Work-in-Process Inventory was 65% complete for materials and 75% complete for conversion costs. This means that for the ending inventory _____ % of the materials and _____ % of the conversion costs were added during April.

   c. On March 31, the Cooking Department beginning Work-in-Process Inventory was 70% complete for materials and 80% complete for conversion costs. This means that for the beginning inventory _____ % of the materials and _____ % of the conversion costs were added during April.

   d. On April 30, the Cooking Department ending Work-in-Process Inventory was 55% complete for materials and 80% complete for conversion costs. This means that for the ending inventory _____ % of the materials and _____ % of the conversion costs were added during April.

2. Use the information in the table and the information in Requirement 1 to compute the equivalent units of production for transferred in costs, direct materials, and conversion costs for both the Mixing and the Cooking Departments.

> Problems **Group A**

For all Problems, assume the weighted-average method is to be used unless you are told otherwise.

P20-29A Preparing a production cost report, no beginning WIP or costs transferred in

Abby Electronics makes DVD players in three processes: assembly, programming, and packaging. Direct materials are added at the beginning of the assembly process. Conversion costs are incurred evenly throughout the process. The Assembly Department had no Work-in-Process Inventory on October 31. In mid-November, Abby Electronics started production on 101,000 DVD players. Of this number, 76,900 DVD players were assembled during November and transferred out to the Programming Department. The November 30 Work-in-Process Inventory in the Assembly Department was 35% of the way through the assembly process. Direct materials costing $375,720 were placed in production in Assembly during November, direct labor of $157,500 was assigned, and manufacturing overhead of $98,505 was allocated to that department.

Requirements

1. Prepare a production cost report for the Assembly Department for November.

2. Prepare a T-account for Work-in-Process Inventory—Assembly to show its activity during November, including the November 30 balance.

Learning Objectives 2, 3

1. Cost per EUP for DM $3.72
2. WIP Balance $114,957

Learning Objectives 2, 3, 4

1. Total Cost per EUP $2.60

P20-30A Preparing a production cost report, no beginning WIP or costs transferred in; journal entries

Allen Paper Co. produces the paper used by wallpaper manufacturers. Allen's four-stage process includes mixing, cooking, rolling, and cutting. During March, the Mixing Department started and completed mixing for 4,500 rolls of paper. The department started but did not finish the mixing for an additional 500 rolls, which were 20% complete with respect to both direct materials and conversion work at the end of March. Direct materials and conversion costs are incurred evenly throughout the mixing process. The Mixing Department incurred the following costs during March:

Work-in-Process Inventory—Mixing	
Bal. March 1	0
Direct materials	5,520
Direct labor	580
Manufacturing overhead	5,860

Requirements

1. Prepare a production cost report for the Mixing Department for March.

2. Journalize all transactions affecting the company's mixing process during March, including those already posted.

Learning Objectives 2, 3, 4

1. Total EUP for CC 2,850
3. WIP Balance $1,145

P20-31A Preparing a production cost report, two materials added at different points, no beginning WIP or costs transferred in; journal entries

White's Exteriors produces exterior siding for homes. The Preparation Department begins with wood, which is chopped into small bits. At the end of the process, an adhesive is added. Then the wood/adhesive mixture goes on to the Compression Department, where the wood is compressed into sheets. Conversion costs are added evenly throughout the preparation process. January data for the Preparation Department are as follows:

UNITS	
Beginning Work-in-Process Inventory	0 sheets
Started in production	3,500 sheets
Completed and transferred out to Compression in January	2,500 sheets
Ending Work-in-Process Inventory (35% of the way through the preparation process)	1,000 sheets
COSTS	
Beginning Work-in-Process Inventory	$ 0
Costs added during January:	
Wood	2,905
Adhesives	1,925
Direct labor	665
Manufacturing overhead allocated	1,900
Total costs	$ 7,395

Requirements

1. Prepare a production cost report for the Preparation Department for January. (*Hint*: Each direct material added at a different point in the production process requires its own equivalent units of production computation.)

2. Prepare the journal entry to record the cost of the sheets completed and transferred out to the Compression Department.

3. Post the journal entries to the Work-in-Process Inventory—Preparation T-account. What is the ending balance?

P20-32A Preparing production cost report, second department with beginning WIP; journal entries

Learning Objectives 2, 3, 4

1. Cost per EUP DM $24.00

Claudia Carpet manufactures broadloom carpet in seven processes: spinning, dyeing, plying, spooling, tufting, latexing, and shearing. In the Dyeing Department, direct materials (dye) are added at the beginning of the process. Conversion costs are incurred evenly throughout the process. Information for November 2016 follows:

UNITS	
Beginning Work-in-Process Inventory	55 rolls
Transferred in from Spinning Department during November	560 rolls
Completed during November	490 rolls
Ending Work-in-Process Inventory (80% complete for conversion work)	125 rolls
COSTS	
Beginning Work-in-Process Inventory (transferred in costs, $3,500; materials costs, $1,750; conversion costs, $5,420)	$ 10,670
Transferred in from Spinning Department	18,025
Materials costs added during November	13,010
Conversion costs added during November (manufacturing wages, $8,120; manufacturing overhead allocated, $45,460)	53,580

Requirements

1. Prepare the November production cost report for Claudia's Dyeing Department.

2. Journalize all transactions affecting Claudia's Dyeing Department during November, including the entries that have already been posted.

P20-33A Preparing production cost report, second department with beginning WIP; decision making

Learning Objectives 2, 3, 5

1. Total cost per EUP for CC $10.00

Sea Bound uses three processes to manufacture lifts for personal watercraft: forming a lift's parts from galvanized steel, assembling the lift, and testing the completed lift. The lifts are transferred to Finished Goods Inventory before shipment to marinas across the country.

CHAPTER 20

Sea Bound's Testing Department requires no direct materials. Conversion costs are incurred evenly throughout the testing process. Other information follows for the month of August:

UNITS	
Beginning Work-in-Process Inventory	2,200 units
Transferred in from Assembling Department during the period	7,100 units
Completed during the period	4,200 units
Ending Work-in-Process Inventory (40% complete for conversion work)	5,100 units
COSTS	
Beginning Work-in-Process Inventory (transferred in costs, $93,800; conversion costs, $18,200)	$ 112,000
Transferred in from the Assembly Department during the period	706,000
Conversion costs added during the period	44,200

The cost transferred into Finished Goods Inventory is the cost of the lifts transferred out of the Testing Department.

Requirements

1. Prepare a production cost report for the Testing Department.

2. What is the cost per unit for lifts completed and transferred out to Finished Goods Inventory? Why would management be interested in this cost?

Learning Objective 6
Appendix 20A

1. Total EUP for CC 3,780

P20A-34A Preparing production cost report, second department, with beginning WIP and transferred in costs, journal entries, FIFO method

Vero, Inc. manufactures tire tubes in a two-stage process that includes assembly and sealing. The Sealing Department tests the tubes and adds a puncture-resistant coating to each tube to prevent air leaks.

The direct materials (coating) are added at the end of the sealing process. Conversion costs are incurred evenly throughout the process. Work in process of the Sealing Department on February 29, 2016, consisted of 1,000 tubes that were 70% of the way through the production process. The beginning balance in Work-in-Process Inventory—Sealing was $26,700, which consisted of $11,100 in transferred in costs and $15,600 in conversion costs. During March, 4,800 tubes were transferred in from the Assembly Department. The Sealing Department transferred 3,600 tubes to Finished Goods Inventory in March, and 2,200 were still in process on March 31. This ending inventory was 40% of the way through the sealing process. Vero uses FIFO process costing.

At March 31, before recording the transfer of costs from the Sealing Department to Finished Goods Inventory, the Vero general ledger included the following account:

Work-in-Process Inventory—Sealing

Balance, Feb. 29	26,700
Transferred in from Assembly	48,000
Direct materials	18,000
Direct labor	29,550
Manufacturing overhead	27,150

Requirements

1. Prepare a production cost report for the Sealing Department for March.

2. Journalize all transactions affecting the Sealing Department during March, including the entries that have already been posted.

P20A-35A Preparing a production cost report, second department with beginning WIP; recording transactions

Work Problem P20-32A using the FIFO method. The Dyeing Department beginning work in process of 55 units is 40% complete as to conversion costs. Round equivalent unit of production costs to four decimal places.

Learning Objective 6
Appendix 20A

1. Total EUP for DM 560

> Problems **Group B**

For all Problems, assume the weighted-average method is to be used unless you are told otherwise.

P20-36B Preparing a production cost report, no beginning WIP or cost transferred in

Lori Electronics makes DVD players in three processes: assembly, programming, and packaging. Direct materials are added at the beginning of the assembly process. Conversion costs are incurred evenly throughout the process. The Assembly Department had no Work-in-Process Inventory on March 31. In mid-April, Lori Electronics started production on 95,000 DVD players. Of this number, 68,000 DVD players were assembled during April and transferred out to the Programming Department. The April 30 Work-in-Process Inventory in the Assembly Department was 30% of the way through the assembly process. Direct materials costing $280,250 were placed in production in Assembly during April, direct labor of $152,712 was assigned, and manufacturing overhead of $69,500 was allocated to that department.

Learning Objectives 2, 3

1. Total cost per EUP $5.87
2. WIP Balance $103,302

Requirements

1. Prepare a production cost report for the Assembly Department for April.

2. Prepare a T-account for Work-in-Process Inventory—Assembly to show its activity during April, including the April 30 balance.

P20-37B Preparing a production cost report, no beginning WIP or costs transferred in; journal entries

Neal Paper Co. produces the paper used by wallpaper manufacturers. Neal's four-stage process includes mixing, cooking, rolling, and cutting. During September, the Mixing Department started and completed mixing for 4,420 rolls of paper. The department started but did not finish the mixing for an additional 600 rolls, which were 20% complete with respect to both direct materials and conversion work at the end of September. Direct materials and conversion costs are incurred evenly throughout the mixing process. The Mixing Department incurred the following costs during September:

Learning Objectives 2, 3, 4

1. Cost per EUP DM $1.25

Work-in-Process Inventory—Mixing	
Bal. Sep. 1	0
Direct materials	5,675
Direct labor	570
Manufacturing overhead	6,240

Requirements

1. Prepare a production cost report for the Mixing Department for September.

2. Journalize all transactions affecting the company's mixing process during September, including those already posted.

Learning Objectives 2, 3, 4

1. Total cost per EUP $2.26
3. WIP Balance $1,836

P20-38B Preparing a production cost report, two materials added at different points, no beginning WIP or costs transferred in; journal entries

John's Exteriors produces exterior siding for homes. The Preparation Department begins with wood, which is chopped into small bits. At the end of the process, an adhesive is added. Then the wood/adhesive mixture goes on to the Compression Department, where the wood is compressed into sheets. Conversion costs are added evenly throughout the preparation process. January data for the Preparation Department are as follows:

UNITS	
Beginning Work-in-Process Inventory	0 sheets
Started in production	3,700 sheets
Completed and transferred out to Compression in January	2,000 sheets
Ending Work-in-Process Inventory (30% of the way through the preparation process)	1,700 sheets
COSTS	
Beginning Work-in-Process Inventory	$ 0
Costs added during January:	
Wood	3,108
Adhesives	1,240
Direct labor	558
Manufacturing overhead allocated	1,450
Total costs	$ 6,356

Requirements

1. Prepare a production cost report for the Preparation Department for January. (*Hint:* Each direct material added at a different point in the production process requires its own equivalent unit of production computation.)

2. Prepare the journal entry to record the cost of the sheets completed and transferred out to the Compression Department.

3. Post the journal entries to the Work-in-Process Inventory—Preparation T-account. What is the ending balance?

P20-39B Preparing a production cost report, second department with beginning WIP; journal entries

Learning Objectives 2, 3, 4

1. Cost per EUP DM $21.00

Carrie Carpet manufactures broadloom carpet in seven processes: spinning, dyeing, plying, spooling, tufting, latexing, and shearing. In the Dyeing Department, direct materials (dye) are added at the beginning of the process. Conversion costs are incurred evenly throughout the process. Information for July 2016 follows:

UNITS	
Beginning Work-in-Process Inventory	75 rolls
Transferred in from Spinning Department during July	560 rolls
Completed during July	500 rolls
Ending Work-in-Process Inventory (80% complete for conversion work)	135 rolls
COSTS	
Beginning Work-in-Process Inventory (transferred in costs, $4,400; materials costs, $1,575; conversion costs, $5,199)	$ 11,174
Transferred in from Spinning Department	21,000
Materials costs added during July	11,760
Conversion costs added during July (manufacturing wages, $8,445; manufacturing overhead allocated, $43,508)	51,953

Requirements

1. Prepare a production cost report for Carrie's Dyeing Department for July.
2. Journalize all transactions affecting Carrie's Dyeing Department during July, including the entries that have already been posted.

P20-40B Preparing a production cost report, second department with beginning WIP; decision making

Learning Objectives 2, 3, 5

1. Cost per EUP CC $15.00

Lake Bound uses three processes to manufacture lifts for personal watercrafts: forming a lift's parts from galvanized steel, assembling the lift, and testing the completed lift. The lifts are transferred to finished goods before shipment to marinas across the country.

Lake Bound's Testing Department requires no direct materials. Conversion costs are incurred evenly throughout the testing process. Other information follows for October 2016:

UNITS	
Beginning Work-in-Process Inventory	2,100 units
Transferred in from Assembling Department during the period	7,300 units
Completed during the period	4,300 units
Ending Work-in-Process Inventory (40% complete for conversion work)	5,100 units
COSTS	
Beginning Work-in-Process Inventory (transferred in costs, $93,200; conversion costs, $18,300)	$ 111,500
Transferred in from the Assembly Department during the period	687,000
Conversion costs added during the period	76,800

CHAPTER 20

The cost transferred into Finished Goods Inventory is the cost of the lifts transferred out of the Testing Department. Lake Bound uses weighted-average process costing.

Requirements

1. Prepare a production cost report for the Testing Department.

2. What is the cost per unit for lifts completed and transferred out to Finished Goods Inventory? Why would management be interested in this cost?

Learning Objective 6
Appendix 20A

1. Cost per EUP CC $19.0000

P20A-41B **Preparing a production cost report, second department, with beginning WIP and transferred in costs, FIFO method**

Vuma, Inc. manufactures tire tubes in a two-stage process that includes assembly and sealing. The Sealing Department tests the tubes and adds a puncture-resistant coating to each tube to prevent air leaks.

The direct materials (coating) are added at the end of the sealing process. Conversion costs are incurred evenly throughout the process. Work in process of the Sealing Department on March 31, 2016, consisted of 400 tubes that were 30% of the way through the production process. The beginning balance in Work-in-Process Inventory—Sealing was $27,800, which consisted of $10,500 in transferred in costs and $17,300 in conversion costs. During April, 3,000 tubes were transferred in from the Assembly Department. The Sealing Department transferred 2,800 tubes to Finished Goods Inventory in April, and 600 were still in process on April 30. This ending inventory was 80% of the way through the sealing process. Vuma uses FIFO process costing.

At April 30, before recording the transfer of costs from the Sealing Department to Finished Goods Inventory, the Vuma general ledger included the following account:

Work-in-Process Inventory—Sealing	
Balance, Mar. 31	27,800
Transferred in from Assembly	48,000
Direct materials	22,400
Direct labor	19,850
Manufacturing overhead	40,190

Requirements

1. Prepare a production cost report for the Sealing Department for April.

2. Journalize all transactions affecting the Sealing Department during April, including the entries that have already been posted.

Learning Objective 6
Appendix 20A

1. Cost per EUP DM $21.0000

P20A-42B **Preparing a production cost report, second department with beginning WIP; journal entries**

Work Problem P20-39B using the FIFO method. The Dyeing Department beginning work in process of 75 units is 80% complete as to conversion costs. Round equivalent unit costs to four decimal places.

CRITICAL THINKING

> Decision Case 20-1

Billy Davidson operates Billy's Worm Farm in Mississippi. Davidson raises worms for fishing. He sells a box of 20 worms for $12.60. Davidson has invested $400,000 in the worm farm. He had hoped to earn a 24% annual rate of return (net income divided by total assets), which works out to a 2% monthly return on his investment. After looking at the farm's bank balance, Davidson fears he is not achieving this return. To evaluate the farm's performance, he prepared the following production cost report. The Finished Goods Inventory is zero because the worms ship out as soon as they reach the required size. Monthly operating expenses total $2,000 (in addition to the costs below).

BILLY'S WORM FARM
Production Cost Report—BROODING DEPARTMENT
Month Ended June 30, 2016

UNITS	Whole Units	Equivalent Units Transferred In	Equivalent Units Direct Materials	Equivalent Units Conversion Costs
Units to account for:				
Beginning work-in-process	9,000			
Transferred in	21,000			
Total units to account for	30,000			
Units accounted for:				
Completed and transferred out	20,000	20,000	20,000	20,000
Ending work-in-process	10,000	10,000	6,000	3,600
Total units accounted for	30,000	30,000	26,000	23,600

COSTS	Transferred In	Direct Materials	Conversion Costs	Total Costs
Costs to account for:				
Beginning work-in-process	$ 21,000	$ 39,940	$ 5,020	$ 65,960
Costs added during period	46,200	152,460	56,340	255,000
Total costs to account for	67,200	192,400	61,360	320,960
Divided by: Total EUP	÷ 30,000	÷ 26,000	÷ 23,600	
Cost per equivalent unit	$ 2.24	$ 7.40	$ 2.60	$ 12.24
Costs accounted for:				
Completed and transferred out	$ 44,800	$ 148,000	$ 52,000	$ 244,800
Ending work-in-process	22,400	44,400	9,360	76,160
Total costs accounted for	$ 67,200	$ 192,400	$ 61,360	$ 320,960

Requirements

Billy Davidson has the following questions about the farm's performance during June.

1. What is the cost per box of worms sold? (*Hint:* This is the unit cost of the boxes completed and shipped out of brooding.)

2. What is the gross profit per box?

3. How much operating income did Billy's Worm Farm make in June?

4. What is the return on Davidson's investment of $400,000 for the month of June? (Compute this as June's operating income divided by Davidson's $400,000 investment, expressed as a percentage.)

5. What monthly operating income would provide a 2% monthly rate of return? What price per box would Billy's Worm Farm have had to charge in June to achieve a 2% monthly rate of return?

> Ethical Issue 20-1

Rick Pines and Joe Lopez are the plant managers for High Mountain Lumber's particle board division. High Mountain Lumber has adopted a just-in-time management philosophy. Each plant combines wood chips with chemical adhesives to produce particle board to order, and all product is sold as soon as it is completed. Laura Green is High Mountain Lumber's regional controller. All of High Mountain Lumber's plants and divisions send Green their production and cost information. While reviewing the numbers of the two particle board plants, she is surprised to find that both plants estimate their ending Work-in-Process Inventories at 75% complete, which is higher than usual. Green calls Lopez, whom she has known for some time. He admits that to ensure their division would meet its profit goal and that both he and Pines would make their bonus (which is based on division profit), they agreed to inflate the percentage completion. Lopez explains, "Determining the percent complete always requires judgment. Whatever the percent complete, we'll finish the Work-in-Process Inventory first thing next year."

Requirements

1. How would inflating the percentage completion of ending Work-in-Process Inventory help Pines and Lopez get their bonus?

2. The particle board division is the largest of High Mountain Lumber's divisions. If Green does not correct the percentage completion of this year's ending Work-in-Process Inventory, how will the misstatement affect High Mountain Lumber's financial statements?

3. Evaluate Lopez's justification, including the effect, if any, on next year's financial statements.

4. Address the following: What is the ethical issue? What are the options? What are the potential consequences? What should Green do?

MyAccountingLab For a wealth of online resources, including exercises, problems, media, and immediate tutorial help, please visit http://www.myaccountinglab.com.

> Quick Check Answers

1. c **2.** a **3.** b **4.** d **5.** b **6.** a **7.** d **8.** c **9.** b **10.** c **11A.** a

Cost-Volume-Profit Analysis 21

Which Items Should Be Marked Down?

Charlene walks out of the summer heat into the cool, air-conditioned electronics store. She tries to envision how the store will look in a few months during the holiday season when the decorations will be up. She watches customers browsing and interacting with the sales staff. She notices which areas of the store are busy and which ones have little activity. Recent sales reports indicate touch screen computer tablets and HDTVs are the fast-moving items, and the in-store activity mirrors those reports.

Even though it is only July, Charlene has to make decisions now for the sales planned for November and December. Charlene is a buyer for the store. It is her job to ensure that the store has ample inventory to satisfy customers' needs. Charlene must decide which items should be featured on Black Friday, the day after Thanksgiving, which has become one of the busiest shopping days of the year. How low should the sales prices go for these featured items? If the sales prices are lowered, the gross profit on those items will also decrease. Will an increase in sales volume make up for the decreased gross profit per item? Will discounting certain items draw customers into the store to purchase other items that have a larger gross profit? If the company makes early buying commitments, can Charlene negotiate better deals that will decrease its costs and therefore increase profits?

Charlene's decisions could have a major impact on her company. For many retailers, the sales made in November and December determine the profitability for the year. Charlene needs a management tool, like *cost-volume-profit analysis*, to assist her in making these planning decisions.

What Is Cost-Volume-Profit Analysis?

Have you ever wondered how companies such as Best Buy Co. Inc. determine which items to feature in their major sales events? How can they afford to sell certain items at such a low price on Black Friday or Cyber Monday? What effect do the sales have on overall profits?

Best Buy opened its first store in 1966 in St. Paul, Minnesota. The company now has almost 1,500 domestic stores, almost 2,000 total stores worldwide, and about 140,000 employees. Its 2013 consolidated statement of earnings reports more than $42 billion in revenues with a gross profit percentage of 22.8% and an operating income percentage of 2.7%. These percentages have been fairly consistent for the years 2007–2013. Best Buy has to consider how changes in sales prices will affect sales volume and its overall profits, which is often done by using cost-volume-profit analysis.

Cost-volume-profit analysis is not only for merchandising companies. It can also be used by manufacturing and service companies. Let's take a closer look at this powerful management tool.

Chapter 21 Learning Objectives

1 Determine how changes in volume affect costs

2 Calculate operating income using contribution margin and contribution margin ratio

3 Use cost-volume-profit (CVP) analysis for profit planning

4 Use CVP analysis to perform sensitivity analysis

5 Use CVP analysis to calculate margin of safety, operating leverage, and multiproduct breakeven points

6 Distinguish between variable costing and absorption costing (Appendix 21A)

7 Compute operating income using variable costing and absorption costing (Appendix 21A)

HOW DO COSTS BEHAVE WHEN THERE IS A CHANGE IN VOLUME?

Learning Objective 1

Determine how changes in volume affect costs

Some costs, such as cost of goods sold, increase as the volume of sales increases. Other costs, such as straight-line depreciation expense, are not affected by volume changes. Managers need to know how a business's costs are affected by changes in its volume of activity, such as number of products produced and sold, in order to make good decisions about the business. Let's look at three different types of costs:

- Variable costs
- Fixed costs
- Mixed costs

We will again use Smart Touch Learning, our fictitious company, to illustrate the concepts. Smart Touch Learning manufactures touch screen tablet computers that are preloaded with the company's e-learning software.

Variable Costs

Variable Cost

A cost that increases or decreases *in total* in direct proportion to increases or decreases in the volume of activity.

Variable costs are costs that increase or decrease *in total* in direct proportion to increases or decreases in the volume of activity. Volume is the measure or degree of an activity of a business action that affects costs—the more volume, the more costs incurred. Some activities that are affected by changes in volume include selling, producing, driving, and calling. The volume of activities can be measured in many different ways, such as number of units sold, number of units produced, number of miles driven by a delivery vehicle, and number of phone calls placed.

The direct materials used in the production of tablet computers are a variable cost for Smart Touch Learning. For example, each tablet computer requires a battery. If batteries cost $55 each, then the production of each tablet increases the total cost incurred by $55. The following chart shows the cost for batteries at different levels of activity:

Number of Tablets Produced	Variable Cost per Tablet	Total Variable Cost
0 tablets	$ 55	$ 0
25 tablets	55	1,375
50 tablets	55	2,750
75 tablets	55	4,125
100 tablets	55	5,500

As you can see, the total variable cost of batteries increases proportionately as the number of tablets produced increases. But the battery cost per tablet does not change. Exhibit 21-1 graphs the total variable cost for batteries as the number of tablets produced increases from 0 to 100.

Exhibit 21-1 | **Total Variable Cost of Batteries**

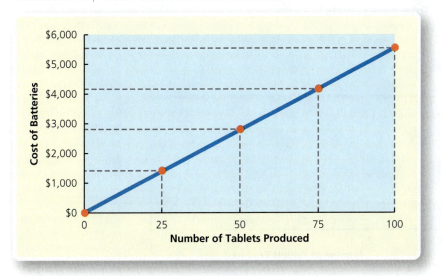

If there are no tablets manufactured, Smart Touch Learning incurs no battery cost, so the total variable cost line begins at the bottom left corner. This point is called the origin, and it represents zero volume and zero cost. The slope of the variable cost line is the change in total battery cost (on the vertical axis) divided by the change in the number of tablets produced (on the horizontal axis). The slope of the graph equals the variable cost per unit. In Exhibit 21-1, the slope of the variable cost line is $55 per tablet because Smart Touch Learning spends $55 on the battery for each tablet produced.

Exhibit 21-1 shows how the total variable cost of batteries varies directly with the number of tablets produced. But, again, note that the per tablet cost remains constant at $55.

Remember this important fact about variable costs: Total variable costs fluctuate with changes in volume, but the variable cost per unit remains constant.

As shown in the preceding example, direct materials are a variable cost for a manufacturing company. Direct labor is also a variable cost. Manufacturing overhead usually includes both variable costs and fixed costs. Let's look at fixed costs next to learn how they differ from variable costs.

Fixed Costs

In contrast to variable costs, **fixed costs** are costs that do not change *in total* over wide ranges of volume of activity. Some common fixed costs include rent, salaries, property taxes, and depreciation. Smart Touch Learning's fixed costs include depreciation on the manufacturing plant and equipment. The company has these fixed costs regardless of the number of tablets produced.

Fixed Cost
A cost that remains the same *in total*, regardless of changes over wide ranges of volume of activity.

Suppose Smart Touch Learning incurs $12,000 of fixed costs each month, and the number of monthly tablets produced is between 0 and 100. Exhibit 21-2 graphs total fixed costs as a flat line that intersects the cost axis at $12,000 because Smart Touch Learning will incur the same $12,000 of fixed costs regardless of the number of tablets produced during the month.

Exhibit 21-2 | Total Fixed Costs

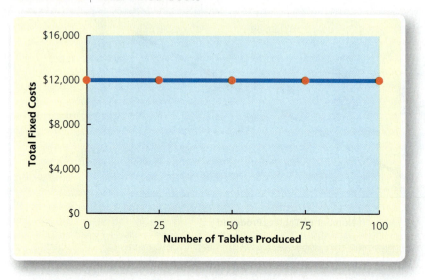

Total fixed costs do not change, as shown in Exhibit 21-2, but the *fixed cost per tablet* depends on the number of tablets produced. If Smart Touch Learning produces 25 tablets, the fixed cost per tablet is $480 ($12,000 / 25 tablets). If the number of tablets produced doubles to 50 tablets, the fixed cost per tablet is cut in half to $240 ($12,000 / 50 tablets). Therefore, the fixed cost per tablet is *inversely* proportional to the number of tablets produced. In other words, as the number of tablets increases, the fixed cost per tablet decreases, as follows:

Total Fixed Costs	Number of Tablets Produced	Fixed Cost per Tablet
$ 12,000	25 tablets	$ 480
12,000	50 tablets	240
12,000	75 tablets	160
12,000	100 tablets	120

Remember this important fact about fixed costs: Total fixed costs remain constant, but the fixed cost per unit is inversely proportional to changes in volume.

Exhibit 21-3 shows a summary of the characteristics of fixed and variable costs.

Exhibit 21-3 | **Characteristics of Variable and Fixed Costs**

	Total Cost	**Cost per Unit**
Variable Costs	Changes *proportionately* to changes in volume • When volume increases, total cost increases • When volume decreases, total cost decreases	Remains constant
Fixed Costs	Remains constant	Changes *inversely* to changes in volume • When volume increases, cost per unit decreases • When volume decreases, cost per unit increases

Mixed Costs

Not all costs can be classified as either fixed or variable. Costs that have both variable and fixed components are called mixed costs. For example, Smart Touch Learning's cell phone provider charges $100 per month to provide the service plus $0.10 for each minute of use. If the cell phone is used for 100 minutes, the company will bill Smart Touch Learning $110 [$100 + (100 minutes × $0.10 per minute)]. The following table shows the cost for the cell phone at different levels of activity:

Are all costs either fixed or variable?

Mixed Cost
A cost that has both fixed and variable components.

Number of Minutes Used	Total Fixed Cost	Total Variable Cost	Total Cost
100 minutes	$ 100	$ 10	$ 110
200 minutes	100	20	120
300 minutes	100	30	130
400 minutes	100	40	140
500 minutes	100	50	150

Exhibit 21-4 (on the next page) shows how Smart Touch Learning can separate its cell phone bill into fixed and variable components. The $100 monthly charge is a fixed cost because it is the same no matter how many minutes the company uses the cell phone. The $0.10-per-minute charge is a variable cost that increases in direct proportion to the number of minutes of use. If Smart Touch Learning uses the phone for 100 minutes, its total variable cost is $10 (100 minutes × $0.10 per minute). If it doubles the use to 200 minutes, total variable cost also doubles to $20 (200 minutes × $0.10 per minute), and the total bill rises to $120 ($100 + $20).

Exhibit 21-4 | **Mixed Costs**

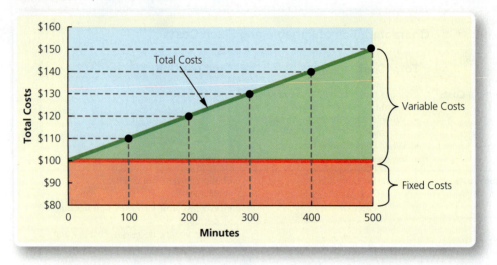

> The cost you incur to operate your car is an example of a mixed cost, relative to miles driven. The more miles you drive, the more you spend on gas and oil changes, so those costs are variable. The cost you incur for insurance, however, is fixed—the amount does not change based on number of miles driven. Therefore, the total cost is mixed—it has both a variable and a fixed component.

High-Low Method

High-Low Method

A method used to separate mixed costs into their variable and fixed components, using the highest and lowest activity levels.

When companies have mixed costs, it is helpful to separate the costs into their variable and fixed components so managers can use the information to make planning and control decisions. Some mixed costs, such as the cell phone cost, are easy to separate; other costs, however, are not as easy to break down.

An easy method to separate mixed costs into variable and fixed components is the **high-low method**. This method requires you to identify the highest and lowest levels of activity over a period of time.

Let's revisit the Smart Touch Learning illustration. A summary of its manufacturing equipment maintenance costs for the past year shows the following costs for each quarter:

	Total Maintenance Cost	Number of Tablets Produced	
1st Quarter	$ 1,630	360 tablets	
2nd Quarter	1,935	415 tablets	
3rd Quarter	1,960	480 tablets ←	Highest Volume
4th Quarter	1,480	240 tablets ←	Lowest Volume

We can use the high-low method, which requires three steps, to estimate Smart Touch Learning's fixed and variable costs of manufacturing equipment maintenance.

Step 1: Identify the highest and lowest levels of activity, and calculate the variable cost per unit.

The highest volume is 480 tablets produced in the third quarter of the year, and the lowest volume is 240 tablets produced in the fourth quarter.

Using the high and low points, find the change in costs and divide by the change in volume of activity.

> **Variable cost per unit = Change in total cost / Change in volume of activity**
> = **(Highest cost − Lowest cost) / (Highest volume − Lowest volume)**
> = ($1,960 − $1,480) / (480 tablets − 240 tablets)
> = $480 / 240 tablets
> = $2 per tablet

Step 2: Calculate the total fixed cost.

> **Total fixed cost = Total mixed cost − Total variable cost**
> = **Total mixed cost − (Variable cost per unit × Number of units)**
> = $1,960 − ($2 per tablet × 480 tablets)
> = $1,960 − $960
> = $1,000

This example uses the highest volume and its mixed cost to calculate the total fixed cost, but you can also use the lowest volume and its mixed cost to calculate the same $1,000 total fixed cost.

> *Rework Step 2 using the lowest point, $1,480 total cost and 240 tablets. Verify for yourself that either point can be used!*

Remember the characteristics of variable and fixed costs: Changes in activity levels do not affect variable cost per unit or total fixed costs; both remain constant. Therefore, once the variable cost per unit is computed, either the highest or the lowest level of volume can be used to calculate the total fixed cost.

Why does Step 2 of the high-low method work with both the highest volume and the lowest volume?

Step 3: Create and use an equation to show the behavior of a mixed cost.

> **Total mixed cost = (Variable cost per unit × Number of units) + Total fixed cost**
> Total manufacturing = ($2 per tablet × Number of tablets) + $1,000
> maintenance cost

Using this equation, the estimated manufacturing equipment maintenance cost for 400 tablets would be as follows:

> **Total manufacturing maintenance cost = ($2 per tablet × Number of tablets) + $1,000**
> = ($2 per tablet × 400 tablets) + $1,000
> = $1,800

This method provides a rough estimate of fixed and variable costs that can be used for planning purposes. The high and low activity volumes become the relevant range, which is discussed in the next section. Managers find the high-low method to be quick and easy, but there are other more complex methods that provide better estimates. One of these methods is regression analysis, which can be completed using spreadsheet software, such as Excel. This method is illustrated in more advanced accounting textbooks, such as cost accounting textbooks.

Relevant Range and Relativity

Relevant Range

The range of volume where total fixed costs and variable cost per unit remain constant.

The **relevant range** is the range of volume where total fixed costs remain constant and the variable cost per unit remains constant. To estimate costs, managers need to know the relevant range because of the following relationships:

- *Total* fixed costs can differ from one relevant range to another.
- The variable cost *per unit* can differ in various relevant ranges.

Exhibit 21-5 shows fixed costs for Smart Touch Learning over three different relevant ranges. If the company expects to produce 2,400 tablets next year, the relevant range is between 2,001 and 4,000 tablets, and managers will plan for fixed costs of $144,000.

Exhibit 21-5 | Relevant Range

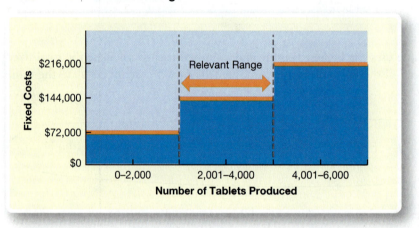

To produce more than 4,000 tablets, Smart Touch Learning will have to expand the company. This will increase total fixed costs for added rent, supervisory salaries, and equipment costs. Exhibit 21-5 shows that total fixed cost increases to $216,000 as the relevant range shifts to this higher band of volume. Conversely, if the company expects to produce fewer than 2,001 tablets, the company will budget only $72,000 of fixed costs. Managers will have to lay off employees or take other actions to cut fixed costs.

Variable cost per unit can also change outside the relevant range. For example, Smart Touch Learning may get a quantity discount for batteries if it purchases more than 4,000 batteries.

We also need to remember that costs are classified as fixed or variable relative to some activity. However, if the frame of reference shifts, then the classification can shift, too. For example, Smart Touch Learning may lease cars for sales representatives to use when making sales calls. The amount of the lease is the same each month, $500. Therefore, relative to the number of tablets produced, the cost is fixed. Increasing or decreasing the number of tablets produced does not change the total amount of the lease. It remains constant at $500 per month. However, relative to the number of sales representatives, the cost is variable as it is directly proportional to the number of sales representatives. If there is one sales representative, the total cost is $500 per month. If there are two sales representatives, then two cars are required and the cost doubles to $1,000 per month. While the cost per unit remains constant, $500 per sales representative, the total cost changes with the change in volume, number of sales representatives.

For all examples and problems in this textbook, when classifying costs as fixed or variable, classify them relative to the number of units produced and sold unless told otherwise.

Following is a list of costs for a furniture manufacturer that specializes in wood tables. Classify each cost as variable, fixed, or mixed relative to the number of tables produced and sold.

1. Wood used to build tables
2. Depreciation on saws and other manufacturing equipment
3. Compensation for sales representatives paid on a salary plus commission basis
4. Supervisor's salary
5. Wages of production workers

Check your answers online in MyAccountingLab or at http://www.pearsonhighered.com/Horngren.

For more practice, see Short Exercises S21-1 through S21-3.   My AccountingLab

WHAT IS CONTRIBUTION MARGIN, AND HOW IS IT USED TO COMPUTE OPERATING INCOME?

Classifying costs as either variable or fixed is referred to as *cost behavior* because changes in volume can have an effect on how the costs behave. That is, the total cost either changes (variable costs) or remains constant (fixed costs). Let's see how managers can use cost behavior to make decisions.

> **Learning Objective 2**
>
> Calculate operating income using contribution margin and contribution margin ratio

Contribution Margin

Contribution margin is the difference between net sales revenue and variable costs. It is called contribution margin because it is the amount that contributes to covering the fixed costs and then to providing operating income. Contribution margin is often expressed in total. For example, if Smart Touch Learning sells 200 tablets for $500 each that incur variable costs of $275 each, then the contribution margin is:

> **Contribution Margin**
>
> The amount that contributes to covering the fixed costs and then to providing operating income. Net sales revenue−Variable costs.

> **Contribution margin = Net sales revenue − Variable costs**
> = ($500 per tablet × 200 tablets) − ($275 per tablet × 200 tablets)
> = $100,000 − $55,000
> = $45,000

Unit Contribution Margin

The previous example calculated contribution margin as a total amount. Contribution margin can also be expressed as a unit amount. Using the same example for Smart Touch Learning, we can express the unit contribution margin as:

> **Unit contribution margin = Net sales revenue per unit − Variable costs per unit**
> = $500 per tablet − $275 per tablet
> = $225 per tablet

The terms *unit contribution margin* and *contribution margin per unit* are used interchangeably.

Contribution Margin Ratio

Contribution Margin Ratio
The ratio of contribution margin to net sales revenue. Contribution margin / Net sales revenue.

A third way to express contribution margin is as a ratio. **Contribution margin ratio** is the ratio of contribution margin to net sales revenue. Because contribution margin is based on sales price and variable costs, which do not change per unit, the ratio can be calculated using either the total amounts or the unit amounts, as illustrated below:

> **Contribution margin ratio = Contribution margin / Net sales revenue**
> = $45,000 / $100,000
> = 45%
> ————————————————————
> = $225 per tablet / $500 per tablet
> = 45%

Contribution Margin Income Statement

A traditional income statement classifies costs by *function*; that is, costs are classified as either product costs or period costs. Remember that *product costs* are those costs that are incurred in the purchase or production of the product sold. For a manufacturing company such as Smart Touch Learning, the product costs are direct materials, direct labor, and manufacturing overhead. These costs accumulate in the inventory accounts until the product is sold. At that point, the costs are transferred to the expense account Cost of Goods Sold. The *period costs* are the selling and administrative costs. This is the format that is required by GAAP, the Generally Accepted Accounting Principles, and the format you have been using in your accounting studies thus far.

Contribution Margin Income Statement
The income statement that groups cost by behavior—variable or fixed—and highlights the contribution margin.

The traditional income statement format does not always provide enough information for managers, so another format is used. A **contribution margin income statement** classifies cost by *behavior*; that is, costs are classified as either variable costs or fixed costs. Exhibit 21-6 illustrates the differences between the two formats.

Exhibit 21-6 | **Traditional Income Statement Versus Contribution Margin Income Statement**

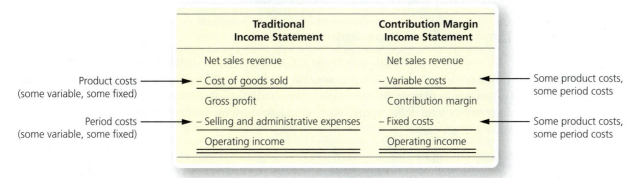

Product costs (some variable, some fixed) →

Traditional Income Statement	Contribution Margin Income Statement
Net sales revenue	Net sales revenue
– Cost of goods sold	– Variable costs
Gross profit	Contribution margin
– Selling and administrative expenses	– Fixed costs
Operating income	Operating income

← Some product costs, some period costs

Period costs (some variable, some fixed) →

← Some product costs, some period costs

Try It!

A furniture manufacturer specializes in wood tables. The tables sell for $100 and incur $40 in variable costs. The company has $6,000 in fixed costs per month.

6. Prepare a contribution margin income statement for one month if the company sells 200 tables.
7. What is the total contribution margin for the month when the company sells 200 tables?
8. What is the unit contribution margin?
9. What is the contribution margin ratio?

Check your answers online in MyAccountingLab or at http://www.pearsonhighered.com/Horngren.

For more practice, see Short Exercises S21-4 and S21-5.   MyAccountingLab

HOW IS COST-VOLUME-PROFIT (CVP) ANALYSIS USED?

Now that you have learned about cost behavior, let's see how managers use this information to make business decisions. **Cost-volume-profit (CVP) analysis** is a planning tool that looks at the relationships among costs and volume and how they affect profits (or losses). CVP is also sometimes referred to as *cost-volume-price analysis* because changes in sales prices also affect profits (or losses). Smart Touch Learning uses CVP analysis to estimate how changes in sales prices, variable costs, fixed costs, and volume will affect profits.

Assumptions

CVP analysis assumes the following for the relevant range:

- The price per unit does not change as volume changes. For example, Smart Touch Learning assumes that all tablets will sell for $500 each.

- Managers can classify each cost as variable, fixed, or mixed.

- The only factor that affects total costs is a change in volume, which increases or decreases variable and mixed costs. Smart Touch Learning assumes the variable cost per tablet is $275.

- Fixed costs do not change. Smart Touch Learning assumes fixed costs are $12,000 per month.

- There are no changes in inventory levels. Smart Touch Learning assumes the number of tablets produced equals the number of tablets sold.

Learning Objective 3
Use cost-volume-profit (CVP) analysis for profit planning

Cost-Volume-Profit (CVP) Analysis
A planning tool that expresses the relationships among costs, volume, and prices and their effects on profits and losses.

Most business conditions do not perfectly meet these general assumptions, so managers regard CVP analysis as approximate, not exact.

Target Profit—Three Approaches

CVP analysis can be used to estimate the amount of sales needed to achieve a target profit. **Target profit** is the operating income that results when sales revenue minus variable and fixed costs equals management's profit goal. Required sales can be expressed as either a number of units or as a total dollar figure. We will look at three methods of estimating sales required to make a target profit:

- Equation approach
- Contribution margin approach
- Contribution margin ratio approach

The Equation Approach

Let's start by expressing income in equation form and then breaking it down into its components:

> Net sales revenue −   Total costs   = Operating income
>
> Net sales revenue − Variable costs − Fixed costs = Operating income

Sales revenue equals the unit sales price ($500 per tablet in this case) multiplied by the number of units (tablets) sold. Variable costs equal variable cost per unit ($275 in this case) times the number of units (tablets) sold. Smart Touch Learning's fixed costs total $12,000 per month. If the company desires to earn $6,000 in profits each month, how many tablets must it sell?

> **Net sales revenue − Variable costs − Fixed costs = Target profit**
> ($500 per unit × Units sold) − ($275 per unit × Units sold) − $12,000 = $ 6,000
> [($500 per unit − $275 per unit) × Units sold] − $12,000 = $ 6,000
> $225 per unit × Units sold = $ 6,000 + $12,000
> $225 per unit × Units sold = $18,000
> Units sold = $18,000 / $225 per unit
> Units sold = 80 units

Be sure to check your calculations. We can prove the required sales by substituting the number of units into the operating income equation and then checking to ensure that this level of sales results in $6,000 in profit.

> **Net sales revenue − Variable costs − Fixed costs = Operating income**
> ($500 per unit × 80 units) − ($275 per unit × 80 units) − $12,000 =
> $40,000 − $22,000 − $12,000 = $6,000

Based on these calculations, then, Smart Touch Learning must sell 80 tablets per month to achieve the target profit of $6,000 per month. Expressed in dollars, the company must have total sales of $40,000 (80 tablets × $500 per tablet).

The Contribution Margin Approach

The contribution margin approach is a shortcut method of computing the required sales in units. Notice in the previous example that the fixed costs plus the target profit ($12,000 + $6,000) was divided by the contribution margin per unit ($225 per unit). We can rewrite the equation approach to derive the following equation:

$$\text{Required sales in units} = \frac{\text{Fixed costs} + \text{Target profit}}{\text{Contribution margin per unit}}$$

Using this formula, we can enter the given amounts to calculate the required sales in units. Notice that the formula is dividing dollars by dollars per unit. When the dollars cancel out during the division process, the result is expressed in units.

$$\text{Required sales in units} = \frac{\text{Fixed costs} + \text{Target profit}}{\text{Contribution margin per unit}}$$
$$= \frac{\$12,000 + \$6,000}{\$225 \text{ per unit}}$$
$$= 80 \text{ units}$$

Previously, we proved our answer using the equation approach. We can also prove our answer using the contribution margin income statement format:

Net sales revenue	($500 per unit × 80 units)	$ 40,000
− Variable costs	($275 per unit × 80 units)	22,000
Contribution margin	($225 per unit × 80 units)	18,000
− Fixed costs		12,000
Operating income		$ 6,000

Contribution Margin Ratio Approach

Companies can use the contribution margin ratio approach to compute required sales in terms of *sales dollars* rather than in units. The formula is the same as using the contribution margin approach, except that the denominator is the contribution margin ratio rather than contribution margin per unit.

We previously computed the contribution margin ratio for Smart Touch Learning as 45%:

$$\text{Contribution margin ratio} = \text{Contribution margin / Net sales revenue}$$
$$= \$225 \text{ per tablet / } \$500 \text{ per tablet}$$
$$= 45\%$$

Notice that when we use the ratio as the denominator in the formula, we are dividing dollars by a percentage. Therefore, the result will be expressed in dollars.

$$\text{Required sales in dollars} = \frac{\text{Fixed costs } + \text{ Target profit}}{\text{Contribution margin ratio}}$$
$$= \frac{\$12,000 + \$6,000}{45\%}$$
$$= \$40,000$$

ETHICS

Did you check the formula?

Donna Dickerson is the assistant controller for a large manufacturing company and works directly under the supervision of the controller, Nicole Randall. While reviewing some documents Nicole prepared, Donna notices a mistake in the target profit calculations. The Excel spreadsheet used to summarize fixed costs has an error in the formula, and some of the individual costs listed are not included in the total. Donna is aware that the target profit calculations are used for planning purposes, so she brings the error to the controller's attention. Nicole doesn't seem concerned. "It doesn't really matter," says Nicole. "Those figures never show up on the financial statements, so a little mistake won't matter." Is Nicole correct? What should Donna do? What would you do?

Solution

Omitting fixed costs from the target profit calculations will understate the amount of sales required to reach the target profit. If required sales are understated, then managers might make decisions that could be detrimental to the company. Donna should convince her supervisor to admit her mistake and provide corrected estimates to managers. If Donna is unable to convince Nicole to admit her mistake, she should discuss the error and the possible consequences with Nicole's supervisor. Failure to report the error is a violation of IMA's credibility standard of ethical practice.

Breakeven Point—A Variation of Target Profit

Breakeven Point
The sales level at which operating income is zero. Total revenues equal total costs.

A variation of the target profit calculation is the breakeven point calculation. The **breakeven point** is the sales level at which the company does not earn a profit or a loss but has an operating income of zero. It is the point at which total revenues equal total costs. The same three approaches can be used. The only difference is that the target profit is $0. Exhibit 21-7 shows the calculation of the breakeven point for Smart Touch Learning using the three approaches.

Exhibit 21-7 | **Breakeven Point Calculations for Smart Touch Learning**

Equation Approach

Net sales revenue − Variable costs − Fixed costs = Target profit

($500 per unit × Units sold) − ($275 per unit × Units sold) − $12,000 = $0

[($500 per unit − $275 per unit) × Units sold] − $12,000 = $0

$225 per unit × Units sold = $12,000

Units sold = $12,000 / $225 per unit

Units sold = 54 units*

Contribution Margin Approach

$$\text{Required sales in units} = \frac{\text{Fixed costs + Target profit}}{\text{Contribution margin per unit}}$$

$$= \frac{\$12,000 + \$0}{\$225 \text{ per unit}}$$

$$= 54 \text{ units*}$$

Contribution Margin Ratio Approach

$$\text{Required sales in dollars} = \frac{\text{Fixed costs + Target profit}}{\text{Contribution margin ratio}}$$

$$= \frac{\$12,000 + \$0}{45\%}$$

$$= \$26,667**$$

*Actual result of 53.3333 rounded up to the next full unit as it is not possible to sell partial tablets.

**Actual result of $26,666.6667 rounded up to next full dollar.

CVP Graph—A Graphic Portrayal

A CVP graph provides a picture that shows how changes in the levels of sales will affect profits. As in the variable, fixed, and mixed cost graphs of Exhibits 21-1, 21-2, and 21-4, the volume of units is on the horizontal axis and dollars are on the vertical axis. The five steps to graph the CVP relationships for Smart Touch Learning are illustrated in Exhibit 21-8 (on the next page).

Exhibit 21-8 | **Cost-Volume-Profit Graph for Smart Touch Learning**

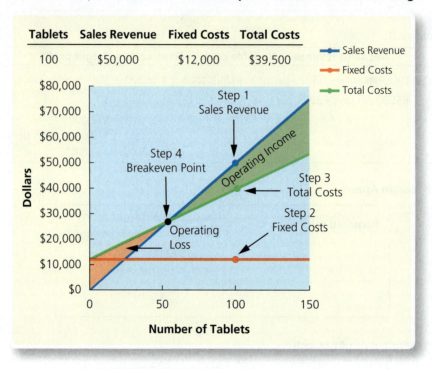

Tablets	Sales Revenue	Fixed Costs	Total Costs
100	$50,000	$12,000	$39,500

Step 1: Choose a sales volume, such as 100 tablets. Plot the point for total sales revenue at that volume: 100 tablets × $500 per tablet = $50,000. Draw the *sales revenue line* from the origin ($0) through the $50,000 point. Why start at the origin? If Smart Touch Learning sells no tablets, there is no revenue.

Step 2: Draw the *fixed cost line*, a horizontal line that intersects the dollars axis at $12,000. The fixed cost line is flat because fixed costs are the same, $12,000, no matter how many tablets are sold.

Step 3: Draw the *total cost line*. Total costs are the sum of variable costs plus fixed costs. Thus, total costs are *mixed*. The total cost line follows the form of the mixed cost line in Exhibit 21-4. Begin by computing total variable costs at the chosen sales volume: 100 tablets × $275 per tablet = $27,500. Add total variable costs to fixed costs: $27,500 + $12,000 = $39,500. Plot the total cost point of $39,500 for 100 tablets. Then draw a line through this point from the $12,000 fixed cost intercept on the dollars vertical axis. This is the *total cost line*. The total cost line starts at the fixed cost line because even if Smart Touch Learning sells no tablets, the company still incurs the $12,000 of fixed costs.

Step 4: Identify the *breakeven point*. The breakeven point is where the sales revenue line intersects the total cost line. This is where revenue exactly equals total costs—at 54 tablets, or $26,667 in sales (based on rounded figures from Exhibit 21-7).

Step 5: Mark the *operating loss* area on the graph. To the left of the breakeven point, total costs exceed sales revenue—leading to an operating loss, indicated by the orange zone. Mark the *operating income* area on the graph. To the right of the breakeven point, the business earns a profit because sales revenue exceeds total costs, as shown by the green zone.

Graphs like Exhibit 21-8 are helpful to managers because the managers can use the graphs to prepare a quick estimate of the profit or loss earned at different levels of sales. The three target profit formulas are also useful, but they only indicate income or loss for a single sales amount.

HOW IS CVP ANALYSIS USED FOR SENSITIVITY ANALYSIS?

Managers often want to predict how changes in sales price, costs, or volume affect their profits. Managers can use CVP relationships to conduct sensitivity analysis. **Sensitivity analysis** is a "what if" technique that estimates profit or loss results if sales price, costs, volume, or underlying assumptions change. Sensitivity analysis allows managers to see how various business strategies will affect how much profit the company will make and, thus, empowers managers with better information for decision making. Let's see how Smart Touch Learning can use CVP analysis to estimate the effects of some changes in its business environment.

Learning Objective 4
Use CVP analysis to perform sensitivity analysis

Sensitivity Analysis
A "what if" technique that estimates profit or loss results if sales price, costs, volume, or underlying assumptions change.

Changes in the Sales Price

Competition in the touch screen tablet computer business is so fierce that Smart Touch Learning believes it must cut the sales price to $475 per tablet to maintain market share. Suppose the company's variable costs remain $275 per tablet and fixed costs stay at $12,000. How will the lower sales price affect the breakeven point?

Using the contribution margin approach, the results are as follows:

$$\text{Required sales in units} = \frac{\text{Fixed costs} + \text{Target profit}}{\text{Contribution margin per unit}}$$

$$= \frac{\$12,000 + \$0}{\$475 \text{ per unit} - \$275 \text{ per unit}}$$

$$= 60 \text{ units}$$

With the original $500 sales price, Smart Touch Learning's breakeven point was 54 tablets. With the new lower sales price of $475 per tablet, the breakeven point increases to 60 tablets. The lower sales price means that each tablet contributes less toward fixed costs, so the company must sell more tablets to break even. Additionally, each unit sold beyond the breakeven point will contribute less to profits due to the lower contribution margin per unit.

Changes in Variable Costs

Return to Smart Touch Learning's original data, disregarding the change made in sales price in the previous example. Assume that one of the company's suppliers raises prices, which increases the variable cost for each tablet to $285 (instead of the original $275). Smart Touch Learning decides it cannot pass this increase on to its customers, so the company holds the price at the original $500 per tablet. Fixed costs remain at $12,000. How many tablets must Smart Touch Learning sell to break even after the supplier raises prices?

$$\text{Required sales in units} = \frac{\text{Fixed cost} + \text{Target profit}}{\text{Contribution margin per unit}}$$

$$= \frac{\$12,000 + \$0}{\$500 \text{ per unit} - \$285 \text{ per unit}}$$

$$= 56 \text{ units*}$$

*rounded up to next full unit

Higher variable costs per tablet reduce Smart Touch Learning's contribution margin per unit from $225 per tablet to $215 per tablet. As a result, the company must sell more tablets to break even—56 rather than the original 54. This analysis shows why managers are particularly concerned with controlling costs during an economic downturn. Increases in costs raise the breakeven point, and a higher breakeven point can lead to problems if demand falls due to a recession.

Of course, a decrease in variable costs would have the opposite effect. Lower variable costs increase the contribution margin on each tablet and, therefore, lower the breakeven point.

Changes in Fixed Costs

Return to Smart Touch Learning's original data, disregarding the changes made in the previous two examples. The company is considering spending an additional $3,000 on Web site banner ads. This would increase fixed costs from $12,000 to $15,000. If the tablets are sold at the original price of $500 each and variable costs remain at $275 per tablet, what is the new breakeven point?

$$\text{Required sales in units} = \frac{\text{Fixed costs} + \text{Target profit}}{\text{Contribution margin per unit}}$$

$$= \frac{\$15,000 + \$0}{\$500 \text{ per unit} - \$275 \text{ per unit}}$$

$$= 67 \text{ units*}$$

*rounded up to next full unit

Higher fixed costs increase the total contribution margin required to break even. In this case, increasing the fixed costs from $12,000 to $15,000 increases the breakeven point to 67 tablets (from the original 54 tablets).

Managers usually prefer a lower breakeven point to a higher one but do not overemphasize this one aspect of CVP analysis. Even though investing in the Web site banner ads increases Smart Touch Learning's breakeven point, the company should pay the extra $3,000 if that would increase both sales and profits.

Exhibit 21-9 shows how all of these changes affect the contribution margin per unit and the breakeven point.

Exhibit 21-9 | **Effects of Changes in Sales Price, Variable Costs, and Fixed Costs**

CAUSE	EFFECT	RESULT
Change	Contribution Margin per Unit	Breakeven Point
Sales price per unit increases	Increases	Decreases
Sales price per unit decreases	Decreases	Increases
Variable cost per unit increases	Decreases	Increases
Variable cost per unit decreases	Increases	Decreases
Total fixed cost increases	No effect	Increases
Total fixed cost decreases	No effect	Decreases

A furniture manufacturer specializes in wood tables. The tables sell for $100 and incur $40 in variable costs. The company has $6,000 in fixed costs per month. Calculate the breakeven point in units under each independent scenario.

14. Variable costs increase by $10 per unit.
15. Fixed costs decrease by $600.
16. Sales price increases by 10%.

Check your answers online in MyAccountingLab or at http://www.pearsonhighered.com/Horngren.

For more practice, see Short Exercises S21-11 and S21-12. MyAccountingLab

WHAT ARE SOME OTHER WAYS CVP ANALYSIS CAN BE USED?

We have learned how CVP analysis can be used for estimating target profits and breakeven points as well as sensitivity analysis. Let's look at three more applications of CVP analysis.

Margin of Safety

The **margin of safety** is the excess of expected sales over breakeven sales. The margin of safety is, therefore, the amount sales can decrease before the company incurs an operating loss. It is the *cushion* between profit and loss.

Managers use the margin of safety to evaluate the risk of both their current operations and their plans for the future. Let's apply the margin of safety to our fictitious company.

Smart Touch Learning's original breakeven point was 54 tablets. Suppose the company expects to sell 100 tablets. The margin of safety can be expressed in units, in dollars, or as a ratio. The margin of safety is:

Learning Objective 5

Use CVP analysis to calculate margin of safety, operating leverage, and multiproduct breakeven points

Margin of Safety
The excess of expected sales over breakeven sales. The amount sales can decrease before the company incurs an operating loss.

Expected sales − Breakeven sales = Margin of safety in units
100 tablets − 54 tablets = 46 tablets

Margin of safety in units × Sales price per unit = Margin of safety in dollars
46 tablets × $500 per tablet = $23,000

Margin of safety in units / Expected sales in units = Margin of safety ratio
46 tablets / 100 tablets = 46%

Sales can drop by 46 tablets, or $23,000, before Smart Touch Learning incurs a loss. This margin of safety is 46% of total expected sales. In other words, the company can lose almost half of its business before incurring an operating loss. That is a comfortable margin of safety.

Both margin of safety and target profit use CVP analysis, but from different perspectives. Margin of safety focuses on the sales part of the equation—that is, how many sales dollars the company is generating above breakeven sales dollars. Conversely, target profit focuses on how much operating income is left over from sales revenue after covering all variable and fixed costs.

If you have done really well on all your assignments in a particular course for the semester and currently have an A, you have created a sort of margin of safety for your grade. That is, by performing above the minimum (C, or breakeven), you have a cushion to help you maintain a passing grade even if you happen to perform poorly on a future assignment.

Operating Leverage

Cost Structure
The proportion of fixed costs to variable costs.

The **cost structure** of a company is the proportion of fixed costs to variable costs. This relationship is important because, depending on the cost structure, small changes in the business environment could have a substantial impact on profits. Companies with higher fixed costs are at greater risk, but they also have the opportunity for greater rewards. Let's compare two companies to see how their cost structures affect their profits when there is a change in sales volume.

Two companies provide horse-drawn carriage tours in Charleston, South Carolina. This is a very competitive business, and both companies charge $25 per person for the tours. Both companies expect to provide tours to 500 passengers during September. Company A has low variable costs and high fixed costs. Company B has the opposite cost structure with high variable costs and low fixed costs. The expected contribution margin income statements for both companies are:

	Company A	Company B
Sales Revenue (500 passengers × $25 per passenger)	$ 12,500	$ 12,500
Variable Cost		
(500 passengers × $5 per passenger)	2,500	
(500 passengers × $15 per passenger)		7,500
Contribution Margin	10,000	5,000
Fixed Costs	6,000	1,000
Operating Income	$ 4,000	$ 4,000

During September, a hurricane threatened the area and many tourists made other travel plans. Both companies had only 400 passengers during the month. Let's look at their actual income statements with this decrease in volume:

	Company A	Company B
Sales Revenue (400 passengers × $25 per passenger)	$ 10,000	$ 10,000
Variable Cost		
(400 passengers × $5 per passenger)	2,000	
(400 passengers × $15 per passenger)		6,000
Contribution Margin	8,000	4,000
Fixed Costs	6,000	1,000
Operating Income	$ 2,000	$ 3,000

Both companies experienced the same decrease in sales volume, but Company B's operating income did not decrease as much as Company A's because of its cost structure.

Companies can predict the expected change in operating income due to a change in sales volume based on their cost structure. **Operating leverage** predicts the effects fixed costs have on changes in operating income when sales volume changes. The **degree of operating leverage** can be measured by dividing the contribution margin by the operating income. Let's calculate the degree of operating leverage of both companies at the 500-passenger volume:

$$\text{Degree of operating leverage} = \frac{\text{Contribution margin}}{\text{Operating income}}$$

Company A $\dfrac{\$10,000}{\$4,000} = 2.50$

Company B $\dfrac{\$5,000}{\$4,000} = 1.25$

Operating Leverage
Effects that fixed costs have on changes in operating income when sales volume changes.

Degree of Operating Leverage
The ratio that measures the effects that fixed costs have on changes in operating income when sales volume changes. Contribution margin / Operating income.

The degree of operating leverage for Company A is 2.50. This means that the percentage change in operating income will be 2.50 times the percentage change in sales. For Company B, the percentage change in sales will have a lesser effect on operating income at 1.25 times the change. Let's calculate the percentage changes to verify these predictions:

		Company A		Company B
Estimated sales		$ 12,500		$ 12,500
Actual sales		(10,000)		(10,000)
Dollar change in sales		$ 2,500		$ 2,500
Percent change in sales	($2,500 / $12,500)	20%	($2,500 / $12,500)	20%
Degree of operating leverage		× 2.50		× 1.25
Predicted percent change in operating income		50%		25%
Estimated operating income		$ 4,000		$ 4,000
Actual operating income		(2,000)		(3,000)
Dollar change in operating income		$ 2,000		$ 1,000
Actual percent change in operating income	($2,000 / $4,000)	50%	($1,000 / $4,000)	25%

The chart on the prior page shows that the degree of operating leverage accurately predicted the effect on operating income when sales volume changed. Notice that Company A had higher fixed costs and, therefore, had a greater decrease in profits when sales decreased. Higher fixed costs create greater risk for the company. When there is a decrease in sales, there is also a decrease in contribution margin to cover the fixed costs and provide operating income. However, a cost structure with high fixed costs has the opposite effect when sales increase. A 20% increase in sales would have had 2.50 times that effect, or 50%, increase in operating income. Therefore, a sales increase of $2,500 ($12,500 × 20%) would have resulted in an increase in operating income of $2,000 ($4,000 × 50%).

> *Prepare an income statement for Company A with a 20% increase in sales. Verify for yourself that the above statement is true!*

Sales Mix

Sales Mix
The combination of products that make up total sales.

Most companies sell more than one product. Sales price and variable costs differ for each product, so each product makes a different contribution to profits. The same CVP formulas we used earlier can apply to a company with multiple products.

To calculate the breakeven point for the company, we must compute the *weighted-average contribution margin* of all the company's products. The sales mix provides the weights that make up total product sales. The weights equal 100% of total product sales. **Sales mix**, or *product mix*, is the combination of products that make up total sales. For example, assume Cool Cat Furniture sold 6,000 cat beds and 4,000 scratching posts during the past year. The sales mix of 6,000 beds and 4,000 posts creates a ratio of 6,000/10,000 or 60% cat beds and 4,000/10,000 or 40% scratching posts. You could also convert this to the least common ratio, as 6/10 is the same as 3/5 cat beds and 4/10 is the same as 2/5 scratching posts. So, we say the sales mix is 3:2, or for every three cat beds sold, Cool Cat expects to sell two scratching posts.

Cool Cat's total fixed costs are $40,000. The cat bed's unit sales price is $44, and variable cost per bed is $24. The scratching post's unit sales price is $100, and variable cost per post is $30. To compute breakeven sales in units for both products, Cool Cat completes the following three steps.

Step 1: Calculate the weighted-average contribution margin per unit as follows:

	Cat Beds	Scratching Posts	Total
Sales price per unit	$ 44	$ 100	
Variable cost per unit	24	30	
Contribution margin per unit	20	70	
Sales mix in units	× 3	× 2	5 units
Contribution margin	$ 60	$ 140	$ 200
Weighted-average contribution margin per unit ($200 per unit / 5 units)			$ 40

Step 2: Calculate the breakeven point in units for the "package" of products:

$$\text{Required sales in units} = \frac{\text{Fixed costs } + \text{ Target profit}}{\text{Weighted-average contribution margin per unit}}$$

$$= \frac{\$40,000 + \$0}{\$40 \text{ per item}}$$

$$= 1,000 \text{ items}$$

Step 3: Calculate the breakeven point in units for each product. Multiply the "package" breakeven point in units by each product's proportion of the sales mix.

Breakeven sales of cat beds	(1,000 items × 3/5)	600 cat beds
Breakeven sales of scratching posts	(1,000 items × 2/5)	400 scratching posts

In this example, the calculations yield round numbers. When the calculations do not yield round numbers, round your answer up to the next whole number.

The overall breakeven point in sales dollars is $66,400:

600 cat beds at $44 sales price each	$ 26,400
400 scratching posts at $100 sales price each	40,000
Total sales revenue	$ 66,400

We can prove this breakeven point by preparing a contribution margin income statement:

	Cat Beds	Scratching Posts	Total
Sales Revenue:			
Cat beds (600 × $44)	$ 26,400		
Scratching posts (400 × $100)		$ 40,000	$ 66,400
Variable Costs:			
Cat beds (600 × $24)	14,400		
Scratching posts (400 × $30)		12,000	26,400
Contribution Margin	$ 12,000	$ 28,000	40,000
Fixed Costs			40,000
Operating Income			$ 0

If the sales mix changes, then Cool Cat can repeat this analysis using new sales mix information to find the breakeven points for each product.

In addition to finding the breakeven point, Cool Cat can also estimate the sales needed to generate a certain level of operating profit. Suppose Cool Cat would like to earn operating income of $20,000. How many units of each product must Cool Cat now sell?

$$\text{Required sales in units} = \frac{\text{Fixed costs} + \text{Target profit}}{\text{Weighted-average contribution margin per unit}}$$

$$= \frac{\$40,000 + \$20,000}{\$40 \text{ per item}}$$

$$= 1{,}500 \text{ items}$$

Breakeven sales of cat beds	(1,500 items × 3/5)	900 cat beds
Breakeven sales of scratching posts	(1,500 items × 2/5)	600 scratching posts

We can prove this planned profit level by preparing a contribution margin income statement:

	Cat Beds	Scratching Posts	Total
Sales Revenue:			
Cat beds (900 × $44)	$ 39,600		
Scratching posts (600 × $100)		$ 60,000	$ 99,600
Variable Costs:			
Cat beds (900 × $24)	21,600		
Scratching posts (600 × $30)		18,000	39,600
Contribution Margin	$ 18,000	$ 42,000	60,000
Fixed Costs			40,000
Operating Income			$ 20,000

DECISIONS

What if we advertise more?

At the weekly executive staff meeting, the topic turned to the most recent income statement. Revenues were down for the third consecutive month. Hogan Wilkerson, the marketing director, suggested a new advertising campaign. "Let me spend an additional $5,000 per month on advertising, and I'll guarantee increased profits," claimed Wilkerson. "The $5,000 in new advertising will increase sales by 15%."

The company's current sales mix provides a weighted-average unit contribution margin of $25 per unit on 2,000 units. Assuming that the sales mix stays the same, should the company spend the additional amount on advertising?

Solution

The additional cost of advertising is a fixed cost because the amount will not change with a change in sales volume. Current sales are 2,000 units. A 15% increase in sales will be 300 additional units

(2,000 units × 15%). Therefore, the additional contribution margin will be $7,500 (300 units × $25 per unit). The increase in contribution margin ($7,500) is more than the increase in fixed costs ($5,000), so profits will increase by $2,500 per month and the advertising campaign should be approved.

Alternate Solution

The sales manager, Cindy Cochran, has a different perspective. Given the current economic conditions, she feels a 15% increase in sales is overly optimistic and 10% is a more realistic estimate. If sales only increase 10%, then the additional sales would be 200 units (2,000 units × 10%) and the additional contribution margin would be $5,000 (200 units × $25 per unit). In that situation, the increase in contribution margin is equal to the increase in costs, and overall profits will not increase.

A furniture manufacturer specializes in wood tables. The tables sell for $100 and incur $40 in variable costs. The company has $6,000 in fixed costs per month. Expected sales are 200 tables per month.

17. Calculate the margin of safety in units.
18. Determine the degree of operating leverage. Use expected sales.
19. The company begins manufacturing wood chairs to match the tables. Chairs sell for $50 each and have variable costs of $30. The new production process increases fixed costs to $7,000 per month. The expected sales mix is one table for every four chairs. Calculate the breakeven point in units.

Check your answers online in MyAccountingLab or at http://www.pearsonhighered.com/Horngren.

For more practice, see Short Exercises S21-13 through S21-16. MyAccountingLab

APPENDIX 21A: Variable Costing

HOW DOES VARIABLE COSTING DIFFER FROM ABSORPTION COSTING?

The purpose of managerial accounting is to provide managers with information that is useful for internal decision making—for planning and controlling decisions. As you have seen, this type of information often differs from the financial accounting information provided to external users, such as investors and creditors. In this appendix, you study two methods of determining the cost of producing products and when each method is appropriate.

Learning Objective 6

Distinguish between variable costing and absorption costing

Absorption Costing

Up to this point, we have illustrated the use of absorption costing when determining the cost of products. **Absorption costing** considers direct materials, direct labor, variable manufacturing overhead, and fixed manufacturing overhead as product costs. This approach is called absorption costing because the products *absorb* all of the manufacturing costs—materials, labor, and overhead. These costs are recorded first as assets in the inventory accounts. Later, when the product is sold, the costs are transferred to the expense account Cost of Goods Sold. Absorption costing is required by the Generally Accepted Accounting Principles (GAAP) for financial statements issued to investors, creditors, and other external users. The external financial statements use the traditional income statement format with a focus on gross profit.

Absorption Costing

The product costing method that assigns direct materials, direct labor, variable manufacturing overhead, and fixed manufacturing overhead to products. Required by GAAP for external reporting.

Variable Costing

Variable costing is an alternative costing method that considers only variable manufacturing costs when determining product costs. Variable costing includes direct materials, direct labor, and variable manufacturing overhead as product costs. Fixed manufacturing overhead is considered a period cost and is expensed in the period in which it is incurred because these costs are incurred whether or not the company manufactures any goods. Variable costing cannot be used for external reporting, but it is useful to managers for planning and controlling. The internal financial statements use the contribution margin income statement format with a focus on contribution margin.

Variable Costing

The product costing method that assigns only variable manufacturing costs to products: direct materials, direct labor, and variable manufacturing overhead. Used for internal reporting.

Exhibit 21A-1 summarizes the differences between absorption costing and variable costing. Key differences between the two methods are highlighted in green.

Exhibit 21A-1 | **Differences Between Absorption Costing and Variable Costing**

	Absorption Costing	Variable Costing
Product Costs	Direct materials Direct labor Variable manufacturing overhead **Fixed manufacturing overhead**	Direct materials Direct labor Variable manufacturing overhead
Period Costs	Variable selling and administrative costs Fixed selling and administrative costs	**Fixed manufacturing overhead** Variable selling and administrative costs Fixed selling and administrative costs
Income Statement Format	Traditional format: Sales Revenue – **Cost of Goods Sold** **Gross Profit** – **Selling and Administrative Costs** Operating Income	Contribution margin format: Sales Revenue – **Variable Costs** **Contribution Margin** – **Fixed Costs** Operating Income

Comparison of Unit Product Costs

To illustrate the difference between absorption costing and variable costing, let's look at Smart Touch Learning. Exhibit 21A-2 summarizes the company's price and cost information, based on its 2018 income statement first illustrated in Chapter 18.

Exhibit 21A-2 | **Smart Touch Learning—Price and Cost Summary**

Units produced	2,000	units
Sales price	$ 500.00	per tablet
Direct materials	150.00	per tablet
Direct labor	75.00	per tablet
Variable manufacturing overhead	20.00	per tablet
Fixed manufacturing overhead	110,000.00	per year
Variable selling and administrative costs	62.50	per tablet
Fixed selling and administrative costs	116,000.00	per year

To determine the unit product cost using absorption costing, add the cost per tablet for the variable manufacturing costs: direct materials ($150.00), direct labor ($75.00), and variable manufacturing overhead ($20.00). Then determine the unit cost of the fixed manufacturing overhead by dividing the total cost ($110,000.00) by the number of units produced (2,000 units) and add it to the variable costs. To determine the unit product cost using variable costing, simply add the cost per tablet for the variable manufacturing costs: direct materials ($150.00), direct labor ($75.00), and variable manufacturing overhead ($20.00). The calculations are summarized in Exhibit 21A-3.

Exhibit 21A-3 | **Comparison of Unit Product Cost Computations—2,000 Units Produced**

		Absorption Costing	Variable Costing
Direct materials		$ 150.00	$ 150.00
Direct labor		75.00	75.00
Variable manufacturing overhead		20.00	20.00
Fixed manufacturing overhead	($110,000 / 2,000 units)	55.00	
Total unit product cost		$ 300.00	$ 245.00

Notice that the selling and administrative costs, both fixed and variable, are not included in the unit product cost calculations. Both costing methods consider selling and administrative costs to be period costs. Variable costing also considers fixed manufacturing overhead to be a period cost while absorption costing considers it to be a product cost.

Try It!

20. Pierce Company had the following costs:

Units produced	500 units
Direct materials	$ 25 per unit
Direct labor	45 per unit
Variable manufacturing overhead	15 per unit
Fixed manufacturing overhead	5,000 per year
Variable selling and administrative costs	30 per unit
Fixed selling and administrative costs	3,200 per year

Calculate the unit product cost using absorption costing and variable costing.

Check your answers online in MyAccountingLab or at http://www.pearsonhighered.com/Horngren.

For more practice, see Short Exercises S21A-17 through S21A-21. MyAccountingLab

HOW DOES OPERATING INCOME DIFFER BETWEEN VARIABLE COSTING AND ABSORPTION COSTING?

Now that you know how to calculate unit product costs using variable costing and absorption costing, let's see the effects the two methods have on calculating operating income. There are three different scenarios to consider:

- Units produced equal units sold
- Units produced are more than units sold
- Units produced are less than units sold

Learning Objective 7

Compute operating income using variable costing and absorption costing

Production Equals Sales

Let's assume that for Year 1 Smart Touch Learning has the following history:

- No beginning balance in Finished Goods Inventory
- Produced 2,000 tablet computers during the year
- Sold 2,000 tablet computers during the year

Based on these assumptions, we can also conclude that Smart Touch Learning has no ending balance in Finished Goods Inventory because the beginning balance was zero and all units produced were sold.

Exhibit 21A-4 shows the income statements for Smart Touch Learning using absorption costing and variable costing. The unit costs and total fixed costs were given or calculated in Exhibits 21A-2 and 21A-3.

Exhibit 21A-4 | **Absorption and Variable Costing: Year 1—Production Equals Sales**

Absorption Costing			
Sales Revenue	(2,000 units × $500.00 per unit)		$ 1,000,000
Cost of Goods Sold	(2,000 units × $300.00 per unit)		600,000
Gross Profit			400,000
Selling and Administrative Costs:			
Variable S&A Costs	(2,000 units × $62.50 per unit)	$ 125,000	
Fixed S&A Costs		116,000	241,000
Operating Income			$ 159,000
Finished Goods Inventory, Ending Balance			$ 0

Variable Costing			
Sales Revenue	(2,000 units × $500.00 per unit)		$ 1,000,000
Variable Costs:			
Variable Manufacturing Costs	(2,000 units × $245.00 per unit)	$ 490,000	
Variable S&A Costs	(2,000 units × $62.50 per unit)	125,000	615,000
Contribution Margin			385,000
Fixed Costs:			
Fixed Manufacturing Costs		110,000	
Fixed S&A Costs		116,000	226,000
Operating Income			$ 159,000
Finished Goods Inventory, Ending Balance			$ 0

As shown in Exhibit 21A-4, when all of the units produced are sold, there is no difference in operating income between the two costing methods. The reason is that all fixed costs are expensed. In other words, because the ending Finished Goods Inventory balance is zero and there are no production costs assigned to the inventory accounts, all costs incurred have been recorded as expenses and deducted from revenues on the income statement.

Production Exceeds Sales

Let's assume that for Year 2 Smart Touch Learning shows the following:

- No beginning balance in Finished Goods Inventory (Year 1 ended with a zero balance; therefore, Year 2 will start with a zero balance)
- Produced 2,500 tablet computers during the year
- Sold 2,000 tablet computers during the year
- Ending balance in Finished Goods Inventory of 500 units (Beginning balance + units produced − units sold = 0 units + 2,500 units − 2,000 units = 500 units)

With the change in number of tablets produced, the unit product costs must be recalculated. The calculations are summarized in Exhibit 21A-5.

Exhibit 21A-5 | **Comparison of Unit Product Cost Computations—2,500 Units Produced**

		Absorption Costing	Variable Costing
Direct materials		$ 150.00	$ 150.00
Direct labor		75.00	75.00
Variable manufacturing overhead		20.00	20.00
Fixed manufacturing overhead	($110,000 / 2,500 units)	44.00	
Total unit product cost		$ 289.00	$ 245.00

The increase in production decreased the total unit product cost from $300 (Exhibit 21A-3) to $289 under absorption costing because the total fixed costs are distributed among a greater number of units.

Suppose you invite a friend for dinner and you make an apple pie. There are only two of you, so you can each have half of the pie.

Now suppose you invite two more friends. There are four people having dinner and still only one pie. Each person can have only a fourth of the pie.

This concept also applies to fixed costs. Total fixed costs stay the same (one whole pie), so the more units produced, the smaller the amount assigned to each unit (smaller piece of pie each).

Exhibit 21A-6 shows the income statements for Smart Touch Learning for Year 2 using absorption costing and variable costing. The unit costs and total fixed costs were given or calculated in Exhibits 21A-2 and 21A-5.

Exhibit 21A-6 | **Absorption and Variable Costing: Year 2—Production Exceeds Sales**

Absorption Costing

Sales Revenue	(2,000 units × $500.00 per unit)		$ 1,000,000
Cost of Goods Sold	(2,000 units × $289.00 per unit)		578,000
Gross Profit			422,000
Selling and Administrative Costs:			
Variable S&A Costs	(2,000 units × $62.50 per unit)	$ 125,000	
Fixed S&A Costs		116,000	241,000
Operating Income			$ 181,000
Finished Goods Inventory, Ending Balance	(500 units × $289.00 per unit)		$ 144,500

Variable Costing

Sales Revenue	(2,000 units × $500.00 per unit)		$ 1,000,000
Variable Costs:			
Variable Manufacturing Costs	(2,000 units × $245.00 per unit)	$ 490,000	
Variable S&A Costs	(2,000 units × $62.50 per unit)	125,000	615,000
Contribution Margin			385,000
Fixed Costs:			
Fixed Manufacturing Costs		110,000	
Fixed S&A Costs		116,000	226,000
Operating Income			$ 159,000
Finished Goods Inventory, Ending Balance	(500 units × $245.00 per unit)		$ 122,500

As shown in Exhibit 21A-6, when more units are produced than sold, operating income is greater under absorption costing. The reason is that with absorption costing some manufacturing fixed costs are still in ending Finished Goods Inventory on the balance sheet and have not been expensed. The difference between the operating incomes for the two methods is $22,000 ($181,000 − $159,000). This is the same difference in ending Finished Goods Inventory ($144,500 − $122,500).

Let's take a closer look at the production costs under the two costing methods. Exhibit 21A-7 illustrates the assignment of production costs in absorption costing and variable costing.

Exhibit 21A-7 | **Year 2: Production Costs in Absorption and Variable Costing—Production Exceeds Sales**

ABSORPTION COSTING				
	Production Costs	**=**	**Ending Inventory**	**+**	**Expensed**
Direct Materials	2,500 units × $150 per unit $375,000	=	500 units × $150 per unit $75,000	+	2,000 units × $150 per unit $300,000
Direct Labor	2,500 units × $75 per unit $187,500	=	500 units × $75 per unit $37,500	+	2,000 units × $75 per unit $150,000
Variable Manufacturing Overhead	2,500 units × $20 per unit $50,000	=	500 units × $20 per unit $10,000	+	2,000 units × $20 per unit $40,000
Fixed Manufacturing Overhead	$110,000	=	$110,000 × (500 units / 2,500 units) $22,000	+	$110,000 × (2,000 units / 2,500 units) $88,000
TOTALS	$722,500	=	$144,500	+	$578,000

VARIABLE COSTING				
	Production Costs	**=**	**Ending Inventory**	**+**	**Expensed**
Direct Materials	2,500 units × $150 per unit $375,000	=	500 units × $150 per unit $75,000	+	2,000 units × $150 per unit $300,000
Direct Labor	2,500 units × $75 per unit $187,500	=	500 units × $75 per unit $37,500	+	2,000 units × $75 per unit $150,000
Variable Manufacturing Overhead	2,500 units × $20 per unit $50,000	=	500 units × $20 per unit $10,000	+	2,000 units × $20 per unit $40,000
Fixed Manufacturing Overhead	$110,000	=	$0	+	$110,000
TOTALS	$722,500	=	$122,500	+	$600,000

In absorption costing, the costs assigned to ending Finished Goods Inventory are greater and the costs expensed are less than the assignment in variable costing when units produced exceed units sold. This is because, in contrast to absorption costing, in variable costing, all fixed manufacturing costs are expensed in the period incurred. Let's see what happens when units sold exceed units produced.

Production Is Less Than Sales

Let's assume that for Year 3 Smart Touch Learning shows the following:

- A beginning balance in Finished Goods Inventory of 500 units that cost $144,500 under absorption costing and $122,500 under variable costing (Year 2's ending balances)
- Produced 1,500 tablet computers during the year
- Sold 2,000 tablet computers during the year

Based on the above assumptions, we can also conclude that Smart Touch has no ending balance in Finished Goods Inventory because the beginning balance was 500 units, which was increased by the 1,500 units produced and decreased by the 2,000 units sold:

> 500 units + 1,500 units − 2,000 units = 0 units

With the change in number of tablets produced, the unit product costs must be recalculated. The calculations are summarized in Exhibit 21A-8 (on the next page).

Exhibit 21A-8 | **Comparison of Unit Product Cost Computations—1,500 Units Produced**

		Absorption Costing	Variable Costing
Direct materials		$ 150.00	$ 150.00
Direct labor		75.00	75.00
Variable manufacturing overhead		20.00	20.00
Fixed manufacturing overhead	($110,000 / 1,500 units)	73.33*	
Total unit product cost		$ 318.33	$ 245.00

*rounded to nearest cent

The decrease in production increased the total unit product cost from $289 (Exhibit 21A-5) to $318.33 under absorption costing because the total fixed costs were distributed among fewer units.

Exhibit 21A-9 shows the income statements for Smart Touch Learning for Year 3 using absorption costing and variable costing. The unit costs and total fixed costs were given or calculated in Exhibits 21A-2 and 21A-8.

Exhibit 21A-9 | **Absorption and Variable Costing: Year 3—Production Is Less Than Sales**

Absorption Costing

Sales Revenue	(2,000 units × $500.00 per unit)		$ 1,000,000
Cost of Goods Sold	(500 units × $289.00 per unit)	$ 144,500	
	(1,500 units × $318.33 per unit)	477,495	621,995
Gross Profit			378,005
Selling and Administrative Costs:			
Variable S&A Costs	(2,000 units × $62.50 per unit)	125,000	
Fixed S&A Costs		116,000	241,000
Operating Income			$ 137,005
Finished Goods Inventory, Ending Balance			$ 0

Variable Costing

Sales Revenue	(2,000 units × $500.00 per unit)		$ 1,000,000
Variable Costs:			
Variable Manufacturing Costs	(2,000 units × $245.00 per unit)	$ 490,000	
Variable S&A Costs	(2,000 units × $62.50 per unit)	125,000	615,000
Contribution Margin			385,000
Fixed Costs:			
Fixed Manufacturing Costs		110,000	
Fixed S&A Costs		116,000	226,000
Operating Income			$ 159,000
Finished Goods Inventory, Ending Balance			$ 0

As shown in Exhibit 21A-9, when more units are sold than produced, operating income is less under absorption costing. The only way to sell more units than were produced is to sell some units that were in inventory at the beginning of the period. Notice the cost of goods sold calculation using absorption costing includes the 500 units in beginning Finished Goods

Inventory at $289.00 per unit, $144,500. This is the amount shown as the ending Finished Goods Inventory for Year 2 in Exhibits 21A-6 and 21A-7. Remember that Year 2's ending inventory becomes Year 3's beginning inventory.

In variable costing, the fixed manufacturing costs for the prior year were expensed in the prior year. Because only variable costs are assigned to the units, the unit product cost is the same for all three accounting periods, $245.00 per unit. Under absorption costing, the units in beginning inventory have manufacturing fixed costs assigned to them. Therefore, the units sold under absorption costing have a higher cost per unit, which increases cost of goods sold and decreases operating income.

Let's take a closer look at the production costs under the two costing methods when production is less than sales. Exhibit 21A-10 illustrates the assignment of production costs in absorption costing and variable costing.

Exhibit 21A-10 | **Year 3: Production Costs in Absorption and Variable Costing—Production Less Than Sales**

ABSORPTION COSTING						
	Production Costs	=	Ending Inventory	+	Expensed	
Beginning Inventory	500 units × $289 per unit $144,500	=	$0	+	500 units × $289 per unit $144,500	
Direct Materials	1,500 units × $150 per unit $225,000	=	$0	+	1,500 units × $150 per unit $225,000	
Direct Labor	1,500 units × $75 per unit $112,500	=	$0	+	1,500 units × $75 per unit $112,500	
Variable Manufacturing Overhead	1,500 units × $20 per unit $30,000	=	$0	+	1,500 units × $20 per unit $30,000	
Fixed Manufacturing Overhead	$110,000	=	$0	+	$110,000*	
TOTALS	$622,000	=	$0	+	$622,000	

*$5 difference due to rounding the per unit fixed cost.
Actual cost: $110,000. Calculated cost: 1,500 units × $73.33 per unit = $109,995

VARIABLE COSTING						
	Production Costs	=	Ending Inventory	+	Expensed	
Beginning Inventory	500 units × $245 per unit $122,500	=	$0	+	500 units × $245 per unit $122,500	
Direct Materials	1,500 units × $150 per unit $225,000	=	$0	+	1,500 units × $150 per unit $225,000	
Direct Labor	1,500 units × $75 per unit $112,500	=	$0	+	1,500 units × $75 per unit $112,500	
Variable Manufacturing Overhead	1,500 units × $20 per unit $30,000	=	$0	+	1,500 units × $20 per unit $30,000	
Fixed Manufacturing Overhead	$110,000	=	$0	+	$110,000	
TOTALS	$600,000	=	$0	+	$600,000	

In absorption costing, the manufacturing costs expensed are greater than the amount expensed in variable costing when units produced are less than sold because the units in beginning inventory under absorption costing were assigned a greater cost in the previous accounting period.

Summary

In the three years illustrated for Smart Touch Learning, the only difference was the number of tablet computers produced. In each year, the number of tablets sold, the sales price per unit, the variable costs per unit, and the total fixed costs were the same. Let's compare the three years to determine why many managers prefer to use variable costing for planning and controlling. Exhibit 21A-11 summarizes the income statements for the three years.

Exhibit 21A-11 | **Absorption and Variable Costing: 3-Year Summary**

Absorption Costing	Year 1	Year 2	Year 3	Total*
Sales Revenue	$ 1,000,000	$ 1,000,000	$ 1,000,000	$ 3,000,000
Cost of Goods Sold	600,000	578,000	621,995	1,800,000
Gross Profit	400,000	422,000	378,005	1,200,000
Selling and Administrative Costs	241,000	241,000	241,000	723,000
Operating Income	$ 159,000	$ 181,000	$ 137,005	$ 477,000
Gross Profit per Unit	$ 200.00	$ 211.00	$ 189.00	

Variable Costing	Year 1	Year 2	Year 3	Total
Sales Revenue	$ 1,000,000	$ 1,000,000	$ 1,000,000	$ 3,000,000
Variable Costs	615,000	615,000	615,000	1,845,000
Contribution Margin	385,000	385,000	385,000	1,155,000
Fixed Costs	226,000	226,000	226,000	678,000
Operating Income	$ 159,000	$ 159,000	$ 159,000	$ 477,000
Contribution Margin per Unit	$ 192.50	$ 192.50	$ 192.50	

*Absorption costing total figures adjusted for $5 rounding error created in Year 3 when fixed cost per unit was rounded.

Suppose the production supervisor receives a bonus based on absorption costing. Will the supervisor increase or decrease production? Based on the summary of income statements presented in Exhibit 21A-11, operating income under absorption costing was greater than operating income under variable costing in Year 2, when production exceeded sales. The production supervisor knows that absorption costing assigns fixed manufacturing overhead to each tablet produced. In absorption costing:

- For every tablet that is produced but not sold, absorption costing "hides" some of the fixed manufacturing overhead in ending Finished Goods Inventory (an asset).
- The more tablets added to ending Finished Goods Inventory, the more fixed manufacturing overhead is "hidden" in ending Finished Goods Inventory at the end of the month.
- The more fixed manufacturing overhead in ending Finished Goods Inventory, the smaller the Cost of Goods Sold and the higher the operating income.

To maximize the bonus under absorption costing, the supervisor may increase production to build up ending Finished Goods Inventory, increase operating income, and therefore increase the bonus. However, this incentive directly conflicts with the just-in-time philosophy, which emphasizes minimal inventory levels. Therefore, many managers prefer to use variable costing to make internal planning and control decisions. The use of variable costing to determine bonuses does not give the incentive to produce more products than needed.

How can using absorption costing affect production levels when determining performance-based bonuses?

Try It!

21. Hayden Company has 50 units in Finished Goods Inventory at the beginning of the accounting period. During the accounting period, Hayden produced 150 units and sold 200 units for $150 each. All units incurred $80 in variable manufacturing costs and $20 in fixed manufacturing costs. Hayden also incurred $7,500 in Selling and Administrative Costs, all fixed. Calculate the operating income for the year using absorption costing and variable costing.

Check your answers online in MyAccountingLab or at http://www.pearsonhighered.com/Horngren.

For more practice, see Short Exercises S21A-22 through S21A-24.   **MyAccountingLab**

REVIEW

> Things You Should Know

1. **How do costs behave when there is a change in volume?**

   - Total variable costs change in direct proportion to changes in volume, but the variable cost per unit remains unchanged.
   - Total fixed costs remain unchanged with changes in volume, but the fixed cost per unit changes inversely.
   - Mixed costs have a variable and fixed component.
   - Mixed costs can be separated into their variable and fixed components using the high-low method.

2. **What is contribution margin, and how is it used to compute operating income?**

   - Contribution margin = Net sales revenue − Variable costs.
   - Contribution margin ratio = Contribution margin / Net sales revenue.
   - The traditional income statement separates costs by function: product costs and period costs.
   - The contribution margin income statement separates costs by behavior—fixed and variable—and highlights contribution margin.

CHAPTER 21

3. **How is cost-volume-profit (CVP) analysis used?**
   - Required sales to obtain a target profit can be calculated using three approaches:
     - Equation approach
     - Contribution margin approach
     - Contribution margin ratio approach
   - Breakeven point is a variation of the target profit approaches where target profit equals $0.
   - CVP graphs are used to make quick estimates of profit levels at various volumes of sales.

4. **How is CVP analysis used for sensitivity analysis?**
   - Increases in sales prices increase contribution margin and decrease the breakeven point.
   - Decreases in sales prices decrease contribution margin and increase the breakeven point.
   - Increases in variable costs decrease contribution margin and increase the breakeven point.
   - Decreases in variable costs increase contribution margin and decrease the breakeven point.
   - Increases in fixed costs have no effect on contribution margin and increase the breakeven point.
   - Decreases in fixed costs have no effect on contribution margin and decrease the breakeven point.

5. **What are some other ways CVP analysis can be used?**
   - Margin of safety
     - The excess of expected sales over breakeven sales.
     - In units: Expected sales in units − Breakeven sales in units.
     - In dollars: Margin of safety in units × Sales price per unit.
     - As a ratio: Margin of safety in units / Expected sales in units.
   - Operating leverage
     - Effects that fixed costs have on changes in operating income when sales volume changes.
     - Degree of operating leverage = Contribution margin / Operating income.
   - Sales mix
     - Calculate the breakeven point with multiple products:
       Step 1: Calculate the weighted-average contribution margin per unit.
       Step 2: Calculate the breakeven point in units for the "package" of products.
       Step 3: Calculate the breakeven point in units for each product. Multiply the "package" breakeven point in units by each product's proportion of the sales mix.

6. **How does variable costing differ from absorption costing? (Appendix 21A)**
   - Absorption costing assigns all production costs to products: direct materials, direct labor, variable manufacturing overhead, and fixed manufacturing overhead.
   - Variable costing assigns only the variable production costs to products: direct materials, direct labor, and variable manufacturing overhead. Fixed manufacturing overhead is considered a period cost.

7. **How does operating income differ between variable costing and absorption costing? (Appendix 21A)**

- When production equals sales, the operating income is the same for both absorption costing and variable costing.

- When production exceeds sales, operating income using absorption costing is greater than when using variable costing.

- When production is less than sales, operating income using absorption costing is less than when using variable costing.

> Summary Problem 21-1

The Sock Company buys hiking socks for $6 per pair and sells them for $10. Management budgets monthly fixed costs of $10,000 for sales volumes between 0 and 12,000 pairs of socks.

Requirements

1. Use both the equation approach and the contribution margin approach to compute the company's monthly breakeven point in units.

2. Use the contribution margin ratio approach to compute the breakeven point in sales dollars.

3. Compute the monthly sales level (in units) required to earn a target operating income of $6,000. Use either the equation approach or the contribution margin approach.

4. Prepare a graph of The Sock Company's CVP relationships, similar to Exhibit 21-8. Draw the sales revenue line, the fixed cost line, and the total cost line. Label the axes, the breakeven point, the operating income area, and the operating loss area.

> Solution

Requirement 1

Equation approach:

Net sales revenue − Variable costs − Fixed costs = Target profit

($10 per unit × Units sold) − ($6 per unit × Units sold) − $10,000 = $ 0

[($10 per unit − $6 per unit) × Units sold] − $10,000 = $ 0

$4 per unit × Units sold = $10,000

Units sold = $10,000 / $4 per unit

Units sold = 2,500 units

Contribution margin approach:

$$\text{Required sales in units} = \frac{\text{Fixed costs} + \text{Target profit}}{\text{Contribution margin per unit}}$$

$$= \frac{\$10,000 + \$0}{\$10 \text{ per unit} - \$6 \text{ per unit}}$$

$$= 2,500 \text{ units}$$

Requirement 2

$$\text{Contribution margin ratio} = \frac{\text{Contribution margin}}{\text{Sales price}} = \frac{\$4}{\$10} = 40\%$$

$$\text{Required sales in dollars} = \frac{\text{Fixed costs} + \text{Target profit}}{\text{Contribution margin ratio}}$$

$$= \frac{\$10,000 + \$0}{40\%}$$

$$= \$25,000$$

This can be confirmed by multiplying the breakeven point in units (as calculated in Requirement 1) by the sales price:

$$2,500 \text{ pairs of socks} \times \$10 \text{ per pair of socks} = \$25,000$$

Requirement 3

Equation approach:

Net sales revenue − Variable costs − Fixed costs = Target profit
($10 per unit × Units sold) − ($6 per unit × Units sold) − $10,000 = $ 6,000
[($10 per unit − $6 per unit) × Units sold] − $10,000 = $ 6,000
$4 per unit × Units sold = $16,000
Units sold = $16,000 / $4 per unit
Units sold = 4,000 units

Contribution margin approach:

$$\text{Required sales in units} = \frac{\text{Fixed costs} + \text{Target profit}}{\text{Contribution margin per unit}}$$

$$= \frac{\$10,000 + \$6,000}{\$4 \text{ per unit}}$$

$$= 4,000 \text{ units}$$

Requirement 4

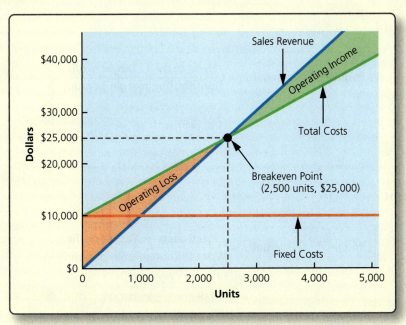

> Summary Problem 21-2

The Sock Company buys hiking socks for $6 per pair and sells them for $10. Management budgets monthly fixed costs of $12,000 for sales volumes between 0 and 12,000 pairs.

Requirements

Consider each of the following questions separately by using the foregoing information each time.

1. Calculate the breakeven point in units.
2. The Sock Company reduces its sales price from $10 per pair to $8 per pair. Calculate the new breakeven point in units.
3. The Sock Company finds a new supplier for the socks. Variable costs will decrease by $1 per pair. Calculate the new breakeven point in units.
4. The Sock Company plans to advertise in hiking magazines. The advertising campaign will increase total fixed costs by $2,000 per month. Calculate the new breakeven point in units.
5. In addition to selling hiking socks, The Sock Company would like to start selling sports socks. The Sock Company expects to sell one pair of hiking socks for every three pairs of sports socks. The Sock Company will buy the sports socks for $4 per pair and sell them for $8 per pair. Total fixed costs will stay at $12,000 per month. Calculate the breakeven point in units for both hiking socks and sports socks.

> Solution

Requirement 1

$$\text{Required sales in units} = \frac{\text{Fixed costs } + \text{ Target profit}}{\text{Contribution margin per unit}}$$

$$= \frac{\$12{,}000 + \$0}{\$10 \text{ per unit} - \$6 \text{ per unit}}$$

$$= 3{,}000 \text{ units}$$

Requirement 2

$$\text{Required sales in units} = \frac{\text{Fixed costs } + \text{ Target profit}}{\text{Contribution margin per unit}}$$

$$= \frac{\$12{,}000 + \$0}{\$8 \text{ per unit} - \$6 \text{ per unit}}$$

$$= 6{,}000 \text{ units}$$

Requirement 3

$$\text{Required sales in units} = \frac{\text{Fixed costs } + \text{ Target profit}}{\text{Contribution margin per unit}}$$

$$= \frac{\$12{,}000 + \$0}{\$10 \text{ per unit} - \$5 \text{ per unit}}$$

$$= 2{,}400 \text{ units}$$

Requirement 4

$$\text{Required sales in units} = \frac{\text{Fixed costs } + \text{ Target profit}}{\text{Contribution margin per unit}}$$

$$= \frac{\$14{,}000 + \$0}{\$10 \text{ per unit} - \$6 \text{ per unit}}$$

$$= 3{,}500 \text{ units}$$

Requirement 5

Step 1: Calculate the weighted-average contribution margin:

	Hiking	Sports	Total
Sales price per unit	$ 10	$ 8	
Variable cost per unit	6	4	
Contribution margin per unit	4	4	
Sales mix in units	× 1	× 3	4 units
Contribution margin	$ 4	$ 12	$ 16
Weighted-average contribution margin per unit ($16 per unit / 4 units)			$ 4

Step 2: Calculate the breakeven point for the "package" of products:

$$\text{Required sales in units} = \frac{\text{Fixed costs} + \text{Target profit}}{\text{Contribution margin per unit}}$$

$$= \frac{\$12,000 + \$0}{\$4 \text{ per unit}}$$

$$= 3,000 \text{ units}$$

Step 3: Calculate the breakeven point for each product:

Breakeven sales of hiking socks	(3,000 items × 1/4)	750 pairs of hiking socks
Breakeven sales of sport socks	(3,000 items × 3/4)	2,250 pairs of sport socks

> Key Terms

Absorption Costing (p. 1123) (Appendix 21A)

Breakeven Point (p. 1112)

Contribution Margin (p. 1107)

Contribution Margin Income Statement (p. 1108)

Contribution Margin Ratio (p. 1108)

Cost Structure (p. 1118)

Cost-Volume-Profit (CVP) Analysis (p. 1109)

Degree of Operating Leverage (p. 1119)

Fixed Cost (p. 1101)

High-Low Method (p. 1104)

Margin of Safety (p. 1117)

Mixed Cost (p. 1103)

Operating Leverage (p. 1119)

Relevant Range (p. 1106)

Sales Mix (p. 1120)

Sensitivity Analysis (p. 1115)

Target Profit (p. 1110)

Variable Cost (p. 1100)

Variable Costing (p. 1123) (Appendix 21A)

> Quick Check

1. For Frank's Funky Sounds, straight-line depreciation on the trucks is a
   a. variable cost.
   b. fixed cost.
   c. mixed cost.
   d. high-low cost.

Learning Objective 1

CHAPTER 21

Learning Objective 1

2. Assume Intervale Railway is considering hiring a reservations agency to handle passenger reservations. The agency would charge a flat fee of $13,000 per month, plus $3 per passenger reservation. What is the total reservation cost if 200,000 passengers take the trip next month?

    a. $613,000   **b.** $3.07   **c.** $600,000   **d.** $13,000

Learning Objective 2

3. If Intervale Railway's fixed costs total $90,000 per month, the variable cost per passenger is $45, and tickets sell for $75, what is the contribution margin per unit and contribution margin ratio?

    a. $45 per passenger; 60%   **c.** $30 per passenger; 40%

    b. $30 per passenger; 60%   **d.** $45 per passenger; 40%

Learning Objective 3

4. If Intervale Railway's fixed costs total $90,000 per month, the variable cost per passenger is $45, and tickets sell for $75, how much revenue must the Railway generate to earn $120,000 in operating income per month?

    a. $350,000   **b.** $210,000   **c.** $7,000   **d.** $525,000

Learning Objective 3

5. If Intervale Railway's fixed costs total $90,000 per month, the variable cost per passenger is $45, and tickets sell for $75, what is the breakeven point in units?

    a. 1,200 passengers   **c.** 225,000 passengers

    b. 2,000 passengers   **d.** 3,000 passengers

Learning Objective 3

6. On a CVP graph, the total cost line intersects the vertical (dollars) axis at

    a. the origin.   **c.** the breakeven point.

    b. the level of the fixed costs.   **d.** the level of the variable costs.

Learning Objective 4

7. If a company increases its sales price per unit for Product A, the new breakeven point will

    a. increase.   **c.** remain the same.

    b. decrease.   **d.** More information is needed.

Learning Objective 4

8. If a company increases its fixed costs for Product B, then the contribution margin per unit will

    a. increase.   **c.** remain the same.

    b. decrease.   **d.** More information needed.

Learning Objective 5

9. The Best Appliances had the following revenue over the past five years:

2011	$ 600,000
2012	700,000
2013	900,000
2014	800,000
2015	1,000,000

To predict revenues for 2016, The Best Appliances uses the average for the past five years. The company's breakeven revenue is $800,000 per year. What is The Best Appliances's predicted margin of safety in dollars for 2016?

    a. $800,000   **b.** $0   **c.** $200,000   **d.** $100,000

10. Rocky Mountain Waterpark sells half of its tickets for the regular price of $75. The other half go to senior citizens and children for the discounted price of $35. Variable cost per guest is $15 for both groups, and fixed costs total $60,000 per month. What is Rocky Mountain's breakeven point in total guests? Regular guests? Discount guests?

   a. 2,000; 1,000; 1,000   c. 750; 375; 375
   b. 800; 400; 400   d. 1,500; 750; 750

Learning Objective 5

Use the following data for questions 11A–12A:

Donovan Company incurred the following costs while producing 500 units: direct materials, $10 per unit; direct labor, $25 per unit; variable manufacturing overhead, $15 per unit; total fixed manufacturing overhead costs, $10,000; variable selling and administrative costs, $5 per unit; total fixed selling and administrative costs, $7,500. There are no beginning inventories.

11A. What is the unit product cost using variable costing?

   a. $50 per unit   c. $70 per unit
   b. $55 per unit   d. $90 per unit

**Learning Objective 6
Appendix 21A**

12A. What is the operating income using variable costing if 450 units are sold for $100 each?

   a. $2,750   b. $5,000   c. $500   d. $2,500

**Learning Objective 7
Appendix 21A**

Check your answers at the end of the chapter.

ASSESS YOUR PROGRESS

> Review Questions

1. What is a variable cost? Give an example.
2. What is a fixed cost? Give an example.
3. What is a mixed cost? Give an example.
4. What is the purpose of using the high-low method?
5. Describe the three steps of the high-low method.
6. What is the relevant range?
7. A chain of convenience stores has one manager per store who is paid a monthly salary. Relative to Store #36 located in Atlanta, Georgia, is the manager's salary fixed or variable? Why?
8. A chain of convenience stores has one manager per store who is paid a monthly salary. Relative to the number of stores, is the manager's salary fixed or variable? Why?
9. What is contribution margin?
10. What are the three ways contribution margin can be expressed?
11. How does a contribution margin income statement differ from a traditional income statement?
12. What is cost-volume-profit analysis?
13. What are the CVP assumptions?

14. What is target profit?

15. What are the three approaches to calculating the sales required to achieve the target profit? Give the formula for each one.

16. Of the three approaches to calculate sales required to achieve target profit, which one(s) calculate the required sales in units and which one(s) calculate the required sales in dollars?

17. What is the breakeven point?

18. Why is the calculation to determine the breakeven point considered a variation of the target profit calculation?

19. On the CVP graph, where is the breakeven point shown? Why?

20. What is sensitivity analysis? How do managers use this tool?

21. What effect does an increase in sales price have on contribution margin? An increase in fixed costs? An increase in variable costs?

22. What is the margin of safety? What are the three ways it can be expressed?

23. What is a company's cost structure? How can cost structure affect a company's profits?

24. What is operating leverage? What does it mean if a company has a degree of operating leverage of 3?

25. How can CVP analysis be used by companies with multiple products?

26A. What is absorption costing?

27A. What is variable costing?

28A. How are absorption costing and variable costing the same? How are they different?

29A. When units produced equal units sold, how does operating income differ between variable costing and absorption costing?

30A. When units produced exceed units sold, how does operating income differ between variable costing and absorption costing? Why?

31A. When units produced are less than units sold, how does operating income differ between variable costing and absorption costing? Why?

32A. Explain why the fixed manufacturing overhead cost per unit changes when there is a change in the number of units produced.

33A. Explain how increasing production can increase gross profit when using absorption costing.

> Short Exercises

Learning Objective 1

S21-1 Identifying variable, fixed, and mixed costs

Philadelphia Acoustics builds innovative speakers for music and home theater systems. Identify each cost as variable (V), fixed (F), or mixed (M), relative to number of speakers produced and sold.

1. Units of production depreciation on routers used to cut wood enclosures.

2. Wood for speaker enclosures.

3. Patents on crossover relays.

4. Total compensation to salesperson who receives a salary plus a commission based on meeting sales goals.

5. Crossover relays.

6. Straight-line depreciation on manufacturing plant.

7. Grill cloth.

8. Cell phone costs of salesperson.

9. Glue.

10. Quality inspector's salary.

S21-2 Identifying variable, fixed, and mixed costs

Learning Objective 1

Holly's Day Care has been in operation for several years. Identify each cost as variable (V), fixed (F), or mixed (M), relative to number of students enrolled.

1. Building rent.

2. Toys.

3. Compensation of the office manager, who receives a salary plus a bonus based on number of students enrolled.

4. Afternoon snacks.

5. Lawn service contract at $200 per month.

6. Holly's salary.

7. Wages of afterschool employees.

8. Drawing paper for student artwork.

9. Straight-line depreciation on furniture and playground equipment.

10. Fee paid to security company for monthly service.

S21-3 Using the high-low method

Learning Objective 1

Mel owns a machine shop. In reviewing the shop's utility bills for the past 12 months, he found that the highest bill of $2,600 occurred in August when the machines worked 1,400 machine hours. The lowest utility bill of $2,300 occurred in December when the machines worked 900 machine hours.

Requirements

1. Calculate the variable rate per machine hour and the total fixed utility cost.

2. Show the equation for determining the total utility cost for the machine shop.

3. If Mel anticipates using 1,000 machine hours in January, predict the shop's total utility bill using the equation from Requirement 2.

S21-4 Calculating contribution margin

Learning Objective 2

Garson Company sells a product for $90 per unit. Variable costs are $60 per unit, and fixed costs are $800 per month. The company expects to sell 540 units in September. Calculate the contribution margin per unit, in total, and as a ratio.

S21-5 Preparing a contribution margin income statement

Learning Objective 2

Gabrick Company sells a product for $30 per unit. Variable costs are $20 per unit, and fixed costs are $2,500 per month. The company expects to sell 560 units in September. Prepare an income statement for September using the contribution margin format.

S21-6 Calculating required sales in units, contribution margin given

Learning Objective 3

Malden, Inc. sells a product with a contribution margin of $60 per unit. Fixed costs are $10,500 per month. How many units must Malden sell to earn an operating income of $15,000?

CHAPTER 21

Learning Objective 3

S21-7 Calculating required sales in units, contribution margin ratio given

Summer Company sells a product with a contribution margin ratio of 60%. Fixed costs are $650 per month. What amount of sales (in dollars) must Summer Company have to earn an operating income of $7,000? If each unit sells for $30, how many units must be sold to achieve the desired operating income?

Learning Objectives 2, 3

S21-8 Computing contribution margin, units to achieve target profit, and breakeven point

Compute the missing amounts for the following table.

	A	B	C
Number of units	870 units	25,000 units	2,800 units
Sales price per unit	$ 1,000	$ 100	$ 160
Variable costs per unit	600	60	80
Total fixed costs	79,200	80,000	64,000
Target profit	268,800	920,000	160,000
Calculate:			
Contribution margin per unit	_____	_____	_____
Contribution margin ratio	_____	_____	_____
Required units to achieve target profit	_____	_____	_____
Required units to break even	_____	_____	_____
Required sales dollars to break even	_____	_____	_____

Use the following information to complete Short Exercises S21-9 through S21-14.

Playtime Park competes with Water World by providing a variety of rides. Playtime Park sells tickets at $60 per person as a one-day entrance fee. Variable costs are $24 per person, and fixed costs are $226,800 per month.

Learning Objectives 2, 3

S21-9 Computing contribution margin per unit, breakeven point in sales units

Compute the contribution margin per unit and the number of tickets Playtime Park must sell to break even. Perform a numerical proof to show that your answer is correct.

Learning Objectives 2, 3

S21-10 Computing contribution margin ratio, breakeven point in sales dollars

Compute Playtime Park's contribution margin ratio. Carry your computation to two decimal places. Use the contribution margin ratio approach to determine the sales revenue Playtime Park needs to break even.

Learning Objective 4

S21-11 Applying sensitivity analysis of changing sales price and variable cost

Using the Playtime Park information presented, do the following tasks.

Requirements

1. Suppose Playtime Park cuts its ticket price from $60 to $54 to increase the number of tickets sold. Compute the new breakeven point in tickets and in sales dollars.

2. Ignore the information in Requirement 1. Instead, assume that Playtime Park increases the variable cost from $24 to $30 per ticket. Compute the new breakeven point in tickets and in sales dollars.

S21-12   Applying sensitivity analysis of changing fixed costs

Learning Objective 4

Refer to the original information (ignoring the changes considered in Short Exercise S21-11). Suppose Playtime Park reduces fixed costs from $226,800 per month to $208,800 per month. Compute the new breakeven point in tickets and in sales dollars.

S21-13   Computing margin of safety

Learning Objective 5

Refer to the original information (ignoring the changes considered in Short Exercises S21-11 and S21-12). If Playtime Park expects to sell 7,000 tickets, compute the margin of safety in tickets and in sales dollars.

S21-14   Computing degree of operating leverage

Learning Objective 5

Refer to the original information (ignoring the changes considered in Short Exercises S21-11 and S21-12). If Playtime Park expects to sell 7,000 tickets, compute the degree of operating leverage. Estimate the operating income if sales increase by 15%.

Use the following information to complete Short Exercises S21-15 and S21-16.

SoakNFun Swim Park sells individual and family tickets. With a ticket, each person receives a meal, three beverages, and unlimited use of the swimming pools. SoakNFun has the following ticket prices and variable costs for 2016:

	Individual	Family
Sales price per ticket	$ 40	$ 120
Variable cost per ticket	25	100

SoakNFun expects to sell one individual ticket for every four family tickets. SoakNFun's total fixed costs are $76,000.

S21-15   Calculating breakeven point for two products

Learning Objective 5

Using the SoakNFun Swim Park information presented, do the following tasks.

Requirements

1. Compute the weighted-average contribution margin per ticket.
2. Calculate the total number of tickets SoakNFun must sell to break even.
3. Calculate the number of individual tickets and the number of family tickets the company must sell to break even.

S21-16   Calculating breakeven point for two products

Learning Objective 5

For 2017, SoakNFun expects a sales mix of four individual tickets for every one family ticket.

Requirements

1. Compute the new weighted-average contribution margin per ticket.
2. Calculate the total number of tickets SoakNFun must sell to break even.
3. Calculate the number of individual tickets and the number of family tickets the company must sell to break even.

Learning Objective 6
Appendix 21A

S21A-17 Classifying costs

Classify each cost by placing an X in the appropriate columns. The first cost is completed as an example.

	Absorption Costing		Variable Costing	
	Product Cost	Period Cost	Product Cost	Period Cost
a. Direct materials	X		X	
b. Direct labor				
c. Variable manufacturing overhead				
d. Fixed manufacturing overhead				
e. Variable selling and administrative costs				
f. Fixed selling and administrative costs				

Use the following information for Short Exercises S21A-18 and S21A-19.

Burlington Company reports the following information for June:

Sales Revenue	$ 745,000
Variable Cost of Goods Sold	240,000
Fixed Cost of Goods Sold	186,000
Variable Selling and Administrative Costs	152,000
Fixed Selling and Administrative Costs	65,000

Learning Objective 6
Appendix 21A

S21A-18 Calculating variable costs

Calculate the contribution margin and operating income for June using variable costing.

Learning Objective 6
Appendix 21A

S21A-19 Calculating absorption costs

Calculate the gross profit and operating income for June using absorption costing.

Use the following information for Short Exercises S21A-20 and S21A-21.

Matthew Company had the following costs:

Units produced	310 units
Direct materials	$ 67 per unit
Direct labor	33 per unit
Variable manufacturing overhead	14 per unit
Fixed manufacturing overhead	6,200 per year
Variable selling and administrative costs	20 per unit
Fixed selling and administrative costs	3,100 per year

Learning Objective 6
Appendix 21A

S21A-20 Computing unit product cost, absorption costing

Calculate the unit product cost using absorption costing. Round your answer to the nearest cent.

S21A-21 Computing unit product cost, variable costing

Learning Objective 6
Appendix 21A

Calculate the unit product cost using variable costing. Round your answer to the nearest cent.

S21A-22 Computing absorption cost per unit

Learning Objective 7
Appendix 21A

Abrey, Inc. has the following cost data for Product X:

Direct materials	$ 41 per unit
Direct labor	60 per unit
Variable manufacturing overhead	8 per unit
Fixed manufacturing overhead	5,000 per year

Calculate the unit product cost using absorption costing when production is 250 units, 500 units, and 2,500 units.

Note: Short Exercise S21A-22 must be completed before attempting Short Exercise S21A-23.

S21A-23 Computing absorption costing gross profit

Learning Objective 7
Appendix 21A

Refer to your answers to Short Exercise S21A-22. Product X sells for $175 per unit. Calculate the gross profit using absorption costing when Abrey:

a. Produces and sells 250 units.

b. Produces 500 units and sells 250 units

c. Produces 2,500 units and sells 250 units.

S21A-24 Computing inventory balances

Learning Objective 7
Appendix 21A

Wong Company reports the following data:

Finished Goods Inventory:	
Beginning balance, in units	500
Units produced	3,100
Units sold	(1,500)
Ending balance, in units	2,100
Production Costs:	
Variable manufacturing costs per unit	$ 65
Total fixed manufacturing costs	40,300

Calculate the product cost per unit and the total cost of the 2,100 units in ending inventory using absorption costing and variable costing.

> Exercises

Learning Objectives 1, 2, 3, 4, 5

E21-25 Using terminology

Match the following terms with the correct definitions:

1. Costs that do not change in total over wide ranges of volume.		a.	Breakeven point
2. Technique that estimates profit or loss results when conditions change.		b.	Contribution margin
3. The sales level at which operating income is zero.		c.	Cost behavior
4. Drop in sales a company can absorb without incurring an operating loss.		d.	Margin of safety
5. Combination of products that make up total sales.		e.	Relevant range
6. Net sales revenue minus variable costs.		f.	Sales mix
7. Describes how a cost changes as volume changes.		g.	Fixed costs
8. Costs that change in total in direct proportion to changes in volume.		h.	Variable costs
9. The band of volume where total fixed costs and variable cost per unit remain constant.		i.	Sensitivity analysis

Learning Objective 1

E21-26 Determining cost behavior

Identify each cost below as variable (V), fixed (F), or mixed (M), relative to units sold. Explain your reason.

Units Sold	25	50	75	100
a. Total phone cost	$ 150	$ 200	$ 250	$ 300
b. Materials cost per unit	35	35	35	35
c. Manager's salary	3,000	3,000	3,000	3,000
d. Depreciation cost per unit	60	30	20	15
e. Total utility cost	400	650	900	1,150
f. Total cost of goods sold	3,125	6,250	9,375	12,500

Learning Objective 1

90 units $52.50

E21-27 Determining fixed cost per unit

For each total fixed cost listed below, determine the fixed cost per unit when sales are 45, 90, and 180 units.

Store rent	$ 1,800
Manager's salary	1,350
Equipment lease	900
Depreciation on fixtures	675

Learning Objective 1

Total VC, 80 units $9,600

E21-28 Determining total variable cost

For each variable cost per unit listed below, determine the total variable cost when units produced and sold are 40, 80, and 160 units.

Direct materials	$ 35
Direct labor	65
Variable overhead	9
Sales commission	11

E21-29 Determining total mixed cost

Robert Street Barber Shop pays $30 per month for water for the first 10,000 gallons and $1.75 per thousand gallons above 10,000 gallons. Calculate the total water cost when the barber shop uses 6,000 gallons, 12,000 gallons, and 17,000 gallons.

Learning Objective 1

17,000 gal. $42.25

E21-30 Determining mixed costs—the high-low method

The manager of Quick Car Inspection reviewed the monthly operating costs for the past year. The costs ranged from $4,400 for 1,400 inspections to $4,200 for 1,000 inspections.

Learning Objective 1

3. $4,300

Requirements

1. Calculate the variable cost per inspection.

2. Calculate the total fixed costs.

3. Write the equation and calculate the operating costs for 1,200 inspections.

4. Draw a graph illustrating the total cost under this plan. Label the axes, and show the costs at 1,000, 1,200, and 1,400 inspections.

E21-31 Calculating contribution margin ratio, preparing contribution margin income statements

For its top managers, Global Travel formats its income statement as follows:

Learning Objective 2

2. $250,000 sales level, VC $87,500

GLOBAL TRAVEL Contribution Margin Income Statement Three Months Ended March 31, 2016	
Sales Revenue	$ 318,500
Variable Costs	111,475
Contribution Margin	207,025
Fixed Costs	175,000
Operating Income	$ 32,025

Global's relevant range is between sales of $250,000 and $360,000.

Requirements

1. Calculate the contribution margin ratio.

2. Prepare two contribution margin income statements: one at the $250,000 sales level and one at the $360,000 sales level. (*Hint:* The proportion of each sales dollar that goes toward variable costs is constant within the relevant range.)

E21-32 Computing contribution margin in total, per unit, and as a ratio

Complete the table below for contribution margin per unit, total contribution margin, and contribution margin ratio:

	A	B	C
Number of units	1,800 units	9,790 units	1,410 units
Sales price per unit	$ 1,900	$ 500	$ 800
Variable costs per unit	1,140	250	480
Calculate:			
Contribution margin per unit	_____	_____	_____
Total contribution margin	_____	_____	_____
Contribution margin ratio	_____	_____	_____

E21-33 Computing breakeven sales

Ten Toes Co. produces sports socks. The company has fixed costs of $75,000 and variable costs of $0.75 per package. Each package sells for $1.50.

Requirements

1. Compute the contribution margin per package and the contribution margin ratio. (Round your answers to two decimal places.)

2. Find the breakeven point in units and in dollars using the contribution margin approach.

E21-34 Computing a change in breakeven sales

Owner Shan Lo is considering franchising her Noodles by Lo restaurant concept. She believes people will pay $6.50 for a large bowl of noodles. Variable costs are $3.25 per bowl. Lo estimates monthly fixed costs for a franchise at $3,000.

Requirements

1. Use the contribution margin ratio approach to find a franchise's breakeven sales in dollars.

2. Lo believes most locations could generate $34,500 in monthly sales. Is franchising a good idea for Lo if franchisees want a minimum monthly operating income of $13,500?

E21-35 Computing breakeven sales and operating income or loss under different conditions

Graham's Steel Parts produces parts for the automobile industry. The company has monthly fixed costs of $630,000 and a contribution margin of 80% of revenues.

Requirements

1. Compute Graham's monthly breakeven sales in dollars. Use the contribution margin ratio approach.

2. Use contribution margin income statements to compute Graham's monthly operating income or operating loss if revenues are $550,000 and if they are $1,010,000.

3. Do the results in Requirement 2 make sense given the breakeven sales you computed in Requirement 1? Explain.

E21-36 Analyzing a cost-volume-profit graph

Learning Objective 3

3. $40,000

John Kyler is considering starting a Web-based educational business, e-Prep MBA. He plans to offer a short-course review of accounting for students entering MBA programs. The materials would be available on a password-protected Web site; students would complete the course through self-study. Kyler would have to grade the course assignments, but most of the work would be in developing the course materials, setting up the site, and marketing. Unfortunately, Kyler's hard drive crashed before he finished his financial analysis. However, he did recover the following partial CVP chart:

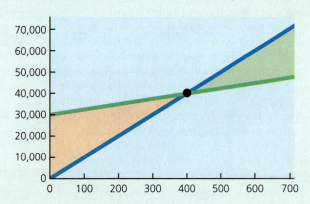

Requirements

1. Label each axis, the sales revenue line, the total costs line, the fixed costs line, the operating income area, and the breakeven point.

2. If Kyler attracts 300 students to take the course, will the venture be profitable?

3. What are the breakeven sales in students and dollars?

E21-37 Using sensitivity analysis

Learning Objective 4

1b. 1,400 students

Intersection Driving School charges $500 per student to prepare and administer written and driving tests. Variable costs of $150 per student include trainers' wages, study materials, and gasoline. Annual fixed costs of $140,000 include the training facility and fleet of cars.

Requirements

1. For each of the following independent situations, calculate the contribution margin per unit and the breakeven point in units by first referring to the original data provided:

   a. Breakeven point with no change in information.
   b. Decrease sales price to $250 per student.
   c. Decrease variable costs to $100 per student.
   d. Decrease fixed costs to $122,500.

2. Compare the impact of changes in the sales price, variable costs, and fixed costs on the contribution margin per unit and the breakeven point in units.

Learning Objective 5

1. $42,500

E21-38 Computing margin of safety

Ricky's Repair Shop has a monthly target profit of $17,000. Variable costs are 60% of sales, and monthly fixed costs are $8,000.

Requirements

1. Compute the monthly margin of safety in dollars if the shop achieves its income goal.

2. Express Ricky's margin of safety as a percentage of target sales.

Learning Objective 5

2. 40.2750%

E21-39 Computing degree of operating leverage

Following is the income statement for Marsden Mufflers for the month of June 2016:

MARSDEN MUFFLERS Contribution Margin Income Statement Month Ended June 30, 2016	
Sales Revenue (280 units × $325)	$ 91,000
Variable Costs (280 units × $150)	42,000
Contribution Margin	49,000
Fixed Costs	12,500
Operating Income	$ 36,500

Requirements

1. Calculate the degree of operating leverage. (Round to four decimal places.)

2. Use the degree of operating leverage calculated in Requirement 1 to estimate the change in operating income if total sales increase by 30% (assuming no change in sales price per unit). (Round interim calculations to four decimal places and final answer to the nearest dollar.)

3. Verify your answer in Requirement 2 by preparing a contribution margin income statement with the total sales increase of 30%.

Learning Objective 5

2. 340 standards

E21-40 Calculating breakeven point for two products

Stewart's Scooters plans to sell a standard scooter for $120 and a chrome scooter for $160. Stewart's purchases the standard scooter for $30 and the chrome scooter for $40. Stewart's expects to sell one standard scooter for every three chrome scooters. Stewart's monthly fixed costs are $85,500.

Requirements

1. How many of each type of scooter must Stewart's Scooters sell each month to break even?

2. How many of each type of scooter must Stewart's Scooters sell each month to earn $67,500?

E21A-41 Using absorption and variable costing

Moffett Company reports the following information for March:

Sales Revenue	$ 72,500
Variable Cost of Goods Sold	14,360
Fixed Cost of Goods Sold	12,100
Variable Selling and Administrative Costs	11,500
Fixed Selling and Administrative Costs	6,400

**Learning Objectives 6, 7
Appendix 21A**

2. CM $46,640

Requirements

1. Calculate the gross profit and operating income for March using absorption costing.
2. Calculate the contribution margin and operating income for March using variable costing.

Use the following information for Exercises E21A-42 and E21A-43.

Organic, Inc. has collected the following data for November (there are no beginning inventories):

Units produced and sold	300 units
Sales price	$ 275 per unit
Direct materials	53 per unit
Direct labor	76 per unit
Variable manufacturing overhead	28 per unit
Fixed manufacturing overhead	4,350 per month
Variable selling and administrative costs	20 per unit
Fixed selling and administrative costs	4,675 per month

E21A-42 Computing absorption costing operating income

Refer to the information for Organic, Inc.

**Learning Objectives 6, 7
Appendix 21A**

1. $171.50

Requirements

1. Using absorption costing, calculate the unit product cost.
2. Prepare an income statement using the traditional format.

E21A-43 Computing variable costing operating income

Refer to the information for Organic, Inc.

**Learning Objectives 6, 7
Appendix 21A**

2. CM $29,400

Requirements

1. Using variable costing, calculate the unit product cost.
2. Prepare an income statement using the contribution margin format.

Learning Objectives 6, 7
Appendix 21A

2. FG $30,000

E21A-44 Preparing variable costing income statements, production exceeds sales

RefreshAde produced 15,000 cases of powdered drink mix and sold 12,000 cases in April 2016. The sales price was $30, variable costs were $13 per case ($10 manufacturing and $3 selling and administrative), and total fixed costs were $70,000 ($45,000 manufacturing overhead and $25,000 selling and administrative). The company had no beginning Finished Goods Inventory.

Requirements

1. Prepare the April income statement using variable costing.

2. Determine the product cost per unit and the total cost of the 3,000 cases in Finished Goods Inventory as of April 30.

Note: Exercise E21A-44 must be completed before attempting Exercise E21A-45.

Learning Objectives 6, 7
Appendix 21A

1. OI $143,000

E21A-45 Preparing absorption costing income statements, production exceeds sales

Refer to Exercise E21A-44.

Requirements

1. Prepare the April income statement using absorption costing.

2. Determine the product cost per unit and the total cost of the 3,000 cases in Finished Goods Inventory as of April 30.

3. Is the April 30 balance in Finished Goods Inventory higher or lower than variable costing? Explain why.

Note: Exercises E21A-44 and E21A-45 must be completed before attempting Exercise E21A-46.

Learning Objectives 6, 7
Appendix 21A

E21A-46 Comparing variable and absorption costing

Refer to Exercises E21A-44 and E21A-45.

Requirements

1. Which costing method produces the highest operating income? Explain why.

2. Which costing method produces the highest April 30 balance in Finished Goods Inventory? Explain why.

Note: Exercise E21A-44 must be completed before attempting Exercise E21A-47.

Learning Objectives 6, 7
Appendix 21A

1. CM $391,000

E21A-47 Preparing variable costing income statements, production less than sales

Refer to your answers to Exercise E21A-44. In May 2016, RefreshAde produced 20,000 cases of powdered drink mix and sold 23,000 cases, of which 3,000 were produced in April. The sales price was $30, variable costs were $13 per case ($10 manufacturing and $3 selling and administrative), and total fixed costs were $70,000 ($45,000 manufacturing and $25,000 selling and administrative).

Requirements

1. Prepare the May income statement using variable costing.

2. Determine the balance in Finished Goods Inventory as of May 31.

Note: Exercise E21A-47 must be completed before attempting Exercise E21A-48.

E21A-48 Preparing absorption costing income statements, production exceeds sales

Refer to Exercise E21A-47.

Learning Objectives 6, 7
Appendix 21A

1. OI $312,000

Requirements

1. Prepare the May income statement using absorption costing.

2. Is operating income using absorption costing higher or lower than variable costing income? Explain why.

3. Determine the balance in Finished Goods Inventory as of May 31.

> Problems Group A

P21-49A Calculating cost-volume-profit elements

The budgets of four companies yield the following information:

Learning Objectives 1, 2

	Company			
	Up	**Down**	**Left**	**Right**
Sales Revenue	$ 2,187,500	$ (d)	$ 375,000	$ (j)
Variable Costs	(a)	77,000	225,000	374,400
Fixed Costs	(b)	216,000	236,000	(k)
Operating Income (Loss)	256,700	(e)	(g)	85,400
Units Sold	125,000	14,000	(h)	(l)
Contribution Margin per Unit	$ 3.50	$ (f)	$ 75.00	$ 18.00
Contribution Margin Ratio	(c)	80%	(i)	20%

Requirements

1. Fill in the blanks for each missing value. (Round the contribution margin per unit to the nearest cent.)

2. Which company has the lowest breakeven point in sales dollars?

3. What causes the low breakeven point?

P21-50A Calculating break even sales and sales to earn a target profit; preparing a contribution margin income statement

British Productions performs London shows. The average show sells 1,000 tickets at $60 per ticket. There are 120 shows per year. No additional shows can be held as the theater is also used by other production companies. The average show has a cast of 60, each earning a net average of $320 per show. The cast is paid after each show. The other variable cost is a program-printing cost of $8 per guest. Annual fixed costs total $459,200.

Learning Objectives 1, 2, 3

4. CM $3,936,000

Requirements

1. Compute revenue and variable costs for each show.

2. Use the equation approach to compute the number of shows British Productions must perform each year to break even.

3. Use the contribution margin ratio approach to compute the number of shows needed each year to earn a profit of $4,264,000. Is this profit goal realistic? Give your reasoning.

4. Prepare British Productions's contribution margin income statement for 120 shows performed in 2016. Report only two categories of costs: variable and fixed.

Learning Objectives 2, 3, 4

2. 65.00%

P21-51A Analyzing CVP relationships

Kincaid Company sells flags with team logos. Kincaid has fixed costs of $639,600 per year plus variable costs of $4.20 per flag. Each flag sells for $12.00.

Requirements

1. Use the equation approach to compute the number of flags Kincaid must sell each year to break even.

2. Use the contribution margin ratio approach to compute the dollar sales Kincaid needs to earn $32,500 in operating income for 2016. (Round the contribution margin ratio to two decimal places.)

3. Prepare Kincaid's contribution margin income statement for the year ended December 31, 2016, for sales of 78,000 flags. (Round your final answers up to the next whole number.)

4. The company is considering an expansion that will increase fixed costs by 17% and variable costs by $0.60 per flag. Compute the new breakeven point in units and in dollars. Should Kincaid undertake the expansion? Give your reasoning. (Round your final answers up to the next whole number.)

Learning Objectives 2, 3, 4

1. 40 trades

P21-52A Computing breakeven sales and sales needed to earn a target profit; graphing CVP relationships; performing sensitivity analysis

American Investor Group is opening an office in Portland, Oregon. Fixed monthly costs are office rent ($8,000), depreciation on office furniture ($1,800), utilities ($2,200), special telephone lines ($1,100), a connection with an online brokerage service ($2,700), and the salary of a financial planner ($19,200). Variable costs include payments to the financial planner (9% of revenue), advertising (11% of revenue), supplies and postage (4% of revenue), and usage fees for the telephone lines and computerized brokerage service (6% of revenue).

Requirements

1. Use the contribution margin ratio approach to compute American's breakeven revenue in dollars. If the average trade leads to $1,250 in revenue for American, how many trades must be made to break even?

2. Use the equation approach to compute the dollar revenues needed to earn a monthly target profit of $14,000.

3. Graph American's CVP relationships. Assume that an average trade leads to $1,250 in revenue for American. Show the breakeven point, the sales revenue line, the fixed cost line, the total cost line, the operating loss area, the operating income area, and the sales in units (trades) and dollars when monthly operating income of $14,000 is earned.

4. Suppose that the average revenue American earns increases to $2,500 per trade. Compute the new breakeven point in trades. How does this affect the breakeven point?

P21-53A Calculating breakeven point for two products, margin of safety, and operating leverage

Learning Objectives 2, 4, 5

2. 12,000 dz. & 3,000 dz.

The contribution margin income statement of Krazy Kustard Donuts for August 2016 follows:

KRAZY KUSTARD DONUTS
Contribution Margin Income Statement
Month Ended August 31, 2016

Sales Revenue		$ 125,000
Variable Costs:		
Cost of Goods Sold	$ 32,100	
Selling Costs	17,100	
Administrative Costs	800	50,000
Contribution Margin		75,000
Fixed Costs:		
Selling Costs	32,400	
Administrative Costs	10,800	43,200
Operating Income		$ 31,800

Krazy Kustard sells four dozen plain donuts for every dozen custard-filled donuts. A dozen plain donuts sells for $4.00, with total variable cost of $1.60 per dozen. A dozen custard-filled donuts sells for $8.00, with total variable cost of $3.20 per dozen.

Requirements

1. Calculate the weighted-average contribution margin.
2. Determine Krazy Kustard's monthly breakeven point in dozens of plain donuts and custard-filled donuts. Prove your answer by preparing a summary contribution margin income statement at the breakeven level of sales. Show only two categories of costs: variable and fixed.
3. Compute Krazy Kustard's margin of safety in dollars for August 2016.
4. Compute the degree of operating leverage for Krazy Kustard Donuts. Estimate the new operating income if total sales increase by 40%. (Round the degree of operating leverage to four decimal places and the final answer to the nearest dollar. Assume the sales mix remains unchanged.)
5. Prove your answer to Requirement 4 by preparing a contribution margin income statement with a 40% increase in total sales. (The sales mix remains unchanged.)

Learning Objectives 6, 7
Appendix 21A

2b. VC $4,750

P21A-54A Preparing variable and absorption costing income statements

Gia's Foods produces frozen meals that it sells for $8 each. The company computes a new monthly fixed manufacturing overhead allocation rate based on the planned number of meals to be produced that month. Assume all costs and production levels are exactly as planned. The following data are from Gia's Foods's first month in business:

	January 2016
Units produced and sold:	
Sales	950 meals
Production	1,150 meals
Variable manufacturing cost per meal	$ 4
Sales commission cost per meal	1
Total fixed manufacturing overhead	690
Total fixed selling and administrative costs	700

Requirements

1. Compute the product cost per meal produced under absorption costing and under variable costing.

2. Prepare income statements for January 2016 using
   a. absorption costing.
   b. variable costing.

3. Is operating income higher under absorption costing or variable costing in January?

Learning Objectives 6, 7
Appendix 21A

1. Absorption costing $19.00

P21A-55A Preparing variable and absorption costing income statements

Game Play manufactures video games that it sells for $39 each. The company uses a fixed manufacturing overhead allocation rate of $6 per game. Assume all costs and production levels are exactly as planned. The following data are from Game Play's first two months in business during 2016:

	October	November
Sales	1,300 units	2,500 units
Production	2,300 units	2,300 units
Variable manufacturing cost per game	$ 13	$ 13
Sales commission cost per game	5	5
Total fixed manufacturing overhead	13,800	13,800
Total fixed selling and administrative costs	8,500	8,500

Requirements

1. Compute the product cost per game produced under absorption costing and under variable costing.

2. Prepare monthly income statements for October and November, including columns for each month and a total column, using these costing methods:
   a. absorption costing.
   b. variable costing.

3. Is operating income higher under absorption costing or variable costing in October? In November? Explain the pattern of differences in operating income based on absorption costing versus variable costing.

4. Determine the balance in Finished Goods Inventory on October 31 and November 30 under absorption costing and variable costing. Compare the differences in inventory balances and the differences in operating income. Explain the differences in inventory balances based on absorption costing versus variable costing.

> Problems **Group B**

P21-56B Calculating cost-volume-profit elements

Learning Objectives 1, 2

The budgets of four companies yield the following information:

	Beach	Lake	Mountain	Valley
			Company	
Sales Revenue	$ 1,531,250	$ (d)	$ 2,340,000	$ (j)
Variable Costs	(a)	79,750	1,872,000	275,600
Fixed Costs	(b)	160,000	112,000	(k)
Operating Income (Loss)	249,700	(e)	(g)	60,700
Units Sold	175,000	11,000	(h)	(l)
Contribution Margin per Unit	$ 3.50	$ (f)	$ 72.00	$ 13.00
Contribution Margin Ratio	(c)	80%	(i)	20%

Requirements

1. Fill in the blanks for each missing value. (Round the contribution margin to the nearest cent.)

2. Which company has the lowest breakeven point in sales dollars?

3. What causes the low breakeven point?

P21-57B Calculating breakeven sales and sales to earn a target profit; preparing a contribution margin income statement

Learning Objectives 1, 2, 3

3. CMR 55.13%

City Productions performs London shows. The average show sells 900 tickets at $65 per ticket. There are 140 shows a year. No additional shows can be held as the theater is also used by other production companies. The average show has a cast of 55, each earning a net average of $330 per show. The cast is paid after each show. The other variable cost is a program-printing cost of $9 per guest. Annual fixed costs total $580,500.

Requirements

1. Compute revenue and variable costs for each show.

2. Use the equation approach to compute the number of shows City Productions must perform each year to break even.

3. Use the contribution margin ratio approach to compute the number of shows needed each year to earn a profit of $4,128,000. Is this profit goal realistic? Give your reasoning.

4. Prepare City Productions's contribution margin income statement for 140 shows performed in 2016. Report only two categories of costs: variable and fixed.

Learning Objectives 2, 3, 4

3. Op. Inc. $(72,000)

P21-58B Analyzing CVP relationships

Allen Company sells flags with team logos. Allen has fixed costs of $583,200 per year plus variable costs of $4.80 per flag. Each flag sells for $12.00.

Requirements

1. Use the equation approach to compute the number of flags Allen must sell each year to break even.

2. Use the contribution margin ratio approach to compute the dollar sales Allen needs to earn $33,000 in operating income for 2016. (Round the contribution margin to two decimal places.)

3. Prepare Allen's contribution margin income statement for the year ended December 31, 2016, for sales of 71,000 flags. (Round your final answers up to the next whole number.)

4. The company is considering an expansion that will increase fixed costs by 21% and variable costs by $0.60 per flag. Compute the new breakeven point in units and in dollars. Should Allen undertake the expansion? Give your reasoning. (Round your final answers up to the next whole number.)

Learning Objectives 2, 3, 4

4. 25 trades

P21-59B Computing breakeven sales and sales needed to earn a target profit; graphing CVP relationships; performing sensitivity analysis

Big Time Investor Group is opening an office in Boise. Fixed monthly costs are office rent ($8,900), depreciation on office furniture ($2,000), utilities ($2,400), special telephone lines ($1,000), a connection with an online brokerage service ($2,800), and the salary of a financial planner ($17,900). Variable costs include payments to the financial planner (8% of revenue), advertising (13% of revenue), supplies and postage (3% of revenue), and usage fees for the telephone lines and computerized brokerage service (6% of revenue).

Requirements

1. Use the contribution margin ratio approach to compute Big Time's breakeven revenue in dollars. If the average trade leads to $1,000 in revenue for Big Time, how many trades must be made to break even?

2. Use the equation approach to compute the dollar revenues needed to earn a monthly target profit of $12,600.

3. Graph Big Time's CVP relationships. Assume that an average trade leads to $1,000 in revenue for Big Time. Show the breakeven point, the sales revenue line, the fixed cost line, the total cost line, the operating loss area, the operating income area, and the sales in units (trades) and dollars when monthly operating income of $12,600 is earned.

4. Suppose that the average revenue Big Time earns increases to $2,000 per trade. Compute the new breakeven point in trades. How does this affect the breakeven point?

P21A-60B Calculating breakeven point for two products, margin of safety, and operating leverage

The contribution margin income statement of Creative Donuts for May 2016 follows:

3. $81,000

CREATIVE DONUTS
Contribution Margin Income Statement
Month Ended May 31, 2016

Sales Revenue		$ 129,000
Variable Costs:		
Cost of Goods Sold	$ 32,300	
Selling Costs	17,200	
Administrative Costs	2,100	51,600
Contribution Margin		77,400
Fixed Costs:		
Selling Costs	21,600	
Administrative Costs	7,200	28,800
Operating Income		$ 48,600

Creative sells two dozen plain donuts for every dozen custard-filled donuts. A dozen plain donuts sells for $4.00, with a variable cost of $1.60 per dozen. A dozen custard-filled donuts sells for $8.00, with a variable cost of $3.20 per dozen.

Requirements

1. Calculate the weighted-average contribution margin.
2. Determine Creative's monthly breakeven point in dozens of plain donuts and custard-filled donuts. Prove your answer by preparing a summary contribution margin income statement at the breakeven level of sales. Show only two categories of costs: variable and fixed.
3. Compute Creative's margin of safety in dollars for May 2016.
4. Compute the degree of operating leverage for Creative Donuts. Estimate the new operating income if total sales increase by 40%. (Round the degree of operating leverage to four decimal places and the final answer to the nearest dollar. Assume the sales mix remains unchanged.)
5. Prove your answer to Requirement 4 by preparing a contribution margin income statement with a 40% increase in total sales. (The sales mix remains unchanged.)

Learning Objectives 6, 7
Appendix 21A

2a. OI $2,730

P21A-61B Preparing variable and absorption costing income statements

Viviana's Foods produces frozen meals that it sells for $11 each. The company computes a new monthly fixed manufacturing overhead allocation rate based on the planned number of meals to be produced that month. Assume all costs and production levels are exactly as planned. The following data are from Viviana's Foods's first month in business:

	January 2016
Units produced and sold:	
Sales	800 meals
Production	1,000 meals
Variable manufacturing cost per meal	$ 5
Sales commission cost per meal	1
Total fixed manufacturing overhead	650
Total fixed selling and administrative costs	750

Requirements

1. Compute the product cost per meal produced under absorption costing and under variable costing.

2. Prepare income statements for January 2016 using
   a. absorption costing.
   b. variable costing.

3. Is operating income higher under absorption costing or variable costing in January?

Learning Objectives 6, 7
Appendix 21A

2b. CM for Nov. $66,700

P21A-62B Preparing variable and absorption costing income statements

Game Depot manufactures video games that it sells for $45 each. The company uses a fixed manufacturing overhead allocation rate of $3 per game. Assume all costs and production levels are exactly as planned. The following data are from Game Depot's first two months in business during 2016:

	October	November
Sales	1,200 units	2,900 units
Production	2,700 units	2,700 units
Variable manufacturing cost per game	$ 15	$ 15
Sales commission cost per game	7	7
Total fixed manufacturing overhead	8,100	8,100
Total fixed selling and administrative costs	8,000	8,000

Requirements

1. Compute the product cost per game produced under absorption costing and under variable costing.

2. Prepare monthly income statements for October and November, including columns for each month and a total column, using these costing methods:
   a. absorption costing.
   b. variable costing.

3. Is operating income higher under absorption costing or variable costing in October? In November? Explain the pattern of differences in operating income based on absorption costing versus variable costing.

4. Determine the balance in Finished Goods Inventory on October 31 and November 30 under absorption costing and variable costing. Compare the differences in inventory balances and the differences in operating income. Explain the differences in inventory balances based on absorption costing versus variable costing.

> Continuing Problem

P21-63 Computing breakeven sales and sales needed to earn a target profit; performing sensitivity analysis

This problem continues the Daniels Consulting situation from Problem P19-40 of Chapter 19. Daniels Consulting provides consulting service at an average price of $120 per hour and incurs variable cost of $60 per hour. Assume average fixed costs are $3,900 a month.

Requirements

1. What is the number of hours that must be billed to reach the breakeven point?

2. If Daniels desires to make a profit of $4,500, how many consulting hours must be completed?

3. Daniels thinks it can reduce fixed cost to $3,190 per month, but variable cost will increase to $62 per hour. What is the new breakeven point in hours?

COMPREHENSIVE PROBLEM

> Comprehensive Problem for Chapters 18–21

The Savannah Shirt Company makes two types of T-shirts: basic and custom. Basic shirts are plain shirts without any screen printing on them. Custom shirts are created using the basic shirts and then adding a custom screen printing design.

The company buys cloth in various colors and then makes the basic shirts in two departments, Cutting and Sewing. The company uses a process costing system (weighted-average method) to determine the production cost of the basic shirts. In the Cutting Department, direct materials (cloth) are added at the beginning of the process and conversion costs are added evenly through the process. In the Sewing Department, no direct materials are added. The only additional material, thread, is considered an indirect material because it cannot be easily traced to the finished product. Conversion costs are added evenly throughout the process in the Sewing Department. The finished basic shirts are sold to retail stores or are sent to the Custom Design Department for custom screen printing.

The Custom Design Department creates custom shirts by adding screen printing to the basic shirt. The department creates a design based on the customer's request and then prints the design using up to four colors. Because these shirts have the custom printing added, which is unique for each order, the additional cost incurred is determined using job order costing, with each custom order considered a separate job.

For March 2016, the Savannah Shirt Company compiled the following data for the Cutting and Sewing Departments:

Department	Item	Amount	Units
Cutting	Beginning balance	$ 0	0 shirts
	Started in March		1,500 shirts
	Direct materials added in March	4,905	
	Conversion costs	2,445	
	Completed and transferred to Sewing	???	1,500 shirts
	Ending balance	0	0 shirts
Sewing	Beginning balance, transferred in, $1,225; conversion costs, $300	1,525	250 shirts
	Transferred in from Cutting	???	???
	Conversion costs added in March	$ 1,650	
	Completed and transferred to Finished Goods	???	1,250 shirts
	Ending balance, 75% complete	???	???

For the same time period, the Savannah Shirt Company compiled the following data for the Custom Design Department:

Job	Quantity	Design Fee	Printing	Status
367	50	Yes	4 colors	Complete
368	250	No	2 colors	Complete
369	150	Yes	3 colors	Complete
370	100	Yes	2 colors	Complete

The Savannah Shirt Company has previously determined that creating and programming the design cost $75 per design. This is a one-time charge. If a customer places another order with the same design, the customer is not charged a second time. Additionally, the cost to print is $0.50 per color per shirt.

Requirements

1. Complete a production cost report for the Cutting Department and the Sewing Department. What is the cost of one basic shirt?

2. Determine the total cost and the average cost per shirt for jobs 367, 368, 369, and 370. If the company set the sales price at 160% of the total cost, determine the total sales price of each job.

3. In addition to the custom jobs, the Savannah Shirt Company sold 1,250 basic shirts (assume the beginning balance in Finished Goods Inventory is sufficient to make these sales, and the unit cost of the basic shirts in Finished Goods Inventory is the same as the unit cost incurred this month). If the company set the sales price at 140% of the cost, determine the sales price per unit, total sales revenue, and the total cost of goods sold for the basic shirts.

4. Calculate the total revenue and total cost of goods sold for all sales, basic and custom.

5. Assume the company sold only basic shirts (no custom designs) and incurred fixed costs of $1,403 per month.

   a. Calculate the contribution margin per unit, contribution margin ratio, required sales in units to break even, and required sales in dollars to break even.
   b. Determine the margin of safety in units and dollars.
   c. Graph Savannah Shirt Company's CVP relationships. Show the breakeven point, the sales revenue line, the fixed cost line, the total cost line, the operating loss area, and the operating income area.
   d. Suppose the Savannah Shirt Company wants to earn an operating income of $4,100 per month. Compute the required sales in units and dollars to achieve this profit goal.

6. The Savannah Shirt Company is considering adding a new product line, a cloth shopping bag with custom screen printing that will be sold to grocery stores. If the current market price of cloth shopping bags is $1.25 and the company desires a net profit of 40%, what is the target cost? The company estimates the full product cost of the cloth bags will be $0.60. Should the company manufacture the cloth bags? Why or why not?

CRITICAL THINKING

> Decision Case 21-1

Steve and Linda Hom live in Bartlesville, Oklahoma. Two years ago, they visited Thailand. Linda, a professional chef, was impressed with the cooking methods and the spices used in Thai food. Bartlesville does not have a Thai restaurant, and the Homs are contemplating opening one. Linda would supervise the cooking, and Steve would leave his current job to be the maître d'. The restaurant would serve dinner Tuesday through Saturday.

Steve has noticed a restaurant for lease. The restaurant has seven tables, each of which can seat four. Tables can be moved together for a large party. Linda is planning two seatings per evening, and the restaurant will be open 50 weeks per year.

The Homs have drawn up the following estimates:

Average revenue, including beverages and desserts	$ 45 per meal
Average cost of food	15 per meal
Chef's and dishwasher's salaries	5,100 per month
Rent (premises, equipment)	4,000 per month
Cleaning (linen, premises)	800 per month
Replacement of dishes, cutlery, glasses	300 per month
Utilities, advertising, telephone	2,300 per month

Requirements

1. Compute the *annual* breakeven number of meals and sales revenue for the restaurant.

2. Compute the number of meals and the amount of sales revenue needed to earn operating income of $75,600 for the year.

3. How many meals must the Homs serve each night to earn their target profit of $75,600?

4. What factors should the Homs consider before they make their decision as to whether to open the restaurant?

> Ethical Issue 21-1

You have just begun your summer internship at Omni Instruments. The company supplies sterilized surgical instruments for physicians. To expand sales, Omni is considering paying a commission to its sales force. The controller, Matthew Barnhill, asks you to compute: (1) the new breakeven sales figure, and (2) the operating profit if sales increase 15% under the new sales commission plan. He thinks you can handle this task because you learned CVP analysis in your accounting class.

You spend the next day collecting information from the accounting records, performing the analysis, and writing a memo to explain the results. The company president is pleased with your memo. You report that the new sales commission plan will lead to a significant increase in operating income and only a small increase in breakeven sales.

The following week, you realize that you made an error in the CVP analysis. You overlooked the sales personnel's $2,800 monthly salaries, and you did not include this fixed selling cost in your computations. You are not sure what to do. If you tell Matthew Barnhill of your mistake, he will have to tell the president. In this case, you are afraid Omni might not offer you permanent employment after your internship.

Requirements

1. How would your error affect breakeven sales and operating income under the proposed sales commission plan? Could this cause the president to reject the sales commission proposal?

2. Consider your ethical responsibilities. Is there a difference between: (a) initially making an error and (b) subsequently failing to inform the controller?

3. Suppose you tell Matthew Barnhill of the error in your analysis. Why might the consequences not be as bad as you fear? Should Barnhill take any responsibility for your error? What could Barnhill have done differently?

4. After considering all the factors, should you inform Barnhill or simply keep quiet?

> Team Project 21-1

Select a nearby company. Arrange an interview for your team with a managerial accountant, a controller, or another accounting/finance officer of the company.

Requirements

Before your team conducts the interview, research the company and answer the following questions:

1. Is this a service, merchandising, or manufacturing company? What is its primary product or service?

2. What are some possible fixed costs this company incurs?

3. What are some possible variable costs this company incurs?

4. Select one of the company's products or services. Estimate the unit contribution margin for the product or service.

At the interview, ask the above questions and compare your team's answers to the company's answers. Then ask the following questions:

5. How does the company determine the sales prices of products and services?

6. What is the company's cost structure? Does the company have relatively high or low fixed costs?

7. What is the company's sales mix? Has the sales mix changed recently? If so, what caused the change?

Your team should summarize your findings in a short paper. Provide any exhibits that enhance your explanations. Provide proper references and a works cited page.

MyAccountingLab   **For a wealth of online resources, including exercises, problems, media, and immediate tutorial help, please visit http://www.myaccountinglab.com.**

> Quick Check Answers

1. b **2.** a **3.** c **4.** d **5.** d **6.** b **7.** b **8.** c **9.** b **10.** d **11A.** a **12A.** a

22 Master Budgets

How Can a Budget Help My Division?

Hanna Kendall sat down at her desk with anticipation. Hanna, the newly promoted manager of her division at B&T Manufacturing, was ready to begin preparing the budget for the next year. At the last B&T division managers' meeting, most of the other managers were grumbling about the process. No one else seemed to like the task, but Hanna felt differently. She remembered from her managerial accounting class that budgeting can have many benefits. When used appropriately, budgets help managers plan and control activities for their divisions by providing guidance and benchmarks for the budgeting period. Hanna considered the budget to be a road map of sorts for her division—a way to know the direction in which the division should

progress and a way to determine whether the division met its goals.

Hanna considered how to begin the process. She knew she needed to study last year's budget prepared by the previous manager, compare it to actual results to see which goals had been met, and consider outside influences such as the economic conditions for B&T's industry. Hanna also wanted to get input from her employees to ensure the goals set for the division were realistic, obtainable, and a source of motivation. Hanna had seen budgets used to punish employees when budget goals were set at an unobtainable level, but she was not that type of manager. Hanna wanted high morale in her division, with everyone working toward the same goals.

What Is a Budget?

A *budget* is a financial plan that managers use to coordinate the business's activities. All types of companies can benefit from using budgets, including service companies such as National HealthCare Corporation (NHC), which provides medical care; merchandising companies such as CVS Caremark Corporation (CVS), which sells medicines and medical supplies; and manufacturing companies such as Abbott Laboratories, which manufactures pharmaceutical products. There are many different types of budgets. Some are for short-term use, and others are for long-term use. Budgets help managers plan for the future, track the progress of their business segments, and take corrective action as needed. Budgeting is an extremely important management tool. In this chapter, we focus on the purposes and types of budgets and the development of one type of budget—the master budget. In later chapters, we focus on how managers can use budgets to control business activities.

Chapter 22 Learning Objectives

1   Describe budgeting objectives, benefits, and procedures and how human behavior influences budgeting

2   Define budget types and the components of the master budget

3   Prepare an operating budget for a manufacturing company

4   Prepare a financial budget for a manufacturing company

5   Describe how information technology can be used in the budgeting process

6   Prepare an operating budget for a merchandising company (Appendix 22A)

7   Prepare a financial budget for a merchandising company (Appendix 22A)

WHY DO MANAGERS USE BUDGETS?

The concept of budgeting is familiar. Financial decisions, large and small, require some planning. For example, as you decide whether to rent an apartment or buy a house, repair your older vehicle or buy a new one, cook at home or eat out, you are considering your financial situation. Perhaps you decide to cook at home in order to save for a down payment on a house, which indicates you have a financial plan to use to meet goals. For many people, however, budgeting is not a formal process where plans are written and carefully followed. This failure to formalize the plans often results in a failure to achieve financial goals.

Companies use budgets for the same reasons as you do in your personal life—to plan and control actions and the related revenues and expenses.

Learning Objective 1

Describe budgeting objectives, benefits, and procedures and how human behavior influences budgeting

Budgeting Objectives

A **budget** is a financial plan that managers use to coordinate a business's activities. Managers use budgets in fulfilling their major responsibilities. First, they develop strategies—overall business goals, such as a goal to expand international operations or a goal to be a value leader in one market while diversifying into other markets. Companies then plan and budget for specific actions to achieve those goals. The next step is to act—to carry out the plans.

After acting, managers compare actual results with the budget and use the information to make control decisions. The feedback allows them to determine what, if any, corrective action to take. If, for example, the company spent more than expected in one area of operations, managers must cut other costs or increase revenues. These decisions then affect the company's future strategies and plans.

Exhibit 22-1 (on the next page) illustrates the process of developing strategies, planning, acting, and controlling. Notice that the process is a loop—the control step is not an end, but an input into the develop strategies step. Successful companies use current period results to help make decisions regarding the company's future.

Budget
A financial plan that managers use to coordinate a business's activities.

Budgeting Benefits

Budgeting requires managers to plan, promotes coordination and communication, and provides a benchmark for evaluating actual performance. The budget really represents the plan the company has in place to achieve its goals.

Exhibit 22-1 | **Budgeting Objectives**

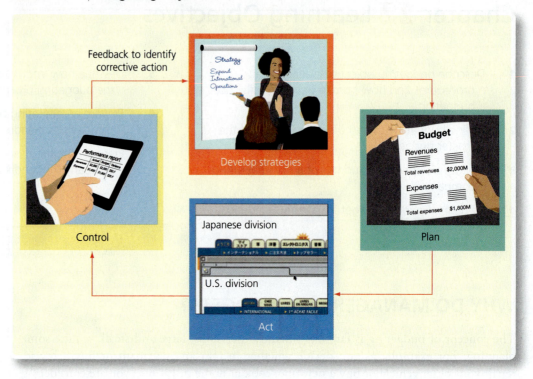

Planning

Budgeting requires managers to plan for the company's future. Decisions are then based on this formalized plan, which helps prevent haphazard decision making. For example, if the company plans to expand into a new market, the budget will include expected funding sources and expenditures for the expansion. Keep in mind, however, that budgets are plans for future activities and may need to be modified. If a company learns of a revenue shortfall, where actual revenues earned are less than budgeted revenues, the company has to modify its plan and devise strategies to increase revenues or cut expenses so the company can achieve its planned goals. The better the plan and the more time the company has to act on the plan, the more likely it will be to find a way to meet the target.

Coordination and Communication

The budget coordinates a company's activities. Creating a budget facilitates coordination and communication by requiring managers at different levels and in different functions across the entire value chain to work together to make a single, unified, comprehensive plan for the business. For example, a company stimulates sales by offering free shipping on orders over a specified dollar amount. If sales increase, the shipping department may have to hire additional employees to handle the increase in shipments. The budget encourages communication among managers to ensure that the extra profits from increased sales outweigh the revenue lost from not charging for shipping.

Benchmarking

Budgets provide a benchmark that motivates employees and helps managers evaluate performance. In most companies, part of the manager's performance evaluation depends on how actual results compare to the budget. Exhibit 22-2 illustrates a performance report for a service company.

Exhibit 22-2 | **Performance Report**

SERVICE COMPANY Income Statement Performance Report For the Month Ended May 31, 2018			
	Actual	**Budget**	**Variance**
Number of services sold	19,000	20,000	(1,000)
Service Revenue	$ 589,000	$ 600,000	$ (11,000)
Variable Expenses:			
Server Space Expense	38,000	45,000	7,000
Commissions Expense	29,450	30,000	550
Total Variable Expenses	67,450	75,000	7,550
Contribution Margin	521,550	525,000	(3,450)
Fixed Expenses:			
Salary Expenses	20,000	20,000	0
Internet Access Expense	18,000	18,000	0
Total Fixed Expenses	38,000	38,000	0
Operating Income	$ 483,550	$ 487,000	$ (3,450)

This report identifies variances—the areas where the actual results differed from the budget. The differences are itemized below:

1. Actual Service Revenue was $11,000 less than budgeted Service Revenue. This was caused by two factors. The company was able to sell at a higher average price per service, $31 per service ($589,000 / 19,000 services), than the $30 per service it planned ($600,000 / 20,000 services). However, the company sold 1,000 fewer services than it planned to sell (19,000 actual services − 20,000 budgeted services). The increase in price per service was not enough to make up for the decrease in the number of services sold.

2. Variable expenses were less than budgeted for both Server Space Expense and Advertising Expense, which creates two favorable variances. Actual Server Space Expense was less than budgeted Server Space Expense because the company sold 1,000 fewer services and because the company reduced the Server Space Expense per service from $2.25 per budgeted service ($45,000 / 20,000 services) to $2.00 per actual service ($38,000 / 19,000 services). Commissions Expense remained constant at 5% of revenues, but due to the $11,000 reduction in revenues, Commissions Expense was $550 less ($11,000 × 5%).

3. Actual fixed expenses were exactly the same as budgeted fixed expenses. Considering this company's fixed expenses, one wouldn't expect these to change unless the company changed the pay rate, number of employees, or negotiated a new contract with its Internet service provider.

After management reviews the variances, the company will want to consider how it can implement new strategies to meet its goals. Can the company increase the number of services sold at the new higher price? Should the company increase its advertising budget in hopes of increasing the number of services sold? Can the company reduce any of its fixed expenses? This type of analysis is covered in greater detail in the next chapter. This chapter concentrates on the development of the budget.

Budgeting Procedures

The budgeting process varies from company to company. For a small company, the process may be relatively simple and somewhat informal. In larger companies, however, the process can be very complex, with a budget committee coordinating the process. To achieve the benefit of motivating employees, the budget should include input from all levels. This requires significant coordination among the company's various business segments. Therefore, the budgeting process usually begins several months before the beginning of the budget period.

Budgeting and Human Behavior

What is the most important part of a budgeting system? It is getting managers and employees to accept the budget so the company can reap the planning, coordination, and control benefits illustrated in Exhibit 22-1.

Few people enjoy having their work monitored and evaluated. If managers use the budget as a benchmark to evaluate employees' performance, managers must first motivate employees to accept the budget's goals. Here is how they can do it:

- Managers must support the budget themselves, or no one else will.
- Managers must show employees how budgets can help them achieve better results.
- Managers must have employees participate in developing the budget so that employees feel the goals are realistic and achievable.

Budgetary Slack
Occurs when managers intentionally understate expected revenues or overstate expected expenses to increase the chances of receiving favorable performance evaluations.

Managers' performance is also evaluated by comparing actual results to the budget. When they develop the company's budget, they may be tempted to participate in budgetary "gaming" and build in budgetary slack. **Budgetary slack** occurs when managers intentionally understate expected revenues or overstate expected expenses. For example, managers might want to budget fewer sales and higher expenses than they expect. This increases the chance that their actual performance will be better than the budget and then they will receive a good evaluation. But adding slack into the budget makes it less accurate—and less useful for planning and control.

Another budgetary game is referred to as *spend it or lose it*. In many companies, if a business segment has a budgeted expense item and does not spend as much as expected for the item, there is a fear the budgeted item will have a lower amount in future budget periods. For example, if the Accounts Payable Department budget allows for $5,000 in Supplies Expense and the department only spends $3,000, then there is a fear the amount will be reduced to $3,000 in the next budget. The employees are then motivated to purchase unneeded supplies, which reduces the operating income for the company.

Try It!

Match the following statements to the appropriate budgeting objective or benefit: developing strategies, planning, acting, controlling, coordinating and communicating, and benchmarking.

1. Managers are required to think about future business activities.
2. Managers use feedback to identify corrective action.
3. Managers use results to evaluate employees' performance.
4. Managers work with managers in other divisions.

Check your answers online in MyAccountingLab or at http://www.pearsonhighered.com/Horngren.

For more practice, see Short Exercise S22-1. **MyAccountingLab**

ETHICS

Do I have to tell my manager?

Lugo Pryor is a sales representative at Rutherford, Inc. Lugo has a reputation of always being able to exceed the sales goal set by his manager, and exceeding the sales goal results in a year-end bonus. Lugo has just received a verbal commitment from a customer for a large order to be processed in the new year. Rutherford has not yet received a purchase order from the customer, but when it arrives, it will increase Lugo's sales by approximately 10% for the year. Lugo has also received the proposed budget for the new year from his manager. Because the purchase order has not been processed, the proposed budget does not include this new order. Lugo smiles. If he can get the budget approved before the purchase order is processed, he will certainly exceed his sales goal for the next year and earn a sizable year-end bonus. Should Lugo tell his manager about the order? What would you do?

Solution

Lugo should tell his manager about the order. Budgets are used for planning decisions. Failure to let the company know about an order of this size could have negative repercussions if the production department is caught off guard and the order cannot be delivered as promised. Also, Lugo's credibility may be compromised when the truth about the order is revealed and his manager discovers the budgeting game Lugo is playing.

ARE THERE DIFFERENT TYPES OF BUDGETS?

There are many different purposes for budgeting; therefore, there are many different types of budgets. Let's look at some different types.

Learning Objective 2
Define budget types and the components of the master budget

Strategic and Operational Budgets

The term *strategic* generally indicates a long-term goal. A company will develop strategies such as becoming the cost leader in a particular market or expanding into international markets. It may take several years to achieve these goals. A **strategic budget** is a long-term financial plan used to coordinate the activities needed to achieve the long-term goals of the company. Strategic budgets often span three to 10 years. Because of their longevity, they often are not as detailed as budgets for shorter periods.

The term *operational* generally indicates a short-term goal. After the company develops strategies and creates a strategic budget, the next step is to plan for shorter periods. An **operational budget** is a short-term financial plan used to coordinate the activities needed to achieve the short-term goals of the company. Operational budgets are most often one year in length but may also span only a week, a month, or a quarter, depending on the company's needs. Operational budgets are generally much more detailed than strategic budgets.

Strategic Budget
A long-term financial plan used to coordinate the activities needed to achieve the long-term goals of the company.

Operational Budget
A short-term financial plan used to coordinate the activities needed to achieve the short-term goals of the company.

Static and Flexible Budgets

A **static budget** is a budget prepared for only one level of sales volume. For example, Smart Touch Learning, the fictitious company we have used to illustrate accounting concepts throughout the textbook, may prepare a budget based on annual sales of 2,000 touch screen tablet computers. All revenue and expense calculations would be based on sales of 2,000 tablets.

A **flexible budget** is a budget prepared for various levels of sales volume. This type of budget is useful for *what if* analysis. Smart Touch Learning may expect to sell 2,000 tablet computers, but a flexible budget showing results for selling 1,600 tablets, 1,800 tablets, 2,000 tablets, 2,200 tablets, and 2,400 tablets allows managers to plan for various sales levels. Flexible budgets are covered in detail in the next chapter.

Static Budget
A budget prepared for only one level of sales volume.

Flexible Budget
A budget prepared for various levels of sales volume.

Master Budgets

Master Budget
The set of budgeted financial statements and supporting schedules for the entire organization; includes the operating budget, capital expenditures budget, and financial budget.

The **master budget** is the set of budgeted financial statements and supporting schedules for the entire organization. Budgeted financial statements are financial statements based on budgeted amounts rather than actual amounts. The master budget is operational and static. Exhibit 22-3 shows the order in which managers prepare the components of the master budget for a manufacturing company such as Smart Touch Learning.

Exhibit 22-3 | **Master Budget Components**

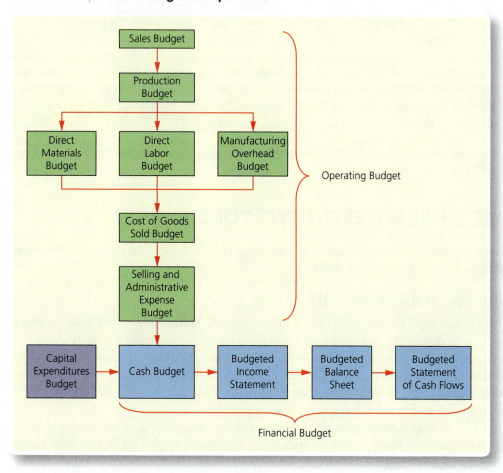

The exhibit shows that the master budget includes three types of budgets:

1. The operating budget
2. The capital expenditures budget
3. The financial budget

> Note the difference between the terms *operational* budget and *operating* budget. The operational budget is a general term referring to a budget length (short-term, one year or less), whereas the operating budget is a specific part of the master budget.

Operating Budget
The set of budgets that projects sales revenue, cost of goods sold, and selling and administrative expenses, all of which feed into the cash budget and then the budgeted financial statements.

The **operating budget** is the set of budgets that projects sales revenue, cost of goods sold, and selling and administrative expenses, all of which feed into the cash budget and then the budgeted financial statements. The first component of the operating budget is the sales budget, the cornerstone of the master budget. Why? Because sales affect most other components of the master budget. The company should not produce products it does not expect to sell. Additionally, variable product and period costs are projected based on sales and production levels. Therefore, the sales budget is the first step in developing the master budget.

The second type of budget is the **capital expenditures budget**. This budget presents the company's plan for purchasing property, plant, equipment, and other long-term assets.

The third type of budget is the financial budget. The **financial budget** includes the cash budget and the budgeted financial statements. Prior components of the master budget provide information for the first element of the financial budget: the cash budget. The **cash budget** details how the business expects to go from the beginning cash balance to the desired ending cash balance and feeds into the budgeted financial statements. These budgeted financial statements look exactly like ordinary financial statements. The only difference is that they list budgeted (projected) amounts rather than actual amounts.

In creating the master budget, managers must think carefully about pricing, product lines, job assignments, needs for additional equipment, and negotiations with banks. Successful managers use this opportunity to make decisions that affect the future course of business.

Capital Expenditures Budget
The budget that presents the company's plan for purchasing property, plant, equipment, and other long-term assets.

Financial Budget
The budget that includes the cash budget and the budgeted financial statements.

Cash Budget
The budget that details how the business expects to go from the beginning cash balance to the desired ending cash balance.

Match the budget types to the definitions.

Budget Types	Definitions
5. Financial	a. Includes sales, production, and cost of goods sold budgets
6. Flexible	b. Long-term budgets
7. Operating	c. Includes only one level of sales volume
8. Operational	d. Includes various levels of sales volumes
9. Static	e. Short-term budgets
10. Strategic	f. Includes the budgeted financial statements

Check your answers online in MyAccountingLab or at http://www.pearsonhighered.com/Horngren.

For more practice, see Short Exercise S22-2. MyAccountingLab

HOW ARE OPERATING BUDGETS PREPARED FOR A MANUFACTURING COMPANY?

To illustrate the preparation of the master budget, we use the fictitious company Smart Touch Learning. As you recall, the company manufactures its own brand of touch screen tablet computers that are preloaded with the company's e-learning software. The master budget is for 2019, prepared by quarter. The balance sheet for December 31, 2018, as shown in Exhibit 22-4 (on the next page), provides some of the data we use in preparing the master budget.

Learning Objective 3
Prepare an operating budget for a manufacturing company

Exhibit 22-4 | Balance Sheet

SMART TOUCH LEARNING Balance Sheet December 31, 2018		
Assets		
Current Assets:		
Cash	$ 15,000	
Accounts Receivable	70,000	
Raw Materials Inventory	30,000	
Finished Goods Inventory	55,000	
Total Current Assets		$ 170,000
Property, Plant, and Equipment:		
Equipment	210,340	
Less: Accumulated Depreciation	(12,000)	198,340
Total Assets		$ 368,340
Liabilities		
Current Liabilities:		
Accounts Payable		$ 20,000
Stockholders' Equity		
Common Stock, no par	$ 300,000	
Retained Earnings	48,340	
Total Stockholders' Equity		348,340
Total Liabilities and Stockholders' Equity		$ 368,340

Sales Budget

The forecast of sales revenue is the cornerstone of the master budget because the level of sales affects expenses and almost all other elements of the master budget. Budgeted total sales for each product equal the sales price multiplied by the expected number of units sold. The sales and marketing teams at Smart Touch Learning project that the company will sell 500 tablet computers in the first quarter of 2019, with sales increasing by 50 tablets each quarter. The tablets sell for $500 each. Exhibit 22-5 shows the sales budget for Smart Touch Learning for 2019. The total sales for the year will be carried to the budgeted income statement.

Exhibit 22-5 | Sales Budget

SMART TOUCH LEARNING Sales Budget For the Year Ended December 31, 2019					
	First Quarter	Second Quarter	Third Quarter	Fourth Quarter	Total
Budgeted tablets to be sold	500	550	600	650	2,300
Sales price per unit	× $500	× $500	× $500	× $500	× $500
Total sales	$ 250,000	$ 275,000	$ 300,000	$ 325,000	$ 1,150,000

Production Budget

The production budget determines the number of tablets to be produced during the year and is the basis for the production costs budgets: direct materials budget, direct labor budget, and manufacturing overhead budget. Additionally, the information is used to complete the cost of goods sold budget.

To calculate the number of tablets to be produced, start with the number of tablets projected to be sold. Add to this amount the desired number of tablets for ending Finished Goods Inventory to calculate the total number of tablets needed. Keep in mind that Smart Touch Learning does not want to end the period with zero inventory; it wants to have enough tablets on hand to begin the next period. The company should have the minimum amount of inventory to be sure the company balances providing goods to customers with turning over the inventory efficiently. Keeping inventory at the minimum level that meets these needs helps reduce inventory storage costs, insurance costs, and warehousing costs, and it reduces the potential for inventory to become obsolete.

After determining the number of tablets needed, subtract the number of tablets already on hand in beginning Finished Goods Inventory. The difference is the number of tablets to be produced. The calculation can be summarized as follows:

> Budgeted tablets to be sold
> + Desired tablets in ending inventory
> Total tablets needed
> − Tablets in beginning inventory
> Budgeted tablets to be produced

The December 31, 2018, balance sheet for Smart Touch Learning shown in Exhibit 22-4 indicates the Finished Goods Inventory account has a balance of $55,000, which consists of 200 tablets at a cost of $275 each. The company desires to have an ending inventory each quarter equal to 20% of the next quarter's sales. Assume the projected number of tablets to be sold during the first quarter of 2020 is 700, 50 more than fourth quarter 2019. Following are the calculations for desired ending inventory:

> First Quarter: Second quarter's sales × 20% = Desired ending inventory
> 550 tablets × 20% = 110 tablets
>
> Second Quarter: Third quarter's sales × 20% = Desired ending inventory
> 600 tablets × 20% = 120 tablets
>
> Third Quarter: Fourth quarter's sales × 20% = Desired ending inventory
> 650 tablets × 20% = 130 tablets
>
> Fourth Quarter: First quarter's sales (2020) × 20% = Desired ending inventory
> 700 tablets × 20% = 140 tablets

Exhibit 22-6 illustrates the production budget for Smart Touch Learning.

Exhibit 22-6 | Production Budget

SMART TOUCH LEARNING Production Budget For the Year Ended December 31, 2019					
	First Quarter	Second Quarter	Third Quarter	Fourth Quarter	Total
Budgeted tablets to be sold	500	550	600	650	2,300
Plus: Desired tablets in ending inventory	110	120	130	140	140
Total tablets needed	610	670	730	790	2,440
Less: Tablets in beginning inventory	200	110	120	130	200
Budgeted tablets to be produced	410	560	610	660	2,240

Don't forget that one period's ending inventory becomes the next period's beginning inventory.

Direct Materials Budget

Smart Touch Learning has determined the number of tablets to be produced each quarter. The next step is to determine the product costs for the tablets, beginning with direct materials costs. The purchasing department has projected that the cost of direct materials is $150 per unit. The company now needs to determine the amount of materials to purchase each quarter. The amount of indirect materials needed for the production of tablet computers has been determined to be insignificant and will therefore not be considered in the calculation. That means that the amount of materials in the Raw Materials Inventory account is assumed to be only direct materials.

Just as the Finished Goods Inventory account must be considered when calculating the amount of tablets to produce, the Raw Materials Inventory account must be considered when calculating the amount of materials to be purchased. The formula is:

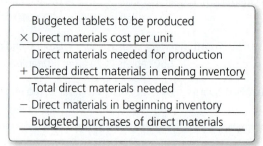

```
    Budgeted tablets to be produced
  × Direct materials cost per unit
    ─────────────────────────────────
    Direct materials needed for production
  + Desired direct materials in ending inventory
    ─────────────────────────────────
    Total direct materials needed
  − Direct materials in beginning inventory
    ─────────────────────────────────
    Budgeted purchases of direct materials
```

The December 31, 2018, balance shown in Exhibit 22-4 places the Raw Materials Inventory balance at $30,000. The company desires the ending balance in Raw Materials

Inventory to be 40% of the next quarter's budgeted production. The desired ending balance for the fourth quarter is $42,600. Following are the calculations for desired ending inventory:

First Quarter: 2nd quarter's production × $150 per unit × 40% = Desired ending inventory
560 tablets × $150 per unit × 40% = $33,600

Second Quarter: 3rd quarter's production × $150 per unit × 40% = Desired ending inventory
610 tablets × $150 per unit × 40% = $36,600

Third Quarter: 4th quarter's production × $150 per unit × 40% = Desired ending inventory
660 tablets × $150 per unit × 40% = $39,600

Fourth Quarter: Amount given   Desired ending inventory
$42,600

Exhibit 22-7 illustrates the direct materials budget for Smart Touch Learning.

Exhibit 22-7 | **Direct Materials Budget**

SMART TOUCH LEARNING Direct Materials Budget For the Year Ended December 31, 2019					
	First Quarter	Second Quarter	Third Quarter	Fourth Quarter	Total
Budgeted tablets to be produced	410	560	610	660	2,240
Direct materials cost per unit	× $150	× $150	× $150	× $150	× $150
Direct materials needed for production	$ 61,500	$ 84,000	$ 91,500	$ 99,000	$ 336,000
Plus: Desired direct materials in ending inventory	33,600	36,600	39,600	42,600	42,600
Total direct materials needed	95,100	120,600	131,100	141,600	378,600
Less: Direct materials in beginning inventory	30,000	33,600	36,600	39,600	30,000
Budgeted purchases of direct materials	$ 65,100	$ 87,000	$ 94,500	$ 102,000	$ 348,600

Direct Labor Budget

The next product cost to consider is direct labor. The production manager projects that each tablet computer will require three hours of direct labor. The personnel manager projects direct labor costs to average $25 per hour. To calculate the direct labor cost, multiply the number of tablets to be produced by the number of projected direct labor hours. Then multiply that total by the average direct cost per hour. Exhibit 22-8 (on the next page) shows the direct labor budget for Smart Touch Learning for 2019.

Exhibit 22-8 | **Direct Labor Budget**

	First Quarter	Second Quarter	Third Quarter	Fourth Quarter	Total
SMART TOUCH LEARNING					
Direct Labor Budget					
For the Year Ended December 31, 2019					
Budgeted tablets to be produced	410	560	610	660	2,240
Direct labor hours per unit	× 3	× 3	× 3	× 3	× 3
Direct labor hours needed for production	1,230	1,680	1,830	1,980	6,720
Direct labor cost per hour	× $25	× $25	× $25	× $25	× $25
Budgeted direct labor cost	$ 30,750	$ 42,000	$ 45,750	$ 49,500	$ 168,000

The various units used in budgeting can be confusing. Notice that the direct labor budget includes tablets produced, direct labor hours per tablet, and direct labor cost per hour. It is extremely important to keep track of the different units and not confuse dollars with other units such as hours or tablets!

Manufacturing Overhead Budget

The last product cost to consider is manufacturing overhead. The production manager worked with the cost accountant to project the variable manufacturing cost at $20 per tablet. Additionally, they project that fixed costs are $12,000 per quarter for depreciation on the manufacturing equipment and $15,440 per quarter for other fixed costs, such as utilities, rent, and property taxes on the manufacturing facility. The manufacturing overhead budget calculates the budgeted overhead cost for the year and also the predetermined overhead allocation rate for the year. The predetermined overhead allocation rate is used to allocate the indirect overhead costs to the tablets produced. Smart Touch Learning uses direct labor hours as the allocation base to allocate overhead costs. As a reminder, the formula to calculate the predetermined overhead allocation rate is:

$$\text{Predetermined Overhead Allocation Rate} = \frac{\text{Total estimated overhead costs}}{\text{Total estimated quantity of the overhead allocation base}}$$

Exhibit 22-9 shows the manufacturing overhead budget for Smart Touch Learning for 2019.

Exhibit 22-9 | **Manufacturing Overhead Budget**

SMART TOUCH LEARNING Manufacturing Overhead Budget For the Year Ended December 31, 2019	First Quarter	Second Quarter	Third Quarter	Fourth Quarter	Total
Budgeted tablets to be produced	410	560	610	660	2,240
VOH* cost per tablet	× $20	× $20	× $20	× $20	× $20
Budgeted VOH	$ 8,200	$ 11,200	$ 12,200	$ 13,200	$ 44,800
Budgeted FOH**					
Depreciation	12,000	12,000	12,000	12,000	48,000
Utilities, insurance, property taxes	15,440	15,440	15,440	15,440	61,760
Total budgeted FOH	27,440	27,440	27,440	27,440	109,760
Budgeted manufacturing overhead costs	$ 35,640	$ 38,640	$ 39,640	$ 40,640	$ 154,560
Direct labor hours (DLHr)	1,230	1,680	1,830	1,980	6,720
Predetermined overhead allocation rate ($154,560 / 6,720 DLHr)					$ 23/DLHr

*VOH – Variable Manufacturing Overhead

**FOH – Fixed Manufacturing Overhead

Cost of Goods Sold Budget

Now that the product costs have been determined, Smart Touch Learning's managers can use them to complete the cost of goods sold budget. Start by calculating the projected cost to produce each tablet in 2019. The total projected manufacturing cost to produce each tablet in 2019 is $294, which is calculated as follows:

Direct materials cost per tablet	$ 150
Direct labor cost per tablet (3 DLHr per tablet × $25 per DLHr)	75
Manufacturing overhead cost per tablet (3 DLHr per tablet × $23 per DLHr)	69
Total projected manufacturing cost per tablet for 2019	$ 294

    Smart Touch Learning uses the first-in, first-out (FIFO) inventory costing method. The production budget illustrated in Exhibit 22-6 shows that the company starts 2019 with 200 tablets in Finished Goods Inventory, and the balance sheet in Exhibit 22-4 shows the beginning Finished Goods Inventory has a total cost of $55,000, which is $275 per tablet. All other tablets sold in 2019 will assume the budgeted production cost of $294 per tablet, as calculated above.

    Referring to the sales budget in Exhibit 22-5, the company projected sales of 500 tablets in the first quarter. **Therefore, using FIFO, 200 tablets will be assigned the beginning inventory costs of $55,000 and the remaining 300 tablets will be assigned the cost of $294 per tablet.** The cost of goods sold budget for Smart Touch Learning for 2019 is shown in Exhibit 22-10 (on the next page).

How do inventory costing methods affect the budgeting process?

Exhibit 22-10 | **Cost of Goods Sold Budget**

SMART TOUCH LEARNING Cost of Goods Sold Budget For the Year Ended December 31, 2019					
	First Quarter	Second Quarter	Third Quarter	Fourth Quarter	Total
Beginning inventory, 200 tablets	$ 55,000				$ 55,000
Tablets produced and sold in 2019 @ $294 each (300, 550, 600, 650 tablets per quarter)	88,200	$ 161,700	$ 176,400	$ 191,100	617,400
Total budgeted cost of goods sold	$ 143,200	$ 161,700	$ 176,400	$ 191,100	$ 672,400

Selling and Administrative Expense Budget

The cost accountant works with the office and sales managers to develop the selling and administrative expense budget. Cost behavior is also considered for this budget, with costs designated as variable or fixed. Smart Touch Learning projects the following selling and administrative costs for 2019:

Salaries Expense, fixed	$ 30,000 per quarter
Rent Expense, fixed	25,000 per quarter
Insurance Expense, fixed	2,500 per quarter
Depreciation Expense, fixed	1,500 per quarter
Supplies Expense, variable	1% of Sales Revenue

To calculate the projected Supplies Expense, multiply the Sales Revenue for each quarter, as calculated in the sales budget in Exhibit 22-5, by 1%.

Quarter	Sales Revenue	Supplies Expense
First	$ 250,000	$ 2,500
Second	275,000	2,750
Third	300,000	3,000
Fourth	325,000	3,250

The selling and administrative expense budget for Smart Touch Learning for 2019 is shown in Exhibit 22-11.

Exhibit 22-11 | **Selling and Administrative Expense Budget**

SMART TOUCH LEARNING Selling and Administrative Expense Budget For the Year Ended December 31, 2019					
	First Quarter	Second Quarter	Third Quarter	Fourth Quarter	Total
Salaries Expense	$ 30,000	$ 30,000	$ 30,000	$ 30,000	$ 120,000
Rent Expense	25,000	25,000	25,000	25,000	100,000
Insurance Expense	2,500	2,500	2,500	2,500	10,000
Depreciation Expense	1,500	1,500	1,500	1,500	6,000
Supplies Expense	2,500	2,750	3,000	3,250	11,500
Total budgeted S&A expense	$ 61,500	$ 61,750	$ 62,000	$ 62,250	$ 247,500

Try It!

11. Kendall Company projects 2017 first quarter sales to be $10,000 and increase by 5% per quarter. Determine the projected sales for 2017 by quarter and in total. Round answers to the nearest dollar.

12. Friedman Company manufactures and sells bicycles. A popular model is the XC. The company expects to sell 1,500 XCs in 2016 and 1,800 XCs in 2017. At the beginning of 2016, Friedman has 350 XCs in Finished Goods Inventory and desires to have 10% of the next year's sales available at the end of the year. How many XCs will Friedman need to produce in 2016?

Check your answers online in MyAccountingLab or at http://www.pearsonhighered.com/Horngren.

For more practice, see Short Exercises S22-3 through S22-8. **My**AccountingLab

HOW ARE FINANCIAL BUDGETS PREPARED FOR A MANUFACTURING COMPANY?

The financial budgets include the cash budget and the budgeted financial statements—budgeted income statement, budgeted balance sheet, and budgeted statement of cash flows. However, before we can begin the cash budget, we have to complete the capital expenditures budget.

Learning Objective 4

Prepare a financial budget for a manufacturing company

Capital Expenditures Budget

Capital expenditures are purchases of long-term assets, such as delivery trucks, computer systems, office furniture, and manufacturing equipment. The decision to purchase these expensive, long-term assets is part of a strategic plan, and this decision-making process is covered in detail in a later chapter. For now, we will assume Smart Touch Learning plans to purchase additional manufacturing equipment on January 2, 2019. The equipment will cost $160,000 and will be paid in two equal installments during the first and second quarters of 2019. The installment payments are included in the cash budget. A separate capital expenditures budget is not illustrated.

Cash Budget

The cash budget pulls information from the other budgets previously prepared and has three sections: cash receipts, cash payments, and short-term financing.

Cash Receipts

The primary source of cash is from customers. The sales budget illustrated in Exhibit 22-5 shows the projected sales by quarter. Smart Touch Learning projects that 30% of the sales will be cash sales, which indicates cash will be collected immediately. The remaining 70% of the sales are expected to be on account. The company expects to collect 60% of the credit sales in the quarter of the sale and 40% in the quarter following the sale. Bad debt expense is not significant and, therefore, is not considered in the budgeting process. The balance sheet for December 31, 2018, shows Accounts Receivable has a balance of $70,000 and this amount is expected to be collected in the first quarter of 2019. Exhibit 22-12 shows the schedule of cash receipts from customers. The total cash receipts from customers for each quarter will be carried to the cash budget. The December 31, 2019, balance in Accounts Receivable will be carried to the budgeted balance sheet.

Exhibit 22-12 | Schedule of Cash Receipts from Customers

	First Quarter	Second Quarter	Third Quarter	Fourth Quarter	Total
Total sales (from Sales Budget, Exhibit 22-5)	$ 250,000	$ 275,000	$ 300,000	$ 325,000	$ 1,150,000
	First Quarter	**Second Quarter**	**Third Quarter**	**Fourth Quarter**	**Total**
Cash Receipts from Customers:					
Accounts Receivable balance, December 31, 2018	$ 70,000				
1st Qtr.—Cash sales (30%)	75,000				
1st Qtr.—Credit sales (70%), 60% collected in 1st qtr.	105,000				
1st Qtr.—Credit sales (70%), 40% collected in 2nd qtr.		$ 70,000			
2nd Qtr.—Cash sales (30%)		82,500			
2nd Qtr.—Credit sales (70%), 60% collected in 2nd qtr.		115,500			
2nd Qtr.—Credit sales (70%), 40% collected in 3rd qtr.			$ 77,000		
3rd Qtr.—Cash sales (30%)			90,000		
3rd Qtr.—Credit sales (70%), 60% collected in 3rd qtr.			126,000		
3rd Qtr.—Credit sales (70%), 40% collected in 4th qtr.				$ 84,000	
4th Qtr.—Cash sales (30%)				97,500	
4th Qtr.—Credit sales (70%), 60% collected in 4th qtr.				136,500	
Total cash receipts from customers	$ 250,000	$ 268,000	$ 293,000	$ 318,000	$ 1,129,000
Accounts Receivable balance, December 31, 2019:					
4th Qtr.—Credit sales (70%), 40% collected in 1st qtr. 2020		$ 91,000			

Cash Payments

Smart Touch Learning has cash payments for capital expenditures, product costs (direct materials purchases, direct labor costs, and manufacturing overhead costs), and selling and administrative expenses. Therefore, the calculations for cash payments require reference to several previously developed budgets.

Direct Materials Exhibit 22-7 shows the purchases of direct materials. All direct materials purchases are on account, and Smart Touch Learning projects payments will be 75% in the quarter of the purchase and 25% in the quarter following the purchase. Reference to the

December 31, 2018, balance sheet shown in Exhibit 22-4 indicates Accounts Payable has a balance of $20,000. This amount will be paid in the first quarter of 2019.

Direct Labor Exhibit 22-8 shows the direct labor costs. Smart Touch Learning pays direct labor costs in the quarter incurred.

Manufacturing Overhead Exhibit 22-9 shows the manufacturing overhead costs. Smart Touch Learning makes cash payments for these costs in the quarter incurred. Keep in mind that we are calculating *cash payments*. Therefore, *non-cash expenses* are not included in the cash budget. The most common non-cash expense is depreciation. The cash outflow for long-term assets, such as manufacturing equipment, is at the time of purchase. Depreciation is the allocation of the asset cost to an expense account over the life of the asset. The allocation does not affect cash and is not included in the cash budget.

Selling and Administrative Expenses Exhibit 22-11 shows the selling and administrative expenses, which Smart Touch Learning pays in the quarter incurred. Again, be sure non-cash expenses, such as the depreciation on the office equipment, are not included in the cash budget.

Income Tax Expense The financial accountant at Smart Touch Learning has projected Income Tax Expense to be $70,000 for the year. Payments will be made in four equal installments during the four quarters.

Capital Expenditures The manufacturing equipment expected to be purchased on January 2, 2019, for $160,000 will be paid in two $80,000 installments in the first and second quarters of 2019.

Exhibit 22-13 (on the next page) shows the schedule of cash payments. The total quarterly cash payments for each category will be carried to the cash budget. The December 31, 2019, balance in Accounts Payable will be carried to the budgeted balance sheet.

Short-Term Financing

The December 31, 2018, balance sheet shown in Exhibit 22-4 shows Cash has a balance of $15,000. Smart Touch Learning's financial accountant recommends maintaining a larger cash balance in the future. The recommended minimum cash balance for 2019 is $30,000. The company has arranged short-term financing through a local bank. The company borrows cash as needed at the beginning of each quarter, in increments of $1,000, in order to maintain the minimum cash balance. Interest is paid on any outstanding principal balance at the beginning of the following quarter at 3% per quarter. Repayments on the principal balance are also made at the beginning of the quarter, in increments of $1,000, as cash is available.

As you learned in financial accounting, percentages related to interest are usually expressed as an amount per year (annual percentage rate or APR). However, note that in this case, the interest rate is expressed as an amount per quarter.

Exhibit 22-13 | **Schedule of Cash Payments**

	First Quarter	Second Quarter	Third Quarter	Fourth Quarter	Total
Total direct materials purchases (Exhibit 22-7)	$ 65,100	$ 87,000	$ 94,500	$ 102,000	$ 348,600
	First Quarter	Second Quarter	Third Quarter	Fourth Quarter	Total
Cash Payments					
Direct Materials:					
Accounts Payable balance, December 31, 2018	$ 20,000				
1st Qtr.—Direct materials purchases (75%)	48,825				
1st Qtr.—Direct materials purchases (25%)		$ 16,275			
2nd Qtr.—Direct materials purchases (75%)		65,250			
2nd Qtr.—Direct materials purchases (25%)			$ 21,750		
3rd Qtr.—Direct materials purchases (75%)			70,875		
3rd Qtr.—Direct materials purchases (25%)				$ 23,625	
4th Qtr.—Direct materials purchases (75%)				76,500	
Total payments for direct materials	**68,825**	**81,525**	**92,625**	**100,125**	**$ 343,100**
Direct Labor (Exhibit 22-8):					
Total payments for direct labor	**30,750**	**42,000**	**45,750**	**49,500**	**168,000**
Manufacturing Overhead (Exhibit 22-9):					
Variable manufacturing overhead	8,200	11,200	12,200	13,200	44,800
Utilities, insurance, property taxes	15,440	15,440	15,440	15,440	61,760
Total payments for manufacturing overhead	**23,640**	**26,640**	**27,640**	**28,640**	**106,560**
Selling and Administrative Expenses (Exhibit 22-11):					
Salaries Expense	30,000	30,000	30,000	30,000	120,000
Rent Expense	25,000	25,000	25,000	25,000	100,000
Insurance Expense	2,500	2,500	2,500	2,500	10,000
Supplies Expense	2,500	2,750	3,000	3,250	11,500
Total payments for S&A expenses	**60,000**	**60,250**	**60,500**	**60,750**	**241,500**
Income Taxes:					
Total payments for income taxes	**17,500**	**17,500**	**17,500**	**17,500**	**70,000**
Capital Expenditures:					
Total payments for capital expenditures	**80,000**	**80,000**			**160,000**
Total cash payments (before interest)	**$ 280,715**	**$ 307,915**	**$ 244,015**	**$ 256,515**	**$ 1,089,160**
Accounts Payable balance, December 31, 2019:					
4th Qtr.—Direct materials purchases, 25% paid in 1st qtr. 2020		$ 25,500			

Now that we have compiled the information needed for cash receipts and cash payments, let's insert those amounts into the cash budget so we can determine the amount of short-term financing needed during 2019. Exhibit 22-14 shows the partially completed cash budget for 2019.

Exhibit 22-14 | **Cash Budget—First Quarter, Before Short-Term Financing Calculations**

SMART TOUCH LEARNING Cash Budget For the Year Ended December 31, 2019	First Quarter	Second Quarter	Third Quarter	Fourth Quarter	Total
Beginning cash balance	$ 15,000				$ 15,000
Cash receipts	250,000	268,000	293,000	318,000	1,129,000
Cash available	265,000				
Cash payments:					
Capital expenditures	80,000	80,000	0	0	160,000
Purchases of direct materials	68,825	81,525	92,625	100,125	343,100
Direct labor	30,750	42,000	45,750	49,500	168,000
Manufacturing overhead	23,640	26,640	27,640	28,640	106,560
Selling and administrative expenses	60,000	60,250	60,500	60,750	241,500
Income taxes	17,500	17,500	17,500	17,500	70,000
Interest expense	0				
Total cash payments	280,715				
Ending cash balance before financing	(15,715)				
Minimum cash balance desired	(30,000)	(30,000)	(30,000)	(30,000)	(30,000)
Projected cash excess (deficiency)	(45,715)				
Financing:					
Borrowing					
Principal repayments					
Total effects of financing					
Ending cash balance					

Notice that the cash payment for interest expense for the first quarter is $0. The December 31, 2018, balance sheet from Exhibit 22-4 does not show Notes Payable or Interest Payable as liabilities. Therefore, no interest is owed at the beginning of the first quarter of 2019. Exhibit 22-14 shows a cash balance before financing of $(15,715), which is the cash available less the cash payments ($265,000 − $280,715). This amount is less than the minimum cash balance desired and creates a cash deficiency of $45,715, which means the company needs to borrow that amount to maintain the minimum desired cash balance of $30,000. The company borrows funds in increments of $1,000, so the amount borrowed is $46,000. Smart Touch Learning will then have an ending cash balance for the first quarter of $30,285:

Ending cash balance before financing	+	Total effects of financing	=	Ending cash balance
$(15,715)	+	$46,000	=	$30,285

The ending cash balance for the first quarter, then, becomes the beginning cash balance for the second quarter. Exhibit 22-15 shows the cash budget completed for the first quarter.

Exhibit 22-15 | **Cash Budget—Second Quarter, Before Short-Term Financing Calculations**

SMART TOUCH LEARNING Cash Budget For the Year Ended December 31, 2019	First Quarter	Second Quarter	Third Quarter	Fourth Quarter	Total
Beginning cash balance	$ 15,000	$ 30,285			$ 15,000
Cash receipts	250,000	268,000	293,000	318,000	1,129,000
Cash available	265,000	298,285			
Cash payments:					
Capital expenditures	80,000	80,000	0	0	160,000
Purchases of direct materials	68,825	81,525	92,625	100,125	343,100
Direct labor	30,750	42,000	45,750	49,500	168,000
Manufacturing overhead	23,640	26,640	27,640	28,640	106,560
Selling and administrative expenses	60,000	60,250	60,500	60,750	241,500
Income taxes	17,500	17,500	17,500	17,500	70,000
Interest expense	0				
Total cash payments	280,715				
Ending cash balance before financing	(15,715)				
Minimum cash balance desired	(30,000)	(30,000)	(30,000)	(30,000)	(30,000)
Projected cash excess (deficiency)	(45,715)				
Financing:					
Borrowing	46,000				
Principal repayments					
Total effects of financing	46,000				
Ending cash balance	$ 30,285				

The amount borrowed at the beginning of the first quarter accrued interest during the quarter and must be paid at the beginning of the second quarter.

Principal ×	Rate	× Time	= Interest Expense
$46,000	× 3% per quarter	× 1 quarter =	$1,380

When the interest payment is recorded for the second quarter, it is determined that Smart Touch Learning again has a cash deficiency and must borrow funds to maintain the minimum cash balance of $30,000. Carefully examine Exhibit 22-16, which shows the first and second quarters after financing and the third quarter before financing.

Exhibit 22-16 | Cash Budget—Third Quarter, Before Short-Term Financing Calculations

	First Quarter	Second Quarter	Third Quarter	Fourth Quarter	Total
SMART TOUCH LEARNING					
Cash Budget					
For the Year Ended December 31, 2019					
Beginning cash balance	$ 15,000	$ 30,285	$ 30,990		$ 15,000
Cash receipts	250,000	268,000	293,000	318,000	1,129,000
Cash available	265,000	298,285	323,990		
Cash payments:					
Capital expenditures	80,000	80,000	0	0	160,000
Purchases of direct materials	68,825	81,525	92,625	100,125	343,100
Direct labor	30,750	42,000	45,750	49,500	168,000
Manufacturing overhead	23,640	26,640	27,640	28,640	106,560
Selling and administrative expenses	60,000	60,250	60,500	60,750	241,500
Income taxes	17,500	17,500	17,500	17,500	70,000
Interest expense	0	1,380			
Total cash payments	280,715	309,295			
Ending cash balance before financing	(15,715)	(11,010)			
Minimum cash balance desired	(30,000)	(30,000)	(30,000)	(30,000)	(30,000)
Projected cash excess (deficiency)	(45,715)	(41,010)			
Financing:					
Borrowing	46,000	42,000			
Principal repayments					
Total effects of financing	46,000	42,000			
Ending cash balance	$ 30,285	$ 30,990			

The calculation for the interest expense for the third quarter is:

Principal	×	**Rate**	× **Time**	= **Interest Expense**
($46,000 + $42,000)	×	3% per quarter	× 1 quarter =	$2,640

After the third quarter interest payment is calculated and the ending cash balance before financing is determined, Smart Touch Learning shows a projected cash excess for the third quarter, as shown in Exhibit 22-17 (on the next page). The cash excess can be used to repay a portion of the amount previously borrowed, again in increments of $1,000.

Exhibit 22-17 shows the completed cash budget. Take time to carefully examine the document to ensure you understand the calculations. The calculation for the interest expense for the fourth quarter is:

Principal	×	**Rate**	× **Time**	= **Interest Expense**
($46,000 + $42,000 − $47,000)	×	3% per quarter	× 1 quarter =	$1,230

Exhibit 22-17 | Completed Cash Budget

	First Quarter	Second Quarter	Third Quarter	Fourth Quarter	Total
SMART TOUCH LEARNING **Cash Budget** **For the Year Ended December 31, 2019**					
Beginning cash balance	$ 15,000	$ 30,285	$ 30,990	$ 30,335	$ 15,000
Cash receipts	250,000	268,000	293,000	318,000	1,129,000
Cash available	265,000	298,285	323,990	348,335	1,144,000
Cash payments:					
Capital expenditures	80,000	80,000	0	0	160,000
Purchases of direct materials	68,825	81,525	92,625	100,125	343,100
Direct labor	30,750	42,000	45,750	49,500	168,000
Manufacturing overhead	23,640	26,640	27,640	28,640	106,560
Selling and administrative expenses	60,000	60,250	60,500	60,750	241,500
Income taxes	17,500	17,500	17,500	17,500	70,000
Interest expense	0	1,380	2,640	1,230	5,250
Total cash payments	280,715	309,295	246,655	257,745	1,094,410
Ending cash balance before financing	(15,715)	(11,010)	77,335	90,590	49,590
Minimum cash balance desired	(30,000)	(30,000)	(30,000)	(30,000)	(30,000)
Projected cash excess (deficiency)	(45,715)	(41,010)	47,335	60,590	19,590
Financing:					
Borrowing	46,000	42,000			88,000
Principal repayments			(47,000)	(41,000)	(88,000)
Total effects of financing	46,000	42,000	(47,000)	(41,000)	0
Ending cash balance	$ 30,285	$ 30,990	$ 30,335	$ 49,590	$ 49,590

Note that the principal repayment in the fourth quarter is only $41,000 even though the company has $60,590 in excess cash. At the beginning of the fourth quarter, the balance on the note is $41,000, which is the total of the amounts borrowed in the first and second quarters less the repayment made in the third quarter ($46,000 + $42,000 − $47,000). Smart Touch Learning will only repay what has been borrowed and now has excess cash to be used for other purposes.

Also, pay special attention to the Total column of the cash budget. You cannot simply add across each row to determine these amounts because this is a summary for the entire year. For example, the beginning cash balance for the year is the same as the beginning cash balance for the first quarter, but not the sum of the beginning balances for each quarter.

The budgeted financial statements are the next step in the budgeting process, and the cash budget provides several amounts needed. The interest expense calculations are carried to the budgeted income statement, and the ending cash balance is carried to the budgeted balance sheet. Smart Touch Learning repaid all amounts borrowed during the year. If those amounts had not been repaid in full, the balance would be carried to the budgeted balance sheet as the balance for Notes Payable.

DECISIONS

Do we really need to budget?

David Sinclair left the budget meeting in a foul mood. "I'm the maintenance supervisor, not an accountant," he mumbled as he walked back to his office. "I've got real work to do. I don't have time to make a budget!" David's company requires all managers to participate in the budgeting process. In fact, all employees are encouraged to participate, not just the managers. But David just can't see the point. According to David, if it's broke, he gets it fixed. Writing numbers on a sheet of paper doesn't get things fixed! What do you think? Should David be required to participate in the budgeting process?

Solution

Budgets should be used to plan and control the company's activities. If the company is large enough to have a maintenance department with a manager, then there is probably a significant amount of upkeep required. David is the person that should

be most familiar with the company's equipment and the cost required to keep the equipment in good repair in order to prevent production shutdowns due to equipment malfunctions. David may be more comfortable tinkering with the machinery, but the company needs to be able to call upon his real-life maintenance experience to ensure that the budget adequately covers the department's needs.

Alternate Solution

David's supervisor should recognize that not all employees have the desire to participate in activities such as budgeting. It is the supervisor's responsibility to ensure that David understands how to use the budget and how it is to his advantage that the budget be as accurate as possible. The better the plan, the better the results. If the company is more profitable due to better planning, all employees will benefit.

Budgeted Income Statement

Smart Touch Learning has now determined all amounts needed to calculate the budgeted net income for 2019. Following is a summary of the sources for these figures:

Account	Budget	Exhibit	Amount
Sales Revenue	Sales	22-5	$ 1,150,000
Cost of Goods Sold	Cost of Goods Sold	22-10	672,400
S&A Expenses	S&A Expense	22-11	247,500
Interest Expense	Cash	22-17	5,250
Income Tax Expense	Cash	22-17	70,000

Be sure to not confuse revenues earned with cash received from customers or expenses incurred with cash payments. The accrual-based income statement reports revenues earned and expenses incurred. The statement of cash flows reports cash receipts and cash payments.

Exhibit 22-18 (on the next page) shows the budgeted income statement for Smart Touch Learning for the year ended December 31, 2019.

Exhibit 22-18 | **Budgeted Income Statement**

SMART TOUCH LEARNING Budgeted Income Statement For the Year Ended December 31, 2019	
Sales Revenue	$ 1,150,000
Cost of Goods Sold	672,400
Gross Profit	477,600
Selling and Administrative Expenses	247,500
Operating Income	230,100
Interest Expense	5,250
Income before Income Taxes	224,850
Income Tax Expense	70,000
Net Income	$ 154,850

Budgeted Balance Sheet

The budgeted balance sheet for Smart Touch Learning at December 31, 2019, will pull amounts from the various budgets previously completed. One remaining calculation is for Retained Earnings. Retained Earnings is increased by the amount of net income earned and decreased by the amount of dividends declared. The net income is shown in Exhibit 22-18, and the company does not project dividends for the year. Following is a summary of the sources for the balance sheet figures:

Account	Source	Exhibit	Amount
Cash	Cash budget	22-17	$ 49,590
Accounts Receivable	Schedule of cash receipts from customers	22-12	91,000
Raw Materials Inventory	Direct materials budget	22-7	42,600
Finished Goods Inventory	Production budget Cost of goods sold budget	22-6 22-10	140 units $ 294 per unit
Equipment	2018 balance sheet Capital expenditures budget	22-4	210,340 160,000
Accumulated Depreciation	2018 balance sheet Manufacturing overhead budget S&A expense budget	22-4 22-9 22-11	12,000 48,000 6,000
Accounts Payable	Schedule of cash payments	22-13	25,500
Common Stock	2018 balance sheet	22-4	300,000
Retained Earnings	2018 balance sheet Budgeted income statement	22-4 22-18	48,340 154,850

Take the time to look at each exhibit referenced on the previous page to ensure you know where each figure came from. Also, keep in mind that the balance sheet only shows the *ending balances* of each account as of December 31, 2019. The budgeted balance sheet for Smart Touch Learning for December 31, 2019, is shown in Exhibit 22-19.

Exhibit 22-19 | **Budgeted Balance Sheet**

SMART TOUCH LEARNING Budgeted Balance Sheet December 31, 2019		
Assets		
Current Assets:		
Cash	$ 49,590	
Accounts Receivable	91,000	
Raw Materials Inventory	42,600	
Finished Goods Inventory (140 units × $294/unit)	41,160	
Total Current Assets		$ 224,350
Property, Plant, and Equipment:		
Equipment ($210,340 + $160,000)	370,340	
Less: Accumulated Depreciation ($12,000 + $48,000 + $6,000)	(66,000)	304,340
Total Assets		**$ 528,690**
Liabilities		
Current Liabilities:		
Accounts Payable		$ 25,500
Stockholders' Equity		
Common Stock, no par	$ 300,000	
Retained Earnings ($48,340 + $154,850)	203,190	
Total Stockholders' Equity		503,190
Total Liabilities and Stockholders' Equity		**$ 528,690**

Budgeted Statement of Cash Flows

The last step in the preparation of the master budget is the budgeted statement of cash flows. The information comes from the cash budget, illustrated in Exhibit 22-17. All cash receipts and disbursements are designated as operating activities, investing activities, or financing activities. The direct method is used and illustrated in Exhibit 22-20 (on the next page).

Exhibit 22-20 | **Budgeted Statement of Cash Flows**

SMART TOUCH LEARNING Budgeted Statement of Cash Flows For the Year Ended December 31, 2019		
Operating Activities:		
Cash receipts from customers	$ 1,129,000	
Cash payments for operating expenses*	(859,160)	
Cash payments for interest expense	(5,250)	
Cash payments for income taxes	(70,000)	
Net cash provided by operating activities		$ 194,590
Investing Activities:		
Cash payments for equipment purchases	(160,000)	
Net cash used for investing activities		(160,000)
Financing Activities:		
Proceeds from issuance of notes payable	88,000	
Payment of notes payable	(88,000)	
Net cash provided by financing activities		0
Net increase in cash		34,590
Cash balance, January 1, 2019		15,000
Cash balance, December 31, 2019		$ 49,590

*Add payments for direct materials, direct labor, overhead, and S&A
expenses ($343,100 + $168,000 + $106,560 + $241,500)

13. Meeks Company has the following sales for the first quarter of 2017:

	January	February	March
Cash sales	$ 5,000	$ 5,500	$ 5,250
Sales on account	15,000	14,000	14,500
Total sales	$ 20,000	$ 19,500	$ 19,750

Sales on account are collected the month after the sale. The Accounts Receivable balance on January 1 is $12,500, the amount of December's sales on account. Calculate the cash receipts from customers for the first three months of 2017.

Check your answers online in MyAccountingLab or at http://www.pearsonhighered.com/Horngren.

For more practice, see Short Exercises S22-9 through S22-11.   MyAccountingLab

HOW CAN INFORMATION TECHNOLOGY BE USED IN THE BUDGETING PROCESS?

Exhibits 22-5 through 22-20 show that managers must prepare many calculations to develop the master budget for a small company such as Smart Touch Learning. Technology makes it more cost effective for managers to

- Conduct sensitivity analysis.
- Combine individual unit budgets to create the companywide master budget.

Sensitivity Analysis

The master budget models the company's *planned* activities. Top management pays special attention to ensure that the results of the budgeted income statement, the budgeted balance sheet, and the budgeted statement of cash flows support key strategies.

Actual results, however, often differ from plans. Management, therefore, wants to know how budgeted income and cash flows would change if key assumptions turned out to be incorrect. We previously defined *sensitivity analysis* as a *what if* technique that asks *what* a result will be *if* a predicted amount is not achieved or *if* an underlying assumption changes. *What if* the stock market crashes? How will this affect Smart Touch Learning's sales? Will it have to postpone a planned expansion? *What* will the company's cash balance be on June 30 *if* the period's sales are 25% cash, not 30% cash? Will Smart Touch Learning have to borrow more cash?

Many companies use computer spreadsheet programs like Excel to prepare master budget schedules and statements. Today, *what if* budget questions are easily answered within Excel with a few keystrokes.

Technology makes it cost effective to perform more comprehensive sensitivity analyses. Armed with a better understanding of how changes in sales and costs are likely to affect the company's bottom line, today's managers can react quickly if key assumptions underlying the master budget (such as sales price or quantity) turn out to be wrong. Summary Problems 22-1 and 22-2 are examples of sensitivity analyses for Smart Touch Learning.

Budgeting Software

Companies with multiple business segments must combine the budget data from each of the segments to prepare the companywide budgeted income statement, budgeted balance sheet, and budgeted statement of cash flows. This process can be difficult for companies whose business segments use different spreadsheets to prepare the budgets.

Companies often turn to budget-management software to solve this problem. Often designed as a component of the company's Enterprise Resource Planning (ERP) system, this software helps managers develop and analyze budgets.

Software also allows managers to conduct sensitivity analyses on their own segment's data. When the manager is satisfied with his or her budget, he or she can easily enter it in the companywide budget. His or her segment's budget automatically integrates with budgets from all other business segments—from around the building, around the state, around the country, or around the world.

Whether at headquarters or on the road, top executives can log into the budget system through the Internet and conduct their own sensitivity analyses on individual business segments' budgets or on the companywide budget. The result is that managers spend less time compiling and summarizing data and more time analyzing and making decisions that ensure the budget leads the company to achieve its key strategic goals.

Try It!

14. Crowley Company projects the following sales:

	January	February	March
Cash sales (25%)	$ 5,000	$ 5,500	$ 6,000
Sales on account (75%)	15,000	16,500	18,000
Total sales	$ 20,000	$ 22,000	$ 24,000

Crowley collects sales on account in the month after the sale. The Accounts Receivable balance on January 1 is $13,500, which represents December's sales on account. Crowley projects the following cash receipts from customers:

	January	February	March
Cash receipts from cash sales	$ 5,000	$ 5,500	$ 6,000
Cash receipts from sales on account	13,500	15,000	16,500
Total cash receipts from customers	$ 18,500	$ 20,500	$ 22,500

Recalculate cash receipts from customers if total sales remain the same but cash sales are only 20% of the total.

Check your answers online in MyAccountingLab or at http://www.pearsonhighered.com/Horngren.

For more practice, see Short Exercises S22-12 and S22-13. MyAccountingLab

Appendix 22A: Budgeting for Merchandising Companies

The chapter illustrated the preparation of the master budget for a manufacturing company. Appendix 22A illustrates the process for a merchandising company. Many of the calculations and budgets are the same, but in some ways, the master budget for a merchandising company is easier to complete. Merchandising companies purchase the products they sell rather than manufacture them. Therefore, the inventory, purchases, and cost of goods sold budget replaces the production budget, direct materials budget, direct labor budget, manufacturing overhead budget, and cost of goods sold budget. Exhibit 22A-1 shows the master budget components for a merchandising company.

Exhibit 22A-1 | **Master Budget Components—Merchandising Company**

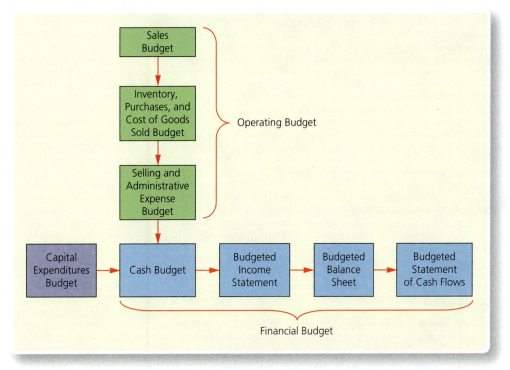

We use Greg's Games, a fictitious company, to illustrate the preparation of the master budget. Greg's Games is a retail chain store that carries a complete line of video and board games. We prepare the master budget for one of the stores in the chain for April, May, June, and July, the main selling season.

HOW ARE OPERATING BUDGETS PREPARED FOR A MERCHANDISING COMPANY?

Exhibit 22A-2 (on the next page) shows the balance sheet for Greg's Games for March 31, 2018. The balance sheet provides some of the data that we use in preparing the master budget.

Learning Objective 6

Prepare an operating budget for a merchandising company

Sales Budget

In a merchandising company, just as with a manufacturing company, the forecast of sales revenue is the cornerstone of the master budget because the level of sales affects expenses and almost all other elements of the master budget. Budgeted total sales for each product equal the sales price multiplied by the expected number of units sold.

Sales in March were $40,000. The sales manager projects the following monthly sales:

April	$ 50,000
May	80,000
June	60,000
July	50,000
August	40,000

Exhibit 22A-2 | **Balance Sheet**

GREG'S GAMES
Balance Sheet
March 31, 2018

Assets		
Current Assets:		
Cash	$ 16,400	
Accounts Receivable	16,000	
Merchandise Inventory	48,000	
Prepaid Insurance	1,800	
Total Current Assets		$ 82,200
Property, Plant, and Equipment:		
Equipment and Fixtures	32,000	
Less: Accumulated Depreciation	(12,800)	19,200
Total Assets		$ 101,400
Liabilities		
Current Liabilities:		
Accounts Payable	$ 16,800	
Salaries and Commissions Payable	4,250	
Total Liabilities		$ 21,050
Stockholders' Equity		
Common Stock, no par	20,000	
Retained Earnings	60,350	
Total Stockholders' Equity		80,350
Total Liabilities and Stockholders' Equity		$ 101,400

Sales are 60% cash and 40% on account. Greg's Games collects all credit sales the month after the sale. The $16,000 balance in Accounts Receivable at March 31, 2018, is March's sales on account (40% of $40,000). There are no other Accounts Receivable. Uncollectible accounts are immaterial and thus aren't included in the master budget. Exhibit 22A-3 shows the sales budget for Greg's Games for the four months. The April through July total budgeted sales of $240,000 are carried to the budgeted income statement.

Exhibit 22A-3 | **Sales Budget**

GREG'S GAMES
Sales Budget
Four Months Ended July 31, 2018

	April	May	June	July	Total
Cash sales (60%)	$ 30,000	$ 48,000	$ 36,000	$ 30,000	$ 144,000
Sales on account (40%)	20,000	32,000	24,000	20,000	96,000
Total budgeted sales	$ 50,000	$ 80,000	$ 60,000	$ 50,000	$ 240,000

Inventory, Purchases, and Cost of Goods Sold Budget

This budget determines cost of goods sold for the budgeted income statement, ending Merchandise Inventory for the budgeted balance sheet, and merchandise inventory purchases for the cash budget. The familiar cost of goods sold computation specifies the relations among these items:

Beginning merchandise inventory + Purchases − Ending merchandise inventory = Cost of goods sold

Beginning merchandise inventory is known from last month's balance sheet, budgeted cost of goods sold averages 70% of sales, and budgeted ending merchandise inventory is a computed amount. Greg's Games minimum merchandise inventory rule is as follows: Ending merchandise inventory should be equal to $20,000 plus 80% of the next month's cost of goods sold. You must solve for the budgeted purchases figure. To do this, rearrange the previous equation to isolate purchases on the left side:

Purchases = Cost of goods sold + Ending merchandise inventory − Beginning merchandise inventory

How much merchandise inventory does Greg's Games need to purchase? Greg's Games should have the minimum amount of merchandise inventory to be sure the company balances providing goods to customers with turning over the merchandise inventory efficiently. Keeping merchandise inventory at the minimum level that meets these needs helps reduce inventory storage costs, insurance costs, and warehousing costs and reduces the potential for merchandise inventory to become obsolete. Exhibit 22A-4 shows Greg's Games merchandise inventory, purchases, and cost of goods sold budget. The beginning balance of Merchandise Inventory for April is the ending balance from the March 31 balance sheet.

Exhibit 22A-4 | **Inventory, Purchases, and Cost of Goods Sold Budget**

GREG'S GAMES
Inventory, Purchases, and Cost of Goods Sold Budget
Four Months Ended July 31, 2018

	April	May	June	July	Total
Cost of goods sold (70% × sales)	$ 35,000	$ 56,000	$ 42,000	$ 35,000	$ 168,000
Plus: Desired ending merchandise inventory					
$20,000 + (80% × COGS for next month)*	64,800	53,600	48,000	42,400	42,400
Total merchandise inventory required	99,800	109,600	90,000	77,400	210,400
Less: Beginning merchandise inventory	48,000	64,800	53,600	48,000	48,000
Budgeted purchases	$ 51,800	$ 44,800	$ 36,400	$ 29,400	$ 162,400

*April: $20,000 + (80% × $56,000) = $64,800
May: $20,000 + (80% × $42,000) = $53,600
June: $20,000 + (80% × $35,000) = $48,000
July: $20,000 + (80% × COGS for August) = $20,000 + (80% × (70% × $40,000)) = $42,400

Selling and Administrative Expense Budget

The monthly payroll for Greg's Games is salaries of $2,500 plus sales commissions equal to 15% of sales. This is a mixed cost, with both a fixed and a variable component. Other monthly expenses are as follows:

Rent Expense	$ 2,000, paid as incurred
Depreciation Expense	$ 500
Insurance Expense	$ 200 expiration of prepaid amount
Miscellaneous Expense	5% of sales, paid as incurred

The selling and administrative expense budget for Greg's Games is shown in Exhibit 22A-5.

Exhibit 22A-5 | **Selling and Administrative Expense Budget**

GREG'S GAMES Selling and Administrative Expense Budget Four Months Ended July 31, 2018					
	April	May	June	July	Total
Variable expenses:					
Commissions Expense (15% of sales)	$ 7,500	$ 12,000	$ 9,000	$ 7,500	$ 36,000
Miscellaneous Expenses (5% of sales)	2,500	4,000	3,000	2,500	12,000
Total variable expenses	10,000	16,000	12,000	10,000	48,000
Fixed expenses:					
Salaries Expense	2,500	2,500	2,500	2,500	10,000
Rent Expense	2,000	2,000	2,000	2,000	8,000
Depreciation Expense	500	500	500	500	2,000
Insurance Expense	200	200	200	200	800
Total fixed expenses	5,200	5,200	5,200	5,200	20,800
Total selling and administrative expenses	$ 15,200	$ 21,200	$ 17,200	$ 15,200	$ 68,800

15A. Camp Company is a sporting goods store. The company sells a tent that sleeps six people. The store expects to sell 250 tents in 2016 and 280 tents in 2017. At the beginning of 2016, Camp Company has 25 tents in Merchandise Inventory and desires to have 5% of the next year's sales available at the end of the year. How many tents will Camp Company need to purchase in 2016?

Check your answer online in MyAccountingLab or at http://www.pearsonhighered.com/Horngren.

For more practice, see Short Exercises S22A-14 through S22A-16. MyAccountingLab

HOW ARE FINANCIAL BUDGETS PREPARED FOR A MERCHANDISING COMPANY?

We continue the budgeting process for Greg's Games by preparing the capital expenditures budget, cash budget, and budgeted financial statements—budgeted income statement, budgeted balance sheet, and budgeted statement of cash flows.

Learning Objective 7

Prepare a financial budget for a merchandising company

Capital Expenditures Budget

Greg's Games plans to purchase a used delivery truck in April, paying $3,000 at the time of the purchase. Because this is the only capital expenditure, a separate budget is not illustrated. The cash payment will be shown on the cash budget.

Cash Budget

The cash budget pulls information from the other budgets previously prepared and has three sections: cash receipts, cash payments, and short-term financing.

Cash Receipts

The primary source of cash is from customers. The sales budget illustrated in Exhibit 22A-3 shows the total sales for the period. Recall that the company's sales are 60% cash and 40% on credit. The 40% credit sales are collected the month after the sale is made. Exhibit 22A-6 shows that April's budgeted cash collections consist of two parts:

1. April's cash sales from the sales budget in Exhibit 22A-3 ($30,000)
2. Collections of March's credit sales ($16,000 Accounts Receivable from the March 31 balance sheet, Exhibit 22A-2).

   This process is repeated for all four months.

Exhibit 22A-6 | **Schedule of Cash Receipts from Customers**

GREG'S GAMES Budgeted Cash Receipts from Customers Four Months Ended July 31, 2018					
	April	May	June	July	Total
Cash sales (60%)	$ 30,000	$ 48,000	$ 36,000	$ 30,000	$ 144,000
Credit sales receipts, one month after sale (40%)	16,000*	20,000	32,000	24,000	92,000
Total cash receipts	$ 46,000	$ 68,000	$ 68,000	$ 54,000	$ 236,000

* March 31 Accounts Receivable (Exhibit 22A-2)

Accounts Receivable balance, July 31:
July sales on account to be collected in August, $20,000

Cash Payments

Greg's Games pays for merchandise inventory purchases 50% during the month of purchase and 50% the month after purchase. Use the inventory, purchases, and cost of goods sold budget from Exhibit 22A-4 to compute budgeted cash payments for purchases of inventory. April's cash payments for purchases consist of two parts:

1. Payment of 50% of March's purchases ($16,800 Accounts Payable balance from the March 31 balance sheet, Exhibit 22A-2).
2. Payment for 50% of April's purchases (50% × $51,800 = $25,900).

This process is repeated for all four months and is illustrated in Exhibit 22A-7.

Exhibit 22A-7 | **Schedule of Cash Payments for Purchases**

GREG'S GAMES Budgeted Cash Payments for Purchases Four Months Ended July 31, 2018					
	April	**May**	**June**	**July**	**Total**
50% of last month's purchases	$ 16,800*	$ 25,900	$ 22,400	$ 18,200	$ 83,300
50% of this month's purchases	25,900	22,400	18,200	14,700	81,200
Total cash payments for purchases	$ 42,700	$ 48,300	$ 40,600	$ 32,900	$ 164,500

* March 31 Accounts Payable (Exhibit 22A-2)

Accounts Payable balance, July 31:
50% of July purchases to be paid in August, $14,700

Use the selling and administrative expense budget (Exhibit 22A-5) and Greg's Games payment information to compute cash payments for selling and administrative expenses. Greg's Games pays half the salaries and commissions in the month incurred and half in the following month. Therefore, at the end of each month, Greg's Games reports Salaries and Commissions Payable equal to half the month's payroll. The $4,250 balance in Salaries and Commissions Payable in the March 31 balance sheet in Exhibit 22A-2 is half the March payroll of $8,500:

March payroll = Salaries + Sales commissions of 15% of sales
= $2,500 + (15% × $40,000)
= $2,500 + $6,000
= $8,500

Why are depreciation expense and insurance expense from the selling and administrative expense budget *excluded* from the budgeted cash payments for selling and administrative expenses?

Recall that the company's selling and administrative expenses also include $2,000 rent, $500 depreciation, $200 of insurance expense, and miscellaneous expenses of 5% of sales for the month. Greg's Games pays all those expenses in the month incurred except for insurance and depreciation. **Recall that the insurance was prepaid insurance, so the cash payment for insurance was made before this budget period; therefore, no cash payment is made for insurance during April–July. Depreciation is a non-cash expense, so it's not included in the budgeted cash payments for selling and administrative operating expenses.** April's cash payments for selling and administrative expenses consist of the following items:

Payment of 50% of March's salaries ($2,500 × 50%) (from March 31 balance sheet, Exhibit 22A-2)	$ 1,250
Payment of 50% of March's commissions ($6,000 × 50%) (from March 31 balance sheet, Exhibit 22A-2)	3,000
Payment of 50% of April's salaries ($2,500 × 50%) (Exhibit 22A-5)	1,250
Payment of 50% of April's commissions ($7,500 × 50%) (Exhibit 22A-5)	3,750
Payment of Rent Expense (Exhibit 22A-5)	2,000
Payment of Miscellaneous Expenses (Exhibit 22A-5)	2,500
Total April cash payments for S&A Expenses	$ 13,750

Exhibit 22A-8 shows the schedule of cash payments for selling and administrative expenses for Greg's Games.

Exhibit 22A-8 | **Schedule of Cash Payments for Selling and Administrative Expenses**

	April	May	June	July	Total
GREG'S GAMES Budgeted Cash Payments for Selling and Administrative Expenses Four Months Ended July 31, 2018					
Variable expenses:					
50% of last month's Commissions Expense	$ 3,000	$ 3,750	$ 6,000	$ 4,500	$ 17,250
50% of this month's Commissions Expense	3,750	6,000	4,500	3,750	18,000
Miscellaneous Expenses	2,500	4,000	3,000	2,500	12,000
Total payments for variable expenses	9,250	13,750	13,500	10,750	47,250
Fixed expenses:					
50% of last month's Salaries Expense	1,250	1,250	1,250	1,250	5,000
50% of this month's Salaries Expense	1,250	1,250	1,250	1,250	5,000
Rent Expense	2,000	2,000	2,000	2,000	8,000
Total payments for fixed expenses	4,500	4,500	4,500	4,500	18,000
Total payments for S&A expenses	$ 13,750	$ 18,250	$ 18,000	$ 15,250	$ 65,250

Salaries and Commissions Payable balance, July 31:
50% of July salaries and commissions to be paid in August, $5,000

Short-Term Financing

Greg's Games requires a minimum cash balance of $10,000 at the end of each month. The store can borrow cash in $1,000 increments at an annual interest rate of 12%. Management borrows no more than the amount needed to maintain the $10,000 minimum ending cash balance. Total interest expense will vary as the amount of borrowing varies from month to month. Notes payable require $1,000 installment payments of principal per month, plus monthly interest on the unpaid principal balance. This is an installment loan; therefore, payments of principal are $1,000 per month even if there is additional excess cash on hand. Borrowing and all principal and interest payments occur at the end of the month.

To prepare the cash budget, start with the beginning cash balance from the March 31 balance sheet (Exhibit 22A-2) and add the budgeted cash receipts (Exhibit 22A-6) to determine the cash available. Then subtract cash payments for purchases (Exhibit 22A-7), selling and administrative expenses (Exhibit 22A-8), and any capital expenditures. This yields the ending cash balance before financing.

Greg's Games requires a minimum ending cash balance of $10,000. April's $2,950 budgeted cash balance before financing falls $7,050 short of the minimum required ($10,000 − $2,950). To be able to access short-term financing, Greg's Games secured a line of credit with the company's bank. Securing this credit in advance is crucial to having the credit available to draw upon when cash shortages arise. Because Greg's Games borrows in $1,000 increments, the company will have to borrow $8,000 to cover April's expected short-fall. The budgeted ending cash balance equals the "ending cash balance before financing," adjusted for the total effects of the financing (an $8,000 inflow in April). Exhibit 22A-9 (on the next page) shows that Greg's Games expects to end April with $10,950 of cash ($2,950 + $8,000). Additionally, when Greg's Games borrows, the amount borrowed is to be paid back in $1,000 installments plus interest at 12% annually. Note that in May, the company begins to pay the $8,000 borrowed in April. Greg's Games must also pay interest at 12%. For May, the interest paid is calculated as $8,000 owed × 12% per year × 1/12 of the year, or $80 interest. For June, the company's interest owed will change because the principal of the note has been paid down by $1,000 in May. June interest is calculated as ($8,000 − $1,000) owed × 12% per year × 1/12 of the year, or $70 interest. For July, interest is ($8,000 − $1,000 − $1,000) owed × 12% per year × 1/12 of the year, or $60 interest. Exhibit 22A-9 shows the cash budget for April, May, June, and July.

Exhibit 22A-9 | **Cash Budget**

GREG'S GAMES Cash Budget Four Months Ended July 31, 2018	April	May	June	July	Total
Beginning cash balance	$ 16,400	$ 10,950	$ 11,320	$ 19,650	$ 16,400
Cash receipts	46,000	68,000	68,000	54,000	236,000
Cash available	62,400	78,950	79,320	73,650	252,400
Cash payments:					
Capital expenditures	3,000	0	0	0	3,000
Purchases of merchandise inventory	42,700	48,300	40,600	32,900	164,500
Selling and administrative expenses	13,750	18,250	18,000	15,250	65,250
Interest expense	0	80	70	60	210
Total cash payments	59,450	66,630	58,670	48,210	232,960
Ending cash balance before financing	2,950	12,320	20,650	25,440	19,440
Minimum cash balance desired	(10,000)	(10,000)	(10,000)	(10,000)	(10,000)
Projected cash excess (deficiency)	(7,050)	2,320	10,650	15,440	9,440
Financing:					
Borrowing	8,000				8,000
Principal repayments		(1,000)	(1,000)	(1,000)	(3,000)
Total effects of financing	8,000	(1,000)	(1,000)	(1,000)	5,000
Ending cash balance	$ 10,950	$ 11,320	$ 19,650	$ 24,440	$ 24,440

The cash balance at the end of July of $24,440 is the Cash balance on the July 31 budgeted balance sheet.

Budgeted Income Statement

Use the sales budget (Exhibit 22A-3); the inventory, purchases, and cost of goods sold budget (Exhibit 22A-4); and the selling and administrative expenses budget (Exhibit 22A-5) to prepare the budgeted income statement. The computation of interest expense as part of the cash budget is also used in the budgeted income statement. Income taxes are ignored in order to simplify the process. Exhibit 22A-10 shows the budgeted income statement for Greg's Games.

Exhibit 22A-10 | **Budgeted Income Statement**

GREG'S GAMES Budgeted Income Statement Four Months Ended July 31, 2018		
Sales Revenue		$ 240,000
Cost of Goods Sold		168,000
Gross Profit		72,000
Selling and Administrative Expenses:		
Commissions Expense	$ 36,000	
Miscellaneous Expense	12,000	
Salaries Expense	10,000	
Rent Expense	8,000	
Depreciation Expense	2,000	
Insurance Expense	800	
Total Selling and Administrative Expenses		68,800
Operating Income		3,200
Interest Expense		210
Net Income		$ 2,990

Budgeted Balance Sheet

To prepare the budgeted balance sheet, project each asset, liability, and stockholders' equity account based on the plans outlined in the previous exhibits. Determine the balance of each account as of July 31, 2018. Following is a summary of the sources for the balance sheet figures:

Account	Source	Exhibit	Amount
Cash	Cash budget	22A-9	$ 24,440
Accounts Receivable	Schedule of cash receipts from customers	22A-6	20,000
Merchandise Inventory	Inventory, purchases, and COGS budget	22A-4	42,400
Prepaid Insurance	March 31 balance sheet	22A-2	1,800
	S&A expense budget	22A-5	800
Equipment	March 31 balance sheet	22A-2	32,000
	Capital expenditures budget		3,000
Accumulated Depreciation	March 31 balance sheet	22A-2	12,800
	S&A expense budget	22A-5	2,000
Accounts Payable	Schedule of cash payments for purchases	22A-7	14,700
Salaries and Commissions Payable	Schedule of cash payments for S&A expenses	22A-8	5,000
Notes Payable	Cash budget	22A-9	5,000
Common Stock	March 31 balance sheet	22A-2	20,000
Retained Earnings	March 31 balance sheet	22A-2	60,350
	Budgeted income statement	22A-10	2,990

Study the budgeted balance sheet in Exhibit 22A-11 to make certain you understand the computation of each figure.

Exhibit 22A-11 | **Budgeted Balance Sheet**

GREG'S GAMES Budgeted Balance Sheet July 31, 2018		
Assets		
Current Assets:		
Cash	$ 24,440	
Accounts Receivable	20,000	
Merchandise Inventory	42,400	
Prepaid Insurance ($1,800 − $800)	1,000	
Total Current Assets		$ 87,840
Property, Plant, and Equipment:		
Equipment and Fixtures ($32,000 + $3,000)	35,000	
Less: Accumulated Depreciation ($12,800 + $2,000)	(14,800)	20,200
Total Assets		$ 108,040
Liabilities		
Current Liabilities:		
Accounts Payable	$ 14,700	
Salaries and Commissions Payable	5,000	
Notes Payable—Short-term	5,000	
Total Liabilities		$ 24,700
Stockholders' Equity		
Common Stock, no par	20,000	
Retained Earnings ($60,350 + $2,990)	63,340	
Total Stockholders' Equity		83,340
Total Liabilities and Stockholders' Equity		$ 108,040

Budgeted Statement of Cash Flows

The final step in the master budget process is preparing the budgeted statement of cash flows. The information comes from the cash budget in Exhibit 22A-9. All cash receipts and disbursements are designated as operating activities, investing activities, or financing activities. Exhibit 22A-12 shows the direct method for a budgeted statement of cash flows for Greg's Games.

Exhibit 22A-12 | **Budgeted Statement of Cash Flows**

GREG'S GAMES Budgeted Statement of Cash Flows Four Months Ended July 31, 2018		
Operating Activities:		
Cash receipts from customers	$ 236,000	
Cash payments for purchases	(164,500)	
Cash payments for S&A expenses	(65,250)	
Cash payments for interest expense	(210)	
Net cash provided by operating activities		$ 6,040
Investing Activities:		
Cash payments for equipment purchases	(3,000)	
Net cash used for investing activities		(3,000)
Financing Activities:		
Proceeds from issuance of notes payable	8,000	
Payment of notes payable	(3,000)	
Net cash provided by financing activities		5,000
Net increase in cash		8,040
Cash balance, April 1, 2018		16,400
Cash balance, July 31, 2018		**$ 24,440**

16A. Connor Company began operations on January 1 and has projected the following selling and administrative expenses:

Rent Expense	$ 1,000 per month, paid as incurred
Utilities Expense	500 per month, paid in month after incurred
Depreciation Expense	300 per month
Insurance Expense	100 per month, 6 months prepaid on January 1

Determine the cash payments for selling and administrative expenses for the first three months of operations.

Check your answers online in MyAccountingLab or at http://www.pearsonhighered.com/Horngren.

For more practice, see Short Exercises S22A-17 through S22A-20. MyAccountingLab

REVIEW

> Things You Should Know

1. Why do managers use budgets?

- Budgeting objectives
  - Develop strategies—overall, long-term business goals
  - Plan—budget for specific actions to achieve goals
  - Act—carry out the plans
  - Control—feedback to identify corrective action (if necessary)
- Budgeting benefits
  - Requires managers to *plan* how to increase sales and how to cut costs
  - Promotes *coordination and communication*, such as communicating the importance of cost-reduction goals
  - Provides a *benchmark* that motivates employees and helps managers evaluate how well employees contributed to the sales growth and cost-reduction goals

2. Are there different types of budgets?

- Strategic budgets—for long-term goals
- Operational budgets—for short-term goals
- Static budgets—for one level of sales volume
- Flexible budgets—for various levels of sales volumes
- Master budgets
  - Set of budgeted financial statements and supporting schedules
  - Operational and static budgets
  - Includes operating budget, capital expenditures budget, and financial budget

3. How are operating budgets prepared for a manufacturing company?

- Sales budget—the cornerstone of the master budget
- Production budget
  - Direct materials budget
  - Direct labor budget
  - Manufacturing overhead budget
- Cost of goods sold budget
- Selling and administrative expense budget

4. How are financial budgets prepared for a manufacturing company?

- Cash budget
  - Cash receipts
  - Cash payments
  - Short-term financing

- Budgeted financial statements
  - Budgeted income statement
  - Budgeted balance sheet
  - Budgeted statement of cash flows

5. How can information technology be used in the budgeting process?

- Sensitivity analysis—*what if* analysis
- Budgeting software allows business segments to integrate individual budgets into the companywide budget.

6. How are operating budgets prepared for a merchandising company? (Appendix 22A)

- Sales budget—the cornerstone of the master budget
- Inventory, purchases, and cost of goods sold budget
- Selling and administrative expense budget

7. How are financial budgets prepared for a merchandising company? (Appendix 22A)

- Cash budget
  - Cash receipts
  - Cash payments
  - Short-term financing
- Budgeted financial statements
  - Budgeted income statement
  - Budgeted balance sheet
  - Budgeted statement of cash flows

> Summary Problem 22-1

Smart Touch Learning has decided to revise its budget to show fourth quarter sales of 700 tablets due to the expectation of increased holiday sales. First quarter sales for the following year are not expected to change.

Requirements

1. Revise the following budgets:
   a. Sales budget (Exhibit 22-5)
   b. Production budget (Exhibit 22-6)
2. Describe how the following budgets will be affected (without revising the budgets):
   a. Direct materials budget
   b. Direct labor budget
   c. Manufacturing overhead budget
   d. Cost of goods sold budget
   e. Selling and administrative expense budget

> Solution

Requirement 1

Revised figures appear in color for emphasis.

a. Revised sales budget

SMART TOUCH LEARNING Revised Sales Budget For the Year Ended December 31, 2019					
	First Quarter	Second Quarter	Third Quarter	Fourth Quarter	Total
Budgeted tablets to be sold	500	550	600	700	2,350
Sales price per unit	× $500	× $500	× $500	× $500	× $500
Total sales	$ 250,000	$ 275,000	$ 300,000	$ 350,000	$1,175,000

b. Revised production budget

SMART TOUCH LEARNING Revised Production Budget For the Year Ended December 31, 2019					
	First Quarter	Second Quarter	Third Quarter	Fourth Quarter	Total
Budgeted tablets to be sold	500	550	600	700	2,350
Plus: Desired tablets in ending inventory	110	120	140*	140	140
Total tablets needed	610	670	740	840	2,490
Less: Tablets in beginning inventory	200	110	120	140	200
Budgeted tablets to be produced	410	560	620	700	2,290

*700 × 20%

Requirement 2

a. Direct materials budget: An increase in production will require more direct materials and, therefore, more purchases of materials.

b. Direct labor budget: An increase in production will require additional labor and, therefore, increase the direct labor costs.

c. Manufacturing overhead budget: An increase in production will require additional variable manufacturing overhead and, therefore, an increase in variable manufacturing overhead costs. Fixed costs will not change unless the increased production takes Smart Touch Learning out of its relevant range.

d. Cost of goods sold budget: An increase in production will decrease the production cost per unit because the fixed costs will be distributed among more units. In other words, the predetermined overhead allocation rate will decrease. The small increase in production will only have a minor effect on production costs, however, because fixed manufacturing overhead costs are a small portion of the total production cost. Therefore, total cost of goods sold will increase due to the increase in units sold.

e. Selling and administrative expense budget: If the increase in sales does not take Smart Touch Learning out of its relevant range, then fixed selling and administrative costs will not change. The variable selling and administrative cost, Supplies, will increase with the increase in sales.

> Summary Problem 22-2

Continue the revised Smart Touch Learning illustration from Summary Problem 22-1. Recall that the fourth quarter sales are revised to 700 tablets with the expectation of increased holiday sales.

Suppose a change in the receipt of cash from sales on account is as follows:

       60% in the month of the sale

       20% in the month after the sale

       19% two months after the sale

       1% never collected

Requirements

1. Revise the schedule of budgeted cash receipts (Exhibit 22-12) to include the increase in fourth quarter sales (from Summary Problem 22-1) and the change in the timing of customer receipts.

2. How will the changes in cash receipts affect the cash budget?

> Solution

Requirement 1

Revised figures appear in color for emphasis.

	First Quarter	Second Quarter	Third Quarter	Fourth Quarter	Total
Total sales (from Summary Problem 22-1)	$ 250,000	$ 275,000	$ 300,000	$ 350,000	$ 1,175,000

	First Quarter	Second Quarter	Third Quarter	Fourth Quarter	Total
Cash Receipts from Customers:					
Accounts Receivable balance, December 31, 2018	$ 70,000				
1st Qtr.—Cash sales (30%)	75,000				
1st Qtr.—Credit sales (70%), 60% collected in 1st qtr.	105,000				
1st Qtr.—Credit sales (70%), 20% collected in 2nd qtr.		$ 35,000			
1st Qtr.—Credit sales (70%), 19% collected in 3rd qtr.			$ 33,250		
2nd Qtr.—Cash sales (30%)		82,500			
2nd Qtr.—Credit sales (70%), 60% collected in 2nd qtr.		115,500			
2nd Qtr.—Credit sales (70%), 20% collected in 3rd qtr.			38,500		
2nd Qtr.—Credit sales (70%), 19% collected in 4th qtr.				$ 36,575	
3rd Qtr.—Cash sales (30%)			90,000		
3rd Qtr.—Credit sales (70%), 60% collected in 3rd qtr.			126,000		
3rd Qtr.—Credit sales (70%), 20% collected in 4th qtr.				42,000	
4th Qtr.—Cash sales (30%)				105,000	
4th Qtr.—Credit sales (70%), 60% collected in 4th qtr.				147,000	
Total cash receipts from customers	$ 250,000	$ 233,000	$ 287,750	$ 330,575	$ 1,101,325

Requirement 2

The decrease in cash receipts will require Smart Touch Learning to borrow more funds on the short-term note payable. Increased borrowing will increase interest expense and decrease net income for the year.

	First Quarter	Second Quarter	Third Quarter	Fourth Quarter	Total
Original budgeted cash receipts	$ 250,000	$ 268,000	$ 293,000	$ 318,000	$ 1,129,000
Revised budgeted cash receipts	250,000	233,000	287,750	330,575	1,101,325
Difference	$ 0	$ (35,000)	$ (5,250)	$ 12,575	$ (27,675)

> Key Terms

Budget (p. 1169)

Budgetary Slack (p. 1172)

Capital Expenditures
   Budget (p. 1175)

Cash Budget (p. 1175)

Financial Budget (p. 1175)

Flexible Budget (p. 1173)

Master Budget (p. 1174)

Operating Budget (p. 1174)

Operational Budget (p. 1173)

Static Budget (p. 1173)

Strategic Budget (p. 1173)

> Quick Check

1. A company can expect to receive which of the following benefits when it starts its budgeting process?

   Learning Objective 1

   a. The budget provides managers with a benchmark against which to compare actual results for performance evaluation.

   b. The planning required to develop the budget helps managers foresee and avoid potential problems before they occur.

   c. The budget helps motivate employees to achieve sales growth and cost-reduction goals.

   d. All of the above

2. A company prepares a five-year budget. This budget would be considered a(n)

   Learning Objective 2

   a. strategic budget   c. master budget
   b. operational budget   d. flexible budget

3. Which of the following is the cornerstone of the master budget?

   Learning Objective 3

   a. The selling and administrative expense budget
   b. The budgeted balance sheet
   c. The sales budget
   d. The production budget

Use the following information to answer questions 4 through 7.

Suppose Iron City manufactures cast iron skillets. One model is a 10-inch skillet that sells for $20. Iron City projects sales of 500 10-inch skillets per month. The production costs are $9 per skillet for direct materials, $1 per skillet for direct labor, and $2 per skillet for manufacturing overhead. Iron City has 50 10-inch skillets in inventory at the beginning of July but wants to have an ending inventory equal to 20% of the next month's sales. Selling and administrative expenses for this product line are $1,500 per month.

4. How many 10-inch skillets should Iron City produce in July?

   Learning Objective 3

   a. 500 skillets   c. 600 skillets
   b. 550 skillets   d. 650 skillets

5. Compute the total amount budgeted for product costs for July.

   Learning Objective 3

   a. $6,000   c. $6,600
   b. $6,500   d. $7,200

Learning Objective 3

6. Compute the budgeted cost of goods sold for July.

   a. $6,000   c. $6,600

   b. $6,500   d. $7,200

Learning Objective 4

7. Compute the budgeted gross profit for July.

   a. $6,000   c. $4,000

   b. $5,000   d. $3,000

Learning Objective 4

8. The budgeted statement of cash flows is part of which element of the master budget?

   a. The financial budget   c. The capital expenditures budget

   b. The operating budget   d. None of the above

Learning Objective 4

9. Which of the following expenses would *not* appear in the cash budget?

   a. Depreciation expense   c. Interest expense

   b. Marketing expense   d. Wages expense

Learning Objective 5

10. Information technology has made it easier for managers to perform all of the following tasks *except*

    a. preparing performance reports that identify variances between actual and budgeted revenues and costs.

    b. combining individual units' budgets into the companywide budget.

    c. sensitivity analyses.

    d. removing budgetary slack from the budget.

Use the following information to answer questions 11A and 12A.

Suppose Mallcentral sells 1,000 hardcover books per day at an average price of $30. Assume that Mallcentral's cost for the books is 75% of the selling price it charges retail customers. Mallcentral has no beginning inventory, but it wants to have a three-day supply of ending inventory. Assume that selling and administrative expenses are $1,000 per day.

Learning Objective 6
Appendix 22A

11A. Compute Mallcentral's budgeted sales for the next (seven-day) week.

   a. $157,500   c. $435,000

   b. $217,000   d. $210,000

Learning Objective 6
Appendix 22A

12A. Determine Mallcentral's budgeted purchases for the next (seven-day) week.

   a. $300,000   c. $157,500

   b. $225,000   d. $75,000

Learning Objective 7
Appendix 22A

13A. The budgeted balance sheet is part of which element of the master budget?

   a. Financial budget   c. Capital expenditures budget

   b. Operating budget   d. None of the above

Check your answers at the end of the chapter.

ASSESS YOUR PROGRESS

> Review Questions

1. List the four budgeting objectives.

2. One benefit of budgeting is coordination and communication. Explain what this means.

3. How is benchmarking beneficial?

4. What is budgetary slack? Why might managers try to build slack into their budgets?

5. Explain the difference between strategic and operational budgets.

6. Explain the difference between static and flexible budgets.

7. What is a master budget?

8. What are the three types of budgets included in the master budget? Describe each type.

9. Why is the sales budget considered the cornerstone of the master budget?

10. What is the formula used to determine the number of units to be produced?

11. What is the formula used to determine the amount of direct materials to be purchased?

12. What are the two types of manufacturing overhead? How do they affect the manufacturing overhead budget calculations?

13. How is the predetermined overhead allocation rate determined?

14. What is the capital expenditures budget?

15. What are the three sections of the cash budget?

16. What are the budgeted financial statements? How do they differ from regular financial statements?

17. What is sensitivity analysis? Why is it important for managers?

18A. How does the master budget for a merchandising company differ from a manufacturing company?

19A. What is the formula used to determine the amount of merchandise inventory to be purchased?

20A. What budgets are included in the financial budget for a merchandising company?

> Short Exercises

S22-1 Budgeting benefits

List the three key benefits companies get from preparing a budget.

Learning Objective 1

S22-2 Budgeting types

Consider the following budgets and budget types.

Learning Objective 2

Cash	Cost of Goods Sold
Flexible	Master
Operational	Sales
Static	Strategic

Which budget or budget type should be used to meet the following needs?

a. Upper management is planning for the next five years.

b. A store manager wants to plan for different levels of sales.

c. The accountant wants to determine if the company will have sufficient funds to pay expenses.

d. The CEO wants to make companywide plans for the next year.

Learning Objective 3

S22-3 Preparing an operating budget—sales budget

Yogi Company manufactures luggage sets. Yogi sells its luggage sets to department stores. Yogi expects to sell 1,650 luggage sets for $320 each in January and 2,050 luggage sets for $320 each in February. All sales are cash only. Prepare the sales budget for January and February.

Learning Objective 3

S22-4 Preparing an operating budget—production budget

Yandell Company expects to sell 1,650 units of finished product in January and 2,000 units in February. The company has 240 units on hand on January 1 and desires to have an ending inventory equal to 60% of the next month's sales. March sales are expected to be 2,050 units. Prepare Yandell's production budget for January and February.

Learning Objective 3

S22-5 Preparing an operating budget—direct materials budget

Yosko expects to produce 1,950 units in January and 2,114 units in February. The company budgets $85 per unit for direct materials. Indirect materials are insignificant and not considered for budgeting purposes. The balance in the Raw Materials Inventory account (all direct materials) on January 1 is $50,000. Yosko desires the ending balance in Raw Materials Inventory to be 40% of the next month's direct materials needed for production. Desired ending balance for February is $51,400. Prepare Yosko's direct materials budget for January and February.

Learning Objective 3

S22-6 Preparing an operating budget—direct labor budget

Yancey Company expects to produce 1,920 units in January and 1,974 units in February. Yancey budgets two direct labor hours per unit. Direct labor costs average $20 per hour. Prepare Yancey's direct labor budget for January and February.

Learning Objective 3

S22-7 Preparing an operating budget—manufacturing overhead budget

Yasmin Company expects to produce 2,110 units in January that will require 6,330 hours of direct labor and 2,280 units in February that will require 6,840 hours of direct labor. Yasmin budgets $8 per unit for variable manufacturing overhead; $1,300 per month for depreciation; and $33,820 per month for other fixed manufacturing overhead costs. Prepare Yasmin's manufacturing overhead budget for January and February, including the predetermined overhead allocation rate using direct labor hours as the allocation base.

Learning Objective 3

S22-8 Preparing an operating budget—cost of goods sold budget

Young Company expects to sell 1,800 units in January and 1,900 units in February. The company expects to incur the following product costs:

Direct materials cost per unit	$ 45
Direct labor cost per unit	64
Manufacturing overhead cost per unit	28

The beginning balance in Finished Goods Inventory is 260 units at $137 each for a total of $35,620. Young uses FIFO inventory costing method. Prepare the cost of goods sold budget for Young for January and February.

S22-9 Preparing a financial budget—schedule of cash receipts

Learning Objective 4

Yeaman expects total sales of $333,000 in January and $407,000 in February. Assume that Yeaman's sales are collected as follows:

- 60% in the month of the sale
- 30% in the month after the sale
- 8% two months after the sales
- 2% never collected

November sales totaled $260,000, and December sales were $330,000. Prepare a schedule of cash receipts from customers for January and February. Round answers to the nearest dollar.

S22-10 Preparing a financial budget—schedule of cash payments

Learning Objective 4

Yada Company budgeted direct materials purchases of $192,340 in January and $138,260 in February. Assume Yada pays for direct materials purchases 30% in the month of purchase and 70% in the month after purchase. The Accounts Payable balance on January 1 is $40,000. Prepare a schedule of cash payments for purchases for January and February. Round to the nearest dollar.

S22-11 Preparing a financial budget—cash budget

Learning Objective 4

Yates has $13,500 in cash on hand on January 1 and has collected the following budget data:

	January	February
Sales	$ 528,000	$ 560,000
Cash receipts from customers	442,400	502,800
Cash payments for direct materials purchases	180,598	160,464
Direct labor costs	135,040	113,792
Manufacturing overhead costs (includes depreciation of $2,100 per month)	55,428	53,436

Assume direct labor costs and manufacturing overhead costs are paid in the month incurred. Additionally, assume Yates has cash payments for selling and administrative expenses including salaries of $45,000 per month plus commissions that are 2% of sales, all paid in the month of sale. The company requires a minimum cash balance of $10,000. Prepare a cash budget for January and February. Round to the nearest dollar. Will Yates need to borrow cash by the end of February?

Note: Short Exercise S22-9 must be completed before attempting Short Exercise S22-12.

Learning Objective 5

S22-12 Using sensitivity analysis in budgeting

Refer to the Yeaman's schedule of cash receipts from customers that you prepared in Short Exercise S22-9. Now assume that Yeaman's sales are collected as follows:

50% in the month of the sale

30% in the month after the sale

18% two months after the sale

2% never collected

Prepare a revised schedule of cash receipts for January and February.

Learning Objective 5

S22-13 Using sensitivity analysis in budgeting

Riverside Sporting Goods Store has the following sales budget:

RIVERSIDE SPORTING GOODS STORE Sales Budget Four Months Ended July 31					
	April	May	June	July	Total
Cash sales (80%)	$ 42,400	$ 67,200	$ 52,800	$ 42,400	$ 204,800
Credit sales (20%)	10,600	16,800	13,200	10,600	51,200
Total sales	$ 53,000	$ 84,000	$ 66,000	$ 53,000	$ 256,000

Suppose June sales are expected to be $82,000 rather than $66,000. Revise Riverside's sales budget.

Learning Objective 6
Appendix 22A

S22A-14 Understanding the components of the master budget

The following are some of the components included in the master budget of a merchandising company.

   a. Budgeted balance sheet

   b. Sales budget

   c. Capital expenditures budget

   d. Budgeted income statement

   e. Cash budget

   f. Inventory, purchases, and cost of goods sold budget

   g. Budgeted statement of cash flows

   h. Selling and administrative expense budget

List the items of the master budget in order of preparation.

Learning Objective 6
Appendix 22A

S22A-15 Preparing an operating budget—sales budget

Climbers sells its rock-climbing shoes worldwide. Climbers expects to sell 4,500 pairs of shoes for $190 each in January and 3,200 pairs of shoes for $230 each in February. All sales are cash only. Prepare the sales budget for January and February.

S22A-16 Preparing an operating budget—inventory, purchases, and cost of goods sold budget

Learning Objective 6
Appendix 22A

Smith Company expects to sell 5,500 units for $195 each for a total of $1,072,500 in January and 3,000 units for $210 each for a total of $630,000 in February. The company expects cost of goods sold to average 70% of sales revenue, and the company expects to sell 4,000 units in March for $210 each. Smith's target ending inventory is $14,000 plus 50% of the next month's cost of goods sold. Prepare Smith's inventory, purchases, and cost of goods sold budget for January and February.

S22A-17 Preparing a financial budget—schedule of cash receipts

Learning Objective 7
Appendix 22A

Packers expects total sales of $697,500 for January and $345,000 for February. Assume that Packers's sales are collected as follows:

60% in the month of the sale

20% in the month after the sale

17% two months after the sale

3% never collected

November sales totaled $389,000, and December sales were $401,000. Prepare a schedule of cash receipts from customers for January and February. Round answers to the nearest dollar.

S22A-18 Preparing a financial budget—schedule of cash payments

Learning Objective 7
Appendix 22A

Johnson Company has budgeted purchases of merchandise inventory of $456,250 in January and $531,250 in February. Assume Johnson pays for inventory purchases 70% in the month of purchase and 30% in the month after purchase. The Accounts Payable balance on December 31 is $97,575. Prepare a schedule of cash payments for purchases for January and February.

S22A-19 Preparing a financial budget—cash budget

Learning Objective 7
Appendix 22A

Williams Company has $14,000 in cash on hand on January 1 and has collected the following budget data:

	January	February
Sales	$ 1,320,000	$ 630,000
Cash receipts from customers	851,370	871,700
Cash payments for merchandise inventory	561,600	532,368

Assume Williams has cash payments for selling and administrative expenses including salaries of $36,000 plus commissions of 3% of sales, all paid in the month of sale. The company requires a minimum cash balance of $10,500. Prepare a cash budget for January and February. Will Williams need to borrow cash by the end of February?

Note: Short Exercise S22A-17 must be completed before attempting Short Exercise S22A-20.

Learning Objective 7
Appendix 22A

S22A-20 Using sensitivity analysis in budgeting

Refer to the Packers schedule of cash receipts from customers that you prepared in Short Exercise S22A-17. Now assume that Packers's sales are collected as follows:

50% in the month of the sale

20% in the month after the sale

25% two months after the sale

5% never collected

Prepare a revised schedule of cash receipts for January and February.

> Exercises

Learning Objective 1

This year Op. Inc. $1,880,000

E22-21 Budgeting benefits

David Rodriguez owns a chain of travel goods stores, Rodriguez Travel Goods. Last year, his sales staff sold 25,000 suitcases at an average sales price of $150. Variable expenses were 60% of sales revenue, and the total fixed expense was $120,000. This year, the chain sold more expensive product lines. Sales were 20,000 suitcases at an average price of $250. The variable expense percentage and the total fixed expenses were the same both years. Rodriguez evaluates the chain manager by comparing this year's operating income with last year's operating income.

Prepare a performance report for this year, similar to Exhibit 22-2, which compares this year's results with last year's results. How would you improve Rodriguez's performance evaluation system to better analyze this year's results?

Learning Objective 2

E22-22 Describing master budget components

Sarah Edwards, division manager for Pillows Plus, is speaking to the controller, Diana Rothman, about the budgeting process. Sarah states, "I'm not an accountant, so can you explain the three main parts of the master budget to me and tell me their purpose?" Answer Sarah's question.

Learning Objective 3

Jul. total sales $23,400

E22-23 Preparing an operating budget—sales budget

Sinclair Company manufactures T-shirts printed with tourist destination logos. The following table shows sales prices and projected sales volume for the summer months:

T-Shirt Sizes	Sales Price	Projected Sales in Units		
		June	July	August
Youth	$ 9	425	675	575
Adult—regular	12	700	700	850
Adult—oversized	17	450	525	475

Prepare a sales budget for Sinclair Company for the three months.

E22-24 Preparing an operating budget—sales and production budgets

Learning Objective 3

May pkg. produced 5,995

Gorman Company manufactures drinking glasses. One unit is a package of eight glasses, which sells for $35. Gorman projects sales for April will be 5,500 packages, with sales increasing by 450 packages per month for May, June, and July. On April 1, Gorman has 125 packages on hand but desires to maintain an ending inventory of 10% of the next month's sales. Prepare a sales budget and a production budget for Gorman for April, May, and June.

E22-25 Preparing an operating budget—direct materials, direct labor, and manufacturing overhead budgets

Learning Objective 3

2nd Qtr. OH $587.50

Trevor, Inc. manufactures model airplane kits and projects production at 500, 570, 300, and 450 kits for the next four quarters. Direct materials are $10 per kit. Indirect materials are considered insignificant and are not included in the budgeting process. Beginning Raw Materials Inventory is $200, and the company desires to end each quarter with 30% of the materials needed for the next quarter's production. Trevor desires a balance of $200 in Raw Materials Inventory at the end of the fourth quarter. Each kit requires 0.75 hours of direct labor at an average cost of $25 per hour. Manufacturing overhead is allocated using direct labor hours as the allocation base. Variable overhead is $0.75 per kit, and fixed overhead is $160 per quarter. Prepare Trevor's direct materials budget, direct labor budget, and manufacturing overhead budget for the year. Round the direct labor hours needed for production, budgeted overhead costs, and predetermined overhead allocation rate to two decimal places. Round other amounts to the nearest whole number.

Note: Exercise E22-25 must be completed before attempting Exercise E22-26.

E22-26 Preparing an operating budget—cost of goods sold budget

Learning Objective 3

3rd Qtr. COGS $20,895

Refer to the budgets prepared in Exercise E22-25. Determine the cost per kit to manufacture the model airplane kits. Trevor projects sales of 400, 100, 700, and 500 kits for the next four quarters. Prepare a cost of goods sold budget for the year. Trevor has no kits in beginning inventory. Round amounts to two decimal places.

E22-27 Preparing a financial budget—schedule of cash receipts, sensitivity analysis

Learning Objectives 4, 5

1. Feb. total cash receipts $11,960

Armand Company projects the following sales for the first three months of the year: $10,600 in January; $12,300 in February; and $12,900 in March. The company expects 60% of the sales to be cash and the remainder on account. Sales on account are collected 50% in the month of the sale and 50% in the following month. The Accounts Receivable account has a zero balance on January 1. Round to the nearest dollar.

Requirements

1. Prepare a schedule of cash receipts for Armand for January, February, and March. What is the balance in Accounts Receivable on March 31?

2. Prepare a revised schedule of cash receipts if receipts from sales on account are 60% in the month of the sale, 30% in the month following the sale, and 10% in the second month following the sale. What is the balance in Accounts Receivable on March 31?

Learning Objective 4

Mar. total cash pmts. $11,600

E22-28 Preparing a financial budget—schedule of cash payments

Armand Company has the following projected costs for manufacturing and selling and administrative expenses:

	Jan.	Feb.	Mar.
Direct materials purchases	$ 3,900	$ 4,100	$ 4,600
Direct labor costs	3,300	3,900	3,500
Depreciation on plant	550	550	550
Utilities for plant	650	650	650
Property taxes on plant	150	150	150
Depreciation on office	550	550	550
Utilities for office	350	350	350
Property taxes on office	180	180	180
Office salaries	3,000	3,000	3,000

All costs are paid in month incurred except: direct materials, which are paid in the month following the purchase; utilities, which are paid in the month after incurred; and property taxes, which are prepaid for the year on January 2. The Accounts Payable and Utilities Payable accounts have a zero balance on January 1. Prepare a schedule of cash payments for Armand for January, February, and March. Determine the balances in Prepaid Property Taxes, Accounts Payable, and Utilities Payable as of March 31.

*Note: Exercises E22-27 and E22-28 must be completed before attempting
Exercise E22-29.*

Learning Objective 4

Feb. ending cash bal. $3,367

E22-29 Preparing the financial budget—cash budget

Use the original schedule of cash receipts completed in Exercise E22-27, Requirement 1, and the schedule of cash payments completed in Exercise E22-28 to complete a cash budget for Armand Company.

Additional information: Armand's beginning cash balance is $3,000, and Armand desires to maintain a minimum ending cash balance of $3,000. Armand borrows cash as needed at the beginning of each month in increments of $1,000 and repays the amounts borrowed in increments of $1,000 at the beginning of months when excess cash is available. The interest rate on amounts borrowed is 8% per year. Interest is paid at the beginning of the month on the outstanding balance from the previous month.

Learning Objective 4

Mar. interest expense $212

E22-30 Preparing the financial budget—cash budget

Harley Company requires a minimum cash balance of $5,000. When the company expects a cash deficiency, it borrows the exact amount required on the first of the month. Expected excess cash is used to repay any amounts owed. Interest owed from the previous month's principal balance is paid on the first of the month at 12% per year. The company has already completed the budgeting process for the first quarter for cash receipts and cash payments for all expenses except interest. Harley does not have any outstanding debt on January 1. Complete the cash budget for the first quarter for Harley Company. Round interest expense to the nearest whole dollar.

HARLEY COMPANY
Cash Budget
For the Three Months Ended March 31

	January	February	March	Total
Beginning balance	5,000			
Cash receipts	18,000	26,000	40,000	84,000
Cash available	23,000			
Cash payments:				
All expenses except interest	35,000	30,000	32,000	97,000
Interest expense	0			
Total cash payments	35,000			
Ending balance before financing				
Minimum cash balance desired	(5,000)	(5,000)	(5,000)	(5,000)
Projected cash excess (deficiency)				
Financing:				
Borrowing				
Principal repayments				
Total effects of financing				
Ending cash balance				

E22-31 Preparing the financial budget—budgeted balance sheet

Berkson, Inc. has the following balance sheet at December 31, 2016:

Learning Objective 4

FG inventory $500

BERKSON, INC.
Balance Sheet
December 31, 2016

Assets

Current Assets:		
Cash	$ 2,100	
Accounts Receivable	900	
Raw Materials Inventory	900	
Finished Goods Inventory	1,650	
Total Current Assets		$ 5,550
Property, Plant, and Equipment:		
Equipment	17,000	
Less: Accumulated Depreciation	(3,500)	13,500
Total Assets		$ 19,050

Liabilities

Current Liabilities:		
Accounts Payable		$ 1,400

Stockholders' Equity

Common Stock, no par	$ 7,000	
Retained Earnings	10,650	
Total Stockholders' Equity		17,650
Total Liabilities and Stockholders' Equity		$ 19,050

Berkson projects the following transactions for 2017:

  Sales on account, $21,000

  Cash receipts from customers from sales on account, $15,800

  Purchase of raw materials on account, $2,000

  Payments on account, $2,000

  Total cost of completed products, $15,150, which includes the following:

   Raw materials used, $2,000

   Direct labor costs incurred and paid, $5,800

   Manufacturing overhead costs incurred and paid, $6,500

   Depreciation on manufacturing equipment, $850

  Cost of goods sold, $16,300

  Selling and administrative costs incurred and paid, $1,000

  Purchase of equipment, paid in 2017, $1,900

Prepare a budgeted balance sheet for Berkson, Inc. for December 31, 2017.

Hint: It may be helpful to trace the effects of each transaction on the accounting equation to determine the ending balance of each account.

E22-32 Using sensitivity analysis

Bolden Company prepared the following budgeted income statement for 2017:

BOLDEN COMPANY Budgeted Income Statement For the Year Ended December 31, 2017	
Unit Sales	1,400
Sales Revenue ($700 per unit)	$ 980,000
Cost of Goods Sold (55% of sales)	539,000
Gross Profit	441,000
Selling and Administrative Expenses (35% of sales)	343,000
Operating Income	$ 98,000

Requirements

1. Prepare a budgeted income statement with columns for 1,300 units, 1,400 units, and 1,600 units sold.

2. How might managers use this type of budgeted income statement?

3. How might spreadsheet software such as Excel assist in this type of analysis?

E22A-33 Preparing an operating budget—inventory, purchases, and cost of goods sold budget

Learning Objective 6
Appendix 22A

Qtr. ended Jun. 30 purchases
$59,000

Stewart, Inc. sells tire rims. Its sales budget for the nine months ended September 30, 2016, follows:

	Quarter Ended			Nine-Month Total
	March 31	**June 30**	**September 30**	
Cash sales, 20%	$ 20,000	$ 30,000	$ 25,000	$ 75,000
Credit sales, 80%	80,000	120,000	100,000	300,000
Total sales	$ 100,000	$ 150,000	$ 125,000	$ 375,000

In the past, cost of goods sold has been 40% of total sales. The director of marketing and the financial vice president agree that each quarter's ending inventory should not be below $10,000 plus 10% of cost of goods sold for the following quarter. The marketing director expects sales of $200,000 during the fourth quarter. The January 1 inventory was $36,000. Prepare an inventory, purchases, and cost of goods sold budget for each of the first three quarters of the year. Compute cost of goods sold for the entire nine-month period.

E22A-34 Preparing an operating budget—selling and administrative expense budget

Learning Objective 6
Appendix 22A

Qtr. ended Mar. 31 total S&A exp.
$21,700

Consider the sales budget presented in Exercise E22A-33. Stewart's selling and administrative expenses include the following:

Rent, $1,100 per month
Salaries, $2,000 per month
Commissions, 4% of sales
Depreciation, $1,800 per month
Miscellaneous expenses, 3% of sales

Prepare a selling and administrative expense budget for each of the three quarters of 2016 and totals for the nine-month period.

E22A-35 Preparing a financial budget—schedule of cash receipts and schedule of cash payments

Learning Objective 7
Appendix 22A

b. Sep. cash recpts. $119,795

Agua Frio is a distributor of bottled water. For each of the items, compute the amount of cash receipts or payments Agua Frio will budget for September. The solution to one item may depend on the answer to an earlier item.

a. Management expects to sell equipment that cost $17,000 at a gain of $3,000. Accumulated depreciation on this equipment is $7,000.

b. Management expects to sell 7,400 cases of water in August and 9,600 cases in September. Each case sells for $13. Cash sales average 30% of total sales, and credit sales make up the rest. Three-fourths of credit sales are collected in the month of the sale, with the balance collected the following month.

c. The company pays rent and property taxes of $3,900 each month. Commissions and other selling expenses average 30% of sales. Agua Frio pays one-half of commissions and other selling expenses in the month incurred, with the balance paid the following month.

Learning Objectives 5, 7
Appendix 22A

1. Feb. ending cash bal. $10,400

E22A-36 Preparing a financial budget—cash budget, sensitivity analysis

Linstead Auto Parts, a family-owned auto parts store, began January with $10,400 cash. Management forecasts that collections from credit customers will be $11,500 in January and $15,500 in February. The store is scheduled to receive $4,500 cash on a business note receivable in January. Projected cash payments include inventory purchases ($12,900 in January and $14,600 in February) and selling and administrative expenses ($2,500 each month).

Linstead Auto Parts's bank requires a $10,000 minimum balance in the store's checking account. At the end of any month when the account balance falls below $10,000, the bank automatically extends credit to the store in multiples of $1,000. Linstead Auto Parts borrows as little as possible and pays back loans in quarterly installments of $1,500, plus 3% APR interest on the entire unpaid principal. The first payment occurs three months after the loan.

Requirements

1. Prepare Linstead Auto Parts's cash budget for January and February.
2. How much cash will Linstead Auto Parts borrow in February if collections from customers that month total $14,500 instead of $15,500?

Learning Objective 7
Appendix 22A

May ending cash bal. $20,000

E22A-37 Preparing a financial budget—cash budget

You recently began a job as an accounting intern at Reed Golf Park. Your first task was to help prepare the cash budget for April and May. Unfortunately, the computer with the budget file crashed, and you did not have a backup or even a paper copy. You ran a program to salvage bits of data from the budget file. After entering the following data in the budget, you may have just enough information to reconstruct the budget.

REED GOLF PARK Cash Budget Two Months Ended May 31		
	April	May
Beginning cash balance	$ 18,500	$?
Cash receipts	?	84,000
Cash from sale of plant assets	0	2,100
Cash available	108,600	?
Cash payments:		
Purchase of inventory	?	46,000
Selling and administrative expenses	47,600	?
Interest expense	?	?
Total cash payments	99,600	?
Ending cash balance before financing	?	22,100
Minimum cash balance desired	(20,000)	(20,000)
Cash excess (deficiency)	?	?
Financing:		
Borrowing	?	?
Principal repayments	?	?
Total effects of financing	?	?
Ending cash balance	?	?

Reed Golf Park eliminates any cash deficiency by borrowing the exact amount needed from First Street Bank, where the current interest rate is 7% per year. Reed Golf Park first pays interest on its outstanding debt at the end of each month. The company then repays all borrowed amounts at the end of the month with any excess cash above the minimum required but after paying monthly interest expenses. Reed does not have any outstanding debt on April 1.

Complete the cash budget. Round interest expense to the nearest whole dollar.

E22A-38 Preparing a financial budget—budgeted balance sheet

Learning Objective 7
Appendix 22A

Cash $7,500

Use the following June actual ending balances and July 31, 2016, budgeted amounts for Ollies to prepare a budgeted balance sheet for July 31, 2016.

a. June 30 Merchandise Inventory balance, $17,760

b. July purchase of Merchandise Inventory, $4,600, paid in cash

c. July payments of Accounts Payable, $8,700

d. June 30 Accounts Payable balance, $10,500

e. June 30 Furniture and Fixtures balance, $34,300; Accumulated Depreciation balance, $29,820

f. June 30 total stockholders' equity balance, $28,120

g. July Depreciation Expense, $800

h. Cost of Goods Sold, 60% of sales

i. Other July expenses, including income tax, $5,000, paid in cash

j. June 30 Cash balance, $11,200

k. July budgeted sales, all on account, $12,200

l. June 30 Accounts Receivable balance, $5,180

m. July cash receipts from collections on account, $14,600

Hint: It may be helpful to trace the effects of each transaction on the accounting equation to determine the ending balance of each account.

> Problems **Group A**

Learning Objective 3

3. POHR $8
4. Adult bats COGS $60,690

P22-39A   Preparing an operating budget—sales, production, direct materials, direct labor, overhead, COGS, and S&A expense budgets

The Huber Batting Company manufactures wood baseball bats. Huber's two primary products are a youth bat, designed for children and young teens, and an adult bat, designed for high school and college-aged players. Huber sells the bats to sporting goods stores, and all sales are on account. The youth bat sells for $35; the adult bat sells for $65. Huber's highest sales volume is in the first three months of the year as retailers prepare for the spring baseball season. Huber's balance sheet for December 31, 2016, follows:

HUBER BATTING COMPANY Balance Sheet December 31, 2016		
Assets		
Current Assets:		
Cash	$ 15,000	
Accounts Receivable	21,600	
Raw Materials Inventory	12,000	
Finished Goods Inventory	17,210	
Total Current Assets		$ 65,810
Property, Plant, and Equipment:		
Equipment	115,000	
Less: Accumulated Depreciation	(20,000)	95,000
Total Assets		**$ 160,810**
Liabilities		
Current Liabilities:		
Accounts Payable		$ 10,500
Stockholders' Equity		
Common Stock, no par	$ 130,000	
Retained Earnings	20,310	
Total Stockholders' Equity		150,310
Total Liabilities and Stockholders' Equity		**$ 160,810**

Other data for Huber Batting Company for the first quarter of 2017:

a. Budgeted sales are 1,300 youth bats and 3,100 adult bats.

b. Finished Goods Inventory on December 31 consists of 650 youth bats at $17 each and 440 adult bats at $14 each.

c. Desired ending Finished Goods Inventory is 100 youth bats and 550 adult bats; FIFO inventory costing method is used.

d. Direct materials cost is $7 per youth bat and $9 per adult bat.

e. Desired ending Raw Materials Inventory is $12,000 (indirect materials are insignificant and not considered for budgeting purposes).

f. Each bat requires 0.5 hours of direct labor; direct labor costs average $15 per hour.

g. Variable manufacturing overhead is $0.50 per bat.

h. Fixed manufacturing overhead includes $600 per quarter in depreciation and $13,260 per quarter for other costs, such as insurance and property taxes.

i. Fixed selling and administrative expenses include $14,000 per quarter for salaries; $3,000 per quarter for rent; $2,000 per quarter for insurance; and $300 per quarter for depreciation.

j. Variable selling and administrative expenses include supplies at 3% of sales.

Requirements

1. Prepare Huber's sales budget for the first quarter of 2017.

2. Prepare Huber's production budget for the first quarter of 2017.

3. Prepare Huber's direct materials budget, direct labor budget, and manufacturing overhead budget for the first quarter of 2017. Round the predetermined overhead allocation rate to two decimal places. The overhead allocation base is direct labor hours.

4. Prepare Huber's cost of goods sold budget for the first quarter of 2017.

5. Prepare Huber's selling and administrative expense budget for the first quarter of 2017.

P22-40A Preparing a financial budget—schedule of cash receipts, schedule of cash payments, cash budget

Humble Company has provided the following budget information for the first quarter of 2016:

Learning Objective 4

1. Total cash pmts. $187,127
2. Ending Cash bal. $25,573

Total sales	$ 208,000
Budgeted purchases of direct materials	40,150
Budgeted direct labor cost	37,300
Budgeted manufacturing overhead costs:	
Variable manufacturing overhead	1,119
Depreciation	1,000
Insurance and property taxes	6,833
Budgeted selling and administrative expenses:	
Salaries expense	6,000
Rent expense	1,500
Insurance expense	1,700
Depreciation expense	200
Supplies expense	10,400

Additional data related to the first quarter of 2016 for Humble Company:

a. Capital expenditures include $37,000 for new manufacturing equipment to be purchased and paid in the first quarter.

b. Cash receipts are 75% of sales in the quarter of the sale and 25% in the quarter following the sale.

c. Direct materials purchases are paid 50% in the quarter purchased and 50% in the next quarter.

d. Direct labor, manufacturing overhead, and selling and administrative costs are paid in the quarter incurred.

e. Income tax expense for the first quarter is projected at $50,000 and is paid in the quarter incurred.

f. Humble Company expects to have adequate cash funds and does not anticipate borrowing in the first quarter.

g. The December 31, 2015, balance in Cash is $40,000, in Accounts Receivable is $16,700, and in Accounts Payable is $15,200.

Requirements

1. Prepare Humble Company's schedule of cash receipts from customers and schedule of cash payments for the first quarter of 2016.

2. Prepare Humble Company's cash budget for the first quarter of 2016.

Learning Objective 4

1. NI $166,300
2. FG inventory $6,650

P22-41A Preparing a financial budget—budgeted income statement, balance sheet, and statement of cash flows

Cooke Company has the following post-closing trial balance on December 31, 2016:

COOKE COMPANY Post-Closing Trial Balance December 31, 2016		
Account	Debit	Credit
Cash	$ 14,000	
Accounts Receivable	15,500	
Raw Materials Inventory	15,000	
Finished Goods Inventory	26,850	
Equipment	160,000	
Accumulated Depreciation		$ 30,000
Accounts Payable		15,200
Common Stock		80,000
Retained Earnings		106,150
Totals	$ 231,350	$ 231,350

The company's accounting department has gathered the following budgeting information for the first quarter of 2017:

Budgeted total sales, all on account	$ 308,500
Budgeted direct materials to be purchased and used	34,000
Budgeted direct labor cost	13,320
Budgeted manufacturing overhead costs:	
Variable manufacturing overhead	2,220
Depreciation	1,200
Insurance and property taxes	1,020
Budgeted cost of goods sold	71,960
Budgeted selling and administrative expenses:	
Salaries expense	6,000
Rent expense	4,500
Insurance expense	1,900
Depreciation expense	500
Supplies expense	12,340
Budgeted cash receipts from customers	262,300
Budgeted income tax expense	45,000
Budgeted purchase and payment for capital expenditures (additional equipment)	37,000

Additional information:

a. Direct materials purchases are paid 60% in the quarter purchased and 40% in the next quarter.

b. Direct labor, manufacturing overhead, selling and administrative costs, and income tax expense are paid in the quarter incurred.

Requirements

1. Prepare Cooke Company's budgeted income statement for the first quarter of 2017.

2. Prepare Cooke Company's budgeted balance sheet as of March 31, 2017.
   Hint: Use the budgeted statement of cash flows prepared in Requirement 3 to determine the Cash balance.

3. Prepare Cooke Company's budgeted statement of cash flows for the first quarter of 2017.

Learning Objectives 3, 4

1. 3rd Qtr. DM purchases $7,380
4th Qtr. total cash pmts. (before
interest) $32,998

**P22-42A Completing a comprehensive budgeting problem—manufacturing
company**

The Grady Tire Company manufactures racing tires for bicycles. Grady sells tires
for $60 each. Grady is planning for the next year by developing a master budget by
quarters. Grady's balance sheet for December 31, 2016, follows:

GRADY TIRE COMPANY Balance Sheet December 31, 2016		
Assets		
Current Assets:		
Cash	$ 55,000	
Accounts Receivable	45,000	
Raw Materials Inventory	900	
Finished Goods Inventory	2,600	
Total Current Assets		$ 103,500
Property, Plant, and Equipment:		
Equipment	155,000	
Less: Accumulated Depreciation	(77,000)	78,000
Total Assets		**$ 181,500**
Liabilities		
Current Liabilities:		
Accounts Payable		$ 6,000
Stockholders' Equity		
Common Stock, no par	$ 110,000	
Retained Earnings	65,500	
Total Stockholders' Equity		175,500
Total Liabilities and Stockholders' Equity		**$ 181,500**

Other data for Grady Tire Company:

a. Budgeted sales are 700 tires for the first quarter and expected to increase by 50 tires
per quarter. Cash sales are expected to be 30% of total sales, with the remaining
70% of sales on account.

b. Finished Goods Inventory on December 31 consists of 100 tires at $26 each.

c. Desired ending Finished Goods Inventory is 20% of the next quarter's sales; first
quarter sales for 2018 are expected to be 900 tires. FIFO inventory costing method
is used.

d. Direct materials cost is $9 per tire.

e. Desired ending Raw Materials Inventory is 20% of the next quarter's direct
materials needed for production; desired ending inventory for December 31
is $900; indirect materials are insignificant and not considered for budgeting
purposes.

f. Each tire requires 0.4 hours of direct labor; direct labor costs average $10 per hour.

g. Variable manufacturing overhead is $4 per tire.

h. Fixed manufacturing overhead includes $3,000 per quarter in depreciation and $1,770 per quarter for other costs, such as utilities, insurance, and property taxes.

i. Fixed selling and administrative expenses include $7,500 per quarter for salaries; $3,000 per quarter for rent; $1,650 per quarter for insurance; and $2,000 per quarter for depreciation.

j. Variable selling and administrative expenses include supplies at 2% of sales.

k. Capital expenditures include $50,000 for new manufacturing equipment, to be purchased and paid in the first quarter.

l. Cash receipts for sales on account are 30% in the quarter of the sale and 70% in the quarter following the sale; December 31, 2016, Accounts Receivable is received in the first quarter of 2017; uncollectible accounts are considered insignificant and not considered for budgeting purposes.

m. Direct materials purchases are paid 70% in the quarter purchased and 30% in the following quarter; December 31, 2016, Accounts Payable is paid in the first quarter of 2017.

n. Direct labor, manufacturing overhead, and selling and administrative costs are paid in the quarter incurred.

o. Income tax expense is projected at $4,000 per quarter and is paid in the quarter incurred.

p. Grady desires to maintain a minimum cash balance of $50,000 and borrows from the local bank as needed in increments of $1,000 at the beginning of the quarter; principal repayments are made at the beginning of the quarter when excess funds are available and in increments of $1,000; interest is 8% per year and paid at the beginning of the quarter based on the amount outstanding from the previous quarter.

Requirements

1. Prepare Grady's operating budget and cash budget for 2017 by quarter. Required schedules and budgets include: sales budget, production budget, direct materials budget, direct labor budget, manufacturing overhead budget, cost of goods sold budget, selling and administrative expense budget, schedule of cash receipts, schedule of cash payments, and cash budget. Manufacturing overhead costs are allocated based on direct labor hours. Round all calculations to the nearest dollar.

2. Prepare Grady's annual financial budget for 2017, including budgeted income statement, budgeted balance sheet, and budgeted statement of cash flows.

P22-43A Using sensitivity analysis

Soya Company prepared the following budgeted income statement for the first quarter of 2016:

SOYA COMPANY Budgeted Income Statement For the Quarter Ended March 31, 2016		January	February	March	Total
Sales Revenue	(20% increase per month)	$ 8,000	$ 9,600	$ 11,520	$ 29,120
Cost of Goods Sold	(40% of sales)	3,200	3,840	4,608	11,648
Gross Profit		4,800	5,760	6,912	17,472
S&A Expenses	($2,000 + 10% of sales)	2,800	2,960	3,152	8,912
Operating Income		2,000	2,800	3,760	8,560
Income Tax Expense	(30% of operating income)	600	840	1,128	2,568
Net Income		$ 1,400	$ 1,960	$ 2,632	$ 5,992

Soya Company is considering two options. Option 1 is to increase advertising by $1,200 per month. Option 2 is to use better-quality materials in the manufacturing process. The better materials will increase the cost of goods sold to 45% but will provide a better product at the same sales price. The marketing manager projects either option will result in sales increases of 25% per month rather than 20%.

Requirements

1. Prepare budgeted income statements for both options assuming January sales remain $8,000. Round all calculations to the nearest dollar.

2. Which option should Soya choose? Explain your reasoning.

P22A-44A Preparing an operating budget—sales budget; inventory, purchases and COGS budget; and S&A expense budget

Learning Objective 6
Appendix 22A

2. May purchases $30,750
3. Apr. total S&A exp. $10,900

Paperclip Office Supply's March 31, 2016, balance sheet follows:

PAPERCLIP OFFICE SUPPLY Balance Sheet March 31, 2016		
Assets		
Current Assets:		
Cash	$ 34,000	
Accounts Receivable	20,000	
Merchandise Inventory	14,500	
Prepaid Insurance	2,400	
Total Current Assets		$ 70,900
Property, Plant, and Equipment:		
Equipment and Fixtures	56,000	
Less: Accumulated Depreciation	(26,000)	30,000
Total Assets		**$ 100,900**
Liabilities		
Current Liabilities:		
Accounts Payable	$ 13,000	
Salaries and Commissions Payable	3,600	
Total Liabilities		$ 16,600
Stockholders' Equity		
Common Stock, no par	12,000	
Retained Earnings	72,300	
Total Stockholders' Equity		84,300
Total Liabilities and Stockholders' Equity		**$ 100,900**

The budget committee of Paperclip Office Supply has assembled the following data:

a. Sales in April are expected to be $60,000. Paperclip forecasts that monthly sales will increase 2% over April sales in May. June's sales will increase by 4% over April sales. July sales will increase 20% over April sales. Cash receipts are 80% in the month of the sale and 20% in the month following the sale.

b. Paperclip maintains inventory of $7,000 plus 25% of the cost of goods sold budgeted for the following month. Cost of goods sold equal 50% of sales revenue. Purchases are paid 30% in the month of the purchase and 70% in the month following the purchase.

c. Monthly salaries amount to $4,000. Sales commissions equal 5% of sales for that month. Salaries and commissions are paid 60% in the month incurred and 40% in the following month.

d. Other monthly expenses are as follows:

- Rent: $2,800, paid as incurred
- Depreciation: $700
- Insurance: $400, expiration of prepaid amount
- Income tax: $1,900, paid as incurred

Requirements

1. Prepare Paperclip's sales budget for April and May 2016. Round *all* amounts to the nearest dollar.

2. Prepare Paperclip's inventory, purchases, and cost of goods sold budget for April and May.

3. Prepare Paperclip's selling and administrative expense budget for April and May.

Learning Objective 7
Appendix 22A

1. Jan. total cash recpts. $68,000
3. Feb. total pmts. for S&A exp. $13,056

P22A-45A Preparing a financial budget—schedule of cash receipts, schedule cash payments, cash budget

Knobbles Company's budget committee provides the following information:

December 31, 2015, account balances:		
Cash		$ 23,000
Accounts Receivable		20,000
Merchandise Inventory		20,000
Accounts Payable		11,500
Salaries and Commissions Payable		2,850

Budgeted amounts for 2016:	January	February
Sales	$ 80,000	$ 81,600
Purchases	40,200	41,000
Commissions Expense	4,000	4,080
Salaries Expense	7,000	7,000
Rent Expense	2,000	2,000
Depreciation Expense	600	600
Insurance Expense	400	400
Income Tax Expense	2,200	2,200

Requirements

1. Prepare the schedule of cash receipts from customers for January and February 2016. Assume cash receipts are 60% in the month of the sale and 40% in the month following the sale.

2. Prepare the schedule of cash payments for purchases for January and February 2016. Assume purchases are paid 60% in the month of purchase and 40% in the month following the purchase.

3. Prepare the schedule of cash payments for selling and administrative expenses for January and February 2016. Assume 25% of the accrual for Salaries and Commissions Payable is for commissions and 75% is for salaries. The December 31 balance will be paid in January. Salaries and commissions are paid 70% in the month incurred and 30% in the following month. Rent and income tax expenses are paid as incurred. Insurance expense is an expiration of the prepaid amount.

4. Prepare the cash budget for January and February 2016. Assume no financing took place.

P22A-46A Preparing a financial budget—budgeted income statement, balance sheet, and statement of cash flows

Learning Objective 7
Appendix 22A

2. RE $101,315
3. Net cash OA $35,442

Grant Company has the following post-closing trial balance on December 31, 2016:

GRANT COMPANY
Post-Closing Trial Balance
December 31, 2016

Account	Debit	Credit
Cash	$ 26,000	
Accounts Receivable	19,000	
Merchandise Inventory	16,500	
Prepaid Insurance	1,600	
Equipment and Fixtures	56,000	
Accumulated Depreciation		$ 15,000
Accounts Payable		16,000
Salaries and Commissions Payable		6,125
Common Stock		17,000
Retained Earnings		64,975
Totals	$ 119,100	$ 119,100

The company's accounting department has gathered the following budgeting information for the first quarter of 2017:

Budgeted total sales, all on account	$ 121,200
Budgeted purchases of merchandise inventory, all on account	60,900
Budgeted cost of goods sold	60,600
Budgeted selling and administrative expenses:	
Commissions expense	6,060
Salaries expense	8,000
Rent expense	4,800
Depreciation expense	400
Insurance expense	200
Budgeted cash receipts from customers	127,960
Budgeted cash payments for merchandise inventory	67,675
Budgeted cash payments for salaries and commissions	15,243
Budgeted income tax expense	4,800

Additional information:

Rent and income tax expenses are paid as incurred. Insurance expense is an expiration of the prepaid amount.

Requirements

1. Prepare a budgeted income statement for the quarter ended March 31, 2017.
2. Prepare a budgeted balance sheet as of March 31, 2017.
3. Prepare a budgeted statement of cash flows for the quarter ended March 31, 2017.

Learning Objectives 6, 7
Appendix 22A

6. Total cash pmts. $81,950
7. NI $1,200

P22A-47A Completing a comprehensive budgeting problem—merchandising company

Professional Printing Supply of Baltimore has applied for a loan. Its bank has requested a budgeted balance sheet at April 30, 2016, and a budgeted statement of cash flows for April. The March 31, 2016, balance sheet follows:

PROFESSIONAL PRINTING SUPPLY		
Balance Sheet		
March 31, 2016		
Assets		
Current Assets:		
Cash	$ 51,000	
Accounts Receivable	14,200	
Merchandise Inventory	12,200	
Total Current Assets		$ 77,400
Property, Plant, and Equipment:		
Equipment and Fixtures	80,400	
Less: Accumulated Depreciation	(12,300)	68,100
Total Assets		$ 145,500
Liabilities		
Current Liabilities:		
Accounts Payable		$ 7,900
Stockholders' Equity		
Common Stock, no par	$ 30,000	
Retained Earnings	107,600	
Total Stockholders' Equity		137,600
Total Liabilities and Stockholders' Equity		$ 145,500

As Professional Printing Supply's controller, you have assembled the following additional information:

a. April dividends of $4,000 were declared and paid.

b. April capital expenditures of $16,600 budgeted for cash purchase of equipment.

c. April depreciation expense, $600.

d. Cost of goods sold, 40% of sales.

e. Desired ending inventory for April is $23,600.

f. April selling and administrative expenses include salaries of $36,000, 40% of which will be paid in cash and the remainder paid next month.

g. Additional April selling and administrative expenses also include miscellaneous expenses of 15% of sales, all paid in April.

h. April budgeted sales, $84,000, 70% collected in April and 30% in May.

i. April cash payments of March 31 liabilities incurred for March purchases of inventory, $7,900.

j. April purchases of inventory, $7,900 for cash and $37,100 on account. Half the credit purchases will be paid in April and half in May.

Requirements

1. Prepare the sales budget for April.

2. Prepare the inventory, purchases, and cost of goods sold budget for April.

3. Prepare the selling and administrative expense budget for April.

4. Prepare the schedule of cash receipts from customers for April.

5. Prepare the schedule of cash payments for selling and administrative expenses for April.

6. Prepare the cash budget for April. Assume the company does not use short-term financing to maintain a minimum cash balance.

7. Prepare the budgeted income statement for April.

8. Prepare the budgeted balance sheet at April 30, 2016.

9. Prepare the budgeted statement of cash flows for April.

> Problems **Group B**

P22-48B Preparing an operating budget—sales, production, direct materials, direct labor, overhead, COGS, and S&A expense budgets

The Haney Batting Company manufactures wood baseball bats. Haney's two primary products are a youth bat, designed for children and young teens, and an adult bat, designed for high school and college-aged players. Haney sells the bats to sporting goods stores, and all sales are on account. The youth bat sells for $35; the adult bat sells for $55. Haney's highest sales volume is in the first three months of the year as retailers prepare for the spring baseball season. Haney's balance sheet for December 31, 2016, follows:

Learning Objective 3

3. POHR $3
4. Adult bats COGS $74,175

HANEY BATTING COMPANY Balance Sheet December 31, 2016		
Assets		
Current Assets:		
Cash	$ 40,000	
Accounts Receivable	17,900	
Raw Materials Inventory	9,000	
Finished Goods Inventory	16,450	
Total Current Assets		$ 83,350
Property, Plant, and Equipment:		
Equipment	140,000	
Less: Accumulated Depreciation	(10,000)	130,000
Total Assets		$ 213,350
Liabilities		
Current Liabilities:		
Accounts Payable		$ 10,500
Stockholders' Equity		
Common Stock, no par	$ 140,000	
Retained Earnings	62,850	
Total Stockholders' Equity		202,850
Total Liabilities and Stockholders' Equity		$ 213,350

Other data for Haney Batting Company for the first quarter of 2017:

a. Budgeted sales are 1,300 youth bats and 3,100 adult bats.

b. Finished Goods Inventory on December 31 consists of 200 youth bats at $11 each and 750 adult bats at $19 each.

c. Desired ending Finished Goods Inventory is 250 youth bats and 550 adult bats; FIFO inventory costing method is used.

d. Direct materials cost is $13 per youth bat and $15 per adult bat.

e. Desired ending Raw Materials Inventory is $9,000 (indirect materials are insignificant and not considered for budgeting purposes).

f. Each bat requires 0.3 hours of direct labor; direct labor costs average $32 per hour.

g. Variable manufacturing overhead is $0.40 per bat.

h. Fixed manufacturing overhead includes $600 per quarter in depreciation and $1,525 per quarter for other costs, such as insurance and property taxes.

i. Fixed selling and administrative expenses include $14,000 per quarter for salaries; $2,500 per quarter for rent; $1,900 per quarter for insurance; and $100 per quarter for depreciation.

j. Variable selling and administrative expenses include supplies at 1% of sales.

Requirements

1. Prepare Haney's sales budget for the first quarter of 2017.

2. Prepare Haney's production budget for the first quarter of 2017.

3. Prepare Haney's direct materials, direct labor budget, and manufacturing overhead budget for the first quarter of 2017. Round the predetermined overhead allocation rate to two decimal places. The overhead allocation base is direct labor hours.

4. Prepare Haney's cost of goods sold budget for the first quarter of 2017.

5. Prepare Haney's selling and administrative expense budget for the first quarter of 2017.

Learning Objective 4

1. Total cash pmts. $179,935
2. Ending Cash bal. $35,765

P22-49B Preparing a financial budget—schedule of cash receipts, schedule of cash payments, cash budget

Sosa Company has provided the following budget information for the first quarter of 2016:

Total sales	$ 297,500
Budgeted purchases of direct materials	39,450
Budgeted direct labor cost	38,880
Budgeted manufacturing overhead costs:	
Variable manufacturing overhead	3,645
Depreciation	600
Insurance and property taxes	9,120
Budgeted selling and administrative expenses:	
Salaries expense	5,000
Rent expense	3,000
Insurance expense	1,200
Depreciation expense	100
Supplies expense	2,975

Additional data related to the first quarter of 2016 for Sosa Company:

a. Capital expenditures include $36,000 for new manufacturing equipment, to be purchased and paid in the first quarter.

b. Cash receipts are 60% of sales in the quarter of the sale and 40% in the quarter following the sale.

c. Direct materials purchases are paid 70% in the quarter purchased and 30% in the next quarter.

d. Direct labor, manufacturing overhead, and selling and administrative costs are paid in the quarter incurred.

e. Income tax expense for the first quarter is projected at $42,000 and is paid in the quarter incurred.

f. Sosa Company expects to have adequate cash funds and does not anticipate borrowing in the first quarter.

g. The December 31, 2015, balance in Cash is $14,000, in Accounts Receivable is $23,200, and in Accounts Payable is $10,500.

Requirements

1. Prepare Sosa Company's schedule of cash receipts from customers and schedule of cash payments for the first quarter of 2016.

2. Prepare Sosa Company's cash budget for the first quarter of 2016.

P22-50B Preparing a financial budget—budgeted income statement, balance sheet, and statement of cash flows

Carson Company has the following post-closing trial balance on December 31, 2016:

Learning Objective 4

1. NI $55,810
2. FG inventory $13,810

CARSON COMPANY Post-Closing Trial Balance December 31, 2016		
Account	**Debit**	**Credit**
Cash	$ 25,000	
Accounts Receivable	21,600	
Raw Materials Inventory	8,000	
Finished Goods Inventory	15,750	
Equipment	140,000	
Accumulated Depreciation		$ 65,000
Accounts Payable		11,600
Common Stock		70,000
Retained Earnings		63,750
Totals	$ 210,350	$ 210,350

The company's accounting department has gathered the following budgeting information for the first quarter of 2017:

Budgeted total sales, all on account	$ 181,500
Budgeted direct materials to be purchased and used	36,350
Budgeted direct labor cost	25,560
Budgeted manufacturing overhead costs:	
Variable manufacturing overhead	1,775
Depreciation	1,200
Insurance and property taxes	2,350
Budgeted cost of goods sold	69,175
Budgeted selling and administrative expenses:	
Salaries expense	7,000
Rent expense	2,000
Insurance expense	1,600
Depreciation expense	100
Supplies expense	1,815
Budgeted cash receipts from customers	175,875
Budgeted income tax expense	44,000
Budgeted purchase and payment for capital expenditures (additional equipment)	38,000

Additional information:

a. Direct materials purchases are paid 60% in the quarter purchased and 40% in the next quarter.

b. Direct labor, manufacturing overhead, selling and administrative costs, and income tax expense are paid in the quarter incurred.

Requirements

1. Prepare Carson Company's budgeted income statement for the first quarter of 2017.

2. Prepare Carson Company's budgeted balance sheet as of March 31, 2017. *Hint:* Use the budgeted statement of cash flows prepared in Requirement 3 to determine the Cash balance.

3. Prepare Carson Company's budgeted statement of cash flows for the first quarter of 2017.

P22-51B Completing a comprehensive budgeting problem—manufacturing company

Learning Objectives 3, 4

The Grilton Tire Company manufactures racing tires for bicycles. Grilton sells tires for $50 each. Grilton is planning for the next year by developing a master budget by quarters. Grilton's balance sheet for December 31, 2016, follows:

1. 3rd Qtr. DM purchases $16,320
4th Qtr. total cash pmts. (before interest) $76,814

GRILTON TIRE COMPANY
Balance Sheet
December 31, 2016

Assets

Current Assets:		
Cash	$ 39,000	
Accounts Receivable	40,000	
Raw Materials Inventory	2,400	
Finished Goods Inventory	8,700	
Total Current Assets		$ 90,100
Property, Plant, and Equipment:		
Equipment	177,000	
Less: Accumulated Depreciation	(42,000)	135,000
Total Assets		$ 225,100

Liabilities

Current Liabilities:		
Accounts Payable		$ 8,000

Stockholders' Equity

Common Stock, no par	$ 130,000	
Retained Earnings	87,100	
Total Stockholders' Equity		217,100
Total Liabilities and Stockholders' Equity		$ 225,100

Other data for Grilton Tire Company:

a. Budgeted sales are 1,500 tires for the first quarter and expected to increase by 200 tires per quarter. Cash sales are expected to be 30% of total sales, with the remaining 70% of sales on account.

b. Finished Goods Inventory on December 31 consists of 300 tires at $29 each.

c. Desired ending Finished Goods Inventory is 40% of the next quarter's sales; first quarter sales for 2018 are expected to be 2,300 tires; FIFO inventory costing method is used.

d. Direct materials cost is $8 per tire.

e. Desired ending Raw Materials Inventory is 30% of the next quarter's direct materials needed for production; desired ending inventory for December 31 is $2,400; indirect materials are insignificant and not considered for budgeting purposes.

f. Each tire requires 0.40 hours of direct labor; direct labor costs average $16 per hour.

g. Variable manufacturing overhead is $2 per tire.

h. Fixed manufacturing overhead includes $4,500 per quarter in depreciation and $26,780 per quarter for other costs, such as utilities, insurance, and property taxes.

i. Fixed selling and administrative expenses include $8,000 per quarter for salaries; $1,800 per quarter for rent; $1,200 per quarter for insurance; and $500 per quarter for depreciation.

j. Variable selling and administrative expenses include supplies at 2% of sales.

k. Capital expenditures include $45,000 for new manufacturing equipment, to be purchased and paid in the first quarter.

l. Cash receipts for sales on account are 60% in the quarter of the sale and 40% in the quarter following the sale; December 31, 2016, Accounts Receivable is received in the first quarter of 2017; uncollectible accounts are considered insignificant and not considered for budgeting purposes.

m. Direct materials purchases are paid 70% in the quarter purchased and 30% in the following quarter; December 31, 2016, Accounts Payable is paid in the first quarter of 2017.

n. Direct labor, manufacturing overhead, and selling and administrative costs are paid in the quarter incurred.

o. Income tax expense is projected at $3,500 per quarter and is paid in the quarter incurred.

p. Grilton desires to maintain a minimum cash balance of $35,000 and borrows from the local bank as needed in increments of $1,000 at the beginning of the quarter; principal repayments are made at the beginning of the quarter when excess funds are available and in increments of $1,000; interest is 6% per year and paid at the beginning of the quarter based on the amount outstanding from the previous quarter.

Requirements

1. Prepare Grilton's operating budget and cash budget for 2017 by quarter. Required schedules and budgets include: sales budget, production budget, direct materials budget, direct labor budget, manufacturing overhead budget, cost of goods sold budget, selling and administrative expense budget, schedule of cash receipts, schedule of cash payments, and cash budget. Manufacturing overhead costs are allocated based on direct labor hours. Round all calculations to the nearest dollar.

2. Prepare Grilton's annual financial budget for 2017, including budgeted income statement, budgeted balance sheet, and budgeted statement of cash flows.

P22-52B Using sensitivity analysis

Shaner Company prepared the following budgeted income statement for the first quarter of 2016:

SHANER COMPANY
Budgeted Income Statement
For the Quarter Ended March 31, 2016

		January	February	March	Total
Sales Revenue	(20% increase per month)	$ 5,000	$ 6,000	$ 7,200	$ 18,200
Cost of Goods Sold	(10% of sales)	500	600	720	1,820
Gross Profit		4,500	5,400	6,480	16,380
S&A Expenses	($2,500 + 10% of sales)	3,000	3,100	3,220	9,320
Operating Income		1,500	2,300	3,260	7,060
Income Tax Expense	(30% of operating income)	450	690	978	2,118
Net Income		$ 1,050	$ 1,610	$ 2,282	$ 4,942

Shaner Company is considering two options. Option 1 is to increase advertising by $900 per month. Option 2 is to use better-quality materials in the manufacturing process. The better materials will increase the cost of goods sold to 15% but will provide a better product at the same sales price. The marketing manager projects either option will result in sales increases of 25% per month rather than 20%.

Requirements

1. Prepare budgeted income statements for both options, assuming January sales remain $5,000. Round all calculations to the nearest dollar.

2. Which option should Shaner choose? Explain your reasoning.

Learning Objective 6
Appendix 22A

2. May purchases $71,750
3. Apr. total S&A exp. $16,000

P22A-53B Preparing an operating budget—sales budget; inventory, purchases and COGS budget; and S&A expense budget

Watercooler Office Supply's March 31, 2016, balance sheet follows:

WATERCOOLER OFFICE SUPPLY
Balance Sheet
March 31, 2016

Assets

Current Assets:		
Cash	$ 35,000	
Accounts Receivable	15,000	
Merchandise Inventory	26,500	
Prepaid Insurance	1,500	
Total Current Assets		$ 78,000
Property, Plant, and Equipment:		
Equipment and Fixtures	56,000	
Less: Accumulated Depreciation	(26,000)	30,000
Total Assets		**$ 108,000**

Liabilities

Current Liabilities:		
Accounts Payable	$ 11,000	
Salaries and Commissions Payable	2,625	
Total Liabilities		$ 13,625

Stockholders' Equity

Common Stock, no par	25,000	
Retained Earnings	69,375	
Total Stockholders' Equity		94,375
Total Liabilities and Stockholders' Equity		**$ 108,000**

The budget committee of Watercooler Office Supply has assembled the following data.

a. Sales in April are expected to be $140,000. Watercooler forecasts that monthly sales will increase 2% over April sales in May. June's sales will increase by 4% over April sales. July sales will increase 20% over April sales. Cash receipts are 80% in the month of the sale and 20% in the month following the sale.

b. Watercooler maintains inventory of $9,000 plus 25% of the cost of goods sold budgeted for the following month. Cost of goods sold equal 50% of sales revenue. Purchases are paid 30% in the month of the purchase and 70% in the month following the purchase.

c. Monthly salaries amount to $5,000. Sales commissions equal 5% of sales for that month. Salaries and commissions are paid 70% in the month incurred and 30% in the following month.

d. Other monthly expenses are as follows:
    • Rent: $3,000, paid as incurred
    • Depreciation: $700
    • Insurance: $300, expiration of prepaid amount
    • Income tax: $2,000, paid as incurred

Requirements

1. Prepare Watercooler's sales budget for April and May 2016. Round *all* amounts to the nearest dollar.

2. Prepare Watercooler's inventory, purchases, and cost of goods sold budget for April and May.

3. Prepare Watercooler's selling and administrative expense budget for April and May.

P22A-54B Preparing a financial budget—schedule of cash receipts, schedule of cash payments, cash budget

Knight Company's budget committee provides the following information:

**Learning Objective 7
Appendix 22A**

1. Feb. total cash recpts. $60,960
3. Feb. total pmts. for S&A exp. $13,018

December 31, 2015, account balances:	
Cash	$ 28,000
Accounts Receivable	20,000
Merchandise Inventory	18,500
Accounts Payable	18,000
Salaries and Commissions Payable	8,400

Budgeted amounts for 2016:	January	February
Sales	$ 60,000	$ 61,200
Purchases	30,150	30,750
Commissions Expense	3,000	3,060
Salaries Expense	7,000	7,000
Rent Expense	3,000	3,000
Depreciation Expense	500	500
Insurance Expense	200	200
Income Tax Expense	1,600	1,600

Requirements

1. Prepare the schedule of cash receipts from customers for January and February 2016. Assume cash receipts are 80% in the month of the sale and 20% in the month following the sale.

2. Prepare the schedule of cash payments for purchases for January and February 2016. Assume purchases are paid 60% in the month of purchase and 40% in the month following the purchase.

3. Prepare the schedule of cash payments for selling and administrative expense for January and February 2016. Assume 25% of the accrual for Salaries and Commissions Payable is for commissions and 75% is for salaries. The December 31 balance will be paid in January. Salaries and commissions are paid 30% in the month incurred and 70% in the following month. Rent and income tax expenses are paid as incurred. Insurance expense is an expiration of the prepaid amount.

4. Prepare the cash budget for January and February. Assume no financing took place.

Learning Objective 7
Appendix 22A

2. RE $75,040
3. Net cash OA $28,004

P22A-55B Preparing a financial budget—budgeted income statement, balance sheet, and statement of cash flows

Green Company has the following post-closing trial balance on December 31, 2016:

GREEN COMPANY Post-Closing Trial Balance December 31, 2016		
Account	**Debit**	**Credit**
Cash	$ 23,000	
Accounts Receivable	12,000	
Merchandise Inventory	16,500	
Prepaid Insurance	1,600	
Equipment and Fixtures	40,000	
Accumulated Depreciation		$ 14,000
Accounts Payable		11,000
Salaries and Commissions Payable		3,200
Common Stock		21,000
Retained Earnings		43,900
Totals	$ 93,100	$ 93,100

The company's accounting department has gathered the following budgeting information for the first quarter of 2017:

Budgeted total sales, all on account	$ 121,200
Budgeted purchases of merchandise inventory, all on account	60,900
Budgeted cost of goods sold	60,600
Budgeted selling and administrative expenses:	
Commissions expense	6,060
Salaries expense	12,000
Rent expense	5,600
Depreciation expense	1,400
Insurance expense	400
Budgeted cash receipts from customers	114,840
Budgeted cash payments for merchandise inventory	59,600
Budgeted cash payments for salaries and commissions	17,636
Budgeted income tax expense	4,000

Additional information:

Rent and income tax expenses are paid as incurred. Insurance expense is an expiration of the prepaid amount.

Requirements

1. Prepare a budgeted income statement for the quarter ended March 31, 2017.

2. Prepare a budgeted balance sheet as of March 31, 2017.

3. Prepare a budgeted statement of cash flows for the quarter ended March 31, 2017.

P22A-56B Completing a comprehensive budgeting problem—merchandising company

**Learning Objectives 6, 7
Appendix 22A**

6. Total cash pmts. $81,700
7. NI $4,300

True Printing Company of Baltimore has applied for a loan. Its bank has requested a budgeted balance sheet at April 30, 2016, and a budgeted statement of cash flows for April. The March 31, 2016, balance sheet follows:

TRUE PRINTING COMPANY
Balance Sheet
March 31, 2016

Assets		
Current Assets:		
Cash	$ 50,300	
Accounts Receivable	17,100	
Merchandise Inventory	12,100	
Total Current Assets		$ 79,500
Property, Plant, and Equipment:		
Equipment and Fixtures	81,200	
Less: Accumulated Depreciation	(12,200)	69,000
Total Assets		$ 148,500
Liabilities		
Current Liabilities:		
Accounts Payable		$ 8,300
Stockholders' Equity		
Common Stock, no par	$ 20,000	
Retained Earnings	120,200	
Total Stockholders' Equity		140,200
Total Liabilities and Stockholders' Equity		$ 148,500

As True Printing's controller, you have assembled the following additional information:

a. April dividends of $3,500 were declared and paid.

b. April capital expenditures of $16,900 budgeted for cash purchase of equipment.

c. April depreciation expense, $200.

d. Cost of goods sold, 40% of sales.

e. Desired ending inventory for April is $24,800.

f. April selling and administrative expenses includes salaries of $39,000, 40% of which will be paid in cash and the remainder paid next month.

g. Additional April selling and administrative expenses also include miscellaneous expenses of 10% of sales, all paid in April.

h. April budgeted sales, $87,000, 60% collected in April and 40% in May.

i. April cash payments of March 31 liabilities incurred for March purchases of inventory, $8,300.

j. April purchases of inventory, $9,900 for cash and $37,600 on account. Half the credit purchases will be paid in April and half in May.

Requirements

1. Prepare the sales budget for April.

2. Prepare the inventory, purchases, and cost of goods sold budget for April.

3. Prepare the selling and administrative expense budget for April.

4. Prepare the schedule of cash receipts from customers for April.

5. Prepare the schedule of cash payments for selling and administrative expenses for April.

6. Prepare the cash budget for April. Assume the company does not use short-term financing to maintain a minimum cash balance.

7. Prepare the budgeted income statement for April.

8. Prepare the budgeted balance sheet at April 30, 2016.

9. Prepare the budgeted statement of cash flows for April.

> Continuing Problem

P22-57 Preparing a financial budget

This problem continues the Daniels Consulting situation from Problem P21-63 of Chapter 21. Assume Daniels Consulting began January with $12,000 cash. Management forecasts that cash receipts from credit customers will be $52,000 in January and $55,000 in February. Projected cash payments include equipment purchases ($16,000 in January and $40,400 in February) and selling and administrative expenses ($6,000 each month).

Daniels's bank requires a $23,000 minimum balance in the firm's checking account. At the end of any month when the account balance falls below $23,000, the bank automatically extends credit to the firm in multiples of $5,000. Daniels borrows as little as possible and pays back loans each month in $1,000 increments, plus 12% interest on the entire unpaid principal. The first payment occurs one month after the loan.

Requirements

1. Prepare Daniels Consulting's cash budget for January and February 2018.

2. How much cash will Daniels borrow in February if cash receipts from customers that month total $30,000 instead of $55,000?

CRITICAL THINKING

> Decision Case 22-1

Each autumn, as a hobby, Anne Magnuson weaves cotton place mats to sell through a local craft shop. The mats sell for $20 per set of four. The shop charges a 10% commission and remits the net proceeds to Magnuson at the end of December. Magnuson has woven and sold 25 sets each year for the past two years. She has enough cotton in inventory to make another 25 sets. She paid $7 per set for the cotton. Magnuson uses a four-harness loom that she purchased for cash exactly two years ago. It is depreciated at the rate of $10 per month. The Accounts Payable balance relates to the cotton inventory and is payable by September 30.

Magnuson is considering buying an eight-harness loom so that she can weave more intricate patterns in linen. The new loom costs $1,000 and would be depreciated at $20 per month. Her bank has agreed to lend her $1,000 at 18% interest per year, with $200 payment of principal, plus accrued interest payable each December 31. Magnuson believes she can weave 15 linen place mat sets in time for the Christmas rush if she does not weave any cotton mats. She predicts that each linen set will sell for $50. Linen costs $18 per set. Magnuson's supplier will sell her linen on credit, payable December 31.

Magnuson plans to keep her old loom whether or not she buys the new loom. The balance sheet for her weaving business at August 31, 2016, is as follows:

ANNE MAGNUSON, WEAVER
Balance Sheet
August 31, 2016

Assets		Liabilities	
Current Assets:		Current Liabilities:	
Cash	$ 25	Account Payable	$ 74
Inventory of cotton	175		
Total Current Assets	200		
Property, Plant, and Equipment:		**Stockholders' Equity**	
Loom	500	Stockholders' Equity	386
Less: Accumulated Depreciation	(240)		
Total PP&E	260		
Total Assets	**$ 460**	Total Liabilities and Stockholders' Equity	**$ 460**

Requirements

1. Prepare a cash budget for the four months ending December 31, 2016, for two alternatives: weaving the place mats in cotton using the existing loom and weaving the place mats in linen using the new loom. For each alternative, prepare a budgeted income statement for the four months ending December 31, 2016, and a budgeted balance sheet at December 31, 2016.

2. On the basis of financial considerations only, what should Magnuson do? Give your reason.

3. What nonfinancial factors might Magnuson consider in her decision?

> Ethical Issue 22-1

Southeast Suites operates a regional hotel chain. Each hotel is operated by a manager and an assistant manager/controller. Many of the staff who run the front desk, clean the rooms, and prepare the breakfast buffet work part time or have a second job, so employee turnover is high.

Assistant manager/controller Terry Dunn asked the new bookkeeper to help prepare the hotel's master budget. The master budget is prepared once a year and is submitted to company headquarters for approval. Once approved, the master budget is used to evaluate the hotel's performance. These performance evaluations affect hotel managers' bonuses, and they also affect company decisions on which hotels deserve extra funds for capital improvements.

When the budget was almost complete, Dunn asked the bookkeeper to increase amounts budgeted for labor and supplies by 15%. When asked why, Dunn responded that hotel manager Clay Murry told her to do this when she began working at the hotel. Murry explained that this budgetary cushion gave him flexibility in running the hotel. For example, because company headquarters tightly controls capital improvement funds, Murry can use the extra money budgeted for labor and supplies to replace broken televisions or pay "bonuses" to keep valued employees. Dunn initially accepted this explanation because she had observed similar behavior at the hotel where she worked previously.

Requirements

Put yourself in Dunn's position. In deciding how to deal with the situation, answer the following questions:

1. What is the ethical issue?
2. What are the options?
3. What are the possible consequences?
4. What should you do?

> Fraud Case 22-1

Patrick works for McGill's Computer Repair, owned and operated by Frank McGill. As a computer technician, Patrick has grown accustomed to friends and family members asking for assistance with their personal computers. In an effort to increase his income, Patrick started a personal computer repair business that he operates out of his home on a part-time basis, working evenings and weekends. Because Patrick is doing this "on the side" for friends and family, he does not want to charge as much as McGill's charges its customers. When Frank McGill assigned Patrick the task of developing the budget for his department, Patrick increased the amount budgeted for computer parts. When the budget was approved, Patrick purchased as many parts as the budget allowed, even when they were not needed. He then took the extra parts home to use in his personal business in an effort to keep his costs down and profits up. So far, no one at McGill's has asked about the parts expense because Patrick has not allowed the actual amount spent to exceed the budgeted amount.

Requirements

1. Why would Patrick's actions be considered fraudulent?
2. What can a company do to protect against this kind of business risk?

MyAccountingLab   For a wealth of online resources, including exercises, problems, media, and immediate tutorial help, please visit http://www.myaccountinglab.com.

> Quick Check Answers

1. d **2.** a **3.** c **4.** b **5.** c **6.** a **7.** c **8.** a **9.** a **10.** d **11A.** d **12A.** b **13A.** a

Flexible Budgets and Standard Cost Systems

Why Are We Not Meeting Our Budget?

Ritchie Billings owns a small food-processing plant in the Midwest. The company specializes in producing flour by processing grains grown by local farmers. The product list includes oat, wheat, soy, and corn flour. Ritchie is looking at the income statement for the past six months and comparing it to the budget. There is a difference between the budgeted operating income and the actual operating income, but Ritchie is having a hard time figuring out why.

Ritchie knows he has been paying the farmers more for grain this year, which has increased the direct materials cost. Also, he has hired some really good workers lately. He is paying them more than expected, and they have been so efficient he did not have to replace one employee who quit. Shouldn't the savings from having one less employee offset the increased wages paid to the other employees? Ritchie also recently replaced a manufacturing machine. The new machine is much more efficient, using less electricity and requiring less maintenance. Where are those cost savings on the income statement?

Ritchie needs a system that will allow him to better analyze the costs his company incurs so he can better understand the effects his decisions have on operating income.

How Much Corn Is in Corn Flakes?

Most production companies have manufacturing standards for both costs and quantities of inputs. For example, consider the Kellogg Company. More than 100 years ago, brothers W. K. Kellogg and Dr. John Harvey Kellogg accidentally flaked wheat berry. Further experimentation led to flaked corn and the recipe for Kellogg's Corn Flakes. Today, the Kellogg Company expects to use a certain quantity of milled corn and sugar for each batch of Corn Flakes it produces. Additionally, the company has expectations about the cost of the milled corn and sugar. Even small changes in these expectations can have a significant effect on profits, so they are closely monitored. In this chapter, you learn how companies such as Kellogg Company can use flexible budgets and standard cost systems to control business activities and take corrective action when needed.

Chapter **23** Learning Objectives

1 Prepare flexible budgets and performance reports using static and flexible budgets	**4** Compute the standard cost variances for manufacturing overhead
2 Identify the benefits of a standard cost system and understand how standards are set	**5** Describe the relationship among and responsibility for the product cost variances
3 Compute the standard cost variances for direct materials and direct labor	**6** Record transactions in a standard cost system and prepare a standard cost income statement

Previously, you learned how managers use budgets for planning and controlling business activities. Exhibit 23-1 illustrates budgeting objectives.

Exhibit 23-1 | **Budgeting Objectives**

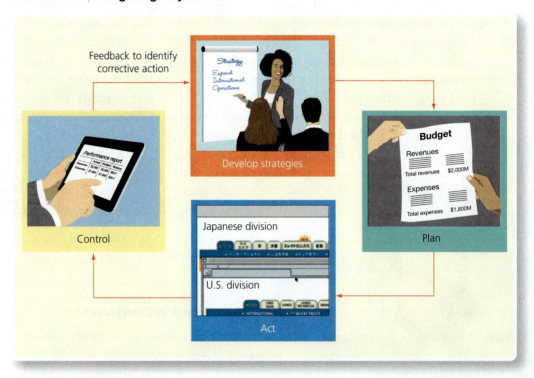

The master budget focuses on the planning step. In this chapter, we focus on the controlling step as we look at the decisions managers make during and after the budgeting period, based on the actual results. Managers may ask:

- Did my division meet its sales goals?
- Have costs increased?
- Sales have dropped, so how do we need to adjust spending?

Businesses often have to make hard decisions. An economic downturn or increased competition may cause a decrease in sales. If that happens, spending must also decrease in order for the company to remain profitable. A budget *variance* is the difference between an *actual* amount and a *budgeted* amount. This chapter shows how managers use variances to control business activities. It is important to know *why* actual amounts differ from the budget. This enables managers to identify problems and decide what action to take.

HOW DO MANAGERS USE BUDGETS TO CONTROL BUSINESS ACTIVITIES?

To illustrate the concepts, we use Cheerful Colors, a fictitious crayon manufacturer. The company begins the manufacturing process by combining direct materials, such as heated liquid paraffin wax and dry pigments. The heated mixture is then poured into molds. After the molds cool, the crayons are removed, inspected, and boxed in bulk. The crayons are then shipped to another facility where paper wrappers are added to each crayon and the crayons are boxed to meet individual customers' needs. Cheerful Colors uses molds that make 100 crayons each and considers each batch of 100 crayons to be one unit for sales and costing purposes.

Learning Objective 1

Prepare flexible budgets and performance reports using static and flexible budgets

Performance Reports Using Static Budgets

Before the beginning of the year, Cheerful Colors's managers prepared a master budget. The master budget is a **static budget**, which means that it is prepared for only *one* level of sales volume. The static budget does not change after it is developed.

Exhibit 23-2 (on the next page) shows a static budget performance report for Cheerful Colors for 2017. The report shows that Cheerful Colors's actual operating income for 2017 is $36,320. This is $2,570 higher than expected from the static budget. This is a $2,570 favorable variance for 2017 operating income. A **variance** is the difference between an actual amount and the budgeted amount. The variances in the third column of Exhibit 23-2 are as follows:

Static Budget
A budget prepared for only one level of sales volume.

Variance
The difference between an actual amount and the budgeted amount; labeled as favorable if it increases operating income and unfavorable if it decreases operating income.

- Favorable (F) if an actual amount *increases* operating income
  - Actual revenue > Budgeted revenue
  - Actual expense < Budgeted expense
- Unfavorable (U) if an actual amount *decreases* operating income
  - Actual revenue < Budgeted revenue
  - Actual expense > Budgeted expense

The variances in Exhibit 23-2 are called **static budget variances**. A static budget variance is the difference between actual results and the expected results in the static budget. Cheerful Colors's static budget variance for operating income is favorable primarily because Cheerful Colors sold 52,000 batches of crayons rather than the 50,000 batches it budgeted to sell during 2017. But there is more to this story. Cheerful Colors needs a *flexible budget* to show budgeted income at different sales levels. Let's see how to prepare and use a flexible budget.

Static Budget Variance
The difference between actual results and the expected results in the static budget.

Performance Reports Using Flexible Budgets

The report in Exhibit 23-2 is hard to analyze because the static budget is based on 50,000 batches of crayons, but the actual results are for 52,000 batches of crayons. This report raises more questions than it answers—for example:

- Why did the $16,500 unfavorable direct materials variance occur?
- Did workers waste materials?
- Did the cost of materials suddenly increase?
- How much of the additional expense arose because Cheerful Colors sold 52,000 batches rather than 50,000 batches?

We need a flexible budget to help answer these questions.

Exhibit 23-2 | **Static Budget Performance Report**

CHEERFUL COLORS Static Budget Performance Report For the Year Ended December 31, 2017			
	Actual Results	Static Budget	Static Budget Variance
Units (Batches of 100)	52,000	50,000	2,000 F
Sales Revenue	$ 384,800	$ 375,000	$ 9,800 F
Variable Costs:			
Manufacturing:			
Direct Materials	104,000	87,500	16,500 U
Direct Labor	145,600	150,000	4,400 F
Variable Overhead	30,160	37,500	7,340 F
Selling and Administrative:			
Supplies	19,200	18,750	450 U
Total Variable Costs	298,960	293,750	5,210 U
Contribution Margin	85,840	81,250	4,590 F
Fixed Costs:			
Manufacturing	23,920	25,000	1,080 F
Selling and Administrative	25,600	22,500	3,100 U
Total Fixed Costs	49,520	47,500	2,020 U
Operating Income	$ 36,320	$ 33,750	$ 2,570 F

Preparing Flexible Budgets

Flexible Budget
A budget prepared for various levels of sales volume.

A **flexible budget** summarizes revenues and expenses for various levels of sales volume within a relevant range. Flexible budgets separate variable costs from fixed costs; the variable costs put the *flex* in the flexible budget. To create a flexible budget, you need to know the following:

- Budgeted selling price per unit
- Variable cost per unit
  - Product costs
    - Direct materials
    - Direct labor
    - Variable manufacturing overhead
  - Variable selling and administrative expenses
- Total fixed costs
  - Fixed manufacturing overhead
  - Fixed selling and administrative expenses
- Different volume levels within the relevant range

Exhibit 23-3 is a flexible budget for Cheerful Colors's revenues and expenses that predicts what will happen if sales reach 48,000 batches, 50,000 batches, or 52,000 batches of crayons during 2017. The budgeted sale price per batch is $7.50. Budgeted variable costs are $1.75 for direct materials, $3.00 for direct labor, $0.75 for variable manufacturing overhead, and 5% of sales revenue for selling and administrative supplies. Budgeted fixed costs are $25,000 for manufacturing overhead and $22,500 for selling and administrative.

Exhibit 23-3 | **Flexible Budget**

CHEERFUL COLORS Flexible Budget For the Year Ended December 31, 2017				
	Budget Amounts per Unit			
Units (Batches of 100)		48,000	50,000	52,000
Sales Revenue	$ 7.50	$ 360,000	$ 375,000	$ 390,000
Variable Costs:				
Manufacturing:				
Direct Materials	1.75	84,000	87,500	91,000
Direct Labor	3.00	144,000	150,000	156,000
Variable Overhead	0.75	36,000	37,500	39,000
Selling and Administrative:				
Supplies	5% of sales	18,000	18,750	19,500
Total Variable Costs		282,000	293,750	305,500
Contribution Margin		78,000	81,250	84,500
Fixed Costs:				
Manufacturing		25,000	25,000	25,000
Selling and Administrative		22,500	22,500	22,500
Total Fixed Costs		47,500	47,500	47,500
Operating Income		$ 30,500	$ 33,750	$ 37,000

Notice in Exhibit 23-3 that sales revenue, variable costs, and contribution margin increase as more batches of crayons are sold, but fixed costs remain constant regardless of the number of crayons sold within the relevant range of 48,000 to 52,000 batches. *Variable cost per unit* and *total fixed costs* remain constant within a specific relevant range of output. Total fixed costs and the variable cost per batch may change outside this range. For example, if Cheerful Colors sells more than the relevant range, it will have to buy or rent additional equipment, which will increase total fixed costs. Cheerful Colors may also have to pay workers for overtime pay, so the variable cost of direct labor may be more than $3.00 per batch.

Budget Variances

It is not enough to know that a variance occurred. Managers must know *why* a variance occurred in order to pinpoint problems and take corrective action. As you can see in Exhibit 23-2, the static budget underestimated both sales and total variable costs. These differences are caused by two primary factors: There is a difference in prices or costs, and/or there is a difference in volume. To develop more useful information, managers divide the static budget variance into two broad categories:

- **Flexible budget variance**—the difference between actual results and the expected results in the flexible budget for the *actual* units sold. The variance arises because the company had different revenues and/or costs than expected for the *actual* units sold. The flexible budget variance occurs because sales price per unit, variable cost per unit, and/or total fixed costs were different than planned on in the budget.

Flexible Budget Variance
The difference between actual results and the expected results in the flexible budget for the *actual* units sold.

Sales Volume Variance
The difference between the expected results in the flexible budget for the *actual* units sold and the static budget.

- **Sales volume variance**—the difference between expected results in the flexible budget for the *actual* units sold and the static budget. This variance arises because the actual number of units sold differed from the number of units on which the static budget was based. Sales volume variance is the volume difference between actual sales and budgeted sales.

Exhibit 23-4 diagrams these variances.

Exhibit 23-4 | Budget Variances

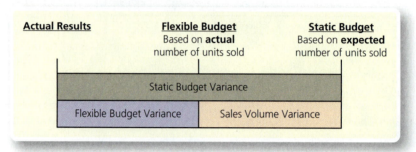

Following are the formulas for computing the two variances for Cheerful Colors:

Flexible Budget Variance	=	Actual Results (based on 52,000 units sold)	−	Flexible Budget (based on 52,000 units sold)
Sales Volume Variance	=	Flexible Budget (based on 52,000 units sold)	−	Static Budget (based on 50,000 units sold)

We have seen that Cheerful Colors budgeted (planned to sell) 50,000 batches of crayons during 2017. Actual sales were 52,000 batches. We need to compute the flexible budget variance and the sales volume variance for Cheerful Colors. Exhibit 23-5 is Cheerful Colors's flexible budget performance report for 2017. Recall that the variances in the second and fourth columns of Exhibit 23-5 are:

- Favorable (F) if an actual amount increases operating income.
- Unfavorable (U) if an actual amount decreases operating income.

Column 1 of the performance report shows the actual results—based on the 52,000 batches of crayons actually sold. These amounts were originally shown in Exhibit 23-2 and are not based on the budget amounts per unit, but are the actual operating revenues and expenses for the period. Actual operating income is $36,320 for 2017.

Column 3 is Cheerful Colors's flexible budget (as shown in Exhibit 23-3) for the 52,000 batches actually sold. Operating income should have been $37,000 based on that level of sales.

Column 5 (originally shown in Exhibit 23-2) gives the static budget for the 50,000 batches expected to have been sold in 2017. Cheerful Colors budgeted earnings of $33,750 before the budgeting period began.

Column 2 is the flexible budget variance and shows operating income is $680 less than Cheerful Colors expected for 52,000 batches of crayons. Managers want to know why operating income did not match the flexible budget.

- Sales revenue was $5,200 less than expected for 52,000 batches.
- Total variable costs were $6,540 less than expected for 52,000 batches.
- Total fixed costs were $2,020 too high for 52,000 batches.

Exhibit 23-5 | **Flexible Budget Performance Report**

	Budget Amounts per Unit	Actual Results	Flexible Budget Variance	Flexible Budget	Sales Volume Variance	Static Budget
		1	2 (1) – (3)	3	4 (3) – (5)	5
Units (Batches of 100)		52,000		52,000		50,000
Sales Revenue	$ 7.50	$ 384,800	$ 5,200 U	$ 390,000	$ 15,000 F	$ 375,000
Variable Costs:						
Manufacturing:						
Direct Materials	1.75	104,000	13,000 U	91,000	3,500 U	87,500
Direct Labor	3.00	145,600	10,400 F	156,000	6,000 U	150,000
Variable Overhead	0.75	30,160	8,840 F	39,000	1,500 U	37,500
Selling and Administrative:						
Supplies	5% of sales	19,200	300 F	19,500	750 U	18,750
Total Variable Costs		298,960	6,540 F	305,500	11,750 U	293,750
Contribution Margin		85,840	1,340 F	84,500	3,250 F	81,250
Fixed Costs:						
Manufacturing		23,920	1,080 F	25,000	0	25,000
Selling and Administrative		25,600	3,100 U	22,500	0	22,500
Total Fixed Costs		49,520	2,020 U	47,500	0	47,500
Operating Income		$ 36,320	$ 680 U	$ 37,000	$ 3,250 F	$ 33,750

CHEERFUL COLORS
Flexible Budget Performance Report
For the Year Ended December 31, 2017

Flexible Budget Variance
$ 680 U

Sales Volume Variance
$ 3,250 F

Static Budget Variance
$ 2,570 F

Managers need to focus on why costs are higher than expected to determine whether the increase is controllable, which means it can be managed, or uncontrollable due to some abnormal or isolated event. Managers also focus on why costs are lower than expected to determine whether, for example, poorer-quality materials were used or standards need to be updated.

Overall, expenses decreased by $4,520 ($6,540 decrease in total variable expenses minus $2,020 increase in total fixed expenses) below the flexible budget, and sales revenue decreased by $5,200, resulting in the overall $680 unfavorable flexible budget variance for operating income.

Column 4 is the sales volume variance, which is the difference between column 3 and column 5. The differences between the static budget and the flexible budget—column 4—arise only because Cheerful Colors sold 52,000 batches of crayons rather than the 50,000 batches it planned to sell. Sales revenue is $15,000 more than Cheerful Colors planned (2,000 more batches sold at $7.50 budgeted sales price). Total variable expenses are $11,750 higher (unfavorable) than planned for the same reason—2,000 more batches sold. Fixed costs are the same for both budgets as the units were within the relevant range. Overall, operating income is favorable by $3,250 because Cheerful Colors sold more crayons than it planned to sell (52,000 batches rather than the 50,000 batches budgeted). Notice that this is also the planned contribution margin difference of $3,250.

The next step is to look deeper into the flexible budget variances to better understand what caused the variances so managers can take corrective action as needed.

Try It!

1. Garland Company expects to sell 600 wreaths in December 2016 but wants to plan for 100 more and 100 less than expected. The wreaths sell for $5.00 each and have variable costs of $2.00 each. Fixed costs are expected to be $500 for the month. Prepare a flexible budget for 500, 600, and 700 wreaths.

Check your answer online in MyAccountingLab or at http://www.pearsonhighered.com/Horngren.

For more practice, see Short Exercises S23-1 through S23-3. MyAccountingLab

WHY DO MANAGERS USE A STANDARD COST SYSTEM TO CONTROL BUSINESS ACTIVITIES?

Learning Objective 2

Identify the benefits of a standard cost system and understand how standards are set

Standard

A price, cost, or quantity that is expected under normal conditions.

Standard Cost System

An accounting system that uses standards for product costs—direct materials, direct labor, and manufacturing overhead.

Most companies use standards to develop budgets. A **standard** is the price, cost, or quantity that is expected under normal conditions. For example, based on Exhibit 23-5, Cheerful Colors expects the direct materials to cost $1.75 per batch of 100 crayons. Therefore, the standard cost for direct materials is $1.75, and that was the amount used to develop both the static and flexible budgets. The terms *standard* and *budget* are sometimes used interchangeably. However, a budget amount generally indicates a total amount, whereas a standard amount is a per unit amount. In the case of direct materials, the standard is $1.75 per batch, and the budgeted amount for 52,000 batches is $91,000 ($1.75 per batch × 52,000 batches).

Cheerful Colors uses a **standard cost system**, which is an accounting system that uses standards for product costs—direct materials, direct labor, and manufacturing overhead. Each input has both a cost standard and an efficiency standard. For example, Cheerful Colors has a standard for the following:

- Cost it pays per pound of paraffin wax (this determines the cost standard)
- Amount of wax it uses for making the crayons (this determines the efficiency standard)

Let's see how managers set these cost and efficiency standards.

Setting Standards

Setting standards can be the most difficult part of using a standard cost system. Setting standards requires coordination and communication among different divisions and functions. For example, the cost standard for direct materials starts with the base purchase cost of each unit of Raw Materials Inventory. Accountants help managers set a cost standard for materials after considering purchase discounts, freight in, and receiving costs. Companies can work with reliable vendors to build relationships that ensure quality and on-time delivery of materials at an affordable cost.

For direct labor, accountants work with human resource managers to determine the cost standard for direct labor. They must consider basic pay rates, payroll taxes, and fringe benefits. Job descriptions reveal the level of experience needed for each task. A big part of this process is ensuring that employees receive training for the job and are paid fairly for the job.

Accountants work with production managers to estimate manufacturing overhead costs. Production managers identify an appropriate allocation base such as direct labor hours or direct labor cost, or they allocate overhead using activity-based costing. Accountants then compute the standard overhead allocation rates. Exhibit 23-6 summarizes the setting of standard costs.

Exhibit 23-6 | **Standard Setting Issues**

	Cost Standards	Efficiency Standards
Direct Materials	Responsibility: Purchasing manager Factors: Purchase cost, discounts, delivery requirements, credit policies	Responsibility: Production manager and engineers Factors: Product specifications, spoilage, production scheduling
Direct Labor	Responsibility: Human resources manager Factors: Wage rate based on experience requirements, payroll taxes, fringe benefits	Responsibility: Production manager and engineers Factors: Time requirements for the production level and employee experience needed
Manufacturing Overhead	Responsibility: Production manager Factors: Nature and amount of resources needed to support activities, such as moving materials, maintaining equipment, and product inspection	

Let's see how Cheerful Colors might determine its production cost standards for materials, labor, and manufacturing overhead.

Cost Standards

The manager in charge of purchasing for Cheerful Colors indicates that the purchase price, net of discounts, is $1.65 per pound of paraffin. Delivery, receiving, and inspection add an average of $0.10 per pound. Cheerful Colors's hourly wage for workers is $10.00, and payroll taxes, and fringe benefits total $2.00 per direct labor hour. Variable manufacturing overhead will total $37,500 based on 50,000 batches of crayons (static budget), fixed manufacturing overhead is $25,000, and overhead is allocated based on 12,500 estimated direct labor hours. Exhibit 23-7 computes Cheerful Colors's cost standards for direct

Exhibit 23-7 | **Standard Cost Calculations**

Direct materials cost standard for paraffin:

Purchase price, net of discounts	$ 1.65 per pound
Delivery, receiving, and inspection	0.10 per pound
Total standard cost per pound of paraffin	**$ 1.75 per pound**

Direct labor cost standard:

Hourly wage	$ 10.00 per direct labor hour
Payroll taxes and fringe benefits	2.00 per direct labor hour
Total standard cost per direct labor hour	**$ 12.00 per direct labor hour**

Variable overhead cost standard:

$$\frac{\text{Estimated variable overhead cost}}{\text{Estimated quantity of allocation base}} = \frac{\$37,500}{12,500 \text{ direct labor hours}} = \textbf{\$ 3.00 per direct labor hour}$$

Fixed overhead cost standard:

$$\frac{\text{Estimated fixed overhead cost}}{\text{Estimated quantity of allocation base}} = \frac{\$25,000}{12,500 \text{ direct labor hours}} = \textbf{\$ 2.00 per direct labor hour}$$

materials, direct labor, and manufacturing overhead based on the static budget of 50,000 batches of crayons.

Efficiency Standards

Production managers and engineers set direct materials and direct labor efficiency standards. Efficiency standards are also called *quantity standards* or *usage standards* because they are a measure of how much *input* should be put into the manufacturing process. In other words, if employees are working efficiently, without spilling or otherwise wasting materials, how much paraffin should Cheerful Colors put into each batch of crayons, the *output*? That amount is the direct materials efficiency standard.

> Be careful to not confuse inputs and outputs. Inputs are what go into making the product and include materials, labor, and overhead. Outputs are the finished products—in this case, crayons. Another way to think about it: Inputs are what go into the factory, and outputs are what come out of the factory.

To set labor standards, companies can analyze every movement in the production process and then take steps to eliminate inefficiencies. For example, to eliminate unnecessary work, machines can be rearranged for better work flow and less materials handling. Companies can also conduct time-and-motion studies to streamline various tasks. For example, a plant can install a conveyer at waist height to minimize bending and lifting.

Companies often develop efficiency standards based on *best practices*. This is often called *benchmarking*. The best practice may be an internal benchmark from other plants or divisions within the company, or it may be an external benchmark from other companies. Internal benchmarks are easy to obtain, but managers can also purchase external benchmark data.

Cheerful Colors has analyzed the manufacturing process and has set the following efficiency standards:

- Direct materials efficiency standard: 1.00 pound of paraffin per batch of crayons
- Direct labor efficiency standard: 0.25 direct labor hours per batch of crayons

Manufacturing overhead is allocated based on direct labor hours, and the efficiency standards for expected direct labor hours have been established, so no additional efficiency standards are required for manufacturing overhead.

Standard Cost System Benefits

Surveys show that the use of standard cost systems is widespread in manufacturing companies in the United States and around the world. Using a standard cost system helps managers:

- Prepare the master budget
- Set target levels of performance for flexible budgets
- Identify performance standards
- Set sales prices of products and services
- Decrease accounting costs

Standard cost systems might appear to be expensive. Indeed, the company must invest up front to develop the standards, and the standards must be updated on a regular basis—at least once per year. But standards can save accounting costs. When integrated with the company's Enterprise Resource Planning (ERP) system, businesses can easily keep track of inventory costs, determine cost and efficiency variances, and make real-time decisions.

Variance Analysis for Product Costs

Once standards are established, managers can use the standards to assign costs to production. At least once per year, managers will compare the actual production costs to the standard costs to locate variances. Exhibit 23-8 shows the formulas for computing the cost and efficiency variances.

Exhibit 23-8 | Cost and Efficiency Variances

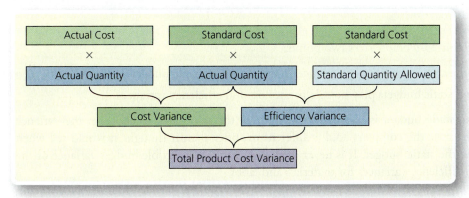

A **cost variance** measures how well the business keeps unit costs of material and labor inputs within standards. As the name suggests, the cost variance is the *difference in costs* (actual cost per unit – standard cost per unit) of an input, multiplied by the *actual quantity* used of the input:

Cost Variance
Measures how well the business keeps unit costs of material and labor inputs within standards.

$$
\begin{aligned}
\text{Cost Variance} &= (\text{Actual Cost} \times \text{Actual Quantity}) - (\text{Standard Cost} \times \text{Actual Quantity}) \\
&= (\text{Actual Cost} - \text{Standard Cost}) \times \text{Actual Quantity} \\
&= (AC - SC) \times AQ
\end{aligned}
$$

An **efficiency variance** measures how well the business uses its materials or human resources. The efficiency variance measures the *difference in quantities* (actual quantity of input used – standard quantity of input allowed for the actual number of units produced), multiplied by the *standard cost per unit* of the input:

Efficiency Variance
Measures how well the business uses its materials or human resources.

$$
\begin{aligned}
\text{Efficiency Variance} &= (\text{Standard Cost} \times \text{Actual Quantity}) - (\text{Standard Cost} \times \text{Standard Quantity}) \\
&= (\text{Actual Quantity} - \text{Standard Quantity}) \times \text{Standard Cost} \\
&= (AQ - SQ) \times SC
\end{aligned}
$$

Exhibit 23-9 shows the relationship among variances and how to separate total flexible budget variances for materials and labor into cost and efficiency variances.

Exhibit 23-9 | **Variance Relationships**

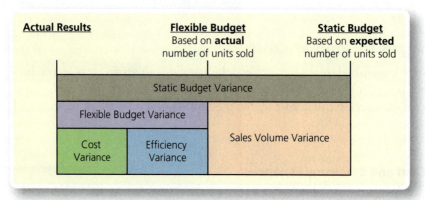

Exhibit 23-9 emphasizes two points:

- First, the cost and efficiency variances add up to the flexible budget variance.
- Second, static budgets play no role in the cost and efficiency variances.

The static budget is used only to compute the sales volume variance, the variance caused because the company sold a different quantity than it thought it would sell when it created the static budget. It is never used to compute the flexible budget variance or the cost and efficiency variances for materials and labor.

DECISIONS

How much time should employees report?

Will Crocker is an accountant at Southeast Accounting, a regional accounting firm headquartered in Charlotte, North Carolina. Accounting personnel at Southeast Accounting are required to report time spent working on clients' accounts. The actual reported time is used to estimate the labor time required for similar jobs for other clients and for subsequent jobs for the same client. Therefore, the reported time has two primary purposes. It is used to determine engagement fees—the amount the client will be charged for the job. It is also used to evaluate personnel efficiency—whether or not the employee is able to complete the job in the expected time.

Will has recently completed an engagement at a client's location. Will's actual time on the engagement was 70 hours, but the engagement was budgeted for 50 hours. Will is reluctant to report the 70 hours actually worked because it will create an unfavorable direct labor efficiency variance. Accountants at Southeast Accounting often report actual engagement time at or just slightly above the budgeted time even if the actual time is substantially more. Should Will report the actual time spent on the engagement or under-report the time to avoid an unfavorable variance?

Solution

Will should report the actual time spent on each engagement. Management, not aware that engagements are taking longer than expected, is routinely underestimating the time needed for the engagements in subsequent years. The employees' actions are causing a never-ending loop—budgeted hours are too low, employees fail to report the actual higher amounts, and, therefore, subsequent budgeted hours are also too low. To help solve the problem, management needs to emphasize the need for accurate figures for budgeting purposes. By continually using inaccurate amounts, the firm is underestimating the cost to complete the engagements, which also causes it to under-charge the clients. This can create serious profitability issues.

Management also needs to work to erase the climate of fear at the firm, where employees feel threatened by the variance system and the impact unfavorable variances could have on their jobs. Variances should be used to investigate and make changes, not punish employees. In the current environment, it is improbable management will collect accurate information from the employees.

Match the definitions to the correct variance.

Variance	Definition
2. Cost variance	a. The difference between the expected results in the flexible budget for the *actual* units sold and the static budget.
3. Efficiency variance	
4. Flexible budget variance	b. The difference between actual results and the expected results in the flexible budget for the *actual* units sold.
5. Sales volume variance	
6. Static budget variance	c. Measures how well the business keeps unit costs of material and labor inputs within standards.
	d. The difference between actual results and the expected results in the static budget.
	e. Measures how well the business uses its materials or human resources.

Check your answers online in MyAccountingLab or at http://www.pearsonhighered.com/Horngren.

For more practice, see Short Exercises S23-4 and S23-5. MyAccountingLab

HOW ARE STANDARD COSTS USED TO DETERMINE DIRECT MATERIALS AND DIRECT LABOR VARIANCES?

Now we'll return to our Cheerful Colors example. Exhibit 23-5, the flexible budget performance report, showed several substantial flexible budget variances, including a $13,000 unfavorable variance for direct materials and a $10,400 favorable variance for direct labor. Exhibit 23-10 summarizes the flexible budget variances for the production costs.

Learning Objective 3

Compute the standard cost variances for direct materials and direct labor

Exhibit 23-10 | **Flexible Budget Variances for Production Costs**

	Budget Amounts per Unit	Actual Results	Flexible Budget Variance	Flexible Budget
Units (Batches of 100)		52,000		52,000
Variable Costs:				
Direct Materials	$ 1.75	$ 104,000	$ 13,000 U	$ 91,000
Direct Labor	3.00	145,600	10,400 F	156,000
Variable Overhead	0.75	30,160	8,840 F	39,000
Fixed Costs:				
Fixed Overhead		23,920	1,080 F	25,000
Totals		$ 303,680	$ 7,320 F	$ 311,000

Both favorable and unfavorable variances should be investigated, if substantial, to determine their causes. **As an example, suppose a company avoided routine maintenance on machinery in order to have a favorable cost variance in the current period. In a later period, the company could have a major breakdown that could have been avoided if the machinery had been properly maintained. The breakdown could require not only a substantial repair bill, but also a halt in production that could lead to lost sales.** Therefore, managers should look at any variance that is significant.

Let's look at the flexible budget variances for direct materials and direct labor and separate them into their two components—cost and efficiency.

Direct Materials Variances

The flexible budget variance for direct materials is $13,000 unfavorable. Additional data concerning direct materials follow, including standards discussed in the previous section:

Direct materials cost standard	$1.75 per pound of paraffin
Direct materials efficiency standard	1.00 pound of paraffin per batch of crayons
Actual amount of paraffin purchased and used	65,000 pounds
Actual cost of paraffin purchased and used	$104,000

Direct Materials Cost Variance

Using the above information, we can determine that Cheerful Colors paid less than expected for the paraffin. The actual cost per pound of paraffin is $1.60 ($104,000 / 65,000 pounds = $1.60 per pound). Using the formula, the direct materials cost variance is $9,750 favorable. The calculation follows:

$$\text{Direct Materials Cost Variance} = (AC - SC) \times AQ$$
$$= (\$1.60 \text{ per pound} - \$1.75 \text{ per pound}) \times 65,000 \text{ pounds}$$
$$= \$9,750 \text{ F}$$

The direct materials cost variance is *favorable* because the purchasing department paid *less* for paraffin than the standard cost.

Direct Materials Efficiency Variance

To calculate the direct materials efficiency variance, the standard quantity of inputs has to be determined. The standard quantity of inputs is the *quantity that should have been used* for the actual units produced. For Cheerful Colors, the standard quantity of inputs (paraffin) that workers should have used for the actual number of crayon batches produced is 52,000 pounds (1.00 pound per batch × 52,000 batches). The direct materials efficiency variance is as follows:

$$\text{Direct Materials Efficiency Variance} = (AQ - SQ) \times SC$$
$$= (65,000 \text{ pounds} - 52,000 \text{ pounds}) \times \$1.75 \text{ per pound}$$
$$= \$22,750 \text{ U}$$

The direct materials efficiency variance is *unfavorable* because workers used *more* paraffin than they planned (budgeted) to use for 52,000 batches of crayons.

Exhibit 23-11 | **Direct Materials Variances**

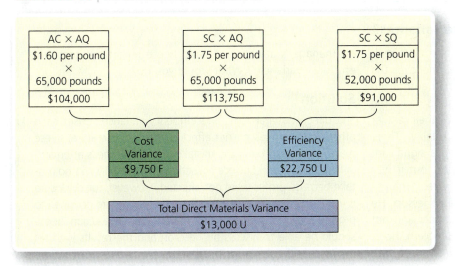

> *Favorable and unfavorable variances are netted together in the same way debits and credits are. Favorable variances are added together to create a total favorable variance. Unfavorable variances are added together to create a total unfavorable variance. But if a favorable and an unfavorable variance exist, the variances are subtracted from each other. The variance is determined to be favorable or unfavorable based on which one is the larger amount.*

Summary of Direct Materials Variances

Exhibit 23-11 summarizes how Cheerful Colors divides the $13,000 unfavorable direct materials flexible budget variance into its cost and efficiency components.

In summary, Cheerful Colors spent $13,000 more than it should have for paraffin because:

- Workers used 13,000 pounds of paraffin more than expected. The inefficient use of the paraffin reduced profits by $22,750, as shown by the unfavorable efficiency variance.
- Cheerful Colors paid $1.60 per pound of paraffin instead of the standard rate of $1.75 per pound—for a favorable cost variance.

Let's consider why each variance may have occurred and who may be responsible.

1. The purchasing manager is in the best position to explain the favorable cost variance. Cheerful Colors's purchasing manager may have negotiated a lower cost for paraffin.
2. The production manager in charge of making crayons can explain why workers used so much paraffin to make the 52,000 batches of crayons. Was the paraffin of lower quality that caused crayons to be rejected? Did workers waste materials? Did the production equipment malfunction? Cheerful Colors's top management needs this information to decide what corrective action to take.

These variances raise questions that can help pinpoint problems. But be careful! A favorable variance does not always mean that a manager did a good job, nor does an unfavorable variance mean that a manager did a bad job. Perhaps Cheerful Colors's purchasing manager got a lower cost by purchasing inferior-quality materials. This could lead to wasted materials and poor-quality crayons. If so, the purchasing manager's decision hurt the company. This illustrates why good managers use variances as a guide for investigation, rather than merely to assign blame, and investigate favorable as well as unfavorable variances.

ETHICS

Do we have to talk about all of these variances?

Reese knew he had made a mistake, but he didn't realize how big his mistake was. Reese was looking over the production reports for the past quarter. He had authorized a purchase of materials that seemed like a good deal—the cost was 40% less than the amount charged by their regular vendor—but the materials had been low quality. There had been a lot of waste. The reports showed a significant unfavorable direct materials efficiency variance, but it was offset by the just-as-significant favorable direct materials cost variance. Reese had learned a valuable lesson. He would take more time to check out new vendors and not make the same mistake again. The current problem, however, was the reports. Reese was scheduled to meet with his manager. He decided the best course of action would be to not discuss the cost and efficiency variances for direct materials, but just focus on the total variance. Reese knew his manager was busy and may never read the detailed reports and find out about the mistake if he didn't bring it to his manager's attention. Should Reese report the cost and efficiency variances? What would you do?

Solution

The direct materials cost and efficiency variances offset each other, so there was no net effect on profits. Therefore, Reese may not need to bring the mistake to his manager's attention. In fact, Reese may convince himself that there really was no mistake because profits were not affected. However, full disclosure is usually the best option. Standard cost systems are designed to provide feedback so managers can take corrective action. Reese should be able to discuss his decision and the results with his manager without fear of punishment. His manager may have some insight that would be beneficial to Reese, and managers tend to respect people who bring their mistakes to their manager's attention and explain what they have learned. Additionally, if Reese does not bring it up and his manager finds out about it later, Reese's integrity may be questioned.

Direct Labor Variances

Cheerful Colors uses a similar approach to analyze the direct labor flexible budget variance. The flexible budget variance for direct labor is $10,400 favorable, as shown in Exhibit 23-10. Additional data concerning direct labor follow, including standards discussed in the previous section:

Direct labor cost standard	$12.00 per DLHr
Direct labor efficiency standard	0.25 DLHr per batch of crayons
Actual amount of direct labor hours	10,400 DLHr
Actual cost of direct labor	$145,600

Direct Labor Cost Variance

Using the above information, we can determine that Cheerful Colors paid more than expected for direct labor. The actual cost per hour of direct labor is $14.00 ($145,600 / 10,400 DLHr = $14.00 per DLHr). Using the formula, the direct labor cost variance is $20,800 unfavorable. The calculation follows:

$$
\begin{aligned}
\text{Direct Labor Cost Variance} &= (AC - SC) \times AQ \\
&= (\$14.00 \text{ per DLHr} - \$12.00 \text{ per DLHr}) \times 10,400 \text{ DLHr} \\
&= \$20,800 \text{ U}
\end{aligned}
$$

The $20,800 direct labor cost variance is *unfavorable* because Cheerful Colors paid workers $2.00 *more* per hour than budgeted ($14.00 actual cost − $12.00 standard cost).

Direct Labor Efficiency Variance

Now let's see how efficiently Cheerful Colors used its labor. The standard quantity of direct labor hours that workers *should have used* to make 52,000 batches of crayons is 0.25 direct labor hours each, or 13,000 total direct labor hours (52,000 batches × 0.25 DLHr per batch). The direct labor efficiency variance is as follows:

$$\text{Direct Labor Efficiency Variance} = (AQ - SQ) \times SC$$
$$= (10{,}400 \text{ DLHr} - 13{,}000 \text{ DLHr}) \times \$12.00 \text{ per DLHr}$$
$$= \$31{,}200 \text{ F}$$

The $31,200 direct labor efficiency variance is *favorable* because laborers actually worked 2,600 *fewer* hours than the flexible budget called for to produce 52,000 batches of crayons.

Summary of Direct Labor Variances

Exhibit 23-12 summarizes how Cheerful Colors divides the $10,400 favorable direct labor flexible budget variance into its cost and efficiency components.

Exhibit 23-12 | **Direct Labor Variances**

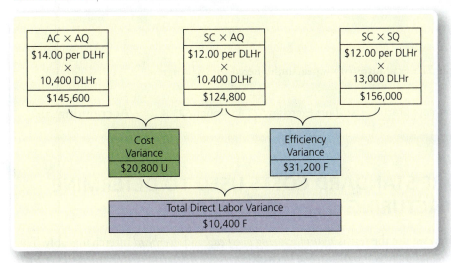

The $10,400 favorable direct labor variance suggests that total labor costs were significantly less than expectations. To manage Cheerful Colors's labor costs, we need to gain more insight:

- Workers made 52,000 batches of crayons in 10,400 hours instead of the budgeted 13,000 hours—for a favorable efficiency variance.
- Cheerful Colors paid its employees an average of $14.00 per hour in 2017 instead of the standard rate of $12.00—for an unfavorable cost variance.

This situation reveals a trade-off. Perhaps Cheerful Colors hired more experienced, and thus more expensive, workers and had an unfavorable cost variance. However, due to more advanced skills, experience, and/or motivation, the workers turned out more work than expected, and the strategy was successful. The overall effect on profits was favorable. This possibility reminds us that managers should take care in using variances to evaluate performance. Managers should always carefully analyze the data before taking action.

Tipton Company manufactures shirts. During June, Tipton made 1,200 shirts and gathered the following additional data:

Direct materials cost standard	$6.00 per yard of fabric
Direct materials efficiency standard	1.50 yards per shirt
Actual amount of fabric purchased and used	1,680 yards
Actual cost of fabric purchased and used	$10,500
Direct labor cost standard	$15.00 per DLHr
Direct labor efficiency standard	2.00 DLHr per shirt
Actual amount of direct labor hours	2,520 DLHr
Actual cost of direct labor	$36,540

Calculate the following variances:

7. Direct materials cost variance
8. Direct materials efficiency variance
9. Total direct materials variance
10. Direct labor cost variance
11. Direct labor efficiency variance
12. Total direct labor variance

Check your answers online in MyAccountingLab or at http://www.pearsonhighered.com/Horngren.

For more practice, see Short Exercises S23-6 through S23-8.   MyAccountingLab

HOW ARE STANDARD COSTS USED TO DETERMINE MANUFACTURING OVERHEAD VARIANCES?

Learning Objective 4

Compute the standard cost variances for manufacturing overhead

In this section, we use the terms *manufacturing overhead* and *overhead* interchangeably. The total overhead variance is the difference between:

Actual overhead cost	and	Standard overhead allocated to production

Exhibit 23-10 shows that Cheerful Colors incurred $30,160 in variable overhead costs and $23,920 in fixed overhead costs. Therefore, total overhead costs incurred are $54,080 ($30,160 + $23,920). The next step is to see how Cheerful Colors allocates overhead in a standard cost system.

Allocating Overhead in a Standard Cost System

In a standard cost system, the manufacturing overhead allocated to production is as follows:

Overhead allocated to production	=	Standard overhead allocation rate	×	Standard quantity of the allocation base allowed for *actual* output

In a standard cost system, the *standard* overhead allocation rate replaces the *predetermined* overhead allocation rate illustrated in previous chapters, but the concept is the same. It is a rate calculated during the budgeting process when other standards are determined.

Let's begin by computing Cheerful Colors's standard variable and fixed overhead allocation rates. Cheerful Colors allocates overhead based on direct labor hours. The static budget that was presented in Exhibit 23-2 indicated expected production would be 50,000 batches of crayons. At that level of production and using the direct labor efficiency standard of 0.25 direct labor hours per batch, Cheerful Colors expected to incur 12,500 direct labor hours, which is calculated as follows:

Budgeted allocation base = 50,000 batches × 0.25 direct labor hours per batch = 12,500 DLHr

The static budget also shows budgeted variable overhead at $37,500 and budgeted fixed overhead at $25,000. We are using *static budget* amounts here because standards are set *before* the budgeting period, so the accountants at Cheerful Colors did not yet know the actual production levels for the year when the standards were set.

The standard overhead allocation rate is calculated as follows:

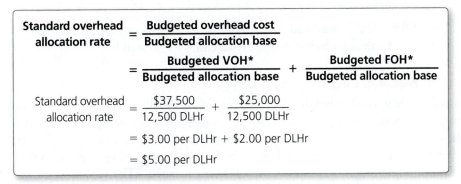

*VOH = Variable overhead; FOH = Fixed overhead

Cheerful Colors used a $3.00 per direct labor hour rate to allocate variable overhead to batches and $2.00 per direct labor hour rate to allocate fixed overhead to batches in 2017. Now, let's analyze the variances for variable and fixed overhead.

Variable Overhead Variances

Cheerful Colors uses a similar approach to analyze the variable overhead flexible budget variance as it did to analyze the direct materials and direct labor variances. Remember, direct materials and direct labor are also variable costs, so the approach is similar.

According to Exhibit 23-10, Cheerful Colors has an $8,840 favorable variable overhead flexible budget variance, which means the company spent less than budgeted. To analyze the favorable variance, Cheerful Colors computes the variable overhead cost and efficiency variances. Recall that the standard cost for variable overhead is $3.00 per direct labor hour, and 13,000 direct labor hours were budgeted for 52,000 batches of crayons in the flexible budget (0.25 DLHr per batch × 52,000 batches). However, actual variable overhead cost was $30,160, and it took 10,400 direct labor hours to make 52,000 batches. To summarize the data for variable overhead:

Variable overhead cost standard	$3.00 per DLHr
Variable overhead efficiency standard	0.25 DLHr per batch of crayons
Actual amount of direct labor hours	10,400 DLHr
Actual cost of variable overhead	$30,160

Variable Overhead Cost Variance

Using the above information, we can determine that Cheerful Colors paid less than expected for variable overhead. The actual cost of variable overhead per hour of direct labor is $2.90 ($30,160 / 10,400 DLHr = $2.90 per DLHr). Using the formula, the variable overhead cost variance is $1,040 favorable. The calculation follows:

> **Variable Overhead Cost Variance = (AC − SC) × AQ**
> = ($2.90 per DLHr − $3.00 per DLHr) × 10,400 DLHr
> = $1,040 F

The $1,040 variable overhead cost variance is *favorable* because Cheerful Colors spent $0.10 *less* per hour than budgeted ($2.90 actual cost − $3.00 standard cost).

Variable Overhead Efficiency Variance

Now let's see how efficiently Cheerful Colors used its variable overhead. Because variable overhead is allocated based on direct labor hours used, this variance will also be favorable, as the direct labor efficiency variance was favorable. The *standard quantity of direct labor hours* that workers should have used to make 52,000 batches of crayons is 13,000 total direct labor hours (52,000 batches × 0.25 DLHr per batch). The variable overhead efficiency variance is as follows:

> **Variable Overhead Efficiency Variance = (AQ − SQ) × SC**
> = (10,400 DLHr − 13,000 DLHr) × $3.00 per DLHr
> = $7,800 F

The $7,800 variable overhead efficiency variance is *favorable* because laborers actually worked 2,600 *fewer* hours than the flexible budget called for to produce 52,000 batches of crayons, and variable overhead is allocated based on direct labor hours.

Summary of Variable Overhead Variances

Exhibit 23-13 summarizes how Cheerful Colors divides the $8,840 favorable variable overhead flexible budget variance into its cost and efficiency components.

Exhibit 23-13 | **Variable Overhead Variances**

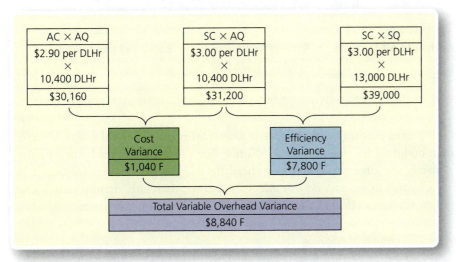

The $8,840 favorable variable overhead variance indicates that variable overhead costs were less than expected. To manage Cheerful Colors's variable overhead costs, we need to get more insight:

- Cheerful Colors incurred $1,040 less than anticipated actual variable overhead costs—for a favorable cost variance.
- Workers made 52,000 batches of crayons in 10,400 hours instead of the budgeted 13,000 hours—for a favorable efficiency variance.

Management may decide that the variable overhead cost variance is sufficiently small and does not warrant investigation. However, they may want to investigate the variance further to determine if the reduction in costs was controllable or if the cost standard needs to be updated.

Fixed Overhead Variances

The three production costs analyzed so far were variable costs, so the analysis was similar for direct materials, direct labor, and variable overhead. However, Cheerful Colors uses a slightly different approach to analyze the fixed overhead variances. Remember that fixed costs are not expected to change *in total* within the relevant range, but they do change *per unit* when there is a change in volume. To analyze fixed overhead costs, we will need three amounts:

- Actual fixed overhead costs incurred
- Budgeted fixed overhead costs
- Allocated fixed overhead costs

Keep in mind that the budgeted amount for fixed overhead is the same in both the static budget and the flexible budget because fixed costs are not expected to change in total when there is a change in volume. Refer to Exhibit 23-5, Flexible Budget Performance Report, to review this concept.

Fixed Overhead Cost Variance

The fixed overhead cost variance measures the difference between *actual* fixed overhead and *budgeted* fixed overhead to determine the controllable portion of total fixed overhead variance. Both of these amounts are given in Exhibit 23-2, Static Budget Performance Report, and Exhibit 23-5, Flexible Budget Performance Report.

> **Fixed Overhead Cost Variance** = **Actual fixed overhead** − **Budgeted fixed overhead**
> = $23,920 − $25,000
> = $1,080 F

The $1,080 fixed overhead cost variance is *favorable* because Cheerful Colors actually spent less than budgeted for fixed overhead. Notice that the fixed overhead cost variance calculated above is the same as the fixed overhead flexible budget variance calculated in Exhibit 23-5. Changes in volume do not affect fixed costs; therefore, there is only a cost effect and not an efficiency effect in the fixed overhead flexible budget variance.

Fixed Overhead Volume Variance

The fixed overhead volume variance measures the difference between the budgeted fixed overhead and the amount of fixed overhead allocated to batches of crayons. Using the standard overhead allocation rate for fixed overhead previously calculated, fixed overhead is allocated at $2.00 per direct labor hour and each batch of crayons has an efficiency standard of 0.25 direct labor hours per batch. Therefore, the amount of fixed overhead allocated is $26,000, as shown below:

> **Overhead allocated to production** = **Standard overhead allocation rate** × **Standard quantity of the allocation base allowed for *actual* output**
> = $2.00 per DLHr × (0.25 DLHr per batch × 52,000 batches)
> = $2.00 per DLHr × 13,000 DLHr
> = $26,000

The fixed overhead volume variance is as follows:

> **Fixed Overhead Volume Variance** = **Budgeted fixed overhead** − **Allocated fixed overhead**
> = $25,000 − $26,000
> = $1,000 F

The $1,000 fixed overhead volume variance is *favorable* because Cheerful Colors produced more batches than budgeted and, therefore, allocated more overhead to crayon batches than the $25,000 budgeted fixed overhead amount. In other words, based on the standard for fixed overhead, Cheerful Colors has overallocated fixed overhead by $1,000.

The fixed overhead volume variance is not a *cost* variance—it is a *volume* variance—and explains why fixed overhead is overallocated or underallocated. Exhibit 23-14 graphs the fixed overhead volume variance for Cheerful Colors. The small blue triangle bordered by the lines representing budgeted fixed overhead, standard fixed overhead allocated, and standard direct labor hours lines represents the favorable fixed overhead volume variance for this example.

Exhibit 23-14 | **Fixed Overhead Volume Variance**

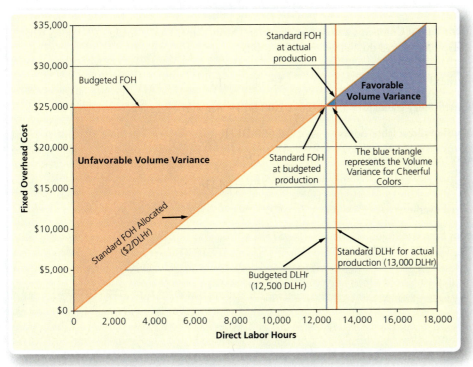

Summary of Fixed Overhead Variances

Exhibit 23-15 summarizes the fixed overhead variances.

To manage Cheerful Colors's fixed overhead costs, we need to get more insight:

- Cheerful Colors incurred $1,080 less than anticipated in fixed overhead costs for a favorable cost variance.
- Workers made 52,000 batches of crayons, which was 2,000 batches more than budgeted and resulted in a $1,000 favorable volume variance.

Management may decide that the fixed overhead cost variance is sufficiently small and does not warrant investigation. However, they may want to investigate the variance further to determine if the reduction in costs was controllable or if the cost standard needs to be updated.

Exhibit 23-15 | **Fixed Overhead Variances**

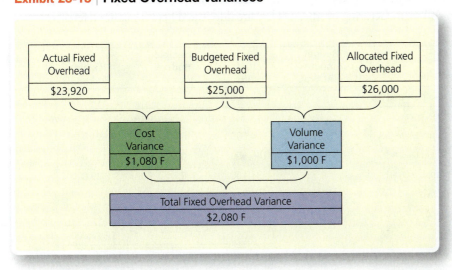

Try It!

This Try It! continues the previous Try It! for Tipton Company, a shirt manufacturer. During June, Tipton made 1,200 shirts but had budgeted production at 1,400 shirts. Tipton gathered the following additional data:

Variable overhead cost standard	$0.50 per DLHr
Direct labor efficiency standard	2.00 DLHr per shirt
Actual amount of direct labor hours	2,520 DLHr
Actual cost of variable overhead	$1,512
Fixed overhead cost standard	$0.25 per DLHr
Budgeted fixed overhead	$700
Actual cost of fixed overhead	$750

Calculate the following variances:

13. Variable overhead cost variance
14. Variable overhead efficiency variance
15. Total variable overhead variance
16. Fixed overhead cost variance
17. Fixed overhead volume variance
18. Total fixed overhead variance

Check your answers online in MyAccountingLab or at http://www.pearsonhighered.com/Horngren.

For more practice, see Short Exercises S23-9 and S23-10. MyAccountingLab

WHAT IS THE RELATIONSHIP AMONG THE PRODUCT COST VARIANCES, AND WHO IS RESPONSIBLE FOR THEM?

Learning Objective 5

Describe the relationship among and responsibility for the product cost variances

Now that we have looked at the individual product cost variances, let's look at the big picture. Exhibit 23-10 showed the flexible budget variances for the product costs—direct materials, direct labor, and manufacturing overhead. They are duplicated here for easier reference:

	Budget Amounts per Unit	Actual Results	Flexible Budget Variance	Flexible Budget
Units (Batches of 100)		52,000		52,000
Variable Costs:				
Direct Materials	$ 1.75	$ 104,000	$ 13,000 U	$ 91,000
Direct Labor	3.00	145,600	10,400 F	156,000
Variable Overhead	0.75	30,160	8,840 F	39,000
Fixed Costs:				
Fixed Overhead		23,920	1,080 F	25,000
Totals		$ 303,680	$ 7,320 F	$ 311,000

The individual variances are summarized here:

Direct materials cost variance	$ 9,750 F
Direct materials efficiency variance	22,750 U
Direct labor cost variance	20,800 U
Direct labor efficiency variance	31,200 F
Variable overhead cost variance	1,040 F
Variable overhead efficiency variance	7,800 F
Fixed overhead cost variance	1,080 F
Fixed overhead volume variance	1,000 F

Variance Relationships

Exhibit 23-16 illustrates the relationships among the various product cost variances. Take time to carefully study the diagram.

Exhibit 23-16 | Product Cost Variance Relationships

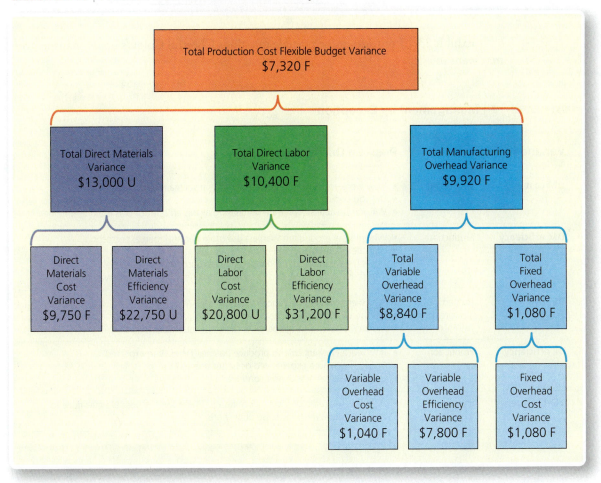

Notice that the fixed overhead volume variance is not included in the diagram. As previously stated, this variance is not a flexible budget variance but a volume variance. It shows how allocating fixed costs on a per unit basis causes a difference between budgeted fixed overhead and allocated fixed overhead. The allocation causes the overallocation or underallocation of fixed manufacturing overhead.

Variance Responsibilities

Management by Exception
When managers concentrate on results that are outside the accepted parameters.

Now that all the variances are summarized, Cheerful Colors can investigate the variances it feels are significant. This is called **management by exception** because managers concentrate on results that are outside the accepted parameters. In other words, managers focus on the exceptions. Exceptions can be expressed as a percentage of a budgeted amount or a dollar amount. Many companies use a combination of percentages and dollar amounts. For example, a company may investigate any variances greater than 10% of the budgeted amount and/or $10,000 or more.

Cheerful Colors investigates any variances greater than $5,000. Therefore, Cheerful Colors will look into the following variances:

Direct materials cost variance	$ 9,750 F
Direct materials efficiency variance	22,750 U
Direct labor cost variance	20,800 U
Direct labor efficiency variance	31,200 F
Variable overhead efficiency variance	7,800 F

Exhibit 23-17 provides some possible questions Cheerful Colors's upper management may want to ask.

Exhibit 23-17 | **Management by Exception**

Variance	Manager	Possible Questions
DM cost	Purchasing	• How were you able to purchase paraffin at such a reduced cost? • Did you compromise on quality? • Will you be able to continue purchasing at this amount or was it a one-time deal?
DM efficiency	Production	• Why did the production workers use more paraffin than expected? • Was there a problem with quality? • Did you have inexperienced workers that caused excessive waste? • Was there some event, such as a large spillage, that caused the variance?
DL cost	Human Resources	• Why were workers paid more than expected? • Did the workers hired have advanced skills? • Did an increase in fringe benefits cause the labor cost to increase?
DL efficiency	Production	• How were workers able to produce batches faster than expected? • Are workers more experienced or better trained? • Can this level of production continue?
VOH efficiency	Production	• VOH was allocated on direct labor hours. Therefore, the possible questions for the DL efficiency variance also apply here.

Try It!

Match the product cost variance with the manager most probably responsible. Some answers may be used more than once. Some answers may not be used.

Variance	Manager
19. Variable overhead cost variance	a. Human resources
20. Direct materials efficiency variance	b. Purchasing
21. Direct labor cost variance	c. Production
22. Fixed overhead cost variance	
23. Direct materials cost variance	

Check your answers online in MyAccountingLab or at http://www.pearsonhighered.com/Horngren.

For more practice, see Short Exercise S23-11.   MyAccountingLab

HOW DO JOURNAL ENTRIES DIFFER IN A STANDARD COST SYSTEM?

Using a standard cost system simplifies the recording process because entries are made at standard costs. Let's look at the various journal entries.

> **Learning Objective 6**
>
> Record transactions in a standard cost system and prepare a standard cost income statement

Journal Entries

Management needs to know about variances to address each problem. Therefore, Cheerful Colors records variances from standards as soon as possible. This means that Cheerful Colors records direct materials cost variances when materials are purchased. It also means that Work-in-Process Inventory is debited at standard input quantities and standard costs as crayons are manufactured. However, because our chapter example for Cheerful Colors was for the year 2017, we will record summary entries.

Transaction 1—Direct Materials Purchased

The journal entry to record direct materials purchased has an emphasis on the *cost* of the materials. Transaction 1 records the debit to Raw Materials Inventory, which is recorded at the actual quantity of paraffin purchases (65,000 pounds) at the *standard cost* ($1.75 per pound). In contrast, the credit to Accounts Payable is for the actual quantity of paraffin purchased (65,000 pounds) at the *actual cost* ($1.60 per pound). This is the actual amount owed to the vendor. Maintaining Raw Materials Inventory at the $1.75 *standard cost* allows Cheerful Colors to record the direct materials cost variance at the time of purchase. Recall that Cheerful Colors's direct materials cost variance was $9,750 favorable. A favorable variance has a credit balance and is a contra expense. An unfavorable variance means more expense has been incurred than planned and would have a debit balance.

> When recording variances, favorable variances are credited and unfavorable variances are debited. Remember that variances are considered favorable if they increase operating income—and operating income is increased with credits (like revenues). Variances are considered unfavorable if they decrease operating income—and operating income is decreased with debits (like expenses).

$$\left.\dfrac{A\uparrow}{RM\uparrow}\right\} = \left\{\dfrac{L\uparrow}{A/P\uparrow} + \dfrac{E\uparrow}{DM\ Cost\ Var.\uparrow}\right.$$

Date	Accounts and Explanation	Debit	Credit
Trans. 1	Raw Materials Inventory (65,000 pounds × $1.75/pound)	113,750	
	Direct Materials Cost Variance		9,750
	Accounts Payable (65,000 pounds × $1.60/pound)		104,000
	Purchased direct materials.		

Transaction 2—Direct Materials Usage

The journal entry to record the direct materials usage has an emphasis on the *quantity* of the materials used. In Transaction 2, Cheerful Colors debits Work-in-Process Inventory for the standard cost at the *standard quantity* of 52,000 pounds of direct materials that should have been used to make 52,000 batches of crayons. This maintains Work-in-Process Inventory at standard cost. Raw Materials Inventory is credited for the *actual quantity* of materials put into production (65,000 pounds) at the standard cost ($1.75 per pound). Cheerful Colors's direct materials efficiency variance was $22,750 unfavorable. An unfavorable variance has a debit balance, which increases expense and decreases profits.

$$\left.\dfrac{A\downarrow}{\substack{WIP\uparrow \\ RM\downarrow}}\right\} = \left\{\dfrac{L}{} + \dfrac{E\downarrow}{DM\ Eff.\ Var.\downarrow}\right.$$

Date	Accounts and Explanation	Debit	Credit
Trans. 2	Work-in-Process Inventory (1 lb./batch × $1.75/lb.× 52,000 batches)	91,000	
	Direct Materials Efficiency Variance	22,750	
	Raw Materials Inventory (65,000 pounds × $1.75/pound)		113,750
	Used direct materials.		

> Direct materials were put into Raw Materials Inventory at actual quantity *purchased* times standard cost, and they are transferred out at actual quantity *used* times standard cost.

Transaction 3—Direct Labor

In Transaction 3, Work-in-Process Inventory is debited for the $12.00 per hour *standard cost* of the 13,000 direct labor hours that should have been used for 52,000 batches, the *standard quantity*. Wages Payable is credited for the *actual cost* (the *actual* hours worked at the *actual* wage rate) because this is the amount Cheerful Colors must pay the workers. The direct labor cost variance is $20,800 unfavorable, a debit amount. The direct labor efficiency variance is credited for the $31,200 favorable variance. This maintains Work-in-Process Inventory at standard cost.

Date	Accounts and Explanation	Debit	Credit
Trans. 3	Work-in-Process Inventory (0.25 DLHr/batch × $12/DLHr × 52,000 batches)	156,000	
	Direct Labor Cost Variance	20,800	
	Direct Labor Efficiency Variance		31,200
	Wages Payable (10,400 DLHr × $14.00/DLHr)		145,600
	Direct labor costs incurred.		

$$\left.\frac{A\uparrow}{WIP\uparrow}\right\} = \left\{\begin{array}{cc} \frac{L\uparrow}{\substack{\text{Wages} \\ \text{Pay.}\uparrow}} + & \frac{E\uparrow}{\substack{\text{DL Cost Var.}\downarrow \\ \text{DL Eff. Var.}\uparrow}} \end{array}\right.$$

Transaction 4—Manufacturing Overhead

Transaction 4 records Cheerful Colors's actual overhead cost for 2017. Manufacturing Overhead is debited for the actual overhead costs: $30,160 actual variable overhead plus $23,920 actual fixed overhead equals $54,080 total manufacturing overhead. Various Accounts is a fictitious account used here to simplify the illustration and may include accounts such as Cash, Accounts Payable, Accumulated Depreciation, Prepaid Insurance, or other accounts related to incurring overhead costs.

Date	Accounts and Explanation	Debit	Credit
Trans. 4	Manufacturing Overhead ($30,160 + $23,920)	54,080	
	Various Accounts		54,080
	Manufacturing overhead costs incurred.		

$$\left.\frac{A\downarrow}{\substack{\text{Accum. Deprn.}\uparrow \\ \text{Cash}\downarrow \\ \text{Prepaid Ins.}\downarrow}}\right\} = \left\{\begin{array}{cc} \frac{L\uparrow}{A/P\uparrow} + & \frac{E\downarrow}{\text{Mfg. OH}\uparrow} \end{array}\right.$$

Transaction 5—Overhead Allocated

Transaction 5 shows the overhead allocated to Work-in-Process Inventory computed as:

$$\begin{array}{cc} \substack{\text{Standard overhead} \\ \text{allocation rate}} \times & \substack{\text{Standard quantity of the allocation} \\ \text{base for actual output}} \\ \end{array}$$
$$\$5.00/\text{DLHr} \times (0.25 \text{ DLHr/batch} \times 52,000 \text{ batches})$$

Date	Accounts and Explanation	Debit	Credit
Trans. 5	Work-in-Process Inventory ($5.00/DLHr × 0.25 DLHr/batch × 52,000 batches)	65,000	
	Manufacturing Overhead		65,000
	Manufacturing overhead costs allocated.		

$$\left.\frac{A\uparrow}{WIP\uparrow}\right\} = \left\{\begin{array}{cc} \frac{L}{} + & \frac{E\uparrow}{\text{Mfg. OH}\downarrow} \end{array}\right.$$

Transaction 6—Completed Goods

Transaction 6 transfers the standard cost of the 52,000 batches of crayons completed during 2017 from Work-in-Process Inventory to Finished Goods Inventory. The amount transferred is the total standard costs for the 52,000 batches: direct materials ($91,000), direct labor ($156,000), and manufacturing overhead ($65,000).

$$\left.\begin{array}{c} A\uparrow\downarrow \\ \hline FG\uparrow \\ WIP\downarrow \end{array}\right\} = \left\{\begin{array}{c} \underline{L} + \underline{E} \\ \\ \end{array}\right.$$

Date	Accounts and Explanation	Debit	Credit
Trans. 6	Finished Goods Inventory	312,000	
	Work-in-Process Inventory		312,000
	Completed goods transferred.		

Transaction 7—Cost of Goods Sold

Transaction 7 transfers the cost of goods sold of the 52,000 batches completed at the standard cost of $6.00 per batch ($312,000 from Transaction 6 divided by 52,000 batches). This transaction assumes all batches produced during 2017 were sold in 2017. The sales journal entry has not been presented for simplicity purposes.

$$\left.\begin{array}{c} A\downarrow \\ \hline FG\downarrow \end{array}\right\} = \left\{\begin{array}{c} \underline{L} + \underline{E\downarrow} \\ COGS\uparrow \end{array}\right.$$

Date	Accounts and Explanation	Debit	Credit
Trans. 7	Cost of Goods Sold	312,000	
	Finished Goods Inventory		312,000
	Cost of sales at standard cost.		

Transaction 8—Adjust Manufacturing Overhead

Transaction 8 adjusts the Manufacturing Overhead account and records the overhead variances. All of the manufacturing overhead variances are favorable, so they are all credited. The debit to Manufacturing Overhead indicates that the actual overhead costs debited to the account were less than the allocated amounts credited to the account, and overhead was overallocated. The account, therefore, had a credit balance and has to be debited to bring it to a zero balance. When overhead is underallocated, then the adjustment to Manufacturing Overhead is a credit, and the net amount of the overhead variances is unfavorable.

$$\left.\begin{array}{c} A \\ \\ \\ \\ \\ \end{array}\right\} = \left\{\begin{array}{c} \underline{L} + \underline{E\uparrow\downarrow} \\ MOH\uparrow \\ VOH\ Cost\ Var.\uparrow \\ VOH\ Eff.\ Var.\uparrow \\ FOH\ Cost\ Var.\uparrow \\ FOH\ Vol.\ Var.\uparrow \end{array}\right.$$

Date	Accounts and Explanation	Debit	Credit
Trans. 8	Manufacturing Overhead	10,920	
	Variable Overhead Cost Variance		1,040
	Variable Overhead Efficiency Variance		7,800
	Fixed Overhead Cost Variance		1,080
	Fixed Overhead Volume Variance		1,000
	To adjust Manufacturing Overhead.		

Exhibit 23-18 shows the relevant Cheerful Colors accounts after posting these entries.

Exhibit 23-18 | Flow of Costs in a Standard Cost System

Raw Materials Inventory			
Trans. 1	113,750	113,750	Trans. 2
Bal.	0		

Work-in-Process Inventory			
Trans. 2	91,000	312,000	Trans. 6
Trans. 3	156,000		
Trans. 5	65,000		
Bal.	0		

Finished Goods Inventory			
Trans. 6	312,000	312,000	Trans. 7
Bal.	0		

Manufacturing Overhead			
Trans. 4	54,080	65,000	Trans. 5
Trans. 8	10,920		
Bal.	0		

Cost of Goods Sold		
Trans. 7	312,000	

Accounts Payable		
	104,000	Trans. 1

Direct Materials Cost Variance		
	9,750	Trans. 1

Direct Materials Efficiency Variance		
Trans. 2	22,750	

Wages Payable		
	145,600	Trans. 3

Direct Labor Cost Variance		
Trans. 3	20,800	

Direct Labor Efficiency Variance		
	31,200	Trans. 3

Various Accounts		
	54,080	Trans. 4

Variable Overhead Cost Variance		
	1,040	Trans. 8

Variable Overhead Efficiency Variance		
	7,800	Trans. 8

Notice that the inventory accounts have a zero balance at the end of 2017. That is because we assumed Cheerful Colors used all materials purchased, completed all units started, and sold all units completed.

Fixed Overhead Cost Variance		
	1,080	Trans. 8

Fixed Overhead Volume Variance		
	1,000	Trans. 8

Standard Cost Income Statement

Cheerful Colors's top management needs to know about the company's cost variances. Exhibit 23-19 (on the next page) shows a standard cost income statement that highlights the variances for management.

First, notice that the operating income shown in Exhibit 23-19 is the same as that shown in Exhibit 23-5, Flexible Budget Performance Report. The standard cost income statement doesn't alter the actual operating income—it simply emphasizes the variances from standard.

The statement starts with sales revenue at standard and subtracts the unfavorable sales revenue variance of $5,200 (from Exhibit 23-5) to yield actual sales revenue. (A favorable sales revenue variance would be added.) Next, the statement shows Cost of Goods Sold at standard cost. Then, the statement separately lists each manufacturing cost variance, followed by Cost of Goods Sold at actual cost. The variances with credit balances are shown in parentheses because they are contra expenses and therefore decrease the expense Cost of Goods Sold.

At the end of the period, all the variance accounts, which are temporary accounts, are closed to zero out their balances.

Exhibit 23-19 | Standard Cost Income Statement

CHEERFUL COLORS Standard Cost Income Statement For the Year Ended December 31, 2017			
Sales Revenue at standard (52,000 batches @ $7.50)			$ 390,000
Sales Revenue Variance*			(5,200)
Sales Revenue at actual			384,800
Cost of Goods Sold at standard (52,000 batches @ $6.00)		$ 312,000	
Manufacturing Cost Variances:			
Direct Materials Cost Variance	$ (9,750)		
Direct Materials Efficiency Variance	22,750		
Direct Labor Cost Variance	20,800		
Direct Labor Efficiency Variance	(31,200)		
Variable Overhead Cost Variance	(1,040)		
Variable Overhead Efficiency Variance	(7,800)		
Fixed Overhead Cost Variance	(1,080)		
Fixed Overhead Volume Variance	(1,000)		
Total Manufacturing Variances		(8,320)	
Cost of Goods Sold at actual			303,680
Gross Profit			81,120
Selling and Administrative Expenses**			44,800
Operating Income			$ 36,320

*From Exhibit 23-5

**$19,200 + $25,600 from Exhibit 23-5

The income statement shows that the net effect of all the manufacturing cost variances is $8,320 favorable. Therefore, 2017's operating income is $8,320 more than it would have been if all the actual manufacturing costs had been equal to their standard costs.

Gunter Company reported the following manufacturing overhead variances.

Variable overhead cost variance	$ 320 F
Variable overhead efficiency variance	458 U
Fixed overhead cost variance	667 U
Fixed overhead volume variance	625 F

24. Record the journal entry to adjust Manufacturing Overhead.
25. Was Manufacturing Overhead overallocated or underallocated?

Check your answers online in MyAccountingLab or at http://www.pearsonhighered.com/Horngren.

REVIEW

> Things You Should Know

1. **How do managers use budgets to control business activities?**

   - Variances are differences between budgeted amounts and actual amounts.
     - Favorable (F) variances increase operating income.
     - Unfavorable (U) variances decrease operating income.
   - A static budget performance report shows the differences between the static budget and actual results.
   - Flexible budgets help managers plan for various levels of sales.
   - A flexible budget performance report shows the following:
     - Flexible budget variance—the differences between the actual results and the flexible budget.
     - Sales volume variance—the differences between the flexible budget and the static budget.

2. **Why do managers use a standard cost system to control business activities?**

   - A standard is a price, cost, or quantity that is expected under normal conditions.
   - A standard cost system uses standards for product costs—direct materials, direct labor, and manufacturing overhead.
   - Managers must establish both cost and efficiency standards.
   - Standard cost systems allow managers to efficiently record transactions related to production.
   - The flexible budget variance can be further broken down into its two components:

   > Cost Variance = (Actual Cost × Actual Quantity) − (Standard Cost × Actual Quantity)
   > = (Actual Cost − Standard Cost) × Actual Quantity
   > = (AC − SC) × AQ

   > Efficiency Variance = (Standard Cost × Actual Quantity) − (Standard Cost × Standard Quantity)
   > = (Actual Quantity − Standard Quantity) × Standard Cost
   > = (AQ − SQ) × SC

   - A cost variance measures the difference in actual and standard costs based on the actual amount used.
   - An efficiency variance measures the difference in the actual amount used and the standard amount based on the standard cost.

3. **How are standard costs used to determine direct materials and direct labor variances?**

   - Direct materials cost variance—measures how well the business keeps unit costs of material inputs within standards.

- Direct materials efficiency variance—measures how well the business uses its materials.

- Direct labor cost variance—measures how well the business keeps unit costs of labor inputs within standards.

- Direct labor efficiency variance—measures how well the business uses its human resources.

4. How are standard costs used to determine manufacturing overhead variances?

- Manufacturing overhead costs are allocated using the standard overhead allocation rate:

$$\text{Standard overhead allocation rate} = \frac{\text{Budgeted overhead cost}}{\text{Budgeted allocation base}}$$

$$= \frac{\text{Budgeted VOH*}}{\text{Budgeted allocation base}} + \frac{\text{Budgeted FOH*}}{\text{Budgeted allocation base}}$$

*VOH = Variable overhead; FOH = Fixed overhead

- Variable overhead cost variance—measures how well the business keeps unit costs of variable overhead inputs within standards.

- Variable overhead efficiency variance—measures how well the business uses its variable overhead inputs.

- Fixed overhead cost variance—measures how well the business keeps fixed overhead within standards.

- Fixed overhead volume variance—measures how fixed overhead is allocated when actual volume is not equal to budgeted volume.

5. What is the relationship among the product cost variances, and who is responsible for them?

- The net amount of the production variances (except the fixed overhead volume variance) equals the total production cost flexible budget variance.

- The fixed overhead volume variance is not a cost variance but a volume variance.

- Various managers are responsible for the variances. Sometimes decisions by one manager may affect variances for another manager (for example, purchasing cheaper materials may cause problems in production).

6. How do journal entries differ in a standard cost system?

- Raw Materials Inventory—actual quantity at standard cost.

- Work-in-Process Inventory, Finished Goods Inventory, and Cost of Goods Sold— standard quantity of inputs allowed for actual outputs, at the standard cost of inputs.

- Favorable variances are credited because they increase operating income.

- Unfavorable variances are debited because they decrease operating income.

- The manufacturing overhead variances account for the difference between the actual costs debited to Manufacturing Overhead and the standard costs allocated by a credit to Manufacturing Overhead.

- A standard cost income statement highlights the variances for management.

> Summary Problem 23-1

Sutherland Company manufactures book bags and has provided the following information for June 2016:

	Actual Results	Static Budget
Units	7,000	8,000
Sales Revenue	$ 87,500	$ 96,000
Variable Expenses	57,400	64,000
Contribution Margin	30,100	32,000
Fixed Expenses	19,000	20,000
Operating Income	$ 11,100	$ 12,000

Requirements

1. Prepare a flexible budget performance report using Exhibit 23-5 as a guide. (*Hint:* You will need to calculate the flexible budget amounts for 7,000 units.)

2. As the company owner, which employees would you praise or criticize after you analyze this performance report?

> Solution

Requirement 1

SUTHERLAND COMPANY
Flexible Budget Performance Report
For the Month Ended June 30, 2016

	Budget Amounts per Unit	1 Actual Results	2 (1) – (3) Flexible Budget Variance	3 Flexible Budget	4 (3) – (5) Sales Volume Variance	5 Static Budget
Units		7,000		7,000		8,000
Sales Revenue	$ 12.00	$ 87,500	$ 3,500 F	$ 84,000	$12,000 U	$ 96,000
Variable Costs	8.00	57,400	1,400 U	56,000	8,000 F	64,000
Contribution Margin		30,100	2,100 F	28,000	4,000 U	32,000
Fixed Costs		19,000	1,000 F	20,000	0	20,000
Operating Income		$ 11,100	$ 3,100 F	$ 8,000	$ 4,000 U	$ 12,000

Flexible Budget Variance
$ 3,100 F

Sales Volume Variance
$ 4,000 U

Static Budget Variance
$ 900 U

Requirement 2

More information is needed to determine which employees to praise or criticize. As the company owner, you should determine the *causes* of the variances before praising or criticizing employees. It is especially important to determine whether the variance is due to factors the manager can control. For example:

- The $1,000 favorable flexible budget variance for fixed costs could be due to a reduction in insurance premiums. Or the savings might have come from delaying a scheduled overhaul of equipment that decreased fixed expenses in the short term but could increase the company's costs in the long run.

- The $4,000 unfavorable sales volume variance for operating income could be due to an ineffective sales staff, or it could be due to a long period of snow that made it difficult for employees to get to work, bringing work to a standstill.

Wise managers use variances to raise questions and direct attention, not to fix blame.

> Summary Problem 23-2

Sutherland Company produced 7,000 book bags in June, and *actual* amounts were as follows:

Direct materials (cloth)	7,400 yards @ $2.00 per yard
Direct labor	2,740 hours @ $10.00 per hour
Variable overhead	$ 5,400
Fixed overhead	11,900

Sutherland's *standards* were as follows:

Direct materials (cloth)	1 yard per book bag @ $2.00 per yard
Direct labor	0.40 direct labor hours per book bag @ $10.50 per direct labor hour
Variable overhead	0.40 direct labor hours per book bag @ $2.00 per direct labor hour
Fixed overhead	$9,600 (0.40 direct labor hours per book bag @ $3.00 per direct labor hour)

Requirements

1. Compute cost and efficiency variances for direct materials, direct labor, and variable overhead.

2. Compute the cost and volume variances for fixed overhead.

> Solution

Requirement 1

Direct Materials Variances

Standard materials allowed = 1 yard per book bag × 7,000 book bags = 7,000 yards

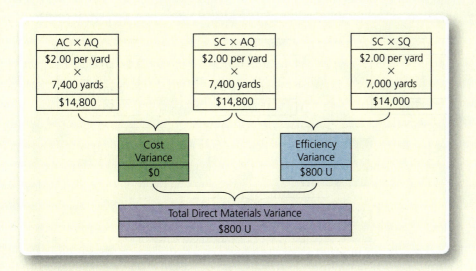

Direct Labor Variances

Standard labor allowed = 0.40 direct labor hours per book bag × 7,000 book bags = 2,800 direct labor hours

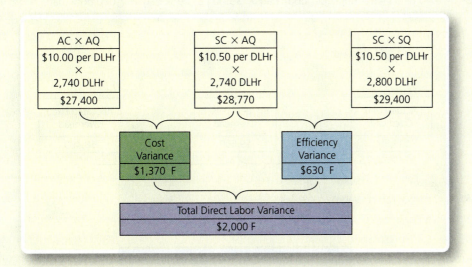

Variable Overhead Variances

Standard labor allowed = 0.40 direct labor hours per book bag × 7,000 book bags = 2,800 direct labor hours

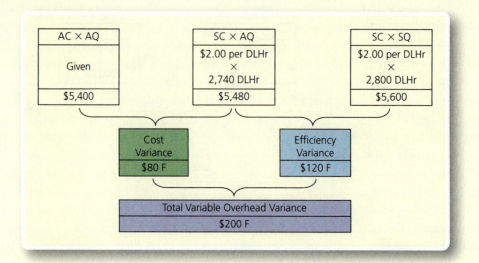

Requirement 2

Fixed Overhead Variances

Fixed overhead allocation = 0.40 direct labor hours per book bag × $3.00 per book bag × 7,000 book bags = $8,400

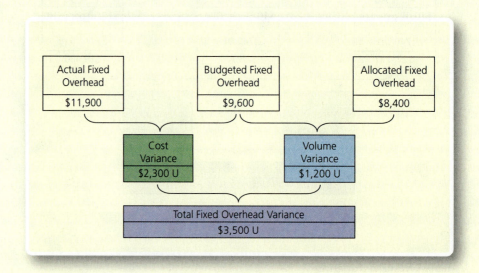

> Key Terms

Cost Variance (p. 1263)

Efficiency Variance (p. 1263)

Flexible Budget (p. 1256)

Flexible Budget Variance (p. 1257)

Management by Exception (p. 1278)

Sales Volume Variance (p. 1258)

Standard (p. 1260)

Standard Cost System (p. 1260)

Static Budget (p. 1255)

Static Budget Variance (p. 1255)

Variance (p. 1255)

> Quick Check

Questions 1–4 rely on the following data.

MajorNet Systems is a start-up company that makes connectors for high-speed Internet connections. The company has budgeted variable costs of $145 for each connector and fixed costs of $7,500 per month. MajorNet's static budget predicted production and sales of 100 connectors in August, but the company actually produced and sold only 84 connectors at a total cost of $21,000.

1. MajorNet's total flexible budget cost for 84 connectors per month is

   Learning Objective 1

   a. $14,500.   c. $19,680.

   b. $12,180.   d. $21,000.

2. MajorNet's sales volume variance for total costs is

   Learning Objective 1

   a. $1,320 U.   c. $2,320 U.

   b. $1,320 F.   d. $2,320 F.

3. MajorNet's flexible budget variance for total costs is

   Learning Objective 1

   a. $1,320 U.   c. $2,320 U.

   b. $1,320 F.   d. $2,320 F.

4. MajorNet Systems's managers could set direct labor standards based on

   Learning Objective 2

   a. time-and-motion studies.   c. benchmarking.

   b. continuous improvement.   d. All of the above.

Questions 5–6 rely on the following data.

MajorNet Systems has budgeted three hours of direct labor per connector, at a standard cost of $17 per hour. During August, technicians actually worked 189 hours completing 84 connectors. All 84 connectors actually produced were sold. MajorNet paid the technicians $17.80 per hour.

5. What is MajorNet's direct labor cost variance for August?

   Learning Objective 3

   a. $67.20 U   c. $201.60 U

   b. $151.20 U   d. $919.80 U

6. What is MajorNet's direct labor efficiency variance for August?

   Learning Objective 3

   a. $919.80 F   c. $1,121.40 F

   b. $1,071.00 F   d. $3,364.20 F

Questions 7–9 rely on the following data.

FrontGrade Systems allocates manufacturing overhead based on machine hours. Each connector should require 11 machine hours. According to the static budget, FrontGrade expected to incur the following:

   1,100 machine hours per month (100 connectors $\times$ 11 machine hours per connector)

   $5,500 in variable manufacturing overhead costs

   $8,250 in fixed manufacturing overhead costs

During August, FrontGrade actually used 1,000 machine hours to make 110 connectors and spent $5,600 in variable manufacturing costs and $8,300 in fixed manufacturing overhead costs.

Learning Objective 4

7. FrontGrade's standard *variable* manufacturing overhead allocation rate is

    a. $5.00 per machine hour.   c. $7.50 per machine hour.

    b. $5.50 per machine hour.   d. $12.50 per machine hour.

Learning Objective 4

8. Calculate the variable overhead cost variance for FrontGrade.

    a. $450 F   c. $1,050 F

    b. $600 U   d. $1,650 F

Learning Objective 4

9. Calculate the variable overhead efficiency variance for FrontGrade.

    a. $450 F   c. $1,050 F

    b. $600 U   d. $1,650 F

Learning Objective 5

10. The person probably most responsible for the direct labor efficiency variance is

    a. the marketing manager.   c. the human resources manager.

    b. the production manager.   d. the purchasing manager.

Learning Objective 6

11. MajorNet Systems's static budget predicted production of and sales of 100 connectors in August, but the company actually produced and sold only 84 connectors. Direct materials were budgeted at $95 per connector. The company purchased and used direct materials that cost $8,148. What is the journal entry for the direct materials used?

Date	Accounts and Explanation	Debit	Credit
a.	Raw Materials Inventory	7,980	
	Direct Materials Cost Variance	168	
	Accounts Payable		8,148
b.	Raw Materials Inventory	7,980	
	Direct Materials Efficiency Variance	168	
	Accounts Payable		8,148
c.	Work-in-Process Inventory	7,980	
	Direct Materials Cost Variance	168	
	Raw Materials Inventory		8,148
d.	Work-in-Process Inventory	7,980	
	Direct Materials Efficiency Variance	168	
	Raw Materials Inventory		8,148

Check your answers at the end of the chapter.

ASSESS YOUR PROGRESS

> Review Questions

1. What is a variance?

2. Explain the difference between a favorable and an unfavorable variance.

3. What is a static budget performance report?

4. How do flexible budgets differ from static budgets?

5. How is a flexible budget used?

6. What are the two components of the static budget variance? How are they calculated?

7. What is a flexible budget performance report?

8. What is a standard cost system?

9. Explain the difference between a cost standard and an efficiency standard. Give an example of each.

10. Give the general formulas for determining cost and efficiency variances.

11. How does the static budget affect cost and efficiency variances?

12. List the direct materials variances, and briefly describe each.

13. List the direct labor variances, and briefly describe each.

14. List the variable overhead variances, and briefly describe each.

15. List the fixed overhead variances, and briefly describe each.

16. How is the fixed overhead volume variance different from the other variances?

17. What is management by exception?

18. List the eight product variances and the manager most likely responsible for each.

19. Briefly describe how journal entries differ in a standard cost system.

20. What is a standard cost income statement?

> Short Exercises

S23-1 Matching terms

Learning Objective 1

Match each term to the correct definition.

Terms:

a. Flexible budget

b. Flexible budget variance

c. Sales volume variance

d. Static budget

e. Variance

Definitions:

1. A summarized budget for several levels of volume that separates variable costs from fixed costs.

2. A budget prepared for only one level of sales.

3. The difference between an actual amount and the budgeted amount.

4. The difference arising because the company actually earned more or less revenue, or incurred more or less cost, than expected for the actual level of output.

5. The difference arising only because the number of units actually sold differs from the static budget units.

Learning Objective 1

S23-2 Preparing flexible budgets

Major, Inc. manufactures travel locks. The budgeted selling price is $15 per lock, the variable cost is $10 per lock, and budgeted fixed costs are $12,000 per month. Prepare a flexible budget for output levels of 3,000 locks and 10,000 locks for the month ended April 30, 2016.

Learning Objective 1

S23-3 Calculating flexible budget variances

Complete the flexible budget variance analysis by filling in the blanks in the partial flexible budget performance report for 9,000 travel locks for Gable, Inc.

GABLE, INC. Flexible Budget Performance Report (partial) For the Month Ended April 30, 2016					
	Actual Results	**Flexible Budget Variance**			**Flexible Budget**
Units	9,000	(a)			9,000
Sales Revenue	$ 135,000	(b)		(c)	$ 117,000
Variable Costs	51,700	(d)		(e)	49,500
Contribution Margin	83,300	(f)		(g)	67,500
Fixed Costs	15,600	(h)		(i)	14,600
Operating Income	$ 67,700	(j)		(k)	$ 52,900

Learning Objective 2

S23-4 Matching terms

Match each term to the correct definition.

Terms:

a. Benchmarking

b. Efficiency variance

c. Cost variance

d. Standard cost

Definitions:

1. Measures whether the quantity of materials or labor used to make the actual number of outputs is within the standard allowed for the number of outputs.

2. Uses standards based on best practice.

3. Measures how well the business keeps unit costs of materials and labor inputs within standards.

4. A price, cost, or quantity that is expected under normal conditions.

Learning Objective 2

S23-5 Identifying the benefits of standard costs

Setting standards for a product may involve many employees of the company. Identify some of the employees who may be involved in setting the standard costs, and describe what their role might be in setting those standards.

Learning Objective 3

S23-6 Calculating materials variances

Goldman, Inc. is a manufacturer of lead crystal glasses. The standard direct materials quantity is 0.7 pound per glass at a cost of $0.30 per pound. The actual result for one month's production of 6,900 glasses was 1.3 pounds per glass, at a cost of $0.40 per pound. Calculate the direct materials cost variance and the direct materials efficiency variance.

S23-7 Calculating labor variances

Goldman, Inc. manufactures lead crystal glasses. The standard direct labor time is 0.5 hours per glass, at a cost of $17 per hour. The actual results for one month's production of 6,900 glasses were 0.2 hours per glass, at a cost of $11 per hour. Calculate the direct labor cost variance and the direct labor efficiency variance.

Note: Short Exercises S23-6 and S23-7 must be completed before attempting Short Exercise S23-8.

S23-8 Interpreting material and labor variances

Refer to your results from Short Exercises S23-6 and S23-7.

Requirements

1. For each variance, who in Goldman's organization is most likely responsible?

2. Interpret the direct materials and direct labor variances for Goldman's management.

S23-9 Computing standard overhead allocation rates

The following information relates to Smithson, Inc.'s overhead costs for the month:

Static budget variable overhead	$8,400
Static budget fixed overhead	$3,600
Static budget direct labor hours	1,200 hours
Static budget number of units	4,800 units

Smithson allocates manufacturing overhead to production based on standard direct labor hours. Compute the standard variable overhead allocation rate and the standard fixed overhead allocation rate.

Note: Short Exercise S23-9 must be completed before attempting Short Exercise S23-10.

S23-10 Computing overhead variances

Refer to the Smithson, Inc. data in Short Exercise S23-9. Last month, Smithson reported the following actual results: actual variable overhead, $10,400; actual fixed overhead, $2,750; actual production of 5,000 units at 0.30 direct labor hours per unit. The standard direct labor time is 0.25 direct labor hours per unit (1,200 static direct labor hours / 4,800 static units).

Requirements

1. Compute the overhead variances for the month: variable overhead cost variance, variable overhead efficiency variance, fixed overhead cost variance, and fixed overhead volume variance.

2. Explain why the variances are favorable or unfavorable.

Learning Objective 5

S23-11 Understanding variance relationships

Complete the table below for the missing variances.

Total Flexible Budget Product Cost Variance					
(a)					
Total Direct Materials Variance		Total Direct Labor Variance		Total Manufacturing Overhead Variance	
(b)		(c)		(d)	
Direct Materials Cost Variance	Direct Materials Efficiency Variance	Direct Labor Cost Variance	Direct Labor Efficiency Variance	Total Variable Overhead Variance	Total Fixed Overhead Variance
$460 F	$245 U	$440 U	$555 F	(e)	(f)
				Variable Overhead Cost Variance / Variable Overhead Efficiency Variance	Fixed Overhead Cost Variance
				$225 U $400 F	$25 F

Learning Objective 6

S23-12 Journalizing materials entries

The following direct materials variance analysis was performed for Jackson.

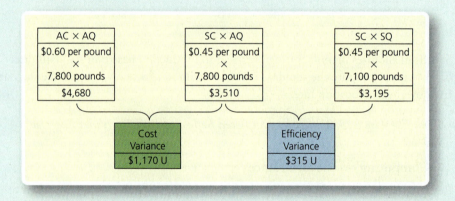

Requirements

1. Record Jackson's direct materials journal entries. Assume purchases were made on account.

2. Explain what management will do with this variance information.

S23-13 Journalizing labor entries

Learning Objective 6

The following direct labor variance analysis was performed for Logan.

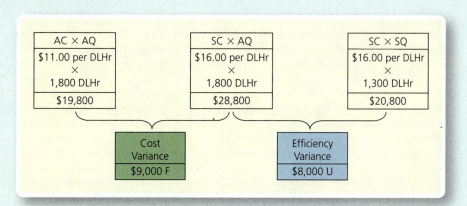

Requirements

1. Record Logan's direct labor journal entry (use Wages Payable).
2. Explain what management will do with this variance information.

S23-14 Preparing a standard cost income statement

Learning Objective 6

Use the following information to prepare a standard cost income statement for Watson Company for 2016.

Cost of Goods Sold at standard	$ 367,000	Direct Labor Efficiency Variance	$ 16,500 F
Sales Revenue at standard	580,000	Variable Overhead Efficiency Variance	3,000 U
Direct Materials Cost Variance	7,400 U	Fixed Overhead Volume Variance	12,400 F
Direct Materials Efficiency Variance	2,200 U	Selling and Administrative Expenses	70,000
Direct Labor Cost Variance	49,000 U	Variable Overhead Cost Variance	1,400 F
Fixed Overhead Cost Variance	1,800 F		

> Exercises

E23-15 Preparing a flexible budget

Learning Objective 1

$203,500 Op. Inc. for 55,000 units

Safe Now sells its main product, ergonomic mouse pads, for $13 each. Its variable cost is $5.30 per pad. Fixed costs are $220,000 per month for volumes up to 65,000 pads. Above 65,000 pads, monthly fixed costs are $275,000. Prepare a monthly flexible budget for the product, showing sales revenue, variable costs, fixed costs, and operating income for volume levels of 35,000, 55,000, and 80,000 pads.

Learning Objective 1

E23-16 Preparing a flexible budget performance report

Cole Pro Company managers received the following incomplete performance report:

COLE PRO COMPANY
Flexible Budget Performance Report
For the Year Ended July 31, 2016

	Actual Results	Flexible Budget Variance	Flexible Budget	Sales Volume Variance	Static Budget
Units	39,000	(a)	39,000	8,000 F	(g)
Sales Revenue	$ 214,000	(b)	$ 214,000	$ 19,000 F	(h)
Variable Expenses	86,000	(c)	80,000	8,000 U	(i)
Contribution Margin	128,000	(d)	134,000	11,000 F	(j)
Fixed Expenses	108,000	(e)	103,000	0	(k)
Operating Income	$ 20,000	(f)	$ 31,000	$ 11,000 F	(l)

Complete the performance report. Identify the employee group that may deserve praise and the group that may be subject to criticism. Give your reasoning.

Learning Objective 1

Flex. Bud. Var. for Op. Inc.
$46,620 F

E23-17 Preparing a flexible budget performance report

Top managers of Stenback Industries predicted 2016 sales of 14,900 units of its product at a unit price of $7.00. Actual sales for the year were 14,300 units at $10.50 each. Variable costs were budgeted at $2.20 per unit, and actual variable costs were $2.30 per unit. Actual fixed costs of $45,000 exceeded budgeted fixed costs by $2,000.

Prepare Stenback's flexible budget performance report. What variance contributed most to the year's favorable results? What caused this variance?

Learning Objectives 2, 3

2. DM Eff. Var. $100 F

E23-18 Defining the benefits of setting cost standards and calculating materials and labor variances

Bargain, Inc. produced 1,000 units of the company's product in 2016. The standard quantity of direct materials was three yards of cloth per unit at a standard cost of $1.00 per yard. The accounting records showed that 2,900 yards of cloth were used and the company paid $1.05 per yard. Standard time was two direct labor hours per unit at a standard rate of $9.75 per direct labor hour. Employees worked 1,800 hours and were paid $9.25 per hour.

Requirements

1. What are the benefits of setting cost standards?
2. Calculate the direct materials cost variance and the direct materials efficiency variance as well as the direct labor cost and efficiency variances.

Learning Objective 3

DL Eff. Var. $1,540 F

E23-19 Calculating materials and labor variances

Pro Fender, which uses a standard cost system, manufactured 20,000 boat fenders during 2016, using 146,000 square feet of extruded vinyl purchased at $1.05 per square foot. Production required 410 direct labor hours that cost $15.00 per hour. The direct materials standard was seven square feet of vinyl per fender, at a standard cost of $1.10 per square foot. The labor standard was 0.026 direct labor hour per fender, at a standard cost of $14.00 per hour.

Compute the cost and efficiency variances for direct materials and direct labor. Does the pattern of variances suggest Pro Fender's managers have been making trade-offs? Explain.

E23-20 Computing overhead variances

Grand Fender is a competitor of Pro Fender from Exercise E23-19. Grand Fender also uses a standard cost system and provides the following information:

Static budget variable overhead	$ 5,630
Static budget fixed overhead	$ 22,520
Static budget direct labor hours	563 hours
Static budget number of units	21,000 units
Standard direct labor hours	0.026 hours per fender

Grand Fender allocates manufacturing overhead to production based on standard direct labor hours. Grand Fender reported the following actual results for 2016: actual number of fenders produced, 20,000; actual variable overhead, $5,200; actual fixed overhead, $24,000; actual direct labor hours, 480.

Requirements

1. Compute the overhead variances for the year: variable overhead cost variance, variable overhead efficiency variance, fixed overhead cost variance, and fixed overhead volume variance.

2. Explain why the variances are favorable or unfavorable.

E23-21 Calculating overhead variances

Good Deal, Inc. is a competitor of Bargain, Inc. from Exercise E23-18. Good Deal also uses a standard cost system and provides the following information:

Static budget variable overhead	$ 1,200
Static budget fixed overhead	$ 1,600
Static budget direct labor hours	800 hours
Static budget number of units	400 units
Standard direct labor hours	2 hours per unit

Good Deal allocates manufacturing overhead to production based on standard direct labor hours. Good Deal reported the following actual results for 2016: actual number of units produced, 1,000; actual variable overhead, $2,400; actual fixed overhead, $2,900; actual direct labor hours, 1,300.

Requirements

1. Compute the variable overhead cost and efficiency variances and fixed overhead cost and volume variances.

2. Explain why the variances are favorable or unfavorable.

Learning Objective 6

GP $244,300

E23-22 Preparing a standard cost income statement

The May 2016 revenue and cost information for Austin Outfitters, Inc. follows:

Sales Revenue (at standard)	$ 580,000
Cost of Goods Sold (at standard)	343,000
Direct Materials Cost Variance	1,200 F
Direct Materials Efficiency Variance	6,000 F
Direct Labor Cost Variance	4,400 U
Direct Labor Efficiency Variance	2,000 F
Variable Overhead Cost Variance	3,000 U
Variable Overhead Efficiency Variance	1,500 U
Fixed Overhead Cost Variance	1,200 U
Fixed Overhead Volume Variance	8,200 F

Prepare a standard cost income statement for management through gross profit. Report all standard cost variances for management's use. Has management done a good or poor job of controlling costs? Explain.

Learning Objective 6

MOH Adj. $1,500 DR

E23-23 Preparing journal entries

Hayesville Company uses a standard cost system and reports the following information for 2016:

Standards:
3 yards of cloth per unit at $1.05 per yard
2 direct labor hours per unit at $10.25 per hour
Overhead allocated at $4.00 per direct labor hour
Actual:
2,700 yards of cloth were purchased at $1.10 per yard
Employees worked 1,300 hours and were paid $9.75 per hour
Actual variable overhead was $4,000
Actual fixed overhead was $2,500

Hayesville Company reported the following variances:

Direct materials cost variance	$ 135 U
Direct materials efficiency variance	315 F
Direct labor cost variance	650 F
Direct labor efficiency variance	7,175 F
Variable overhead cost variance	1,400 U
Variable overhead efficiency variance	1,400 F
Fixed overhead cost variance	200 U
Fixed overhead volume variance	1,700 F

Hayesville produced 1,000 units of finished product in 2016. Record the journal entries to record direct materials, direct labor, variable overhead, and fixed overhead, assuming all expenditures were on account and there were no beginning or ending balances in the inventory accounts (all materials purchased were used in production, and all goods produced were sold). Record the journal entries to record the transfer to Finished Goods Inventory and Cost of Goods Sold (omit the journal entry for Sales Revenue). Adjust the Manufacturing Overhead account.

E23-24 Preparing a standard cost income statement

Learning Objective 6

GP $1,002,990

All-Star Fender, which uses a standard cost system, manufactured 20,000 boat fenders during 2016. The 2016 revenue and cost information for All-Star follows:

Sales Revenue	$ 1,200,000
Cost of Goods Sold (at standard)	191,240
Direct materials cost variance	7,250 F
Direct materials efficiency variance	5,750 U
Direct labor cost variance	440 U
Direct labor efficiency variance	520 F
Variable overhead cost variance	950 U
Variable overhead efficiency variance	400 F
Fixed overhead cost variance	2,240 U
Fixed overhead volume variance	4,560 U

Assume each fender produced was sold for the standard price of $60, and total selling and administrative costs were $350,000. Prepare a standard cost income statement for 2016 for All-Star Fender.

> Problems Group A

P23-25A Preparing a flexible budget performance report

Learning Objective 1

1. Static Bud. Var. for Op. Inc. $20,800 F

Small Talk Technologies manufactures capacitors for cellular base stations and other communications applications. The company's July 2016 flexible budget shows output levels of 7,500, 9,000, and 11,000 units. The static budget was based on expected sales of 9,000 units.

SMALL TALK TECHNOLOGIES
Flexible Budget
For the Month Ended July 31, 2016

	Budget Amount per Unit			
Units		7,500	9,000	11,000
Sales Revenue	$ 24	$ 180,000	$ 216,000	$ 264,000
Variable Expenses	14	105,000	126,000	154,000
Contribution Margin		75,000	90,000	110,000
Fixed Expenses		53,000	53,000	53,000
Operating Income		$ 22,000	$ 37,000	$ 57,000

The company sold 11,000 units during July, and its actual operating income was as follows:

SMALL TALK TECHNOLOGIES
Income Statement
For the Month Ended July 31, 2016

Sales Revenue	$ 271,000
Variable Expenses	159,200
Contribution Margin	111,800
Fixed Expenses	54,000
Operating Income	$ 57,800

Requirements

1. Prepare a flexible budget performance report for July.

2. What was the effect on Small Talk's operating income of selling 2,000 units more than the static budget level of sales?

3. What is Small Talk's static budget variance for operating income?

4. Explain why the flexible budget performance report provides more useful information to Small Talk's managers than the simple static budget variance. What insights can Small Talk's managers draw from this performance report?

Learning Objectives 1, 3, 4

2. VOH Eff. Var. $1,377 U

P23-26A Preparing a flexible budget computing standard cost variances

Kyler Recliners manufactures leather recliners and uses flexible budgeting and a standard cost system. Kyler allocates overhead based on yards of direct materials. The company's performance report includes the following selected data:

		Static Budget (1,025 recliners)	Actual Results (1,005 recliners)
Sales	(1,025 recliners × $495 each)	$ 507,375	
	(1,005 recliners × $485 each)		$ 487,425
Variable Manufacturing Costs:			
Direct Materials	(6,150 yds. @ $8.90/yd.)	54,735	
	(6,300 yds. @ $8.70/yd.)		54,810
Direct Labor	(10,250 DLHr @ $9.00/DLHr)	92,250	
	(9,850 DLHr @ $9.10/DLHr)		89,635
Variable Overhead	(6,150 yds. @ $5.10/yd.)	31,365	
	(6,300 yds. @ $6.50/yd.)		40,950
Fixed Manufacturing Costs:			
Fixed Overhead		62,730	64,730
Total Cost of Goods Sold		241,080	250,125
Gross Profit		$ 266,295	$ 237,300

Requirements

1. Prepare a flexible budget based on the actual number of recliners sold.

2. Compute the cost variance and the efficiency variance for direct materials and for direct labor. For manufacturing overhead, compute the variable overhead cost, variable overhead efficiency, fixed overhead cost, and fixed overhead volume variances. Round to the nearest dollar.

3. Have Kyler's managers done a good job or a poor job controlling materials, labor, and overhead costs? Why?

4. Describe how Kyler's managers can benefit from the standard cost system.

P23-27A Computing standard cost variances and reporting to management

Learning Objectives 3, 4, 5

Smart Hearing manufactures headphone cases. During September 2016, the company produced and sold 108,000 cases and recorded the following cost data:

1. DM Eff. Var. $640 F

Standard Cost Information

	Quantity	Cost
Direct Materials	2 parts	$ 0.16 per part
Direct Labor	0.02 hours	8.00 per hour
Variable Manufacturing Overhead	0.02 hours	9.00 per hour

Fixed Manufacturing Overhead ($33,320 for static budget volume of 98,000 units and 1,960 hours, or $17 per hour)

Actual Cost Information

Direct Materials	(212,000 parts @ $0.21 per part)	$ 44,520
Direct Labor	(1,660 hours @ $8.15 per hour)	13,529
Variable Manufacturing Overhead		8,000
Fixed Manufacturing Overhead		31,000

Requirements

1. Compute the cost and efficiency variances for direct materials and direct labor.

2. For manufacturing overhead, compute the variable overhead cost and efficiency variances and the fixed overhead cost and volume variances.

3. Smart Hearing's management used better quality materials during September. Discuss the trade-off between the two direct material variances.

CHAPTER 23

P23-28A Computing and journalizing standard cost variances

Juda manufactures coffee mugs that it sells to other companies for customizing with their own logos. Juda prepares flexible budgets and uses a standard cost system to control manufacturing costs. The standard unit cost of a coffee mug is based on static budget volume of 59,800 coffee mugs per month:

Direct Materials (0.2 lbs. @ $0.25 per lb.)		$ 0.05
Direct Labor (3 minutes @ $0.13 per minute)		0.39
Manufacturing Overhead:		
Variable (3 minutes @ $0.06 per minute)	$ 0.18	
Fixed (3 minutes @ $0.14 per minute)	0.42	0.60
Total Cost per Coffee Mug		$ 1.04

Actual cost and production information for July 2016 follows:

a. There were no beginning or ending inventory balances. All expenditures were on account.

b. Actual production and sales were 62,500 coffee mugs.

c. Actual direct materials usage was 10,000 lbs. at an actual cost of $0.17 per lb.

d. Actual direct labor usage was 198,000 minutes at a total cost of $29,700.

e. Actual overhead cost was $9,900 variable and $31,000 fixed.

f. Selling and administrative costs were $120,000.

Requirements

1. Compute the cost and efficiency variances for direct materials and direct labor.

2. Journalize the purchase and usage of direct materials and the assignment of direct labor, including the related variances.

3. For manufacturing overhead, compute the variable overhead cost and efficiency variances and the fixed overhead cost and volume variances.

4. Journalize the actual manufacturing overhead and the allocated manufacturing overhead. Journalize the movement of all production costs from Work-in-Process Inventory. Journalize the adjusting of the Manufacturing Overhead account.

5. Juda intentionally hired more highly skilled workers during July. How did this decision affect the cost variances? Overall, was the decision wise?

Note: Problem P23-28A must be completed before attempting Problem P23-29A.

P23-29A Preparing a standard cost income statement

Review your results from Problem P23-28A. Juda's standard and actual sales price per mug is $3. Prepare the standard cost income statement for July 2016.

> Problems Group B

P23-30B Preparing a flexible budget performance report

Cellular Technologies manufactures capacitors for cellular base stations and other communication applications. The company's July 2016 flexible budget shows output levels of 7,500, 9,000, and 11,000 units. The static budget was based on expected sales of 9,000 units.

Learning Objective 1

1. Static Bud. Var. for Op. Inc.
$24,500 F

CHAPTER 23

CELLULAR TECHNOLOGIES Flexible Budget For the Month Ended July 31, 2016	Budget Amounts per Unit			
Units		7,500	9,000	11,000
Sales Revenue	$ 25	$ 187,500	$ 225,000	$ 275,000
Variable Expenses	13	97,500	117,000	143,000
Contribution Margin		90,000	108,000	132,000
Fixed Expenses		56,000	56,000	56,000
Operating Income		$ 34,000	$ 52,000	$ 76,000

The company sold 11,000 units during July, and its actual operating income was as follows:

CELLULAR TECHNOLOGIES Income Statement For the Month Ended July 31, 2016	
Sales Revenue	$ 282,000
Variable Expenses	148,000
Contributions Margin	134,000
Fixed Expenses	57,500
Operating Income	$ 76,500

Requirements

1. Prepare a flexible budget performance report for July 2016.
2. What was the effect on Cellular's operating income of selling 2,000 units more than the static budget level of sales?
3. What is Cellular's static budget variance for operating income?
4. Explain why the flexible budget performance report provides more useful information to Cellular's managers than the simple static budget variance. What insights can Cellular's managers draw from this performance report?

Learning Objectives 1, 3, 4

2. VOH Eff. Var. $1,315 U

P23-31B Preparing a flexible budget and computing standard cost variances

Root Recliners manufactures leather recliners and uses flexible budgeting and a standard cost system. Root allocates overhead based on yards of direct materials. The company's performance report includes the following selected data:

		Static Budget (1,000 recliners)	Actual Results (980 recliners)
Sales	(1,000 recliners × $505 each)	$ 505,000	
	(980 recliners × $490 each)		$ 480,200
Variable Manufacturing Costs:			
Direct Materials	(6,000 yds. @ $8.70/yard)	52,200	
	(6,143 yds. @ $8.50/yard)		52,216
Direct Labor	(10,000 DLHr @ $9.00/DLHr)	90,000	
	(9,600 DLHr @ $9.10/DLHr)		87,360
Variable Overhead	(6,000 yds. @ $5.00/yard)	30,000	
	(6,143 yds. @ $6.40/yard)		39,315
Fixed Manufacturing Costs:			
Fixed Overhead		60,000	62,000
Total Cost of Goods Sold		232,200	240,891
Gross Profit		$ 272,800	$ 239,309

Requirements

1. Prepare a flexible budget based on the actual number of recliners sold.
2. Compute the cost variance and the efficiency variance for direct materials and for direct labor. For manufacturing overhead, compute the variable overhead cost, variable overhead efficiency, fixed overhead cost, and fixed overhead volume variances. Round to the nearest dollar.
3. Have Root's managers done a good job or a poor job controlling materials, labor, and overhead costs? Why?
4. Describe how Root's managers can benefit from the standard cost system.

Learning Objectives 3, 4, 5

1. DM Eff. Var. $300 F

P23-32B Computing standard cost variances and reporting to management

Smart Sets manufactures headphone cases. During September 2016, the company produced 108,000 cases and recorded the following cost data:

Standard Cost Information

	Quantity	Cost
Direct Materials	2 parts	$ 0.15 per part
Direct Labor	0.02 hours	8.00 per hour
Variable Manufacturing Overhead	0.02 hours	9.00 per hour

Fixed Manufacturing Overhead ($31,360 for static budget volume of 98,000 units and 1,960 hours, or $16 per hour)

Actual Information

Direct Materials	(214,000 parts @ $0.20 per part)	$ 42,800
Direct Labor	(1,660 hours @ $8.10 per hour)	13,446
Variable Manufacturing Overhead		14,000
Fixed Manufacturing Overhead		26,000

Requirements

1. Compute the cost and efficiency variances for direct materials and direct labor.

2. For manufacturing overhead, compute the variable overhead cost and efficiency variances and the fixed overhead cost and volume variances.

3. Smart Sets's management used better-quality materials during September. Discuss the trade-off between the two direct material variances.

P23-33B Computing and journalizing standard cost variances

Smith manufactures coffee mugs that it sells to other companies for customizing with their own logos. Smith prepares flexible budgets and uses a standard cost system to control manufacturing costs. The standard unit cost of a coffee mug is based on static budget volume of 59,900 coffee mugs per month:

Learning Objectives 3, 4, 5, 6

3. VOH Cost Var. $2,985 F

Direct Materials (0.2 lbs. @ $0.25 per lb.)		$ 0.05
Direct Labor (3 minutes @ $0.11 per minute)		0.33
Manufacturing Overhead:		
Variable (3 minutes @ $0.06 per minute)	$ 0.18	
Fixed (3 minutes @ $0.13 per minute)	0.39	0.57
Total Cost per Coffee Mug		$ 0.95

Actual cost and production information for July 2016 follows:

a. Actual production and sales were 62,600 coffee mugs.

b. Actual direct materials usage was 10,000 lbs. at an actual cost of $0.17 per lb.

c. Actual direct labor usage of 199,000 minutes at a cost of $27,860.

d. Actual overhead cost was $8,955 variable and $31,945 fixed.

e. Selling and administrative costs were $95,000.

Requirements

1. Compute the cost and efficiency variances for direct materials and direct labor.

2. Journalize the purchase and usage of direct materials and the assignment of direct labor, including the related variances.

3. For manufacturing overhead, compute the variable overhead cost and efficiency variances and the fixed overhead cost and volume variances.

4. Journalize the actual manufacturing overhead and the allocated manufacturing overhead. Journalize the movement of all production from Work-in-Process Inventory. Journalize the adjusting of the Manufacturing Overhead account.

5. Smith intentionally hired more highly skilled workers during July. How did this decision affect the cost variances? Overall, was the decision wise?

Note: Problem P23-33B must be completed before attempting
Problem P23-34B.

Learning Objective 6

COGS at actual $70,460

P23-34B Preparing a standard cost income statement

Review your results from Problem P23-33B. Smith's actual and standard sales price per mug is $5. Prepare the standard cost income statement for July 2016.

> Continuing Problem

P23-35 Calculating materials and labor variances and preparing journal entries

This continues the Daniels Consulting situation from Problem P22-57 of Chapter 22. Assume Daniels has created a standard cost card for each job. Standard direct materials per job include 10 software packages at a cost of $900 per package. Standard direct labor costs per job include 105 hours at $100 per hour. Daniels plans on completing 12 jobs during March 2018.

Actual direct materials costs for March included 90 software packages at a total cost of $81,450. Actual direct labor costs included 110 hours per job at an average rate of $107 per hour. Daniels completed all 12 jobs in March.

Requirements

1. Calculate direct materials cost and efficiency variances.

2. Calculate direct labor cost and efficiency variances.

3. Prepare journal entries to record the use of both materials and labor for March for the company.

CRITICAL THINKING

> Decision Case 23-1

Suppose you manage the local Scoopy's ice cream parlor. In addition to selling ice cream cones, you make large batches of a few flavors of milk shakes to sell throughout the day. Your parlor is chosen to test the company's "Made-for-You" system. This new system enables patrons to customize their milk shakes by choosing different flavors.

Customers like the new system and your staff appears to be adapting, but you wonder whether this new made-to-order system is as efficient as the old system in which you just made a few large batches. Efficiency is a special concern because your performance is evaluated in part on the restaurant's efficient use of materials and labor. Your superiors consider efficiency variances greater than 5% to be unacceptable.

You decide to look at your sales for a typical day. You find that the parlor used 390 pounds of ice cream and 72 hours of direct labor to produce and sell 2,000 shakes. The standard quantity allowed for a shake is 0.2 pound of ice cream and 0.03 hour of direct labor. The standard costs are $1.50 per pound for ice cream and $8 per hour for labor.

Requirements

1. Compute the efficiency variances for direct labor and direct materials.

2. Provide likely explanations for the variances. Do you have reason to be concerned about your performance evaluation? Explain.

3. Write a memo to Scoopy's national office explaining your concern and suggesting a remedy.

> Fraud Case 23-1

Drew Castello, general manager of Sunflower Manufacturing, was frustrated. He wanted the budgeted results, and his staff was not getting them to him fast enough. Drew decided to pay a visit to the accounting office, where Jeff Hollingsworth was supposed to be working on the reports. Jeff had recently been hired to update the accounting system and speed up the reporting process.

"What's taking so long?" Drew asked. "When am I going to get the variance reports?" Jeff sighed and attempted to explain the problem. "Some of the variances appear to be way off. We either have a serious problem in production, or there is an error in the spreadsheet. I want to recheck the spreadsheet before I distribute the report." Drew pulled up a chair, and the two men went through the spreadsheet together. The formulas in the spreadsheet were correct and showed a large unfavorable direct labor efficiency variance. It was time for Drew and Jeff to do some investigating.

After looking at the time records, Jeff pointed out that it was unusual that every employee in the production area recorded exactly eight hours each day in direct labor. Did they not take breaks? Was no one ever five minutes late getting back from lunch? What about clean-up time between jobs or at the end of the day?

Drew began to observe the production laborers and noticed several disturbing items. One employee was routinely late for work, but his time card always showed him clocked in on time. Another employee took 10- to 15-minute breaks every hour, averaging about 1½ hours each day, but still reported eight hours of direct labor each day. Yet another employee often took an extra 30 minutes for lunch, but his time card showed him clocked in on time. No one in the production area ever reported any "down time" when they were not working on a specific job, even though they all took breaks and completed other tasks such as doing clean-up and attending department meetings.

Requirements

1. How might the observed behaviors cause an unfavorable direct labor efficiency variance?

2. How might an employee's time card show the employee on the job and working when the employee was not present?

3. Why would the employees' activities be considered fraudulent?

> Team Project 23-1

Lynx Corp. manufactures windows and doors. Lynx has been using a standard cost system that bases cost and efficiency standards on Lynx's historical long-run average performance. Suppose Lynx's controller has engaged your team of management consultants to advise him or her whether Lynx should use some basis other than historical performance for setting standards.

Requirements

1. List the types of variances you recommend that Lynx compute (for example, direct materials cost variance for glass). For each variance, what specific standards would Lynx need to develop? In addition to cost standards, do you recommend that Lynx develop any nonfinancial standards?

2. There are many approaches to setting standards other than simply using long-run average historical costs and quantities.

   a. List three alternative approaches that Lynx could use to set standards, and explain how Lynx could implement each alternative.

   b. Evaluate each alternative method of setting standards, including the pros and cons of each method.

   c. Write a memo to Lynx's controller detailing your recommendations. First, should Lynx retain its historical data-based standard cost approach? If not, which of the alternative approaches should it adopt?

> Communication Activity 23-1

In 75 words or fewer, explain what a cost variance is and describe its potential causes.

MyAccountingLab   **For a wealth of online resources, including exercises, problems, media, and immediate tutorial help, please visit http://www.myaccountinglab.com.**

> Quick Check Answers

1. c   **2.** d   **3.** a   **4.** d   **5.** b   **6.** b   **7.** a   **8.** b   **9.** c   **10.** b   **11.** d

Cost Allocation and Responsibility Accounting

How Do I Control What I Can't See?

Pierre Simons founded his beverage company, Drake Drink Company, a few years ago, and the company is now expanding. Pierre is making plans to add another soft drink bottling facility. So far, all operations have been in one area, with the corporate office attached to the bottling facility. The new plant, however, will be about 200 miles from the current location. Pierre believes the new location will help the company expand into new markets and decrease shipping costs. The problem is control. How will Pierre oversee operations at a plant 200 miles away?

Cost control at Drake Drink Company has been relatively easy while operating in one location. Direct manufacturing costs of direct materials and direct labor are assigned to the products, and indirect costs of manufacturing overhead are allocated using a predetermined overhead allocation rate. Adding a second location, however, complicates this process. Should the same allocation rate be used

for both locations? Additionally, the corporate office will provide services, such as payroll processing, to both plants. If Pierre wants to know the profitability of each location, then the income statements for each plant should reflect the cost of these services. Pierre must decide how the costs will be allocated.

In addition to concerns about cost control, the Drake Drink Company has reached the point where one person can no longer oversee all of the day-to-day operations. Pierre has to find competent employees to manage the new plant. He also has to develop a system that will allow him to clearly communicate the company's goals to the new managers and monitor the progress at the new plant. Pierre, as a business owner, has profitability goals, but he is also concerned with other aspects of the business. How will he ensure that his new customers are satisfied, proper procedures are followed to ensure safe products are produced, and employees are motivated?

How Is Success Measured?

As companies grow and expand, the management of day-to-day operations has to be delegated—one person cannot continue to oversee every aspect of the business. Consider PepsiCo, Inc. Pepsi-Cola was created in the late 1890s by Caleb Bradham, a New Bern, North Carolina, pharmacist. PepsiCo, Inc. was founded in 1965 with the merger of Pepsi-Cola and Frito-Lay. Through expansion and acquisitions, PepsiCo now has annual revenue of approximately $66 billion and more than 274,000 employees worldwide. How does upper management track the progress of the company? PepsiCo reports the operations of six business segments in its annual report distributed to the public, but internally it has a significant number of subunits that report on their progress. The company has to have a system to ensure that each manager is making decisions that are in the best interest of the whole company, not just his or her department. In this chapter, we look at ways companies can track the progress of each business segment.

Chapter 24 Learning Objectives

1 Assign direct costs and allocate indirect costs using predetermined overhead allocation rates with single and multiple allocation bases

2 Explain why companies decentralize and use responsibility accounting

3 Describe the purpose of performance evaluation systems and how the balanced scorecard helps companies evaluate performance

4 Use responsibility reports to evaluate cost, revenue, and profit centers

5 Use return on investment (ROI) and residual income (RI) to evaluate investment centers

6 Determine how transfer pricing affects decentralized companies (Appendix 24A)

HOW DO COMPANIES ASSIGN AND ALLOCATE COSTS?

Learning Objective 1

Assign direct costs and allocate indirect costs using predetermined overhead allocation rates with single and multiple allocation bases

As you have learned, product costs consist of direct materials, direct labor, and manufacturing overhead. These costs must be traced to each product manufactured. Direct materials costs and direct labor costs can be easily traced to products. Therefore, direct materials costs and direct labor costs are *assigned* to products. Manufacturing overhead costs, also called indirect costs, cannot be cost-effectively traced to products. Examples of manufacturing overhead costs include rent, utilities, insurance, and property taxes on the manufacturing facility; depreciation on the manufacturing equipment; indirect labor, such as production supervisors' salaries; and indirect materials, such as glue, thread, or other materials that cannot be cost-effectively traced to products. Manufacturing overhead costs are *accumulated* in cost pools and then *allocated* to products.

The most accurate overhead allocation can be made only when total overhead costs are known—and that is not until the end of the accounting period. But managers cannot wait that long for product cost information; businesses must, instead, figure out a way to allocate these indirect costs during the accounting period.

In this chapter, we look at three different ways that businesses can allocate indirect costs: single plantwide rate, multiple department rates, and activity-based costing. We start with the simplest method and move to the more complex. With complexity comes more detailed information—which usually leads to better decisions. There are situations, however, when the cost of obtaining more detailed information outweighs the benefits received from the additional information. If that is the situation, then a simpler method may be appropriate.

Smart Touch Learning, the fictitious company we used in previous chapters, is used again here. Smart Touch Learning manufactures its own brand of touch screen tablet computers that are preloaded with the company's e-learning software. Its manufacturing operations have been successful, and the company is now expanding production by producing a premium model in addition to the standard model.

The premium model has several superior features, including a larger screen, faster processor, longer-lasting battery, and specialized software programs. The features included in the premium model trigger some differences in the manufacturing process. For example, smaller circuitry in the hardware components requires the use of refined tools that are capable of more precise calibration. Before beginning production on a batch of tablets, a calibration setup is required. (*Setup* is when the company prepares the manufacturing line—sets it up—to produce a different product.) The calibration setup for premium tablets is performed by workers with specialized skills. Due to their specialized skills, laborers working on the premium model are paid at a higher rate. Furthermore, the operating system on the premium model requires additional software components with a specialized configuration to support the superior hardware features. Due to the specialized configuration, testing the operating system of the premium model takes longer than testing the operating system of the standard model.

The management team has compiled the following information regarding its expectations for the next year:

		Standard Model	Premium Model
Number of units		2,000 units	500 units
Direct materials cost per unit		$ 150.00	$ 200.00
Direct labor cost per unit		$ 88.00	$ 148.00
Total manufacturing overhead	$ 100,000		

The challenge is to determine the best way to *allocate* the $100,000 in manufacturing overhead costs to the 2,500 tablets so the manufacturing cost per unit can be calculated. Managers need to know the product cost to make planning and control decisions.

Single Plantwide Rate

Using a single plantwide rate is the traditional method of allocating manufacturing overhead costs and is the simplest method. In this method, the company calculates the **predetermined overhead allocation rate** before the period begins by selecting one allocation base and using the same base to allocate overhead costs to all units. When Smart Touch Learning was producing only one model of tablets, direct labor cost was used as the allocation base. Retaining direct labor cost as the allocation base, let's calculate the predetermined overhead allocation rate, use the rate to allocate overhead, and determine the total unit cost.

The total estimated overhead costs are given, $100,000. To determine the total estimated direct labor cost, multiply the direct labor cost per unit times the estimated number of units. This must be done for both models.

Predetermined Overhead Allocation Rate
Estimated overhead cost per unit of the allocation base, calculated at the beginning of the accounting period. Total estimated overhead costs / Total estimated quantity of the overhead allocation base.

	Direct labor cost per unit	×	Number of units	=	Total direct labor cost
Standard	$ 88 per unit	×	2,000 units	=	$ 176,000
Premium	$ 148 per unit	×	500 units	=	74,000
Total					$ 250,000

We now have the amounts needed to calculate the predetermined overhead allocation rate.

$$\text{Predetermined overhead allocation rate} = \frac{\text{Total estimated overhead costs}}{\text{Total estimated quantity of the overhead allocation base}}$$

$$= \frac{\$100,000 \text{ total estimated overhead costs}}{\$250,000 \text{ total estimated direct labor costs}} = 40\% \text{ of direct labor costs}$$

The manufacturing overhead costs can now be allocated to each model by multiplying the predetermined overhead allocation rate by the actual quantity of the allocation base used by the product.

	Predetermined overhead allocation rate	×	Actual quantity of the allocation base used	=	Allocated manufacturing overhead cost
Standard	40%	×	$ 176,000 direct labor	=	$ 70,400
Premium	40%	×	$ 74,000 direct labor	=	29,600
Total					$ 100,000

Note that the predetermined overhead allocation rate is multiplied by the actual *quantity of the allocation base used. In this illustration (and in the illustrations of the additional two methods discussed), we have made the assumption that the* estimated *quantity of the allocation base used and the* actual *quantity of the allocation base used are the same. This simplifies the illustration.*

To determine the unit cost of the manufacturing overhead, we divide each product's total manufacturing overhead cost by the associated number of units. We can then add the manufacturing overhead unit cost to the direct materials unit cost and the direct labor unit cost to determine the total unit cost.

	Standard Model	Premium Model
Total manufacturing overhead	$ 70,400	$ 29,600
÷ Number of units	÷ 2,000 units	÷ 500 units
Manufacturing overhead cost per unit	$ 35.20	$ 59.20
Direct materials cost per unit	$ 150.00	$ 200.00
Direct labor cost per unit	88.00	148.00
Manufacturing overhead cost per unit	35.20	59.20
Total cost per unit	$ 273.20	$ 407.20

Because direct labor cost is the single allocation base for all products, Smart Touch Learning allocates far more *total* dollars of overhead cost to the standard model than to the premium model, $70,400 compared with $29,600. However, total dollars of overhead are spread over more tablets, which is why the *per unit* cost of overhead is less for the standard model than for the premium model, $35.20 compared with $59.20.

Using a single plantwide rate is simple, but it may not be accurate. Using direct labor costs as the allocation base may distort the unit costs of the two models. For example, we know that the premium model requires workers with advanced skills who are paid at a higher rate. The higher labor cost for the premium model resulted in more overhead cost per unit being allocated to that model. Does the fact that the premium model workers earn more result in the premium model using more resources that would cause an increase in overhead costs? In other words, is there a relationship between labor cost and overhead cost? If so, then it is appropriate to use direct labor cost as the allocation base. If not, another allocation method is needed.

Multiple Department Rates

A modification of the overhead allocation method using a single plantwide rate is using multiple predetermined overhead allocation rates that have different allocation bases. This method is more complex, but it may be more accurate. The allocation process is the same, except now there are multiple cost pools and multiple allocation bases.

Smart Touch Learning has determined that the manufacturing process can be separated into two main departments. In the first department, Production, the tablet parts are assembled. In the second department, Software, the software is installed and tested. Management has further separated the overhead costs into two cost pools—one pool for the overhead costs associated with the Production Department and another pool for the overhead costs associated with the Software Department.

After careful analysis, Smart Touch Learning has decided that machine usage is the primary cost driver for the Production Department. In other words, the company feels there is a direct relationship between the number of hours the machines are used and the amount of overhead costs incurred. Therefore, it has decided to use machine hours for the allocation base for the Production Department. Smart Touch Learning has also decided that direct labor costs are the primary cost driver for the Software Department and has decided to use direct labor cost as the allocation base for that department. Exhibit 24-1 summarizes the allocation process for Smart Touch Learning using different allocation bases for each department.

Exhibit 24-1 | Overhead Allocation Process Using Department Rates

Allocation Process	Departments	
	Production Department	**Software Department**
Step 1: Identify departments and estimate their total overhead costs.	$80,000 estimated total overhead costs	$20,000 estimated total overhead costs
Step 2: Identify the allocation base for each department and estimate the total quantity of each allocation base.	**Machine hours (MHr)** Standard: 15,000 MHr Premium: 5,000 MHr Total: 20,000 MHr	**Direct labor cost** Standard: $ 22,000 Premium: 9,250 Total: $ 31,250
Step 3: Compute the predetermined overhead allocation rate for each department.	$80,000 / 20,000 MHr = $4.00/MHr	$20,000 / $31,250 = 64% of direct labor cost
Step 4: Allocate indirect costs to the cost object.	**Standard:** $4.00/MHr × 15,000 MHr = $60,000 **Premium:** $4.00/MHr × 5,000 MHr = $20,000	**Standard:** 64% of direct labor costs × $22,000 = $14,080 **Premium:** 64% of direct labor costs × $9,250 = $5,920

Total Cost

To determine the unit cost of the manufacturing overhead, we divide the total cost by the number of units. We can then add the manufacturing overhead unit cost to the direct materials and direct labor unit costs to determine the total unit cost.

	Standard Model	Premium Model
Manufacturing overhead—Production	$ 60,000	$ 20,000
Manufacturing overhead—Software	14,080	5,920
Total manufacturing overhead	$ 74,080	$ 25,920
÷ Number of units	÷ 2,000 units	÷ 500 units
Manufacturing overhead cost per unit	$ 37.04	$ 51.84
Direct materials cost per unit	$ 150.00	$ 200.00
Direct labor cost per unit (Production and Software Departments)	88.00	148.00
Manufacturing overhead cost per unit	37.04	51.84
Total cost per unit	$ 275.04	$ 399.84

Analysis

Now that we have computed an estimated cost per unit using two different methods, let's compare the results.

	Standard Model	Premium Model
Total estimated cost per unit:		
Single plantwide allocation rate	$ 273.20	$ 407.20
Multiple department allocation rates	275.04	399.84
Difference	$ (1.84)	$ 7.36

Using a more refined allocation system with multiple allocation rates shows the standard model costs slightly more than originally thought, whereas the premium model costs less than originally thought. The differences may not seem significant, but in today's competitive market, even slight differences can make an impact. Managers need better data to set prices and identify the most profitable products. Let's look at one more allocation method, activity-based costing, which refines the allocation process even more than using departmental allocation rates.

Activity-Based Costing

Before business got so competitive, managers could limit their focus to a broad business function, such as production, and use a single plantwide rate or multiple department rates to allocate manufacturing overhead costs to their inventory. But today's business environment calls for more refined cost accounting. This is especially important when production includes manufacturing products that require different resources or different amounts of the various resources. Smart Touch Learning is now facing this situation—its two primary products require different amounts of the resources. As we stated previously, the premium model of the touch screen tablet computer requires the calibration setup to be performed by higher-paid workers with specialized skills, and the operating system testing process takes longer than testing the standard model due to the specialized configuration. Additionally, the premium model is produced in smaller batches because the quantity of sales is lower than the standard model (500 units compared with 2,000 units).

Companies like Smart Touch Learning, with diverse products, can obtain better costing information by using activity-based costing and activity-based management. **Activity-based management (ABM)** focuses on the primary activities the business performs, determines the costs of the activities, and then uses the cost information to make decisions that will lead to improved customer satisfaction and greater profits. The costs of the activities (rather than the overhead costs of the plant or departments) become the building blocks for allocating indirect costs to products and services. The process of first determining the costs of the activities to then determine the cost of products and services is called **activity-based costing (ABC)**.

In ABC, each activity has its own (usually unique) allocation base, often called a *cost driver*. Exhibit 24-2 shows some representative activities and allocation bases.

Activity-Based Management (ABM)
Using activity-based cost information to make decisions that improve customer satisfaction while also increasing profits.

Activity-Based Costing (ABC)
Focuses on the costs of activities as the building blocks for allocating indirect costs to products and services.

Exhibit 24-2 | Examples of Activities and Allocation Bases

Activity	Allocation Base
Quality Inspection—Inspecting raw materials or finished products	Number of inspections
Warranty Services—Providing service for defective products	Number of service calls
Shipping—Shipping finished products to customers	Number of pounds of product shipped
Setup—Setting up machines for production	Number of batches
Machining—Machine usage	Number of machine hours
Purchasing—Purchasing raw materials	Number of purchase orders

> You go to a restaurant with three of your friends, and the waiter brings one bill for $100. You had the special and ordered water to drink. The meal you ordered cost only $15. Your friends ordered appetizers and drinks with their meals. How do you split the bill? Because four of you had dinner together, do you pay 1/4 of the bill, $25, or do you pay based on the cost of what you ordered, $15? Paying based on what you ordered is the key to activity-based costing. Production costs are allocated based on the amount of each activity of production that the products use.

An activity-based costing system is developed in four steps. Exhibit 24-3 summarizes the steps for Smart Touch Learning.

Exhibit 24-3 | **Activity-Based Costing for Smart Touch Learning**

ABC Step	Application		
Step 1: Identify *activities* and estimate their total costs.	**Setup** $15,000	**Production** $65,000	**Testing** $20,000
Step 2: Identify the allocation base for each *activity* and estimate the total quantity of each allocation base.	**Number of batches** Standard: 40 batches Premium: 20 batches Total: 60 batches	**Direct labor hours (DLHr)** Standard: 10,000 DLHr Premium: 2,500 DLHr Total: 12,500 DLHr	**Number of tests** Standard: 7,750 tests Premium: 2,250 tests Total: 10,000 tests
Step 3: Compute the predetermined overhead allocation rate for each *activity*.	$15,000 / 60 batches = $250/batch	$65,000 / 12,500 DLHr = $5.20/DLHr	$20,000 / 10,000 tests = $2.00/test
Step 4: Allocate indirect costs to the cost object.	**Standard:** $250/batch × 40 batches = $10,000 **Premium:** $250/batch × 20 batches = $5,000	**Standard:** $5.20/DLHr × 10,000 DLHr = $52,000 **Premium:** $5.20/DLHr × 2,500 DLHr = $13,000	**Standard:** $2.00/test × 7,750 tests = $15,500 **Premium:** $2.00/test × 2,250 tests = $4,500

Step 1: Identify Activities and Estimate Their Total Costs

The first step in developing an activity-based costing system is to identify the activities that will be used to allocate the manufacturing overhead. Analyzing all the activities required for a product or service forces managers to think about how each activity might be improved—or whether it is necessary at all.

The Smart Touch Learning management team has carefully analyzed the production process. It has determined there are three activities in the production process that incur the majority of the manufacturing overhead costs. Therefore, Smart Touch Learning will create three cost pools to accumulate the overhead costs. The first activity is setup. Before a batch of tablets can be manufactured, the machines must be properly calibrated. After the setup activity is complete, the tablets can be produced. Production is the second activity. The third activity is testing the operating system. The managers at Smart Touch Learning then looked at the manufacturing overhead costs incurred by these three activities and estimated each activity would incur the following overhead costs during the next year:

Activity	Estimated Overhead Cost
Setup	$ 15,000
Production	65,000
Testing	20,000
Total	$ 100,000

Exhibit 24-4 shows the difference between Smart Touch Learning's traditional system and its ABC system.

Exhibit 24-4 | **Overview of Smart Touch Learning's Traditional and ABC Systems**

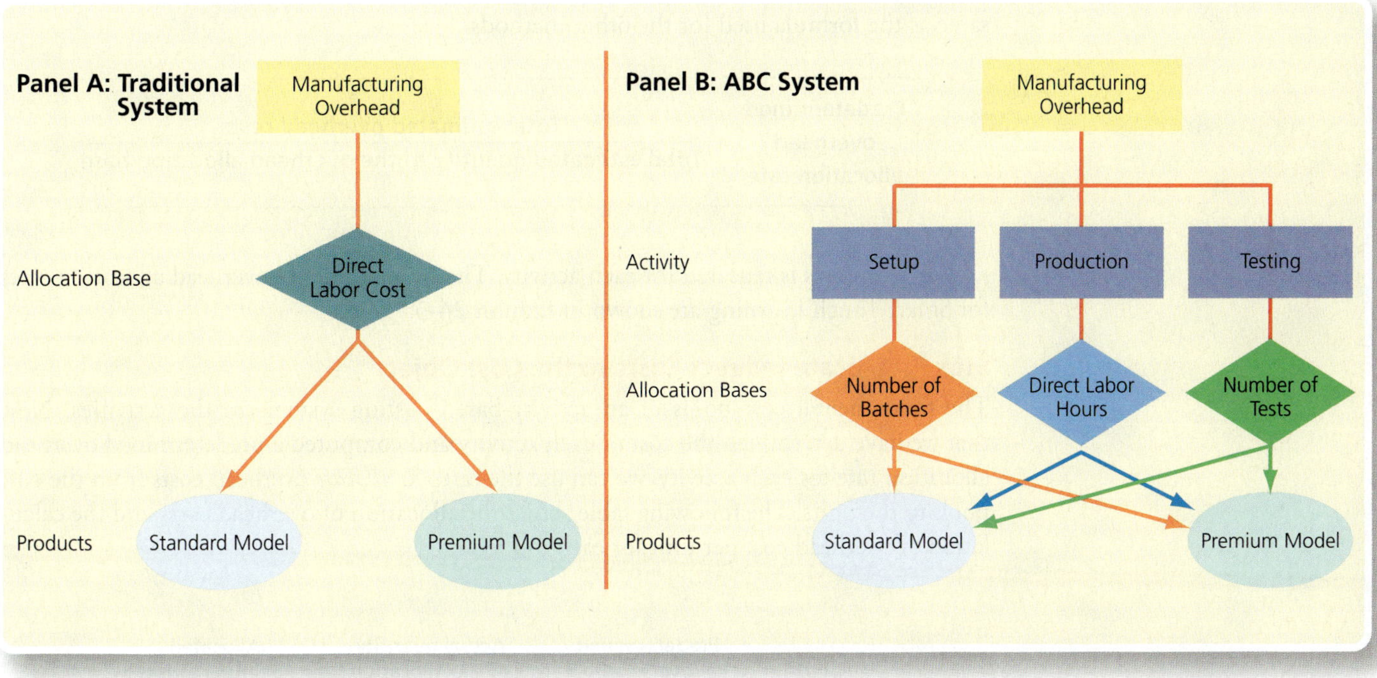

Step 2: Identify the Allocation Base for Each Activity and Estimate the Total Quantity of Each Allocation Base

Because allocation bases may differ for different activities, this step must be completed for each activity.

Setup Smart Touch Learning has determined that the allocation base for setup is number of batches. The standard model is normally produced in batches of 50 units. Therefore, the production of 2,000 units would require 40 batches (2,000 units / 50 units per batch). The premium model is normally produced in batches of 25 units. Therefore, the production of 500 units would require 20 batches (500 units / 25 units per batch).

Production Smart Touch Learning has determined that the allocation base for production is direct labor hours. Note that the company is not using direct labor *costs* but direct labor *hours*. Analysis of the process indicated that the overhead costs were related to the time it took to process the units through the activity, not how much the workers were paid. Both models require an average of five hours of labor to assemble. Therefore, the standard model is expected to require 10,000 labor hours during the next year (2,000 units × 5 hours per unit) and the premium model is expected to require 2,500 hours (500 units × 5 hours per unit).

Testing Smart Touch Learning has determined that the allocation base for testing is the number of testing operations performed. Units are randomly selected for testing, with the premium units tested more often than the standard units due to their complexity. Based on the number of units to be produced, the production manager estimates the standard model units to have 7,750 tests during the year and the premium model to have 2,250 tests, for a total of 10,000 tests.

Step 3: Compute the Predetermined Overhead Allocation Rate for Each Activity

The formula to compute the predetermined overhead allocation rate for each activity is the same as the formula used for the other methods.

$$\text{Predetermined overhead allocation rate} = \frac{\text{Total estimated overhead costs}}{\text{Total estimated quantity of the overhead allocation base}}$$

The process is repeated for each activity. The predetermined overhead allocation rates for Smart Touch Learning are shown in Exhibit 24-3.

Step 4: Allocate Indirect Costs to the Cost Object

The fundamental cost pools of an activity-based costing system are the activities. Now that we have determined the cost of each activity and computed a predetermined overhead allocation rate for each activity, we can use the rates to *allocate* overhead costs from the cost pools to the units. The following table shows the allocation of overhead costs and the calculation of overhead cost per unit for each model:

	Predetermined overhead allocation rate	×	Actual quantity of the allocation base used	=	Allocated manufacturing overhead cost
STANDARD					
Setup	$250.00 per batch	×	40 batches	=	$ 10,000
Production	$ 5.20 per DLHr	×	10,000 DLHr	=	52,000
Testing	$ 2.00 per test	×	7,750 tests	=	15,500
Total manufacturing overhead					$ 77,500
÷ Number of units					÷ 2,000 units
Manufacturing overhead cost per unit					$ 38.75
PREMIUM					
Setup	$250.00 per batch	×	20 batches	=	$ 5,000
Production	$ 5.20 per DLHr	×	2,500 DLHr	=	13,000
Testing	$ 2.00 per test	×	2,250 tests	=	4,500
Total manufacturing overhead					$ 22,500
÷ Number of units					÷ 500 units
Manufacturing overhead cost per unit					$ 45.00

The total production cost of each model, including direct materials, direct labor, and manufacturing overhead costs, is shown below:

	Standard Model	Premium Model
Direct materials cost per unit	$ 150.00	$ 200.00
Direct labor cost per unit	88.00	148.00
Manufacturing overhead cost per unit	38.75	45.00
Total cost per unit	$ 276.75	$ 393.00

Traditional Costing Systems Compared with ABC Systems

Let's compare the estimated cost per unit calculated with the three different systems.

	Standard Model	Premium Model
Single plantwide allocation rate		
Direct materials cost per unit	$ 150.00	$ 200.00
Direct labor cost per unit	88.00	148.00
Manufacturing overhead cost per unit	35.20	59.20
Total cost per unit	$ 273.20	$ 407.20
Multiple department allocation rates		
Direct materials cost per unit	$ 150.00	$ 200.00
Direct labor cost per unit	88.00	148.00
Manufacturing overhead cost per unit	37.04	51.84
Total cost per unit	$ 275.04	$ 399.84
Activity-based allocation rates		
Direct materials cost per unit	$ 150.00	$ 200.00
Direct labor cost per unit	88.00	148.00
Manufacturing overhead cost per unit	38.75	45.00
Total cost per unit	$ 276.75	$ 393.00

With each refinement of the costing system, from a single plantwide allocation rate to multiple department allocation rates to activity-based allocation rates, the cost per unit of the standard model increased while the cost per unit of the premium model decreased. **Activity-based costs are more accurate because ABC considers the resources (activities) each product actually uses.** Allocating overhead based on labor costs distorted the cost of the premium units. This happened because the laborers working on premium units are paid more due to their advanced skills, which increased the cost of the direct labor on the premium models. However, the higher direct labor cost does not have a direct cause-and-effect relationship on the overhead costs. Other factors, such as smaller batches and increased testing, do have an effect.

Which cost calculation is most accurate?

> It is important to note that the total overhead cost did not change, only the allocation of the total overhead to the two different types of tablets. Total overhead allocated in all three methods is $100,000.

Try It!

Newton Company has analyzed its production process and identified two primary activities. These activities, their allocation bases, and their estimated costs are listed below.

Activity	Allocation Base	Estimated Activity	Estimated Costs
Purchasing	Number of purchase orders	200 purchase orders	$ 10,000
Materials handling	Number of parts	15,000 parts	$ 7,500

The company manufactures two products: Regular and Super. The products use the following resources in March:

	Regular	Super
Number of purchase orders	5 purchase orders	7 purchase orders
Number of parts	600 parts	750 parts

1. Compute the predetermined overhead allocation rates using activity-based costing.
2. Determine the amount of overhead allocated to Regular products in March.
3. Determine the amount of overhead allocated to Super products in March.

Check your answers online in MyAccountingLab or at http://www.pearsonhighered.com/Horngren.

For more practice, see Short Exercises S24-1 through S24-3. **My**Accounting**Lab**

WHY DO DECENTRALIZED COMPANIES NEED RESPONSIBILITY ACCOUNTING?

Learning Objective 2

Explain why companies decentralize and use responsibility accounting

Centralized Company

A company in which major planning and controlling decisions are made by top management.

Decentralized Company

A company that is divided into business segments, with segment managers making planning and controlling decisions for their segments.

In a small company, the owner or top manager often makes all planning and controlling decisions. Small companies are most often considered to be **centralized companies** because centralized decision making is easier due to the smaller scope of their operations. However, when a company grows, it is impossible for a single person to manage the entire organization's daily operations. Therefore, most companies decentralize as they grow. **Decentralized companies** split their operations into different segments, such as departments or divisions. Top management delegates decision-making responsibility to the segment managers. Top management determines the type of decentralization that best suits the company's strategy. For example, decentralization may be based on geographic area (domestic and international), customer base (commercial and residential), product line (motorcycles and all-terrain vehicles), business function (sales and service), or some other business characteristic.

Advantages of Decentralization

Decentralization offers several advantages to large companies, including the following:

- **Frees top management time.** By delegating responsibility for daily operations to business segment managers, top management can concentrate on long-term strategic planning and higher-level decisions that affect the entire company.

- **Supports use of expert knowledge.** Decentralization allows top management to hire the expertise each business segment needs to excel in its own specific operations. For example, decentralizing by state allows companies to hire managers with specialized knowledge of consumer demand for products or services, demographics, or the laws in each state. Such specialized knowledge can help segment managers make better decisions than could the company's top managers about product and business improvements within the business segment.

- **Improves customer relations.** Segment managers focus on just one segment of the company. Therefore, they can maintain closer contact with important customers than can upper management. Thus, decentralization often leads to improved customer relations and quicker customer response time.

- **Provides training.** Decentralization also provides segment managers with training and experience necessary to become effective top managers. For example, companies often choose CEOs based on their past performance as division managers.

- **Improves motivation and retention.** Empowering segment managers to make decisions increases managers' motivation and retention. This improves job performance and satisfaction.

Disadvantages of Decentralization

Despite its advantages, decentralization can also cause potential problems, including the following:

- **Duplication of costs.** Decentralization may cause the company to duplicate certain costs or assets. For example, each business segment may hire its own payroll department and purchase its own payroll software. Companies can often avoid such duplications by providing centralized services. For example, a hotel chain might segment its business by property, yet each property might share one centralized reservations office and one centralized Web site.

- **Problems achieving goal congruence.** Goal congruence occurs when segment managers' goals align with top management's goals. Decentralized companies often struggle to achieve goal congruence. Segment managers may not fully understand the "big picture" of the company. They may make decisions that are good for their division but could harm another division or the rest of the company. For example, the purchasing department might buy cheaper components to decrease product cost. However, cheaper components might hurt the product line's quality. As a result, the company's brand, *as a whole*, might suffer. Later in this chapter, we see how managerial accountants can design performance evaluation systems that encourage goal congruence.

Goal Congruence
Aligning the goals of business segment managers and other subordinates with the goals of top management.

Although we've discussed some disadvantages of decentralization, it's important to note that the advantages of decentralization usually outweigh the disadvantages.

Responsibility Accounting

Decentralized companies delegate responsibility for specific decisions to each subunit, creating responsibility centers. A **responsibility center** is a part of the organization for which a manager has decision-making authority and accountability for the results of those decisions. We again use the fictitious company Smart Touch Learning. As you recall, Smart Touch Learning manufactures its own brand of touch screen tablet computers that are preloaded with the company's e-learning software. The e-learning software is also sold independently.

Responsibility Center
A part of the organization for which a manager has decision-making authority and accountability for the results of those decisions.

Each manager is responsible for planning and controlling some part of the company's activities. Lower-level managers are often responsible for budgeting and controlling costs of a single value-chain function. For example, one manager is responsible for planning and controlling the *production* of Smart Touch Learning's tablet computers at the plant, while another manager is responsible for planning and controlling the *distribution* of the product to customers. Lower-level managers report to higher-level managers, who have broader responsibilities. Managers in charge of production and distribution report to senior managers responsible for profits earned by an entire product line.

Responsibility Centers

Decentralized companies need a way to evaluate their various responsibility centers. A **responsibility accounting system** is a system for evaluating the performance of each responsibility center and its manager. The goal of the system's performance reports is to provide relevant information to the managers empowered to make decisions. There are four types of responsibility centers:

- Cost center
- Revenue center
- Profit center
- Investment center

Responsibility Accounting System
A system for evaluating the performance of each responsibility center and its manager.

Cost Center In a **cost center**, the manager is only responsible for controlling costs. Manufacturing operations, such as the tablet computer production line at Smart Touch Learning, are cost centers. The line foreman controls costs by monitoring materials costs, repair and maintenance costs, employee costs, and employee efficiency. The foreman is *not* responsible for generating revenues because he or she is not involved in selling the product. The plant manager evaluates the foreman on his or her ability to control *costs* by comparing actual costs to budgeted costs. Responsibility reports for cost centers include only costs.

Cost Center
A responsibility center whose manager is only responsible for controlling costs.

Revenue Center In a **revenue center**, the manager is only responsible for generating revenues. A kiosk that sells sunglasses at a local mall is an example of a revenue center. The business is a part of a chain, so the local manager does not control costs. The merchandise inventory is purchased by a central purchasing department, and rent paid to the mall is negotiated by the corporate office. Company procedures indicate only one employee should be in the booth, so the local manager has little control over wages expense. The primary responsibility of the manager is to generate revenues by selling sunglasses. Therefore, the kiosk is considered a revenue center. Responsibility reports for a revenue center include only revenues.

Revenue Center
A responsibility center whose manager is only responsible for generating revenue.

Profit Center In a **profit center**, the manager is responsible for generating revenues and controlling costs and, therefore, profits. The manager responsible for a grocery store is accountable for increasing sales revenue *and* controlling costs to achieve the profit goals. The manager controls costs by ordering sufficient merchandise inventory to meet sales demand without having excessive spoilage from outdated food products and scheduling workers to have sufficient customer service without paying more than necessary in wages. Profit center responsibility reports include both revenues and expenses to show the profit center's operating income.

Profit Center
A responsibility center whose manager is responsible for generating revenue and controlling costs and, therefore, profits.

Investment Center In an **investment center**, the manager is responsible for generating profits and efficiently managing the center's invested capital. Managers of investment centers, for example division managers of a chain of stores, are responsible for (1) generating sales, (2) controlling expenses, (3) managing the amount of capital required to earn the income, and (4) planning future investments for growth and expansion of the company. The division manager has limited funds and has to decide which store will receive a renovation and when a new computerized inventory system will be installed. These long-term investments, also called *capital investments* and *invested capital*, are purchased with the intent to increase profits, so the investment center manager is evaluated on how well the center uses the investments to generate profits. Investment center responsibility reports include profits as well as return on investment (ROI) and residual income (RI) measures, which are covered later in the chapter.

Exhibit 24-5 summarizes the types of responsibility centers, their managers' responsibilities, and their responsibility reports.

Investment Center
A responsibility center whose manager is responsible for generating profits and efficiently managing the center's invested capital.

Exhibit 24-5 | **Responsibility Centers**

Responsibility Center	Manager's Responsibility	Responsibility Report
Cost Center	Controlling costs	Compares actual costs to budgeted costs
Revenue Center	Generating revenues	Compares actual revenues to budgeted revenues
Profit Center	Producing profits through generating revenues and controlling costs	Compares actual revenues and costs to budgeted revenues and costs
Investment Center	Producing profits and efficiently managing the center's invested capital	Compares actual profits to budgeted profits and measures return on investment and residual income

Responsibility Reports

Exhibit 24-6 shows how an organization like Smart Touch Learning might assign responsibility.

Exhibit 24-6 | **Smart Touch Learning Organization Chart (Partial)**

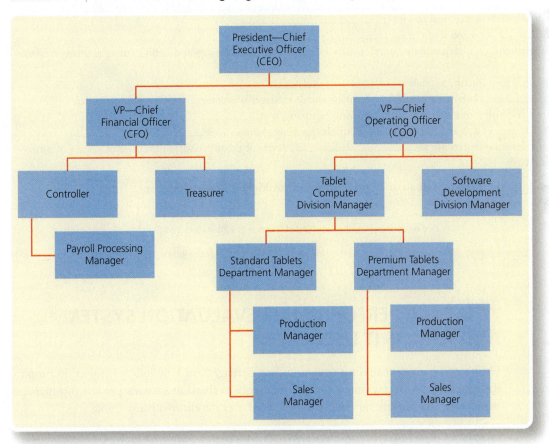

At the top level, the President—Chief Executive Officer (CEO) oversees each of the two vice presidents. The Vice President—Chief Operating Officer (COO) oversees two divisions. Division managers generally have broad responsibility, including deciding how to use assets to maximize return on investment. Most companies classify divisions as *investment centers*.

Each division manager supervises all the activities in that division. Exhibit 24-6 shows that the Tablet Computer Division manager oversees the production of two product lines—standard tablets and premium tablets. Product lines are generally considered *profit centers*. Thus, the manager of the standard tablets product line is responsible for evaluating lower-level managers of both:

- *Cost centers*—such as plants that make standard tablets
- *Revenue centers*—such as managers responsible for selling standard tablets

Fill in the blanks with the phrase that best completes the sentence. Some phrases may be used more than once and some not at all.

Phrases:

cost center	revenue center
investment center	lower
profit center	higher
responsibility center	

4. The maintenance department at the local zoo is a(n) _____.
5. The concession stand at the local zoo is a(n) _____.
6. The menswear department of a department store, which is responsible for buying and selling merchandise, is a(n) _____.
7. The production line at a manufacturing plant is a(n) _____.
8. A(n) _____ is any segment of the business whose manager is accountable for specific activities.
9. A brand of soft drink, a division of a beverage manufacturing company, is a(n) _____.
10. The sales manager in charge of a shoe company's northwest sales territory oversees a(n) _____.
11. Managers of cost and revenue centers are at _____ levels of the organization than are managers of profit and investment centers.

Check your answers online in MyAccountingLab or at http://www.pearsonhighered.com/Horngren.

For more practice, see Short Exercises S24-4 and S24-5.   MyAccountingLab

WHAT IS A PERFORMANCE EVALUATION SYSTEM, AND HOW IS IT USED?

Learning Objective 3

Describe the purpose of performance evaluation systems and how the balanced scorecard helps companies evaluate performance

Once a company decentralizes operations, top management is no longer involved in running the subunits' day-to-day operations. **Performance evaluation systems** provide top management with a framework for maintaining control over the entire organization.

Goals of Performance Evaluation Systems

Performance Evaluation System
A system that provides top management with a framework for maintaining control over the entire organization.

When companies decentralize, top management needs a system to communicate its goals to subunit managers. Additionally, top management needs to determine whether the decisions being made at the subunit level are effectively meeting company goals. Let's look at the primary goals of performance evaluation systems.

Promoting Goal Congruence and Coordination

As previously mentioned, decentralization increases the difficulty of achieving goal congruence. Segment managers may not always make decisions consistent with the overall goals of the organization. A company will be able to achieve its goals only if each unit moves, in a synchronized fashion, toward the overall company goals. The performance evaluation system should provide incentives for coordinating the subunits' activities and direct them toward achieving the overall company goals.

Communicating Expectations

To make decisions that are consistent with the company's goals, segment managers must know the goals and the specific part their unit plays in attaining those goals. The performance evaluation system should spell out the unit's most critical objectives. Without a clear picture of what upper management expects, segment managers have little to guide their daily operating decisions.

Motivating Segment Managers

Segment managers are usually motivated to make decisions that will help to achieve top management's expectations. For additional motivation, upper management may offer bonuses to segment managers who meet or exceed performance targets. Top management must exercise extreme care in setting performance targets. For example, managers measured solely by their ability to control costs may take whatever actions are necessary to achieve that goal, including sacrificing quality or customer service. Such actions would *not* be in the best interests of the company as a whole. Therefore, upper management must consider the ramifications of the performance targets it sets for segment managers.

Providing Feedback

As noted previously, in decentralized companies, top management is not involved in the day-to-day operations of each subunit. Performance evaluation systems provide upper management with the feedback it needs to maintain control over the entire organization, even though it has delegated responsibility and decision-making authority to segment managers. If targets are not met at the unit level, upper management will take corrective actions, ranging from modifying unit goals (if the targets were unrealistic) to replacing the segment manager (if the targets were achievable but the manager failed to reach them).

Benchmarking

Performance evaluation results are often used for benchmarking, which is the practice of comparing the company's achievements against the best practices in the industry. Companies also benchmark performance against the subunit's past performance. Historical trend data (measuring performance over time) help managers assess whether their decisions are improving, having no effect on, or adversely affecting subunit performance. Some companies also benchmark performance against other subunits with similar characteristics. Comparing results against industry benchmarks, however, is often more revealing than comparing results against budgets or past performance. To survive, a company must keep up with its competitors. Benchmarking helps the company determine whether it is performing at least as well as its competitors.

Limitations of Financial Performance Measurement

In the past, performance measurement revolved almost entirely around *financial* performance. On the one hand, this focus makes sense because the ultimate goal of a company is to generate profit. On the other hand, *current* financial performance tends to reveal the results of *past* actions rather than indicate *future* performance. For this reason, financial measures tend to be **lag indicators** (after the fact) rather than **lead indicators** (future predictors). Management needs to know the results of past decisions, but it also needs

Lag Indicator
A performance measure that indicates past performance.

Lead Indicator
A performance measure that forecasts future performance.

to know how current decisions may affect the future. To adequately assess the company, managers need both lead indicators and lag indicators.

Another limitation of financial performance measures is that they tend to focus on the company's short-term achievements rather than on long-term performance because financial statements are prepared on a monthly, quarterly, or annual basis. To remain competitive, top management needs clear signals that assess and predict the company's performance over longer periods of time.

Due to the limitations of financial performance measures, companies need to also use operational performance measures in their performance evaluation systems.

The Balanced Scorecard

Balanced Scorecard
The performance evaluation system that requires management to consider both financial performance measures and operational performance measures when judging the performance of a company and its subunits.

In the early 1990s, Robert Kaplan and David Norton introduced the **balanced scorecard**.[1] The balanced scorecard is a performance evaluation system that requires management to consider *both* financial performance measures (lag indicators) and operational performance measures (lead indicators) when judging the performance of a company and its subunits. These measures should be linked with the company's goals and its strategy for achieving those goals. The balanced scorecard represents a major shift in corporate performance measurement. Rather than treating financial indicators as the sole measure of performance, companies recognize that they are only one measure among a broader set. Keeping score of operating measures *and* traditional financial measures gives management a "balanced" view of the organization because management needs to consider other critical factors, such as customer satisfaction, operational efficiency, and employee excellence. Management uses *key performance indicators*—such as customer satisfaction ratings and revenue growth—to measure critical factors that affect the success of the company. **Key performance indicators (KPIs)** are summary performance measures that help managers assess whether the company is achieving its goals.

Key Performance Indicator (KPI)
A summary performance measure that helps managers assess whether the company is achieving its goals.

The balanced scorecard views the company from four different perspectives, each of which evaluates a specific aspect of organizational performance:

- Financial perspective
- Customer perspective
- Internal business perspective
- Learning and growth perspective

The company's strategy affects and, in turn, is affected by all four perspectives. There is a cause-and-effect relationship linking the four perspectives.

Companies that adopt the balanced scorecard usually have specific goals they wish to achieve within each of the four perspectives. Once management clearly identifies the goals, it develops KPIs that can assess how well the goals are being achieved. That is, it measures actual results of KPIs against goal KPIs. The difference is the variance. Management can focus attention on the most critical variances and prevent information overload. Management should take care to use only a few KPIs for each perspective. Let's look at each of the perspectives and discuss the links among them.

Financial Perspective

This perspective helps managers answer the question "How do we look to investors and creditors?" The ultimate goal of for-profit companies is to generate income. Therefore, company strategy revolves around increasing the company's profits through increasing revenue growth and productivity. Companies grow revenue by introducing new products, gaining new customers, and increasing sales to existing customers. Companies increase

[1] Robert Kaplan and David Norton, "The Balanced Scorecard—Measures That Drive Performance," *Harvard Business Review on Measuring Corporate Performance* (Boston: Harvard Business School Press, 1998): 123–145; Robert Kaplan and David Norton, *Translating Strategy into Action: The Balanced Scorecard* (Boston: Harvard Business School Press, 1996).

productivity through reducing costs and using the company's assets more efficiently. The financial perspective focuses management's attention on KPIs that assess financial objectives, such as revenue growth and cost cutting. The latter portion of this chapter discusses the most commonly used financial perspective KPIs in detail.

Customer Perspective

This perspective helps managers evaluate the question "How do customers see us?" Customer satisfaction is critical to achieving the company's financial goals outlined in the financial perspective of the balanced scorecard. Customers are typically concerned with four specific product or service attributes: (1) the product's price, (2) the product's quality, (3) the service quality at the time of sale, and (4) the product's delivery time. Because each of these attributes is critical to making the customer happy, most companies have specific objectives for each of these attributes.

Internal Business Perspective

This perspective helps managers address the question "At what business processes must we excel to meet customer and financial objectives?" The answer to this question incorporates three factors: innovation, operations, and post-sales service. All three factors critically affect customer satisfaction, which will affect the company's financial success.

Satisfying customers once does not guarantee future success, which is why the first important factor of the internal business perspective is innovation. Customers' needs and wants constantly change. Just a few years ago, smartphones and tablet computers did not exist. Companies must continually improve existing products and develop new products to succeed in the future.

The second important factor of the internal business perspective is operations. Lean and effective internal operations allow the company to meet customers' needs and expectations and remain competitive.

The third factor of the internal business perspective is post-sales service. Claims of excellent post-sales service help to generate more sales.

Learning and Growth Perspective

This perspective helps managers assess the question "How can we continue to improve and create value?" The learning and growth perspective focuses on three factors: (1) employee capabilities, (2) information system capabilities, and (3) the company's "climate for action." The learning and growth perspective lays the foundation needed to improve internal business operations, sustain customer satisfaction, and generate financial success. Without skilled employees, updated technology, and a positive corporate culture, the company will not be able to meet the objectives of the other perspectives.

Let's consider each of these factors. First, because most routine work is automated, employees are freed up to be critical and creative thinkers who, therefore, can help achieve the company's goals. The learning and growth perspective measures employees' skills, knowledge, motivation, and empowerment. Second, employees need timely and accurate information on customers, internal processes, and finances; therefore, KPIs measure the maintenance and improvement of the company's information system. Finally, management must create a corporate culture that supports and encourages communication, change, and growth. For example, a company may use the balanced scorecard to communicate strategy to every employee and to show each employee how his or her daily work contributes to company success. Exhibit 24-7 (on the next page) summarizes the balanced scorecard and gives examples of KPIs for each perspective.

So far, we have looked at why companies decentralize, why they need to measure subunit performance, and how the balanced scorecard can help provide key operational measures. Next, we focus on how companies measure the financial perspective of the balanced scorecard.

Exhibit 24-7 | **Balanced Scorecard**

Perspective	Strategy	Common Key Performance Indicators (KPIs)
Financial	Increase company profits through increasing revenue growth and productivity	• Net income • Sales revenue growth • Gross margin growth • Cash flow • Return on investment • Residual income
Customer	Improve customer satisfaction for long-term success	• Customer satisfaction ratings • Percentage of market share • Increase in number of customers • Number of repeat customers • Number of customer complaints • Rate of on-time deliveries • Percentage of sales returns
Internal Business	Improve internal efficiency and effectiveness to achieve profitability and customer satisfaction through: • Innovation • Operations • Post-sales service	• Number of new products developed • New-product development time • Manufacturing cycle time • Defect rate • Number of units produced per hour • Number of warranty claims received • Average repair time • Average wait time for a customer service representative
Learning and Growth	Retain skilled employees, update technology, and create a positive corporate culture to provide a foundation for improved internal operations, sustain customer satisfaction, and generate financial success	• Hours of employee training • Number of cross-trained employees • Percentage of computer downtime • Percentage of processes with real-time feedback on quality, cycle time, and cost • Employee satisfaction • Employee turnover • Number of employee suggestions implemented

ETHICS

Is the customer always right?

Leigh Conkin manages a Pickens Steak House, and she is going through the customer comment cards completed over the past weekend and finds another complaint from Mr. McNeill. Every time he comes into the restaurant, he completes a customer comment card, and every time he makes negative comments about the food and the service. This card gave his dining experience a rating of 2 out of 5 points. Leigh's performance evaluation includes a key performance indicator for customer satisfaction, and Leigh is required to forward customer comment cards to the corporate office. Almost all of the comment cards for her restaurant are positive, with ratings of 4 or 5, but Mr. McNeill's ratings are having a major impact on her average because the ratings are so low and because there are so many of them. "Obviously, the man can't be that unhappy," Leigh thought. "Otherwise, he wouldn't eat here two or three times every week. I just won't send in any more of his cards." Is Leigh making the right decision? What should she do? What would you do?

Solution

Leigh has an obligation to submit the comment cards as required. She should also contact Mr. McNeill to discuss his dining experiences, if company policy allows it. Perhaps there is something she can do to make his experience better that would result in better comments. It is also possible Mr. McNeill is gaming the restaurant—recording complaints even though the food and service are satisfactory. Many companies attempt to create goodwill by offering coupons for free products or services to customers who file complaints. By leaving negative comments, Mr. McNeill may be hoping for a free meal. Leigh should also contact her manager to explain the situation and ask that the comments from this one customer not be considered for her evaluation. However, even if the request is denied, Leigh should not withhold the information from the company. To withhold the information is a credibility violation. To be credible, information should be communicated fairly and objectively and all relevant information should be disclosed.

Classify each key performance indicator according to the balanced scorecard perspective it addresses. Choose from the following: financial perspective, customer perspective, internal business perspective, or learning and growth perspective.

12. Number of repeat customers
13. Employee turnover
14. Revenue growth
15. Number of on-time deliveries
16. Number of defects found during the manufacturing process

Check your answers online in MyAccountingLab or at http://www.pearsonhighered.com/Horngren.

For more practice, see Short Exercises S24-6 and S24-7. MyAccountingLab

HOW DO COMPANIES USE RESPONSIBILITY ACCOUNTING TO EVALUATE PERFORMANCE IN COST, REVENUE, AND PROFIT CENTERS?

Learning Objective 4
Use responsibility reports to evaluate cost, revenue, and profit centers

In this part of the chapter, we take a more detailed look at how companies measure the financial perspective of the balanced scorecard for different business segments of the company. We focus now on the financial performance measurement of each type of responsibility center.

Responsibility accounting performance reports capture the financial performance of cost, revenue, and profit centers. Recall that performance reports compare *actual* results with *budgeted* amounts and display a variance, or difference, between the two amounts. Because *cost centers* are only responsible for controlling costs, their performance reports include only information on actual costs versus budgeted *costs*. Likewise, performance reports for *revenue centers* contain only actual revenue versus budgeted *revenue*. However, *profit centers* are responsible for both controlling costs and generating revenue. Therefore, their performance reports contain actual and budgeted information on both their *revenues* and *costs*.

A unique factor of responsibility accounting performance reports is the focus on *responsibility* and *controllability*. Because the responsibility accounting performance reports are used for performance evaluation, the focus is only on what the manager has responsibility for and control over. It is not logical to evaluate a manager on items he or she cannot control or is not responsible for.

Controllable Versus Noncontrollable Costs

A **controllable cost** is one that the manager has the power to influence by his or her decisions. All costs are ultimately controllable at the upper levels of management, but controllability decreases as responsibility decreases. That means lower-level management has responsibility for a limited amount of costs. Responsibility accounting attempts to associate costs with the manager who has control over the cost. Results are shown on a responsibility accounting performance report, usually called a responsibility report. Responsibility reports are completed for each manager of a business segment.

Let's consider the production manager at Smart Touch Learning. This manager is responsible for efficiently and cost-effectively producing quality products. The production manager is, therefore, responsible for controlling the direct materials usage by properly training production workers, thus avoiding waste. On the other hand, the production manager does not make investment decisions, such as the decision to replace older, inefficient manufacturing equipment with new equipment. That type of decision is made at a higher level of management. Therefore, a responsibility report for the production manager

Controllable Cost
A cost that a manager has the power to influence by his or her decisions.

would not include depreciation expense on the manufacturing equipment because that cost is beyond his or her control. Likewise, the manager does not control his or her own salary, so that item would also not be listed on the report.

Responsibility Reports

Let's look at responsibility reports for cost, revenue, and profit centers.

Cost Centers

Cost center responsibility reports typically focus on the *flexible budget variance*—the difference between actual results and the flexible budget. Recall that a flexible budget uses standard (budgeted) costs at the actual level of activity. Therefore, the flexible budget variance highlights the differences caused by changes in cost, not by changes in sales or production volume. Exhibit 24-8 illustrates

Exhibit 24-8 | **Performance Report Versus Responsibility Report—Cost Center**

SMART TOUCH LEARNING Payroll Processing Department Performance Report For the Month Ended July 31, 2018				
	Actual Results	Flexible Budget	Flexible Budget Variance	% Variance*
Salaries	$ 3,000	$ 3,000	$ 0	0.0%
Wages	15,500	15,000	500 U	3.3% U
Payroll Benefits	6,100	5,000	1,100 U	22.0% U
Equipment Depreciation	3,000	3,000	0	0.0%
Supplies	1,850	2,000	150 F	7.5% F
Other Expenses	1,900	2,000	100 F	5.0% F
Total Expenses	$ 31,350	$ 30,000	$ 1,350 U	4.5% U

* % Variance = Flexible Budget Variance / Flexible Budget

SMART TOUCH LEARNING Payroll Processing Department Responsibility Report For the Month Ended July 31, 2018				
	Actual Results	Flexible Budget	Flexible Budget Variance	% Variance*
Wages	$ 15,500	$ 15,000	$ 500 U	3.3% U
Supplies	1,850	2,000	150 F	7.5% F
Other Expenses	1,900	2,000	100 F	5.0% F
Total Expenses	$ 19,250	$ 19,000	$ 250 U	1.3% U

* % Variance = Flexible Budget Variance / Flexible Budget

Notice that the 1.3% variance for Total Expenses is not the net of the % Variance for each expense: (3.3%) + 7.5% + 5.0% ≠ 1.3%. This is an example of a horizontal analysis, which is the difference between two amounts divided by the base amount. In this case, the difference is the Flexible Budget Variance and the base amount is the Flexible Budget.

the difference between a *performance report* and *responsibility report* for a cost center using the regional payroll processing department of Smart Touch Learning. Because the payroll processing department only incurs costs and does not generate revenue, it is classified as a cost center.

The performance report shows all costs incurred by the department. This report is useful when management needs to know the full cost of operating the department. For example, if Smart Touch Learning is considering outsourcing payroll and eliminating the department, then management needs the full cost information to make the decision. (This type of decision is covered later in the short-term business decisions chapter.) However, if Smart Touch Learning wants to evaluate the performance of the department manager, then the responsibility report is more useful. Notice the items that are included in the performance report but are *not* included in the responsibility report:

- Salaries—The department manager does not control his or her own salary.

- Payroll Benefits—Costs such as health insurance are determined at a higher level and are not controlled by the department manager. Other payroll costs, such as payroll taxes, are determined by law and also are not controlled by the department manager.

- Equipment Depreciation—The department manager does not have the authority to make investment decisions and, therefore, is not held responsible for the cost.

Managers use *management by exception* to determine which variances in the responsibility report are worth investigating. Management by exception directs management's attention to important differences between actual and budgeted amounts. For example, management may investigate only variances that exceed a certain dollar amount (for example, more than $1,000) or a certain percentage of the budgeted figure (for example, more than 10%). Smaller variances signal that operations are close to target and do not require management's immediate attention. Companies that use standard costs can compute cost and efficiency variances to better understand why significant flexible budget variances occurred.

Revenue Centers

Revenue center responsibility reports often highlight both the flexible budget variance and the sales volume variance. The responsibility report for the Premium Tablet Sales Department of Smart Touch Learning might look similar to Exhibit 24-9, with detailed sales volume and revenue shown for each type of premium tablet computer sold. The Sales Department is part of the Premium Tablet Department (for simplicity, the exhibit shows volume and revenue for only one item).

Exhibit 24-9 | Responsibility Report—Revenue Center

SMART TOUCH LEARNING Premium Tablet Sales Department Responsibility Report For the Month Ended July 31, 2018					
	Actual Sales	Flexible Budget Variance	Flexible Budget	Sales Volume Variance	Static Budget
Number of Premium Tablets	90	0	90	10 F	80
Sales Revenue	$ 47,250	$ 2,250 F	$ 45,000	$ 5,000 F	$ 40,000

Recall that the sales volume variance is due strictly to volume differences—selling more or fewer units than originally planned. The flexible budget variance, however, is due strictly to differences in the sales price—selling units for a higher or lower price than originally planned. Both the sales volume variance and the flexible budget variance help revenue center managers understand why they have exceeded or fallen short of budgeted revenue.

Profit Centers

Managers of profit centers are responsible for both generating revenue and controlling costs, so their performance reports include both revenues and expenses. Exhibit 24-10 shows an example of a profit center *performance* report for the Standard Tablet Computer Department.

Exhibit 24-10 | Performance Report—Profit Center

SMART TOUCH LEARNING Standard Tablet Department Performance Report For the Month Ended July 31, 2018				
	Actual	Flexible Budget	Flexible Budget Variance	% Variance
Sales Revenue	$ 5,243,600	$ 5,000,000	$ 243,600 F	4.9% F
Variable Expenses	4,183,500	4,000,000	183,500 U	4.6% U
Contribution Margin	1,060,100	1,000,000	60,100 F	6.0% F
Traceable Fixed Expenses	84,300	75,000	9,300 U	12.4% U
Department Segment Margin	$ 975,800	$ 925,000	$ 50,800 F	5.5% F

Notice how this profit center performance report contains a line called "Traceable Fixed Expenses." Recall that one drawback of decentralization is that subunits may duplicate costs or assets. Many companies avoid this problem by providing centralized service departments where several subunits, such as profit centers, share assets or costs. For example, the payroll processing cost center shown in Exhibit 24-8 serves all of Smart Touch Learning. In addition to centralized payroll departments, companies often provide centralized human resource departments, legal departments, and information systems.

When subunits share centralized services, management must decide how to allocate those costs to the various segments that utilize their services. If the costs are not allocated, the subunit's performance report will *not* include any charge for using those services. However, if they are allocated, the performance report will show a charge for the traceable portion of those expenses, as shown in Exhibit 24-10.

Most companies charge subunits for their use of centralized services because the subunit would incur a cost to buy those services on its own. For example, if Smart Touch Learning did not operate a centralized payroll department, the Standard Tablet Department would have to hire its own payroll processing personnel and purchase computers, payroll software, and supplies necessary to process the department's payroll. As an alternative, it could outsource payroll to an outside company. In either event, the department would incur a cost for processing payroll. It only seems fair that the department is charged for using the centralized payroll processing department.

Keep in mind, however, that even if the department is charged for the services, the charge would most likely be included in the department's *performance* report but not be included in the department's *responsibility* report. Responsibility accounting holds the manager with the most influence for the cost accountable for the cost. The manager for the Standard Tablet Department would most likely not have any control over cost decisions made for the payroll processing department. Exhibit 24-11 shows the responsibility report for the department. Notice that the traceable fixed expenses are not included.

Exhibit 24-11 | **Responsibility Report—Profit Center**

SMART TOUCH LEARNING
Standard Tablet Department Responsibility Report
For the Month Ended July 31, 2018
	Actual	**Flexible Budget**	**Flexible Budget Variance**	**% Variance**
Sales Revenue	$ 5,243,600	$ 5,000,000	$ 243,600 F	4.9% F
Variable Expenses	4,183,500	4,000,000	183,500 U	4.6% U
Contribution Margin	$ 1,060,100	$ 1,000,000	$ 60,100 F	6.0% F

DECISIONS

Am I responsible for what I can't control?

Fraser Marrero is the sales representative for the northwest territory of Tidwell, Inc. Tidwell considers each sales territory a business segment. The company provides each sales representative with a monthly income statement for his or her territory, and sales representatives are evaluated based on these statements. Tidwell also has a bonus system. Year-end bonuses for sales representatives are determined based on the success of the sales territory.

Fraser is taking some time to analyze his income statements for the first nine months of the fiscal year. Fraser has worked hard to build better relationships with existing customers while also adding new customers. The sales revenue for his territory has been steadily increasing. Unfortunately, the operating income for the territory has not shown much improvement. Fraser has had some increases in travel costs, but they have been in line with the increases in sales. Other costs, however, have increased significantly. The income statements show the allocation of corporate administrative costs such as salaries for office personnel and depreciation on office equipment.

"How am I ever going to earn a bonus with all these additional costs?" Fraser wondered. "I don't have any control over them, but I still seem to be held responsible for them. I need to talk to the sales manager."

Fraser schedules a meeting with the sales manager, Tony Voss. How should the sales manager respond?

Solution

All employees need to understand the goals of the company and work toward achieving them. Tony should explain why Fraser is being evaluated the way that he is so he can work to improve his performance, which should also benefit the company as a whole. The sales manager should explain that sales territories are expected to generate enough sales to cover their own territory's costs, a portion of the corporate overhead costs, and also contribute toward companywide profits. Fraser receives benefits from the corporate office, such as payroll processing, customer order processing, and collections of accounts receivable from his customers. Therefore, it is appropriate for a portion of the corporate costs to be allocated to his territory. The current reporting system allows upper management to determine which territories are achieving the company's overall profitability goals.

Alternate Solution

Fraser has a right to question the sales manager about the evaluation system. Fraser should be evaluated only on those items that he has control over, which is a key component of responsibility accounting. If the corporate office installs a new computer system, which increases depreciation, the current system allocates a portion to his territory, causing an increase in expenses and a decrease in operating income. Fraser, however, has no control over this decision and should not be held responsible for it. Fraser should request that Tidwell, Inc. not only provide the performance reports it is currently generating, but also responsibility reports for each territory. The responsibility reports should include only those items the sales representatives have significant control over and are able to influence. Performance evaluations should be based on the responsibility reports.

Summary

Regardless of the type of responsibility center, responsibility reports should focus on information, not blame. Analyzing budget variances helps managers understand the underlying *reasons* for the unit's performance. Once management understands these reasons, it may be able to take corrective actions. Some variances are, however, uncontrollable. For example, the 2010 BP oil spill in the Gulf of Mexico caused damage to many businesses along the coast as well as environmental damage to the wetlands and wildlife. Consequently, the cost of seafood from the Gulf of Mexico increased because of the decreased supply. These cost increases resulted in unfavorable cost variances for many restaurants and seafood retailers. Managers should not be held accountable for conditions they cannot control. Responsibility accounting can help managers identify the causes of variances, thereby allowing them to determine what was controllable and what was not.

We have just looked at the detailed financial information presented in responsibility reports. In addition to these *detailed* reports, upper management often uses *summary* measures—financial KPIs—to assess the financial performance of cost, revenue, and profit centers. Examples include the *cost per unit of output* (for cost centers), *revenue growth* (for revenue centers), and *gross margin growth* (for profit centers). KPIs such as these are used to address the financial perspective of the balanced scorecard for cost, revenue, and profit centers. In the next section, we look at the most commonly used KPIs for investment centers.

Match the responsibility center to the correct responsibility report.

Responsibility Centers

17. Cost center
18. Revenue center
19. Profit center

Responsibility Reports

a. Includes flexible budget variances for revenues and costs.
b. Includes flexible budget variances for costs.
c. Includes flexible budget variances and sales volume variances for revenues.

Check your answers online in MyAccountingLab or at http://www.pearsonhighered.com/Horngren.

For more practice, see Short Exercise S24-8.   MyAccountingLab

HOW DOES PERFORMANCE EVALUATION IN INVESTMENT CENTERS DIFFER FROM OTHER CENTERS?

Learning Objective 5

Use return on investment (ROI) and residual income (RI) to evaluate investment centers

Investment centers are typically large divisions of a company. The duties of an investment center manager are similar to those of a CEO. The CEO is responsible for maximizing income, in relation to the company's invested capital, by using company assets efficiently. Likewise, investment center managers are responsible for not only generating profit, but also making the best use of the investment center's assets.

For example, an investment center manager has the authority to open new stores or close existing stores. The manager may also decide how much inventory to hold, what types of investments to make, how aggressively to collect accounts receivable, and whether to invest in new equipment. In other words, the manager has decision-making responsibility over all of the center's assets, both current and long-term.

Companies cannot evaluate investment centers the way they evaluate profit centers, based only on operating income, because operating income does not indicate how *efficiently* the segment is using its assets. The financial evaluation of investment centers must measure two factors: (1) how much operating income the segment is generating and (2) how efficiently the segment is using its assets.

Consider Smart Touch Learning. In addition to its Tablet Computer Division, it also has an online e-Learning Division. Operating income, average total assets, and net sales for the two divisions for July follow:

	e-Learning Division	Tablet Computer Division
Operating income	$ 450,000	$ 975,800
Average total assets	2,500,000	6,500,000
Net sales	7,500,000	5,243,600

Based on operating income alone, the Tablet Computer Division (with operating income of $975,800) appears to be more profitable than the e-Learning Division (with operating income of $450,000). However, this comparison is misleading because it does not consider the assets invested in each division. The Tablet Computer Division has more assets than does the e-Learning Division.

To adequately evaluate an investment center's financial performance, companies need summary performance measures—or KPIs—that include *both* the division's operating income *and* its assets. In the next sections, we discuss two commonly used performance measures: return on investment (ROI) and residual income (RI). Both measures incorporate both the division's assets and its operating income. For simplicity, we leave the term *divisional* or *investment center* out of the equations. However, keep in mind that all of the equations use investment center data when evaluating an investment center's performance. Also, each ratio has been rounded to the nearest full percentage.

Return on Investment (ROI)

Return on investment (ROI) is one of the most commonly used KPIs for evaluating an investment center's financial performance. ROI is a measure of profitability and efficiency. Companies typically define ROI as follows:

$$ROI = \frac{Operating\ income}{Average\ total\ assets}$$

Return on Investment (ROI)
A measure of profitability and efficiency. Operating income / Average total assets.

ROI measures the amount of operating income an investment center earns relative to the amount of its average total assets. The ROI formula focuses on the amount of operating income earned before considering other revenue/expense items (such as interest expense) by utilizing the average total assets employed for the year. Each division's ROI is calculated as follows:

$$e\text{-Learning Division's ROI} = \frac{\$450,000}{\$2,500,000} = 0.18 = 18\%$$

$$\text{Tablet Computer Division's ROI} = \frac{\$975,800}{\$6,500,000} = 0.15 = 15\%$$

Although the Tablet Computer Division has a higher operating income than the e-Learning Division, the Tablet Computer Division is actually *less* profitable than the e-Learning Division when we consider that the Tablet Computer Division requires more average total assets to generate its operating income.

In addition to comparing ROI across divisions, management also compares a division's ROI across time to determine whether the division is becoming more or less profitable in relation to its average total assets. Additionally, management often benchmarks divisional ROI with other companies in the same industry to determine how each division is performing compared to its competitors.

To determine what is driving a division's ROI, management often restates the ROI equation in its expanded form. Notice that Net sales is incorporated in the denominator of the first term and in the numerator of the second term. When the two terms are multiplied together, Net sales cancels out, leaving the original ROI formula.

Why do managers rewrite the ROI formula this way?

$$\text{ROI} = \frac{\text{Operating income}}{\text{Net sales}} \times \frac{\text{Net sales}}{\text{Average total assets}} = \frac{\text{Operating income}}{\text{Average total assets}}$$

Expanding the equation this way helps managers better understand how they can improve their ROI. The first term in the expanded equation is called the **profit margin ratio**:

$$\text{Profit margin ratio} = \frac{\text{Operating income}}{\text{Net sales}}$$

Profit Margin Ratio
A profitability measure that shows how much operating income is earned on every dollar of net sales. Operating income / Net sales.

The profit margin ratio shows how much operating income the division earns on every $1.00 of sales, so this term focuses on profitability. Each division's profit margin ratio is calculated as follows:

$$\text{e-Learning Division's profit margin ratio} = \frac{\text{Operating income}}{\text{Net sales}} = \frac{\$450,000}{\$7,500,000} = 0.06 = 6\%$$

$$\text{Tablet Computer Division's profit margin ratio} = \frac{\text{Operating income}}{\text{Net sales}} = \frac{\$975,800}{\$5,243,600} = 0.19 = 19\%$$

The e-Learning Division has a profit margin ratio of 6%, meaning that it earns operating income of $0.06 on every $1.00 of sales. The Tablet Computer Division, however, is much more profitable with a profit margin ratio of 19%, earning $0.19 on every $1.00 of sales.

Asset turnover ratio is the second term of the expanded ROI equation:

Asset Turnover Ratio
Measures how efficiently a business uses its average total assets to generate sales. Net sales / Average total assets.

$$\text{Asset turnover ratio} = \frac{\text{Net sales}}{\text{Average total assets}}$$

The asset turnover ratio shows how efficiently a division uses its average total assets to generate sales. Rather than focusing on profitability, the asset turnover ratio focuses on efficiency. Each division's asset turnover ratio is calculated as follows:

$$\text{e-Learning Division's asset turnover ratio} = \frac{\text{Net sales}}{\text{Average total assets}} = \frac{\$7,500,000}{\$2,500,000} = 3.00$$

$$\text{Tablet Computer Division's asset turnover ratio} = \frac{\text{Net sales}}{\text{Average total assets}} = \frac{\$5,243,600}{\$6,500,000} = 0.81$$

The e-Learning Division has an asset turnover ratio of 3. This means that the e-Learning Division generates $3.00 of sales with every $1.00 of average total assets. The Tablet Computer Division's asset turnover ratio is only 0.81. The Tablet Computer Division generates only

$0.81 of sales with every $1.00 of average total assets. The e-Learning Division uses its average total assets much more efficiently in generating sales than the Tablet Computer Division.

Putting the two terms back together in the expanded ROI equation gets the following:

	Profit margin ratio	×	Asset turnover ratio	= ROI
e-Learning Division	6%	×	3.00	= 18%
Tablet Computer Division	19%	×	0.81	= 15%

As you can see, the expanded ROI equation gives management more insight into the division's ROI. Management can now see that the Tablet Computer Division is more profitable on its sales (profit margin ratio of 19%) than the e-Learning Division (profit margin ratio of 6%), but the e-Learning Division is doing a better job of generating sales with its average total assets (asset turnover ratio of 3.00) than the Tablet Computer Division (asset turnover ratio of 0.81). Consequently, the e-Learning Division has a higher ROI of 18%.

If managers are not satisfied with their division's asset turnover ratio rate, how can they improve it? They might try to eliminate nonproductive assets, for example, by being more aggressive in collecting accounts receivables, by decreasing inventory levels, or by disposing of unnecessary plant assets. Or they might decide to change the retail store layout to increase sales.

What if management is not satisfied with the current profit margin ratio? To increase the profit margin ratio, management must increase the operating income earned on every dollar of sales. Management may cut product costs or selling and administrative costs, but it needs to be careful when trimming costs. Cutting costs in the short term can hurt long-term ROI. For example, sacrificing quality or cutting back on research and development could decrease costs in the short run but may hurt long-term sales. The balanced scorecard helps management carefully consider the consequences of cost-cutting measures before acting on them.

ROI has one major drawback. Evaluating division managers based solely on ROI gives them an incentive to adopt *only* projects that will maintain or increase their current ROI. Suppose that top management has set a companywide target ROI of 16%. Both divisions are considering investing in in-store video display equipment that shows customers how to use featured products. This equipment would increase sales because customers would be more likely to buy the products when they see the infomercials. The equipment would cost each division $100,000 and is expected to provide each division with $17,000 of annual operating income. The *equipment's* ROI is as follows:

$$\text{Equipment ROI} = \frac{\$17,000}{\$100,000} = 0.17 = 17\%$$

Upper management would want the divisions to invest in this equipment because the equipment will provide a 17% ROI, which is higher than the 16% target rate. But what will the managers of the divisions do? Because the Tablet Computer Division currently has an ROI of 15%, the new equipment (with its 17% ROI) will *increase* the division's *overall* ROI. Therefore, the Tablet Computer Division manager will buy the equipment.

However, the e-Learning Division currently has an ROI of 18%. If the e-Learning Division invests in the equipment, its *overall* ROI will *decrease*. Therefore, the manager of the e-Learning Division will probably turn down the investment. In this case, goal congruence is *not* achieved—only one division will invest in equipment. Yet top management wants both divisions to invest in the equipment because the equipment return exceeds the 16% target ROI. Next, we discuss a performance measure that overcomes this problem with ROI.

Residual Income (RI)

Residual Income (RI)
A measure of profitability and efficiency computed as actual operating income less a specified minimum acceptable operating income.

Residual income (RI) is another commonly used KPI for evaluating an investment center's financial performance. Similar to ROI, RI considers both the division's operating income and its average total assets. RI measures the division's profitability and the efficiency with which the division uses its average total assets. RI also incorporates another piece of information: top management's target rate of return (such as the 16% target rate of return in the previous example). The target rate of return is the minimum acceptable rate of return that top management expects a division to earn with its average total assets. You will learn how to calculate target rate of return in your finance class. For now, we provide the target rate of return for you.

RI compares the division's actual operating income with the minimum operating income expected by top management *given the size of the division's average total assets*. RI is the "extra" operating income above the minimum operating income. A positive RI means that the division's operating income exceeds top management's target rate of return. A negative RI means the division is not meeting the target rate of return. Let's look at the RI equation and then calculate the RI for both divisions using the 16% target rate of return from the previous example.

$$\text{RI} = \text{Operating income} - \text{Minimum acceptable operating income}$$
$$\text{RI} = \text{Operating income} - (\text{Target rate of return} \times \text{Average total assets})$$

In this equation, the minimum acceptable operating income is defined as top management's target rate of return multiplied by the division's average total assets. Therefore,

$$
\begin{aligned}
\text{e-Learning Division's RI} &= \$450{,}000 - (16\% \times \$2{,}500{,}000) \\
&= \$450{,}000 - \$400{,}000 \\
&= \$50{,}000
\end{aligned}
$$

The positive RI indicates that the e-Learning Division exceeded top management's 16% target rate of return expectations. The RI calculation also confirms what we learned about the e-Learning Division's ROI. Recall that the e-Learning Division's ROI was 18%, which is higher than the target rate of return of 16%.

Now let's calculate the RI for the Tablet Computer Division:

$$
\begin{aligned}
\text{Tablet Computer Division's RI} &= \$975{,}800 - (16\% \times \$6{,}500{,}000) \\
&= \$975{,}800 - \$1{,}040{,}000 \\
&= \$(64{,}200)
\end{aligned}
$$

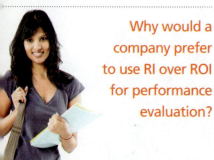

Why would a company prefer to use RI over ROI for performance evaluation?

The Tablet Computer Division's RI is negative. This means that the Tablet Computer Division did not use its average total assets as effectively as top management expected. Recall that the Tablet Computer Division's ROI of 15% fell short of the target rate of return of 16%.

A company may prefer to use RI over ROI for performance evaluation because RI is more likely to lead to goal congruence than ROI. Consider the video display equipment that both divisions could buy. In both divisions, the equipment is expected to generate a 17% return. If the divisions were evaluated based on ROI, we learned that the Tablet Computer Division would buy the equipment because it would increase the division's ROI. The e-Learning Division, on the other hand, probably would not buy the equipment because it would lower the division's ROI.

However, if management evaluates divisions based on RI rather than ROI, what would the divisions do? The answer depends on whether the project yields a positive or negative RI. Recall that the equipment would cost each division $100,000 but would provide $17,000 of operating income each year. The RI provided by *just* the equipment would be as follows:

$$
\begin{aligned}
\text{Equipment RI} &= \$17{,}000 - (16\% \times \$100{,}000) \\
&= \$17{,}000 - \$16{,}000 \\
&= \$1{,}000
\end{aligned}
$$

If purchased, this equipment would *improve* each division's current RI by $1,000 each year. As a result, both divisions would be motivated to invest in the equipment. Goal congruence is achieved because both divisions would take the action that top management desires. That is, both divisions would invest in the equipment.

Another benefit of RI is that management may set different target returns for different divisions. For example, management might require a higher target rate of return from a division operating in a riskier business environment. If the tablet computer industry were riskier than the e-learning industry, top management might decide to set a higher target rate of return—perhaps 17%—for the Tablet Computer Division.

Exhibit 24-12 summarizes the KPIs for investment centers.

Exhibit 24-12 | **Investment Center KPIs**

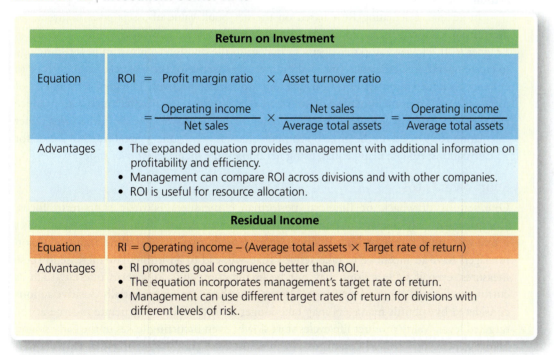

	Return on Investment
Equation	$\text{ROI} = \text{Profit margin ratio} \times \text{Asset turnover ratio}$ $= \dfrac{\text{Operating income}}{\text{Net sales}} \times \dfrac{\text{Net sales}}{\text{Average total assets}} = \dfrac{\text{Operating income}}{\text{Average total assets}}$
Advantages	• The expanded equation provides management with additional information on profitability and efficiency. • Management can compare ROI across divisions and with other companies. • ROI is useful for resource allocation.

	Residual Income
Equation	$\text{RI} = \text{Operating income} - (\text{Average total assets} \times \text{Target rate of return})$
Advantages	• RI promotes goal congruence better than ROI. • The equation incorporates management's target rate of return. • Management can use different target rates of return for divisions with different levels of risk.

Limitations of Financial Performance Measures

We have looked at two KPIs (ROI and RI) commonly used to evaluate the financial performance of investment centers. As discussed in the following sections, all of these measures have drawbacks that management should keep in mind when evaluating the financial performance of investment centers.

Measurement Issues

The ROI and RI calculations appear to be very straightforward; however, management must make some decisions before these measures can be calculated. For example, both use the term *average total assets*. Recall that total assets is a balance sheet amount, which means that it is a snapshot at any given point in time. Because the total assets amount will be *different* at the beginning of the period and at the end of the period, most companies choose to use a simple average of the two amounts in their ROI and RI calculations.

Management must also decide if it really wants to include *all* assets in the average total asset calculation. Many large businesses are continually buying land on which to build future retail outlets. Until those stores are built and opened, the land (including any construction in progress) is a nonproductive asset, which is not adding to the company's operating income. Including nonproductive assets in the average total asset calculation drives down the ROI and RI results. Therefore, some companies do not include nonproductive assets in these calculations.

Another asset measurement issue is whether to use the gross book value of assets (the historical cost of the assets) or the net book value of assets (historical cost less accumulated depreciation). Many companies use the net book value of assets because the amount is consistent with and easily pulled from the balance sheet. Because depreciation expense factors into the company's operating income, the net book value concept is also consistent with the measurement of operating income. However, using the net book value of assets has a definite drawback. Over time, the net book value of assets decreases because accumulated depreciation continues to grow until the assets are fully depreciated. Therefore, ROI and RI get *larger* over time *because of depreciation* rather than because of actual improvements in operations. In addition, the rate of this depreciation effect depends on the depreciation method used.

In general, calculating ROI based on the net book value of assets gives managers an incentive to continue using old, outdated equipment because its low net book value results in a higher ROI. However, top management may want the division to invest in new technology to create operational efficiency (internal business perspective of the balanced scorecard) or to enhance its information systems (learning and growth perspective). The long-term effects of using outdated equipment may be devastating, as competitors use new technology to produce at lower costs and sell at lower prices. Therefore, to create *goal congruence*, some firms prefer calculating ROI based on the gross book value of assets. The same general rule holds true for RI calculations: All else being equal, using net book value increases RI over time.

Short-Term Focus

One serious drawback of financial performance measures is their short-term focus. Companies usually prepare responsibility reports and calculate ROI and RI figures over a one-year time frame or less. If upper management uses a short time frame, division managers have an incentive to take actions that will lead to an immediate increase in these measures, even if such actions may not be in the company's long-term interest (such as cutting back on R&D or advertising). On the other hand, some potentially positive actions considered by subunit managers may take longer than one year to generate income at the targeted level. Many product life cycles start slowly, even incurring losses in the early stages, before generating profit. If managers are measured on short-term financial performance only, they may not introduce new products because they are not willing to wait several years for the positive effect to show up in their financial performance measures.

As a potential remedy, management can measure financial performance using a longer time horizon, such as three to five years. Extending the time frame gives subunit managers the incentive to think long term, rather than short term, and make decisions that will positively affect the company over the next several years.

The limitations of financial performance measures reinforce the importance of the balanced scorecard. The deficiencies of financial measures can be overcome by taking a broader view of performance—including KPIs from all four balanced scorecard perspectives rather than concentrating on only the financial measures.

Try It!

Padgett Company has compiled the following data:

Net sales	$ 1,000,000
Operating income	60,000
Average total assets	400,000
Management's target rate of return	12%

Calculate the following amounts for Padgett:

20. Profit margin ratio
21. Asset turnover ratio
22. Return on investment
23. Residual income

Check your answers online in MyAccountingLab or at http://www.pearsonhighered.com/Horngren.

For more practice, see Short Exercises S24-9 through S24-12. MyAccountingLab

APPENDIX 24A: Transfer Pricing

HOW DO TRANSFER PRICES AFFECT DECENTRALIZED COMPANIES?

When companies decentralize, one responsibility center may transfer goods to another responsibility center within the company. For example, the e-Learning Division at Smart Touch Learning transfers e-Learning software to the Tablet Computer Division. When this happens, a transaction must be recorded for each division, and the company must determine the amount of the transaction. The **transfer price** is the transaction amount of one unit of goods when the transaction occurs between divisions within the same company. The challenge is determining the amount of the transfer price.

> **Learning Objective 6**
> Determine how transfer pricing affects decentralized companies
>
> **Transfer Price**
> The transaction amount of one unit of goods when the transaction occurs between divisions within the same company.

Objectives in Setting Transfer Prices

The primary objective in setting transfer prices is to achieve goal congruence by selecting a price that will maximize overall company profits. A secondary objective is to evaluate the managers of the responsibility centers involved. Achieving these objectives can be challenging because the managers have different objectives for their divisions. The manager of the division selling the product wants the highest transfer price in order to increase revenues for that division, which will increase division profits. The manager of the purchasing division wants the lowest transfer price in order to decrease costs, which will increase profits for that division. If one manager wants the highest transfer price and the other manager wants the lowest transfer price, there is a conflict.

In many cases, the amount of the transfer price does not affect overall company profits because it is revenue for one division and an expense for the other division. Therefore, when profits for all divisions are consolidated, the amounts offset each other and the net effect is zero. In other cases, however, the amount of the transfer price does affect overall profits, so the company needs to have an established system that encourages goal congruence. Let's look at some different scenarios to understand how transfer prices should be determined.

Setting Transfer Prices

The e-Learning Division of Smart Touch Learning develops and sells online courses in accounting, economics, marketing, and management. The courses sell for $100 each; therefore, the market price is $100. Based on current production, the total cost of production is $80, of which $60 is variable cost and $20 is fixed cost. Therefore, the contribution margin per unit is $40 as shown below:

Sales Price per Unit	$ 100
Variable Cost per Unit	60
Contribution Margin per Unit	$ 40

The Tablet Computer Division of Smart Touch Learning loads the courses on the tablet computers prior to selling them. The two divisions are investment centers, so each division records transactions independently. Therefore, the transfer of courses from one division to the other is a sale for the e-Learning Division and a purchase for the Tablet Computer Division. How much should the Tablet Computer Division pay for the courses?

The transfer price should be an amount between the market price of $100 and the variable cost of $60. The Tablet Computer Division would not be willing to pay more than $100 as that is the amount the product can be purchased for in the market (making the assumption that similar courses can be purchased from other vendors and Smart Touch Learning is willing to load courses from other vendors on its tablets). The e-Learning Division would not be willing to sell for less than $60 because any amount less than that will cause a negative contribution margin. The range of $60 to $100 is the negotiable range for the transfer price. Exhibit 24A-1 illustrates the negotiable range.

Exhibit 24A-1 | **Transfer Price Negotiable Range**

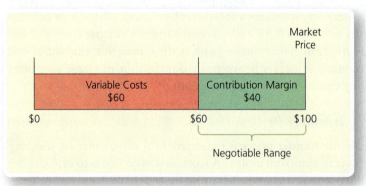

Operating at Capacity

If the e-Learning Division is operating at capacity, it is producing and selling all the courses it is capable of without expanding the facility and adding more employees and/or equipment. In this case, the division has to make a choice about whom to sell to: customers outside the company or the Tablet Computer Division. Because the division has a choice of customers, the transfer price should be a **market-based transfer price**—the sales price Smart Touch Learning charges customers outside the company, which is the market price.

Market-Based Transfer Price
A transfer price based on the current market value of the goods.

If the e-Learning Division sells for less than the market price, then it will have a decrease in contribution margin and company profits will decrease. The lost contribution margin becomes an opportunity cost for the division. An **opportunity cost** is the benefit given up by choosing an alternative course of action.

Opportunity Cost
The benefit given up by choosing an alternative course of action.

Operating Below Capacity

If the e-Learning Division is operating below capacity, then it should be willing to sell courses to the Tablet Computer Division at any amount equal to or above the variable cost of $60. Selling at any price above $60 will create more contribution margin for the division to help cover fixed costs and thereafter increase profits. A **cost-based transfer price** considers the cost of the goods when determining the price. In this situation, the managers can negotiate a transfer price that is satisfactory to both divisions. The price could be the variable cost, the full cost including the variable cost and the fixed cost, or the cost plus a markup.

Cost-Based Transfer Price
A transfer price based on the cost of producing the goods.

If Smart Touch Learning allows the division managers to negotiate a cost-based transfer price, the company should consider using *standard* costs rather than *actual* costs. Otherwise, the selling division has no motivation to control costs. For example, if the negotiated price is the actual variable cost plus a 10% markup, the e-Learning Division will always report a positive contribution margin because the sales price will always be more than the variable cost. There is no incentive for the division to monitor and control the costs of materials, labor, or variable overhead. However, if the transfer price is based on standard costs, the e-Learning Division has an incentive to control costs. Failure to control costs may result in losses for the division and a poor evaluation for the division manager.

Other Issues

There are other issues involved with transfer costs that are beyond the scope of this course. For example, international companies must consider the income tax consequences if tax rates vary between the divisions involved in the transfer. There are legal and ethical issues involved when companies attempt to evade paying income taxes by using transfer prices that shift profits to the division based in the country with the lowest tax rate.

In some cases, it is difficult to determine a market price. For example, if a division of a company manufactures a component of a product that is used only in the company's own products, then there is no outside source to purchase from or an outside market to sell to. A cost-based transfer price would have to be used.

Other issues are nonfinancial. For example, a division may decide to purchase from an outside vendor rather than another division within the company. In that case, the product may be of lower quality or there may be delays in shipping.

Sheffield Company manufactures power tools. The Electric Drill Division (an investment center) can purchase the motors for the drills from the Motor Division (another investment center) or from an outside vendor. The cost to purchase from the outside vendor is $20. The Motor Division also sells to outside customers. The motor needed by the Electric Drill Division sells for $25 to outside customers and has a variable cost of $15. The Motor Division has excess capacity.

24A. If Sheffield Company allows division managers to negotiate transfer prices, what is the minimum amount the manager of the Motor Division should consider?

25A. What is the maximum transfer price the manager of the Electric Drill Division should consider?

Check your answers online in MyAccountingLab or at http://www.pearsonhighered.com/Horngren.

For more practice, see Short Exercise S24A-13   MyAccountingLab

REVIEW

> Things You Should Know

1. How do companies assign and allocate costs?

- Direct materials and direct labor can be easily traced to products, so they are *assigned*.
- Manufacturing overhead, an indirect cost, cannot be easily traced and is *allocated*.

$$\text{Predetermined overhead allocation rate} = \frac{\text{Total estimated overhead costs}}{\text{Total estimated quantity of the overhead allocation base}}$$

$$\text{Allocated manufacturing overhead cost} = \text{Predetermined overhead allocation rate} \times \text{Actual quantity of the allocation base used}$$

- Activity-based costing (ABC) requires 4 steps:

  Step 1: Identify activities and estimate their total costs.

  Step 2: Identify the allocation base for each activity and estimate the total quantity of each allocation base.

  Step 3: Compute the predetermined overhead allocation rate for each activity.

  Step 4: Allocate indirect costs to the cost object.

2. Why do decentralized companies need responsibility accounting?

- Decentralized companies are divided into segments with segment managers making planning and controlling decisions for their segments.
- Advantages of decentralization
  - Frees top management time
  - Supports use of expert knowledge
  - Improves customer relations
  - Provides training
  - Improves motivation and retention
- Disadvantages of decentralization
  - Duplication of costs
  - Problems achieving goal congruence
- Responsibility accounting systems evaluate the performance of each responsibility center and its manager.
- Responsibility centers
  - Cost centers—responsible for controlling costs
  - Revenue centers—responsible for generating revenue
  - Profit centers—responsible for controlling costs and generating revenue
  - Investment centers—responsible for controlling costs, generating revenue, and efficiently managing the division's invested capital

3. **What is a performance evaluation system, and how is it used?**

- Performance evaluation system—a system that provides a framework for maintaining control over the entire organization
- Goals of performance evaluation systems
  - Promoting goal congruence and coordination
  - Communicating expectations
  - Motivating segment managers and other employees
  - Providing feedback
  - Benchmarking
- The balanced scorecard measures both financial and nonfinancial measures within four perspectives:
  - Financial perspective
  - Customer perspective
  - Internal business perspective
  - Learning and growth perspective

4. **How do companies use responsibility accounting to evaluate performance in cost, revenue, and profit centers?**

- Managers should be evaluated based only on controllable costs—those they have the power to influence by their decisions.
- Responsibility reports
  - Cost centers—focus on the flexible budget variances of controllable costs
  - Revenue centers—focus on flexible budget variances and sales volume variances of revenues
  - Profit centers—focus on flexible budget variances of revenues and controllable costs

5. **How does performance evaluation in investment centers differ from other centers?**

- Evaluated on both profitability and efficiency
  - Profitability—ability to generate operating income
  - Efficiency—use of assets
- Return on investment (ROI) = Operating income / Average total assets
- ROI can be expanded into two components
  - Profit margin ratio = Operating income / Net sales
  - Asset turnover ratio = Net sales / Average total assets
  - ROI = Profit margin ratio × Asset turnover ratio
- Residual income (RI) = Operating income − Minimum acceptable operating income
- Residual income (RI) = Operating income − (Target rate of return × Average total assets)
- Limitations of financial performance measures
  - Measurement issues—determining the amount to use for average total assets
  - Short-term focus—may cause managers to make decisions that increase measures in the short term but hurt the company in the long term

6. How do transfer prices affect decentralized companies? (Appendix 24A)

- The transfer price is the transaction amount of one unit of goods when the transaction occurs between divisions within the same company.

- Transfer prices should be set to achieve goal congruence.

- Market-based transfer prices are appropriate when the selling division is operating at capacity.

- Cost-based transfer prices are appropriate when the selling division is operating below capacity.

- The transfer price negotiable range is the variable cost to the market price.

> Summary Problem 24-1

Indianapolis Auto Parts (IAP) has a Seat Assembly Department that uses activity-based costing. IAP's system has the following activities:

Activity	Allocation Base	Cost Allocation Rate
Purchasing	Number of purchase orders	$ 50.00 per purchase order
Assembling	Number of parts	$ 0.50 per part
Packaging	Number of finished seats	$ 1.00 per finished seat

Each baby seat has 20 parts. Direct materials cost per seat is $15. Direct labor cost per seat is $10. Suppose an automobile manufacturer has asked IAP for a bid on 50,000 built-in baby seats that would be installed as an option on its SUVs. IAP will use a total of 200 purchase orders if the bid is accepted.

Requirements

1. Compute the total cost IAP will incur to (a) purchase the needed materials and then (b) assemble and (c) package 50,000 baby seats. Also, compute the average cost per seat.

2. For bidding, IAP adds a 30% markup to total cost. What total price will IAP bid for the entire order?

3. Suppose that instead of an ABC system, IAP has a traditional product costing system that allocates indirect costs other than direct materials and direct labor at the rate of $65 per direct labor hour. The baby seat order will require 10,000 direct labor hours. What price will IAP bid using this system's total cost assuming a 30% markup to total cost?

4. Use your answers to Requirements 2 and 3 to explain how ABC can help IAP make a better decision about the bid price.

> Solution

Requirement 1

Direct materials, 50,000 seats × $15.00 per seat	$ 750,000
Direct labor, 50,000 seats × $10.00 per seat	500,000
Activity costs:	
Purchasing, 200 purchase orders × $50.00 per purchase order	10,000
Assembling, 50,000 seats × 20 parts per seat × $0.50 per part	500,000
Packaging, 50,000 seats × $1.00 per seat	50,000
Total cost of order	$ 1,810,000
Divide by number of seats	÷ 50,000
Average cost per seat	$ 36.20

Requirement 2

Bid price (ABC system): $1,810,000 × 130%	$ 2,353,000

Requirement 3

Direct materials, 50,000 seats × $15.00 per seat	$ 750,000
Direct labor, 50,000 seats × $10.00 per seat	500,000
Indirect costs, 10,000 direct labor hours × $65.00 per direct labor hour	650,000
Total cost of order	$ 1,900,000
Bid price (Traditional system): $1,900,000 × 130%	$ 2,470,000

Requirement 4

IAP's bid would be $117,000 higher using the traditional system than using ABC ($2,470,000 − $2,353,000). Assuming the ABC system more accurately captures the costs caused by the order, the traditional system over-costs the order. This leads to a higher bid price and reduces IAP's chance of winning the order. The ABC system can increase IAP's chance of winning the order by bidding a lower price.

> Summary Problem 24-2

Swift Company has three divisions and expects each division to earn a 16% target rate of return. The company had the following results last year:

Division	Profit margin ratio	Asset turnover ratio	ROI
1	7.2%	2.737	19.7%
2	11.7%	1.584	18.5%

Division 3 reported the following data:

Operating income	$ 1,450,000
Average total assets	16,100,000
Net sales	26,500,000

Requirements

1. Compute Division 3's profit margin ratio, asset turnover ratio, and ROI. Round your results to three decimal places. Interpret the results in relation to the other two divisions.

2. Compute and interpret Division 3's RI.

3. What can you conclude based on the financial performance KPIs?

> Solution

Requirement 1

$$\frac{\text{Division 3's}}{\text{profit margin ratio}} = \frac{\text{Operating income}}{\text{Net sales}} = \frac{\$1,450,000}{\$26,500,000} = 0.055 = 5.5\%$$

$$\frac{\text{Division 3's}}{\text{asset turnover ratio}} = \frac{\text{Net sales}}{\text{Average total assets}} = \frac{\$26,500,000}{\$16,100,000} = 1.646$$

$$\text{Division 3's ROI} = \text{Profit margin ratio} \times \text{Asset turnover ratio}$$
$$= 5.5\% \times 1.646 = 0.091 = 9.1\%$$

Division 3 is far from meeting top management's expectations. Its ROI is only 9.1%. The profit margin ratio of 5.5% is significantly lower than the other two divisions. Additionally, the asset turnover ratio (1.646) is much lower than Division 1's but slightly higher than Division 2's. This means that Division 3 is not generating sales from its average total assets as efficiently as Division 1 but is more efficient than Division 2. Division management needs to consider ways to increase the efficiency with which it uses divisional average total assets and increase profitability.

Requirement 2

$$\text{RI} = \text{Operating income} - (\text{Target rate of return} \times \text{Average total assets})$$
$$= \$1,450,000 - (16\% \times \$16,100,000)$$
$$= \$1,450,000 - \$2,576,000$$
$$= \$(1,126,000)$$

The negative RI confirms the ROI results: The division is not meeting management's target rate of return.

Requirement 3

Both investment center financial performance KPIs (ROI and RI) point to the same conclusion: Division 3 is not meeting financial expectations. Either top management's and stakeholders' expectations are unrealistic or the division is not *currently* performing up to par. Recall, however, that financial performance measures tend to be lag indicators—measuring the results of decisions made in the past. The division's manager may currently be implementing new initiatives to improve the division's future profitability. Lead indicators should be used to project whether such initiatives are pointing the division in the right direction.

> Key Terms

Activity-Based Costing (ABC) (p. 1317)

Activity-Based Management (ABM) (p. 1317)

Asset Turnover Ratio (p. 1338)

Balanced Scorecard (p. 1328)

Centralized Company (p. 1322)

Controllable Cost (p. 1331)

Cost-Based Transfer Price (p. 1345) (Appendix 24A)

Cost Center (p. 1324)

Decentralized Company (p. 1322)

Goal Congruence (p. 1323)

Investment Center (p. 1324)

Key Performance Indicator (KPI) (p. 1328)

Lag Indicator (p. 1327)

Lead Indicator (p. 1327)

Market-Based Transfer Price (p. 1344) (Appendix 24A)

Opportunity Cost (p. 1345) (Appendix 24A)

Performance Evaluation System (p. 1326)

Predetermined Overhead Allocation Rate (p. 1313)

Profit Center (p. 1324)

Profit Margin Ratio (p. 1338)

Residual Income (RI) (p. 1340)

Responsibility Accounting System (p. 1324)

Responsibility Center (p. 1323)

Return on Investment (ROI) (p. 1337)

Revenue Center (p. 1324)

Transfer Price (p. 1343) (Appendix 24A)

> Quick Check

1. Which statement is *false*?

   a. Using a single plantwide overhead allocation rate is the simplest method of allocating overhead costs.

   b. An allocation system that uses departmental overhead allocation rates is more refined than one that uses a plantwide overhead allocation rate.

   c. Allocation focuses on indirect costs.

   d. The predetermined overhead allocation rate is based on actual costs.

   Learning Objective 1

2. Which is *not* one of the potential advantages of decentralization?

   a. Improves motivation and retention

   b. Supports use of expert knowledge

   c. Improves customer relations

   d. Increases goal congruence

   Learning Objective 2

3. The Quaker Foods division of PepsiCo is most likely treated as a(n)

   a. revenue center.

   b. cost center.

   c. investment center.

   d. profit center.

   Learning Objective 2

4. Which of the following is *not* a goal of performance evaluation systems?

   a. Promoting goal congruence and coordination

   b. Communicating expectations

   c. Providing feedback

   d. Reprimanding unit managers

   Learning Objective 3

Learning Objective 3

5. Which of the following balanced scorecard perspectives essentially asks, "Can we continue to improve and create value?"

a. Customer

c. Financial

b. Learning and growth

d. Internal business

Learning Objective 4

6. The performance evaluation of a cost center is typically based on its

a. sales volume variance.

c. static budget variance.

b. ROI.

d. flexible budget variance.

The following data apply to questions 7 through 10.

Assume the Residential Division of Kipper Faucets had the following results last year:

Net sales	$ 4,160,000
Operating income	1,040,000
Average total assets	5,200,000
Management's target rate of return	18%

Learning Objective 5

7. What is the division's profit margin ratio?

a. 400%

c. 25%

b. 20%

d. 80%

Learning Objective 5

8. What is the division's asset turnover ratio?

a. 0.20

c. 1.25

b. 0.80

d. 0.25

Learning Objective 5

9. What is the division's ROI?

a. 20%

c. 500%

b. 25%

d. 80%

Learning Objective 5

10. What is the division's RI?

a. $(140,000)

c. $140,000

b. $104,000

d. $(104,000)

Learning Objective 6
Appendix 24A

11A. Penn Company has a division that manufactures a component that sells for $50 and has variable costs of $25 and fixed costs of $10. Another division wants to purchase the component. What is the minimum transfer price if the division is operating at capacity?

a. $10

c. $35

b. $25

d. $50

Check your answers at the end of the chapter.

ASSESS YOUR PROGRESS

> Review Questions

1. What is the formula to compute the predetermined overhead allocation rate?

2. How is the predetermined overhead allocation rate used to allocate overhead?

3. Describe how a single plantwide overhead allocation rate is used.

4. Why is using a single plantwide overhead allocation rate not always accurate?

5. Why is the use of departmental overhead allocation rates considered a refinement over the use of a single plantwide overhead allocation rate?

6. What is activity-based management? How is it different from activity-based costing?

7. How many cost pools are in an activity-based costing system?

8. What are the four steps to developing an activity-based costing system?

9. Why is ABC usually considered more accurate than traditional costing methods?

10. Explain the difference between a centralized company and a decentralized company.

11. List the advantages of decentralization.

12. List the disadvantages of decentralization.

13. What is goal congruence?

14. Usually, which outweighs the other in decentralization—advantages or disadvantages?

15. What is the purpose of a responsibility accounting system?

16. What is a responsibility center?

17. List the four types of responsibility centers, and briefly describe each.

18. What is a performance evaluation system?

19. What are the goals of a performance evaluation system?

20. Explain the difference between a lag indicator and a lead indicator.

21. How is the use of a balanced scorecard as a performance evaluation system helpful to companies?

22. What is a key performance indicator?

23. What are the four perspectives of the balanced scorecard? Briefly describe each.

24. Explain the difference between a controllable and a noncontrollable cost.

25. What is the typical focus of responsibility reports for cost centers, revenue centers, and profit centers?

26. What are two key performance indicators used to evaluate investment centers?

27. Describe the two ways ROI can be calculated.

28. What does ROI measure?

29. What is the biggest disadvantage of using ROI to evaluate investment centers?

30. How is RI calculated?

31. What does RI measure?

32. What is the biggest advantage of using RI to evaluate investment centers?

33. What are some limitations of financial performance measures?

34A. What is a transfer price?

35A. Explain the difference between market-based transfer prices and cost-based transfer prices.

36A. How does capacity affect transfer pricing decisions?

> ## Short Exercises

Learning Objective 1

S24-1 Computing single plantwide overhead allocation rates

The Oakman Company manufactures products in two departments: Mixing and Packaging. The company allocates manufacturing overhead using a single plantwide rate with direct labor hours as the allocation base. Estimated overhead costs for the year are $920,000, and estimated direct labor hours are 400,000. In October, the company incurred 55,000 direct labor hours.

Requirements

1. Compute the predetermined overhead allocation rate. Round to two decimal places.
2. Determine the amount of overhead allocated in October.

Learning Objective 1

S24-2 Computing departmental overhead allocation rates

The Oakman Company (see Short Exercise S24-1) has refined its allocation system by separating manufacturing overhead costs into two cost pools—one for each department. The estimated costs for the Mixing Department, $620,000, will be allocated based on direct labor hours, and the estimated direct labor hours for the year are 200,000. The estimated costs for the Packaging Department, $300,000, will be allocated based on machine hours, and the estimated machine hours for the year are 60,000. In October, the company incurred 16,000 direct labor hours in the Mixing Department and 15,000 machine hours in the Packaging Department.

Requirements

1. Compute the predetermined overhead allocation rates. Round to two decimal places.
2. Determine the total amount of overhead allocated in October.

Learning Objective 1

S24-3 Computing indirect manufacturing costs per unit, traditional and ABC

The following information is provided for Space Antenna Corp., which manufactures two products: Lo-Gain antennas and Hi-Gain antennas for use in remote areas.

Activity	Cost	Allocation Base
Setup	$ 51,000	Number of setups
Machine maintenance	39,000	Number of machine hours
Total indirect manufacturing costs	$ 90,000	

	Lo-Gain	Hi-Gain	Total
Direct labor hours	1,700	2,300	4,000
Number of setups	50	50	100
Number of machine hours	1,800	1,200	3,000

Space Antenna plans to produce 175 Lo-Gain antennas and 350 Hi-Gain antennas.

Requirements

1. Compute the ABC indirect manufacturing cost per unit for each product.

2. Compute the indirect manufacturing cost per unit using direct labor hours for the single plantwide predetermined overhead allocation rate.

S24-4 Explaining decentralization

Learning Objective 2

Decentralization divides company operations into various reporting units. Most decentralized subunits can be described as one of four different types of responsibility centers.

Requirements

1. Explain why companies decentralize. Describe some typical methods of decentralization.

2. List the four most common types of responsibility centers, and describe their responsibilities.

S24-5 Classifying responsibility centers

Learning Objective 2

Each of the following managers works for a national chain of hotels and has been given certain decision-making authority. Classify each of the managers according to the type of responsibility center he or she manages.

a. Manager of the Central Reservation Office

b. Managers of various corporate-owned hotel locations

c. Manager of the H1 Corporate Division

d. Manager of the Housekeeping Department at one hotel

e. Manager of the H2 Corporate Division

f. Manager of the complimentary breakfast buffet at one hotel

S24-6 Explaining why companies use performance evaluation systems

Learning Objective 3

Well-designed performance evaluation systems accomplish many goals. Consider the following actions, and state which goal is being achieved by the action:

a. Comparing targets to actual results

b. Providing subunit managers with performance targets

c. Comparing actual results with industry standards

d. Providing bonuses to subunit managers who achieve performance targets

e. Aligning subunit performance targets with company strategy

f. Comparing actual results of competitors

g. Taking corrective actions

h. Using the adage "you get what you measure" when designing the performance evaluation system

S24-7 Describing the balanced scorecard and identifying key performance indicators for each perspective

Learning Objective 3

Consider the following key performance indicators, and classify each according to the balanced scorecard perspective it addresses. Choose from financial perspective, customer perspective, internal business perspective, or learning and growth perspective.

a. Number of employee suggestions implemented

b. Revenue growth

CHAPTER 24

c. Number of on-time deliveries

d. Percentage of sales force with access to real-time inventory levels

e. Customer satisfaction ratings

f. Number of defects found during manufacturing

g. Number of warranty claims

h. Return on investment

i. Variable cost per unit

j. Percentage of market share

k. Number of hours of employee training

l. Number of new products developed

m. Yield rate (number of units produced per hour)

n. Average repair time

o. Employee satisfaction

p. Number of repeat customers

Learning Objective 4

S24-8 Using performance reports to evaluate cost, revenue, and profit centers

Management by exception is a term often used in performance evaluation. Describe management by exception and how it is used in the evaluation of cost, revenue, and profit centers.

Learning Objective 5

S24-9 Evaluating investment centers

Consider the following data, and determine which of the corporate divisions is more profitable. Explain your reasoning.

	Domestic	International
Operating income	$ 8,000,000	$ 10,000,000
Average total assets	21,000,000	38,000,000

Learning Objective 5

S24-10 Using ROI and RI to evaluate investment centers

Accel Sports Company makes snowboards, downhill skis, cross-country skis, skateboards, surfboards, and inline skates. The company has found it beneficial to split operations into two divisions based on the climate required for the sport: Snow Sports and Non-snow Sports. The following divisional information is available for the past year:

	Net Sales	Operating Income	Average Total Assets	ROI
Snow Sports	$ 5,100,000	$ 969,000	$ 4,100,000	23.6%
Non-snow Sports	8,000,000	1,520,000	6,000,000	25.3%

Accel's management has specified a 15% target rate of return. Calculate each division's profit margin ratio. Interpret your results.

Note: Short Exercise S24-10 must be completed before attempting Short Exercise S24-11.

S24-11 Using ROI and RI to evaluate investment centers

Learning Objective 5

Refer to the information in Short Exercise S24-10.

Requirements

1. Compute each division's asset turnover ratio (round to two decimal places). Interpret your results.

2. Use your answers to Requirement 1, along with the profit margin ratio, to recalculate ROI using the expanded formula. Do your answers agree with the basic ROI in Short Exercise S24-10?

Note: Short Exercise S24-10 must be completed before attempting Short Exercise S24-12.

S24-12 Using ROI and RI to evaluate investment centers

Learning Objective 5

Refer to the information in Short Exercise S24-10. Compute each division's RI. Interpret your results. Are your results consistent with each division's ROI?

S24A-13 Transfer pricing

Learning Objective 6
Appendix 24A

Henderson Company manufactures electronics. The Calculator Division (an investment center) manufactures handheld calculators. The division can purchase the batteries used in the calculators from the Battery Division (another investment center) or from an outside vendor. The cost to purchase batteries from the outside vendor is $5. The transfer price to purchase from the Battery Division is $6. The Battery Division also sells to outside customers. The sales price is $6, and the variable cost is $3. The Battery Division has excess capacity.

Requirements

1. Should the Calculator Division purchase from the Battery Division or the outside vendor?

2. If Henderson Company allows division managers to negotiate transfer prices, what is the maximum transfer price the manager of the Calculator Division should consider?

3. What is the minimum transfer price the manager of the Battery Division should consider?

4. Does your answer to Requirement 3 change if the Battery Division is operating at capacity?

> Exercises

E24-14 Computing and using single plantwide overhead allocation rate

Learning Objective 1

Basic $234,000

Aragon makes handheld calculators in two models: basic and professional. Aragon estimated $851,500 of manufacturing overhead and 655,000 machine hours for the year. The basic model actually consumed 180,000 machine hours, and the professional model consumed 475,000 machine hours.

Compute the predetermined overhead allocation rate using machine hours (MHr) as the allocation base. How much overhead is allocated to the basic model? To the professional model?

Learning Objective 1

Professional, total OH $644,000

E24-15 Computing and using departmental overhead allocation rates

Aragon (see Exercise E24-14) makes handheld calculators in two models—basic and professional—and wants to refine its costing system by allocating overhead using departmental rates. The estimated $851,500 of manufacturing overhead has been divided into two cost pools: Assembly Department and Packaging Department. The following data have been compiled:

	Assembly Department	Packaging Department	Total
Overhead costs	$ 550,000	$ 301,500	$ 851,500
Machine hours:			
Basic Model	145,000 MHr	35,000 MHr	180,000 MHr
Professional Model	355,000 MHr	120,000 MHr	475,000 MHr
Direct labor hours:			
Basic Model	40,000 DLHr	80,000 DLHr	120,000 DLHr
Professional Model	317,500 DLHr	422,500 DLHr	740,000 DLHr

Compute the predetermined overhead allocation rates using machine hours as the allocation base for the Assembly Department and direct labor hours for the Packaging Department. How much overhead is allocated to the basic model? To the professional model?

Learning Objective 1

1. POHR machine setup $320 per setup

E24-16 Computing product costs in an activity-based costing system

Farrington, Inc. uses activity-based costing to account for its chrome bumper manufacturing process. Company managers have identified four manufacturing activities: materials handling, machine setup, insertion of parts, and finishing. The budgeted activity costs for 2016 and their allocation bases are as follows:

Activity	Total Budgeted Cost	Allocation Base
Materials handling	$ 6,000	Number of parts
Machine setup	3,200	Number of setups
Insertion of parts	51,000	Number of parts
Finishing	80,000	Finishing direct labor hours
Total	$ 140,200	

Farrington expects to produce 500 chrome bumpers during the year. The bumpers are expected to use 4,000 parts, require 10 setups, and consume 1,000 hours of finishing time.

Requirements

1. Compute the predetermined overhead allocation rate for each activity.
2. Compute the expected indirect manufacturing cost of each bumper.

E24-17 Computing product costs in traditional and activity-based costing systems

Learning Objective 1

Erickson Company manufactures wheel rims. The controller expects the following ABC allocation rates for 2016:

2. Standard $236.80

Activity	Allocation Base	Predetermined Overhead Allocation Rate
Materials handling	Number of parts	$ 3.00 per part
Machine setup	Number of setups	600.00 per setup
Insertion of parts	Number of parts	27.00 per part
Finishing	Number of finishing hours	80.00 per hour

Erickson produces two wheel rim models: standard and deluxe. Expected data for 2016 are as follows:

	Standard	Deluxe
Parts per rim	2.0	9.0
Setups per 500 rims	14.0	14.0
Finishing hours per rim	2.0	2.5
Total direct hours per rim	3.0	5.0

The company expects to produce 500 units of each model during the year.

Requirements

1. Compute the total estimated indirect manufacturing cost for 2016.

2. Compute the estimated ABC indirect manufacturing cost per unit of each model. Carry each cost to the nearest cent.

3. Prior to 2016, Erickson used a direct labor hour single plantwide overhead allocation rate system. Compute the predetermined overhead allocation rate based on direct labor hours for 2016. Use this rate to determine the estimated indirect manufacturing cost per wheel rim for each model, to the nearest cent.

E24-18 Identifying responsibility centers after decentralization

Learning Objective 2

Grandpa Jim's Cookie Company sells homemade cookies made with organic ingredients. His sales are strictly Web based. The business is taking off more than Grandpa Jim ever expected, with orders coming from across the country from both consumers and corporate event planners. Grandpa decides to decentralize and hires a full-time baker who will manage production and product costs and a Web site designer/sales manager who will focus on increasing sales through the Web site. Grandpa Jim can no longer handle the business on his own, so he hires a business manager to work with the other employees to ensure the company is best utilizing its assets to produce profit. Grandpa will then have time to focus on new product development.

Now that Grandpa Jim's Cookie Company has decentralized, identify the type of responsibility center that each manager is managing.

Learning Objective 3

E24-19 Explaining why companies use performance evaluation systems

Financial performance is measured in many ways.

Requirements

1. Explain the difference between lag and lead indicators.
2. The following is a list of financial measures. Indicate whether each is a lag or a lead indicator:
   a. Income statement shows net income of $100,000
   b. Listing of next week's orders of $50,000
   c. Trend showing that average hits on the redesigned Web site are increasing at 5% per week
   d. Price sheet from vendor reflecting that cost per pound of sugar for the next month is $2
   e. Contract signed last month with large retail store that guarantees a minimum shelf space for Grandpa's Overloaded Chocolate Cookies for the next year

Learning Objective 3

E24-20 Explaining why companies use performance evaluation systems

Well-designed performance evaluation systems accomplish many goals. Describe the potential benefits performance evaluation systems offer.

Learning Objective 3

E24-21 Describing the balanced scorecard and identifying key performance indicators for each perspective

Consider the following key performance indicators, and classify each indicator according to the balanced scorecard perspective it addresses. Choose from the financial perspective, customer perspective, internal business perspective, and the learning and growth perspective.

a. Number of customer complaints
b. Number of information system upgrades completed
c. Residual income
d. New product development time
e. Employee turnover rate
f. Percentage of products with online help manuals
g. Customer retention
h. Percentage of compensation based on performance
i. Percentage of orders filled each week
j. Gross margin growth
k. Number of new patents
l. Employee satisfaction ratings
m. Manufacturing cycle time (average length of production process)
n. Earnings growth
o. Average machine setup time
p. Number of new customers
q. Employee promotion rate
r. Cash flow from operations
s. Customer satisfaction ratings

t. Machine downtime

u. Finished products per day per employee

v. Percentage of employees with access to upgraded system

w. Wait time per order prior to start of production

E24-22 Using responsibility reports to evaluate cost, revenue, and profit centers

One subunit of Xtreme Sports Company had the following financial results last month:

Learning Objective 4

1. Direct Materials 8.05% U

(Requirement 1 only)

Xtreme—Subunit X	Actual Results	Flexible Budget	Flexible Budget Variance (F or U)	% Variance (F or U)
Direct Materials	$ 28,200	$ 26,100		
Direct Labor	13,500	14,200		
Indirect Labor	26,500	23,500		
Utilities	12,700	11,600		
Depreciation	26,000	26,000		
Repairs and Maintenance	4,000	5,000		
Total	$ 110,900	$ 106,400		

Requirements

1. Complete the performance evaluation report for this subunit. Enter the variance percent as a percentage rounded to two decimal places.

2. Based on the data presented, what type of responsibility center is this subunit?

3. Which items should be investigated if part of management's decision criteria is to investigate all variances exceeding $2,500 or 10%?

4. Should only unfavorable variances be investigated? Explain.

E24-23 Using responsibility reports to evaluate cost, revenue, and profit centers

The accountant for a subunit of Accel Sports Company went on vacation before completing the subunit's monthly responsibility report. This is as far as she got:

Learning Objective 4

Accel—Subunit X Revenue by Product	Actual Results	Flexible Budget Variance	Flexible Budget	Sales Volume Variance	Static Budget
Downhill-RI	$ 323,000	(a)	(b)	$ 20,000 F	$ 298,000
Downhill-RII	152,000	(c)	$ 164,000	(d)	147,000
Cross-EXI	281,000	$ 1,000 U	282,000	(e)	300,000
Cross-EXII	253,000	(f)	248,000	16,500 U	264,500
Snow-LXI	426,000	4,000 F	(g)	(h)	405,000
Total	$ 1,435,000	(i)	(j)	(k)	$ 1,414,500

Requirements

1. Complete the responsibility report for this subunit.

2. Based on the data presented, what type of responsibility center is this subunit?

3. Which items should be investigated if part of management's decision criteria is to investigate all variances exceeding $10,000?

Learning Objective 5

1. Residential's ROI 32.50%

E24-24 Using ROI and RI to evaluate investment centers

Zoes, a national manufacturer of lawn-mowing and snow-blowing equipment, segments its business according to customer type: professional and residential. The following divisional information was available for the past year:

	Net Sales	Operating Income	Average Total Assets
Residential	$ 540,000	$ 58,500	$ 180,000
Professional	1,070,000	152,000	380,000

Management has a 23% target rate of return for each division.

Requirements

1. Calculate each division's ROI. Round all of your answers to four decimal places.

2. Calculate each division's profit margin ratio. Interpret your results.

3. Calculate each division's asset turnover ratio. Interpret your results.

4. Use the expanded ROI formula to confirm your results from Requirement 1. What can you conclude?

Note: Exercise E24-24 must be completed before attempting Exercise E24-25.

Learning Objective 5

Professional's RI $64,600

Learning Objective 6
Appendix 24A

E24-25 Using ROI and RI to evaluate investment centers

Refer to the data in Exercise E24-24. Calculate each division's RI. Interpret your results.

E24A-26 Determining transfer pricing

The Watkins Company is decentralized, and divisions are considered investment centers. Watkins specializes in sports equipment, and one division manufactures netting that is used for basketball hoops, soccer goals, and other sports equipment. The Netting Division reports the following information for a heavy-duty basketball hoop net:

Sales Price per Unit	$ 18
Variable Cost per Unit	6
Contribution Margin per Unit	$ 12

The Basketball Equipment Division can purchase a similar heavy-duty net from an outside vendor for $15.

Requirements

1. Determine the negotiable range for the transfer price.

2. What is the minimum transfer price the Netting Division should consider if operating at capacity? Below capacity?

3. What is the maximum transfer price the Basketball Equipment Division should consider?

> Problems Group A

P24-27A Comparing costs from ABC and single-rate systems

Crescent Pharmaceuticals manufactures an over-the-counter allergy medication. The company sells both large commercial containers of 1,000 capsules to health care facilities and travel packs of 20 capsules to shops in airports, train stations, and hotels. The following information has been developed to determine if an activity-based costing system would be beneficial:

Learning Objective 1

2. Travel packs $1.80

Activity	Estimated Indirect Cost	Allocation Base	Estimated Quantity of Allocation Base
Materials handling	$ 96,000	Number of kilos	24,000 kilos
Packaging	207,000	Number of machine hours	4,140 hours
Quality assurance	124,500	Number of samples	2,075 samples
Total indirect costs	$ 427,500		

Actual production information includes the following:

	Commercial Containers	Travel Packs
Units produced	4,000 containers	54,000 packs
Weight in kilos	14,000	5,400
Machine hours	3,000	540
Number of samples	400	810

Requirements

1. Compute the predetermined overhead allocation rate for each activity.

2. Use the predetermined overhead allocation rates to compute the activity-based costs per unit of the commercial containers and the travel packs. Round to two decimal places. (*Hint:* First compute the total activity-based costs allocated to each product line, and then compute the cost per unit.)

3. Crescent's original single plantwide overhead allocation rate costing system allocated indirect costs to products at $153.00 per machine hour. Compute the total indirect costs allocated to the commercial containers and to the travel packs under the original system. Then compute the indirect cost per unit for each product. Round to two decimal places.

4. Compare the indirect activity-based costs per unit to the indirect costs per unit from the traditional system. How have the unit costs changed? Explain why the costs changed.

1. Sales $24,000 F

P24-28A Integrating decentralization and performance evaluation systems

One subunit of Field Sports Company had the following financial results last month:

Subunit X	Actual Results	Flexible Budget	Flexible Budget Variance (F or U)	% Variance (F or U)
Sales	$ 474,000	$ 450,000		
Variable Expenses	261,000	252,000		
Contribution Margin	213,000	198,000		
Traceable Fixed Expenses	37,000	26,000		
Divisional Segment Margin	$ 176,000	$ 172,000		

Requirements

1. Complete the performance evaluation report for this subunit (round to two decimal places).

2. Based on the data presented and your knowledge of the company, what type of responsibility center is this subunit?

3. Which items should be investigated if part of management's decision criteria is to investigate all variances equal to or exceeding $4,000 *and* exceeding 10% (both criteria must be met)?

4. Should only unfavorable variances be investigated? Explain.

5. Is it possible that the variances are due to a higher-than-expected sales volume? Explain.

6. Will management place equal weight on each of the variances exceeding $4,000? Explain.

7. Which balanced scorecard perspective is being addressed through this performance report? In your opinion, is this performance report a lead or a lag indicator? Explain.

8. List one key performance indicator for the three other balanced scorecard perspectives. Make sure to indicate which perspective is being addressed by the indicators you list.

P24-29A Using ROI and RI to evaluate investment centers

Consider the following condensed financial statements of Safe Money, Inc. The company's target rate of return is 20%.

Learning Objective 5

3. Asset turnover ratio 18.00

SAFE MONEY, INC. Income Statement For the Year Ended December 31, 2016	
Sales Revenue	$ 9,000,000
Cost of Goods Sold	5,200,000
Gross Profit	3,800,000
Operating Expenses	3,350,000
Operating Income	450,000
Other Expenses: Interest Expense	(31,000)
Income Before Income Tax Expense	419,000
Income Tax Expense	146,650
Net Income	$ 272,350

SAFE MONEY, INC. Comparative Balance Sheet As of December 31, 2016, and 2015		
	2016	2015
Assets		
Cash	$ 73,000	$ 61,000
Accounts Receivable	58,200	26,800
Supplies	1,800	1,200
Property, Plant, and Equipment, net	304,000	211,000
Patents, net	153,000	110,000
Total Assets	$ 590,000	$ 410,000
Liabilities and Stockholders' Equity		
Accounts Payable	$ 26,000	$ 28,000
Short-term Notes Payable	145,000	51,000
Long-term Notes Payable	193,000	123,500
Common Stock, no Par	205,000	197,000
Retained Earnings	21,000	10,500
Total Liabilities and Stockholders' Equity	$ 590,000	$ 410,000

Requirements

1. Calculate the company's ROI. Round all of your answers to four decimal places.
2. Calculate the company's profit margin ratio. Interpret your results.
3. Calculate the company's asset turnover ratio. Interpret your results.
4. Use the expanded ROI formula to confirm your results from Requirement 1. Interpret your results.
5. Calculate the company's RI. Interpret your results.

P24-30A Using ROI and RI to evaluate investment centers

Bear Paints is a national paint manufacturer and retailer. The company is segmented into five divisions: Paint Stores (branded retail locations), Consumer (paint sold through home improvement stores), Automotive (sales to auto manufacturers), International, and Administration. The following is selected divisional information for its two largest divisions: Paint Stores and Consumer.

Learning Objective 5

4. Paint Stores's ROI 34.16%

	Net Sales	Operating Income	Average Total Assets
Paint Stores	$ 3,960,000	$ 480,000	$ 1,405,000
Consumer	1,295,000	186,000	1,580,000

Management has specified a 21% target rate of return.

CHAPTER 24

Requirements

1. Calculate each division's ROI. Round all of your answers to four decimal places.

2. Calculate each division's profit margin ratio. Interpret your results.

3. Calculate each division's asset turnover ratio. Interpret your results.

4. Use the expanded ROI formula to confirm your results from Requirement 1. Interpret your results.

5. Calculate each division's RI. Interpret your results, and offer a recommendation for any division with negative RI.

6. Describe some of the factors that management considers when setting its minimum target rate of return.

Learning Objective 6
Appendix 24A

2. Total CM $124,200

P24A-31A Determining transfer pricing

The Costa Company is decentralized, and divisions are considered investment centers. Costa has one division that manufactures oak dining room chairs with upholstered seat cushions. The Chair Division cuts, assembles, and finishes the oak chairs and then purchases and attaches the seat cushions. The Chair Division currently purchases the cushions for $18 from an outside vendor. The Cushion Division manufactures upholstered seat cushions that are sold to customers outside the company. The Chair Division currently sells 1,800 chairs per quarter, and the Cushion Division is operating at capacity, which is 1,800 cushions per quarter. The two divisions report the following information:

Chair Division		Cushion Division	
Sales Price per Chair	$ 110	Sales Price per Cushion	$ 34
Variable Cost (other than cushion)	25	Variable Cost per Cushion	16
Variable Cost (cushion)	18		
Contribution Margin per Chair	$ 67	Contribution Margin per Cushion	$ 18

Requirements

1. Determine the total contribution margin for Costa Company for the quarter.

2. Assume the Chair Division purchases the 1,800 cushions needed from the Cushion Division at its current sales price. What is the total contribution margin for each division and the company?

3. Assume the Chair Division purchases the 1,800 cushions needed from the Cushion Division at its current variable cost. What is the total contribution margin for each division and the company?

4. Review your answers for Requirements 1, 2, and 3. What is the best option for Costa Company?

5. Assume the Cushion Division has capacity of 3,600 cushions per quarter and can continue to supply its outside customers with 1,800 cushions per quarter and also supply the Chair Division with 1,800 cushions per quarter. What transfer price should Costa Company set? Explain your reasoning. Using the transfer price you determined, calculate the total contribution margin for the quarter.

> Problems Group B

P24-32B Comparing costs from ABC and single-rate systems

Learning Objective 1

2. Travel packs $1.70

Haywood Pharmaceuticals manufactures an over-the-counter allergy medication. The company sells both large commercial containers of 1,000 capsules to health care facilities and travel packs of 20 capsules to shops in airports, train stations, and hotels. The following information has been developed to determine if an activity-based costing system would be beneficial:

Activity	Estimated Indirect Cost	Allocation Base	Estimated Quantity of Allocation Base
Materials handling	$ 96,000	Number of kilos	24,000 kilos
Packaging	219,000	Number of machine hours	5,475 hours
Quality assurance	112,500	Number of samples	1,875 samples
Total indirect costs	$ 427,500		

Other production information includes the following:

	Commercial Containers	Travel Packs
Units produced	3,000 containers	57,000 packs
Weight in kilos	13,500	5,700
Machine hours	2,250	570
Number of samples	300	855

Requirements

1. Compute the predetermined overhead allocation rate for each activity.

2. Use the predetermined overhead allocation rates to compute the activity-based costs per unit of the commercial containers and the travel packs. Round to two decimal places. (*Hint*: First compute the total activity-based costs allocated to each product line, and then compute the cost per unit.)

3. Haywood's original single plantwide overhead allocation rate system allocated indirect costs to products at $151.00 per machine hour. Compute the total indirect costs allocated to the commercial containers and to the travel packs under the original system. Then compute the indirect cost per unit for each product. Round to two decimal places.

4. Compare the indirect activity-based costs per unit to the indirect costs per unit from the traditional system. How have the unit costs changed? Explain why the costs changed as they did.

Learning Objectives 2, 3, 4

1. CM $15,000 F

P24-33B Integrating decentralization and performance evaluation systems

One subunit of Zone Sports Company had the following financial results last month:

Subunit X	Actual Results	Flexible Budget	Flexible Budget Variance (F or U)	% Variance (F or U)
Sales	$ 479,000	$ 451,000		
Variable Expenses	264,000	251,000		
Contribution Margin	215,000	200,000		
Traceable Fixed Expenses	40,000	28,000		
Divisional Segment Margin	$ 175,000	$ 172,000		

Requirements

1. Complete the performance evaluation report for this subunit (round to two decimal places).

2. Based on the data presented and your knowledge of the company, what type of responsibility center is this subunit?

3. Which items should be investigated if part of management's decision criteria is to investigate all variances equal to or exceeding $6,000 *and* exceeding 10% (both criteria must be met)?

4. Should only unfavorable variances be investigated? Explain.

5. Is it possible that the variances are due to a higher-than-expected sales volume? Explain.

6. Will management place equal weight on each of the variances exceeding $6,000? Explain.

7. Which balanced scorecard perspective is being addressed through this performance report? In your opinion, is this performance report a lead or a lag indicator? Explain.

8. List one key performance indicator for the three other balanced scorecard perspectives. Make sure to indicate which perspective is being addressed by the indicators you list.

P24-34B Using ROI and RI to evaluate investment centers

Learning Objective 5

Consider the following condensed financial statements of Sure Life, Inc. The company's target rate of return is 30%.

2. Profit margin ratio 10.00%

SURE LIFE, INC. Income Statement For the Year Ended December 31, 2016	
Sales Revenue	$ 3,000,000
Cost of Goods Sold	2,650,000
Gross Profit	350,000
Operating Expenses	50,000
Operating Income	300,000
Other Expenses: Interest Expense	(29,000)
Income Before Income Tax Expense	271,000
Income Tax Expense	94,850
Net Income	$ 176,150

SURE LIFE, INC. Comparative Balance Sheet As of December 31, 2016, and 2015		
	2016	2015
Assets		
Cash	$ 71,000	$ 59,000
Accounts Receivable	56,200	24,800
Supplies	3,800	3,200
Property, Plant, and Equipment, net	308,000	213,000
Patents, net	149,000	112,000
Total Assets	$ 588,000	$ 412,000
Liabilities and Stockholders' Equity		
Accounts Payable	$ 24,000	$ 26,000
Short-term Notes Payable	143,000	49,000
Long-term Notes Payable	191,000	121,500
Common Stock, no Par	211,000	207,000
Retained Earnings	19,000	8,500
Total Liabilities and Stockholders' Equity	$ 588,000	$ 412,000

Requirements

1. Calculate the company's ROI. Round all of your answers to four decimal places.
2. Calculate the company's profit margin ratio. Interpret your results.
3. Calculate the company's asset turnover ratio. Interpret your results.
4. Use the expanded ROI formula to confirm your results from Requirement 1. Interpret your results.
5. Calculate the company's RI. Interpret your results.

P24-35B Using ROI and RI to evaluate investment centers

Learning Objective 5

Benjamin Doore is a national paint manufacturer and retailer. The company is segmented into five divisions: Paint Stores (branded retail locations), Consumer (paint sold through home improvement stores), Automotive (sales to auto manufacturers), International, and Administration. The following is selected divisional information for its two largest divisions: Paint Stores and Consumer:

3. Consumer's asset turnover ratio 0.8076

	Net Sales	Operating Income	Average Total Assets
Paint Stores	$ 4,010,000	$ 482,000	$ 1,385,000
Consumer	1,280,000	185,000	1,585,000

Management has specified a 19% target rate of return.

Requirements

1. Calculate each division's ROI. Round all of your answers to four decimal places.
2. Calculate each division's profit margin ratio. Interpret your results.

3. Calculate each division's asset turnover ratio. Interpret your results.

4. Use the expanded ROI formula to confirm your results from Requirement 1. Interpret your results.

5. Calculate each division's RI. Interpret your results, and offer a recommendation for any division with negative RI.

6. Describe some of the factors that management considers when setting its minimum target rate of return.

Learning Objective 6
Appendix 24A

3. Total CM $21,600

P24A-36B Determining transfer pricing

The Greco Company is decentralized, and divisions are considered investment centers. Greco has one division that manufactures oak dining room chairs with upholstered seat cushions. The Chair Division cuts, assembles, and finishes the oak chairs and then purchases and attaches the seat cushions. The Chair Division currently purchases the cushions for $20 from an outside vendor. The Cushion Division manufactures upholstered seat cushions that are sold to customers outside the company. The Chair Division currently sells 900 chairs per quarter, and the Cushion Division is operating at capacity, which is 900 cushions per quarter. The two divisions report the following information:

Chair Division		Cushion Division	
Sales Price per Chair	$ 85	Sales Price per Cushion	$ 22
Variable Cost (other than cushion)	51	Variable Cost per Cushion	10
Variable Cost (cushion)	20		
Contribution Margin per Chair	$ 14	Contribution Margin per Cushion	$ 12

Requirements

1. Determine the total contribution margin for Greco Company for the quarter.

2. Assume the Chair Division purchases the 900 cushions needed from the Cushion Division at its current sales price. What is the total contribution margin for each division and the company?

3. Assume the Chair Division purchases the 900 cushions needed from the Cushion Division at its current variable cost. What is the total contribution margin for each division and the company?

4. Review your answers for Requirements 1, 2, and 3. What is the best option for Greco Company?

5. Assume the Cushion Division has capacity of 1,800 cushions per quarter and can continue to supply its outside customers with 900 cushions per quarter and also supply the Chair Division with 900 cushions per quarter. What transfer price should Greco Company set? Explain your reasoning. Using the transfer price you determined, calculate the total contribution margin for the quarter.

> Continuing Problem

P24-37 Using ROI and RI to evaluate investment centers

This problem continues the Daniels Consulting situation from Problem P23-35 of Chapter 23. Daniels Consulting reported 2018 sales of $3,200,000 and operating income of $185,600. Average total assets during 2018 were $640,000. Daniels's target rate of return is 17%.

Calculate Daniels's profit margin ratio, asset turnover ratio, ROI, and RI for 2018.

COMPREHENSIVE PROBLEM

> Comprehensive Problem for Chapters 22–24

The Thompson Toy Company manufactures toy building block sets for children. Thompson is planning for 2017 by developing a master budget by quarters. Thompson's balance sheet for December 31, 2016, follows:

THOMPSON TOY COMPANY Balance Sheet December 31, 2016		
Assets		
Current Assets:		
Cash	$ 27,000	
Accounts Receivable	35,000	
Raw Materials Inventory	1,000	
Finished Goods Inventory	3,200	
Total Current Assets		$ 66,200
Property, Plant, and Equipment:		
Equipment	177,000	
Less: Accumulated Depreciation	(39,000)	138,000
Total Assets		**$ 204,200**
Liabilities		
Current Liabilities:		
Accounts Payable		$ 11,000
Stockholders' Equity		
Common Stock, no par	$ 100,000	
Retained Earnings	93,200	
Total Stockholders' Equity		193,200
Total Liabilities and Stockholders' Equity		**$ 204,200**

Other budget data for Thompson Toy Company:

a. Budgeted sales are 500 sets for the first quarter and expected to increase by 100 sets per quarter. Cash sales are expected to be 40% of total sales, with the remaining 60% of sales on account. Sets are budgeted to sell for $70 per set.

b. Finished Goods Inventory on December 31, 2016, consists of 100 sets at $32 each.

c. Desired ending Finished Goods Inventory is 30% of the next quarter's sales; first quarter sales for 2018 are expected to be 900 sets. FIFO inventory costing method is used.

d. Direct materials cost is $10 per set.

e. Desired ending Raw Materials Inventory is 10% of the next quarter's direct materials needed for production; desired ending inventory for December 31, 2017, is $1,000; indirect materials are insignificant and not considered for budgeting purposes.

f. Each set requires 0.20 hours of direct labor; direct labor costs average $10 per hour.

g. Variable manufacturing overhead is $2 per set.

h. Fixed manufacturing overhead includes $4,000 per quarter in depreciation and $1,540 per quarter for other costs, such as utilities, insurance, and property taxes.

i. Fixed selling and administrative expenses include $8,500 per quarter for salaries; $2,400 per quarter for rent; $750 per quarter for insurance; and $1,500 per quarter for depreciation.

j. Variable selling and administrative expenses include supplies at 1% of sales.

k. Capital expenditures include $30,000 for new manufacturing equipment, to be purchased and paid for in the first quarter.

l. Cash receipts for sales on account are 30% in the quarter of the sale and 70% in the quarter following the sale; Accounts Receivable balance on December 31, 2016, is expected to be received in the first quarter of 2017; uncollectible accounts are considered insignificant and not considered for budgeting purposes.

m. Direct materials purchases are paid 90% in the quarter purchased and 10% in the following quarter; Accounts Payable balance on December 31, 2016, is expected to be paid in the first quarter of 2017.

n. Direct labor, manufacturing overhead, and selling and administrative costs are paid in the quarter incurred.

o. Income tax expense is projected at $3,500 per quarter and is paid in the quarter incurred.

p. Thompson desires to maintain a minimum cash balance of $25,000 and borrows from the local bank as needed in increments of $1,000 at the beginning of the quarter; principal repayments are made at the beginning of the quarter when excess funds are available and in increments of $1,000; interest is 5% per year and paid at the beginning of the quarter based on the amount outstanding from the previous quarter.

Requirements

1. Prepare Thompson's operating budget and cash budget for 2017 by quarter. Required schedules and budgets include: sales budget, production budget, direct materials budget, direct labor budget, manufacturing overhead budget, cost of goods sold budget, selling and administrative expense budget, schedule of cash receipts, schedule of cash payments, and cash budget. Manufacturing overhead costs are allocated based on direct labor hours.

2. Prepare Thompson's annual financial budget for 2017, including budgeted income statement, budgeted balance sheet, and budgeted statement of cash flows.

3. Thompson sold 3,000 sets in 2017, and its actual operating income was as follows:

THOMPSON TOY COMPANY Income Statement For the Year Ended December 31, 2017		
Sales Revenue		$ 210,000
Cost of Goods Sold:		
Variable	$ 42,720	
Fixed	20,000	62,720
Gross Profit		147,280
Selling and Administrative Expenses:		
Variable	2,100	
Fixed	52,600	54,700
Operating Income		92,580
Interest Expense		500
Income Before Income Taxes		92,080
Income Tax Expense		20,000
Net Income		$ 72,080

Prepare a flexible budget performance report through operating income for 2017. Show product costs separately from selling and administrative costs. To simplify the calculations due to sets in beginning inventory having a different cost than those produced and sold in 2017, assume the following product costs:

	Variable	Fixed	Total
Static budget	$ 36,040	$ 22,160	$ 58,200
Flexible budget	41,640	22,160	63,800

4. What was the effect on Thompson's operating income of selling 400 sets more than the static budget level of sales?

5. What is Thompson's static budget variance for operating income?

6. Explain why the flexible budget performance report provides more useful information to Thompson's managers than the static budget performance report. What insights can Thompson's managers draw from this performance report?

7. During 2017, Thompson recorded the following cost data:

Standard Cost Information

	Quantity	Cost
Direct Materials	5 pounds per set	$ 2.00 per pound
Direct Labor	0.20 hours per set	$ 10.00 per hour
Variable Manufacturing Overhead	0.20 hours per set	$ 10.00 per hour
Fixed Manufacturing Overhead	0.20 hours per set	$ 40.00 per hour
Static budget amount: $22,160		

Actual Cost Information

Direct Materials	(14,750 pounds @ $2.10 per pound)	$ 30,975
Direct Labor	(580 hours @ $10.50 per hour)	6,090
Variable Manufacturing Overhead	(580 hours @ $9.75 per hour)	5,655
Fixed Manufacturing Overhead		20,000

Compute the cost and efficiency variances for direct materials and direct labor.

8. For manufacturing overhead, compute the variable overhead cost and efficiency variances and the fixed overhead cost and volume variances.

9. Prepare the standard cost income statement for 2017.

10. Calculate Thompson's ROI for 2017. To calculate average total assets, use the December 31, 2016, balance sheet for the beginning balance and the budgeted balance sheet for December 31, 2017, for the ending balance. Round all of your answers to four decimal places.

11. Calculate Thompson's profit margin ratio for 2017. Interpret your results.

12. Calculate Thompson's asset turnover ratio for 2017. Interpret your results.

13. Use the expanded ROI formula to confirm your results from Requirement 10. Interpret your results.

14. Thompson's management has specified a 20% target rate of return. Calculate Thompson's RI for 2017. Interpret your results.

CRITICAL THINKING

> Decision Case 24-1

Colgate-Palmolive Company operates two product segments. Go to the company Web site (**http://www.colgatepalmolive.com**), and then click on the "For Investors" link. From there, go to the SEC filings and select "10-K reports." Select the Annual Report filed February 20, 2014, for the year ended December 31, 2013. The necessary information will be in Note 15 (pages 86–89).

Requirements

1. What are the two product segments? Gather data about each segment's net sales, operating income, and identifiable assets for 2013.

2. Calculate ROI for each segment for 2013.

3. Which segment has the highest ROI? Explain why.

4. If you were on the top management team and could allocate extra funds to only one division, which division would you choose? Why?

> Ethical Issue 24-1

Dixie Irwin is the department manager for Religious Books, a manufacturer of religious books that are sold through Internet companies. Irwin's bonus is based on reducing production costs.

   Irwin has identified a supplier, Cheap Paper, that can provide paper products at a 10% cost reduction. The paper quality is not the same as that of the current paper used in production. If Irwin uses the supplier, she will certainly achieve her personal bonus goals; however, other company goals may be in jeopardy. What is the ethical issue? Identify the key performance issues at risk, and recommend a plan of action for Irwin.

> Fraud Case 24-1

Everybody knew Ed McAlister was a brilliant businessman. He had taken a small garbage collection company in Kentucky and built it up to be one of the largest and most profitable waste management companies in the Midwest. But when he was convicted of a massive financial fraud, what surprised everyone was how crude and simple the scheme was. To keep the earnings up and the stock prices soaring, he and his co-workers came up with an almost foolishly simple scheme: First, they doubled the useful lives of the dumpsters. That allowed them to cut depreciation expense in half. The following year, they simply increased the estimated salvage value of the dumpsters, allowing them to further reduce depreciation expense. With thousands of dumpsters spread over 14 states, these simple adjustments gave the company an enormous boost to the bottom line. When it all came tumbling down, McAlister had to sell everything he owned to pay for his legal costs and was left with nothing.

Requirements

1. If an asset has either too long a useful life or too high an estimated salvage value, what happens, from an accounting perspective, when that asset is worn out and has to be disposed of?

2. Do the rules of GAAP (Generally Accepted Accounting Principles) mandate specific lives for different types of assets?

3. How might either too long a useful life or too high an estimated salvage value affect key performance indicators such as return on investment and residual income?

> Team Project 24-1

Each group should identify one public company's product to evaluate. The team should gather all the information it can about the product.

Requirement

Develop a list of key performance indicators for the product.

> Communication Activity 24-1

In 150 words or fewer, list each of the four perspectives of the balanced scorecard. Give an example of one KPI from each of the perspectives, and explain what measure the KPI provides for a retailing business.

MyAccountingLab For a wealth of online resources, including exercises, problems, media, and immediate tutorial help, please visit http://www.myaccountinglab.com.

> Quick Check Answers

1. d **2.** d **3.** c **4.** d **5.** b **6.** d **7.** c **8.** b **9.** a **10.** b **11A.** d

Short-Term Business Decisions

Will Someone Clean Up This Mess?

Woody Styles looked at his apartment. It was a mess. Attending college full time and working part time didn't leave much time for cleaning. The "dust bunnies" were threatening to take over, and the kitchen floor was rather sticky. Woody didn't like his living conditions, but he also didn't want to use his scheduled study time to clean the apartment. Woody decided the best choice was to outsource the cleaning by hiring a cleaning company to come in every couple of weeks.

Woody was familiar with the concept of outsourcing from his brother Allen, the design manager at Abraham Airplane Company. Allen's job includes analyzing the prototypes of newly created airplanes and gliders to determine which parts should be manufactured in Abraham's manufacturing facilities and which ones should be outsourced to a third-party vendor. Allen has to decide whether Abraham's employees have the expertise to make the part and whether Abraham's equipment is adequate. Often, it is more economical to contract with another company to produce the parts, such as the tires on the landing gear, than it is to buy the needed equipment and train employees to use it efficiently and effectively.

Woody decided to analyze his outsourcing decision. He researched the cost of a cleaning service and compared it to the hours he would have to work at his part-time job to pay for the service. Woody decided the best short-term decision was to clean the apartment himself, but he looked forward to outsourcing the job when he graduated and began working full time.

How Do Managers Make Decisions?

Managers have to make business decisions every day, such as whom to sell to, how much to charge, which products to make, and when it is better to buy a product or service rather than producing it in-house. The Boeing Company is the world's largest aerospace company and the leading manufacturer of commercial airplanes and defense, space, and security systems. The company employs more than 168,000 people in more than 65 countries. Recently, the Boeing Commercial Airline division has focused its new product development on the Boeing 787 Dreamliner, which has had record-breaking customer orders. The first customer delivery was in September 2011. On January 16, 2013, the Federal Aviation Administration (FAA) issued an emergency airworthiness directive ordering all U.S.-based airlines to ground their Boeing 787s due to the risk of a battery overheating or catching fire. The batteries were outsourced and produced by a third-party vendor. Boeing made modifications to the batteries, and the planes were flying again in about three months. The decision to outsource can have a lasting impact on a company's reputation and overall profitability, but Boeing's response was quick—and hopefully the company will not experience any long-term negative effects. These are the types of decisions that we will evaluate in this chapter.

Chapter 25 Learning Objectives

1	Identify information that is relevant for making short-term decisions	**3**	Make decisions about dropping a product, product mix, and sales mix
2	Make regular and special pricing decisions	**4**	Make outsourcing and processing further decisions

In previous chapters, we saw how managers use cost behavior to determine a company's breakeven point, estimate the sales volume needed to achieve target profits, prepare budgets, and evaluate performance. In this chapter, we see how managers use their knowledge of cost behavior to make short-term business decisions, such as whether to accept an order with special pricing or drop an unprofitable product. The decisions we discuss in this chapter pertain to short periods of time, usually one year or less. In the next chapter, we discuss longer-term decisions. Before we look at some typical short-term decisions in detail, let's consider a manager's decision-making process and the information managers need to evaluate their options.

HOW IS RELEVANT INFORMATION USED TO MAKE SHORT-TERM DECISIONS?

Learning Objective 1

Identify information that is relevant for making short-term decisions

Exhibit 25-1 illustrates how managers make decisions among alternative courses of action. Managerial accountants help with the third step: gather and analyze *relevant information* to compare alternatives.

Exhibit 25-1 | How Managers Make Decisions

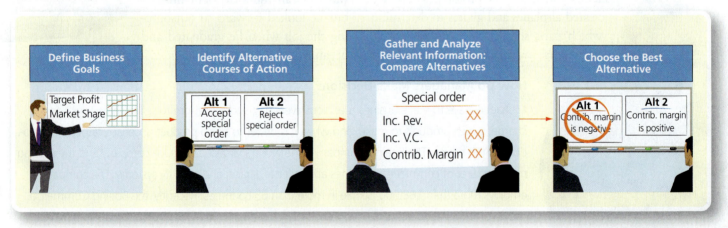

Relevant Information

Relevant Information
Expected future data that differ among alternatives.

Relevant Cost
A cost that is relevant to a particular decision because it is a future cost and differs among alternatives.

When managers make decisions, they focus on information that is relevant to the decisions. **Relevant information** is expected *future* data that *differ* among alternatives. **Relevant costs** are costs that are relevant to a particular decision. To illustrate, if the fictitious company Smart Touch Learning was considering purchasing a new delivery truck and was choosing between two different models, the cost of the trucks, the sales tax, and the insurance premium costs would all be relevant because these costs are *future* costs (after Smart Touch Learning decides which truck to buy) and *differ between alternatives* (each truck model has a different invoice price, sales tax, and insurance premium). These costs are *relevant* because they can affect the decision of which truck to purchase.

Irrelevant costs are costs that *do not* affect the decision. For example, if the two truck models have similar fuel efficiency and maintenance ratings, we do not expect the truck operating costs to differ between those two alternatives. Because these costs do not differ, they do not affect Smart Touch Learning's decision. In other words, they are *irrelevant* to the decision.

Sunk costs are costs that were incurred in the *past* and cannot be changed regardless of which future action is taken. Sunk costs are always irrelevant to the decision. This does not mean we cannot learn from past decisions—managers should always consider the results of past decisions when making future decisions. However, because sunk costs are already spent, the cost is not relevant to future decision making. For example, perhaps Smart Touch Learning wants to trade in its current truck when the company buys the new truck. The amount Smart Touch Learning paid for the current truck—which the company bought for $15,000 a year ago—is a sunk cost. No decision made *now* can alter the sunk costs spent in the past. All the company can do *now* is keep the current truck, trade it in, or sell it for the best price the company can get—even if that price is substantially less than what Smart Touch Learning originally paid for the truck.

What *is* relevant is the amount Smart Touch Learning can receive if it sells the truck in the future. Suppose that one dealership offers an $8,000 trade-in value for the truck, but another dealership offers $10,000. Because the amounts differ and the transaction will take place in the future, the trade-in value *is* relevant to Smart Touch Learning's decision. The same principle applies to all situations—*only relevant data affect decisions*.

Relevant Nonfinancial Information

Nonfinancial, or qualitative, factors also play a role in managers' decisions and, as a result, can be relevant. For example, closing manufacturing plants and laying off employees can seriously hurt employee morale. The decision to buy or subcontract a product or service rather than produce it in-house can reduce control over delivery time or product quality. Offering discounted prices to select customers can upset regular customers and tempt them to take their business elsewhere. **Managers must always consider the potential quantitative *and* qualitative effects of their decisions.**

Managers who ignore qualitative factors can make serious mistakes. For example, the City of Nottingham, England, spent $1.6 million on 215 solar-powered parking meters after seeing how well the parking meters worked in countries along the Mediterranean Sea. However, they did not consider that British skies are typically overcast. The result was that the meters did not always work because of the lack of sunlight. The city *lost* money because people parked for free! Relevant qualitative information has the same characteristics as relevant financial information. The qualitative effect occurs in the *future* and *differs* between alternatives. In the parking meter example, the amount of *future* sunshine required by the meters *differed* between the alternatives. The mechanical meters did not require any sunshine, but the solar-powered meters needed a lot of sunshine.

Differential Analysis

A common approach to making short-term business decisions is called **differential analysis**. In this approach, the emphasis is on the difference in operating income between the alternative approaches. Differential analysis is also sometimes called *incremental analysis*. Instead of looking at the company's *entire* income statement under each decision alternative, we just look at how operating income would *differ* under each alternative. Using this approach, we leave out irrelevant information—the revenues and

---

Irrelevant Cost
A cost that does not affect the decision because it is not in the future or does not differ among alternatives.

Sunk Cost
A cost that was incurred in the past and cannot be changed regardless of which future action is taken.

Is relevant information always financial?

Differential Analysis
A method that looks at how operating income would differ under each decision alternative; leaves out irrelevant information.

costs that will not differ between alternatives. In this chapter, we consider several kinds of short-term business decisions:

• Regular and special pricing
• Dropping unprofitable products and segments, product mix, and sales mix
• Outsourcing and processing further

As you study these decisions, keep in mind the two keys in analyzing short-term business decisions:

1. **Focus on relevant revenues, costs, and profits.** Irrelevant information only clouds the picture and creates information overload.
2. **Use a contribution margin approach that separates variable costs from fixed costs.** Because fixed costs and variable costs behave differently, they must be analyzed separately. Traditional income statements, which blend fixed and variable costs together, can mislead managers. Contribution margin income statements, which isolate costs by behavior (variable or fixed), help managers gather the cost behavior information they need. Keep in mind that manufacturing costs per unit are mixed costs, too—so they can also mislead managers. If you use manufacturing costs per unit in your analysis, be sure to first separate the unit cost into its fixed and variable portions.

We use these two keys in each decision.

Try It!

Doherty Company is considering replacing the individual printers each employee in the corporate office currently uses with a network printer located in a central area. The network printer is more efficient and would, therefore, cost less to operate than the individual printers. However, most of the office staff think having to use a centralized printer would be inconvenient. They prefer to have individual printers located at each desk. Identify the following information as financial or nonfinancial and relevant or irrelevant. The first item has been completed as an example.

	Financial	Nonfinancial	Relevant	Irrelevant
1. Amount paid for current printers	✓			✓
2. Resale value of current printers				
3. Cost of new printer				
4. Operating costs of current printers				
5. Operating costs of new printer				
6. Employee morale				

Check your answers online in MyAccountingLab or at http://www.pearsonhighered.com/Horngren.

For more practice, see Short Exercise S25-1. MyAccountingLab

HOW DOES PRICING AFFECT SHORT-TERM DECISIONS?

We start our discussion on decision making by looking at regular pricing decisions and special pricing decisions. In the past, managers did not consider pricing to be a short-term decision. However, product life cycles are getting shorter in most industries. Companies often sell products for only a few months before replacing them with an updated model, even if the updating is small. The clothing and technology industries have always had short life cycles. Even auto and housing styles change frequently. Pricing has become a shorter-term decision than it was in the past.

Learning Objective 2
Make regular and special pricing decisions

Setting Regular Prices

There are three basic questions managers must answer when setting regular prices for their products or services:

- What is the company's target profit?
- How much will customers pay?
- Is the company a price-taker or a price-setter for this product or service?

The answers to these questions are complex and ever changing. Stockholders expect the company to achieve certain profits. Economic conditions, historical company earnings, industry risk, competition, and new business developments all affect the level of profit that stockholders expect. Stockholders usually tie their profit expectations to the amount of assets invested in the company. For example, stockholders may expect a 10% annual return on investment (ROI). A company's stock price tends to decline if it does not meet target profits, so managers must keep costs low while generating enough revenue to meet target profits.

This leads to the second question: How much will customers pay? Managers cannot set prices above what customers are willing to pay, or sales volume will decline. The amount customers will pay depends on the competition, the product's uniqueness, the effectiveness of marketing campaigns, general economic conditions, and so forth.

To address the third pricing question, whether a company is a price-taker or a price-setter, imagine a horizontal line with price-takers at one end and price-setters at the other end. A company falls somewhere along this line for each of its products and services. Companies are **price-takers** when they have little or no control over the prices of their products or services and *take* the price set by the market. This occurs when their products and services are *not* unique or when competition is intense. Examples include food commodities (milk and corn), natural resources (oil and lumber), and generic consumer products and services (paper towels, dry cleaning, and banking).

Companies are **price-setters** when they have more control over pricing—in other words, they can *set the price* to some extent. Companies are price-setters when their products are unique, which results in less competition. Unique products, such as original art and jewelry, specially manufactured machinery, patented perfume scents, and the latest technological gadget, can command higher prices.

Obviously, managers would rather be price-setters than price-takers. To gain more control over pricing, companies try to differentiate their products. They want to make their products unique in terms of features, service, or quality or at least make the buyer *think* their product is unique or somehow better. Companies achieve this differentiation partly through their advertising efforts. Consider Nike's athletic shoes, Starbucks's coffee, Kleenex's tissues, Tylenol's acetaminophen, Capital One's credit cards, Shell's gas, Abercrombie and Fitch's jeans—the list goes on and on. Are these products really better or significantly different from their lower-priced competitors? It is possible. If these companies can make customers *believe* that this is true, they will gain more control over their pricing because

Price-Taker
A company that has little control over the prices of its products and services because its products and services are not unique or competition is intense.

Price-Setter
A company that has control over the prices of its products and services because its products and services are unique and there is little competition.

customers are willing to pay *more* for their product or service. What is the downside? These companies must charge higher prices or sell more just to cover their advertising costs.

A company's approach to pricing depends on whether it is on the price-taking or price-setting side of the spectrum. Price-takers emphasize a target-pricing approach. Price-setters emphasize a cost-plus pricing approach. Keep in mind that most companies provide many products and services; a company may be a price-taker for some products and a price-setter for other products. Therefore, managers tend to use both approaches to some extent. Exhibit 25-2 summarizes the difference between price-takers and price-setters.

Exhibit 25-2 | Price-Takers Versus Price-Setters

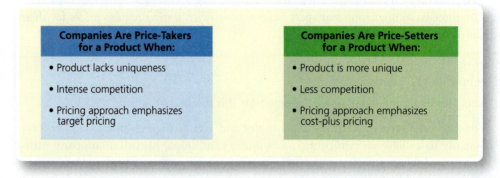

Companies Are Price-Takers for a Product When:	Companies Are Price-Setters for a Product When:
• Product lacks uniqueness	• Product is more unique
• Intense competition	• Less competition
• Pricing approach emphasizes target pricing	• Pricing approach emphasizes cost-plus pricing

Target Pricing

When a company is a price-taker, it emphasizes a target-pricing approach to managing costs and profits. The basic profit calculation is:

$$\begin{array}{r} \text{Revenues} \\ - \text{ Costs} \\ \hline \text{Profits} \end{array}$$

This formula can be rewritten as follows to solve for costs:

$$\begin{array}{r} \text{Revenues} \\ - \text{ Profits} \\ \hline \text{Costs} \end{array}$$

Target Pricing
A method to manage costs and profits by determining the target full product cost. Revenue at market price − Desired profit = Target full product cost.

Target Full Product Cost
The full cost to develop, produce, and deliver the product or service.

Target pricing starts with the market price of the product (the price customers are willing to pay) and then subtracts the company's desired profit to determine the maximum allowed **target full product cost**—the *full* cost to develop, produce, and deliver the product or service. Target pricing is sometimes called *target costing* because the desired target cost is derived from the target price. Modifying the above equation, we reach the target pricing formula:

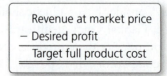

$$\begin{array}{r} \text{Revenue at market price} \\ - \text{ Desired profit} \\ \hline \text{Target full product cost} \end{array}$$

In this relationship, the sales price is *taken* from the market. It is the amount set by the market—the maximum amount customers are willing to pay. The company has no control over this amount and, therefore, must focus on controlling costs to obtain the desired profit. Recall that a product's *full* cost contains all elements from the value chain—both product costs (direct materials, direct labor, and manufacturing overhead) and period costs (selling and administrative costs). Both product costs and period costs include fixed and variable costs. If the product's current cost is higher than the target full product cost, the company must find ways to reduce the product's cost or it will not meet its profit goals. Managers often use activity-based costing along with value engineering (as discussed in a previous chapter) to find ways to cut costs.

Let's return to Smart Touch Learning, a fictitious company that manufactures tablet computers. Assume that tablet computers sold by Smart Touch Learning are a commodity and that the current market price is $500 per tablet. Exhibit 25-3 shows the expected operating income for Smart Touch Learning for 2017 for 2,400 tablets.

How will I know the revenue at market price?

Exhibit 25-3 | **Smart Touch Learning's Budgeted Income Statement**

SMART TOUCH LEARNING Budgeted Income Statement Year Ended December 31, 2017		
Sales Revenue		$ 1,200,000
Variable Costs:		
Manufacturing	$ 588,000	
Selling & Administrative	150,000	738,000
Contribution Margin		462,000
Fixed Costs:		
Manufacturing	110,000	
Selling & Administrative	116,000	226,000
Operating Income		$ 236,000

Because the tablets are a commodity, Smart Touch Learning will emphasize a target-pricing approach. Assume the company's stockholders expect a 10% annual return on the company's assets (ROI). If the company has $2,500,000 average assets, the desired profit is $250,000 ($2,500,000 × 10%). The target full product cost at the current sales volume of 2,400 tablets is calculated as follows:

Revenue at market price	(2,400 tablets @ $500 each, from Exhibit 25-3)	$ 1,200,000
Less: Desired profit	(calculated above)	250,000
Target full product cost		$ 950,000

Once we know the target full product cost, we can analyze the fixed and variable cost components separately. Can Smart Touch Learning make and sell 2,400 tablets at a full product cost of $950,000? We know from Smart Touch Learning's contribution margin income statement (Exhibit 25-3) that the company's variable costs are $307.50 per unit ($738,000 / 2,400 tablets). This variable cost per unit includes both manufacturing costs and selling and administrative costs. We also know the company incurs $226,000 in fixed costs in its current relevant range. Again, some fixed costs stem from manufacturing and some from selling and administrative activities. *In setting regular sales prices, companies must cover **all** of their costs—whether the costs are product or period, fixed or variable.*

Making and selling 2,400 tablets currently cost the company $964,000 [(2,400 units × $307.50 variable cost per unit) + $226,000 of fixed costs], which is $14,000 more than the target full product cost of $950,000. What options does Smart Touch Learning have?

1. Accept the lower operating income of $236,000, which is a 9.44% return on investment ($236,000 operating income / $2,500,000 average assets), not the 10% target return required by stockholders.
2. Reduce fixed costs by $14,000 or more.
3. Reduce variable costs by $14,000 or more.
4. Attempt to increase sales volume. If the company has excess manufacturing capacity, making and selling more units would only affect variable costs; however, it would mean that current fixed costs are spread over more units. Therefore, total cost per unit would decrease and profits would increase.
5. Change or add to its product mix (covered later in this chapter).
6. Attempt to differentiate its tablet computer from the competition to gain more control over sales prices (become a price-setter).
7. A combination of the above strategies that would increase revenues and/or decrease costs by $14,000.

Smart Touch Learning's managers can use cost-volume-profit (CVP) analysis, as you learned in a previous chapter, to determine how many tablets the company would have to sell to achieve its target profit. The company would have to consider how to increase demand for the tablets and the additional costs that would be incurred, such as advertising costs. Managers do not have an easy task when the current cost exceeds the target full product cost. Sometimes companies just cannot compete given the current market price. If that is the case, they may have no other choice than to quit making that product. (This decision is also covered later in the chapter.)

Cost-Plus Pricing

When a company is a price-setter, it emphasizes a cost-plus approach to pricing. This pricing approach is essentially the *opposite* of the target-pricing approach. **Cost-plus pricing** starts with the company's full product costs (as a given) and *adds* its desired profit to determine a cost-plus price.

> **Cost-Plus Pricing**
> A method to manage costs and profits by determining the price. Full product cost + Desired profit = Cost-plus price.

Full product cost
+ Desired profit
Cost-plus price

As you can see, it is the basic profit calculation rearranged to solve for the revenue figure—price.

When the product is unique, the company has more control over pricing—but the company still needs to make sure that the cost-plus price is not higher than what customers are willing to pay. Let's go back to our Smart Touch Learning example. This time, assume the tablet computers benefit from brand recognition due to the company's preloaded e-learning software so the company has some control over the price it charges for its tablets.

Using a cost-plus pricing approach, assuming the current level of sales, and a desired profit of 10% of average assets, the cost-plus price is $506, calculated as follows:

Current variable costs	($307.50 per tablet × 2,400 tablets)	$ 738,000
Plus: Fixed costs		226,000
Full product cost		964,000
Plus: Desired profit	(10% × $2,500,000 average assets)	250,000
Target revenue		$ 1,214,000
Divided by number of tablets		÷ 2,400 units
Cost-plus price per tablet		$ 506 per unit*

*rounded

If the current market price for generic tablet computers is $500, as we assumed earlier, can Smart Touch Learning sell its brand-name tablet computers for $506 or more? Probably. The answer depends on how well the company has been able to differentiate its product or brand name. The company may use focus groups or marketing surveys to find out how customers would respond to its cost-plus price. The company may find out that its cost-plus price is too high, or it may find that it could set the price even higher without losing sales.

Notice how pricing decisions (1) focus on relevant information and (2) use a contribution margin approach that separates variable costs from fixed costs—our two keys to decision making. In pricing decisions, all cost information is relevant because the company must cover *all* costs along the value chain before it can generate a profit. However, we still need to consider variable costs and fixed costs separately because they behave differently at different volumes.

To maximize the effectiveness of pricing decisions, our pricing decision rule is as follows:

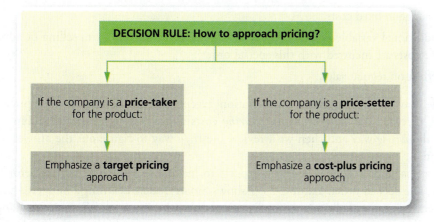

Special Pricing

A special pricing decision occurs when a customer requests a one-time order at a *reduced* sales price. Before agreeing to the special deal, management must consider the following questions:

• Does the company have the excess capacity available to fill the order?

• Will the reduced sales price be high enough to cover the *differential* costs of filling the order?

• Will the special order affect regular sales in the long run?

First, managers must consider available manufacturing capacity. If the company is already using all its existing manufacturing capacity and selling all units made at its *regular* sales price, it would not be as profitable to fill a special order at a *reduced* sales price. Therefore, available excess capacity is a necessity for accepting a special order. This is true for service firms as well as manufacturers.

Second, managers need to consider whether the special reduced sales price is high enough to cover the *differential* costs of filling the special order. Differential costs are the costs that are different if the alternative is chosen. The special price *must* be greater than the variable costs of filling the order or the company will incur a loss on the deal. In other words, the special order must provide a *positive* contribution margin.

Additionally, the company must consider differential fixed costs. If the company has excess capacity, fixed costs probably will not be affected by producing more units (or delivering more service). However, in some cases, management may have to incur some other fixed costs to fill the special order, such as additional insurance premiums or the purchase of special equipment. If so, they need to consider whether the special sales price is high enough to generate a positive contribution margin *and* cover the additional fixed costs.

Finally, managers need to consider whether the special order will affect regular sales in the long run. Will regular customers find out about the special order and demand a lower price? Will the special order customer come back *again and again*, asking for the same reduced price? Will the special order price start a price war with competitors? Managers should determine the answers to these questions and consider how customers will respond. Managers may decide that any profit from the special sales order is not worth these risks.

Let's consider a special pricing example. Smart Touch Learning normally sells its tablet computers for $500 each. Assume that a company has offered Smart Touch Learning $68,750 for 250 tablets, or $275 per tablet. The special pricing requested is substantially less than the regular sales price. Additional information about this sale includes:

- Production will use manufacturing capacity that would otherwise be idle (excess capacity).
- No change in fixed costs.
- No additional variable *nonmanufacturing* expenses (because no extra selling or administrative costs are incurred with this special order).
- No effect on regular sales.

We have addressed every consideration except one: Is the special sales price high enough to cover the variable *manufacturing* costs associated with the order? First, we'll review the *wrong* way and then we'll review the *right* way to figure out the answer to this question.

Suppose Smart Touch Learning expects to make and sell 2,400 tablets before considering the special order. Exhibit 25-4 shows Smart Touch Learning's budgeted income statement using the traditional income statement on the left side of Exhibit 25-4 and the contribution margin income statement on the right (as previously shown in Exhibit 25-3).

The traditional format income statement shows product cost of $290.83 per tablet ($698,000 COGS / 2,400 tablets = $290.83 per tablet, rounded). A manager who does not examine these numbers carefully may believe that Smart Touch Learning should *not* accept the special order at a sales price of $275.00 because each tablet costs $290.83 to manufacture. But appearances can be deceiving! Recall that the manufacturing cost per unit for the tablet is a *mixed* cost, containing both fixed and variable cost components. To correctly answer our question, we need to find only the *variable* portion of the manufacturing unit cost.

**Exhibit 25-4 | Smart Touch Learning's Budgeted Income Statement—
Traditional and Contribution Margin Formats**

**SMART TOUCH LEARNING
Budgeted Income Statement
Year Ended December 31, 2017**

Traditional Format		Contribution Margin Format		
Sales Revenue	$ 1,200,000	Sales Revenue		$ 1,200,000
Cost of Goods Sold	698,000	Variable Costs:		
Gross Profit	502,000	Manufacturing	$ 588,000	
Selling and Administrative Expenses	266,000	Selling & Administrative	150,000	738,000
Operating Income	$ 236,000	Contribution Margin		462,000
		Fixed Costs:		
		Manufacturing	110,000	
		Selling & Administrative	116,000	226,000
		Operating Income		$ 236,000

The right side of Exhibit 25-4 shows the contribution margin income statement that separates variable expenses from fixed expenses. The contribution margin income statement allows us to see that the *variable* manufacturing cost per tablet is only $245 ($588,000 / 2,400 tablets = $245 per tablet). The special sales price of $275 per tablet is *higher* than the variable manufacturing cost of $245. Therefore, the special order will provide a positive contribution margin of $30 per tablet ($275 − $245). Because the special order is for 250 tablets, Smart Touch Learning's total contribution margin should increase by $7,500 (250 tablets × $30 per tablet) if it accepts this order.

Using a differential analysis approach, Smart Touch Learning compares the additional revenues from the special order with the additional expenses to see if the special order will contribute to profits. These are the amounts that will be different if the order is accepted. Exhibit 25-5 shows that the special sales order will increase revenue by $68,750 (250 tablets × $275) but will also increase variable manufacturing costs by $61,250 (250 tablets × $245). As a result, Smart Touch Learning's contribution margin will increase by

Exhibit 25-5 | Differential Analysis of Special Pricing Decision

Expected increase in revenue	(250 tablets × $275)	$ 68,750
Expected increase in variable manufacturing costs	(250 tablets × $245)	(61,250)
Expected *increase* in operating income	(250 tablets × $ 30)	$ 7,500

In differential analysis, items are shown with their effect on profits. The increase in revenues will increase profits, so it is shown as a positive amount. The increase in costs will decrease profits, so it is shown as a negative amount.

$7,500, as previously shown. The other costs shown in Exhibit 25-4 are not relevant to the decision. Variable selling and administrative expenses will be the same whether or not Smart Touch Learning accepts the special order because Smart Touch Learning made no special efforts to acquire this sale. Fixed manufacturing costs will not change because Smart Touch Learning has enough idle capacity to produce 250 extra tablets without needing additional facilities. Fixed selling and administrative expenses will not be affected by this special order, either. Because there are no additional fixed costs, the total increase in contribution margin flows directly to operating income. As a result, the special sales order will increase operating income by $7,500.

Notice that the analysis follows the two keys to making short-term business decisions discussed earlier: (1) Focus on relevant data (revenues and costs that *will change* if Smart Touch Learning accepts the special order) and (2) use of a contribution margin approach that separates variable costs from fixed costs.

To summarize, for special pricing decisions, the decision rule is as follows:

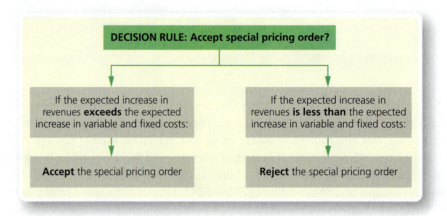

DECISIONS

Should we accept this order?

Jeff Sylvester is a sales representative for Angelfish to Zebras, a manufacturer of stuffed animals. The company sells the stuffed animals to retailers, such as department stores and toy stores. Jeff enjoys his job—he's a good salesman, and he likes selling a product that makes children happy. Jeff recently received a request from a new customer for a special promotion. The store wants Angelfish to Zebras to manufacture a teddy bear wearing a shirt with the store's logo. The store will sell the bears only during a three-week period coinciding with the store's 25th anniversary and will provide the shirts. The store has asked for a special price on the bears, 20% less than Angelfish to Zebras's regular price. The store has justified its request by stating it is a one-time deal because the store does not usually sell stuffed animals and Angelfish to Zebras will not incur any selling costs. Jeff needs to decide whether to accept the sales order. The bears would be made during the company's slow period, after the rush of the holiday season, so capacity is not a problem. Should Jeff accept the order?

Solution

Based on the information given, it appears fixed costs would not change if the order is accepted because the order is for a current product and the manufacturing facility has excess capacity. Additionally, there would be no change in selling and administrative costs. Therefore, the only differential costs would be the variable manufacturing costs. If the reduced sales price is greater than the variable manufacturing costs, then Jeff should accept the order.

Alternative Solution

The marketing manager may have another perspective. The company should carefully consider its existing customers. What if Angelfish to Zebras's other customers find out about the deal? Would they expect the same low sales price? If so, can the company afford to sell to regular customers at such a low price? These questions should be answered before a final decision is made.

HOW DO MANAGERS DECIDE WHICH PRODUCTS TO PRODUCE AND SELL?

Deciding which products to produce and sell is a major managerial decision. If manufacturing capacity is limited, managers must decide which products to produce. If shelf space is limited in the stores, then managers must decide which products to display and sell. Also, managers must often decide whether to drop products, departments, or territories that are not as profitable as desired. Let's look at how these decisions are made.

> **Learning Objective 3**
> Make decisions about dropping a product, product mix, and sales mix

Dropping Unprofitable Products and Segments

Some of the questions managers must consider when deciding whether to drop a product or a business segment, such as a department or territory, include:

- Does the product or segment provide a positive contribution margin?
- Will fixed costs continue to exist, even if the company drops the product or segment?
- Are there any direct fixed costs that can be avoided if the company drops the product or segment?
- Will dropping the product or segment affect sales of the company's other products?
- What would the company do with the freed manufacturing capacity or store space?

Once again, we follow the two key guidelines for short-term business decisions: (1) Focus on relevant data and (2) use a contribution margin approach. The relevant financial data are still the changes in revenues and expenses, but now we are considering a *decrease* in volume rather than an *increase*, as we did in the special pricing decision. In the following example, we consider how managers decide to drop a product. Managers would use the same process in deciding whether to drop a business segment, such as a department or territory.

Earlier, we focused on one of Smart Touch Learning's products—the Standard Tablet. Now we focus on two of its products—the Standard Tablet and the Premium Tablet. Exhibit 25-6 (on the next page) shows the company's budgeted contribution margin income statement by product, assuming fixed costs are shared by both products. The middle column shows the income for the Standard Tablets, as previously shown in Exhibit 25-4. Because the Premium Tablet product line, as shown in the third column, has an operating *loss* of $5,000, management is considering dropping the product.

Exhibit 25-6 | **Budgeted Income Statement by Product**

	Total	Standard Tablets	Premium Tablets
SMART TOUCH LEARNING Budgeted Income Statement Year Ended December 31, 2017			
Sales Revenue	$ 1,430,000	$ 1,200,000	$ 230,000
Variable Costs:			
Manufacturing	706,000	588,000	118,000
Selling & Administrative	172,000	150,000	22,000
Total Variable Costs	878,000	738,000	140,000
Contribution Margin	552,000	462,000	90,000
Fixed Costs:			
Manufacturing	180,000	110,000	70,000
Selling & Administrative	141,000	116,000	25,000
Total Fixed Costs	321,000	226,000	95,000
Operating Income (Loss)	$ 231,000	$ 236,000	$ (5,000)

The first question management should ask is "Does the product provide a positive contribution margin?" If the product has a negative contribution margin, then the product is not even covering its variable costs. Therefore, the company should drop the product. However, if the product has a positive contribution margin, then it is *helping* to cover some of the company's fixed costs. In Smart Touch Learning's case, the Premium Tablets provide a positive contribution margin of $90,000. Smart Touch Learning's managers now need to consider fixed costs.

The Effect of Fixed Costs

Smart Touch Learning could allocate fixed costs in many different ways, and each way would allocate a different amount of fixed costs to each product. For example, fixed costs could be allocated using a traditional method with direct labor hours as the allocation base, by using activity-based costing, or by using some other method. However, in the short term, many fixed costs remain unchanged in total regardless of how they are allocated to products or other cost objects. Therefore, allocated fixed costs are *irrelevant* except for any amounts that will change because of the decision that is made. What is relevant are the following:

1. Will the fixed costs continue to exist *even if* the product is dropped?
2. Are there any *direct* fixed costs of the Premium Tablets that can be avoided if the product is dropped?

Let's consider various assumptions when dropping products.

Fixed Costs Will Continue to Exist and Will Not Change Fixed costs that will continue to exist even after a product is dropped are often called *unavoidable* fixed costs. Unavoidable fixed costs are *irrelevant* to the decision because they *will not change* if the company drops the product. Let's assume that all of Smart Touch Learning's total fixed costs of $321,000 will continue to exist even if the company drops the Premium Tablets. Also assume that Smart Touch Learning makes the Premium Tablets in the same plant using the same machinery as the Standard Tablets. Thus, only the contribution margin the Premium Tablets provide is relevant. If Smart Touch Learning drops the Premium Tablets, it will lose the $90,000 contribution margin.

The differential analysis shown in Exhibit 25-7 verifies the loss. If Smart Touch Learning drops the Premium Tablets, revenue will decrease by $230,000, but variable expenses will decrease by only $140,000, resulting in a net $90,000 decrease in operating income. Because fixed costs are unaffected, they are not included in the analysis. This analysis suggests that management should *not* drop Premium Tablets. It is actually more beneficial for Smart Touch Learning to lose $5,000 on the product line than to drop the Premium Tablets and lose $90,000 in total operating income.

Exhibit 25-7 | Differential Analysis of Dropping a Product When Fixed Costs Will *Not* Change

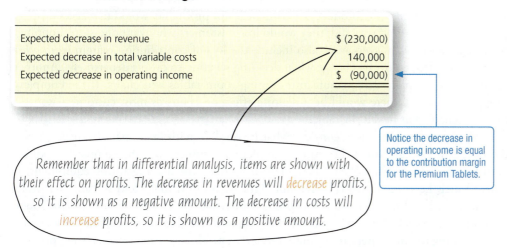

Expected decrease in revenue	$ (230,000)
Expected decrease in total variable costs	140,000
Expected *decrease* in operating income	$ (90,000)

Remember that in differential analysis, items are shown with their effect on profits. The decrease in revenues will decrease profits, so it is shown as a negative amount. The decrease in costs will increase profits, so it is shown as a positive amount.

Notice the decrease in operating income is equal to the contribution margin for the Premium Tablets.

Direct Fixed Costs Will Change In this scenario, instead assume Smart Touch Learning manufactures the Premium Tablets in a separate facility. If the product line is dropped, the lease on the facility can be terminated and the company will be able to avoid all fixed costs except $3,000. In this situation, $92,000 of the fixed costs belong *only* to the Premium Tablet product line ($95,000 total fixed costs − $3,000 unavoidable fixed costs = $92,000 avoidable fixed costs). These would be direct fixed costs of the Premium Tablets only.[1] Therefore, $92,000 of fixed costs are avoidable fixed costs and *are relevant* to the decision because they would change (go away) if the product line were dropped.

Exhibit 25-8 (on the next page) shows that, in this situation, operating income will *increase* by $2,000 if Smart Touch Learning drops the Premium Tablets. Revenues will decline by $230,000, but expenses will decline even more—by $232,000. The result is a net increase to operating income of $2,000. This analysis suggests that management should drop the Premium Tablets.

---

[1] To aid in decision making, companies should separate direct fixed costs from indirect fixed costs on their contribution margin income statements. Companies should *assign direct fixed costs* to the appropriate product and *not allocate indirect fixed costs* among products.

Exhibit 25-8 | **Differential Analysis of Dropping a Product When Fixed Costs *Will* Change**

Expected decrease in revenue		$ (230,000)
Expected decrease in total variable costs	$ 140,000	
Expected decrease in fixed costs	92,000	
Expected decrease in total costs		232,000
Expected *increase* in operating income		$ 2,000

Other Considerations

Management must also consider whether dropping the product or segment would hurt other product sales. In the examples given so far, we assumed that dropping the Premium Tablets would not affect Smart Touch Learning's other product sales. However, think about a grocery store. Even if the produce department is not profitable, would managers drop it? Probably not, because if they did, they would lose customers who want one-stop shopping. In such situations, managers must also include the loss of contribution margin from *other* departments affected by the change when deciding whether to drop a department. Another example is a company that manufactures dining room tables and chairs. If the company dropped the tables, there would be a definite effect on chairs as most customers want to purchase chairs that match the table.

Management should also consider what it could do with freed manufacturing capacity. In the first Smart Touch Learning example, we assumed that the company produces both Standard Tablets and Premium Tablets using the same manufacturing equipment. If Smart Touch Learning drops the Premium Tablets, could it make and sell another product using the freed machine hours? Is product demand strong enough that Smart Touch Learning could make and sell more of the Standard Tablets? Managers should consider whether using the machinery to produce a different product or expanding existing product lines would be more profitable than using the machinery to produce Premium Tablets.

Short-term business decisions should take into account all costs affected by the choice of action. Managers must ask the following questions: What total costs—variable and fixed—will change? Are there additional environmental costs (for example, waste water disposal) that should be considered? As Exhibits 25-7 and 25-8 show, the key to deciding whether to drop products or segments is to compare the lost revenue against the costs that can be saved and to consider what would be done with the freed capacity. The decision rule is as follows:

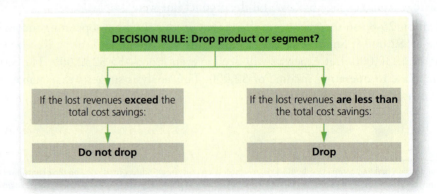

Product Mix

Companies do not have unlimited resources. **Constraints** that restrict the production or sale of a product vary from company to company. For a manufacturer like Smart Touch Learning, the production constraint may be labor hours, machine hours, or available materials. For a merchandiser, the primary constraint is display space. Other companies are constrained by sales demand. Competition may be stiff, and so the company may be able to sell only a limited number of units. In such cases, the company produces only as much as it can sell. However, if a company can sell all the units it can produce, which products should it emphasize? For which items should production be increased? Companies facing constraints consider the following questions:

- What constraint(s) stop(s) the company from making (or displaying) all the units the company can sell?
- Which products offer the highest contribution margin per unit of the constraint?
- Would emphasizing one product over another affect fixed costs?

Constraint
A factor that restricts the production or sale of a product.

Let's return to our Smart Touch Learning example. Assume the company can sell all the Standard Tablets and Premium Tablets it produces, but it has only 19,500 machine hours of manufacturing capacity, and the company uses the same machines to make both types of tablets. In this case, machine hours is the constraint. Note that this is a short-term decision because in the long run, Smart Touch Learning could expand its production facilities to meet sales demand if it made financial sense to do so. The data in Exhibit 25-9 suggest that Premium Tablets are more profitable than Standard Tablets as the Premium Tablets have a higher contribution margin per unit and a higher contribution margin ratio.

Exhibit 25-9 | **Smart Touch Learning's Contribution Margin per Product**

	Standard Tablet	Premium Tablet
Sales price per tablet	$ 500.00	$ 575.00
Variable costs per tablet	307.50	350.00
Contribution margin per tablet	**$ 192.50**	**$ 225.00**
Contribution margin ratio:		
Standard: $192.50 / $500.00	38.50%	
Premium: $225.00 / $575.00		39.13%*

*rounded

However, an important piece of information is missing—the time it takes to make each product. Assume that Standard Tablets require 7.5 machine hours to produce, and Premium Tablets require 10.0 machine hours to produce. *The company will incur the same fixed costs either way, so fixed costs are irrelevant.* Which product should it emphasize?

To maximize profits when fixed costs are irrelevant, follow the decision rule:

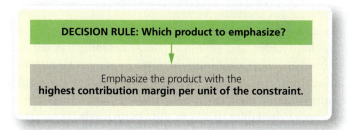

DECISION RULE: Which product to emphasize?

↓

Emphasize the product with the
highest contribution margin per unit of the constraint.

Because *machine hours* is the constraint, Smart Touch Learning needs to figure out which product has the *highest contribution margin per machine hour*. Exhibit 25-10 illustrates the calculation for the contribution margin per machine hour for each product.

Exhibit 25-10 | **Smart Touch Learning's Contribution Margin per Machine Hour**

	Standard Tablet	Premium Tablet
(1) Hours required to produce one tablet	7.5000	10.0000
(2) Tablets produced per hour [1 hour / (1)]	0.1333*	0.1000
(3) Contribution margin per tablet	$ 192.50	$ 225.00
Contribution margin per machine hour [(2) × (3)]	$ 25.66*	$ 22.50

*rounded

Standard Tablets have a higher contribution margin per machine hour, $25.66, than Premium Tablets, $22.50. Smart Touch Learning will earn more profit by producing Standard Tablets. Why? Because even though Standard Tablets have a lower contribution margin *per tablet*, Smart Touch Learning can make more Standard Tablets than Premium Tablets in the 19,500 available machine hours and generate more total contribution margin. Exhibit 25-11 proves that Smart Touch Learning earns more total profit by making Standard Tablets. Multiplying the contribution margin per machine hour by the available number of machine hours shows that Smart Touch Learning can earn $500,370 of contribution margin by producing only Standard Tablets but only $438,750 by producing only Premium Tablets.

Exhibit 25-11 | **Total Contribution Margin with Machine Hour Constraint**

	Standard Tablet	Premium Tablet
Contribution margin per machine hour	$ 25.66*	$ 22.50
Available capacity—number of machine hours	× 19,500	× 19,500
Total contribution margin at full capacity	$ 500,370	$ 438,750

*rounded

To maximize profits, Smart Touch Learning should make 2,600 Standard Tablets (19,500 machine hours available / 7.5 machine hours required per Standard Tablet) and zero Premium Tablets. Smart Touch Learning should not make Premium Tablets because for every machine hour spent making Premium Tablets, Smart Touch Learning would *give up* $3.16 of contribution margin ($25.66 per machine hour for Standard Tablets versus $22.50 per machine hour for Premium Tablets).

We made two assumptions here: (1) Smart Touch Learning's sales of other products will not be hurt by this decision and (2) Smart Touch Learning can sell as many Standard Tablets as it can produce. Let's challenge these assumptions. First, how could making only Standard Tablets hurt sales of other products? The retailers who display Smart Touch Learning tablet computers in their stores may want a choice in products so customers can compare and choose the tablet that best suits their needs. If Smart Touch Learning produces only one type of tablet, retailers may be reluctant to display the brand. Sales of Standard Tablets might fall if Smart Touch Learning no longer offers Premium Tablets.

Let's challenge our second assumption. Smart Touch Learning had only budgeted sales of 2,400 Standard Tablets and has the capacity to produce 2,600 (19,500 machine hours available / 7.5 machine hours required per Standard Tablet). Suppose that a new competitor has decreased the demand for Smart Touch Learning's Standard Tablets and now the company expects to sell only 2,000 Standard Tablets. Smart Touch Learning should only make as many Standard Tablets as it can sell and use the remaining machine hours to produce Premium Tablets. How will this constraint in sales demand change profitability?

Recall from Exhibit 25-11 that Smart Touch Learning will make $500,370 of contribution margin by using all 19,500 machine hours to produce Standard Tablets. However, if Smart Touch Learning makes only 2,000 Standard Tablets, it will use only 15,000 machine hours (2,000 Standard Tablets × 7.5 machine hours required per Standard Tablet). That leaves 4,500 machine hours (19,500 machine hours − 15,000 machine hours) available for making Premium Tablets, which will allow the company to make 450 Premium Tablets (4,500 machine hours / 10.0 machine hours required per Premium Tablet). Smart Touch Learning's new contribution margin will be $486,150, as shown in Exhibit 25-12.

Exhibit 25-12 | Total Contribution Margin with Machine Hour Constraint and Limited Market

	Standard Tablet	Premium Tablet	Total
Contribution margin per machine hour	$ 25.66*	$ 22.50	
Machine hours devoted to product	× 15,000	× 4,500	19,500
Total contribution margin at full capacity	$ 384,900	$ 101,250	$ 486,150

*rounded

Because of the change in product mix, Smart Touch Learning's total contribution margin will fall from $500,370 to $486,150, a $14,220 decrease. Smart Touch Learning had to give up $3.16 of contribution margin per machine hour ($25.66 − $22.50) on the 4,500 hours it spent producing Premium Tablets rather than Standard Tablets. However, Smart Touch Learning had no choice—the company would have incurred an *actual loss* from producing Standard Tablets that it could not sell. If Smart Touch Learning had produced 2,600 Standard Tablets but sold only 2,000, the company would have spent $184,500 to make the unsold tablets (600 Standard Tablets × $307.50 variable cost per Standard Tablet) yet received no sales revenue from them.

What about fixed costs? In most cases, changing the product mix emphasis in the short run will not affect fixed costs, so fixed costs are irrelevant. However, it is possible that fixed costs could differ by emphasizing a different product mix. What if Smart Touch Learning had a month-to-month lease on a production machine used only for making Premium Tablets? If Smart Touch Learning made only Standard Tablets, it could *avoid* the production equipment cost. However, if Smart Touch Learning makes any Premium Tablets, it needs the equipment. In this case, the fixed costs become relevant because they differ between alternative product mixes (Premium Tablets only *versus* Standard Tablets only *versus* both products).

Notice that the analysis again follows the two guidelines for short-term business decisions: (1) Focus on relevant data (only those revenues and costs that differ) and (2) use a contribution margin approach, which separates variable costs from fixed costs.

Sales Mix

The previous illustrations focused on production constraints for a manufacturing company. Merchandising companies also have constraints, with display space as the most common constraint. Merchandisers are constrained by the size of their stores, and managers must choose which products to display.

Because Smart Touch Learning's Standard and Premium Tablets require the same amount of shelf space, let's consider Bragg Company, a fictitious company that operates gift shops in airports. Airport gift shops are fairly small, and Bragg has only 48 linear feet of bookshelves in each store. The following chart shows the *average* sales price, cost of purchasing the books, which is a variable cost, and contribution margin for hardcover and paperback books:

	Hardcover Books	Paperback Books
Sales Price	$ 28.00	$ 12.00
Variable Cost	19.60	7.20
Contribution Margin	$ 8.40	$ 4.80

Fixed costs are not affected by the choice of products to display. Based only on this information, it is apparent that hardcover books have a higher contribution margin per unit and should be the product emphasized. However, managers also have to consider the constraint of limited shelf space. Management at Bragg has determined that each linear foot of bookshelves can display 10 hardcover books or 20 paperback books. Remember that the decision rule for constraints is to *emphasize the product with the highest contribution margin per unit of the constraint.* Exhibit 25-13 shows the total contribution margin with the display space constraint.

Exhibit 25-13 | **Total Contribution Margin with Display Space Constraint**

	Hardcover Books	Paperback Books
Contribution margin per book	$ 8.40	$ 4.80
Books per linear foot of display space	× 10	× 20
Total contribution margin per linear foot of display space	$ 84.00	$ 96.00

Bragg can generate more profits per foot of shelving if paperback books are displayed. Therefore, the company should emphasize paperback books. However, Bragg should also consider the market—what do airport shoppers want? Bragg can display twice as many paperback books than hardcover books. Will the increased variety of titles displayed increase sales and inventory turnover? Will it lose sales if only paperback books are displayed? Other factors must also be considered when making sales mix decisions.

McCollum Company manufactures two products. Both products have the same sales price, and the volume of sales is equivalent. However, due to the difference in production processes, Product A has higher variable costs and Product B has higher fixed costs. Management is considering dropping Product B because that product line has an operating loss.

McCOLLUM COMPANY Income Statement Month Ended June 30, 2016			
	Total	Product A	Product B
Sales Revenue	$ 150,000	$ 75,000	$ 75,000
Variable Costs	90,000	55,000	35,000
Contribution Margin	60,000	20,000	40,000
Fixed Costs	50,000	5,000	45,000
Operating Income/(Loss)	$ 10,000	$ 15,000	$ (5,000)

9. If fixed costs cannot be avoided, should McCollum drop Product B? Why or why not?
10. If 50% of Product B's fixed costs are avoidable, should McCollum drop Product B? Why or why not?

Check your answers online in MyAccountingLab or at http://www.pearsonhighered.com/Horngren.

For more practice, see Short Exercises S25-4 and S25-5. MyAccountingLab

HOW DO MANAGERS MAKE OUTSOURCING AND PROCESSING FURTHER DECISIONS?

Now let's consider some short-term management decisions regarding how products are produced, such as whether the company should outsource a component of the finished product or sell a product as it is or process it further.

Learning Objective 4

Make outsourcing and processing further decisions

Outsourcing

Many companies choose to outsource products or services. For example, a hotel chain may outsource its reservation system. This allows the company to concentrate on its primary function—serving the needs of its guests—rather than purchasing and operating an extensive computerized reservation system. By outsourcing, the hotel chain is taking advantage of another company's expertise, which allows it to focus on its core business function. Outsourcing decisions are often called make-or-buy decisions because managers must decide whether to buy a component product or service or produce it in-house. The heart of these decisions is *how best to use available resources.*

Smart Touch Learning is deciding whether to make the casings for its tablet computers in-house or to outsource them to Crump Casings, a company that specializes in producing

casings for computers, cell phones, and other electronic products. Smart Touch Learning's cost to produce 2,400 casings is as follows:

Direct materials	$ 15,600
Direct labor	7,200
Variable manufacturing overhead	13,200
Fixed manufacturing overhead	19,200
Total manufacturing cost	$ 55,200
Number of casings	÷ 2,400
Cost per casing	$ 23

Crump Casings offers to sell Smart Touch Learning the casings for $21 each. Should Smart Touch Learning make the casings or buy them from Crump Casings? Smart Touch Learning's $23 cost per unit to make the casing is $2 higher than the cost of buying it from Crump Casings. Initially, it seems that Smart Touch Learning should outsource the casings, but the correct answer is not so simple because manufacturing costs per unit contain both fixed and variable components. In deciding whether to outsource, managers must assess fixed and variable costs separately. Some of the questions managers must consider when deciding whether to outsource include:

• How do the company's variable costs compare with the outsourcing costs?

• Are any fixed costs avoidable if the company outsources?

• What could the company do with the freed manufacturing capacity?

How do these considerations apply to Smart Touch Learning? By purchasing the casings, Smart Touch Learning can avoid all variable manufacturing costs—$15,600 of direct materials, $7,200 of direct labor, and $13,200 of variable manufacturing overhead. In total, the company will save $36,000 in variable manufacturing costs, or $15 per casing ($36,000 / 2,400 casings). However, Smart Touch Learning will have to pay the variable outsourcing cost of $21 per unit, or $50,400 for the 2,400 casings. Based only on variable costs, the lower cost alternative is to manufacture the casings in-house. However, managers must still consider fixed costs.

Assume, first, that Smart Touch Learning cannot avoid any of the fixed costs by outsourcing. In this case, the company's fixed costs are irrelevant to the decision because Smart Touch Learning would continue to incur $19,200 of fixed costs either way (the fixed costs do not differ between alternatives). Smart Touch Learning should continue to make its own casings because the variable cost of outsourcing the casings, $50,400, exceeds the variable cost of making the casings, $36,000. Exhibit 25-14 shows the differential analysis for the outsourcing decision.

Exhibit 25-14 | **Differential Analysis for Outsourcing Decision When Fixed Costs Will _Not_ Change**

Casing Costs	Make Casings	Outsource Casings	Difference (Make – Outsource)
Variable costs:			
Direct materials	$ 15,600		$ 15,600
Direct labor	7,200		7,200
Variable manufacturing overhead	13,200		13,200
Purchase cost ($21 × 2,400 casings)		$ 50,400	(50,400)
Total differential cost of casings	$ 36,000	$ 50,400	$ (14,400)

The Difference column shows the effect on profits. If Smart Touch Learning buys the casings, it will save (not spend, avoid) the variable manufacturing costs. If the company saves costs, that will increase profits, so the difference is shown as a positive amount. The amount spent to buy the casings is a cost that will decrease profits, so it is shown as a negative amount.

However, what if Smart Touch Learning can avoid some fixed costs by outsourcing the casings? Assume that management can reduce fixed overhead cost by $12,000 by outsourcing the casings. Smart Touch Learning will still incur $7,200 of fixed overhead ($19,200 − $12,000) if it outsources the casings. In this case, fixed costs become relevant to the decision because they differ between alternatives. Exhibit 25-15 shows the differential analysis when fixed costs will change.

Exhibit 25-15 | **Differential Analysis for Outsourcing Decision When Fixed Costs _Will_ Change**

Casing Costs	Make Casings	Outsource Casings	Difference (Make – Outsource)
Variable costs:			
Direct materials	$ 15,600		$ 15,600
Direct labor	7,200		7,200
Variable manufacturing overhead	13,200		13,200
Fixed manufacturing overhead costs	12,000		12,000
Purchase cost ($21 × 2,400 casings)		$ 50,400	(50,400)
Total differential cost of casings	$ 48,000	$ 50,400	$ (2,400)

Another way to think about it: Should Smart Touch Learning spend $50,400 in order to save $48,000? Absolutely not!

Exhibit 25-15 shows that even with the $12,000 reduction in fixed costs, it would still cost Smart Touch Learning less to make the casings than to buy them from Crump Casings. The net savings from making the casings is $2,400. Exhibit 25-15 also shows that outsourcing decisions follow our two key guidelines for short-term business decisions: (1) Focus on relevant data (differences in costs in this case) and (2) use a contribution margin approach that separates variable costs from fixed costs.

Note how the unit cost—which does *not* separate costs according to behavior—can be deceiving. If Smart Touch Learning's managers made their decision by comparing the total manufacturing cost per casing ($23) to the outsourcing unit cost per casing ($21), they would have incorrectly decided to outsource. Recall that the manufacturing unit cost ($23) contains both fixed and variable components, whereas the outsourcing cost ($21) is strictly variable. To make the correct decision, Smart Touch Learning had to separate the two cost components and analyze them separately.

Our decision rule for outsourcing is as follows:

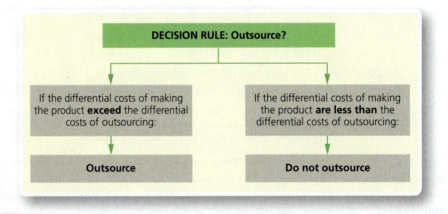

We have not considered what Smart Touch Learning could do with the freed manufacturing capacity it would have if it outsourced the casings. The analysis in Exhibit 25-15 assumes there is no other use for the production facilities if Smart Touch Learning buys the casings from Crump Casings. But suppose Smart Touch Learning has an opportunity to use its freed-up facilities to make another product, which has an expected profit of $30,000. Now, Smart Touch Learning must consider its **opportunity cost**—the benefit given up by choosing an alternative course of action. In this case, Smart Touch Learning's opportunity cost of making the casings is the $30,000 profit it gives up if it does not free its production facilities to make the new product.

Smart Touch Learning's managers must now consider three alternatives:

1. Use the facilities to make the casings.
2. Buy the casings and leave facilities idle (continue to assume $12,000 of avoidable fixed costs from outsourcing casings).
3. Buy the casings and use facilities to make the new product (continue to assume $12,000 of avoidable fixed costs from outsourcing casings).

The alternative with the lowest *net* cost is the best use of Smart Touch Learning's facilities. Exhibit 25-16 compares the three alternatives.

In this scenario, Smart Touch Learning should buy the casings from Crump Casings and use the freed manufacturing capacity to make the new product. If Smart Touch Learning makes the casings or if it buys the casings from Crump Casings but leaves its production facilities idle, it will give up the opportunity to earn an additional $30,000.

Opportunity Cost
The benefit given up by choosing an alternative course of action.

Exhibit 25-16 | **Differential Analysis for Outsourcing Decision When Fixed Costs *Will* Change and Opportunity Cost Exists**

	Make Casings	Outsource Casings	
		Facilities Idle	Make New Product
Expected cost of 2,400 casings (from Exhibit 25-15)	$ 48,000	$ 50,400	$ 50,400
Expected *profit* from new product			(30,000)
Expected **net cost** of obtaining 2,400 casings	$ 48,000	$ 50,400	$ 20,400

> This analysis shows the net cost of the three alternatives. The $30,000 of expected profit from using the freed manufacturing space will increase overall profits if the company chooses to buy the casings, thereby decreasing net costs.

Smart Touch Learning's managers should consider qualitative factors as well as revenue and cost differences in making their final decision. For example, Smart Touch Learning's managers may believe they can better control quality by making the casings themselves. This is an argument for Smart Touch Learning to continue making the casings.

Outsourcing decisions are increasingly important in today's global economy. In the past, make-or-buy decisions often ended up as "make" because coordination, information exchange, and paperwork problems made buying from suppliers too inconvenient. Now, companies can use the Internet to tap into information systems of suppliers and customers located around the world. Paperwork vanishes, and information required to satisfy the strictest JIT delivery schedule is available in real time. As a result, companies are focusing on their core competencies and are outsourcing more functions.

ETHICS

Is this cost too good to be true?

Dale Tripp, purchasing manager at ABC Products, reviewed the cost report one more time. Dale's brother-in-law, Kyle Marcum, wanted Dale to accept a bid from his company to supply a component to a product ABC manufactured. Kyle assured Dale the component was top quality and on-time delivery would never be a problem. Dale was uncertain, however, because the cost Kyle quoted was significantly lower than ABC's current cost to produce the part. Dale had heard rumors in the past that Kyle's company would "lowball" offers to win bids and then raise prices soon after. Dale is concerned Kyle's company will sell the component at the low cost for only a short period of time and then start charging an amount that is higher than ABC's current cost to produce the component. What should Dale do? What would you do?

Solution

Dale should discuss the bid with his supervisor and make sure his supervisor is aware the bid is from a company owned by his brother-in-law. Failure to disclose the relationship may cause Dale's supervisor to question Dale's integrity if the fact is uncovered at a later date. Dale should also discuss the rumors he has heard. While there may not be any truth to them, Dale should not withhold the information. If ABC decides to accept the bid, then Dale should ask for a contract that would guarantee the cost for a specific period of time. The contract would protect ABC from unexpected cost increases.

Sell or Process Further

At what point in processing should a company sell its product? Many companies, especially in the food processing and natural resource industries, face this business decision. Companies in these industries process a raw material (milk, corn, livestock, crude oil, and lumber, to name a few) to a point before it is saleable. For example, a dairy processor pasteurizes raw milk before it is saleable. The company must then decide whether it should sell the pasteurized milk as is or process it further into other dairy products, such as reduced-fat milk, butter, sour cream, cheese, and other dairy products. Some questions managers consider when deciding whether to sell as is or process further include:

- How much revenue will the company receive if it sells the product as is?
- How much revenue will the company receive if it sells the product after processing it further?
- How much will it cost to process the product further?

Consider one of Smart Touch Learning's sell or process further decisions. Suppose Smart Touch Learning can sell its tablet computers as is or add front-accessible USB ports to the tablets. The cost to add the USB ports is $5. This cost includes the cost of the modified casing, the USB component, and the labor to add the component. This feature is very popular with customers, and tablets with this feature sell for $20 more than tablets without the feature. Exhibit 25-17 shows the differential analysis for this decision.

Exhibit 25-17 | **Differential Analysis for Sell or Process Further Decision**

	Sell	Process Further	Difference
Expected revenue from selling (2,400 tablets × $500 each)	$ 1,200,000		
Expected revenue from selling (2,400 tablets × $520 each)		$ 1,248,000	$ 48,000
Additional costs of processing (2,400 tablets × $5 each)		(12,000)	(12,000)
Total net revenue	$ 1,200,000	$ 1,236,000	$ 36,000

Joint Cost
A cost of a production process that yields multiple products.

Notice that Smart Touch Learning's managers do *not* consider the other costs incurred in producing the tablets, $964,000 as shown in Exhibit 25-3 ($738,000 variable costs + $226,000 fixed costs). These costs are **joint costs**—costs of a production process that yields multiple products. (In this case, the multiple products are the tablets without the feature and the tablets with the feature.) Joint costs are *sunk* costs. Recall from our previous discussion that a sunk cost is a past cost that cannot be changed regardless of which future action the company takes. Smart Touch Learning has incurred the joint costs, regardless of whether it sells the tablets as is or processes them further by adding the front-accessible USB ports. Therefore, the joint costs are *not* relevant to the decision. Exhibit 25-18 illustrates joint costs.

Exhibit 25-18 | **Joint Costs**

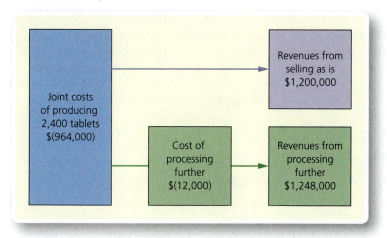

By analyzing only the relevant costs in Exhibit 25-17, managers see that they can increase profit by $36,000 if they add the USB ports. The $48,000 additional revenue ($1,248,000 − $1,200,000) outweighs the additional $12,000 cost of the extra processing.

Thus, the decision rule is as follows:

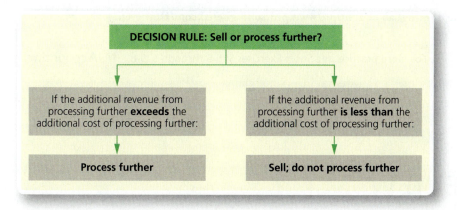

Recall that our keys to decision making include: (1) Focusing on relevant information and (2) using a contribution margin approach that separates variable costs from fixed costs. The analysis in Exhibit 25-18 includes only those *future* costs and revenues that *differ* between alternatives. We assumed Smart Touch Learning already has the equipment and labor necessary to add the additional feature to the tablets. Because fixed costs would not differ between alternatives, they were irrelevant. However, if Smart Touch Learning has to acquire equipment to add the feature, the extra fixed costs would be relevant. Once again, we see that fixed costs are relevant only if they *differ* between alternatives.

Try It!

Grimm Company makes wedding cakes. The company is considering buying the cakes rather than baking them, which will allow it to concentrate on decorating. The company averages 100 wedding cakes per year and incurs the following costs from baking wedding cakes:

Direct materials	$ 500
Direct labor	1,000
Variable manufacturing overhead	200
Fixed manufacturing overhead	1,200
Total manufacturing cost	$ 2,900
Number of cakes	÷ 100
Cost per cake	$ 29

Fixed costs are primarily the depreciation on kitchen equipment such as ovens and mixers. Grimm expects to retain the equipment. Grimm can buy the cakes for $25.

11. Should Grimm make the cakes or buy them? Why?
12. If Grimm decides to buy the cakes, what are some qualitative factors that Grimm should also consider?

Check your answers online in MyAccountingLab or at http://www.pearsonhighered.com/Horngren.

For more practice, see Short Exercises S25-6 through S25-8. MyAccountingLab

REVIEW

> Things You Should Know

1. **How is relevant information used to make short-term decisions?**

   ■ Decision making is a four-step process:
   • Define business goals.
   • Identify alternative courses of action.
   • Gather and analyze relevant information; compare alternatives.
   • Choose the best alternative.

   ■ Relevant information is expected *future* data that *differ* among alternatives.

   ■ Sunk costs occurred in the past and cannot be changed; therefore, they are irrelevant in making decisions.

   ■ Qualitative factors are nonfinancial and can also be relevant.

   ■ Differential analysis emphasizes the differences in operating income under each alternative.

- Two keys in analyzing short-term business decisions are:
  - Focus on relevant revenues, costs, and profits.
  - Use a contribution margin approach that separates variable costs from fixed costs.

2. How does pricing affect short-term decisions?

- When setting *regular* prices, managers should consider the following:
  - What is the company's target profit?
  - How much will customers pay?
  - Is the company a price-taker or a price-setter for this product or service?
- Price-takers have little control over the prices of their products and services because they are not unique or competition is intense.
  - Price-takers must "take" the market price.
  - The pricing approach emphasizes target pricing where:

    Revenue at market price − Desired profit = Target full product cost.
- Price-setters have more control over the prices of their products because they are unique and there is little competition.
  - Price-setters can "set" the market price.
  - The pricing approach emphasizes cost-plus pricing where:

    Full product cost + Desired profit = Cost-plus price.
- When setting *special* prices, managers should consider the following:
  - Does the company have the excess capacity available to fill the order?
  - Will the reduced sales price be high enough to cover the *differential* costs of filling the order?
  - Will the special order affect regular sales in the long run?
- Remember the special pricing decision rule:
  - If the expected increase in revenues **exceeds** the expected increase in variable and fixed costs, **accept** the special pricing order.
  - If the expected increase in revenues **is less than** the expected increase in variable and fixed costs, **reject** the special pricing order.

3. How do managers decide which products to produce and sell?

- When deciding whether to drop a product or a business segment, such as a department or territory, questions managers should answer include the following:
  - Does the product or segment provide a positive contribution margin?
  - Will fixed costs continue to exist even if the company drops the product or segment?
  - Are there any direct fixed costs that can be avoided if the company drops the product or segment?
  - Will dropping the product or segment affect sales of the company's other products?
  - What would the company do with the freed manufacturing capacity or store space?
- Remember the decision rule for dropping a product or segment:
  - If the lost revenues **exceed** the total cost savings, **do not drop** the product or segment.
  - If the lost revenues **are less than** the total cost savings, **drop** the product or segment.

CHAPTER 25

- Companies facing constraints consider the following questions:
  - What constraint(s) stop(s) the company from making (or displaying) all the units the company can sell?
  - Which products offer the highest contribution margin per unit of the constraint?
  - Would emphasizing one product over another affect fixed costs?
- Remember the decision rule for which product to emphasize: Emphasize the product with the **highest contribution margin per unit of the constraint**.
- For merchandising companies, display space is often the most common constraint.

4. **How do managers make outsourcing and processing further decisions?**

- Some of the questions managers must consider when deciding whether to outsource include the following:
  - How do the company's variable costs compare with the outsourcing costs?
  - Are any fixed costs avoidable if the company outsources?
  - What could the company do with the freed manufacturing capacity?
- Remember the outsourcing decision rule:
  - If the differential costs of making the product **exceed** the differential costs of outsourcing, **outsource**.
  - If the differential costs of making the product **are less than** the differential costs of outsourcing, **do not outsource**.
- Some questions managers consider when deciding whether to sell as is or process further include:
  - How much revenue will the company receive if it sells the product as is?
  - How much revenue will the company receive if it sells the product after processing it further?
  - How much will it cost to process the product further?
- Joint costs, the cost of production that yields multiple products, are sunk costs and, therefore, are not relevant to the decision of processing further.
- Remember the sell or process further decision rule:
  - If the additional revenue from processing further **exceeds** the additional cost of processing further, **process further**.
  - If the additional revenue from processing further **is less than** the additional cost of processing further, **sell—do not process further**.

> Summary Problem 25-1

MC Alexander Industries makes tennis balls. Its only plant can produce as many as 2,500,000 cans of tennis balls per year. Current production is 2,000,000 cans. Annual manufacturing, selling, and administrative fixed costs total $700,000. The variable cost of making and selling each can of tennis balls is $1.00. Stockholders expect a 12% annual return on the company's $3,000,000 of assets.

Requirements

1. What is MC Alexander's current full product cost of making and selling 2,000,000 cans of tennis balls? What is the current full *unit* product cost of each can of tennis balls?

2. Assume MC Alexander is a price-taker, and the current market price is $1.45 per can of tennis balls (the price at which manufacturers sell to retailers). What is the *target* full product cost of producing and selling 2,000,000 cans of tennis balls? Given MC Alexander's current costs, will the company reach the stockholders' profit goals?

3. If MC Alexander cannot change its fixed costs, what is the target variable cost per can of tennis balls?

4. Suppose MC Alexander could spend an extra $100,000 on advertising to differentiate its product so that it could be a price-setter. Assuming the original volume and costs, plus the $100,000 of new advertising costs, what cost-plus price will MC Alexander want to charge for a can of tennis balls?

5. Nelson, Inc. has just asked MC Alexander to supply the company with 400,000 cans of tennis balls at a special order price of $1.20 per can. Nelson wants MC Alexander to package the tennis balls under the Nelson label (MC Alexander will imprint the Nelson logo on each tennis ball and can). MC Alexander will have to spend $10,000 to change the packaging machinery. Assuming the original volume and costs, should MC Alexander accept this special order? (Assume MC Alexander will incur variable selling costs as well as variable manufacturing costs related to this order.)

> Solution

Requirement 1

The full product cost per unit is as follows:

Fixed costs	$ 700,000
Plus: Total variable costs (2,000,000 cans × $1.00 per can)	2,000,000
Total full product costs	$ 2,700,000
Divided by the number of cans	÷ 2,000,000
Full product cost per can	$ 1.35

Requirement 2

The target full product cost is as follows:

Revenue at market price	(2,000,000 cans × $1.45 per can)	$ 2,900,000
Less: Desired profit	(12% × $3,000,000 of assets)	360,000
Target full product cost		$ 2,540,000

MC Alexander's current total full product costs ($2,700,000 from Requirement 1) are $160,000 higher than the target full product cost ($2,540,000). If MC Alexander cannot reduce product costs, it will not be able to meet stockholders' profit expectations.

CHAPTER 25

Requirement 3

Assuming MC Alexander cannot reduce its fixed costs, the target variable cost per can is as follows:

Target full product cost (from Requirement 2)	$ 2,540,000
Less: Fixed costs	700,000
Target total variable costs	$ 1,840,000
Divided by the number of cans	÷ 2,000,000
Target variable cost per can	$ 0.92

Because MC Alexander cannot reduce its fixed costs, it needs to reduce variable costs by $0.08 per can ($1.00 − $0.92) to meet its profit goals. This would require an 8% cost reduction, which may not be possible.

Requirement 4

If MC Alexander can differentiate its tennis balls, it will gain more control over pricing. The company's new cost-plus price would be as follows:

Current total costs (from Requirement 1)	$ 2,700,000
Plus: Additional cost of advertising	100,000
Plus: Desired profit (from Requirement 2)	360,000
Target revenue	$ 3,160,000
Divided by the number of cans	2,000,000
Cost-plus price per can	$ 1.58

MC Alexander must study the market to determine whether retailers would pay $1.58 per can of tennis balls.

Requirement 5

Nelson's special order price ($1.20) is less than the current full product cost of each can of tennis balls ($1.35 from Requirement 1). However, this should not influence management's decision. MC Alexander could fill Nelson's special order using existing excess capacity. MC Alexander takes a differential analysis approach to its decision, comparing the extra revenue with the differential costs of accepting the order. Variable costs will increase if MC Alexander accepts the order, so the variable costs are relevant. Only the *additional* fixed costs of changing the packaging machine ($10,000) are relevant because all other fixed costs will remain unchanged.

Revenue from special order	(400,000 cans × $1.20 per can)	$ 480,000
Less: Variable costs of special order	(400,000 cans × $1.00 per can)	400,000
Contribution margin from special order		80,000
Less: Additional fixed costs of special order		10,000
Operating income provided by special order		$ 70,000

MC Alexander should accept the special order because it will increase operating income by $70,000. However, MC Alexander also needs to consider whether its regular customers will find out about the special price and demand lower prices, too.

> Summary Problem 25-2

Shelly's Shades produces standard and deluxe sunglasses:

	Standard	Deluxe
Sales price per pair	$ 20	$ 30
Variable expenses per pair	16	21

The company has 15,000 machine hours available. In one machine hour, Shelly's can produce 70 pairs of the standard model or 30 pairs of the deluxe model.

Requirements

1. Which model should Shelly's emphasize?
2. Shelly's also produces a third product: sport sunglasses. Shelly's incurs the following costs for 20,000 pairs of its sport sunglasses:

Direct materials	$ 20,000
Direct labor	80,000
Variable manufacturing overhead	40,000
Fixed manufacturing overhead	80,000
Total manufacturing cost	$ 220,000
Divided by number of pairs	÷ 20,000
Cost per pair	$ 11

Another manufacturer has offered to sell similar sunglasses to Shelly's for $10 per unit, a total purchase cost of $200,000. If Shelly's outsources *and* leaves its plant idle, it can save $50,000 of fixed overhead costs. Or it can use the freed manufacturing facilities to make other products that will contribute $70,000 to profits. In this case, the company will not be able to avoid any fixed costs. Identify and analyze the alternatives. What is the best course of action?

> Solution

Requirement 1

	Standard		Deluxe	
Sales price per pair	$	20	$	30
Less: Variable expenses per pair		16		21
Contribution margin per pair	$	4	$	9
Units produced each machine hour		× 70		× 30
Contribution margin per machine hour	$	280	$	270
Capacity—number of machine hours		× 15,000		× 15,000
Total contribution margin at full capacity	$ 4,200,000		$ 4,050,000	

Decision: Emphasize the standard model because it has the higher contribution margin per unit of the constraint—machine hours.

Requirement 2

		Buy Sunglasses	
	Make Sunglasses	Facilities Idle	Make Other Products
Relevant Costs:			
Direct materials	$ 20,000		
Direct labor	80,000		
Variable overhead	40,000		
Fixed overhead	50,000		$ 50,000
Purchase cost (20,000 pairs × $10 per pair)		$ 200,000	200,000
Total cost of obtaining sunglasses	190,000	200,000	250,000
Profit from other products			(70,000)
Net cost of obtaining sunglasses	$ 190,000	$ 200,000	$ 180,000

Decision: Shelly's should buy the sunglasses from the outside supplier and use the freed manufacturing facilities to make other products.

> Key Terms

Constraint (p. 1393)

Cost-Plus Pricing (p. 1384)

Differential Analysis (p. 1379)

Irrelevant Cost (p. 1379)

Joint Cost (p. 1402)

Opportunity Cost (p. 1400)

Price-Setter (p. 1381)

Price-Taker (p. 1381)

Relevant Cost (p. 1378)

Relevant Information (p. 1378)

Sunk Cost (p. 1379)

Target Full Product Cost (p. 1382)

Target Pricing (p. 1382)

> Quick Check

Learning Objective 1

1. In making short-term business decisions, what should you do?
   a. Use a traditional costing approach.
   b. Focus on total costs.
   c. Separate variable from fixed costs.
   d. Focus only on quantitative factors.

Learning Objective 1

2. Which of the following is relevant to Kitchenware.com's decision to accept a special order at a lower sale price from a large customer in China?
   a. The cost of shipping the order to the customer
   b. The cost of Kitchenware.com's warehouses in the United States
   c. Founder Eric Crowley's salary
   d. Kitchenware.com's investment in its Web site

3. Which of the following costs are irrelevant to business decisions?   **Learning Objective 1**

   a. Avoidable costs   **c.** Sunk costs

   b. Costs that differ between alternatives   **d.** Variable costs

4. When making decisions, managers should consider   **Learning Objective 1**

   a. revenues that differ between alternatives.

   b. costs that do not differ between alternatives.

   c. only variable costs.

   d. sunk costs in their decisions.

5. When pricing a product or service, managers must consider which of the following?   **Learning Objective 2**

   a. Only period costs   **c.** Only variable costs

   b. Only manufacturing costs   **d.** All costs

6. When companies are price-setters, their products and services   **Learning Objective 2**

   a. are priced by managers using a target-pricing emphasis.

   b. tend to have a lot of competitors.

   c. tend to be commodities.

   d. tend to be unique.

7. In deciding whether to drop its electronics product line, Smith Company should consider   **Learning Objective 3**

   a. how dropping the electronics product line would affect sales of its other products.

   b. the costs it could save by dropping the product line.

   c. the revenues it would lose from dropping the product line.

   d. All of the above.

8. In deciding which product lines to emphasize when a production constraint exists, the company should focus on the product line that has the highest   **Learning Objective 3**

   a. contribution margin per unit of product.

   b. contribution margin per unit of the constraint.

   c. profit per unit of product.

   d. contribution margin ratio.

9. When making outsourcing decisions, which of the following is true?   **Learning Objective 4**

   a. Expected use of the freed capacity is irrelevant.

   b. The variable cost of producing the product in-house is relevant.

   c. The total manufacturing unit cost of making the product in-house is relevant.

   d. Avoidable fixed costs are irrelevant.

10. When deciding whether to sell as is or process a product further, managers should ignore which of the following?   **Learning Objective 4**

    a. The costs of processing the product thus far

    b. The cost of processing further

    c. The revenue if the product is sold as is

    d. The revenue if the product is processed further

Check your answers at the end of the chapter.

CHAPTER 25

ASSESS YOUR PROGRESS

> Review Questions

1. List the four steps in short-term decision making. At which step are managerial accountants most involved?

2. What makes information relevant to decision making?

3. What makes information irrelevant to decision making?

4. What are sunk costs? Give an example.

5. When is nonfinancial information relevant?

6. What is differential analysis?

7. What are the two keys in short-term decision making?

8. What questions should managers answer when setting regular prices?

9. Explain the difference between price-takers and price-setters.

10. What is target pricing? Who uses it?

11. What does the target full product cost include?

12. What is cost-plus pricing? Who uses it?

13. What questions should managers answer when considering special pricing orders?

14. When completing a differential analysis, when are the differences shown as positive amounts? As negative amounts?

15. When should special pricing orders be accepted?

16. What questions should managers answer when considering dropping a product or segment?

17. Explain why a segment with an operating loss can cause the company to have a decrease in total operating income if the segment is dropped.

18. What is a constraint?

19. What questions should managers answer when facing constraints?

20. What is the decision rule concerning products to emphasize when facing a constraint?

21. What is the most common constraint faced by merchandisers?

22. What is outsourcing?

23. What questions should managers answer when considering outsourcing?

24. What questions should managers answer when considering selling a product as is or processing further?

25. What are joint costs? How do they affect the sell or process further decision?

26. What is the decision rule for selling a product as is or processing it further?

> Short Exercises

Learning Objective 1

S25-1 Describing and identifying information relevant to business decisions

You are trying to decide whether to trade in your inkjet printer for a more recent model. Your usage pattern will remain unchanged, but the old and new printers use different ink cartridges.

Indicate if the following items are relevant or irrelevant to your decision:

a. The price of the new printer

b. The price paid for the old printer

c. The trade-in value of the old printer

d. Paper cost

e. The difference between ink cartridges' costs

S25-2 Making pricing decisions

Learning Objective 2

Mountain Run operates a Rocky Mountain ski resort. The company is planning its lift ticket pricing for the coming ski season. Investors would like to earn a 12% return on investment on the company's $111,000,000 of assets. The company primarily incurs fixed costs to groom the runs and operate the lifts. Mountain Run projects fixed costs to be $37,000,000 for the ski season. The resort serves about 680,000 skiers and snowboarders each season. Variable costs are about $8 per guest. Currently, the resort has such a favorable reputation among skiers and snowboarders that it has some control over the lift ticket prices.

Requirements

1. Would Mountain Run emphasize target pricing or cost-plus pricing? Why?

2. If other resorts in the area charge $80 per day, what price should Mountain Run charge?

Note: Short Exercise S25-2 must be completed before attempting Short Exercise S25-3.

S25-3 Making pricing decisions

Learning Objective 2

Refer to details about Mountain Run from Short Exercise S25-2. Assume that Mountain Run's reputation has diminished and other resorts in the vicinity are charging only $80 per lift ticket. Mountain Run has become a price-taker and will not be able to charge more than its competitors. At the market price, Mountain Run managers believe they will still serve 680,000 skiers and snowboarders each season.

Requirements

1. If Mountain Run cannot reduce its costs, what profit will it earn? State your answer in dollars and as a percent of assets. Will investors be happy with the profit level?

2. Assume Mountain Run has found ways to cut its fixed costs to $36,320,000. What is its new target variable cost per skier/snowboarder?

CHAPTER 25

Learning Objective 3

S25-4 Making dropping a product or segment decisions

Gila Fashions operates three departments: Men's, Women's, and Accessories. Departmental operating income data for the third quarter of 2016 are as follows:

GILA FASHIONS
Income Statement
For the Quarter Ended September 30, 2016

| | Department | | | Total |
	Men's	Women's	Accessories	
Sales Revenue	$ 103,000	$ 56,000	$ 97,000	$ 256,000
Variable Costs	63,000	32,000	94,000	189,000
Contribution Margin	40,000	24,000	3,000	67,000
Fixed Costs	22,000	16,000	21,000	59,000
Operating Income (Loss)	$ 18,000	$ 8,000	$ (18,000)	$ 8,000

Assume that the fixed costs assigned to each department include only direct fixed costs of the department:

- Salary of the department's manager
- Cost of advertising directly related to that department

If Gila Fashions drops a department, it will not incur these fixed costs. Under these circumstances, should Gila Fashions drop any of the departments? Give your reasoning.

Learning Objective 3

S25-5 Making product mix decisions

ContainAll produces plastic storage bins for household storage needs. The company makes two sizes of bins: large (50 gallon) and regular (35 gallon). Demand for the products is so high that ContainAll can sell as many of each size as it can produce. The company uses the same machinery to produce both sizes. The machinery can be run for only 2,800 hours per period. ContainAll can produce 11 large bins every hour, whereas it can produce 17 regular bins in the same amount of time. Fixed costs amount to $130,000 per period. Sales prices and variable costs are as follows:

	Regular	Large
Sales price per unit	$ 8.90	$ 10.80
Variable costs per unit	3.70	4.10

Requirements

1. Which product should ContainAll emphasize? Why?
2. To maximize profits, how many of each size bin should ContainAll produce?
3. Given this product mix, what will the company's operating income be?

Learning Objective 4

S25-6 Making outsourcing decisions

Suppose Brady House restaurant is considering whether to (1) bake bread for its restaurant in-house or (2) buy the bread from a local bakery. The chef estimates that variable costs of making each loaf include $0.54 of ingredients, $0.25 of variable overhead (electricity to run the oven), and $0.72 of direct labor for kneading and forming the loaves. Allocating fixed overhead (depreciation on the kitchen equipment and building) based on direct labor, Brady House assigns $1.05 of fixed overhead per loaf. None of the fixed costs are avoidable. The local bakery would charge $1.70 per loaf.

Requirements

1. What is the full product unit cost of making the bread in-house?
2. Should Brady House bake the bread in-house or buy from the local bakery? Why?
3. In addition to the financial analysis, what else should Brady House consider when making this decision?

S25-7 Making outsourcing decisions

Learning Objective 4

Delila Nailey manages a fleet of 325 delivery trucks for Yankee Corporation. Nailey must decide whether the company should outsource the fleet management function. If she outsources to Fleet Management Services (FMS), FMS will be responsible for maintenance and scheduling activities. This alternative would require Nailey to lay off her five employees. However, her own job would be secure; she would be Yankee's liaison with FMS. If she continues to manage the fleet, she will need fleet-management software that costs $10,000 per year to lease. FMS offers to manage this fleet for an annual fee of $265,000. Nailey performed the following analysis:

	Retain In-House	Outsource to FMS	Difference
Annual leasing fee for software	$ 10,000		$ 10,000
Annual maintenance of trucks	145,000		145,000
Total annual salaries of five laid-off employees	160,000		160,000
Fleet Management Service's annual fee		$ 265,000	(265,000)
Total differential cost of outsourcing	$ 315,000	$ 265,000	$ 50,000

Requirements

1. Which alternative will maximize Yankee's short-term operating income?
2. What qualitative factors should Yankee consider before making a final decision?

S25-8 Making sell or process further decisions

Learning Objective 4

Chocolicious processes cocoa beans into cocoa powder at a processing cost of $10,300 per batch. Chocolicious can sell the cocoa powder as is, or it can process the cocoa powder further into either chocolate syrup or boxed assorted chocolates. Once processed, each batch of cocoa beans would result in the following sales revenue:

Cocoa powder	$ 14,500
Chocolate syrup	104,000
Boxed assorted chocolates	196,000

The cost of transforming the cocoa powder into chocolate syrup would be $67,000. Likewise, the company would incur a cost of $179,000 to transform the cocoa powder into boxed assorted chocolates. The company president has decided to make boxed assorted chocolates due to their high sales value and to the fact that the cocoa bean processing cost of $10,300 eats up most of the cocoa powder profits.

Has the president made the right or wrong decision? Explain your answer. Be sure to include the correct financial analysis in your response.

> ## Exercises

Learning Objective 1

E25-9 Describing and identifying information relevant to business decisions

Dan Jacobs, production manager for GreenLife, invested in computer-controlled production machinery last year. He purchased the machinery from Superior Design at a cost of $3,000,000. A representative from Superior Design has recently contacted Dan because the company has designed an even more efficient piece of machinery. The new design would double the production output of the year-old machinery but would cost GreenLife another $4,500,000. Jacobs is afraid to bring this new equipment to the company president's attention because he convinced the president to invest $3,000,000 in the machinery last year.

Explain what is relevant and irrelevant to Jacobs's dilemma. What should he do?

Learning Objective 2

1. $2,750

E25-10 Making special pricing decisions

Suppose the Baseball Hall of Fame in Cooperstown, New York, has approached Hungry-Cardz with a special order. The Hall of Fame wishes to purchase 55,000 baseball card packs for a special promotional campaign and offers $0.33 per pack, a total of $18,150. Hungry-Cardz's total production cost is $0.53 per pack, as follows:

Variable costs:	
Direct materials	$ 0.13
Direct labor	0.04
Variable overhead	0.11
Fixed overhead	0.25
Total cost	$ 0.53

Hungry-Cardz has enough excess capacity to handle the special order.

Requirements

1. Prepare a differential analysis to determine whether Hungry-Cardz should accept the special sales order.

2. Now assume that the Hall of Fame wants special hologram baseball cards. Hungry-Cardz will spend $5,000 to develop this hologram, which will be useless after the special order is completed. Should Hungry-Cardz accept the special order under these circumstances, assuming no change in the special pricing of $0.33 per pack?

Learning Objective 2

1. $475,000

E25-11 Making special pricing decisions

Tolman Sunglasses sell for about $154 per pair. Suppose that the company incurs the following average costs per pair:

Direct materials	$ 39
Direct labor	16
Variable manufacturing overhead	9
Variable selling expenses	3
Fixed manufacturing overhead	25*
Total cost	$ 92

*$2,250,000 Total fixed manufacturing overhead / 90,000 Pairs of sunglasses

Tolman has enough idle capacity to accept a one-time-only special order from Alaska Shades for 25,000 pairs of sunglasses at $83 per pair. Tolman will not incur any variable selling expenses for the order.

Requirements

1. How would accepting the order affect Tolman's operating income? In addition to the special order's effect on profits, what other (longer-term qualitative) factors should Tolman's managers consider in deciding whether to accept the order?

2. Tolman's marketing manager, Peter Kyler, argues against accepting the special order because the offer price of $83 is less than Tolman's $92 cost to make the sunglasses. Kyler asks you, as one of Tolman's staff accountants, to explain whether his analysis is correct. What would you say?

E25-12 Making pricing decisions

Learning Objective 2

3. Desired profit $32,480

Rouse Builders builds 1,500-square-foot starter tract homes in the fast-growing suburbs of Atlanta. Land and labor are cheap, and competition among developers is fierce. The homes are a standard model, with any upgrades added by the buyer after the sale. Rouse Builders's costs per developed sublot are as follows:

Land	$ 51,000
Construction	121,000
Landscaping	5,000
Variable selling costs	4,000

Rouse Builders would like to earn a profit of 16% of the variable cost of each home sold. Similar homes offered by competing builders sell for $202,000 each. Assume the company has no fixed costs.

Requirements

1. Which approach to pricing should Rouse Builders emphasize? Why?

2. Will Rouse Builders be able to achieve its target profit levels?

3. Bathrooms and kitchens are typically the most important selling features of a home. Rouse Builders could differentiate the homes by upgrading the bathrooms and kitchens. The upgrades would cost $22,000 per home but would enable Rouse Builders to increase the selling prices by $38,500 per home. (Kitchen and bathroom upgrades typically add about 175% of their cost to the value of any home.) If Rouse Builders makes the upgrades, what will the new cost-plus price per home be? Should the company differentiate its product in this manner?

CHAPTER 25

Learning Objective 3

1. $(33,000)

(Requirement 1 only)

E25-13 Making dropping a product decisions

Top managers of Best Video are alarmed by their operating losses. They are considering dropping the DVD product line. Company accountants have prepared the following analysis to help make this decision:

BEST VIDEO Income Statement For the Year Ended December 31, 2016			
	Total	**Blu-ray Discs**	**DVD Discs**
Sales Revenue	$ 432,000	$ 309,000	$ 123,000
Variable Costs	240,000	150,000	90,000
Contribution Margin	192,000	159,000	33,000
Fixed Costs:			
Manufacturing	134,000	75,000	59,000
Selling and Administrative	69,000	52,000	17,000
Total Fixed Expenses	203,000	127,000	76,000
Operating Income (Loss)	$ (11,000)	$ 32,000	$ (43,000)

Total fixed costs will not change if the company stops selling DVDs.

Requirements

1. Prepare a differential analysis to show whether Best Video should drop the DVD product line.

2. Will dropping DVDs add $43,000 to operating income? Explain.

Note: Exercise E25-13 must be completed before attempting Exercise E25-14.

Learning Objective 3

1. $12,000

E25-14 Making dropping a product decisions

Refer to Exercise E25-13. Assume that Best Video can avoid $45,000 of fixed costs by dropping the DVD product line (these costs are direct fixed costs of the DVD product line).

Prepare a differential analysis to show whether Best Video should stop selling DVDs.

E25-15 Making product mix decisions

Learning Objective 3

2. CM per MHr, Regular $393

Tread Mile produces two types of exercise treadmills: regular and deluxe. The exercise craze is such that Tread Mile could use all its available machine hours to produce either model. The two models are processed through the same production departments. Data for both models are as follows:

	Per Unit	
	Deluxe	**Regular**
Sales Price	$ 1,040	$ 570
Costs:		
Direct Materials	300	90
Direct Labor	78	190
Variable Manufacturing Overhead	276	92
Fixed Manufacturing Overhead*	120	40
Variable Operating Expenses	115	67
Total Costs	889	479
Operating Income	$ 151	$ 91

*allocated on the basis of machine hours

Requirements

1. What is the constraint?
2. Which model should Tread Mile produce? (*Hint:* Use the allocation of fixed manufacturing overhead to determine the proportion of machine hours used by each product.)
3. If Tread Mile should produce both models, compute the mix that will maximize operating income.

E25-16 Making sales mix decisions

Learning Objective 3

CM per sq. ft., Designer $4.40

Cole sells both designer and moderately priced fashion accessories. Top management is deciding which product line to emphasize. Accountants have provided the following data:

	Per Item	
	Designer	**Moderately Priced**
Average Sales Price	$ 195	$ 79
Average Variable Costs	85	21
Average Contribution Margin	110	58
Average Fixed Costs (allocated)	20	5
Average Operating Income	$ 90	$ 53

The Cole store in Grand Junction, Colorado, has 13,000 square feet of floor space. If Cole emphasizes moderately priced goods, it can display 780 items in the store. If Cole emphasizes designer wear, it can display only 520 designer items. These numbers are also the average monthly sales in units.

Prepare an analysis to show which product the company should emphasize.

Learning Objective 3

1. CM per linear ft., Licious-Ade
12-oz. can $5.10

E25-17 Making sales mix decisions

Each morning, Joel Rowe stocks the drink case at Joel's Beach Hut in Myrtle Beach, South Carolina. The drink case has 100 linear feet of refrigerated drink space. Each linear foot can hold either six 12-ounce cans or three 20-ounce bottles.

Joel's Beach Hut sells three types of cold drinks:

> **1.** Licious-Ade in 12-oz. cans for $1.30 per can
>
> **2.** Licious-Ade in 20-oz. bottles for $1.70 per bottle
>
> **3.** Pep-Cola in 20-oz. bottles for $2.30 per bottle

Joel's Beach Hut pays its suppliers:

> **1.** $0.45 per 12-oz. can of Licious-Ade
>
> **2.** $0.60 per 20-oz. bottle of Licious-Ade
>
> **3.** $0.90 per 20-oz. bottle of Pep-Cola

Joel's Beach Hut's monthly fixed costs include:

Hut rental	$ 385
Refrigerator rental	75
Joel's salary	1,650
Total fixed costs	$ 2,110

Joel's Beach Hut can sell all the drinks stocked in the display case each morning.

Requirements

1. What is Joel's Beach Hut's constraining factor? What should Joel stock to maximize profits?

2. Suppose Joel's Beach Hut refuses to devote more than 65 linear feet to any individual product. Under this condition, how many linear feet of each drink should Joel's stock? How many units of each product will be available for sale each day?

Learning Objective 4

Differential cost $1.50

E25-18 Making outsourcing decisions

Eclipse Systems manufactures an optical switch that it uses in its final product. The switch has the following manufacturing costs per unit:

Direct Materials	$ 11.00
Direct Labor	4.50
Variable Overhead	6.00
Fixed Overhead	8.00
Manufacturing Product Cost	$ 29.50

Another company has offered to sell Eclipse Systems the switch for $20.00 per unit. If Eclipse Systems buys the switch from the outside supplier, the idle manufacturing facilities cannot be used for any other purpose, yet none of the fixed costs are avoidable.

Prepare an outsourcing analysis to determine whether Eclipse Systems should make or buy the switch.

Note: Exercise E25-18 must be completed before attempting Exercise E25-19.

E25-19 Making outsourcing decisions

Learning Objective 4

1. Outsource and make new product $1,350,000

Refer to Exercise E25-18. Eclipse Systems needs 80,000 optical switches. By outsourcing them, Eclipse Systems can use its idle facilities to manufacture another product that will contribute $250,000 to operating income.

Requirements

1. Identify the expected net costs that Eclipse Systems will incur to acquire 80,000 switches under three alternative plans.

2. Which plan makes the best use of Eclipse System's facilities? Support your answer.

E25-20 Making sell or process further decisions

Learning Objective 4

Total net rev. difference $4,104

Naturalplus processes organic milk into plain yogurt. Naturalplus sells plain yogurt to hospitals, nursing homes, and restaurants in bulk, one-gallon containers. Each batch, processed at a cost of $820, yields 1,200 gallons of plain yogurt. Naturalplus sells the one-gallon tubs for $5 each and spends $0.10 for each plastic tub. Naturalplus has recently begun to reconsider its strategy. Naturalplus wonders if it would be more profitable to sell individual-size portions of fruited organic yogurt at local food stores. Naturalplus could further process each batch of plain yogurt into 25,600 individual portions (3/4 cup each) of fruited yogurt. A recent market analysis indicates that demand for the product exists. Naturalplus would sell each individual portion for $0.54. Packaging would cost $0.08 per portion, and fruit would cost $0.07 per portion. Fixed costs would not change.

Should Naturalplus continue to sell only the gallon-size plain yogurt (sell as is) or convert the plain yogurt into individual-size portions of fruited yogurt (process further)? Why?

> Problems **Group A**

P25-21A Identifying relevant information and making pricing decisions

Learning Objectives 1, 2

2. $9,400

Deep Blue manufactures flotation vests in Charleston, South Carolina. Deep Blue's contribution margin income statement for the month ended December 31, 2016, contains the following data:

DEEP BLUE Income Statement For the Month Ended December 31, 2016	
Sales in Units	30,000
Sales Revenue	$ 480,000
Variable Costs:	
Manufacturing	150,000
Selling and Administrative	110,000
Total Variable Costs	260,000
Contribution Margin	220,000
Fixed Costs:	
Manufacturing	121,000
Selling and Administrative	85,000
Total Fixed Costs	206,000
Operating Income	$ 14,000

CHAPTER 25

Suppose Overboard wishes to buy 4,700 vests from Deep Blue. Deep Blue will not incur any variable selling and administrative expenses on the special order. The Deep Blue plant has enough unused capacity to manufacture the additional vests. Overboard has offered $7 per vest, which is below the normal sales price of $16.

Requirements

1. Identify each cost in the income statement as either relevant or irrelevant to Deep Blue's decision.

2. Prepare a differential analysis to determine whether Deep Blue should accept this special sales order.

3. Identify long-term factors Deep Blue should consider in deciding whether to accept the special sales order.

Learning Objective 2

4. $4.39 per unit

P25-22A Making pricing decisions

Happy Gardener operates a commercial plant nursery where it propagates plants for garden centers throughout the region. Happy Gardener has $4,800,000 in assets. Its yearly fixed costs are $650,000, and the variable costs for the potting soil, container, label, seedling, and labor for each gallon-size plant total $1.90. Happy Gardener's volume is currently 480,000 units. Competitors offer the same plants, at the same quality, to garden centers for $4.25 each. Garden centers then mark them up to sell to the public for $9 to $12, depending on the type of plant.

Requirements

1. Happy Gardener's owners want to earn a 11% return on investment on the company's assets. What is Happy Gardener's target full product cost?

2. Given Happy Gardener's current costs, will its owners be able to achieve their target profit?

3. Assume Happy Gardener has identified ways to cut its variable costs to $1.75 per unit. What is its new target fixed cost? Will this decrease in variable costs allow the company to achieve its target profit?

4. Happy Gardener started an aggressive advertising campaign strategy to differentiate its plants from those grown by other nurseries. Happy Gardener does not expect volume to be affected, but it hopes to gain more control over pricing. If Happy Gardener has to spend $90,000 this year to advertise and its variable costs continue to be $1.75 per unit, what will its cost-plus price be? Do you think Happy Gardener will be able to sell its plants to garden centers at the cost-plus price? Why or why not?

P25-23A Making dropping a product decisions

Learning Objective 3

2b: $(31,000)

Members of the board of directors of Safety Step have received the following operating income data for the year ended May 31, 2016:

SAFETY STEP Income Statement For the Year Ended May 31, 2016			
	Product Line		
	Industrial Systems	Household Systems	Total
Sales Revenue	$ 340,000	$ 370,000	$ 710,000
Cost of Goods Sold:			
Variable	35,000	46,000	81,000
Fixed	240,000	69,000	309,000
Total Cost of Goods Sold	275,000	115,000	390,000
Gross Profit	65,000	255,000	320,000
Selling and Administrative Expenses:			
Variable	63,000	75,000	138,000
Fixed	41,000	25,000	66,000
Total Selling and Administrative Expenses	104,000	100,000	204,000
Operating Income (Loss)	$ (39,000)	$ 155,000	$ 116,000

Members of the board are surprised that the industrial systems product line is not profitable. They commission a study to determine whether the company should drop the line. Company accountants estimate that dropping industrial systems will decrease fixed cost of goods sold by $84,000 and decrease fixed selling and administrative expenses by $11,000.

Requirements

1. Prepare a differential analysis to show whether Safety Step should drop the industrial systems product line.

2. Prepare contribution margin income statements to show Safety Step's total operating income under the two alternatives: (a) with the industrial systems line and (b) without the line. Compare the *difference* between the two alternatives' income numbers to your answer to Requirement 1.

3. What have you learned from the comparison in Requirement 2?

Learning Objective 3

2. CM, Deluxe $1,680

P25-24A Making product mix decisions

Brill, located in Port St. Lucie, Florida, produces two lines of electric toothbrushes: deluxe and standard. Because Brill can sell all the toothbrushes it can produce, the owners are expanding the plant. They are deciding which product line to emphasize. To make this decision, they assemble the following data:

	Per Unit	
	Deluxe Toothbrush	Standard Toothbrush
Sales price	$ 80	$ 52
Variable costs	20	15
Contribution margin	$ 60	$ 37
Contribution margin ratio	75.0%	71.2%

After expansion, the factory will have a production capacity of 5,000 machine hours per month. The plant can manufacture either 58 standard electric toothbrushes or 28 deluxe electric toothbrushes per machine hour.

Requirements

1. Identify the constraining factor for Brill.

2. Prepare an analysis to show which product line to emphasize.

Learning Objective 4

1. $(9,600)

P25-25A Making outsourcing decisions

Wild Ride manufactures snowboards. Its cost of making 1,900 bindings is as follows:

Direct materials	$ 17,600
Direct labor	3,500
Variable overhead	2,050
Fixed overhead	7,000
Total manufacturing costs for 1,900 bindings	$ 30,150

Suppose Lancaster will sell bindings to Wild Ride for $16 each. Wild Ride would pay $2 per unit to transport the bindings to its manufacturing plant, where it would add its own logo at a cost of $0.50 per binding.

Requirements

1. Wild Ride's accountants predict that purchasing the bindings from Lancaster will enable the company to avoid $2,400 of fixed overhead. Prepare an analysis to show whether Wild Ride should make or buy the bindings.

2. The facilities freed by purchasing bindings from Lancaster can be used to manufacture another product that will contribute $3,200 to profit. Total fixed costs will be the same as if Wild Ride had produced the bindings. Show which alternative makes the best use of Wild Ride's facilities: (a) make bindings, (b) buy bindings and leave facilities idle, or (c) buy bindings and make another product.

P25-26A Making sell or process further decisions

Learning Objective 4

3. $(12,200)

Rouse Petroleum has spent $205,000 to refine 62,000 gallons of petroleum distillate, which can be sold for $6.30 per gallon. Alternatively, Rouse can process the distillate further and produce 56,000 gallons of cleaner fluid. The additional processing will cost $1.80 per gallon of distillate. The cleaner fluid can be sold for $9.00 per gallon. To sell the cleaner fluid, Rouse must pay a sales commission of $0.10 per gallon and a transportation charge of $0.15 per gallon.

Requirements

1. Diagram Rouse's decision alternatives, using Exhibit 25-18 as a guide.

2. Identify the sunk cost. Is the sunk cost relevant to Rouse's decision?

3. Should Rouse sell the petroleum distillate or process it into cleaner fluid? Show the expected net revenue difference between the two alternatives.

> Problems **Group B**

P25-27B Identifying relevant information and making pricing decisions

Learning Objectives 1, 2

2. $32,900

Summer Fun manufactures flotation vests in Tampa, Florida. Summer Fun's contribution margin income statement for the month ended December 31, 2016, contains the following data:

SUMMER FUN Income Statement For the Month Ended December 31, 2016	
Sales in Units	31,000
Sales Revenue	$ 465,000
Variable Costs:	
Manufacturing	93,000
Selling and Administrative	111,000
Total Variable Costs	204,000
Contribution Margin	261,000
Fixed Costs:	
Manufacturing	121,000
Selling and Administrative	86,000
Total Fixed Expenses	207,000
Operating Income	$ 54,000

Suppose Overtown wishes to buy 4,700 vests from Summer Fun. Summer Fun will not incur any variable selling and administrative expenses on the special order. The Summer Fun plant has enough unused capacity to manufacture the additional vests. Overtown has offered $10 per vest, which is below the normal sale price of $15.

Requirements

1. Identify each cost in the income statement as either relevant or irrelevant to Summer Fun's decision.

2. Prepare a differential analysis to determine whether Summer Fun should accept this special sales order.

3. Identify long-term factors Summer Fun should consider in deciding whether to accept the special sales order.

Learning Objective 2

4. $4.46 per unit

P25-28B Making pricing decisions

Plants Plus operates a commercial plant nursery, where it propagates plants for garden centers throughout the region. Plants Plus has $4,950,000 in assets. Its yearly fixed costs are $650,000, and the variable costs for the potting soil, container, label, seedling, and labor for each gallon-size plant total $1.90. Plants Plus's volume is currently 490,000 units. Competitors offer the same plants, at the same quality, to garden centers for $4.25 each. Garden centers then mark them up to sell to the public for $7 to $10, depending on the type of plant.

Requirements

1. Plants Plus's owners want to earn an 11% return on the company's assets. What is Plants Plus's target full product cost?

2. Given Plants Plus's current costs, will its owners be able to achieve their target profit?

3. Assume Plants Plus has identified ways to cut its variable costs to $1.75 per unit. What is its new target fixed cost? Will this decrease in variable costs allow the company to achieve its target profit?

4. Plants Plus started an aggressive advertising campaign strategy to differentiate its plants from those grown by other nurseries. Plants Plus does not expect volume to be affected, but it hopes to gain more control over pricing. If Plants Plus has to spend $135,000 this year to advertise and its variable costs continue to be $1.75 per unit, what will its cost-plus price be? Do you think Plants Plus will be able to sell its plants to garden centers at the cost-plus price? Why or why not?

Learning Objective 3

2b. $(42,000)

P25-29B Making dropping a product decisions

Members of the board of directors of Security Systems have received the following operating income data for the year ended March 31, 2016:

SECURITY SYSTEMS Income Statement For the Month Ended March 31, 2016			
	Product Line		
	Industrial Systems	Household Systems	Total
Sales Revenue	$ 350,000	$ 380,000	$ 730,000
Cost of Goods Sold:			
Variable	34,000	48,000	82,000
Fixed	260,000	65,000	325,000
Total Cost of Goods Sold	294,000	113,000	407,000
Gross Profit	56,000	267,000	323,000
Selling and Administrative Expenses:			
Variable	62,000	75,000	137,000
Fixed	43,000	27,000	70,000
Total Selling and Administrative Expenses	105,000	102,000	207,000
Operating Income (Loss)	$ (49,000)	$ 165,000	$ 116,000

Members of the board are surprised that the industrial systems product line is losing money. They commission a study to determine whether the company should drop the line. Company accountants estimate that dropping industrial systems will decrease fixed cost of goods sold by $84,000 and decrease fixed selling and administrative expenses by $12,000.

Requirements

1. Prepare a differential analysis to show whether Security Systems should drop the industrial systems product line.

2. Prepare contribution margin income statements to show Security Systems's total operating income under the two alternatives: (a) with the industrial systems line and (b) without the line. Compare the *difference* between the two alternatives' income numbers to your answer to Requirement 1.

3. What have you learned from this comparison in Requirement 2?

P25-30B Making product mix decisions

Brann, located in San Antonio, Texas, produces two lines of electric toothbrushes: deluxe and standard. Because Brann can sell all the toothbrushes it can produce, the owners are expanding the plant. They are deciding which product line to emphasize. To make this decision, they assemble the following data:

	Per Unit	
	Deluxe Toothbrush	Standard Toothbrush
Sales price	$ 80	$ 54
Variable expense	22	17
Contribution margin	$ 58	$ 37
Contribution margin ratio	72.5%	68.5%

After expansion, the factory will have a production capacity of 4,800 machine hours per month. The plant can manufacture either 50 standard electric toothbrushes or 40 deluxe electric toothbrushes per machine hour.

Requirements

1. Identify the constraining factor for Brann.

2. Prepare an analysis to show which product line the company should emphasize.

P25-31B Making outsourcing decisions

Winter Sports manufactures snowboards. Its cost of making 2,100 bindings is as follows:

Direct materials	$ 17,600
Direct labor	2,600
Variable overhead	2,120
Fixed overhead	6,800
Total manufacturing costs for 2,100 bindings	$ 29,120

Learning Objective 3

2. CM, Deluxe $2,320

Learning Objective 4

1. $(12,120)

Suppose Lewis will sell bindings to Winter Sports for $15 each. Winter Sports would pay $2 per unit to transport the bindings to its manufacturing plant, where it would add its own logo at a cost of $0.40 per binding.

Requirements

1. Winter Sports's accountants predict that purchasing the bindings from Lewis will enable the company to avoid $2,100 of fixed overhead. Prepare an analysis to show whether Winter Sports should make or buy the bindings.

2. The facilities freed by purchasing bindings from Lewis can be used to manufacture another product that will contribute $3,100 to profit. Total fixed costs will be the same as if Winter Sports had produced the bindings. Show which alternative makes the best use of Winter Sports's facilities: (a) make bindings, (b) buy bindings and leave facilities idle, or (c) buy bindings and make another product.

Learning Objective 4

3. $(42,970)

P25-32B Making sell or process further decisions

McKnight Petroleum has spent $207,000 to refine 64,000 gallons of petroleum distillate, which can be sold for $6.20 per gallon. Alternatively, McKnight can process the distillate further and produce 53,000 gallons of cleaner fluid. The additional processing will cost $1.85 per gallon of distillate. The cleaner fluid can be sold for $9.20 per gallon. To sell the cleaner fluid, McKnight must pay a sales commission of $0.13 per gallon and a transportation charge of $0.16 per gallon.

Requirements

1. Diagram McKnight's decision alternatives, using Exhibit 25-18 as a guide.

2. Identify the sunk cost. Is the sunk cost relevant to McKnight's decision?

3. Should McKnight sell the petroleum distillate or process it into cleaner fluid? Show the expected net revenue difference between the two alternatives.

> Continuing Problem

P25-33 Making sell or process further decisions

This problem continues the Daniels Consulting situation from Problem P24-37 of Chapter 24. Daniels Consulting provides consulting services at an average price of $150 per hour and incurs variable costs of $75 per hour. Assume average fixed costs are $5,250 a month.

Daniels has developed new software that will revolutionize billing for companies. Daniels has already invested $300,000 in the software. It can market the software as is at $40,000 per client and expects to sell to 12 clients. Daniels can develop the software further, adding integration to Microsoft products at an additional development cost of $150,000. The additional development will allow Daniels to sell the software for $49,000 each but to 16 clients.

Should Daniels sell the software as is or develop it further?

CRITICAL THINKING

> Ethical Issue 25-1

Mary Tan is the controller for Duck Associates, a property management company in Portland, Oregon. Each year, Tan and payroll clerk Toby Stock meet with the external auditors about payroll accounting. This year, the auditors suggest that Tan consider outsourcing Duck Associates's payroll accounting to a company specializing in payroll processing services. This would allow Tan and her staff to focus on their primary responsibility: accounting for the properties under management. At present, payroll requires 1.5 employee positions—payroll clerk Toby Stock and a bookkeeper who spends half her time entering payroll data in the system.

Tan considers this suggestion, and she lists the following items relating to outsourcing payroll accounting:

a. The current payroll software that was purchased for $4,000 three years ago would not be needed if payroll processing were outsourced.

b. Duck Associates's bookkeeper would spend half her time preparing the weekly payroll input form that is given to the payroll processing service. She is paid $450 per week.

c. Duck Associates would no longer need payroll clerk Toby Stock, whose annual salary is $42,000.

d. The payroll processing service would charge $2,000 per month.

Requirements

1. Would outsourcing the payroll function increase or decrease Duck Associates's operating income?

2. Tan believes that outsourcing payroll would simplify her job, but she does not like the prospect of having to lay off Stock, who has become a close personal friend. She does not believe there is another position available for Stock at his current salary. Can you think of other factors that might support keeping Stock, rather than outsourcing payroll processing? How should each of the factors affect Tan's decision if she wants to do what is best for Duck Associates and act ethically?

> Team Project 25-1

Ledfords is a chain of home improvement stores. Suppose Ledfords is trying to decide whether to produce its own line of Formica countertops, cabinets, and picnic tables. Assume Ledford would incur the following unit costs in producing its own product lines:

	Countertops	Cabinets	Picnic Tables
Direct materials per unit	$ 15	$ 10	$ 25
Direct labor per unit	10	5	15
Variable manufacturing overhead per unit	5	2	6

Rather than making these products, assume that Ledfords could buy them from outside suppliers. Suppliers would charge Ledfords $40 per countertop, $25 per cabinet, and $65 per picnic table. Whether Ledfords makes or buys these products, assume that the company expects the following annual sales:

- Countertops—487,200 at $130 each
- Cabinets—150,000 at $75 each
- Picnic tables—100,000 at $225 each

Assume that Ledfords has a production facility with excess capacity that could be used to produce these products with no additional fixed costs. If making is sufficiently more profitable than outsourcing, Ledfords will start production of the new line of products. The president of Ledfords has asked your consulting group for a recommendation.

Requirements

1. Are the following items relevant or irrelevant in Ledfords's decision to build a new plant that will manufacture its own products?

   a. The unit sales prices of the countertops, cabinets, and picnic tables (the sales prices that Ledfords charges its customers)
   b. The prices outside suppliers would charge Ledfords for the three products if Ledfords decides to outsource the products rather than make them
   c. The direct materials, direct labor, and variable overhead Ledfords would incur to manufacture the three product lines
   d. The president's salary

2. Determine whether Ledfords should make or outsource the countertops, cabinets, and picnic tables. In other words, what is the annual difference in operating income if Ledfords decides to make rather than outsource each of these three products?

3. Write a memo giving your recommendation to Ledfords's president. The memo should clearly state your recommendation, along with a brief summary of the reasons for your recommendation.

MyAccountingLab For a wealth of online resources, including exercises, problems, media, and immediate tutorial help, please visit http://www.myaccountinglab.com.

> Quick Check Answers

1. c **2.** a **3.** c **4.** a **5.** d **6.** d **7.** d **8.** b **9.** b **10.** a

Capital Investment Decisions

If I Build It, Will They Buy?

Cody Thacker stands in the parking lot of the newest location of Thacker's C-Store, watching the new customers coming in for their first visit to his 10th store. Cody is pleased with the volume of traffic at the new convenience store. Opening a new store is a large investment and somewhat of a gamble. The previous new store, Store #9, is not doing well. Cody got a great deal on the land but failed to fully evaluate the market. Store #9 does not have the customer volume it needs to make it a profitable location, the workforce is limited, and employee turnover is a huge problem.

Fortunately, Cody learned from the mistake and was more careful when selecting this latest location. Before making the final decision on the location of Store #10, Cody considered the area's population to ensure the store would have the needed customer volume and workforce. He also analyzed the other types of stores in the area, paying particular attention to the locations of competitors' convenience stores, which could affect his ability to attract customers and workers. So far, he is not having problems getting qualified, reliable workers. Morale is high, and the employees are cheerful. The gas pumps are busy, and the traffic inside at the food and beverage counters is brisk. Cody feels his investment in land, building construction, equipment, and inventory at this C-Store is going to generate a good return. He hopes the profits from his current stores will allow him to open Store #11 within the next year.

Where Should We Expand?

All companies have to make investment decisions, such as deciding when to expand, replace equipment, and upgrade technology. Making wise decisions concerning investments in long-term assets is crucial to the long-term success of businesses. QuikTrip Corporation was founded in 1958 with one convenience store in Tulsa, Oklahoma. Fifty years later, in 2008, QuikTrip opened its 500th store. The company now has more than 690 stores in 11 states and more than 16,000 employees. QuikTrip has a stated goal of being the dominant convenience/gasoline retailer in each market through key, high-volume locations. To obtain this goal, QuikTrip has to be selective in its expansion. Each potential location has to be carefully evaluated, and the company has to have a selection process in place to determine new locations.

The focus of this chapter is on learning some methods of analyzing potential investment opportunities so the investments chosen meet a company's needs and provide the best return on investment.

Chapter 26 Learning Objectives

1 Describe the importance of capital investments and the capital budgeting process

2 Use the payback and the accounting rate of return methods to make capital investment decisions

3 Use the time value of money to compute the present values of lump sums and annuities

4 Use discounted cash flow methods to make capital investment decisions

WHAT IS CAPITAL BUDGETING?

Learning Objective 1
Describe the importance of capital investments and the capital budgeting process

Capital Asset
An operational asset used for a long period of time.

Capital Investment
The acquisition of a capital asset.

Capital Budgeting
The process of planning to invest in long-term assets in a way that returns the most profitability to the company.

In financial accounting, you learned how to account for **capital assets**—the operational assets businesses use for long periods of time. Examples include buildings, manufacturing equipment, and office furniture. The assets are considered *operational* assets because they are used in the day-to-day operations of the business in its efforts to generate revenues. They are called capital assets because they are *capitalized*, which means they are recorded as long-term assets when acquired and depreciated over their useful lives. Remember that depreciation is the allocation of a capital asset's cost over its useful life. Depreciation for capital assets used in production, such as manufacturing equipment and the factory building, is accumulated in Manufacturing Overhead. The cost is transferred through the inventory accounts and eventually to Cost of Goods Sold, which is an expense account. Depreciation for the capital assets not used in production, such as office furniture and the corporate office building, is recorded as Depreciation Expense, a selling and administrative expense. Either way, the cost is expensed over the useful life of the asset.

When a capital asset is acquired, by purchase or construction, the company is making a **capital investment**. The focus of this chapter is on how companies make capital investment decisions. The process of making capital investment decisions is often referred to as **capital budgeting**, which is planning for investments in long-term assets in a way that returns the most profitability to the company. Capital budgeting is critical to the business because these investments affect operations for many years and usually require large sums of cash.

Capital investment decisions affect all businesses as they try to become more efficient by automating production and implementing new technologies. Grocers and retailers have invested in expensive checkout machines that allow customers to self-scan their purchases, and airlines have invested in kiosks that allow passengers to self-check-in. These new technologies require substantial cash investments. How do managers decide whether these expansions in plant and equipment will be good investments? They use capital investment analysis. Some large companies employ staff solely dedicated to capital budgeting analysis. They spend thousands of hours per year determining which capital investments to pursue.

The Capital Budgeting Process

Previously, when you learned how to complete the master budget, we discussed the budgeting objectives: to develop strategy, plan, act, and control. The same objectives apply to capital budgeting, but the planning process is more involved due to the long-term nature of the assets. Exhibit 26-1 illustrates the capital budgeting process.

Exhibit 26-1 | Capital Budgeting Process

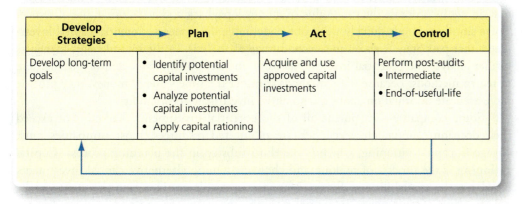

The first step in the capital budgeting process is to develop strategies. These are the long-term goals of the business, such as expanding international operations or being a value leader in one market while diversifying into other markets. This step is the same for all budgeting—short-term, intermediate, and long-term. After companies develop strategies, the next steps are to plan and budget for specific actions to achieve those goals.

The second step in the capital budgeting process is the planning process, which has three substeps. The first is to identify potential capital investments—for example, new technology and equipment that may make the company more efficient, competitive, and/or profitable. Employees, consultants, and outside vendors often offer capital investment proposals to management. After identifying potential capital investments, the second substep is to analyze the investments using one or more capital budgeting methods. In this chapter, we discuss four popular methods of analyzing potential capital investments:

1. Payback
2. Accounting rate of return (ARR)
3. Net present value (NPV)
4. Internal rate of return (IRR)

The first two methods, payback and accounting rate of return, are fairly quick and easy, and they work well for capital investments that have a relatively short life span, such as computer equipment and software that may have a useful life of only three to five years. Payback and accounting rate of return are also used to screen potential investments from those that are less desirable. Payback provides management with valuable information on how fast the cash invested will be recouped. The accounting rate of return shows the effect of the investment on the company's accrual-based income.

However, these two methods are inadequate if the capital investments have a longer life span because these methods do not consider the time value of money. The last two methods, net present value and internal rate of return, factor in the time value of money so they are more appropriate for longer-term capital investments, such as Smart Touch Learning's expansion to manufacturing tablet computers. Management often uses a combination of methods to make final capital investment decisions.

Capital budgeting is not an exact science. Although the calculations these methods require may appear precise, remember that they are based on estimates—predictions about an uncertain future. These estimates must consider many unknown factors, such as changing consumer preferences, competition, the state of the economy, and government regulations. The further into the future the decision extends, the more likely that actual results will differ from predictions. This makes long-term decisions riskier than short-term decisions.

The analysis of capital investments sometimes involves a two-stage process. In the first stage, managers screen the potential capital investments using one or both of the methods that do *not* incorporate the time value of money—payback and accounting rate of return. These simple methods quickly weed out undesirable investments. Potential capital investments that pass Stage 1 go on to a second stage of analysis. In the second stage, managers further analyze the potential investments using the net present value and/or internal rate of return methods. Because these methods consider the time value of money, they provide more accurate information about the potential investment's profitability.

Some companies can pursue all of the potential investments that meet or exceed their decision criteria. However, because of limited resources, most companies must engage in capital rationing, which is the third substep in the planning process. **Capital rationing** is the process of ranking and choosing among alternative capital investments based on the availability of funds. Managers must determine if and when to make specific capital investments, so capital rationing occurs when the company has limited cash available to invest in long-term assets. For example, management may decide to wait three years to buy a certain piece of equipment because it considers other investments more important. In the intervening three years, the company will reassess whether it should still invest in the equipment. Perhaps technology has changed and even better equipment is available. Perhaps consumer tastes have changed so the company no longer needs the equipment. Because of changing factors, long-term capital budgets are usually revised from year to year.

The third step in the capital budgeting process is to act—acquire and use the capital assets selected in the capital rationing process. The assets are used to generate revenues and contribute to company profits.

The fourth step in the capital budgeting process is control. In the short-term operational budgeting process, the control step is called *variance analysis*. Capital budgeting has a similar process. After acquiring and using the capital assets, companies compare the actual results from the investments to the projected results. The comparisons are called **post-audits**, and they help companies determine whether the investments are going as planned and deserve continued support or whether they should abandon the projects and dispose of the assets. Post-audits should be routinely performed during the life of the project, not just at the end of the project life span. The intermediate post-audits allow managers to make adjustments to the projects during their lifetimes. Managers also use feedback from post-audits to better estimate projections for future projects. If managers expect routine post-audits, they will more likely submit realistic estimates with their capital investment proposals.

Notice in Exhibit 26-1 that the control step loops back to the first step: develop strategies. The post-audits help mangers learn from their decisions and make adjustments as needed. The adjustments are then considered when developing new strategies. Also, keep in mind that capital investments are long-term investments and managers must monitor multiple, overlapping investments. For example, the decision to build a new manufacturing facility may be a 30-year project, whereas the manufacturing equipment needed in the new facility may be projected to last only 15 years. Meanwhile, the computer system may need to be upgraded every two to three years and replaced every five or six years. Capital budgeting is a complex process.

Focus on Cash Flows

Generally Accepted Accounting Principles (GAAP) are based on accrual accounting, but capital budgeting focuses on cash flows. The desirability of a capital asset depends on its ability to generate *net cash inflows*—that is, cash inflows in excess of cash outflows—over the asset's useful life. Recall that operating income based on accrual accounting contains non-cash expenses, such as depreciation expense and bad debts expense. These expenses decrease operating income but do not require a cash outlay. The capital investment's net cash inflows, therefore, will differ from its operating income. Of the four capital budgeting methods covered in this chapter, only the accounting rate of return method uses accrual-based accounting income. The other three methods use the investment's projected net cash inflows.

Cash *inflows* include future cash revenue generated from the investment, any future savings in ongoing cash operating costs resulting from the investment, and any future residual value of the asset. Cash inflows are projected by employees from production, marketing, materials management, accounting, and other departments to aid managers in estimating the projected cash flows. Good estimates are a critical part of making the best decisions.

To determine the investment's net cash inflows, the cash inflows are *netted* against the investment's future cash outflows, such as the investment's ongoing cash operating costs and cash paid for refurbishment, repairs, and maintenance costs. The initial investment itself is also a significant cash outflow. However, in our calculations, *we will always consider the amount of the investment separately from all other cash flows related to the investment.* The projected net cash inflows are given in our examples and in the assignment material. In reality, much of capital investment analysis revolves around projecting these figures as accurately as possible using input from employees throughout the organization—production, marketing, and so forth—depending on the type of capital investment. Exhibit 26-2 summarizes the common cash inflows and outflows from capital investments.

What do the projected net cash inflows include?

Exhibit 26-2 | **Capital Investment Cash Flows**

Cash Inflows	Cash Outflows
Revenue generated from investment	Initial investment (acquisition cost)
Savings in operating costs	Additional operating costs
Residual value	Refurbishment, repairs, and maintenance

Exhibit 26-3 illustrates the life cycle of capital investments, with the time line representing multiple years.

Exhibit 26-3 | **Life Cycle of Capital Investments**

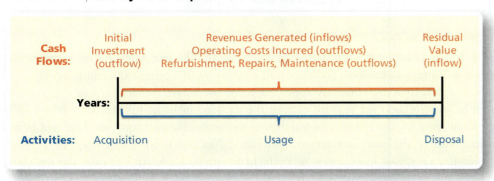

Match the following business activities to the steps in capital budgeting process:

Steps in the capital budgeting process:

- **a.** Develop strategies
- **b.** Plan
- **c.** Act
- **d.** Control

Business activities:

1. A manager evaluates progress one year into the project.
2. Employees submit suggestions for new investments.
3. The company builds a new factory.
4. Top management attends a retreat to set long-term goals.
5. Proposed investments are analyzed.
6. Proposed investments are ranked.
7. New equipment is purchased.

Check your answers online in MyAccountingLab or at http://www.pearsonhighered.com/Horngren.

For more practice, see Short Exercise S26-1.   MyAccountingLab

HOW DO THE PAYBACK AND ACCOUNTING RATE OF RETURN METHODS WORK?

Learning Objective 2

Use the payback and the accounting rate of return methods to make capital investment decisions

The primary focus of the rest of the chapter is learning how to analyze potential capital investments. We begin with two capital investment analysis methods that companies use to evaluate shorter capital investment choices (three to five years) and initially screen longer capital investment choices—payback and accounting rate of return.

Payback

Payback

A capital investment analysis method that measures the length of time it takes to recover, in net cash inflows, the cost of the initial investment.

Payback is a capital investment analysis method that measures the length of time it takes to recover, in net cash inflows, the cost of the initial investment. The initial investment is also called the *capital outlay*. All else being equal, the shorter the payback period, the more attractive the asset. Computing the payback depends on whether net cash inflows are equal each year or differ over time. We consider each, in turn.

Payback with Equal Annual Net Cash Inflows

Smart Touch Learning is considering investing $240,000 in hardware and software to provide a business-to-business (B2B) portal. Employees throughout the company will use the B2B portal to access company-approved suppliers. Smart Touch Learning expects the portal to save $60,000 per year for each of the six years of its useful life. The savings will arise from reducing the number of purchasing personnel the company employs and from reduced costs on the goods and services purchased. Net cash inflows arise from an increase in revenues, a decrease in expenses, or both. In Smart Touch Learning's case, the net cash inflows result from lower expenses.

When net cash inflows are equal each year, managers compute the payback with the following formula:

$$\text{Payback} = \frac{\text{Amount invested}}{\text{Expected annual net cash inflow}}$$

Smart Touch Learning computes the investment's payback as follows:

$$\text{Payback for B2B portal} = \frac{\$240,000}{\$60,000 \text{ per year}} = 4 \text{ years}$$

Smart Touch Learning expects to recoup the $240,000 investment in the B2B portal by the end of year 4, when the accumulated net cash inflows total $240,000.

Smart Touch Learning is also considering whether to, instead, invest $240,000 to upgrade its Web site. The company expects the upgraded Web site to generate $80,000 in net cash inflows each year of its three-year life. The payback is computed as follows:

$$\text{Payback for Web site upgrade} = \frac{\$240,000}{\$80,000 \text{ per year}} = 3 \text{ years}$$

Smart Touch Learning will recoup the $240,000 investment for the Web site upgrade by the end of year 3, when the accumulated net cash inflows total $240,000. The Web site upgrade project has a shorter payback period than the B2B project—three years compared with four years. Therefore, based on this method of analysis, the Web site upgrade is a more attractive project. Exhibit 26-4 summarizes the payback calculations.

Exhibit 26-4 | **Payback—Equal Annual Net Cash Inflows**

Net Cash Outflows		Net Cash Inflows			
		B2B Portal		Web Site Upgrade	
Year	Amount Invested	Annual	Accumulated	Annual	Accumulated
0	$ 240,000				
1		$ 60,000	$ 60,000	$ 80,000	$ 80,000
2		60,000	120,000	80,000	160,000
3		60,000	180,000	80,000	240,000
4		60,000	240,000		
5		60,000	300,000		
6		60,000	360,000		

Payback with Unequal Net Cash Inflows

The payback equation only works when net cash inflows are the same each period. When periodic cash flows are unequal, you must total net cash inflows until the amount invested is recovered. Assume that Smart Touch Learning is considering an alternate investment, the Z80 portal. The Z80 portal differs from the B2B portal and the Web site upgrade in two respects: (1) It has *unequal* net cash inflows during its life, and (2) it has a $30,000 residual value at the end of its life. The Z80 portal will generate net cash inflows of $100,000 in year 1, $80,000 in year 2, $50,000 each year in years 3 and 4, $40,000 each in years 5 and 6, and $30,000 in residual value when the equipment is sold at the end of the project's useful life. Exhibit 26-5 shows the payback schedule for these unequal annual net cash inflows.

Exhibit 26-5 | Payback—Unequal Annual Net Cash Inflows

Year	Net Cash Outflows Z80 Portal Amount Invested	Net Cash Inflows Z80 Portal Annual	Net Cash Inflows Z80 Portal Accumulated
0	$ 240,000		
1		$ 100,000	$ 100,000
2		80,000	180,000
3		50,000	230,000
4		50,000	280,000
5		40,000	320,000
6		40,000	360,000
6 (Residual value)		30,000	390,000

By the end of year 3, the company has recovered $230,000 of the $240,000 initially invested, so it is only $10,000 short of payback. Because the expected net cash inflow in year 4 is $50,000, by the end of year 4 the company will have recovered *more* than the initial investment. Therefore, the payback is somewhere between three and four years. Assuming that the cash flow occurs evenly throughout the fourth year, the payback is calculated as follows:

$$\text{Payback for Z80 portal} = 3 \text{ years} + \frac{\$10,000 \text{ (amount needed to complete recovery in year 4)}}{\$50,000 \text{ (net cash inflow in year 4)}} = 3.2 \text{ years}$$

Based on the payback method alone, the projects would be ranked as follows:

Rank	Project	Payback Period
1	Web site upgrade	3.0 years
2	Z80 portal	3.2 years
3	B2B portal	4.0 years

Criticism of Payback

A major criticism of the payback method is that it focuses only on time to recover the initial investment, not on profitability. The payback considers only those cash flows that occur *during* the payback period. This method ignores any cash flows that occur *after* that period. For example, Exhibit 26-4 shows that the B2B portal will continue to generate net cash inflows for two years after its payback. These additional net cash inflows amount to $120,000 ($60,000 × 2 years), yet the payback method ignores this extra cash. A similar situation occurs with the Z80 portal. As shown in Exhibit 26-5, the Z80 portal will provide an additional $150,000 of net cash inflows ($390,000 total accumulated cash inflows – $240,000 amount invested), including residual value, after its payback of 3.2 years. However, the Web site upgrade's useful life, as shown in Exhibit 26-4, is the same as its payback (three years). No cash flows are ignored, yet the Web site will merely cover its cost and provide no profit. Because this is the case, the company has no financial reason to invest in the Web site.

Exhibit 26-6 compares the payback of the three investments. As the exhibit illustrates, the payback method does not consider the asset's profitability. The method only tells management how quickly it will recover the cash invested. Even though the Web site upgrade has the shortest payback, both the B2B portal and the Z80 portal are better investments because they provide profit. The key point is that the investment with the shortest payback is best *only if all other factors are the same*. **Therefore, managers usually use the payback method as a screening device to eliminate investments that will take too long to recoup the initial investment. They rarely use payback as the sole method for deciding whether to invest in the asset.** Managers also use accounting rate of return, net present value, and internal rate of return to evaluate capital investments.

If the payback method doesn't consider profitability, why do managers use it?

Exhibit 26-6 | **Comparing Payback Periods Between Investments**

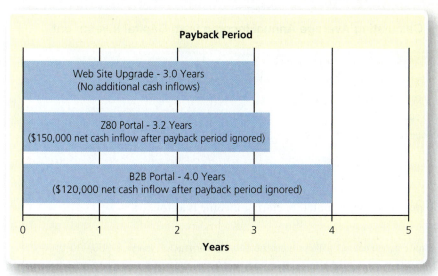

When using the payback method, managers are guided by the following the decision rule:

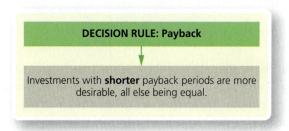

DECISION RULE: Payback

Investments with **shorter** payback periods are more desirable, all else being equal.

Accounting Rate of Return (ARR)

Companies are in business to earn profits. The **accounting rate of return (ARR)** is a capital investment analysis method that measures the profitability of an investment. The formula for calculating ARR is:

$$ARR = \frac{\text{Average annual operating income}}{\text{Average amount invested}}$$

Accounting Rate of Return (ARR)
A capital investment analysis method that measures the profitability of an investment. Average annual operating income / Average amount invested.

Notice that ARR focuses on the *operating income*, not the net cash inflow, that an asset generates. ARR measures the average annual rate of return over the asset's entire life, so it is sometimes called *average rate of return* or *annual rate of return*. Also, notice the similarity to ROI—return on investment—used to evaluate investment centers. The primary difference is ARR is used to evaluate the lifetime return of an investment and ROI is used to evaluate an annual return.

Let's first consider investments with no residual value. Recall the B2B portal, which costs $240,000, has equal annual net cash inflows of $60,000, a six-year useful life, and no (zero) residual value.

Let's look at the average annual operating income in the numerator first. The average annual operating income of an asset is simply the asset's total operating income over the course of its operating life divided by its lifespan (number of years). Operating income is based on *accrual accounting*. Therefore, any non-cash expenses, such as depreciation expense, must be subtracted from the asset's net cash inflows to arrive at its operating income. Exhibit 26-7 displays the formula for calculating average annual operating income.

Exhibit 26-7 | Calculating Average Annual Income from Capital Investment

Total net cash inflows during operating life of the asset	A
Less: Total depreciation during operating life of the asset (Cost – Residual Value)	B
Total operating income during operating life	(A – B)
Divide by: Asset's operating life in years	C
Average annual operating income from asset	[(A – B) / C]

The B2B portal's average annual operating income is as follows:

Total net cash inflows during operating life of the asset ($60,000 per year × 6 years)	$ 360,000
Less: Total depreciation during operating life of the asset ($240,000 – $0)	240,000
Total operating income during operating life	120,000
Divide by: Asset's operating life in years	÷ 6 years
Average annual operating income from asset	$ 20,000

Now let's look at the denominator of the ARR equation. The *average* amount invested in an asset is its book value at the beginning of the asset's useful life plus the book value at the end of the asset's useful life divided by 2. Another way to say that is the asset's initial cost plus the asset's residual value divided by 2. Remember that book value is cost less accumulated depreciation. Therefore, the book value of the asset decreases each year because of the annual depreciation.

Because the B2B portal does not have a residual value, the *average* amount invested is $120,000:

> Average amount invested = (Amount invested + Residual value) / 2
> = ($240,000 + $0) / 2
> = $120,000

We calculate the B2B portal's ARR as follows:

$$\text{ARR of B2B portal} = \frac{\text{Average annual operating income}}{\text{Average amount invested}}$$
$$= \frac{\$20,000}{\$120,000} = 0.167 = 16.7\%$$

Now consider the Z80 portal. Recall that the Z80 portal differed from the B2B portal only in that it had unequal net cash inflows during its life and a $30,000 residual value at the end of its life. Its average annual operating income is calculated as follows:

Total net cash inflows during operating life of the asset	$ 360,000
(Add inflows from each year, not including residual value)	
Less: Total depreciation during operating life of the asset ($240,000 − $30,000)	210,000
Total operating income during operating life	150,000
Divide by: Asset's operating life in years	÷ 6 years
Average annual operating income from asset	$ 25,000

Notice that the Z80 portal's average annual operating income of $25,000 is higher than the B2B portal's operating income of $20,000. Because the Z80 portal has a residual value at the end of its life, less depreciation is expensed each year, leading to a higher average annual operating income.

Now let's calculate the denominator of the ARR equation, the average amount invested in the asset. For the Z80 portal, the average asset investment is as follows:

$$\text{Average amount invested} = \text{(Amount invested + Residual value) / 2}$$
$$= (\$240,000 + \$30,000) / 2$$
$$= \$135,000$$

We calculate the Z80 portal's ARR as follows:

$$\text{ARR of Z80 portal} = \frac{\text{Average annual operating income}}{\text{Average amount invested}}$$
$$= \frac{\$25,000}{\$135,000} = 0.185 = 18.5\%$$

Companies that use the ARR method set a minimum required accounting rate of return. If Smart Touch Learning requires an ARR of at least 20%, then its managers would not approve an investment in the B2B portal or the Z80 portal because the ARR for both investments is less than 20%.

The decision rule is as follows:

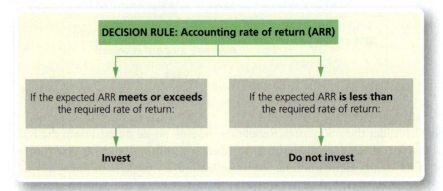

DECISIONS

Where did these numbers come from?

The management team at Browne and Browne (BnB) is deep in the budgeting process. Strategic goals have been finalized, and capital investments are being evaluated. Every department within BnB can submit potential investments. Predicted future cash flows and initial investment figures are given to the accounting department for evaluation using various capital investment analysis methods. Then the department representatives can present the proposals to the management team.

Daryl Baez is a new manager at BnB and just completed his presentation for replacing some aging equipment. He felt prepared and did not expect many questions, but the team members had several. Their primary concern is the calculations for future net cash inflows. Daryl explained that the vendor provided the figures for reduced operating costs based on the efficiency of the new equipment. Should the management team be concerned about the predictions? What should Daryl do? What would you do?

Solution

Capital investments involve large sums of cash, and decisions affect operations for many years. Therefore, the management team should be concerned about the validity of the predictions. Inaccurate predictions could have a long-term, negative impact on profits. If Daryl's only source is the sales representative trying to make the sale, the figures may not be accurate. Daryl should conduct his own research. He could contact current users of the equipment and ask for their feedback. He could look for reviews in trade magazines. Diligence on his part before the purchase will ensure the figures are accurate, satisfy the management team, and help BnB generate higher returns on investments.

Lockwood Company is considering a capital investment in machinery:

Initial investment	$ 600,000
Residual value	50,000
Expected annual net cash inflows	100,000
Expected useful life	8 years
Required rate of return	12%

8. Calculate the payback.
9. Calculate the ARR. Round the percentage to two decimal places.
10. Based on your answers to the above questions, should Lockwood invest in the machinery?

Check your answers online in MyAccountingLab or at http://www.pearsonhighered.com/Horngren.

For more practice, see Short Exercises S26-2 through S26-8. MyAccountingLab

WHAT IS THE TIME VALUE OF MONEY?

A dollar received today is worth more than a dollar to be received in the future because you can invest today's dollar and earn additional interest so you'll have more cash in the future. The fact that invested cash earns interest over time is called the *time value of money*. This concept explains why we would prefer to receive cash sooner rather than later. The time value of money means that the timing of capital investments' net cash inflows is important. Two methods of capital investment analysis incorporate the time value of money: the net present value (NPV) and internal rate of return (IRR). This section reviews the time value of money to make sure you have a firm foundation for discussing these two methods.

Time Value of Money Concepts

The time value of money depends on several key factors:

1. The principal amount (*p*)
2. The number of periods (*n*)
3. The interest rate (*i*)

The principal (*p*) refers to the amount of the investment or borrowing. Because this chapter deals with capital investments, we will primarily discuss the principal in terms of investments. However, the same concepts apply to borrowings, such as mortgages payable and bonds payable, which we covered in the financial accounting chapters. We state the principal as either a single lump sum or an annuity. For example, if you win the lottery, you have the choice of receiving all the winnings now (a single lump sum) or receiving series of equal payments for a period of time in the future (an annuity). An **annuity** is a stream of *equal cash payments* made at *equal time intervals*.[1] For example, $100 cash received per month for 12 months is an annuity. Capital investments also have lump sums and annuities. For example, consider the Smart Touch Learning's Web site upgrade project from the previous section of the chapter. The amount initially invested in the project, $240,000, is a lump sum because it is a one-time payment. However, the annual cash inflows of $80,000 per year for three years is an annuity. We consider both types of cash flows in capital investment decisions.

Annuity
A stream of equal cash payments made at equal time intervals.

The number of periods (*n*) is the length of time from the beginning of the investment until termination. All else being equal, the shorter the investment period, the lower the total amount of interest earned. If you withdraw your savings after four years rather than five years, you will earn less interest. In this chapter, the number of periods is stated in years.[2]

The interest rate (*i*) is the annual percentage earned on the investment. Interest can be computed as either simple interest or compound interest.

Simple Interest Versus Compound Interest

Simple interest means that interest is calculated *only* on the principal amount. **Compound interest** means that interest is calculated on the principal *and* on all previously earned interest. *Compound interest assumes that all interest earned will remain invested and earn additional interest at the same interest rate.* Exhibit 26-8 (on the next page) compares simple interest of 6% on a five-year, $10,000 investment with interest compounded yearly (rounded to the nearest dollar). As you can see, the amount of compound interest earned yearly grows as the base on which it is calculated (principal plus cumulative interest to date) grows. Over the life of this investment, the total amount of compound interest is more

Simple Interest
Interest calculated only on the principal amount.

Compound Interest
Interest calculated on the principal and on all previously earned interest.

---

[1] An *ordinary annuity* is an annuity in which the installments occur at the *end* of each period. An *annuity due* is an annuity in which the installments occur at the beginning of each period. Throughout this chapter, we use ordinary annuities because they are better suited to capital budgeting cash flow assumptions.

[2] The number of periods can also be stated in days, months, or quarters. If one of these methods is used, the interest rate needs to be adjusted to reflect the number of time periods in the year.

than the total amount of simple interest. Most investments yield compound interest, so we assume compound interest, rather than simple interest, for the rest of this chapter.

Exhibit 26-8 | **Simple Interest Versus Compound Interest—$10,000 at 6% for 5 Years**

Year	Simple Interest Calculation	Simple Interest	Compound Interest Calculation	Compound Interest
1	$10,000 × 6%	$ 600	$10,000 × 6%	$ 600
2	$10,000 × 6%	600	($10,000 + $600) × 6%	636
3	$10,000 × 6%	600	($10,000 + $600 + $636) × 6%	674*
4	$10,000 × 6%	600	($10,000 + $600 + $636 + $674) × 6%	715
5	$10,000 × 6%	600	($10,000 + $600 + $636 + $674 + $715) × 6%	758
	Total interest	**$ 3,000**	**Total interest**	**$ 3,383**

*all calculations rounded to the nearest dollar for the rest of this chapter

Present Value Factors

The future value or present value of an investment simply refers to the value of an investment at different points in time. We can calculate the future value or the present value of any investment by knowing (or assuming) information about the three factors we listed earlier: (1) the principal amount, (2) the number of periods, and (3) the interest rate. For example, in Exhibit 26-8, we calculated the interest that would be earned on (1) a $10,000 principal, (2) invested for five years, (3) at 6% interest. The future value of the investment is simply its worth at the end of the five-year time frame—the original principal *plus* the interest earned. In our example, the future value of the investment is as follows:

$$\text{Future value} = \text{Principal} + \text{Interest earned}$$
$$= \$10,000 + \$3,383$$
$$= \$13,383$$

If we invest $10,000 *today*, its *present value* is simply $10,000. So another way of stating the future value is as follows:

$$\text{Future value} = \text{Present value} + \text{Interest earned}$$

We can rearrange the equation as follows:

$$\text{Present value} = \text{Future value} - \text{Interest earned}$$
$$\$10,000 = \$13,383 - \$3,383$$

The only difference between present value and future value is the amount of interest that is earned in the intervening time span.

Calculating each period's compound interest, as we did in Exhibit 26-8, and then adding it to the present value to determine the future value (or subtracting it from the future value to determine the present value) is tedious. Fortunately, mathematical formulas have been developed that specify future values and present values for unlimited combinations of interest rates (i) and time periods (n). Separate formulas exist for single lump sum investments and annuities.

These formulas are programmed into most business calculators, so the user only needs to correctly enter the principal amount, interest rate, and number of time periods to find present or future values. These formulas are also programmed into spreadsheet functions in Microsoft Excel. In this section of the chapter, we use present value tables. (The Excel formulas are illustrated later in the chapter. Note that because the table values are rounded, the Excel results will differ slightly.) The present value tables contain the results of the formulas for various interest rate and time period combinations.

The formulas and resulting tables are shown in Appendix B at the end of this book:

1. **Present Value of $1** (Appendix B, Table B-1)—*used to calculate the value today of one future amount (a lump sum)*
2. **Present Value of Ordinary Annuity of $1** (Appendix B, Table B-2)—*used to calculate the value today of a series of equal future amounts (annuities)*

Take a moment to look at these tables because we are going to use them throughout the rest of the chapter. Note that the columns are interest rates (i) and the rows are periods (n).

The data in each table, known as present value factors (PV factors), are for an investment (or loan) of $1. To find the present value of an amount other than $1, multiply the PV factor by the future amount.

The annuity tables are derived from the lump sum tables. For example, the Annuity PV factors (in the Present Value of Ordinary Annuity of $1 table) are the *sums* of the PV factors found in the Present Value of $1 tables for a given number of time periods. The annuity tables allow us to perform one-step calculations rather than separately computing the present value of each annual cash installment and then summing the individual present values.

Present Value of a Lump Sum

The process for calculating present values is often called *discounting future cash flows* because future amounts are discounted (interest removed) to their present value. Let's consider the investment in Exhibit 26-8. The future value of the investment is $13,383. So the question is, "How much would I have to invest today (in the present time) to have $13,383 five years in the future if I invested at 6%?" Let's calculate the present value using PV factors.

> Present value = Future value × PV factor for i = 6%, n = 5

We determine the PV factor from the table labeled Present Value of $1 (Appendix B, Table B-1). We use this table for lump sum amounts. We look down the 6% column and across the 5 periods row and find the PV factor is 0.747. We finish our calculation as follows:

> **Present value = Future value × PV factor for i = 6%, n = 5**
> = $13,383 × 0.747
> = $9,997

Notice the calculation is off by $3 due to rounding ($10,000 − $9,997). The PV factors are rounded to three decimal places, so the calculations may not be exact. Also, the interest calculations in Exhibit 26-8 were rounded to the nearest dollar. Therefore, there are two rounding issues in this calculation. However, we do have the answer to our question: If approximately $9,997 is invested today at 6% for five years, at the end of five years, the investment will grow to $13,383. Or, conversely, if we expect to receive $13,383 five years from now, its equivalent (discounted) value today is $9,997.

Present Value of an Annuity

Let's now assume that instead of receiving a lump sum at the end of the five years, you will receive $2,000 at the end of each year. This is a series of equal payments ($2,000) over equal intervals (years), so it is an annuity. How much would you have to invest today to receive these payments, assuming an interest rate of 6%?

We determine the annuity PV factor from the table labeled Present Value of Ordinary Annuity of $1 (Appendix B, Table B-2). We use this table for annuities. We look down the 6% column and across the 5 periods row and find the annuity PV factor is 4.212. We finish our calculation as follows:

> Present value = Amount of each cash inflow × Annuity PV factor for i = 6%, n = 5
> = $2,000 × 4.212
> = $8,424

This means that an investment today of $8,424 at 6% will yield total payments of $10,000 over five years ($2,000 per year × 5 years). The reason is that interest is being earned on principal that is left invested each year. Let's verify the calculation.

Year	[1] Beginning Balance Previous [4]	[2] Interest [1] × 6%	[3] Withdrawal $2,000	[4] Ending Balance [1] + [2] − [3]
0				$ 8,424
1	$ 8,424	$ 505	$ 2,000	6,929
2	6,929	416	2,000	5,345
3	5,345	321	2,000	3,666
4	3,666	220	2,000	1,886
5	1,886	114*	2,000	0

*rounded up by $1

The chart shows that the initial investment of $8,424 is invested for one year, earning $505 in interest. At the end of that period, the first withdrawal of $2,000 takes place, leaving a balance of $6,929 ($8,424 + $505 − $2,000). At the end of the five years, the ending balance is $0, proving that the PV of the $2,000 annuity is $8,424.

Summary

Let's assume you have just won the lottery after purchasing one $5 lottery ticket. The state offers you the following three payout options for your after-tax prize money:

> Option 1: $1,000,000 now
> Option 2: $150,000 at the end of each year for the next 10 years ($1,500,000 total)
> Option 3: $2,000,000 at the end of 10 years

Which alternative should you take? You might be tempted to wait 10 years to "double" your winnings. You may be tempted to take the cash now and spend it. However, assume you plan to prudently invest all money received—no matter when you receive it—so that you have financial flexibility in the future (for example, for buying a house, retiring early, or taking exotic vacations). How can you choose among the three payment alternatives, when the total amount of each option varies ($1,000,000 versus $1,500,000 versus $2,000,000) and the timing of the cash flows varies (now versus some each year versus later)? Comparing these three options is like comparing apples to oranges—we just cannot do it—unless we find some common basis for comparison. Our common basis for comparison will be the prize-money's worth at a certain point in time—namely, today. In other words, if we convert each payment option to its *present value*, we can compare apples to apples.

We already know the principal amount and timing of each payment option, so the only assumption we will have to make is the interest rate. The interest rate will vary, depending on the amount of risk you are willing to take with your investment. Riskier investments (such as stock investments) command higher interest rates; safer investments (such as FDIC-insured bank deposits) yield lower interest rates. Let's say that after investigating possible investment alternatives, you choose an investment contract with an 8% annual return. We already know that the present value of Option #1 is $1,000,000 because we would receive that $1,000,000 today. Let's convert the other two payment options to their present values so that we can compare them. We will need to use the Present Value of Ordinary Annuity of $1 table (Appendix B, Table B-2) to convert payment Option #2 (because it is an annuity—a series of equal cash payments made at equal intervals) and the Present Value of $1 table (Appendix B, Table B-1) to convert payment Option #3 (because it is a lump sum). To obtain the PV factors, we will look down the 8% column and across the 10 periods row. Then we finish the calculations as follows:

Option 2:

Present value = Amount of each cash inflow × Annuity PV factor for *i* = 8%, *n* = 10
= $150,000 × 6.710
= $1,006,500

Option 3:

Present value = Principal × PV factor for *i* = 8%, *n* = 10
= $2,000,000 × 0.463
= $926,000

Exhibit 26-9 shows that we have converted each payout option to a common basis—its worth *today*—so we can make a valid comparison among the options. Based on this comparison, you should choose Option #2 because its worth, in today's dollars, is the highest of the three options.

Exhibit 26-9 | **Present Value of Lottery Payout Options**

Payment Options	Present Value of Lottery Payout (*i* = 8%, *n* = 10)
Option #1	$ 1,000,000
Option #2	1,006,500
Option #3	926,000

The lottery problem is a good example of how businesses use discounted cash flows to analyze capital investments. Companies make initial investments to purchase the assets. The initial investment is already in present value, similar to Lottery Option 1. The purpose of the investments is to increase cash flows in the future, but those future cash flows have to be discounted back to their present value in order to compare them to the initial investment already in present value, similar to Lottery Option 2. Some investments also have a residual value, meaning the company can sell the assets at the end of their useful lives and receive a lump sum cash inflow in the future, similar to Lottery Option 3.

Now that you have reviewed time value of money concepts, in the next section we discuss the two capital investment analysis methods that incorporate the time value of money: net present value (NPV) and internal rate of return (IRR).

Calculate the present value of the following future cash flows, rounding all calculations to the nearest dollar:

11. $5,000 received in three years with interest of 10%
12. $5,000 received in each of the following three years with interest of 10%
13. Payments of $2,000, $3,000, and $4,000 received in years 1, 2, and 3, respectively, with interest of 7%

Check your answers online in MyAccountingLab or at http://www.pearsonhighered.com/Horngren.

For more practice, see Short Exercises S26-9 and S26-10. MyAccountingLab

HOW DO DISCOUNTED CASH FLOW METHODS WORK?

Learning Objective 4

Use discounted cash flow methods to make capital investment decisions

Neither payback nor ARR recognizes the time value of money. That is, these methods fail to consider the *timing* of the net cash inflows an asset generates. *Discounted cash flow methods*—the net present value (NPV) and the internal rate of return (IRR) methods—overcome this weakness. These methods incorporate compound interest by assuming that companies will reinvest future cash flows when they are received. Many service, merchandising, and manufacturing firms use discounted cash flow methods to make capital investment decisions.

The NPV and IRR methods rely on present value calculations to compare the amount of the investment (the investment's initial cost) with its expected net cash inflows. Recall that an investment's *net cash inflows* include all *future* cash flows related to the investment, such as future increased sales or cost savings, netted against the investment's cash operating costs. Because the cash outflow for the investment occurs *now*, but the net cash inflows from the investment occur in the *future*, companies can make only valid "apple-to-apple" comparisons if they convert the cash flows to the *same point in time*—namely the present value. Companies use the present value to make the comparison (rather than the future value) because the investment's initial cost is already stated at its present value.[3]

If the present value of the investment's net cash inflows exceeds the initial cost of the investment, that's a good investment. In terms of our earlier lottery example, the lottery

---

[3] If the investment is to be purchased through lease payments, rather than a current cash outlay, we would still use the current cash price of the investment as its initial cost. If no current cash price is available, we would discount the future lease payments back to their present value to estimate the investment's current cash price.

ticket turned out to be a good investment because the present value of its net cash inflows (the present value of the lottery payout under *any* of the three payout options) exceeded the cost of the investment (the lottery ticket cost $5 to purchase). Let's begin our discussion by taking a closer look at the NPV method.

Net Present Value (NPV)

Smart Touch Learning is considering expanding production to include laptop computers and desktop computers, with each product considered a separate potential capital investment project. The projects each require the purchase of one specialized machine. Each machine costs $1,000,000, has a five-year life, and has zero residual value. The two projects have different patterns of predicted net cash inflows, as shown in Exhibit 26-10.

Exhibit 26-10 | Expected Cash Inflows for Two Projects

	Annual Net Cash Inflows	
Year	Laptop Computers	Desktop Computers
1	$ 305,450	$ 500,000
2	305,450	350,000
3	305,450	300,000
4	305,450	250,000
5	305,450	40,000
Total	$ 1,527,250	$ 1,440,000

The laptop project generates more net cash inflows, but the desktop project brings in cash sooner. To decide how attractive each investment is, we find its net present value. **Net present value (NPV)** is a capital investment analysis method that measures the *net difference* between the present value of the investment's net cash inflows and the investment's initial cost. We *discount* the net cash inflows—just as we did in the lottery example—using Smart Touch Learning's minimum required rate of return. This rate is called the **discount rate** because it is the interest rate used for the present value calculations. The discount rate is the interest rate that discounts or reduces future amounts to their lesser value in the present (today). It is also called the *required rate of return* or *hurdle rate* because the investment must meet or exceed this rate to be acceptable. The discount rate depends on the riskiness of investments. The higher the risk, the higher the discount rate. Smart Touch Learning's discount rate for these investments is 14%.

Net Present Value (NPV)
A capital investment analysis method that measures the net difference between the present value of the investment's net cash inflows and the investment's cost.

Discount Rate
Management's minimum desired rate of return on a capital investment.

To help you understand what a discount (hurdle) rate is, visualize a runner jumping over a hurdle at a track—the hurdle is the minimum height the runner must jump. The hurdle rate is the minimum rate that the investment must achieve.

Next we compare the present value of the net cash inflows to the investment's initial cost to decide which projects meet or exceed management's minimum desired rate of return. In other words, management is deciding whether the $1,000,000 investment is worth more (because the company would give it up now to invest in the project) or whether the project's future net cash inflows are worth more. Management can make a valid comparison only between the two sums of money by comparing them at the *same* point in time—namely, at their present value.

NPV with Equal Periodic Net Cash Inflows

Smart Touch Learning expects the laptop project to generate $305,450 of net cash inflows each year for five years. Because these cash flows are equal in amount and occur every year, they are an annuity. Therefore, we use the Present Value of Ordinary Annuity of $1 table (Appendix B, Table B-2) to find the appropriate Annuity PV factor for $i = 14\%$, $n = 5$.

The present value of the net cash inflows from Smart Touch Learning's laptop project is as follows:

> **Present value = Amount of each cash inflow × Annuity PV factor for $i = 14\%$, $n = 5$**
> = $305,450 × 3.433
> = $1,048,610

Next we simply subtract the investment's initial cost of $1,000,000 from the present value of the net cash inflows of $1,048,610. The difference of $48,610 is the *net* present value (NPV), as shown below:

Years		Net Cash Inflow	Annuity PV Factor ($i = 14\%$, $n = 5$)	Present Value
1–5	Present value of annuity	$305,450	3.433	$ 1,048,610
0	Initial investment			(1,000,000)
	Net present value of the laptop project			$ 48,610

A *positive* NPV means that the project earns *more than* the required rate of return. A negative NPV means that the project earns *less than* the required rate of return. This leads to the following decision rule:

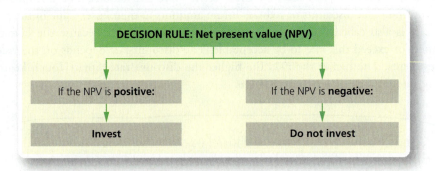

In Smart Touch Learning's case, the laptop project is an attractive investment. The $48,610 positive NPV means that the laptop project earns *more than* Smart Touch Learning's 14% required rate of return.

Another way managers can use present value analysis is to start the capital budgeting process by computing the total present value of the net cash inflows from the project to determine the *maximum* the company can invest in the project and still earn the required rate of return. For Smart Touch Learning, the present value of the net cash inflows is $1,048,610.

This means that Smart Touch Learning can invest a maximum of $1,048,610 and still earn the 14% target rate of return. (If Smart Touch Learning invests $1,048,610, the NPV will be $0 and the return will be exactly 14%.) Because Smart Touch Learning's managers believe they can undertake the project for $1,000,000, the project is an attractive investment.

NPV with Unequal Periodic Net Cash Inflows

In contrast to the laptop project, the net cash inflows of the desktop project are unequal—$500,000 in year 1, $350,000 in year 2, and so on—because the company expects to have higher sales volume in the early years of the project than in later years. Because these amounts vary by year, Smart Touch Learning's managers *cannot* use the annuity table to compute the present value of the desktop project. They must compute the present value of each individual year's net cash inflows *separately* (as separate lump sums received in different years), using the Present Value of $1 table (Appendix B, Table B-1). The net cash inflow received in year 1 is discounted using a PV factor of $i = 14\%$, $n = 1$, while the $350,000 net cash inflow received in year 2 is discounted using a PV factor of $i = 14\%$, $n = 2$, and so forth. After separately discounting each of the five years' net cash inflows, we add each result to find that the *total* present value of the desktop project's net cash inflows is $1,078,910. Finally we subtract the investment's cost of $1,000,000 to arrive at the desktop project's NPV: $78,910.

Years		Net Cash Inflow	PV Factor ($i = 14\%$)	Present Value
	Present value of each year's inflow:			
1	($n = 1$)	$ 500,000	0.877	$ 438,500
2	($n = 2$)	350,000	0.769	269,150
3	($n = 3$)	300,000	0.675	202,500
4	($n = 4$)	250,000	0.592	148,000
5	($n = 5$)	40,000	0.519	20,760
	Total PV of cash inflows			1,078,910
0	Initial investment			(1,000,000)
	Net present value of the desktop project			$ 78,910

Because the NPV is positive, Smart Touch Learning expects the desktop project to earn more than the 14% required rate of return, making this an attractive investment.

Our calculations show that both the laptop and desktop projects have positive NPVs. Therefore, both are attractive investments. Because resources are limited, companies are not always able to invest in all capital assets that meet their investment criteria. As mentioned earlier, this is called *capital rationing*. For example, Smart Touch Learning may not have the funds to invest in both the desktop and laptop projects at this time. In this case, Smart Touch Learning should choose the desktop project because it yields a higher NPV. The desktop project should earn an additional $78,910 beyond the 14% required rate of return, while the laptop project returns an additional $48,610.

This example illustrates an important point. The laptop project promises more *total* net cash inflows. But the *timing* of the desktop cash flows—loaded near the beginning of the project—gives the desktop investment a higher NPV. The desktop project is more attractive because of the time value of money. Its dollars, which are received sooner, are worth more now than the more distant dollars of the laptop project.

NPV of a Project with Residual Value

Many assets yield cash inflows at the end of their useful lives because they have residual value. Companies discount an investment's residual value to its present value when determining the *total* present value of the project's net cash inflows. The residual value is discounted as a single lump sum—not an annuity—because it will be received only once, when the asset is sold. In short, it is just another type of cash inflow of the project.

Suppose Smart Touch Learning expects that the laptop project equipment will be worth $100,000 at the end of its five-year life. To determine the laptop project's NPV, we discount the residual value of $100,000 using the Present Value of $1 table ($i = 14\%$, $n = 5$) located in Appendix B, Table B-1. We then *add* its present value of $51,900 to the present value of the laptop project's other net cash inflows we calculated previously ($1,048,610). This gives the new net present value calculation as shown here:

Years		Net Cash Inflow	Annuity PV Factor ($i = 14\%$, $n = 5$)	PV Factor ($i = 14\%$, $n = 5$)	Present Value
1–5	Present value of annuity	$305,450	3.433		$ 1,048,610
5	Present value of residual value	100,000		0.519	51,900
	Total PV of cash inflows				1,100,510
0	Initial investment				(1,000,000)
	Net present value of the laptop project				$ 100,510

Because of the expected residual value, the laptop project is now more attractive than the desktop project. If Smart Touch Learning could pursue only the laptop or desktop project because of capital rationing, Smart Touch Learning would now choose the laptop project because its NPV of $100,510 is higher than the desktop project's NPV of $78,910 and both projects require the same investment of $1,000,000.

Profitability Index

If Smart Touch Learning had to choose between the laptop and desktop project, the company would choose the desktop project in the first scenario because it yields a higher NPV ($78,910) and the laptop project in the second scenario because it yields a higher NPV when the residual value is considered ($100,510). However, comparing the NPV of the two projects is *only* valid because both projects require the same initial cost—$1,000,000. In contrast, Exhibit 26-11 summarizes three capital investment options faced by Smart Touch Learning. Each capital project requires a different initial investment. All three projects are attractive because each yields a positive NPV. Assuming Smart Touch Learning can invest in only one project at this time, which one should it choose? Project B yields the highest NPV, but it also requires a larger initial investment than the alternatives.

Exhibit 26-11 | Smart Touch Learning Capital Investment Options

Cash Flows	Project A	Project B	Project C
Present value of net cash inflows	$ 150,000	$ 238,000	$ 182,000
Initial investment	(125,000)	(200,000)	(150,000)
Net present value (NPV)	$ 25,000	$ 38,000	$ 32,000

To choose among the projects, Smart Touch Learning computes the profitability index (also known as the *present value index*). The **profitability index** computes the number of dollars returned for every dollar invested, *with all calculations performed in present value dollars*. The profitability index is computed as follows:

> Profitability Index = Present value of net cash inflows / Initial investment

Profitability Index
Computes the number of dollars returned for every dollar invested, with all calculations performed in present value dollars. Present value of net cash inflows / Initial investment.

The profitability index allows us to compare alternative investments in present value terms (like the NPV method), but it also considers differences in the investments' initial cost. Let's compute the profitability index for all three alternatives.

Project	Present value of net cash inflows	/	Initial investment	=	Profitability Index
A	$ 150,000	/	$ 125,000	=	1.20
B	238,000	/	200,000	=	1.19
C	182,000	/	150,000	=	**1.21**

The profitability index shows that Project C is the best of the three alternatives because it returns $1.21 (in present value dollars) for every $1.00 invested. Projects A and B return slightly less.

Let's also compute the profitability index for Smart Touch Learning's laptop and desktop projects (using the first scenario, without the residual value for the laptop project):

Project	Present value of net cash inflows	/	Initial investment	=	Profitability Index
Laptop	$ 1,048,610	/	$ 1,000,000	=	1.049
Desktop	1,078,910	/	1,000,000	=	**1.079**

The profitability index confirms our prior conclusion that the desktop project is more profitable than the laptop project. The desktop project returns $1.079 (in present value dollars) for every $1.00 invested (beyond the 14% return already used to discount the cash flows). We did not need the profitability index to determine that the desktop project was preferable because both projects required the same investment ($1,000,000). Because Smart Touch Learning chose the desktop project over the laptop project, the laptop project is the opportunity cost. *Opportunity cost* is the benefit foregone by choosing an alternative course of action.

ETHICS

How do I get my project approved?

Everyone at Timmons Company is feeling the squeeze. Economic conditions are not good, sales are down, and many capital investments are delayed. Grayson Ham really wants to get his project approved. He has been trying for three years to get the new manufacturing machine. Grayson is convinced the new machine will pay for itself in a few short years due to its greater efficiency. The current machine is a dinosaur—gobbling up electricity and replacement parts. Operating costs are outrageous! Grayson decides the best way to get a new machine is to "enhance" the numbers a little bit. If Grayson overstates the efficiency of the new machine, increasing the predicted future net cash inflows, he feels sure his project will get moved up the list—and he'll finally get the machine. What should Grayson do? What would you do?

Solution

Grayson should not overstate the predicted future net cash inflows. Timmons needs to make decisions that are best for the company as a whole, not just one department. If Grayson overstates the net cash inflows to get his project approved, another more profitable project may be rejected. In tough economic times, the decision could have a significant effect on the company. Grayson should present his project with figures that are as accurate as possible. To do otherwise could cause upper management to question his integrity and competence if his project is selected and it does not perform as expected. Grayson's enhancement will most likely be discovered during a post-audit.

Internal Rate of Return (IRR)

Internal Rate of Return (IRR)
The rate of return, based on discounted cash flows, of a capital investment. The interest rate that makes the NPV of the investment equal to zero.

Another discounted cash flow method for capital budgeting is the internal rate of return. The **internal rate of return (IRR)** is the rate of return, based on discounted cash flows, of a capital investment. *It is the interest rate that makes the NPV of the investment equal to zero.*

Let's look at this concept in another light by substituting in the definition of NPV:

> NPV = Present value of net cash inflows − Initial investment
>
> *If:*
>
> NPV = 0
>
> *then:*
>
> Initial investment = Present value of net cash inflows

When NPV is calculated, the PV factor is selected using the company's required rate of return. If the NPV is positive, then you know the actual rate of return is greater than the required rate of return and it is an acceptable project. However, you do not know the actual rate of return, only that it is greater than the required rate. If the NPV is zero, then you know the actual rate is equal to the required rate. The actual rate of return is called the *internal rate of return*. In other words, the IRR is the *interest rate* that makes the initial cost of the investment equal to the present value of the investment's net cash inflows, which means the NPV is zero. The higher the IRR, the more desirable the project.

IRR with Equal Periodic Net Cash Inflows

Let's first consider Smart Touch Learning's laptop project, which would cost $1,000,000 and result in five equal yearly net cash inflows of $305,450. We compute the IRR of an investment with equal periodic cash flows (annuity) by taking the following steps:

1. The IRR is the interest rate that makes the cost of the investment *equal to* the present value of the investment's net cash inflows, so we set up the following equation:

> Initial investment = PV of net cash inflows
>
> Initial investment = Amount of each cash inflow × Annuity PV factor (i = ?, n = given)

2. Next we plug in the information we do know—the investment cost, $1,000,000, the equal annual net cash inflows, $305,450, but assume there is no residual value, and the number of periods (five years):

> **Initial investment = Amount of each cash inflow × Annuity PV factor (i = ?, n = given)**
>
> $1,000,000 = $305,450 × Annuity PV factor (i =?, n = 5)

3. We then rearrange the equation and solve for the Annuity PV factor (i = ?, n = 5):

> **Annuity PV factor (i = ?, n = 5) = Initial investment / Amount of each cash inflow**
>
> = $1,000,000 / $305,450
>
> = 3.274

4. Finally we find the interest rate that corresponds to this Annuity PV factor. Turn to the Present Value of Ordinary Annuity of $1 table (Appendix B, Table B-2). Scan the row corresponding to the project's expected life—five years, in our example. Choose the column(s) with the number closest to the Annuity PV factor you calculated in step 3. The 3.274 annuity PV factor is in the 16% column. Therefore, the IRR of the laptop project is 16%. Smart Touch Learning expects the project to earn an internal rate of return of 16% over its life. We can confirm this result by using a 16% discount rate to calculate the project's NPV and prove the amount is zero. In other words, 16% is the discount rate that makes the investment cost equal to the present value of the investment's net cash inflows.

Years		Net Cash Inflow	Annuity PV Factor (i = 16%, n = 5)	Present Value
1–5	Present value of annuity	$305,450	3.274	$ 1,000,000*
0	Initial investment			(1,000,000)
	Net present value of the laptop project			$ 0

*slight rounding of $43

To decide whether the project is acceptable, compare the IRR with the minimum desired rate of return. The decision rule is as follows:

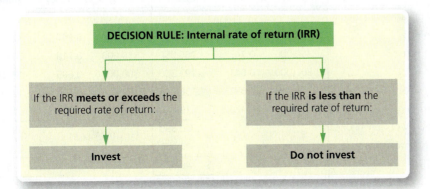

DECISION RULE: Internal rate of return (IRR)

If the IRR **meets or exceeds** the required rate of return: → **Invest**

If the IRR **is less than** the required rate of return: → **Do not invest**

Recall that Smart Touch Learning's required rate of return, or discount rate, is 14%. Because the laptop project's IRR (16%) is higher than the hurdle rate (14%), Smart Touch Learning would invest in the project.

In the laptop project, the exact Annuity PV factor (3.274) appears in the Present Value of an Ordinary Annuity of $1 table (Appendix B, Table B-2). Many times, the exact factor will not appear in the table. For example, let's find the IRR of Smart Touch Learning's B2B portal from Exhibit 26-4. Recall the B2B portal had a six-year life with annual net cash inflows of $60,000. The investment costs $240,000. We find its Annuity PV factor using the same steps:

> **Annuity PV factor ($i = ?$, $n = 6$) = Initial investment / Amount of each cash inflow**
>
> = $240,000 / $60,000
>
> = 4.000

Now look in the Present Value of Ordinary Annuity of $1 table in the row marked 6 periods (Appendix B, Table B-2). You will not see 4.00 under any column. The closest two factors are 3.889 (at 14%) and 4.111 (at 12%). Thus, the B2B portal's IRR must be somewhere between 12% and 14%. If we need a more precise figure, we could interpolate, or use a business calculator or Microsoft Excel, to find the portal's exact IRR of 12.978%. If Smart Touch Learning had a 14% required rate of return, it would *not* invest in the B2B portal because the portal's IRR is less than 14%.

IRR with Unequal Periodic Net Cash Flows

Because the desktop project has unequal cash inflows, Smart Touch Learning cannot use the Present Value of Ordinary Annuity of $1 table to find the asset's IRR. Rather, Smart Touch Learning must use a trial-and-error procedure to determine the discount rate making the project's NPV equal to zero. For example, because the company's minimum required rate of return is 14%, Smart Touch Learning might start by calculating whether the desktop project earns at least 14%. Recall from the NPV calculation that the desktop's NPV using a 14% discount rate is $78,910. Because the NPV is *positive*, the IRR must be *higher* than 14%. Smart Touch Learning continues the trial-and-error process using *higher* discount rates until the company finds the rate that brings the net present value of the desktop project to *zero*. The table below shows the NPV calculations using discount rates of 16% and 18%. At 18%, the NPV is $3,980, which is very close to zero. Thus, the IRR must be slightly higher than 18%. If we use a business calculator or Excel, rather than the trial-and-error procedure, we would find the IRR is 18.23%.

Years		Net Cash Inflow	PV Factor ($i = 16\%$)	Present Value	Net Cash Inflow	PV Factor ($i = 18\%$)	Present Value
	PV of each year's inflow:						
1	($n = 1$)	$ 500,000	0.862	$ 431,000	$ 500,000	0.847	$ 423,500
2	($n = 2$)	350,000	0.743	260,050	350,000	0.718	251,300
3	($n = 3$)	300,000	0.641	192,300	300,000	0.609	182,700
4	($n = 4$)	250,000	0.552	138,000	250,000	0.516	129,000
5	($n = 5$)	40,000	0.476	19,040	40,000	0.437	17,480
	Total PV of cash inflows			1,040,390			1,003,980
0	Initial investment			(1,000,000)			(1,000,000)
	NPV			$ 40,390			$ 3,980

The desktop's internal rate of return is higher than Smart Touch Learning's 14% required rate of return, so the desktop project is acceptable.

Comparing Capital Investment Analysis Methods

We have discussed four capital budgeting methods commonly used by companies to make capital investment decisions. Two of these methods do not incorporate the time value of money: payback and ARR. The discounted cash flow methods are superior because they consider both the time value of money and profitability. These methods compare an investment's initial cost with its future net cash inflows—all converted to the *same point in time*—the present value. Profitability is built into the discounted cash flow methods because they consider *all* cash inflows and outflows over the project's life. Exhibit 26-12 compares the four methods of capital investment analysis.

Exhibit 26-12 | Comparison of Capital Investment Analysis Methods

	Payback	Accounting Rate of Return (ARR)	Net Present Value (NPV)	Internal Rate of Return (IRR)
Focus	The time it takes to recover the company's initial cash investment	How the investment will affect operating income	The difference between the PV of the net cash inflows and the initial cash investment	The rate of return, based on discounted cash flows, of a capital investment
Strengths	• Simple to compute • Highlights risks of investments with longer cash recovery periods	• The only method that uses accrual accounting figures • Measures the profitability of the asset over its entire life	• Incorporates the time value of money • Considers the asset's net cash flows over its entire life • Indicates whether the asset will earn the company's minimum required rate of return	• Incorporates the time value of money • Considers the asset's net cash flows over its entire life • Computes the project's unique rate of return • No additional steps needed for capital rationing decisions
Weaknesses	• Ignores the time value of money • Ignores any cash flows occurring after the payback period, including any residual value	• Ignores the time value of money	• The profitability index should be computed for capital rationing decisions when the assets require different initial investments	• Difficult to calculate accurately without a business calculator or computer software

Managers often use more than one method to gain different perspectives on risks and returns. For example, Smart Touch Learning could decide to pursue capital projects with positive NPVs, provided that those projects have a payback of less than or equal to four years.

Sensitivity Analysis

The examples of capital investment analysis methods illustrated in the chapter used the present value tables located in Appendix B. These calculations can also be completed using a business calculator with NPV and IRR functions. Using computer spreadsheet software, such as Microsoft Excel, can be more beneficial, however, because it allows for easy manipulation of the figures to perform sensitivity analysis. Remember that sensitivity analysis is a "what if" technique that shows how results differ when underlying assumptions change. Capital budgeting decisions affect cash flows far into the future. Smart Touch Learning managers might want to know whether their decision would be affected by any of their major assumptions. Examples include changing the discount rate from 14% to 12% or 16% or increasing or decreasing the net cash inflows by 10%. After reviewing the basic information for NPV analysis, managers perform sensitivity analyses to recalculate and review the results.

Let's use Excel to calculate the NPV and IRR of the two projects Smart Touch Learning is considering: laptop computers and desktop computers. Recall that both projects require an initial investment of $1,000,000 and have no residual value. Their annual net cash inflows are:

	Annual Net Cash Inflows	
Year	Laptop Computers	Desktop Computers
1	$ 305,450	$ 500,000
2	305,450	350,000
3	305,450	300,000
4	305,450	250,000
5	305,450	40,000
Total	$ 1,527,250	$ 1,440,000

One method of setting up Excel spreadsheets is to have areas of the spreadsheet designated for inputs and outputs. Cells for entering the inputs are at the top of the spreadsheet. Cells with formulas to calculate the outputs are in a section below the inputs. All outputs are calculated by Excel based on the formulas entered, which reference the cells with the inputs. This method of setup allows the user to make changes to any input cell and have Excel automatically recalculate the outputs. Exhibit 26-13 shows the Excel spreadsheet set up in this manner with Smart Touch Learning's capital investment analysis for the two projects.

Exhibit 26-13 | **Capital Investment Analysis Using Excel**

	A	B	C	D	E	F
		Chapter 26 - Capital Investment Decisions - M..				
	File Home Insert Page Layout Formulas Data Review View PDF Acrobat					
	B26	f_x				
1	Smart Touch Learning					
2	Capital Investment Analysis					
3						
4	Project:	Laptops		Desktops		
5						
6	INPUTS:					
7	Useful Life (in years)	5		5		
8	Discount rate	14%		14%		
9						
10	Initial Investment	$ (1,000,000)		$ (1,000,000)		
11	Cash Inflows:					
12	Year 1	305,450		500,000		
13	Year 2	305,450		350,000		
14	Year 3	305,450		300,000		
15	Year 4	305,450		250,000		
16	Year 5	305,450		40,000		
17	Totals	$ 1,527,250		$ 1,440,000		
18						
19	OUTPUTS:					
20	NPV	$48,635		$79,196		
21	IRR	16.01%		18.23%		
22						
	Results / Formulas					
	Ready		100%			

Notice that the initial investment is entered as a negative amount because it is a cash outflow and the cash inflows are entered as positive amounts. In the output section, Excel calculated the NPV of the laptop project as $48,635, which is $25 more than the amount previously calculated using the PV tables ($48,610). The difference is because the PV factors in the tables are rounded to three decimal places. The difference for the desktop project is higher, $286 ($79,196 − $78,910). However, for a project with an investment of $1,000,000, this difference is less than 0.03% ($286 / $1,000,000) and should not be considered significant.

Exhibit 26-14 (on the next page) shows the formulas used to calculate the NPV and IRR of the two projects.

Exhibit 26-14 | Excel Formulas

	A	B	C	D
1	Smart Touch Learning			
2	Capital Investment Analysis			
3				
4	Project:	Laptops		Desktops
5				
6	INPUTS:			
7	Useful Life (in years)	5		5
8	Discount rate	0.14		0.14
9				
10	Initial Investment	-1000000		-1000000
11	Cash Inflows:			
12	Year 1	305450		500000
13	Year 2	305450		350000
14	Year 3	305450		300000
15	Year 4	305450		250000
16	Year 5	305450		40000
17	Totals	=SUM(B12:B16)		=SUM(D12:D16)
18				
19	OUTPUTS:			
20	NPV	=NPV(B8,B12:B16)+B10		=NPV(D8,D12:D16)+D10
21	IRR	=IRR(B10:B16)		=IRR(D10:D16)
22				

The formula to calculate NPV is = NPV(rate,value1,value2,...). For the laptop project, the discount rate is entered in cell B8 and the cash inflows are in cells B12 through B16. Notice that the initial investment amount in cell B10 is added. Excel calculated the PV of the cash inflows and then added the negative amount of the cash outflow to determine the NPV:

$$=NPV(B8,B12:B16)+B10$$

The IRR formula includes the range of all the cash flows, including the initial investment. Keep in mind that it is imperative to list the cash flows in the proper order! The time value of money considers the timing of the cash flows, and Excel is calculating the NPV and IRR based on the order of the entries.

Now that the spreadsheet is set up, Smart Touch Learning can easily change any amounts in the input section to complete a sensitivity analysis. Also, the spreadsheet can be used to analyze any other projects by simply changing the inputs. If other projects have longer lives, then rows can be inserted to accommodate the additional cash inflows and then the formulas adjusted to include those rows.

Try setting up the spreadsheet as shown. Then change some inputs—such as the discount rate—to see how the results change.

Capital Rationing

We have mentioned capital rationing several times, but it is worthwhile to revisit the topic. Most companies have limited resources and have to make hard decisions about which projects to pursue and which ones to delay or reject. These decisions are not just based on the quantitative factors of payback, ARR, NPV, and IRR. Qualitative factors must also be considered. For example, a company may choose manufacturing equipment with a lower NPV because it is more environmentally friendly or accept a project that is not profitable but adds value to the community. Companies should also consider the opportunity costs of rejecting certain projects and the possibility of lost business if there is a negative public perception of the company's choices. Exhibit 26-15 shows a decision tree for capital rationing.

Exhibit 26-15 | **Decision Tree for Capital Rationing**

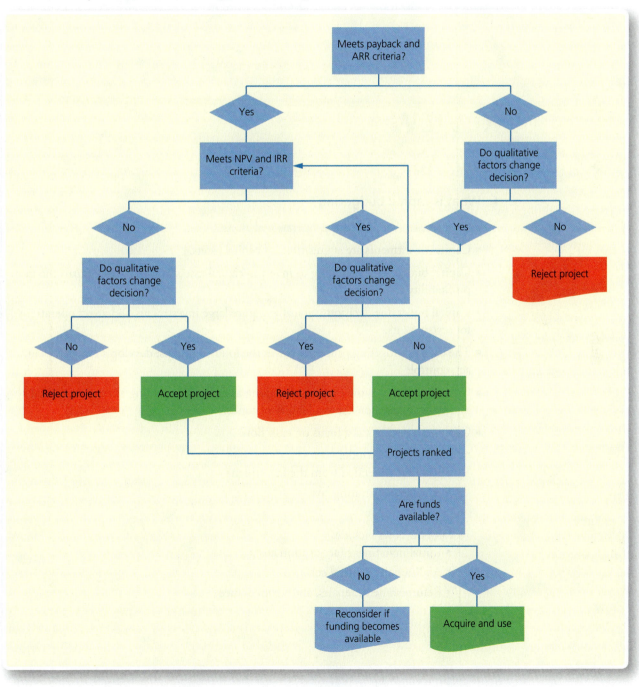

Cornell Company is considering a project with an initial investment of $596,500 that is expected to produce cash inflows of $125,000 for nine years. Cornell's required rate of return is 12%.

14. What is the NPV of the project?
15. What is the IRR of the project?
16. Is this an acceptable project for Cornell?

Check your answers online in MyAccountingLab or at http://www.pearsonhighered.com/Horngren.

For more practice, see Short Exercises S26-11 through S26-14.   MyAccountingLab

REVIEW

> Things You Should Know

1. What is capital budgeting?

- Capital assets are long-term, operational assets.

- Capital investments are acquisitions of capital assets.

- Capital budgeting is planning to invest in capital assets in a way that returns the most profitability to the company.

- Capital budgeting decisions typically require large investments and affect operations for several years.

- The capital budgeting process involves the following steps: develop strategies, plan, act, control.

- Capital rationing is the process of ranking and choosing among alternative capital investments based on the availability of funds.

- Capital budgeting has a focus on cash flows.
  - Cash inflows include:
    - Revenue generated from the investment
    - Savings in operating costs
    - Residual value
  - Cash outflows include:
    - Initial investment (acquisition cost)
    - Additional operating costs
    - Refurbishment, repairs, and maintenance

2. How do the payback and accounting rate of return methods work?

- Payback is a capital investment analysis method that measures the length of time it takes to recover, in net cash inflows, the cost of the initial investment.

  - If net cash inflows are equal:

$$\text{Payback} = \frac{\text{Amount invested}}{\text{Expected annual net cash inflow}}$$

  - If net cash inflows are unequal:
    - Add accumulated net cash inflows for full years before complete recovery, then:

$$\text{Payback} = \text{Full years} + \frac{\text{Amount needed to complete recovery in next year}}{\text{Net cash inflow in next year}}$$

  - Criticisms of payback:
    - Focus is on time, not profitability
    - Ignores cash flows after payback period

  - Decision rule: Investments with **shorter** payback periods are more desirable, all else being equal.

- Accounting rate of return (ARR) is a capital investment analysis method that measures the profitability of an investment.

$$\text{ARR} = \frac{\text{Average annual operating income}}{\text{Average amount invested}}$$

  - Uses operating income rather than cash flows.
  - Decision rule: If the expected ARR **meets or exceeds** the required rate of return, invest in the asset.

3. What is the time value of money?

- The fact that invested money earns interest over time is called the *time value of money*. This concept explains why we would prefer to receive cash sooner rather than later.
- Lump sum payments are one-time cash payments.
- Annuities are streams of equal cash payments made at equal time intervals.
- Simple interest means that interest is calculated *only* on the principal amount.
- Compound interest means that interest is calculated on the principal *and* on all previously earned interest.
- To calculate the present value of a lump sum, use the following equation:

$$\text{Present value} = \text{Future value} \times \text{PV factor for } i = ?, n = ?$$

- To calculate the present value of an annuity, use this equation:

$$\text{Present value} = \text{Amount of each cash inflow} \times \text{Annuity PV factor for } i = ?, n = ?$$

4. How do discounted cash flow methods work?

- Discounted cash flow methods incorporate compound interest and make comparisons by converting all cash flows to the *same point in time*—namely the present value.

- Net Present Value (NPV) analysis is a capital investment analysis method that measures the net difference between the present value of the investment's net cash inflows and the investment's cost.

  - Discount rate is management's minimum desired rate of return on a capital investment and is used to select the present value factors used when calculating the net present value of a project.

  - Decision rule: If the NPV is **positive**, invest in the capital asset.

  - The profitability index computes the number of dollars returned for every dollar invested, *with all calculations performed in present value dollars*. It is useful to rank projects of different sizes.

  > Profitability Index = Present value of net cash inflows / Initial investment

- Internal rate of return (IRR) is the rate of return, based on discounted cash flows, of a capital investment. *It is the interest rate that makes the NPV of the investment equal to zero.*

  - If net cash inflows are equal:
    - Determine the annuity PV factor using this equation:

  > Annuity PV factor (i = ?, n = given) = Initial investment / Amount of each cash inflow

    - Use the Present Value of an Ordinary Annuity of $1 table to find the factor closest to the result to estimate the IRR.

  - If net cash inflows are unequal, use the following methods:
    - A trial-and-error method can be used to estimate the IRR.
    - To find an exact IRR, use a business calculator or spreadsheet software, such as Excel.

  - Decision rule: If the IRR **meets or exceeds** the required rate of return, invest in the asset.

- Review Exhibit 26-12 for a comparison of the four capital investment analysis methods.

- Sensitivity analysis allows managers to evaluate differences when underlying assumptions change.

- Using spreadsheet software, such as Excel, allows for quicker, more precise analysis and easier sensitivity analysis.

- Capital rationing occurs when funds for capital investments are limited.

  - Quantitative and qualitative factors should be considered.

  - Review Exhibit 26-15 for a capital rationing decision tree.

> Summary Problem 26-1

Dyno-max is considering buying a new water treatment system for its plant in Austin, Texas. The company screens its potential capital investments using the payback and accounting rate of return methods. If a potential investment has a payback of less than four years and a minimum 12% accounting rate of return, it will be considered further. The data for the water treatment system follow:

Cost of water treatment system	$ 48,000
Estimated residual value	0
Estimated annual net cash inflow (each year for 5 years) from anticipated environmental cleanup savings	13,000
Estimated useful life	5 years

Requirements

1. Compute the water treatment system's payback.
2. Compute the water treatment system's ARR.
3. Should Dyno-max turn down this investment proposal or consider it further?

> Solution

Requirement 1

$$\text{Payback} = \frac{\text{Amount invested}}{\text{Expected annual net cash inflow}}$$

$$= \frac{\$48,000}{\$13,000} = 3.7 \text{ years (rounded)}$$

Requirement 2

Total net cash inflows during operating life of the asset ($13,000 per year × 5 years)	$ 65,000
Less: Total depreciation during operating life of the asset ($48,000 − $0)	48,000
Total operating income during operating life	17,000
Divide by: Asset's operating life in years	÷ 5 years
Average annual operating income from asset	$ 3,400

$$\text{ARR} = \frac{\$3,400}{(\$48,000 + \$0)/2} = \frac{\$3,400}{\$24,000} = 0.142 = 14.2\%$$

Requirement 3

Decision: The water treatment system proposal passes both initial screening tests. The payback is slightly less than four years, and the accounting rate of return is higher than 12%. Dyno-max should further analyze the proposal using a method that incorporates the time value of money.

> Summary Problem 26-2

Recall from Summary Problem 26-1 that Dyno-max is considering buying a new water treatment system. The investment proposal passed the initial screening tests (payback and accounting rate of return) so the company now wants to analyze the proposal using the discounted cash flow methods. Recall that the water treatment system costs $48,000, has a five-year life, and has no residual value. The estimated net cash inflows from environmental cleanup savings are $13,000 per year over its life. The company's required rate of return is 16%.

Requirements

1. Compute the water treatment system's NPV.

2. Find the water treatment system's IRR (exact percentage is not required).

3. Should Dyno-max buy the water treatment system? Why?

> Solution

Requirement 1

Years		Net Cash Inflow	Annuity PV Factor ($i = 16\%, n = 5$)	Present Value
1–5	Present value of annuity	$13,000	3.274	$ 42,562
0	Initial investment			(48,000)
	Net present value			$ (5,438)

Requirement 2

Annuity PV factor (i = ?, n = 5) = Initial investment / Amount of each cash inflow

= $48,000 / $13,000

= 3.692

Because the cash flows occur for five years, we look for the PV factor 3.692 in the row marked $n = 5$ on the Present Value of Ordinary Annuity of $1 table (Appendix B, Table B-2). The PV factor is 3.605 at 12% and 3.791 at 10%. Therefore, the water treatment system has an IRR that falls between 10% and 12%. (*Optional:* Using a business calculator or Excel, we find an 11.04% internal rate of return.)

Requirement 3

Decision: Dyno-max should not buy the water treatment system. It has a negative NPV, and its IRR falls below the company's required rate of return. Both methods consider profitability and the time value of money. Because the savings came mainly from the estimated environmental cleanup savings, the company may want to study this issue further to ensure all environmental savings, both short-term and long-term, were considered in the initial evaluation.

> Key Terms

Accounting Rate of Return (ARR) (p. 1439)

Annuity (p. 1443)

Capital Asset (p. 1432)

Capital Budgeting (p. 1432)

Capital Investment (p. 1432)

Capital Rationing (p. 1434)

Compound Interest (p. 1443)

Discount Rate (p. 1449)

Internal Rate of Return (IRR) (p. 1454)

Net Present Value (NPV) (p. 1449)

Payback (p. 1436)

Post-Audit (p. 1434)

Profitability Index (p. 1453)

Simple Interest (p. 1443)

> Quick Check

1. What is the second step of capital budgeting?

   a. Gathering the money for the investment

   b. Identifying potential projects

   c. Getting the accountant involved

   d. All of the above

Learning Objective 1

2. Which of the following methods does not consider the investment's profitability?

   a. ARR

   b. Payback

   c. NPV

   d. IRR

Learning Objective 2

3. Suppose Francine Dunkelberg's Sweets is considering investing in warehouse-management software that costs $550,000, has $75,000 residual value, and should lead to cost savings of $130,000 per year for its five-year life. In calculating the ARR, which of the following figures should be used as the equation's denominator (average amount invested in the asset)?

   a. $275,000

   b. $237,500

   c. $625,000

   d. $312,500

Learning Objective 2

4. Your rich aunt has promised to give you $2,000 per year at the end of each of the next four years to help you pay for college. Using a discount rate of 12%, the present value of the gift can be stated as

   a. PV = $2,000 (PV factor, $i = 4\%$, $n = 12$).

   b. PV = $2,000 (Annuity PV factor, $i = 12\%$, $n = 4$).

   c. PV = $2,000 (Annuity FV factor, $i = 12\%$, $n = 4$).

   d. PV = $2,000 \times 12\% \times 4$.

Learning Objective 3

5. Which of the following affects the present value of an investment?

   a. The type of investment (annuity versus single lump sum)

   b. The number of time periods (length of the investment)

   c. The interest rate

   d. All of the above

Learning Objective 3

CHAPTER 26

Learning Objective 4

6. Which of the following is true regarding capital rationing decisions?

   a. Companies should always choose the investment with the highest NPV.

   b. Companies should always choose the investment with the highest ARR.

   c. Companies should always choose the investment with the shortest payback.

   d. None of the above

Learning Objective 4

7. In computing the IRR on an expansion at Mountain Creek Resort, Vernon Valley would consider all of the following *except*

   a. present value factors.

   b. depreciation on the assets built in the expansion.

   c. predicted cash inflows over the life of the expansion.

   d. the cost of the expansion.

Learning Objective 4

8. The IRR is

   a. the interest rate at which the NPV of the investment is zero.

   b. the firm's hurdle rate.

   c. the same as the ARR.

   d. None of the above

Learning Objective 4

9. Which of the following is the most reliable method for making capital budgeting decisions?

   a. ARR method

   b. Post-audit method

   c. NPV method

   d. Payback method

Learning Objective 4

10. Ian Corp. is considering two expansion projects. The first project streamlines the company's warehousing facilities. The second project automates inventory utilizing bar code scanners. Both projects generate positive NPV, yet Ian Corp. only chooses the bar coding project. Why?

    a. The payback is greater than the warehouse project's life.

    b. The internal rate of return of the warehousing project is less than the company's required rate of return for capital projects.

    c. The company is practicing capital rationing.

    d. All of the above are true.

Check your answers at the end of the chapter.

ASSESS YOUR PROGRESS

> Review Questions

1. Explain the difference between capital assets, capital investments, and capital budgeting.

2. Describe the capital budgeting process.

3. What is capital rationing?

4. What are post-audits? When are they conducted?

5. List some common cash inflows from capital investments.

6. List some common cash outflows from capital investments.

7. What is the payback method of analyzing capital investments?

8. How is payback calculated with equal net cash inflows?

9. How is payback calculated with unequal net cash inflows?

10. What is the decision rule for payback?

11. What are some criticisms of the payback method?

12. What is the accounting rate of return?

13. How is ARR calculated?

14. What is the decision rule for ARR?

15. Why is it preferable to receive cash sooner rather than later?

16. What is an annuity? How does it differ from a lump sum payment?

17. How does compound interest differ from simple interest?

18. Explain the difference between the present value factor tables—Present Value of $1 and Present Value of Ordinary Annuity of $1.

19. How is the present value of a lump sum determined?

20. How is the present value of an annuity determined?

21. Why are net present value and internal rate of return considered discounted cash flow methods?

22. What is net present value?

23. What is the decision rule for NPV?

24. What is the profitability index? When is it used?

25. What is the internal rate of return?

26. How is IRR calculated with equal net cash inflows?

27. How is IRR calculated with unequal net cash inflows?

28. What is the decision rule for IRR?

29. How can spreadsheet software, such as Excel, help with sensitivity analysis?

30. Why should both quantitative and qualitative factors be considered in capital investment decisions?

CHAPTER 26

> Short Exercises

Learning Objective 1

S26-1 Outlining the capital budgeting process

Review the following activities of the capital budgeting process:

a. Budget capital investments.

b. Project investments' cash flows.

c. Perform post-audits.

d. Make investments.

e. Use feedback to reassess investments already made.

f. Identify potential capital investments.

g. Screen/analyze investments using one or more of the methods discussed.

Place the activities in sequential order as they occur in the capital budgeting process.

Learning Objective 2

S26-2 Using payback to make capital investment decisions

Carter Company is considering three investment opportunities with the following payback periods:

	Project A	Project B	Project C
Payback period	2.7 years	6.4 years	3.8 years

Use the decision rule for payback to rank the projects from most desirable to least desirable, all else being equal.

Learning Objective 2

S26-3 Using accounting rate of return to make capital investment decisions

Carter Company is considering three investment opportunities with the following accounting rates of return:

	Project X	Project Y	Project Z
ARR	13.25%	6.58%	10.47%

Use the decision rule for ARR to rank the projects from most desirable to least desirable. Carter Company's required rate of return is 8%.

Learning Objective 2

S26-4 Using the payback and accounting rate of return methods to make capital investment decisions

Consider how Stenback Valley Snow Park Lodge could use capital budgeting to decide whether the $11,000,000 Snow Park Lodge expansion would be a good investment. Assume Stenback Valley's managers developed the following estimates concerning the expansion:

Number of additional skiers per day	116 skiers
Average number of days per year that weather conditions allow skiing at Stenback Valley	143 days
Useful life of expansion (in years)	8 years
Average cash spent by each skier per day	$ 244
Average variable cost of serving each skier per day	82
Cost of expansion	11,000,000
Discount rate	12%

Assume that Stenback Valley uses the straight-line depreciation method and expects the lodge expansion to have a residual value of $600,000 at the end of its eight-year life.

Requirements

1. Compute the average annual net cash inflow from the expansion.
2. Compute the average annual operating income from the expansion.

Note: Short Exercise S26-4 must be completed before attempting Short Exercise S26-5.

S26-5 Using the payback method to make capital investment decisions

Learning Objective 2

Refer to the Stenback Valley Snow Park Lodge expansion project in Short Exercise S26-4. Compute the payback for the expansion project. Round to one decimal place.

Note: Short Exercise S26-4 must be completed before attempting Short Exercise S26-6.

S26-6 Using the ARR method to make capital investment decisions

Learning Objective 2

Refer to the Stenback Valley Snow Park Lodge expansion project in Short Exercise S26-4. Calculate the ARR. Round to two decimal places.

Note: Short Exercises S26-4, S26-5, and S26-6 must be completed before attempting Short Exercise S26-7.

S26-7 Using the payback and ARR methods to make capital investment decisions

Learning Objective 2

Refer to the Stenback Valley Snow Park Lodge expansion project in Short Exercise S26-4 and your calculations in Short Exercises S26-5 and S26-6. *Assume the expansion has zero residual value.*

Requirements

1. Will the payback change? Explain your answer. Recalculate the payback if it changes. Round to one decimal place.
2. Will the project's ARR change? Explain your answer. Recalculate ARR if it changes. Round to two decimal places.
3. Assume Stenback Valley screens its potential capital investments using the following decision criteria:

Maximum payback period	5.0 years
Minimum accounting rate of return	18.00%

Will Stenback Valley consider this project further or reject it?

CHAPTER 26

Learning Objective 2

S26-8 Using the payback and ARR methods to make capital investment decisions

Suppose Stenback Valley is deciding whether to purchase new accounting software. The payback for the $30,050 software package is five years, and the software's expected life is seven years. Stenback Valley's required rate of return for this type of project is 9.0%. Assuming equal yearly cash flows, what are the expected annual net cash savings from the new software?

Learning Objective 3

S26-9 Using the time value of money

Use the Present Value of $1 table (Appendix B, Table B-1) to determine the present value of $1 received one year from now. Assume a 12% interest rate. Use the same table to find the present value of $1 received two years from now. Continue this process for a total of five years. Round to three decimal places.

Requirements

1. What is the *total* present value of the cash flows received over the five-year period?
2. Could you characterize this stream of cash flows as an annuity? Why or why not?
3. Use the Present Value of Ordinary Annuity of $1 table (Appendix B, Table B-2) to determine the present value of the same stream of cash flows. Compare your results to your answer to Requirement 1.
4. Explain your findings.

Learning Objective 3

S26-10 Using the time value of money

Your grandfather would like to share some of his fortune with you. He offers to give you money under one of the following scenarios (you get to choose):

1. $8,550 per year at the end of each of the next seven years
2. $48,350 (lump sum) now
3. $100,250 (lump sum) seven years from now

Requirements

1. Calculate the present value of each scenario using an 8% discount rate. Which scenario yields the highest present value? Round to nearest whole dollar.
2. Would your preference change if you used a 12% discount rate?

Note: Short Exercise S26-4 must be completed before attempting Short Exercise S26-11.

Learning Objective 4

S26-11 Using NPV to make capital investment decisions

Refer to the Stenback Valley Snow Park Lodge expansion project in Short Exercise S26-4. What is the project's NPV (round to nearest dollar)? Is the investment attractive? Why or why not?

Note: Short Exercise S26-4 must be completed before attempting Short Exercise S26-12.

Learning Objective 4

S26-12 Using NPV to make capital investment decisions

Refer to Short Exercise S26-4. *Assume the expansion has no residual value.* What is the project's NPV (round to nearest dollar)? Is the investment attractive? Why or why not?

Note: Short Exercise S26-4 must be completed before attempting Short Exercise S26-13.

S26-13 Using IRR to make capital investment decisions

Learning Objective 4

Refer to Short Exercise S26-4. *Continue to assume that the expansion has no residual value.* What is the project's IRR? Is the investment attractive? Why or why not?

S26-14 Using NPV to make capital investment decisions

Learning Objective 4

Castle is considering an investment opportunity with the following expected net cash inflows: Year 1, $230,000; Year 2, $170,000; Year 3, $110,000. The company uses a discount rate of 9%, and the initial investment is $345,000. Calculate the NPV of the investment. Should the company invest in the project? Why or why not?

> Exercises

E26-15 Defining capital investments and the capital budgeting process

Learning Objectives 1, 2, 4

Match each definition with its capital budgeting method.

METHODS

1. Accounting rate of return
2. Internal rate of return
3. Net present value
4. Payback

DEFINITIONS

a. Is only concerned with the time it takes to get cash outflows returned.

b. Considers operating income but not the time value of money in its analyses.

c. Compares the present value of cash outflows to the present value of cash inflows to determine investment worthiness.

d. The true rate of return an investment earns.

E26-16 Defining capital investment terms

Learning Objectives 1, 2, 4

Fill in each statement with the appropriate capital investment analysis method: Payback, ARR, NPV, or IRR. Some statements may have more than one answer.

a. _____ is (are) more appropriate for long-term investments.

b. _____ highlights risky investments.

c. _____ shows the effect of the investment on the company's accrual-based income.

d. _____ is the interest rate that makes the NPV of an investment equal to zero.

e. _____ requires management to identify the discount rate when used.

f. _____ provides management with information on how fast the cash invested will be recouped.

g. _____ is the rate of return, using discounted cash flows, a company can expect to earn by investing in the asset.

h. _____ does not consider the asset's profitability.

i. _____ uses accrual accounting rather than net cash inflows in its computation.

Learning Objective 2

E26-17 Using payback to make capital investment decisions

Consider the following three projects. All three have an initial investment of $500,000.

	Net Cash Inflows					
	Project L		Project M		Project N	
Year	Annual	Accumulated	Annual	Accumulated	Annual	Accumulated
1	$ 100,000	$ 100,000	$ 50,000	$ 50,000	$ 250,000	$ 250,000
2	100,000	200,000	150,000	200,000	250,000	500,000
3	100,000	300,000	200,000	400,000		
4	100,000	400,000	100,000	500,000		
5	100,000	500,000	150,000	650,000		
6	100,000	600,000				
7	100,000	700,000				
8	100,000	800,000				

Requirements

1. Determine the payback period of each project. Rank the projects from most desirable to least desirable based on payback.

2. Are there other factors that should be considered in addition to the payback period?

Learning Objective 2

4.1 yrs.

E26-18 Using payback to make capital investment decisions

White Co. is considering acquiring a manufacturing plant. The purchase price is $1,350,000. The owners believe the plant will generate net cash inflows of $329,000 annually. It will have to be replaced in six years. Use the payback method to determine whether White should purchase this plant. Round to one decimal place.

Learning Objective 2

5.3 yrs.

E26-19 Using payback to make capital investment decisions

Rapp Hardware is adding a new product line that will require an investment of $1,418,000. Managers estimate that this investment will have a 10-year life and generate net cash inflows of $310,000 the first year, $290,000 the second year, and $250,000 each year thereafter for eight years. Compute the payback period. Round to one decimal place.

Note: Exercise S26-19 must be completed before attempting Exercise S26-20.

Learning Objective 2

16.67%

E26-20 Using ARR to make capital investment decisions

Refer to the Rapp Hardware information in Exercise E26-19. Assume the project has no residual value. Compute the ARR for the investment. Round to two places.

Learning Objective 3

2. $143,208

E26-21 Using the time value of money

Sharon wants to take the next five years off work to travel around the world. She estimates her annual cash needs at $34,000 (if she needs more, she will work odd jobs). Sharon believes she can invest her savings at 8% until she depletes her funds.

Requirements

1. How much money does Sharon need now to fund her travels?

2. After speaking with a number of banks, Sharon learns she will only be able to invest her funds at 6%. How much does she need now to fund her travels?

E26-22 Using the time value of money

Congratulations! You have won a state lottery. The state lottery offers you the following (after-tax) payout options:

Option #1:	$11,000,000 after five years
Option #2:	$2,000,000 per year for five years
Option #3:	$10,000,000 after three years

Assuming you can earn 10% on your funds, which option would you prefer?

Learning Objective 3

Option #2 $7,582,000

E26-23 Using NPV to make capital investment decisions

Eon Industries is deciding whether to automate one phase of its production process. The manufacturing equipment has a six-year life and will cost $920,000. Projected net cash inflows are as follows:

Year 1	$ 261,000
Year 2	254,000
Year 3	227,000
Year 4	211,000
Year 5	201,000
Year 6	175,000

Learning Objective 4

2. Equip. with refurb. $(74,219) NPV

Requirements

1. Compute this project's NPV using Eon's 16% hurdle rate. Should Eon invest in the equipment?

2. Eon could refurbish the equipment at the end of six years for $104,000. The refurbished equipment could be used one more year, providing $77,000 of net cash inflows in year 7. Additionally, the refurbished equipment would have a $51,000 residual value at the end of year 7. Should Eon invest in the equipment and refurbish it after six years? (*Hint:* In addition to your answer to Requirement 1, discount the additional cash outflow and inflows back to the present value.)

E26-24 Using NPV and profitability index to make capital investment decisions

Use the NPV method to determine whether Juda Products should invest in the following projects:

- *Project A*: Costs $290,000 and offers seven annual net cash inflows of $57,000. Juda Products requires an annual return of 14% on investments of this nature.

- *Project B*: Costs $395,000 and offers 10 annual net cash inflows of $70,000. Juda Products demands an annual return of 12% on investments of this nature.

Learning Objective 4

1. Project B $500 NPV

Requirements

1. What is the NPV of each project? Assume neither project has a residual value. Round to two decimal places.

2. What is the maximum acceptable price to pay for each project?

3. What is the profitability index of each project? Round to two decimal places.

CHAPTER 26

Learning Objective 4

Project A 8%–9% IRR

E26-25 Using IRR to make capital investment decisions

Refer to the data regarding Juda Products in Exercise E26-24. Compute the IRR of each project, and use this information to identify the better investment.

Learning Objective 4

E26-26 Using capital rationing to make capital investment decisions

Back Manufacturing is considering three capital investment proposals. At this time, Back only has funds available to pursue one of the three investments.

	Equipment A	Equipment B	Equipment C
Present value of net cash inflows	$ 1,695,378	$ 1,969,888	$ 2,169,724
Initial investment	(1,356,302)	(1,601,535)	(1,903,267)
NPV	$ 339,076	$ 368,353	$ 266,457

Which investment should Back pursue at this time? Why?

Learning Objective 4

E26-27 Using capital rationing to make capital investment decisions

Mountain Manufacturing is considering the following capital investment proposals. Mountain's requirement criteria include a maximum payback period of five years and a required rate of return of 12.5%. Determine if each investment is acceptable or should be rejected (ignore qualitative factors). Rank the acceptable investments in order from most desirable to least desirable.

Project	A	B	C	D	E
Payback	3.15 years	4.20 years	2.00 years	3.25 years	5.00 years
NPV	$ 10,250	$ 42,226	$ (10,874)	$ 36,251	$ 0
IRR	13.0%	14.2%	8.5%	14.0%	12.5%
Profitability Index	1.54	1.92	0.75	2.86	1.00

> **Problems Group A**

Learning Objective 3

1. $2,026,805

P26-28A Using the time value of money

You are planning for a very early retirement. You would like to retire at age 40 and have enough money saved to be able to withdraw $215,000 per year for the next 30 years (based on family history, you think you will live to age 70). You plan to save by making 10 equal annual installments (from age 30 to age 40) into a fairly risky investment fund that you expect will earn 10% per year. You will leave the money in this fund until it is completely depleted when you are 70 years old.

Requirements

1. How much money must you accumulate by retirement to make your plan work? (*Hint:* Find the present value of the $215,000 withdrawals.)

2. How does this amount compare to the total amount you will withdraw from the investment during retirement? How can these numbers be so different?

P26-29A Using payback, ARR, NPV, IRR, and profitability index to make capital investment decisions

Learning Objectives 2, 4

1. 26.35% ARR; 1.28 profitability index

Water Country is considering purchasing a water park in Atlanta, Georgia, for $1,850,000. The new facility will generate annual net cash inflows of $475,000 for eight years. Engineers estimate that the facility will remain useful for eight years and have no residual value. The company uses straight-line depreciation, and its stockholders demand an annual return of 12% on investments of this nature.

Requirements

1. Compute the payback, the ARR, the NPV, the IRR, and the profitability index of this investment.

2. Recommend whether the company should invest in this project.

P26-30A Using payback, ARR, NPV, IRR, and profitability index to make capital investment decisions

Learning Objectives 2, 4

1. Plan A 1.19 profitability index; Plan B $(755,780) NPV

Lados operates a chain of sandwich shops. The company is considering two possible expansion plans. Plan A would open eight smaller shops at a cost of $8,600,000. Expected annual net cash inflows are $1,600,000, with zero residual value at the end of 10 years. Under Plan B, Lados would open three larger shops at a cost of $8,300,000. This plan is expected to generate net cash inflows of $1,090,000 per year for 10 years, the estimated useful life of the properties. Estimated residual value for Plan B is $1,300,000. Lados uses straight-line depreciation and requires an annual return of 9%.

Requirements

1. Compute the payback, the ARR, the NPV, and the profitability index of these two plans.

2. What are the strengths and weaknesses of these capital budgeting methods?

3. Which expansion plan should Lados choose? Why?

4. Estimate Plan A's IRR. How does the IRR compare with the company's required rate of return?

P26-31A Using payback, ARR, and NPV with unequal cash flows

Learning Objectives 2, 4

1. Refurbish $116,260 NPV; Purchase 4.2 years payback

Mandel Manufacturing, Inc. has a manufacturing machine that needs attention. The company is considering two options. Option 1 is to refurbish the current machine at a cost of $1,100,000. If refurbished, Mandel expects the machine to last another eight years and then have no residual value. Option 2 is to replace the machine at a cost of

$2,200,000. A new machine would last 10 years and have no residual value. Mandel expects the following net cash inflows from the two options:

Year	Refurbish Current Machine	Purchase New Machine
1	$ 280,000	$ 260,000
2	500,000	740,000
3	380,000	620,000
4	260,000	500,000
5	140,000	380,000
6	140,000	380,000
7	140,000	380,000
8	140,000	380,000
9		380,000
10		380,000
Total	$ 1,980,000	$ 4,400,000

Mandel uses straight-line depreciation and requires an annual return of 16%.

Requirements

1. Compute the payback, the ARR, the NPV, and the profitability index of these two options.

2. Which option should Mandel choose? Why?

Learning Objective 4

1. Plan Beta 20.58% IRR
3. Plan Alpha $369,461 NPV

P26-32A Using Excel to solve for NPV and IRR

Langley Company is considering two capital investments. Both investments have an initial cost of $6,000,000 and total net cash inflows of $14,000,000 over 10 years. Langley requires a 20% rate of return on this type of investment. Expected net cash inflows are as follows:

Year	Plan Alpha	Plan Beta
1	$ 1,400,000	$ 1,400,000
2	1,400,000	1,700,000
3	1,400,000	2,000,000
4	1,400,000	1,700,000
5	1,400,000	1,400,000
6	1,400,000	1,000,000
7	1,400,000	700,000
8	1,400,000	400,000
9	1,400,000	100,000
10	1,400,000	3,600,000
Total	$ 14,000,000	$ 14,000,000

Requirements

1. Use Excel to compute the NPV and IRR of the two plans. Which plan, if any, should the company pursue?

2. Explain the relationship between NPV and IRR. Based on this relationship and the company's required rate of return, are your answers as expected in Requirement 1? Why or why not?

3. After further negotiating, the company can now invest with an initial cost of $5,500,000. Recalculate the NPV and IRR. Which plan, if any, should the company pursue?

> Problems **Group B**

P21-33B Using the time value of money

Learning Objective 3

1. $2,249,170

You are planning for an early retirement. You would like to retire at age 40 and have enough money saved to be able to withdraw $230,000 per year for the next 40 years (based on family history, you think you will live to age 80). You plan to save by making 10 equal annual installments (from age 30 to age 40) into a fairly risky investment fund that you expect will earn 10% per year. You will leave the money in this fund until it is completely depleted when you are 80 years old.

Requirements

1. How much money must you accumulate by retirement to make your plan work? (*Hint:* Find the present value of the $230,000 withdrawals.)

2. How does this amount compare to the total amount you will withdraw from the investment during retirement? How can these numbers be so different?

P26-34B Using payback, ARR, NPV, IRR, and profitability index to make capital investment decisions

Learning Objectives 2, 4

1. 25.99% ARR; 1.36 profitability index

Splash City is considering purchasing a water park in Omaha, Nebraska, for $1,910,000. The new facility will generate annual net cash inflows of $487,000 for eight years. Engineers estimate that the facility will remain useful for eight years and have no residual value. The company uses straight-line depreciation, and its stockholders demand an annual return of 10% on investments of this nature.

Requirements

1. Compute the payback, the ARR, the NPV, the IRR, and the profitability index of this investment.

2. Recommend whether the company should invest in this project.

P26-35B Using payback, ARR, NPV, IRR, and profitability index to make capital investment decisions

Learning Objectives 2, 4

1. Plan A 1.10 profitability index; Plan B $(955,800) NPV

Lolas operates a chain of sandwich shops. The company is considering two possible expansion plans. Plan A would open eight smaller shops at a cost of $8,550,000. Expected annual net cash inflows are $1,525,000, with zero residual value at the end of 10 years. Under Plan B, Lolas would open three larger shops at a cost of $8,340,000. This plan is expected to generate net cash inflows of $1,120,000 per year for 10 years, which is the estimated useful life of the properties. Estimated residual value for Plan B is $1,300,000. Lolas uses straight-line depreciation and requires an annual return of 10%

Requirements

1. Compute the payback, the ARR, the NPV, and the profitability index of these two plans.

2. What are the strengths and weaknesses of these capital budgeting methods?

3. Which expansion plan should Lolas choose? Why?

4. Estimate Plan A's IRR. How does the IRR compare with the company's required rate of return?

Learning Objectives 2, 4

1. Refurbish $(29,750) NPV; Purchase 3.7 years payback

P26-36B Using payback, ARR, and NPV with unequal cash flows

Gaynor Manufacturing, Inc. has a manufacturing machine that needs attention. The company is considering two options. Option 1 is to refurbish the current machine at a cost of $1,600,000. If refurbished, Gaynor expects the machine to last another eight years and then have no residual value. Option 2 is to replace the machine at a cost of $3,800,000. A new machine would last 10 years and have no residual value. Gaynor expects the following net cash inflows from the two options:

Year	Refurbish Current Machine	Purchase New Machine
1	$ 400,000	$ 2,700,000
2	370,000	450,000
3	320,000	400,000
4	270,000	350,000
5	220,000	300,000
6	220,000	300,000
7	220,000	300,000
8	220,000	300,000
9		300,000
10		300,000
Total	$ 2,240,000	$ 5,700,000

Gaynor uses straight-line depreciation and requires an annual return of 10%.

Requirements

1. Compute the payback, the ARR, the NPV, and the profitability index of these two options.

2. Which option should Gaynor choose? Why?

Learning Objective 4

1. Plan Beta 11.23% IRR
3. Plan Alpha $115,654 NPV

P26-37B Using Excel to solve for NPV and IRR

Whitley Company is considering two capital investments. Both investments have an initial cost of $5,000,000 and total net cash inflows of $8,000,000 over 10 years.

Whitley requires a 10% rate of return on this type of investment. Expected net cash inflows are as follows:

Year	Plan Alpha	Plan Beta
1	$ 800,000	$ 800,000
2	800,000	1,100,000
3	800,000	1,400,000
4	800,000	1,100,000
5	800,000	800,000
6	800,000	600,000
7	800,000	500,000
8	800,000	400,000
9	800,000	300,000
10	800,000	1,000,000
Total	$ 8,000,000	$ 8,000,000

Requirements

1. Use Excel to compute the NPV and IRR of the two plans. Which plan, if any, should the company pursue?

2. Explain the relationship between NPV and IRR. Based on this relationship and the company's required rate of return, are your answers as expected in Requirement 1? Why or why not?

3. After further negotiating, the company can now invest with an initial cost of $4,800,000. Recalculate the NPV and IRR. Which plan, if any, should the company pursue?

> Continuing Problem

P26-38 Using payback, ARR, NPV, and IRR to make capital investment decisions

This problem continues the Daniels Consulting situation from Problem P25-33 of Chapter 25. Daniels Consulting is considering purchasing two different types of servers. Server A will generate net cash inflows of $26,000 per year and have a zero residual value. Server A's estimated useful life is three years, and it costs $44,000.

Server B will generate net cash inflows of $28,000 in year 1, $11,000 in year 2, and $5,000 in year 3. Server B has a $5,000 residual value and an estimated life of three years. Server B also costs $44,000. Daniels's required rate of return is 14%.

Requirements

1. Calculate payback, accounting rate of return, net present value, and internal rate of return for both server investments. Use Microsoft Excel to calculate NPV and IRR.

2. Assuming capital rationing applies, which server should Daniels invest in?

COMPREHENSIVE PROBLEM

> Comprehensive Problem for Chapters 25–26

David Dennison, majority stockholder and president of Dennison, Inc., is working with his top managers on future plans for the company. As the company's managerial accountant, you've been asked to analyze the following situations and make recommendations to the management team.

Requirements

1. Division A of Dennison, Inc. has $4,950,000 in assets. Its yearly fixed costs are $650,000, and the variable costs of its product line are $1.40 per unit. The division's volume is currently 480,000 units. Competitors offer a similar product, at the same quality, to retailers for $3.75 each. Dennison's management team wants to earn a 10% return on investment on the division's assets.

   a. What is Division A's target full product cost?

   b. Given the division's current costs, will Division A be able to achieve its target profit?

   c. Assume Division A has identified ways to cut its variable costs to $1.25 per unit. What is its new target fixed cost? Will this decrease in variable costs allow the division to achieve its target profit?

   d. Division A is considering an aggressive advertising campaign strategy to differentiate its product from its competitors. The division does not expect volume to be affected, but it hopes to gain more control over pricing. If Division A has to spend $105,000 next year to advertise and its variable costs continue to be $1.25 per unit, what will its cost-plus price be? Do you think Division A will be able to sell its product at the cost-plus price? Why or why not?

2. The division manager of Division B received the following operating income data for the past year:

DIVISION B OF DENNISON, INC. Income Statement For the Year Ended December 31, 2016			
	Product Line		
	T205	**B179**	**Total**
Sales Revenue	$ 300,000	$ 330,000	$ 630,000
Cost of Goods Sold:			
Variable	36,000	48,000	84,000
Fixed	210,000	66,000	276,000
Total Cost of Goods Sold	246,000	114,000	360,000
Gross Profit	54,000	216,000	270,000
Selling and Administrative Expenses:			
Variable	62,000	72,000	134,000
Fixed	43,000	24,000	67,000
Total Selling and Administrative Expenses	105,000	96,000	201,000
Operating Income (Loss)	$ (51,000)	$ 120,000	$ 69,000

The manager of the division is surprised that the T205 product line is not profitable. The division accountant estimates that dropping the T205 product line will decrease fixed cost of goods sold by $83,000 and decrease fixed selling and administrative expenses by $14,000.

   a. Prepare a differential analysis to show whether Division B should drop the T205 product line.

   b. What is your recommendation to the manager of Division B?

3. Division C also produces two product lines. Because the division can sell all of the product it can produce, Dennison is expanding the plant and needs to decide which product line to emphasize. To make this decision, the division accountant assembled the following data:

	Per Unit	
	K707	**G582**
Sales price	$ 82	$ 48
Variable costs	25	19
Contribution margin	$ 57	$ 29
Contribution margin ratio	69.5%	60.4%

After expansion, the factory will have a production capacity of 4,600 machine hours per month. The plant can manufacture either 26 units of K707s or 50 units of G582s per machine hour.

   a. Identify the constraining factor for Division C.

   b. Prepare an analysis to show which product line to emphasize.

4. Division D is considering two possible expansion plans. Plan A would expand a current product line at a cost of $8,500,000. Expected annual net cash inflows are $1,525,000, with zero residual value at the end of 10 years. Under Plan B, Division D would begin producing a new product at a cost of $8,300,000. This plan is expected to generate net cash inflows of $1,070,000 per year for 10 years, the estimated useful life of the product line. Estimated residual value for Plan B is $990,000. Division D uses straight-line depreciation and requires an annual return of 10%.

   a. Compute the payback, the ARR, the NPV, and the profitability index for both plans.

   b. Compute the estimated IRR of Plan A.

   c. Use Excel to verify the NPV calculations in Requirement 4(a) and the actual IRR for the two plans. How does the IRR of each plan compare with the company's required rate of return?

   d. Division D must rank the plans and make a recommendation to Dennison's top management team for the best plan. Which expansion plan should Division D choose? Why?

CHAPTER 26

CRITICAL THINKING

> Ethical Issue 26-1

Spencer Wilkes is the marketing manager at Darby Company. Last year, Spencer recommended the company approve a capital investment project for the addition of a new product line. Spencer's recommendation included predicted cash inflows for five years from the sales of the new product line. Darby Company has been selling the new products for almost one year. The company has a policy of conducting annual post-audits on capital investments, and Spencer is concerned about the one-year post-audit because sales in the first year have been lower than he estimated. However, sales have been increasing for the last couple of months, and Spencer expects that by the end of the second year, actual sales will exceed his estimates for the first two years combined.

Spencer wants to shift some sales from the second year of the project into the first year. Doing so will make it appear that his cash flow predictions were accurate. With accurate estimates, he will be able to avoid a poor performance evaluation. Spencer has discussed his plan with a couple of key sales representatives, urging them to report sales in the current month that will not be shipped until a later month. Spencer has justified this course of action by explaining that there will be no effect on the annual financial statements because the project year does not coincide with the fiscal year—by the time the accounting year ends, the sales will have actually occurred.

Requirements

1. What is the fundamental ethical issue? Who are the affected parties?

2. If you were a sales representative at Darby Company, how would you respond to Spencer's request? Why?

3. If you were Spencer's manager and you discovered his plan, how would you respond?

4. Are there other courses of action Spencer could take?

> Fraud Case 26-1

John Johnson is the majority stockholder in Johnson's Landscape Company, owning 52% of the company's stock. John asked his accountant to prepare a capital investment analysis for the purchase of new mowers. John used the analysis to persuade a loan officer at the local bank to loan the company $100,000. Once the loan was secured, John used the cash to remodel his home, updating the kitchen and bathrooms, installing new flooring, and adding a pool.

Requirements

1. Are John's actions fraudulent? Why or why not? Does John's percentage of ownership affect your answer?

2. What steps could the bank take to prevent this type of activity?

> Team Project 26-1

Assume you are preparing to move into a new neighborhood. You are considering renting or buying. Divide your team into two groups.

Requirements

1. Group 1 will analyze the renting option. A suitable rental is available for $500 per month, and you expect rent to increase by $50 per month per year. Prepare a schedule showing rent payments for the next 15 years. To simplify the problem, assume rent is paid annually. Using 5% as the discount rate, determine the present value of the rent payments. Round present value amounts to the nearest dollar.

2. Group 2 will analyze the buying option. A suitable purchase will require financing $105,876 at 5%. Annual payments for 15 years will be $10,200 (annual payments assumed to simplify the problem). Calculate the present value of the payments. Additionally, using Excel with appropriate formulas, prepare a payment schedule with the following columns (year 1 is completed as an example):

Year	Beginning Balance	Payment	Applied to Interest	Applied to Principal	Ending Balance
0					$ 105,876
1	$ 105,876	$ 10,200	$ 5,294	$ 4,906	100,970

3. After each group has prepared its schedule, meet as a full team to discuss the analyses. What is the total cash paid out for each option? What is the present value of the cash paid out for each option? Explain the implications of the previous two answers. Are there other factors that should be considered before deciding to rent or buy?

> Communication Activity 26-1

In 100 words or fewer, explain the difference between NPV and IRR.

MyAccountingLab   **For a wealth of online resources, including exercises, problems, media, and immediate tutorial help, please visit http://www.myaccountinglab.com.**

> Quick Check Answers

1. b **2.** b **3.** d **4.** b **5.** d **6.** d **7.** b **8.** a **9.** c **10.** c

CHAPTER 26

UNITED STATES SECURITIES AND EXCHANGE COMMISSION

Washington, D.C. 20549

FORM 10-K/A
Amendment No. 1

(Mark One)

☒ ANNUAL REPORT PURSUANT TO SECTION 13 OR 15(d) OF THE SECURITIES EXCHANGE ACT OF 1934.

For the fiscal year ended September 28, 2013

OR

☐ TRANSITION REPORT PURSUANT TO SECTION 13 OR 15(d) OF THE SECURITIES EXCHANGE ACT OF 1934.

For the transition period from   to

Commission file number 1-12340

GREEN MOUNTAIN COFFEE ROASTERS, INC.

(Exact name of registrant as specified in its charter)

Delaware	03-0339228
(State or other jurisdiction of incorporation or organization)	(I.R.S. Employer Identification No.)

33 Coffee Lane, Waterbury, Vermont 05676
(Address of principal executive offices) (zip code)

(802) 244-5621
(Registrants' telephone number, including area code)
(Former name, former address and former fiscal year, if changed since last report.)

Securities registered pursuant to Section 12(b) of the Act:

Title of each class	Name of each exchange on which registered
Common Stock, $0.10 par value per share	The Nasdaq Global Select Market

Securities registered pursuant to Section 12(g) of the Act: NONE

Indicate by check mark if the registrant is a well-known seasoned issuer, as defined in Rule 405 of the Securities Act.   Yes ☒   No ☐

Indicate by check mark if the registrant is not required to file reports pursuant to Section 13 or Section 15(d) of the Act.   Yes ☐   No ☒

Indicate by check mark whether the registrant (1) has filed all reports required to be filed by Section 13 or 15(d) of the Securities Exchange Act of 1934 during the preceding 12 months (or for such shorter period that the registrant was required to file such reports), and (2) has been subject to such filing requirements for the past 90 days.   Yes ☒   No ☐

Indicate by check mark whether the registrant has submitted electronically and posted on its corporate Web site, if any, every Interactive Data File required to be submitted and posted pursuant to Rule 405 of Regulation S-T (§232.405 of this chapter) during the preceding 12 months (or for such shorter period that the registrant was required to submit and post such files).   Yes ☒   No ☐

Indicate by check mark if disclosure of delinquent filers pursuant to Item 405 of Regulation S-K is not contained herein, and will not be contained, to the best of registrant's knowledge, in definitive proxy or information statements incorporated by reference in Part III of this Form 10-K or any amendment to this Form 10-K.   ☐

Indicate by check mark whether the registrant is a large accelerated filer, an accelerated filer, a non-accelerated filer, or a smaller reporting company. See the definitions of "large accelerated filer," "accelerated filer" and "smaller reporting company" in Rule 12b-2 of the Exchange Act.

Large accelerated filer ☒   Accelerated filer   ☐

Non-accelerated filer   ☐
(Do not check if a smaller reporting company)   Smaller Reporting Company ☐

Indicate by check mark whether the registrant is a shell company (as defined in Rule 12b-2 of the Exchange Act).   Yes ☐   No ☒

The aggregate market value of the voting stock of the registrant held by non-affiliates of the registrant on March 30, 2013 was approximately $7,923,000,000 based upon the closing price of such stock on March 29, 2013.

As of November 13, 2013, 149,030,940 shares of common stock of the registrant were outstanding.

EXPLANATORY NOTE

This Amendment No. 1 ("Amendment No. 1") to the Annual Report on Form 10-K of Green Mountain Coffee Roasters, Inc. (together with its subsidiaries, the "Company," "we," "our," or "us") for the fiscal year ended September 28, 2013 as filed with the SEC on November 20, 2013 (the "2013 Annual Report"), is being filed solely to insert conformed signatures to each of Exhibits 23, 31-1, 31-2, 32-1 and 32-2, which conformed signatures were inadvertently omitted from the initial filing.

This Amendment No. 1 does not amend, modify or update any other portion of the 2013 Annual Report. Additionally, except as specifically referenced herein, this Amendment No. 1 does not reflect any event occurring after the time the 2013 Annual Report was filed on November 20, 2013.

DOCUMENTS INCORPORATED BY REFERENCE

Portions of the registrant's definitive Proxy Statement for the 2014 Annual Meeting of Stockholders to be filed with the Securities and Exchange Commission pursuant to Regulation 14A not later than 120 days after the end of the fiscal year covered by this Form 10-K, are incorporated by reference in Part III, Items 10-14 of this Form 10-K.

Report of Independent Registered Public Accounting Firm

To the Board of Directors and the Stockholders
of Green Mountain Coffee Roasters, Inc.

In our opinion, the consolidated financial statements listed in the accompanying index present fairly, in all material respects, the financial position of Green Mountain Coffee Roasters, Inc. and its subsidiaries at September 28, 2013 and September 29, 2012, and the results of their operations and their cash flows for each of the three years in the period ended September 28, 2013 in conformity with accounting principles generally accepted in the United States of America. In addition, in our opinion, the financial statement schedule listed in the accompanying index presents fairly, in all material respects, the information set forth therein when read in conjunction with the related consolidated financial statements. Also in our opinion, the Company maintained, in all material respects, effective internal control over financial reporting as of September 28, 2013, based on criteria established in *Internal Control—Integrated Framework* (1992) issued by the Committee of Sponsoring Organizations of the Treadway Commission (COSO). The Company's management is responsible for these financial statements and financial statement schedule, for maintaining effective internal control over financial reporting and for its assessment of the effectiveness of internal control over financial reporting, included in Management's Report on Internal Control over Financial Reporting appearing under Item 9A. Our responsibility is to express opinions on these financial statements, on the financial statement schedule, and on the Company's internal control over financial reporting based on our integrated audits. We conducted our audits in accordance with the standards of the Public Company Accounting Oversight Board (United States). Those standards require that we plan and perform the audits to obtain reasonable assurance about whether the financial statements are free of material misstatement and whether effective internal control over financial reporting was maintained in all material respects. Our audits of the financial statements included examining, on a test basis, evidence supporting the amounts and disclosures in the financial statements, assessing the accounting principles used and significant estimates made by management, and evaluating the overall financial statement presentation. Our audit of internal control over financial reporting included obtaining an understanding of internal control over financial reporting, assessing the risk that a material weakness exists, and testing and evaluating the design and operating effectiveness of internal control based on the assessed risk. Our audits also included performing such other procedures as we considered necessary in the circumstances. We believe that our audits provide a reasonable basis for our opinions.

A company's internal control over financial reporting is a process designed to provide reasonable assurance regarding the reliability of financial reporting and the preparation of financial statements for external purposes in accordance with generally accepted accounting principles. A company's internal control over financial reporting includes those policies and procedures that (i) pertain to the maintenance of records that, in reasonable detail, accurately and fairly reflect the transactions and dispositions of the assets of the company; (ii) provide reasonable assurance that transactions are recorded as necessary to permit preparation of financial statements in accordance with generally accepted accounting principles, and that receipts and expenditures of the company are being made only in accordance with authorizations of management and directors of the company; and (iii) provide reasonable assurance regarding prevention or timely detection of unauthorized acquisition, use, or disposition of the company's assets that could have a material effect on the financial statements.

Because of its inherent limitations, internal control over financial reporting may not prevent or detect misstatements. Also, projections of any evaluation of effectiveness to future periods are subject to the risk that controls may become inadequate because of changes in conditions, or that the degree of compliance with the policies or procedures may deteriorate.

/s/ PricewaterhouseCoopers LLP

Boston, Massachusetts
November 20, 2013

GREEN MOUNTAIN COFFEE ROASTERS, INC.

CONSOLIDATED BALANCE SHEETS
(Dollars in thousands)

	September 28, 2013	September 29, 2012
Assets		
Current assets:		
Cash and cash equivalents	$ 260,092	$ 58,289
Restricted cash and cash equivalents	560	12,884
Receivables, less uncollectible accounts and return allowances of $33,640 and $34,517 at September 28, 2013 and September 29, 2012, respectively	467,976	363,771
Inventories	676,089	768,437
Income taxes receivable	11,747	32,943
Other current assets	46,891	35,019
Deferred income taxes, net	58,137	51,613
Total current assets	1,521,492	1,322,956
Fixed assets, net	985,563	944,296
Intangibles, net	435,216	498,352
Goodwill	788,184	808,076
Deferred income taxes, net	149	—
Other long-term assets	30,944	42,109
Total assets	$ 3,761,548	$ 3,615,789
Liabilities and Stockholders' Equity		
Current liabilities:		
Current portion of long-term debt	$ 12,929	$ 6,691
Current portion of capital lease and financing obligations	1,760	3,057
Accounts payable	312,170	279,577
Accrued expenses	242,427	171,450
Income tax payable	—	29,322
Deferred income taxes, net	233	245
Other current liabilities	27,544	29,645
Total current liabilities	597,063	519,987
Long-term debt, less current portion	160,221	466,984
Capital lease and financing obligations, less current portion	76,061	54,794
Deferred income taxes, net	252,867	270,348
Other long-term liabilities	28,721	32,544
Commitments and contingencies (See Notes 5 and 19)		
Redeemable noncontrolling interests	11,045	9,904
Stockholders' equity:		
Preferred stock, $0.10 par value: Authorized—1,000,000 shares; No shares issued or outstanding	—	—
Common stock, $0.10 par value: Authorized—500,000,000 shares; Issued and outstanding—150,265,809 and 152,680,855 shares at September 28, 2013 and September 29, 2012, respectively	15,026	15,268
Additional paid-in capital	1,387,322	1,464,560
Retained earnings	1,252,407	771,200
Accumulated other comprehensive (loss) income	(19,185)	10,200
Total stockholders' equity	$ 2,635,570	$ 2,261,228
Total liabilities and stockholders' equity	$ 3,761,548	$ 3,615,789

The accompanying Notes to Consolidated Financial Statements are an integral part of these financial statements.

GREEN MOUNTAIN COFFEE ROASTERS, INC.

CONSOLIDATED STATEMENTS OF OPERATIONS
(Dollars in thousands except per share data)

	Fiscal years ended		
	September 28, 2013	September 29, 2012	September 24, 2011
Net sales	$ 4,358,100	$ 3,859,198	$ 2,650,899
Cost of sales	2,738,714	2,589,799	1,746,274
Gross profit	1,619,386	1,269,399	904,625
Selling and operating expenses	560,430	481,493	348,696
General and administrative expenses	293,729	219,010	187,016
Operating income	765,227	568,896	368,913
Other income, net	960	1,819	648
Gain (loss) on financial instruments, net	5,513	(4,945)	(6,245)
(Loss) gain on foreign currency, net	(12,649)	7,043	(2,912)
Gain on sale of subsidiary	—	26,311	—
Interest expense	(18,177)	(22,983)	(57,657)
Income before income taxes	740,874	576,141	302,747
Income tax expense	(256,771)	(212,641)	(101,699)
Net Income	$ 484,103	$ 363,500	$ 201,048
Net income attributable to noncontrolling interests	871	872	1,547
Net income attributable to GMCR	$ 483,232	$ 362,628	$ 199,501
Basic income per share:			
Basic weighted average shares outstanding	149,638,636	154,933,948	146,214,860
Net income per common share—basic	$ 3.23	$ 2.34	$ 1.36
Diluted income per share:			
Diluted weighted average shares outstanding	152,801,493	159,075,646	152,142,434
Net income per common share—diluted	$ 3.16	$ 2.28	$ 1.31

The accompanying Notes to Consolidated Financial Statements are an integral part of these financial statements.

GREEN MOUNTAIN COFFEE ROASTERS, INC.
CONSOLIDATED STATEMENTS OF COMPREHENSIVE INCOME
(Dollars in thousands)

	Fiscal years ended								
	September 28, 2013			September 29, 2012			September 24, 2011		
	Pre-tax	Tax (expense) benefit	After-tax	Pre-tax	Tax (expense) benefit	After-tax	Pre-tax	Tax (expense) benefit	After-tax
Net income			$ 484,103			$ 363,500			$ 201,048
Other comprehensive income (loss):									
Cash flow hedges:									
Unrealized losses arising during the period	$ (3,732)	$ 1,489	$ (2,243)	$ (1,234)	$ 498	$ (736)	$ (7,521)	$ 3,035	$ (4,486)
Losses reclassified to net income	1,484	(599)	885	1,359	(549)	810	419	(169)	250
Foreign currency translation adjustments	(28,742)	—	(28,742)	25,353	—	25,353	(8,895)	—	(8,895)
Other comprehensive (loss) income	$ (30,990)	$ 890	$ (30,100)	$ 25,478	$ (51)	$ 25,427	$ (15,997)	$ 2,866	$ (13,131)
Total comprehensive income			454,003			388,927			187,917
Total comprehensive income attributable to noncontrolling interests			156			1,524			1,361
Total comprehensive income attributable to GMCR			$ 453,847			$ 387,403			$ 186,556

The accompanying Notes to Consolidated Financial Statements are an integral part of these financial statements.

GREEN MOUNTAIN COFFEE ROASTERS, INC.
CONSOLIDATED STATEMENTS OF CHANGES IN STOCKHOLDERS' EQUITY
For the three fiscal years in the period ended September 28, 2013 (Dollars in thousands)

	Common stock		Additional paid-in capital	Retained earnings	Accumulated other comprehensive income (loss)	Stockholders' Equity
	Shares	Amount				
Balance at September 25, 2010	132,823,585	$13,282	$473,749	$213,844	$(1,630)	$699,245
Sale of common stock for private placement	9,174,991	918	290,178	—	—	291,096
Options exercised	2,839,426	284	11,096	—	—	11,380
Issuance of common stock under employee stock purchase plan	148,917	15	5,933	—	—	5,948
Issuance of common stock for public equity offering	9,479,544	948	646,415	—	—	647,363
Stock compensation expense	—	—	10,361	—	—	10,361
Tax benefit from exercise of options	—	—	61,670	—	—	61,670
Deferred compensation expense	—	—	214	—	—	214
Adjustment of redeemable noncontrolling interests to redemption value	—	—	—	(1,618)	—	(1,618)
Other comprehensive loss net of tax	—	—	—	—	(12,945)	(12,945)
Net income	—	—	—	199,501	—	199,501
Balance at September 24, 2011	154,466,463	$15,447	$1,499,616	$411,727	$(14,575)	$1,912,215
Options exercised	940,369	94	3,300	—	—	3,394
Issuance of common stock under employee stock purchase plan	301,971	30	8,668	—	—	8,698
Restricted stock awards and units	55,747	5	(5)	—	—	—
Issuance of common stock under deferred compensation plan	37,005	4	(4)	—	—	—
Repurchase of common stock	(3,120,700)	(312)	(76,158)	—	—	(76,470)
Stock compensation expense	—	—	17,868	—	—	17,868
Tax benefit from equity-based compensation plans	—	—	11,064	—	—	11,064
Deferred compensation expense	—	—	211	—	—	211
Adjustment of redeemable noncontrolling interests to redemption value	—	—	—	(3,155)	—	(3,155)
Other comprehensive income, net of tax	—	—	—	—	24,775	24,775
Net income	—	—	—	362,628	—	362,628
Balance at September 29, 2012	152,680,855	$15,268	$1,464,560	$771,200	$10,200	$2,261,228
Options exercised	2,849,308	285	19,532	—	—	19,817
Issuance of common stock under employee stock purchase plan	343,678	34	9,926	—	—	9,960
Restricted stock awards and units	34,761	3	(3)	—	—	—
Repurchase of common stock	(5,642,793)	(564)	(187,714)	—	—	(188,278)
Stock compensation expense	—	—	26,081	—	—	26,081
Tax benefit from equity-based compensation plans	—	—	54,706	—	—	54,706
Deferred compensation expense	—	—	234	—	—	234
Adjustment of redeemable noncontrolling interests to redemption value	—	—	—	(2,025)	—	(2,025)
Other comprehensive loss, net of tax	—	—	—	—	(29,385)	(29,385)
Net income	—	—	—	483,232	—	483,232
Balance at September 28, 2013	150,265,809	$15,026	$1,387,322	$1,252,407	$(19,185)	$2,635,570

The accompanying Notes to Consolidated Financial Statements are an integral part of these financial statements.

GREEN MOUNTAIN COFFEE ROASTERS, INC.
CONSOLIDATED STATEMENTS OF CASH FLOWS
(Dollars in thousands)

| | Fiscal years ended | | |
	September 28, 2013	September 29, 2012	September 24, 2011
Cash flows from operating activities:			
Net income	$ 484,103	$ 363,500	$ 201,048
Adjustments to reconcile net income to net cash provided by operating activities:			
Depreciation and amortization of fixed assets	183,814	135,656	72,297
Amortization of intangibles	45,379	45,991	41,339
Amortization deferred financing fees	7,125	6,050	6,158
Loss on extinguishment of debt	—	—	19,732
Unrealized loss (gain) on foreign currency, net	9,159	(6,557)	1,041
(Gain) loss on disposal of fixed assets	(85)	2,517	884
Gain on sale of subsidiary, excluding transaction costs	—	(28,914)	—
Provision for doubtful accounts	689	3,197	2,584
Provision for sales returns	79,747	107,436	64,457
(Gain) loss on derivatives, net	(4,507)	6,310	3,292
Excess tax benefits from equity-based compensation plans	(54,699)	(12,070)	(67,813)
Deferred income taxes	(17,701)	60,856	(8,828)
Deferred compensation and stock compensation	26,315	18,079	10,575
Other	844	(672)	(6,142)
Changes in assets and liabilities, net of effects of acquisition:			
Receivables	(187,221)	(159,317)	(157,329)
Inventories	87,677	(92,862)	(375,709)
Income tax payable/receivable, net	46,290	16,457	63,487
Other current assets	(12,668)	(6,900)	(715)
Other long-term assets, net	3,915	(469)	(11,454)
Accounts payable and accrued expenses	133,532	17,125	134,035
Other current liabilities	3,100	(2,718)	(3,118)
Other long-term liabilities	1,161	5,090	10,964
Net cash provided by operating activities	835,969	477,785	785
Cash flows from investing activities:			
Change in restricted cash	3,005	(2,875)	2,074
Acquisition of LVH Holdings, Inc. (Van Houtte), net of cash acquired	—	—	(907,835)
Proceeds from the sale of the subsidiary, net of cash acquired	—	137,733	—
Capital expenditures for fixed assets	(232,780)	(401,121)	(283,444)
Other investing activities	4,208	618	1,533
Net cash used in investing activities	(225,567)	(265,645)	(1,187,672)

The accompanying Notes to Consolidated Financial Statements are an integral part of these financial statements.

GREEN MOUNTAIN COFFEE ROASTERS, INC.

CONSOLIDATED STATEMENTS OF CASH FLOWS (CONTINUED)
(Dollars in thousands)

	Fiscal years ended		
	September 28, 2013	September 29, 2012	September 24, 2011
Cash flows from financing activities:			
Net change in revolving line of credit	(226,210)	(108,727)	333,835
Proceeds from issuance of common stock under compensation plans	29,777	12,092	17,328
Proceeds from issuance of common stock for private placement	—	—	291,096
Proceeds from issuance of common stock for public equity offering	—	—	673,048
Financing costs in connection with public equity offering	—	—	(25,685)
Repurchase of common stock	(188,278)	(76,470)	—
Excess tax benefits from equity-based compensation plans	54,699	12,070	67,813
Payments on capital lease and financing obligations	(8,288)	(7,558)	(8)
Proceeds from borrowings of long-term debt	—	—	796,375
Deferred financing fees	—	—	(46,009)
Repayment of long-term debt	(71,620)	(7,814)	(906,885)
Other financing activities	(1,406)	3,283	(1,063)
Net cash (used in) provided by financing activities	(411,326)	(173,124)	1,199,845
Change in cash balances included in current assets held for sale	—	5,160	(5,160)
Effect of exchange rate changes on cash and cash equivalents	2,727	1,124	790
Net increase in cash and cash equivalents	201,803	45,300	8,588
Cash and cash equivalents at beginning of period	58,289	12,989	4,401
Cash and cash equivalents at end of period	$ 260,092	$ 58,289	$ 12,989
Supplemental disclosures of cash flow information:			
Cash paid for interest	$ 9,129	$ 20,783	$ 33,452
Cash paid for income taxes	$ 223,580	$ 136,407	$ 58,182
Fixed asset purchases included in accounts payable and not disbursed at the end of each year	$ 30,451	$ 56,127	$ 25,737
Noncash financing and investing activity:			
Fixed assets acquired under capital lease and financing obligations	$ 27,791	$ 66,531	$ —
Settlement of acquisition-related liabilities through release of restricted cash	$ 9,227	$ 18,788	$ —

The accompanying Notes to Consolidated Financial Statements are an integral part of these financial statements.

GREEN MOUNTAIN COFFEE ROASTERS, INC.

NOTES TO CONSOLIDATED FINANCIAL STATEMENTS

1. Nature of Business and Organization

Green Mountain Coffee Roasters, Inc. (together with its subsidiaries, "the Company") is a leader in the specialty coffee and coffeemaker businesses. Green Mountain Coffee Roasters, Inc. is a Delaware corporation.

The Company manages its operations through two business segments, its United States operations within the Domestic segment and its Canadian operations within the Canada segment. The Company distributes its products in two channels: at-home ("AH") and away-from-home ("AFH").

The Domestic segment sells single cup brewers, accessories, and sources, produces and sells coffee, hot cocoa, teas and other beverages in K-Cup® and Vue® packs ("portion packs") and coffee in more traditional packaging including bags and fractional packs to retailers including supermarkets, department stores, mass merchandisers, club stores, and convenience stores; to restaurants, hospitality accounts, office coffee distributors, and partner brand owners; and to consumers through Company websites. Substantially all of the Domestic segment's distribution to major retailers is processed by fulfillment entities which receive and fulfill sales orders and invoice certain retailers primarily in the AH channel. The Domestic segment also earns royalty income from K-Cup® packs sold by a third-party licensed roaster.

The Canada segment sells single cup brewers, accessories, and sources, produces and sells coffee and teas and other beverages in portion packs and coffee in more traditional packaging including bags, cans and fractional packs under a variety of brands to retailers including supermarkets, department stores, mass merchandisers, club stores, through office coffee services to offices, convenience stores, restaurants, hospitality accounts, and to consumers through its website. The Canada segment included Filterfresh through October 3, 2011, the date of sale (see Note 3, *Acquisitions and Divestitures*).

The Company's fiscal year ends on the last Saturday in September. Fiscal years 2013, 2012 and 2011 represent the years ended September 28, 2013, September 29, 2012 and September 24, 2011, respectively. Fiscal years 2013 and 2011 each consist of 52 weeks and fiscal 2012 consisted of 53 weeks.

2. Significant Accounting Policies

Use of estimates

The preparation of financial statements in conformity with accounting principles generally accepted in the United States of America requires the Company to make estimates and assumptions that affect amounts reported in the accompanying Consolidated Financial Statements. Significant estimates and assumptions by management affect the Company's inventory, deferred tax assets, allowance for sales returns, warranty reserves and certain accrued expenses, goodwill, intangible and long-lived assets and stock-based compensation.

Although the Company regularly assesses these estimates, actual results could differ from these estimates. Changes in estimates are recorded in the period they become known. The Company bases its estimates on historical experience and various other assumptions that it believes to be reasonable under the circumstances.

Principles of Consolidation

The Consolidated Financial Statements include the accounts of the Company and all of the entities in which the Company has a controlling financial interest, most often because the Company holds a majority voting/ownership interest. All significant intercompany transactions and accounts are eliminated in consolidation.

Noncontrolling Interests

Noncontrolling interests ("NCI") are evaluated by the Company and are shown as either a liability, temporary equity (shown between liabilities and equity) or as permanent equity depending on the nature of the redeemable features at amounts based on formulas specific to each entity. Generally, mandatorily redeemable NCI's are classified as liabilities and non-mandatorily redeemable NCI's are classified as either temporary or permanent equity. Redeemable NCIs that are not mandatorily redeemable are classified outside of shareholders' equity in the Consolidated Balance Sheets as temporary equity under the caption, *Redeemable noncontrolling interests,* and are measured at their redemption values at the end of each period. If the redemption value is greater than the carrying value, an adjustment is recorded in retained earnings to record the NCI at its redemption value. Redeemable NCIs that are mandatorily redeemable are classified as a liability in the Consolidated Balance Sheets under either *Other current liabilities* or *Other long-term liabilities*, depending on the remaining duration until settlement, and are measured at the amount of cash that would be paid if settlement occurred at the balance sheet date based on the formula in the Share Purchase and Sale Agreement dated June 22, 2012, with any change from the prior period recognized as interest expense. See Note 8, *Noncontrolling Interests* in the Consolidated Financial Statements included in this Annual Report for further information.

GREEN MOUNTAIN COFFEE ROASTERS, INC.

NOTES TO CONSOLIDATED FINANCIAL STATEMENTS—(Continued)

Net income attributable to NCIs reflects the portion of the net income (loss) of consolidated entities applicable to the NCI shareholders in the accompanying Consolidated Statements of Operations. The net income attributable to NCIs is classified in the Consolidated Statements of Operations as part of consolidated net income and deducted from total consolidated net income to arrive at the net income attributable to the Company.

If a change in ownership of a consolidated subsidiary results in a loss of control or deconsolidation, any retained ownership interests are remeasured with the gain or loss reported to net earnings.

Business Combinations

The Company uses the acquisition method of accounting for business combinations and recognizes assets acquired and liabilities assumed measured at their fair values on the date acquired. Goodwill represents the excess of the purchase price over the fair value of the net assets. The fair values of the assets and liabilities acquired are determined based upon the Company's valuation. The valuation involves making significant estimates and assumptions which are based on detailed financial models including the projection of future cash flows, the weighted average cost of capital and any cost savings that are expected to be derived in the future.

Cash and Cash Equivalents

The Company considers all highly liquid investments purchased with an original maturity of three months or less to be cash equivalents. Cash and cash equivalents include money market funds which are carried at cost, plus accrued interest, which approximates fair value. The Company does not believe that it is subject to any unusual credit or market risk.

Restricted Cash and Cash Equivalents

Restricted cash and cash equivalents represents cash that is not available for use in our operations. Restricted cash of $0.6 million and $12.9 million as of September 28, 2013 and September 29, 2012, respectively. The restricted cash balance as of September 29, 2012 consisted primarily of cash placed in escrow related to our acquisition of Van Houtte, and was released during fiscal 2013.

Allowance for Doubtful Accounts

A provision for doubtful accounts is provided based on a combination of historical experience, specific identification and customer credit risk where there are indications that a specific customer may be experiencing financial difficulties.

Inventories

Inventories consist primarily of green and roasted coffee, including coffee in portion packs, purchased finished goods such as coffee brewers, and packaging materials. Inventories are stated at the lower of cost or market. Cost is being measured using an adjusted standard cost method which approximates FIFO (first-in, first-out). The Company regularly reviews whether the net realizable value of its inventory is lower than its carrying value. If the valuation shows that the net realizable value is lower than the carrying value, the Company takes a charge to cost of sales and directly reduces the carrying value of the inventory.

The Company estimates any required write downs for inventory obsolescence by examining its inventories on a quarterly basis to determine if there are indicators that the carrying values exceed net realizable value. Indicators that could result in additional inventory write downs include age of inventory, damaged inventory, slow moving products and products at the end of their life cycles. While management believes that inventory is appropriately stated at the lower of cost or market, significant judgment is involved in determining the net realizable value of inventory.

Financial Instruments

The Company enters into various types of financial instruments in the normal course of business. Fair values are estimated based on assumptions concerning the amount and timing of estimated future cash flows and assumed discount rates reflecting varying degrees of perceived risk. Cash, cash equivalents, accounts receivable, accounts payable and accrued expenses are reported at carrying value and approximate fair value due to the short maturity of these instruments. Long-term debt is also reported at carrying value, which approximates fair value due to the fact that the interest rate on the debt is based on variable interest rates.

GREEN MOUNTAIN COFFEE ROASTERS, INC.

NOTES TO CONSOLIDATED FINANCIAL STATEMENTS—(Continued)

The fair values of derivative financial instruments have been determined using market information and valuation methodologies. Changes in assumptions or estimates could affect the determination of fair value; however, management does not believe any such changes would have a material impact on the Company's financial condition, results of operations or cash flows. The fair values of short-term investments and derivative financial instruments are disclosed in Note 12, *Fair Value Measurements*, in the Consolidated Financial Statements included in this Annual Report.

Derivative Instruments

The Company enters into over-the-counter derivative contracts based on coffee futures ("coffee futures") to hedge against price increases in price-to-be-fixed coffee purchase commitments and anticipated coffee purchases. Coffee purchases are generally denominated in the U.S. dollar. The Company also enters into interest rate swap agreements to mitigate interest rate risk associated with the Company's variable-rate borrowings and foreign currency forward contracts to hedge the purchase and payment of certain green coffee purchase commitments as well as certain recognized liabilities in currencies other than the Company's functional currency. All derivatives are recorded at fair value. Interest rate swaps, coffee futures, and certain foreign currency forward contracts which hedge the purchase and payment of green coffee purchase commitments are designated as cash flow hedges with the effective portion of the change in the fair value of the derivative instrument recorded as a component of other comprehensive income ("OCI") and subsequently reclassified into net earnings when the hedged exposure affects net earnings. Foreign currency forward contracts which hedge certain recognized liabilities denominated in non-functional currencies are designated as fair value hedges with the changes in the fair value of these instruments along with the changes in the fair value of the hedged liabilities recognized in *gain or loss on foreign currency, net* in the Consolidated Statements of Operations.

Effectiveness is determined by how closely the changes in the fair value of the derivative instrument offset the changes in the fair value of the hedged item. The ineffective portion of the change in the fair value of the derivative instrument is recorded directly to earnings.

The Company formally documents hedging instruments and hedged items, and measures at each balance sheet date the effectiveness of its hedges. When it is determined that a derivative is not highly effective, the derivative expires, or is sold or terminated, or the derivative is discontinued because it is unlikely that a forecasted transaction will occur, the Company discontinues hedge accounting prospectively for that specific hedge instrument.

The Company also enters into certain foreign currency and interest rate derivative contracts to hedge certain foreign currency exposures that are not designated as hedging instruments for accounting purposes. These contracts are recorded at fair value, with the changes in fair value recognized in *gain (loss) on financial instruments, net* in the Consolidated Statements of Operations.

The Company does not engage in speculative transactions, nor does it hold derivative instruments for trading purposes. See Note 11, *Derivative Financial Instruments* and Note 14, *Stockholders' Equity* in the Consolidated Financial Statements included in this Annual Report for further information.

Deferred Financing Costs

Deferred financing costs consist primarily of commitment fees and loan origination fees and are being amortized over the respective life of the applicable debt using a method that approximates the effective interest rate method. Deferred financing costs included in *Other long-term assets* in the accompanying Consolidated Balance Sheets as of September 28, 2013 and September 29, 2012 were $15.2 million and $22.3 million, respectively.

Goodwill and Intangibles

Goodwill is tested for impairment annually at the end of the Company's fiscal year or whenever events or changes in circumstances indicate that the carrying value may not be recoverable. Goodwill is assigned to reporting units for purposes of impairment testing. A reporting unit is the same as an operating segment or one level below an operating segment. The Company may assess qualitative factors to determine if it is more likely than not (i.e., a likelihood of more than 50%) that the fair value of a reporting unit is less than its carrying amount, including goodwill. If the Company determines that it is not more likely than not that the fair value of a reporting unit is less than its carrying amount, no further testing is necessary. If, however, the Company determines that it is more likely than not that the fair value of a reporting unit is less than its carrying amount, the Company performs the first step of a two-step goodwill impairment test. The assessment of qualitative factors is optional and at the Company's discretion. The Company may bypass the qualitative assessment for any reporting unit in any period and perform the first step of the quantitative goodwill

GREEN MOUNTAIN COFFEE ROASTERS, INC.

NOTES TO CONSOLIDATED FINANCIAL STATEMENTS—(Continued)

impairment test. The Company may resume performing the qualitative assessment in any subsequent period. The first step is a comparison of each reporting unit's fair value to its carrying value. The Company estimates fair value based on discounted cash flows. The reporting unit's discounted cash flows require significant management judgment with respect to sales forecasts, gross margin percentages, selling, operating, general and administrative ("SG&A") expenses, capital expenditures and the selection and use of an appropriate discount rate. The projected sales, gross margin and SG&A expense rate assumptions and capital expenditures are based on the Company's annual business plan or other forecasted results. Discount rates reflect market-based estimates of the risks associated with the projected cash flows directly resulting from the use of those assets in operations. The estimates of fair value of reporting units are based on the best information available as of the date of the assessment. If the carrying value of a reporting unit exceeds its estimated fair value in the first step, a second step is performed, which requires the Company to allocate the fair value of the reporting unit derived in the first step to the fair value of the reporting unit's net assets, with any fair value in excess of amounts allocated to such net assets representing the implied fair value of goodwill for that reporting unit. If the implied fair value of the goodwill is less than the book value, goodwill is impaired and is written down to the implied fair value amount.

Intangible assets that have finite lives are amortized over their estimated economic useful lives on a straight line basis. Intangible assets that have indefinite lives are not amortized and are tested for impairment annually or whenever events or changes in circumstances indicate that the carrying value may not be recoverable. Similar to the qualitative assessment for goodwill, the Company may assess qualitative factors to determine if it is more likely than not (i.e., a likelihood of more than 50%) that the fair value of the indefinite-lived intangible asset is less than its carrying amount. If the Company determines that it is not more likely than not that the fair value of the indefinite-lived intangible asset is less than its carrying amount, no further testing is necessary. If, however, the Company determines that it is more likely than not that the fair value of the indefinite-lived intangible asset is less than its carrying amount, the Company compares the fair value of the indefinite-lived asset with its carrying amount. If the carrying value of an individual indefinite-lived intangible asset exceeds its fair value, the individual indefinite-lived intangible asset is written down by an amount equal to such excess. The assessment of qualitative factors is optional and at the Company's discretion. The Company may bypass the qualitative assessment for any indefinite-lived intangible asset in any period and resume performing the qualitative assessment in any subsequent period.

Impairment of Long-Lived Assets

When facts and circumstances indicate that the carrying values of long-lived assets, including fixed assets, may be impaired, an evaluation of recoverability is performed by comparing the carrying value of the assets, at an asset group level, to undiscounted projected future cash flows in addition to other quantitative and qualitative analyses. When assessing impairment, property, plant and equipment assets are grouped at the lowest level for which there are identifiable cash flows that are largely independent of other groups of assets. Upon indication that the carrying value of such assets may not be recoverable, the Company recognizes an impairment loss as a charge against current operations. Long-lived assets to be disposed of are reported at the lower of the carrying amount or fair value, less estimated costs to sell. The Company makes judgments related to the expected useful lives of long-lived assets and its ability to realize undiscounted cash flows in excess of the carrying amounts of such assets which are affected by factors such as the ongoing maintenance and improvements of the assets, changes in economic conditions and changes in operating performance.

Fixed Assets

Fixed assets are carried at cost, net of accumulated depreciation. Expenditures for maintenance, repairs and renewals of minor items are expensed as incurred. Expenditures for refurbishments and improvements that significantly improve the productive capacity or extend the useful life of an asset are capitalized. Depreciation is calculated using the straight-line method over the assets' estimated useful lives. The cost and accumulated depreciation for fixed assets sold, retired, or otherwise disposed of are relieved from the accounts, and the resultant gains and losses are reflected in income.

The Company follows an industry-wide practice of purchasing and loaning coffee brewing and related equipment to wholesale customers. These assets are also carried at cost, net of accumulated depreciation.

Depreciation costs of manufacturing and distribution assets are included in cost of sales on the Consolidated Statements of Operations. Depreciation costs of other assets, including equipment on loan to customers, are included in selling and operating expenses on the Consolidated Statements of Operations.

GREEN MOUNTAIN COFFEE ROASTERS, INC.

NOTES TO CONSOLIDATED FINANCIAL STATEMENTS—(Continued)

Leases

Occasionally, the Company is involved in the construction of leased properties. Due to the extent and nature of that involvement, the Company is deemed the owner during the construction period and is required to capitalize the construction costs on the Consolidated Balance Sheets along with a corresponding financing obligation for the project costs that are incurred by the lessor. Upon completion of the project, a sale-leaseback analysis is performed to determine if the Company can record a sale to remove the assets and related obligation and record the lease as either an operating or capital lease obligation. If the Company is precluded from derecognizing the assets when construction is complete due to continuing involvement beyond a normal leaseback, the lease is accounted for as a financing transaction and the recorded asset and related financing obligation remain on the Consolidated Balance Sheet. Accordingly, the asset is depreciated over its estimated useful life in accordance with the Company's policy. If the Company is not considered the owner of the land, a portion of the lease payments is allocated to ground rent and treated as an operating lease. The portion of the lease payment allocated to ground rental expense is based on the fair value of the land at the commencement of construction. Lease payments allocated to the buildings are recognized as reductions to the financing obligation and interest expense. See Note 19, *Commitments and Contingencies*, for further information.

Leases that qualify as capital leases are recorded at the lower of the fair value of the asset or the present value of the future minimum lease payments over the lease term generally using the Company's incremental borrowing rate. Assets leased under capital leases are included in fixed assets and generally are depreciated over the lease term. Lease payments under capital leases are recognized as a reduction of the capital lease obligation and interest expense.

All other leases are considered operating leases. Assets subject to an operating lease are not recorded on the balance sheet. Lease payments are recognized on a straight-line basis as rent expense over the expected lease term.

Revenue Recognition

Revenue from sales of single cup brewer systems, coffee and other specialty beverages in portion packs, and coffee in more traditional packaging including whole bean and ground coffee selections in bags and ground coffee in fractional packs is recognized when title and risk of loss passes to the customer, which generally occurs upon shipment or delivery of the product to the customer as defined by the contractual shipping terms. Shipping charges billed to customers are also recognized as revenue, and the related shipping costs are included in cost of sales. Cash received in advance of product delivery is recorded in deferred revenue, which is included in other current liabilities on the accompanying Consolidated Balance Sheets, until earned.

The majority of the Company's distribution to major retailers is processed by fulfillment entities. The fulfillment entities receive and fulfill sales orders and invoice certain retailers. All product shipped by the Company to the fulfillment entities are owned by the Company and included in inventories on the accompanying consolidated balance sheets. The Company recognizes revenue when delivery of the product from the fulfillment entity to the retailer has occurred based on the contractual shipping terms and when all other revenue recognition criteria are met.

Sales of single cup brewers, portion packs and other products are recognized net of any discounts, returns, allowances and sales incentives, including coupon redemptions and rebates. The Company estimates the allowance for returns using an average return rate based on historical experience and an evaluation of contractual rights or obligations. The Company routinely participates in trade promotion programs with customers, including customers whose sales are processed by the fulfillment entities, whereby customers can receive certain incentives and allowances which are recorded as a reduction to sales when the sales incentive is offered and committed to or, if the incentive relates to specific sales, at the later of when that revenue is recognized or the date at which the sales incentive is offered. These incentives include, but are not limited to, cash discounts and volume based incentive programs. Allowances to customers that are directly attributable and supportable by customer promotional activities are recorded as selling expenses at the time the promotional activity occurs.

Roasters licensed by the Company to manufacture and sell K-Cup® packs, both to the Company for resale and to their other coffee customers, are obligated to pay a royalty to the Company upon shipment to their customer. The Company records royalty revenue upon shipment of K-Cup® packs by licensed roasters to third-party customers as set forth under the terms and conditions of various licensing agreements. For shipments of K-Cup® packs to the Company for resale, this royalty payment is recorded as a reduction to the carrying value of the related K-Cup® packs in inventory and as a reduction to cost of sales when sold through to third-party customers by the Company.

GREEN MOUNTAIN COFFEE ROASTERS, INC.
NOTES TO CONSOLIDATED FINANCIAL STATEMENTS—(Continued)

Cost of Sales

Cost of sales for the Company consists of the cost of raw materials including coffee beans, hot cocoa, flavorings and packaging materials; a portion of our rental expense; production, warehousing and distribution costs which include salaries; distribution and merchandising personnel; leases and depreciation on facilities and equipment used in production; the cost of brewers manufactured by suppliers; third-party fulfillment charges; receiving, inspection and internal transfer costs; warranty expense; freight, duties and delivery expenses; and certain third-party royalty charges. All shipping and handling expenses are also included as a component of cost of sales.

Product Warranty

The Company provides for the estimated cost of product warranties in cost of sales, at the time product revenue is recognized. Warranty costs are estimated primarily using historical warranty information in conjunction with current engineering assessments applied to the Company's expected repair or replacement costs. The estimate for warranties requires assumptions relating to expected warranty claims which can be impacted significantly by quality issues.

Advertising Costs

The Company expenses the costs of advertising the first time the advertising takes place, except for direct mail campaigns targeted directly at consumers, which are expensed over the period during which they are expected to generate sales. As of September 28, 2013 and September 29, 2012, prepaid advertising costs of $4.1 million and $2.4 million, respectively, were recorded in *Other current assets* in the accompanying Consolidated Balance Sheets. Advertising expense totaled $193.2 million, $147.7 million, and $90.8 million, for fiscal years 2013, 2012, and 2011, respectively.

Income Taxes

The Company recognizes deferred tax assets and liabilities for the expected future tax benefits or consequences of temporary differences between the financial statement carrying amounts of existing assets and liabilities, and their respective tax bases. Deferred tax assets and liabilities are measured using enacted tax rates in effect for the year in which those temporary differences are expected to be recovered or settled. Judgment is required in determining the provision for income taxes and related accruals, deferred tax assets and liabilities. These include establishing a valuation allowance related to the ability to realize certain deferred tax assets. The Company currently believes that future earnings and current tax planning strategies will be sufficient to recover substantially all of the Company's recorded net deferred tax assets. To the extent future taxable income against which these assets may be applied is not sufficient, some portion or all of our recorded deferred tax assets would not be realizable.

Accounting for uncertain tax positions also requires significant judgments, including estimating the amount, timing and likelihood of ultimate settlement. Although the Company believes that its estimates are reasonable, actual results could differ from these estimates. The Company uses a more-likely-than-not measurement attribute for all tax positions taken or expected to be taken on a tax return in order for those tax positions to be recognized in the financial statements.

Stock-Based Compensation

The Company measures the cost of employee services received in exchange for an award of equity instruments based on the grant-date fair value of the award. Equity awards consist of stock options, restricted stock units ("RSUs"), restricted stock awards ("RSAs"), and performance stock units ("PSUs"). The cost is recognized over the period during which an employee is required to provide service in exchange for the award.

The Company measures the fair value of stock options using the Black-Scholes model and certain assumptions, including the expected life of the stock options, an expected forfeiture rate and the expected volatility of its common stock. The expected life of options is estimated based on options vesting periods, contractual lives and an analysis of the Company's historical experience. The expected forfeiture rate is based on the Company's historical employee turnover experience and future expectations. The risk-free interest rate is based on the U.S. Treasury rate over the expected life. The Company uses a blended historical volatility to estimate expected volatility at the measurement date. The fair value of RSUs, RSAs and PSUs is based on the closing price of the Company's common stock on the grant date.

GREEN MOUNTAIN COFFEE ROASTERS, INC.

NOTES TO CONSOLIDATED FINANCIAL STATEMENTS—(Continued)

Foreign Currency Translation and Transactions

The financial statements of the Company's foreign subsidiaries are translated into the reporting currency of the Company which is the U.S. dollar. The functional currency of certain of the Company's foreign subsidiaries is the local currency of the subsidiary. Accordingly, the assets and liabilities of the Company's foreign subsidiaries are translated into U.S. dollars using the exchange rate in effect at each balance sheet date. Revenue and expense accounts are generally translated using the average rate of exchange during the period. Foreign currency translation adjustments are accumulated as a component of other comprehensive income or loss as a separate component of stockholders' equity. Gains and losses arising from transactions denominated in currencies other than the functional currency of the entity are charged directly against earnings in the Consolidated Statement of Operations. Gains and losses arising from transactions denominated in foreign currencies are primarily related to inter- company loans that have been determined to be temporary in nature, cash, long-term debt and accounts payable denominated in non-functional currencies.

Significant Customer Credit Risk and Supply Risk

The majority of the Company's customers are located in the U.S. and Canada. With the exception of M.Block & Sons ("MBlock") as described below, concentration of credit risk with respect to accounts receivable is limited due to the large number of customers in various channels comprising the Company's customer base. The Company does not require collateral from customers as ongoing credit evaluations of customers' payment histories are performed. The Company maintains reserves for potential credit losses and such losses, in the aggregate, have not exceeded management's expectations.

The Company procures the majority of the brewers it sells from one third-party brewer manufacturer. Purchases from this brewer manufacturer amounted to approximately $637.0 million, $721.3 million and $545.3 million in fiscal years 2013, 2012 and 2011, respectively.

The Company primarily relies on MBlock to process the majority of sales orders for our AH single serve business with retailers in the United States. The Company is subject to significant credit risk regarding the creditworthiness of MBlock and, in turn, the creditworthiness of the retailers. Sales processed by MBlock to retailers amounted to $1,600.2 million, $1,458.4 million and $997.0 million for fiscal years 2013, 2012 and 2011, respectively. The Company's account receivables due from MBlock amounted to $157.4 million and $133.1 million at September 28, 2013 and September 29, 2012, respectively.

Sales to customers that represented more than 10% of the Company's net sales included Wal-Mart Stores, Inc. and affiliates ("Wal-Mart"), representing approximately 14% and 12% of consolidated net sales for fiscal years 2013 and 2012, respectively; Costco Wholesale Corporation and affiliates ("Costco"), representing approximately 11% of consolidated net sales for fiscal 2013; and Bed Bath & Beyond, Inc., and affiliates ("Bed Bath & Beyond"), representing approximately 11% of consolidated net sales for fiscal 2011. For Wal-Mart and Bed Bath & Beyond, the majority of U.S. sales are processed through MBlock whereby MBlock is the vendor of record. Starting in fiscal 2012, for U.S. sales to Costco, the Company became the vendor of record and although the sales are processed through MBlock, the Company records the account receivables from the customer and pays MBlock for their fulfillment services. The Company's account receivables due from Costco amounted to $65.7 million, net of allowances, at September 28, 2013.

Research & Development

Research and development charges are expensed as incurred. These expenses amounted to $57.7 million, $41.7 million and $17.7 million in fiscal years 2013, 2012 and 2011, respectively. These costs primarily consist of salary and consulting expenses and are recorded in selling and operating expenses in each respective segment of the Company.

Recent Accounting Pronouncements

In July 2013, the Financial Accounting Standards Board (the "FASB") issued an Accounting Standards Update ("ASU") No. 2013-11, "Presentation of an Unrecognized Tax Benefit When a Net Operating Loss Carryforward, a Similar Tax Loss, or a Tax Credit Carryforward Exists" ("ASU 2013-11"). ASU 2013-11 was issued to eliminate diversity in practice regarding the presentation of unrecognized tax benefits when a net operating loss carryforward, a similar tax loss, or a tax credit carryforward exists. Under ASU 2013-11, an unrecognized tax benefit, or a portion of an unrecognized tax benefit, should be presented in the financial statements as a reduction to a deferred tax asset for a net operating loss carryforward, a similar tax loss, or a tax credit carryforward. Otherwise, to the extent a net operating loss carryforward, a similar tax loss, or a tax credit carryforward is not available at the reporting date under the tax law of the applicable jurisdiction to settle any additional income taxes that would result from the disallowance of a tax position or the tax law of the applicable jurisdiction does not require the entity to use, and the entity does not intend to use, the deferred tax asset for such purpose, the unrecognized tax benefit should be presented in the financial statements as a liability and should not be combined with deferred tax assets. The amendments in this ASU are effective prospectively for reporting periods beginning after December 15, 2013, and early adoption is permitted. The adoption of ASU 2013-11 is not expected to have a material impact on the Company's net income, financial position or cash flows.

In March 2013, the FASB issued ASU No. 2013-05, "Foreign Currency Matters (Topic 830): Parent's Accounting for the Cumulative Translation Adjustment upon Derecognition of Certain Subsidiaries or Groups of Assets within a Foreign Entity or of an Investment in a Foreign Entity" ("ASU 2013-05"). ASU 2013-05 provides clarification regarding whether Subtopic 810-10, Consolidation—Overall, or Subtopic 830-30, Foreign Currency Matters— Translation of Financial Statements, applies to the release of cumulative translation adjustments into net income when a reporting entity either sells a part or all of its investment in a foreign entity or ceases to have a controlling financial interest in a subsidiary or group of assets that constitute a business within a foreign entity. The amendments in this ASU are effective prospectively for reporting periods beginning after December 15, 2013, and early adoption is permitted. The adoption of ASU 2013-05 is not expected to have a material impact on the Company's net income, financial position or cash flows.

In February 2013, the FASB issued ASU No. 2013-04, "Liabilities (Topic 405): Obligations Resulting from Joint and Several Liability Arrangements for Which the Total Amount of the Obligation Is Fixed at the Reporting Date" ("ASU 2013-04"). ASU 2013-04 provides guidance for the recognition, measurement and disclosure of obligations resulting from joint and several liability arrangements for which the total amount of the obligation within the scope of this ASU is fixed at the reporting date. The guidance requires an entity to measure those obligations as the sum of the amount the reporting entity agreed to pay on the basis of its arrangement among its co-obligors as well as any additional amount the reporting entity expects to pay on behalf of its co-obligors. ASU 2013-04 also requires an entity to disclose the nature and amount of those obligations. The amendments in this ASU are effective for reporting periods beginning after December 15, 2013, with early adoption permitted. Retrospective application is required. The adoption of ASU 2013-04 is not expected to have a material impact on the Company's net income, financial position or cash flows.

In February 2013, the FASB issued ASU No. 2013-02, "Comprehensive Income (Topic 220): Reporting of Amounts Reclassified Out of Accumulated Comprehensive Income" ("ASU 2013-02"). ASU 2013-02 requires an entity to report the effect of significant reclassifications out of accumulated other comprehensive income on the respective line items in net income if the amount being reclassified is required under GAAP to be reclassified in its entirety to net income. For significant items not reclassified in their entirety to net income in the same reporting period, an entity is required to cross- reference other disclosures that provide additional detail about those amounts. The amendments in this ASU are effective for annual reporting periods, and interim periods within those annual reporting periods, beginning after December 15, 2012, which for the Company will be the first quarter of fiscal 2014. The adoption of ASU 2013-02 is not expected to have an impact on the Company's net income, financial position or cash flows.

In December 2011, the FASB issued ASU No. 2011-11, "Disclosures about Offsetting Assets and Liabilities," ("ASU 2011-11") that provides amendments for disclosures about offsetting assets and liabilities. The amendments require an entity to disclose information about offsetting and related arrangements to enable users of its financial statements to understand the effect of those arrangements on its financial position. Entities are required to disclose both gross information and net information about both instruments and transactions eligible for offset in the statement of financial position and instruments and transactions subject to an agreement similar to a master netting arrangement. On January 31, 2013, the FASB issued ASU No. 2013-01, "Clarifying the Scope of Disclosures about Offsetting Assets and Liabilities," which clarified that the scope of the disclosures is limited to include derivatives, sale and repurchase agreements and reverse sale and repurchase agreements, and securities borrowing and securities lending arrangements. The amendments are effective for annual reporting periods beginning on or after January 1, 2013, and interim periods within those annual periods. Disclosures required by the amendments should be provided retrospectively for all comparative periods presented. For the Company, the amendments are effective for the fiscal year ending September 27, 2014 (fiscal year 2014). The adoption of ASU 2011-11 is not expected to have a material impact on the Company's disclosures.

GREEN MOUNTAIN COFFEE ROASTERS, INC.

NOTES TO CONSOLIDATED FINANCIAL STATEMENTS—(Continued)

3. Acquisitions and Divestitures

Fiscal 2012

On October 3, 2011, all the outstanding shares of Van Houtte USA Holdings, Inc., also known as the Van Houtte U.S. Coffee Service business or the "Filterfresh" business, were sold to ARAMARK Refreshment Services, LLC ("ARAMARK") in exchange for $149.5 million in cash. Approximately $4.4 million of cash was transferred to ARAMARK as part of the sale and $7.4 million was repaid to ARAMARK upon finalization of the purchase price, resulting in a net cash inflow related to the Filterfresh sale of $137.7 million. The Company recognized a gain on the sale of $26.3 million during the thirteen weeks ended December 24, 2011. Filterfresh had been included in the Canada segment.

As of September 24, 2011, all the assets and liabilities relating to the Filterfresh business were reported in the Consolidated Balance Sheet as assets and liabilities held-for-sale.

Filterfresh revenues and net income included in the Company's consolidated statement of operations were as follows (dollars in thousands, except per share data):

	For the period September 25, 2011 through October 3, 2011 (date of sale)	For the period December 17, 2010 (date of acquisition through) September 24, 2011
Net sales	$ 2,286	$ 90,855
Net income	$ 229	$ 12,263
Less income attributable to noncontrolling interests	20	1,051
Net income attributable to GMCR	$ 209	$ 11,212
Diluted net income per share	$ —	$ 0.07

After the disposition, the Company continues to sell coffee and brewers to Filterfresh, which prior to the sale of Filterfresh were eliminated and were not reflected in the Consolidated Statement of Operations. For fiscal 2012, the Company's sales to Filterfresh through October 3, 2011 (date of sale) that were eliminated in consolidation were $0.6 million. For fiscal 2011, the Company's sales to Filterfresh during the period December 17, 2010 (date of acquisition) through September 24, 2011 that were eliminated in consolidation were $22.2 million.

Fiscal 2011

LJVH Holdings, Inc. (including subsidiaries—Van Houtte)

On December 17, 2010, the Company acquired all of the outstanding capital stock of LJVH Holdings, Inc. ("LJVH" and together with its subsidiaries, "Van Houtte"), a coffee roaster headquartered in Montreal, Quebec, for $907.8 million, net of cash acquired. The acquisition was financed with cash on hand and a $1,450.0 million credit facility. Van Houtte's functional currency is the Canadian dollar. Van Houtte's operations are included in the Canada segment.

At the time of the acquisition, the Company accounted for all the assets relating to the Filterfresh business as held-for-sale.

The Van Houtte acquisition was accounted for under the acquisition method of accounting. The total purchase price of $907.8 million, net of cash acquired, was allocated to Van Houtte's net tangible assets and identifiable intangible assets based on their estimated fair values as of December 17, 2010. The fair value assigned to identifiable intangible assets acquired was determined primarily by using an income approach. The allocation of the purchase price is based upon a valuation determined using management's and the Company's estimates and assumptions. The table below represents the allocation of the purchase price to the acquired net assets of Van Houtte (in thousands):

	Total	Van Houtte Canadian Operations	Filterfresh Assets Held For Sale
Restricted cash	$ 500	$ 500	$ —
Accounts receivable	61,130	47,554	13,576
Inventories	42,958	36,691	6,267
Income taxes receivable	2,260	2,190	70
Deferred income taxes	4,903	3,577	1,326
Other current assets	5,047	4,453	594
Fixed assets	143,928	110,622	33,306
Intangible assets	375,099	355,549	19,550
Goodwill	472,331	409,493	62,838
Other long-term assets	1,577	962	615
Accounts payable and accrued expenses	(54,502)	(46,831)	(7,671)
Other short-term liabilities	(4,330)	(3,404)	(926)
Income taxes payable	(1,496)	(1,496)	—
Deferred income taxes	(117,086)	(104,866)	(12,220)
Notes payable	(2,914)	(1,770)	(1,144)
Other long-term liabilities	(2,452)	(1,683)	(769)
Non-controlling interests	(19,118)	(9,529)	(9,589)
	$ 907,835	$ 802,012	$ 105,823

The purchase price allocated to Filterfresh was the fair value, less the estimated direct costs to sell Filterfresh established at the acquisition date. The fair value of Filterfresh was estimated using an income approach, specifically the discounted cash flow ("DCF") method. Under the DCF method the fair value is calculated by discounting the projected after-tax cash flows for the business to present value. The income approach includes assumptions about the amount and timing of future cash flows using projections and other estimates. A discount rate based on an appropriate weighted average cost of capital was applied to the estimated future cash flows to estimate the fair value.

An income approach, specifically the DCF method, was used to value the noncontrolling interests.

Amortizable intangible assets acquired, valued at the date of acquisition, include approximately $263.1 million for customer relationships, $10.9 million for trademarks and trade names, $1.4 million for franchises and $0.3 million for technology. Indefinite-lived intangible assets acquired include approximately $99.4 million for the Van Houtte trademark which is not amortized. The definite lived intangible assets classified as held-for-sale were not amortized and approximated $19.5 million. Amortizable intangible assets are amortized on a straight-line basis over their respective useful lives, and the weighted-average amortization period is 10.8 years.

The cost of the acquisition in excess of the fair market value of the tangible and intangible assets acquired less liabilities assumed represents acquired goodwill. The acquisition of Van Houtte provides the Company with an expanded Canadian presence and manufacturing and distribution synergies, which provide the basis of the goodwill recognized with respect to the Van Houtte Canadian operations. As discussed above, the purchase price allocated to Filterfresh was the fair value, less the estimated direct costs to sell Filterfresh established at the acquisition date. The excess of the purchase price (fair value) allocated to Filterfresh over the fair value of the net tangible and identifiable intangible assets represents goodwill. Goodwill and intangible assets are reported in the Canada segment. The goodwill and intangible assets recognized are not deductible for tax purposes.

Acquisition costs were expensed as incurred and totaled approximately $10.7 million for the fiscal year ended September 24, 2011 and are included in general and administrative expenses for the Company.

Approximately $9.3 million of the purchase price was held in escrow at September 29, 2012 and was included in restricted cash. A corresponding amount of $9.3 million was included in other current liabilities as of September 29, 2012. None of the purchase price remained in escrow as of September 28, 2013, and therefore, there were no corresponding amounts included in other current liabilities.

GREEN MOUNTAIN COFFEE ROASTERS, INC.

NOTES TO CONSOLIDATED FINANCIAL STATEMENTS—(Continued)

The acquisition was completed on December 17, 2010 and accordingly results of operations from such date have been included in the Company's Statement of Operations. For fiscal 2011, the Van Houtte operations contributed an additional $321.4 million of consolidated revenue and $20.2 million of income before income taxes.

4. Segment Reporting

The Company has historically managed its operations through three business segments: the Specialty Coffee business unit ("SCBU"), the Keurig business unit ("KBU") and the Canadian business unit. Effective as of and as initially disclosed on May 8, 2013, the Company's Board of Directors authorized and approved a reorganization which consolidated U.S. operations to bring greater organizational efficiency and coordination across the Company. Due to this combination, the results of U.S. operations, formerly reported in the SCBU and KBU segments, are reported in one segment ("Domestic") and the results of Canadian operations are reported in the "Canada" segment. The Company's Chief Executive Officer ("CEO") serves as the Company's chief operating decision maker ("CODM") and there are two operating and reportable segments, Domestic and Canada.

As a result of the consolidation of U.S. operations, the Company has recast all historical segment results in order to: i) provide data that is on a basis consistent with the Company's new structure; ii) remove total assets from the Company's segment disclosures as only consolidated asset information is provided to and used by the CODM for use in decision making (in connection with the reorganization, segment asset information is neither provided to nor used by the CODM); and iii) reflect all sustainability expenses in Corporate as the Company no longer allocates those expenses to its operating segments.

For a description of the operating segments, see Note 1, *Nature of Business and Organization*.

Management evaluates the performance of the Company's operating segments based on several factors, including net sales to external customers and operating income. Net sales are recorded on a segment basis and intersegment sales are eliminated as part of the financial consolidation process. Operating income represents gross profit less selling, operating, general and administrative expenses. The Company's manufacturing operations occur within both the Domestic and Canada segments, and the costs of manufacturing are recognized in cost of sales in the operating segment in which the sale occurs. Information system technology services are mainly centralized while finance and accounting functions are primarily decentralized. Expenses consisting primarily of compensation and depreciation related to certain centralized administrative functions including information system technology are allocated to the operating segments. Expenses not specifically related to an operating segment are presented under "Corporate Unallocated." Corporate Unallocated expenses are comprised mainly of the compensation and other related expenses of certain of the Company's senior executive officers and other selected employees who perform duties related to the entire enterprise. Corporate Unallocated expenses also include depreciation for corporate headquarters, sustainability expenses, interest expense not directly attributable to an operating segment, the majority of foreign exchange gains or losses, legal expenses and compensation of the Board of Directors. The Company does not disclose assets or property additions by segment as only consolidated asset information is provided to the CODM for use in decision making.

Effective for the first quarter of fiscal 2013, the Company changed its measure for reporting segment profitability and for evaluating segment performance and the allocation of Company resources from income before taxes to operating income (loss). Prior to the first quarter of fiscal 2013, the Company disclosed each operating and reportable segment's income before taxes to report segment profitability. Segment disclosures for prior periods have been recast to reflect operating income by segment in place of income before taxes. The CODM measures segment performance based upon operating income which excludes interest expense and interest expense is not provided to the CODM by segment. Accordingly, interest expense by segment is no longer presented.

Effective with the beginning of the Company's third quarter of fiscal 2011, sales between operating segments are recorded at cost and the Domestic segment no longer records royalty income from the Canada segment on shipments of portion packs. Prior to the third quarter of fiscal 2011, the Company recorded intersegment sales and purchases of brewer and K-Cup® packs at a markup. As a result of the change, intersegment sales have no impact on segment operating income (loss) and effective with the first quarter of fiscal 2013, the Company no longer discloses intersegment sales. Each operating segment's net sales for fiscal years 2013 and 2012 include only net sales to external customers.

The selected financial data for segment disclosures for fiscal 2011 was not recast for the above changes related to intersegment sales and royalty income. The following table summarizes the approximate net effect of the above changes on segment income before taxes for fiscal 2013, 2012 and 2011 as a result of the above changes (in thousands). The net

NOTES TO CONSOLIDATED FINANCIAL STATEMENTS—(Continued)

effect represents the net mark-up on sales between the segments as well as the Domestic segment royalty income on the sale of portion packs by the Canada segment. The Company used historical mark-up percentages and royalty rates to calculate the net effect.

Increase (decrease) in operating income (loss)	Fiscal 2013	Fiscal 2012	Fiscal 2011
Domestic	$ (38,755)	$ 20,068	$ (29,584)
Canada	39,057	(19,084)	22,157
Corporate—Unallocated	—	—	—
Eliminations	(302)	(984)	7,427
Consolidated	$ —	$ —	$ —

The following tables summarize selected financial data for segment disclosures for fiscal 2013, 2012 and 2011.

	For Fiscal 2013 (Dollars in thousands)			
	Domestic	Canada	Corporate-Unallocated	Consolidated
Net sales	$ 3,725,008	$ 633,092	$ —	$ 4,358,100
Operating income (loss)	$ 826,092	$ 87,674	$ (148,539)	$ 765,227
Depreciation and amortization	$ 162,359	$ 65,334	$ 1,500	$ 229,193
Stock compensation expense	$ 9,909	$ 2,519	$ 13,653	$ 26,081

	For Fiscal 2012 (Dollars in thousands)			
	Domestic	Canada	Corporate-Unallocated	Consolidated
Net sales	$ 3,233,674	$ 625,524	$ —	$ 3,859,198
Operating Income (loss)	$ 576,949	$ 76,198	$ (84,251)	$ 568,896
Depreciation and amortization	$ 116,722	$ 62,984	$ 1,941	$ 181,647
Stock compensation expense	$ 7,808	$ 1,890	$ 8,170	$ 17,868

	For Fiscal 2011 (Dollars in thousands)				
	Domestic	Canada	Corporate-Unallocated	Eliminations	Consolidated
Sales to unaffiliated customers	$ 2,152,432	$ 498,467	$ —	$ —	$ 2,650,899
Intersegment sales	$ 36,855	$ 98,347	$ —	$ (135,202)	$ —
Net sales	$ 2,189,287	$ 596,814	$ —	$ (135,202)	$ 2,650,899
Operating Income	$ 399,638	$ 67,727	$ (73,259)	$ (25,193)	$ 368,913
Depreciation and amortization	$ 68,439	$ 45,193	$ 4	$ —	$ 113,636
Stock compensation expense	$ 5,519	$ 470	$ 4,372	$ —	$ 10,361

NOTES TO CONSOLIDATED FINANCIAL STATEMENTS—(Continued)

Geographic Information

Net sales are attributed to countries based on the location of the customer. Information concerning net sales of principal geographic areas is as follows (in thousands):

	Fiscal 2013	Fiscal 2012	Fiscal 2011
Net Sales:			
United States	$ 3,721,182	$ 3,248,543	$ 2,248,811
Canada	634,360	609,828	400,682
Other	2,558	827	1,406
	$ 4,358,100	$ 3,859,198	$ 2,650,899

Sales to customers that represented more than 10% of the Company's net sales included Wal-Mart, representing approximately 14% and 12% of consolidated net sales for fiscal years 2013 and 2012, respectively, Costco, representing approximately 11% of consolidated net sales for fiscal 2013, and Bed Bath & Beyond, representing approximately 11% of consolidated net sales for fiscal 2011. Sales to Wal-Mart in fiscal years 2013 and 2012 were through both segments; sales to Costco in fiscal 2013 were through both segments; and sales to Bed Bath & Beyond, Inc., in fiscal 2011 were primarily through the Domestic segment.

Information concerning long-lived assets of principal geographic area is as follows (in thousands) as of:

	September 28, 2013	September 29, 2012
Fixed Assets, net:		
United States	$ 844,471	$ 783,075
Canada	135,440	143,640
Other	5,652	17,581
	$ 985,563	$ 944,296

Net Sales by Major Product Category

Net sales by major product category (in thousands):

	Fiscal 2013	Fiscal 2012	Fiscal 2011
Portion Packs	$ 3,187,350	$ 2,708,886	$ 1,704,021
Brewers and Accessories	827,570	759,805	524,709
Other Products and Royalties	343,180	390,507	422,169
	$ 4,358,100	$ 3,859,198	$ 2,650,899

5. Inventories

Inventories consisted of the following (in thousands) as of:

	September 28, 2013	September 29, 2012
Raw materials and supplies	$ 182,882	$ 229,927
Finished goods	493,207	538,510
	$ 676,089	$ 768,437

GREEN MOUNTAIN COFFEE ROASTERS, INC.

NOTES TO CONSOLIDATED FINANCIAL STATEMENTS—(Continued)

As of September 28, 2013, the Company had approximately $245.1 million in green coffee purchase commitments, of which approximately 84% had a fixed price. These commitments primarily extend through fiscal 2015. The value of the variable portion of these commitments was calculated using an average "C" price of coffee of $1.24 per pound at September 28, 2013. In addition to its green coffee commitments, the Company had approximately $141.8 million in fixed price brewer and related accessory purchase commitments and $536.1 million in production raw materials commitments at September 28, 2013. The Company believes, based on relationships established with its suppliers, that the risk of non-delivery on such purchase commitments is remote.

As of September 28, 2013, minimum future inventory purchase commitments were as follows (in thousands):

Fiscal Year	Inventory Purchase Obligations
2014	$ 456,955
2015	124,588
2016	119,565
2017	110,837
2018	111,086
	$ 923,031

6. Fixed Assets

Fixed assets consisted of the following (in thousands) as of:

	Useful Life in Years	September 28, 2013	September 29, 2012
Production equipment	1–15	$ 680,457	$ 544,491
Coffee service equipment	3–7	59,169	63,722
Computer equipment and software	1–6	146,246	111,441
Land	Indefinite	11,520	11,740
Building and building improvements	4–30	134,495	83,172
Furniture and fixtures	1–15	33,975	28,477
Vehicles	4–5	11,786	10,306
Leasehold improvements	1–20 or remaining life of lease, whichever is less	98,990	72,755
Assets acquired under capital leases	5–15	41,200	51,047
Construction-in-progress		202,940	234,442
Total fixed assets		$ 1,420,778	$ 1,211,593
Accumulated depreciation		(435,215)	(267,297)
		$ 985,563	$ 944,296

Assets acquired under capital leases, net of accumulated amortization, were $36.9 million and $47.0 million at September 28, 2013 and September 29, 2012, respectively.

Total depreciation and amortization expense relating to all fixed assets was $183.8 million, $135.7 million and $72.3 million for fiscal years 2013, 2012, and 2011, respectively.

Assets classified as construction-in-progress are not depreciated, as they are not ready for productive use.

GREEN MOUNTAIN COFFEE ROASTERS, INC.

NOTES TO CONSOLIDATED FINANCIAL STATEMENTS—(Continued)

As of September 28, 2013, construction-in-progress includes $21.1 million relating to properties under construction where the Company is deemed to be the accounting owner, even though the Company is not the legal owner. See footnote 19, *Commitments and Contingencies*.

During fiscal years 2013, 2012 and 2011, $6.1 million, $2.8 million, and $2.6 million, respectively, of interest expense was capitalized.

7. Goodwill and Intangible Assets

The following represented the change in the carrying amount of goodwill by segment for fiscal 2013 and 2012 (in thousands):

	Domestic	Canada	Total
Balance as of September 24, 2011	$ 386,416	$ 402,889	$ 789,305
Reassignment of Timothy's goodwill	(17,063)	17,063	—
Foreign currency effect	—	18,771	18,771
Balance as of September 29, 2012	$ 369,353	$ 438,723	$ 808,076
Foreign currency effect	—	(19,892)	(19,892)
Balance as of September 28, 2013	$ 369,353	$ 418,831	$ 788,184

Indefinite-lived intangible assets included in the Canada operating segment consisted of the following (in thousands) as of:

	September 28, 2013	September 29, 2012
Trade names	$ 97,740	$ 102,381

Effective May 8, 2013, the Company combined the results of its U.S. operations, formerly reported in the SCBU and KBU segments, into one Domestic segment.

Effective September 25, 2011, Timothy's is included in the Canada segment. Prior to September 25, 2011, Timothy's was included in the Domestic segment. This resulted in a re-assignment of goodwill of $17.1 million from the Domestic segment to the Canada segment using a relative fair value approach. The amount of goodwill reassigned was determined based on the relative fair values of Timothy's and the Domestic segment.

The Company conducted its annual impairment test of goodwill and indefinite-lived intangible assets as of September 28, 2013, and elected to bypass the optional qualitative assessment and performed a quantitative impairment test. Goodwill was evaluated for impairment at the following reporting unit levels:

- Domestic
- Canada—Roasting and Retail
- Canada—Coffee Services Canada

For the goodwill impairment test, the fair value of the reporting units was estimated using the Discounted Cash Flow ("DCF") method. A number of significant assumptions and estimates are involved in the application of the DCF method including discount rate, sales volume and prices, costs to produce and working capital changes. For the indefinite-lived intangible assets impairment test, the fair value of the trade name was estimated using the Relief-from-Royalty Method. This method estimates the savings in royalties the Company would otherwise have had to pay if it did not own the trade name and had to license the trade name from a third-party with rights of use substantially equivalent to ownership. The fair value of the trade name is the present value of the future estimated after-tax royalty payments avoided by ownership, discounted at an appropriate, risk-adjusted rate of return. For goodwill and indefinite-lived intangible impairment tests, the Company used a royalty rate of 3.0%, an income tax rate of 38.0% for the United States and 27.5% for Canada, and discount rates ranging from 13% to 14%. There was no impairment of goodwill or indefinite-lived intangible assets in fiscal years 2013, 2012, or 2011.

NOTES TO CONSOLIDATED FINANCIAL STATEMENTS—(Continued)

Intangible Assets Subject to Amortization

Definite-lived intangible assets consisted of the following (in thousands) as of:

		September 28, 2013		September 29, 2012	
	Useful Life in Years	Gross Carrying Amount	Accumulated Amortization	Gross Carrying Amount	Accumulated Amortization
Acquired technology	4–10	$ 21,609	$ (17,123)	$ 21,622	$ (15,433)
Customer and roaster agreements	8–11	26,977	(19,750)	27,323	(16,796)
Customer relationships	2–16	414,967	(113,061)	430,178	(79,168)
Trade names	9–11	37,200	(13,353)	38,000	(9,785)
Non-compete agreements	2–5	374	(364)	374	(344)
Total		$ 501,127	$ (163,651)	$ 517,497	$ (121,526)

Definite-lived intangible assets are amortized on a straight-line basis over the period of expected economic benefit. Total amortization expense was $45.4 million, $46.0 million, and $41.3 million for fiscal years 2013, 2012, and 2011, respectively. The weighted average remaining life for definite-lived intangibles at September 28, 2013 is 8.3 years.

The estimated aggregate amortization expense over each of the next five years and thereafter, is as follows (in thousands):

2014	$ 44,361
2015	42,807
2016	42,081
2017	40,686
2018	40,686
Thereafter	126,855

8. Noncontrolling Interests

The changes in the liability and temporary equity attributable to redeemable NCIs for the three fiscal years in the period ended September 28, 2013 are as follows (in thousands):

	Liability attributable to mandatorily redeemable noncontrolling interests	Equity attributable to redeemable noncontrolling interests
Balance at September 25, 2010	$ —	$ —
Purchase noncontrolling interests	—	19,118
Net income	—	1,547
Adjustment to redemption value	—	1,618
Cash distributions	—	(1,063)
Other comprehensive loss, net of tax	—	(186)
Balance at September 24, 2011	$ —	$ 21,034
Disposition of noncontrolling interest	—	(10,331)
Redeemable noncontrolling interest reclassified to other long-term liabilities	4,708	(4,708)
Net income	60	812
Adjustment to redemption value	167	3,155
Cash distributions	(204)	(513)
Other comprehensive loss, net of tax	197	455
Balance at September 29, 2012	$ 4,928	$ 9,904
Net income	462	409
Adjustment to redemption value	372	2,025
Cash distributions	(583)	(823)
Other comprehensive loss, net of tax	(245)	(470)
Balance at September 28, 2013	$ 4,934	$ 11,045

As of September 28, 2013 and September 29, 2012, the liability attributable to mandatorily redeemable noncontrolling interests was included as a component of *Other current liabilities* and *Other long-term liabilities*, respectively, in the Consolidated Balance Sheets.

9. Product Warranties

The Company offers a one-year warranty on all Keurig® Single Cup brewers it sells. The Company provides for the estimated cost of product warranties, primarily using historical information and current repair or replacement costs, at the time product revenue is recognized. Brewer failures may arise in the later part of the warranty period, and actual warranty costs may exceed the reserve. As the Company has grown, it has added significantly to its product testing, quality control infrastructure and overall quality processes. Nevertheless, as the Company continues to innovate, and its products become more complex, both in design and componentry, product performance may tend to modulate, causing warranty rates to possibly fluctuate going forward. As a result, future warranty claims rates may be higher or lower than the Company is currently experiencing and for which the Company is currently providing in its warranty reserve.

The changes in the carrying amount of product warranties for fiscal years 2013 and 2012 are as follows (in thousands):

	Fiscal 2013	Fiscal 2012
Balance, beginning of year	$ 20,218	$ 14,728
Provision related to current period	20,447	47,026
Change in estimate	(12,720)	(1,287)
Usage	(20,141)	(40,249)
Balance, end of year	$ 7,804	$ 20,218

GREEN MOUNTAIN COFFEE ROASTERS, INC.

NOTES TO CONSOLIDATED FINANCIAL STATEMENTS—(Continued)

During fiscal years 2013 and 2012, the Company recovered approximately $0.8 million and $8.3 million respectively, as reimbursement from suppliers related to warranty issues. The recoveries are under an agreement with a supplier and are recorded as a reduction to warranty expense. The recoveries are not reflected in the provision charged to income in the table above.

10. Long-Term Debt

Long-term debt outstanding consists of the following (in thousands) as of:

	September 28, 2013	September 29, 2012
Revolving credit facility, USD	$ —	$ 120,000
Revolving credit facility, multicurrency	—	108,787
Term loan A	170,937	242,188
Other	2,213	2,700
Total long-term debt	$ 173,150	$ 473,675
Less current portion	12,929	6,691
Long-term portion	$ 160,221	$ 466,984

Under the Company's current credit facility ("Restated Credit Agreement"), the Company maintains senior secured credit facilities consisting of (i) an $800.0 million U.S. revolving credit facility, (ii) a $200.0 million alternative currency revolving credit facility, and (iii) a term loan A facility. The Restated Credit Agreement also provides for an increase option for an aggregate amount of up to $500.0 million.

The term loan A facility requires quarterly principal repayments. The term loan and revolving credit borrowings bear interest at a rate equal to an applicable margin plus, at our option, either (a) a eurodollar rate determined by reference to the cost of funds for deposits for the interest period and currency relevant to such borrowing, adjusted for certain costs, or (b) a base rate determined by reference to the highest of (1) the federal funds rate plus 0.50%, (2) the prime rate announced by Bank of America, N.A. from time to time and (3) the eurodollar rate plus 1.00%. The applicable margin under the Restated Credit Agreement with respect to term loan A and revolving credit facilities is a percentage per annum varying from 0.5% to 1.0% for base rate loans and 1.5% to 2.0% for eurodollar loans, based upon the Company's leverage ratio. The Company's average effective interest rate as of September 28, 2013 and September 29, 2012 was 3.5% and 2.9%, respectively, excluding amortization of deferred financing charges and including the effect of interest swap agreements. The Company also pays a commitment fee of 0.2% on the average daily unused portion of the revolving credit facilities.

All the assets of the Company and its domestic wholly-owned material subsidiaries are pledged as collateral under the Restated Credit Agreement. The Restated Credit Agreement contains customary negative covenants, subject to certain exceptions, including limitations on: liens; investments; indebtedness; merger and consolidations; asset sales; dividends and distributions or repurchases of the Company's capital stock; transactions with affiliates; certain burdensome agreements; and changes in the Company's lines of business.

The Restated Credit Agreement requires the Company to comply on a quarterly basis with a consolidated leverage ratio and a consolidated interest coverage ratio. As of September 28, 2013 and throughout fiscal year 2013, the Company was in compliance with these covenants. In addition, the Restated Credit Agreement contains certain mandatory prepayment requirements and customary events of default.

As of September 28, 2013 and September 29, 2012, outstanding letters of credit under the Restated Credit Agreement, totaled $5.0 million and $3.7 million, respectively. No amounts have been drawn against the letters of credit as of September 28, 2013 and September 29, 2012.

In connection with the Restated Credit Agreement, the Company incurred debt issuance costs of $46.0 million which were deferred and included in *Other Long-Term Assets* on the Consolidated Balance Sheet and amortized as interest expense over the life of the respective loan using a method that approximates the effective interest rate method. The Company incurred a loss of $19.7 million in fiscal 2011 primarily on the extinguishment of the term loan B facility under the credit agreement that immediately preceded the Restated Credit Agreement ("Credit Agreement")

GREEN MOUNTAIN COFFEE ROASTERS, INC.

NOTES TO CONSOLIDATED FINANCIAL STATEMENTS—(Continued)

and the extinguishment of a former credit facility that preceded the Credit Agreement resulting from the write-off of debt issuance costs and the original issue discount. The loss on the extinguishment of debt is included in *Interest Expense* on the Consolidated Statements of Operations.

The Company enters into interest rate swap agreements to limit a portion of its exposure to variable interest rates by entering into interest rate swap agreements which effectively fix the rates. In accordance with the interest rate swap agreements and on a monthly basis, interest expense is calculated based on the floating 30-day Libor rate and the fixed rate. If interest expense as calculated is greater based on the 30-day Libor rate, the interest rate swap counterparty pays the difference to the Company; if interest expense as calculated is greater based on the fixed rate, the Company pays the difference to the interest rate swap counterparty. See Note 11, *Derivative Financial Instruments*.

Below is a summary of the Company's derivative instruments in effect as of September 28, 2013 mitigating interest rate exposure of variable-rate borrowings (in thousands):

Derivative Instrument	Hedged Transaction	Notional Amount of Underlying Debt	Fixed Rate Received	Maturity (Fiscal Year)
Swap	30-day Libor	20,000	2.54%	2016
Swap	30-day Libor	30,000	2.54%	2016
Swap	30-day Libor	50,000	2.54%	2016
Swap	30-day Libor	30,000	2.54%	2016
		$ 130,000		

In fiscal years 2013, 2012 and 2011 the Company paid approximately $3.4 million, $4.7 million and $3.8 million, respectively, in additional interest expense pursuant to the interest rate swap agreements.

Maturities

Scheduled maturities of long-term debt are as follows (in thousands):

Fiscal Year	
2014	$ 12,929
2015	19,165
2016	140,064
2017	377
2018	395
Thereafter	220
	$ 173,150

11. Derivative Financial Instruments

Cash Flow Hedges

The Company is exposed to certain risks relating to ongoing business operations. The primary risks that are mitigated by financial instruments are interest rate risk, commodity price risk and foreign currency exchange rate risk. The Company uses interest rate swaps to mitigate interest rate risk associated with the Company's variable-rate borrowings, enters into coffee futures contracts to hedge future coffee purchase commitments of green coffee with the objective of minimizing cost risk due to market fluctuations, and uses foreign currency forward contracts to hedge the purchase and payment of green coffee purchase commitments denominated in non-functional currencies.

The Company designates these contracts as cash flow hedges and measures the effectiveness of these derivative instruments at each balance sheet date. The changes in the fair value of these instruments are classified in accumulated other comprehensive income (loss). The gains or loss on these instruments is reclassified from OCI into earnings in the same period or periods during which the hedged transaction affects earnings. If it is determined that a derivative is not highly effective, the gain or loss is reclassified into earnings.

GREEN MOUNTAIN COFFEE ROASTERS, INC.

NOTES TO CONSOLIDATED FINANCIAL STATEMENTS—(Continued)

Fair Value Hedges

The Company enters into foreign currency forward contracts to hedge certain recognized liabilities in currencies other than the Company's functional currency. The Company designates these contracts as fair value hedges and measures the effectiveness of the derivative instruments at each balance sheet date. The changes in the fair value of these instruments along with the changes in the fair value of the hedged liabilities are recognized in net gains or losses on foreign currency on the consolidated statements of operations.

Other Derivatives

The Company is also exposed to certain foreign currency and interest rate risks on an intercompany note with a foreign subsidiary denominated in Canadian currency. At September 28, 2013, the Company has approximately two years remaining on a CDN $120.0 million, Canadian cross currency swap to exchange interest payments and principal on the intercompany note. This cross currency swap is not designated as a hedging instrument for accounting purposes and is recorded at fair value, with the changes in fair value recognized in the Consolidated Statements of Operations. Gains and losses resulting from the change in fair value are largely offset by the financial impact of the remeasurement of the intercompany note. In accordance with the cross currency swap agreement, on a quarterly basis, the Company pays interest based on the three month Canadian Bankers Acceptance rate and receives interest based on the three month U.S. Libor rate. The Company incurred $1.7 million, $1.8 million, and $1.2 million in additional interest expense pursuant to the cross currency swap agreement during fiscal 2013, 2012, and 2011 respectively.

In conjunction with the repayment of the Company's term loan B facility under the Credit Agreement (See Note 10, *Long-Term Debt*), the interest rate cap previously used to mitigate interest rate risk associated with the Company's variable-rate borrowings on the term loan B no longer qualified for hedge accounting treatment. As a result, a loss of $0.4 million, gross of tax, was reclassified from OCI to income during fiscal 2011.

The Company occasionally enters into foreign currency forward contracts and coffee futures contracts that qualify as derivatives, and are not designated as hedging instruments for accounting purposes in addition to the foreign currency forward contracts and coffee futures contracts noted above. Contracts that are not designated as hedging instruments are recorded at fair value with the changes in fair value recognized in the Consolidated Statements of Operations.

The Company does not hold or use derivative financial instruments for trading or speculative purposes.

The Company is exposed to credit loss in the event of nonperformance by the counterparties to these financial instruments, however, nonperformance is not anticipated.

The following table summarizes the fair value of the Company's derivatives included on the Consolidated Balance Sheets (in thousands) as of:

	September 28, 2013	September 29, 2012	Balance Sheet Classification
Derivatives designated as hedges:			
Interest rate swaps	$ (6,004)	$ (9,019)	Other current liabilities
Coffee futures	(3,809)	(342)	Other current liabilities
Foreign currency forward contracts	(141)	—	Other current liabilities
Foreign currency forward contracts	13	—	Other current assets
	(9,941)	(9,361)	
Derivatives not designated as hedges:			
Cross currency swap	(1,253)	(7,242)	Other current liabilities
	(1,253)	(7,242)	
Total	$ (11,194)	$ (16,603)	

GREEN MOUNTAIN COFFEE ROASTERS, INC.

NOTES TO CONSOLIDATED FINANCIAL STATEMENTS—(Continued)

The following table summarizes the coffee futures contracts outstanding as of September 28, 2013 (in thousands, except for average contract price and "C" price):

Coffee Pounds	Average Contract Price	"C" Price	Maturity	Fair Value of Futures Contracts
375	$ 1.50	$ 1.14	December 2013	$ (138)
5,887	$ 1.39	$ 1.17	March 2014	(1,308)
11,438	$ 1.30	$ 1.19	May 2014	(1,222)
10,875	$ 1.32	$ 1.21	July 2014	(1,141)
28,575				$ (3,809)

The following table summarizes the coffee futures contracts outstanding as of September 29, 2012 (in thousands, except for average contract price and "C" price):

Coffee Pounds	Average Contract Price	"C" Price	Maturity	Fair Value of Futures Contracts
938	$ 1.92	$ 1.74	December 2012	$ (169)
938	$ 1.96	$ 1.78	March 2013	(171)
675	$ 1.80	$ 1.80	May 2013	(1)
375	$ 1.83	$ 1.83	July 2013	$ (1)
262	$ 1.86	$ 1.86	September 2013	$ 0
3,188				$ (342)

The following table summarizes the amount of gain (loss), gross of tax, on financial instruments that qualify for hedge accounting included in OCI (in thousands):

	Fiscal 2013	Fiscal 2012	Fiscal 2011
Cash Flow Hedges:			
Interest rate swaps	$ 3,014	$ 1,250	$ (7,928)
Coffee futures	(6,617)	(2,484)	407
Forward currency forward contracts	(129)	—	—
Total	$ (3,732)	$ (1,234)	$ (7,521)

The following table summarizes the amount of gain (loss), gross of tax, reclassified from OCI to income (in thousands):

	Fiscal 2013	Fiscal 2012	Fiscal 2011	
Interest rate cap	$ —	$ —	$ (392)	Gain (loss) on financial instruments, net
Coffee futures	(1,482)	(1,359)	(27)	Cost of Sales
Forward currency forward contracts	(2)	—	—	(Loss) gain on foreign currency, net
Total	$ (1,484)	$ (1,359)	$ (419)	

The Company expects to reclassify $3.5 million of losses, net of tax, from OCI to earnings on coffee derivatives within the next twelve months.

See note 14, *Stockholders' Equity* for a reconciliation of derivatives in beginning accumulated other comprehensive income (loss) to derivatives in ending accumulated other comprehensive income (loss).

GREEN MOUNTAIN COFFEE ROASTERS, INC.

NOTES TO CONSOLIDATED FINANCIAL STATEMENTS—(Continued)

The following table summarizes the amount of gain (loss), gross of tax, on fair value hedges and related hedged items (in thousands):

	Fiscal 2013	Fiscal 2012	Fiscal 2011	Location of gain (loss) recognized in income on derivative
Foreign currency forward contracts				
Net loss on hedging derivatives	$ (10)	$ (48)	$ —	(Loss) gain on foreign currency, net
Net gain on hedged items	$ 10	$ 48	$ —	(Loss) gain on foreign currency, net

Net losses on financial instruments not designated as hedges for accounting purposes recorded in gain (loss) on financial instruments, net, is as follows (in thousands):

	Fiscal 2013	Fiscal 2012	Fiscal 2011
Net gain (loss) on cross currency swap	$ 5,513	$ (4,918)	$ (2,324)
Net gain (loss) on coffee futures	—	7	(250)
Net loss on interest rate cap	—	(34)	(615)
Net loss on foreign currency option and forward contracts	—	—	(3,056)
Total	$ 5,513	$ (4,945)	$ (6,245)

The net loss on foreign currency contracts were primarily related to contracts entered into to mitigate the risk associated with the Canadian denominated purchase price of Van Houtte in fiscal 2011.

12. Fair Value Measurements

The Company measures fair value as the selling price that would be received for an asset, or paid to transfer a liability, in the principal or most advantageous market on the measurement date. The hierarchy established by the Financial Accounting Standards Board prioritizes fair value measurements based on the types of inputs used in the valuation technique. The inputs are categorized into the following levels:

Level 1—Observable inputs such as quoted prices in active markets for identical assets or liabilities.

Level 2—Inputs other than quoted prices that are observable, either directly or indirectly, which include quoted prices for similar assets or liabilities in active markets and quoted prices for identical assets or liabilities in markets that are not active.

Level 3—Unobservable inputs not corroborated by market data, therefore requiring the entity to use the best available information, including management assumptions.

The following table summarizes the fair values and the levels used in fair value measurements as of September 28, 2013 for the Company's financial (liabilities) assets (in thousands):

	Fair Value Measurements Using		
	Level 1	Level 2	Level 3
Derivatives:			
Interest rate swaps	$ —	$ (6,004)	$ —
Cross currency swap	—	(1,253)	—
Coffee futures	—	(3,809)	—
Foreign currency forward contracts	—	(128)	—
Total	$ —	$ (11,194)	$ —

GREEN MOUNTAIN COFFEE ROASTERS, INC.

NOTES TO CONSOLIDATED FINANCIAL STATEMENTS—(Continued)

The following table summarizes the fair values and the levels used in fair value measurements as of September 29, 2012 for the Company's financial liabilities (in thousands):

	Fair Value Measurements Using		
	Level 1	Level 2	Level 3
Derivatives:			
Interest rate swaps	$ —	$ (9,019)	$ —
Cross currency swap	—	(7,242)	—
Coffee futures	—	(342)	—
Foreign currency forward contracts	—	—	—
Total	$ —	$ (16,603)	$ —

Level 2 derivative financial instruments use inputs that are based on market data of identical (or similar) instruments, including forward prices for commodities, interest rates curves and spot prices that are in observable markets. Derivatives recorded on the balance sheet are at fair value with changes in fair value recorded in OCI for cash flow hedges and in the Consolidated Statements of Operations for fair value hedges and derivatives that do not qualify for hedge accounting treatment.

Derivatives

Derivative financial instruments include coffee futures contracts, interest rate swap agreements, a cross-currency swap agreement and foreign currency forward contracts. The Company has identified significant concentrations of credit risk based on the economic characteristics of the instruments that include interest rates, commodity indexes and foreign currency rates and selectively enters into the derivative instruments with counterparties using credit ratings.

To determine fair value, the Company utilizes the market approach valuation technique for coffee futures and foreign currency forward contracts and the income approach for interest rate and cross currency swap agreements. The Company's fair value measurements include a credit valuation adjustment for the significant concentrations of credit risk.

As of September 28, 2013, the amount of loss estimated by the Company due to credit risk associated with the derivatives for all significant concentrations was not material based on the factors of an industry recovery rate and a calculated probability of default.

Long-Term Debt

The carrying value of long-term debt was $173.2 million and $473.7 million as of September 28, 2013 and September 29, 2012, respectively. The inputs to the calculation of the fair value of long-term debt are considered to be Level 2 within the fair value hierarchy, as the measurement of fair value is based on the net present value of calculated interest and principal payments, using an interest rate derived from a fair market yield curve adjusted for the Company's credit rating. The carrying value of long-term debt approximates fair value as the interest rate on the debt is based on variable interest rates that reset every 30 days.

GREEN MOUNTAIN COFFEE ROASTERS, INC.

NOTES TO CONSOLIDATED FINANCIAL STATEMENTS—(Continued)

13. Income Taxes

Income before income taxes and the provision for income taxes for fiscal years 2013, 2012 and 2011, consist of the following (in thousands):

	Fiscal 2013	Fiscal 2012	Fiscal 2011
Income before income taxes:			
United States	$ 675,438	$ 486,258	$ 248,108
Foreign	65,436	89,883	54,639
Total income before income taxes	$ 740,874	$ 576,141	$ 302,747
Income tax expense:			
United States federal:			
Current	$ 202,006	$ 75,932	$ 75,225
Deferred	(8,654)	74,042	(3,327)
	193,352	149,974	71,898
State and local:			
Current	47,930	40,270	13,939
Deferred	(1,695)	(712)	(1,758)
	46,235	39,558	12,181
Total United States	239,587	189,532	84,079
Foreign:			
Current	29,901	26,860	21,306
Deferred	(12,717)	(3,751)	(3,686)
Total foreign	17,184	23,109	17,620
Total income tax expense	$ 256,771	$ 212,641	$ 101,699

Net deferred tax liabilities consist of the following (in thousands) as of:

	September 28, 2013	September 29, 2012
Deferred tax assets:		
Section 263A capitalized expenses	$ 1,876	$ 2,150
Deferred hedging losses	4,774	3,919
Deferred compensation	13,632	11,534
Net operating loss carryforward	—	1,017
Capital loss carryforward	1,418	1,418
Valuation allowance—capital loss carryforward	(1,418)	(1,418)
Warranty, obsolete inventory and bad debt allowance	32,692	27,421
Tax credit carryforwards	3,651	3,301
Other reserves and temporary differences	15,558	12,412
Gross deferred tax assets	72,183	61,754
Deferred tax liabilities:		
Prepaid expenses	(2,994)	(2,367)
Depreciation	(125,504)	(123,044)
Intangible assets	(138,262)	(144,329)
Other reserves and temporary differences	(237)	(10,994)
Gross deferred tax liabilities	(266,997)	(280,734)
Net deferred tax liabilities	$ (194,814)	$ (218,980)

GREEN MOUNTAIN COFFEE ROASTERS, INC.

NOTES TO CONSOLIDATED FINANCIAL STATEMENTS—(Continued)

A reconciliation for continuing operations between the amount of reported income tax expense and the amount computed using the U.S. Federal Statutory rate of 35% is as follows (in thousands):

	Fiscal 2013	Fiscal 2012	Fiscal 2011
Tax at U.S. Federal Statutory rate	$ 259,306	$ 201,692	$ 105,961
Increase (decrease) in rates resulting from:			
Foreign tax rate differential	(13,087)	(18,072)	(9,289)
Non-deductible stock compensation expense	2,700	1,024	1,761
State taxes, net of federal benefit	31,869	27,114	11,276
Provincial taxes	7,878	10,591	6,309
Domestic production activities deduction	(23,558)	(9,245)	(7,831)
Acquisition costs	—	—	4,158
Federal tax credits	(4,506)	(282)	(962)
Release of capital loss valuation allowance	—	(3,071)	(6,194)
Other	(3,831)	2,890	(3,490)
Tax at effective rates	$ 256,771	$ 212,641	$ 101,699

As of September 28, 2013, the Company had a $17.7 million state capital loss carryforward and a state net operating loss carryforward of $11.5 million available to be utilized against future taxable income for years through fiscal 2015 and 2029, respectively, subject to annual limitation pertaining to change in ownership rules under the Internal Revenue Code of 1986, as amended (the "Code"). Based upon earnings history, the Company concluded that it is more likely than not that the net operating loss carryforward will be utilized prior to its expiration but that the capital loss carryforward will not. The Company has recorded a $1.4 million valuation allowance against the entire deferred tax asset balance for the capital loss carryforward

The total amount of unrecognized tax benefits as of September 28, 2013 and September 29, 2012 was $23.3 million and $24.0 million, respectively. The amount of unrecognized tax benefits at September 28, 2013 that would impact the effective tax rate if resolved in favor of the Company is $19.7 million. As a result of prior acquisitions, the Company is indemnified for up to $16.6 million of the total reserve balance, and the indemnification is capped at CDN $37.9 million. If these unrecognized tax benefits are resolved in favor of the Company, the associated indemnification receivable, recorded in other long-term assets would be reduced accordingly. As of September 28, 2013 and September 29, 2012, accrued interest and penalties of $2.0 million and $0.6 million, respectively, were included in the Consolidated Balance Sheets. The Company recognizes interest and penalties in income tax expense. The Company released $1.5 million of unrecognized tax benefits in the fourth quarter of fiscal 2013 due to the expiration of the statute of limitations. Income tax expense included $0.4 million, $0.2 million and $0.3 million of interest and penalties for fiscal 2013, 2012, and 2011, respectively.

A reconciliation of increases and decreases in unrecognized tax benefits, including interest and penalties, is as follows (in thousands):

	Fiscal 2013	Fiscal 2012	Fiscal 2011
Gross tax contingencies—balance, beginning of year	$ 23,956	$ 24,419	$ 5,480
Increases from positions taken during prior periods	438	2,864	—
Decreases from positions taken during prior periods	—	(4,093)	(236)
Increases from positions taken during current periods	2,709	906	19,175
Decreases resulting from the lapse of the applicable statute of limitations	(3,820)	(140)	—
Gross tax contingencies—balance, end of year	$ 23,283	$ 23,956	$ 24,419

The Company expects to release $3.4 million of unrecognized tax benefits during fiscal 2014 due to the expiration of the statute of limitations.

As of September 28, 2013, the Company had approximately $155.5 million of undistributed international earnings, most of which are Canadian-sourced. With the exception of the repayment of intercompany debt, all earnings of the Company's foreign subsidiaries are considered indefinitely reinvested and no U.S. deferred taxes have been provided on those earnings. If these amounts were distributed to the U.S. in the form of dividends or otherwise, the Company would be subject to additional U.S. income taxes, which could be material. Determination of the amount of any unrecognized deferred income tax on these earnings is not practicable because such liability, if any, is dependent on circumstances existing if and when remittance occurs.

In the normal course of business, the Company is subject to tax examinations by taxing authorities both inside and outside the United States. The Company is currently being examined by the Internal Revenue Service for its fiscal year ended September 25, 2010. With some exceptions, the Company is no longer subject to examinations with respect to returns filed for fiscal years prior to 2006.

14. Stockholders' Equity

Stock Issuances

On May 11, 2011, the Company issued 9,479,544 shares of its common stock, par value $0.10 per share, at $71.00 per share, which included 1,290,000 shares purchased by the underwriters pursuant to an overallotment option. The Company also completed a concurrent private placement of 608,342 shares of its common stock to Luigi Lavazza S.p.A. ("Lavazza") at $68.34 per share, pursuant to the Common Stock Purchase Agreement entered into between the Company and Lavazza on May 6, 2011 in accordance with the September 28, 2010 agreement discussed below. The aggregate net proceeds to the Company from the public offering and concurrent private placement were approximately $688.9 million, net of underwriting discounts and commissions and offering expenses. The Company used the proceeds to repay a portion of the outstanding debt under its credit facility and for general corporate purposes.

On September 28, 2010, the Company sold 8,566,649 shares of its common stock, par value $0.10 per share, to Lavazza for aggregate gross proceeds of $250.0 million. The sale was recorded to stockholders' equity net of transaction related expenses of approximately $0.5 million. The shares were sold pursuant to a Common Stock Purchase Agreement which contains a five-and-one-half-year standstill period, subject to certain exceptions, during which Lavazza is prohibited from increasing its ownership of Common Stock or making any proposals or announcements relating to extraordinary Company transactions. The standstill is subject to additional exceptions after a one-year period, including Lavazza's right to purchase additional shares up to 15% of the Company's outstanding shares.

Stock Repurchase Program

On July 30, 2012, the Board of Directors authorized a program for the Company to repurchase up to $500.0 million of the Company's common shares over the next two years, at such times and prices as determined by the Company's management. Consistent with Delaware law, any repurchased shares are constructively retired and returned to an unissued status. Accordingly, the par value of repurchased shares is deducted from common stock and excess repurchase price over the par value is deducted from additional paid-in capital and from retained earnings if additional paid-in capital is depleted. As of September 28, 2013, $235.3 million remained available for shares to be repurchased under current authorization by our Board of Directors.

	Fiscal 2013	Fiscal 2012
Number of shares acquired	5,642,793	3,120,700
Average price per share of acquired shares	$ 33.37	$ 24.50
Total cost of acquired shares (in thousands)	$ 188,278	$ 76,470

Subsequent to the fiscal year ended September 28, 2013, the Company repurchased an additional 1,348,883 of common shares, leaving $137.8 million available for shares to be repurchased under current authorization by the Company's Board of Directors.

GREEN MOUNTAIN COFFEE ROASTERS, INC.

NOTES TO CONSOLIDATED FINANCIAL STATEMENTS—(Continued)

Accumulated Other Comprehensive Income (Loss)

The following table provides the changes in the components of accumulated other comprehensive income (loss), net of tax (in thousands):

	Cash Flow Hedges	Translation	Accumulated Other Comprehensive Income (Loss)
Balance at September 25, 2010	$ (1,630)	$ —	$ (1,630)
Other comprehensive loss during the period	(4,236)	(8,709)	(12,945)
Balance at September 24, 2011	(5,866)	(8,709)	(14,575)
Other comprehensive income during the period	74	24,701	24,775
Balance at September 29, 2012	(5,792)	15,992	10,200
Other comprehensive loss during the period	(1,358)	(28,027)	(29,385)
Balance at September 28, 2013	$ (7,150)	$ (12,035)	$ (19,185)

The unfavorable translation adjustment change during fiscal year 2013 and 2011 was primarily due to the weakening of the Canadian dollar against the U.S. dollar. The favorable translation adjustment change during fiscal year 2012 was primarily due to the strengthening of the Canadian against the U.S. dollar. See also Note 11, *Derivative Financial Instruments*.

15. Employee Compensation Plans

Equity-Based Incentive Plans

On March 16, 2006, stockholders of the Company approved the Company's 2006 Incentive Plan (the "2006 Plan"). The 2006 Plan was amended on March 13, 2008 and on March 11, 2010 to increase the total shares of common stock authorized for issuance to 13,200,000. As of September 28, 2013, 4,537,397 shares of common stock were available for grant for future equity-based compensation awards under the plan.

On September 25, 2001, the Company registered on Form S-8 the 2000 Stock Option Plan (the "2000 Plan"). The plan expired in October 2010. Grants under the 2000 Plan generally expire ten years after the grant date, or earlier if employment terminates. As of September 28, 2013, there were no options for shares of common stock available for grant under this plan.

In connection with the acquisition of Keurig, the Company assumed the existing outstanding unvested option awards of the Keurig, Incorporated Fifth Amended and Restated 1995 Stock Option Plan (the "1995 Plan") and the Keurig, Incorporated 2005 Stock Option Plan (the "2005 Plan"). No shares under either the 1995 Plan or the 2005 Plan were eligible for post-acquisition awards. As of September 28, 2013 and September 29, 2012, 0 and 2,776 options, respectively, out of the 1,386,933 options for shares of common stock granted were outstanding under the 1995 Plan. As of September 28, 2013 and September 29, 2012, 28,749 options and 37,313 options, respectively, out of the 1,490,577 options granted for shares of common stock were outstanding under the 2005 Plan. All awards assumed in the acquisition were initially granted with a four-year vesting schedule.

On May 3, 2007, Mr. Lawrence Blanford commenced his employment as the President and Chief Executive Officer of the Company. Pursuant to the terms of the employment, the Company made an inducement grant on May 4, 2007, to Mr. Blanford of a non-qualified option to purchase 945,000 shares of the Company's common stock, with an exercise price equal to fair market value on the date of the grant. The shares subject to the option vested in 20% installments on each of the first five anniversaries of the date of the grant.

On November 3, 2008, Ms. Michelle Stacy commenced her employment as the President of Keurig, Incorporated. Pursuant to the terms of the employment, the Company made an inducement grant on November 3, 2008, to Ms. Stacy of a non-qualified option to purchase 157,500 shares of the Company's common stock, with an exercise price equal to fair market value on the date of the grant. The shares subject to the option vested in 25% installments on each of the first four anniversaries of the date of the grant.

GREEN MOUNTAIN COFFEE ROASTERS, INC.

NOTES TO CONSOLIDATED FINANCIAL STATEMENTS—(Continued)

On February 9, 2009, Mr. Howard Malovany commenced his employment as the Vice President, Corporate General Counsel and Secretary of the Company. Pursuant to the terms of the employment, the Company made an inducement grant on February 9, 2009, to Mr. Malovany of a non-qualified option to purchase 157,500 shares of the Company's common stock, with an exercise price equal to fair market value on the date of the grant. The shares subject to the option vested in 25% installments on each of the first four anniversaries of the date of the grant.

On December 17, 2010, Mr. Gérard Geoffrion commenced his employment as the President of the Canada segment. Pursuant to the terms of the employment, the Company made an inducement grant on December 17, 2010, to Mr. Geoffrion of a non-qualified option to purchase 35,000 shares of the Company's common stock, with an exercise price equal to fair market value on the date of the grant. The shares subject to the option vest in 25% installments on each of the first four anniversaries of the date of the grant, provided that Mr. Geoffrion remains employed with the Company on each vesting date.

On December 22, 2010, the Company made an inducement grant to Mr. Sylvain Toutant, Chief Operating Officer of the Canada segment, of a non-qualified option to purchase 20,000 shares of the Company's common stock, with an exercise price equal to fair market value on the date of the grant. The shares subject to the option vest in 25% installments on each of the first four anniversaries of the date of the grant, provided that Mr. Toutant remains employed with the Company on each vesting date.

On February 17, 2011, Ms. Linda Longo-Kazanova commenced her employment as the Vice President, Chief Human Resources Officer. Pursuant to the terms of the employment, the Company made an inducement grant on February 17, 2011, to Ms. Longo-Kazanova of a non-qualified option to purchase 30,000 shares of the Company's common stock, with an exercise price equal to fair market value on the date of the grant. The shares subject to the option vest in 25% installments on each of the first four anniversaries of the date of the grant, provided that Ms. Longo-Kazanova remains employed with the Company on each vesting date.

Under the 2000 Plan, the option price for each incentive stock option was not less than the fair market value per share of common stock on the date of grant, with certain provisions which increased the option price of an incentive stock option to 110% of the fair market value of the common stock if the grantee owned in excess of 10% of the Company's common stock at the date of grant. The 2006 Plan requires the exercise price for all awards requiring exercise to be no less than 100% of fair market value per share of common stock on the date of grant, with certain provisions which increase the option price of an incentive stock option to 110% of the fair market value of the common stock if the grantee owns in excess of 10% of the Company's common stock at the date of grant. Options under the 2000 Plan and the 2006 Plan become exercisable over periods determined by the Board of Directors, generally in the range of three to five years.

Option activity is summarized as follows:

	Number of Shares	Weighted Average Exercise Price (per share)
Outstanding at September 29, 2012	7,470,975	$ 12.56
Granted	474,236	$ 45.48
Exercised	(2,849,308)	$ 6.95
Forfeited/expired	(73,563)	$ 49.53
Outstanding at September 28, 2013	5,022,340	$ 18.30
Exercisable at September 28, 2013	3,958,017	$ 10.70

The following table summarizes information about stock options that have vested and are expected to vest at September 28, 2013:

Number of options outstanding	Weighted average remaining contractual life (in years)	Weighted average exercise price	Intrinsic value at September 28, 2013 (in thousands)
5,011,076	4.81	$ 18.24	$ 284,095

GREEN MOUNTAIN COFFEE ROASTERS, INC.

NOTES TO CONSOLIDATED FINANCIAL STATEMENTS—(Continued)

The following table summarizes information about stock options exercisable at September 28, 2013:

Number of options exercisable	Weighted average remaining contractual life (in years)	Weighted average exercise price	Intrinsic value at September 28, 2013 (in thousands)
3,958,017	3.90	$ 10.70	$ 254,162

Compensation expense is recognized only for those options expected to vest, with forfeitures estimated based on the Company's historical employee turnover experience and future expectations.

The Company uses a blend of recent and historical volatility to estimate expected volatility at the measurement date. The expected life of options is estimated based on options vesting periods, contractual lives and an analysis of the Company's historical experience.

The intrinsic values of options exercised during fiscal years 2013, 2012 and 2011 were approximately $165.5 million, $46.6 million and $221.8 million, respectively. The Company's policy is to issue new shares upon exercise of stock options.

The grant-date fair value of employee share options and similar instruments is estimated using the Black-Scholes option-pricing model with the following assumptions for grants issued during fiscal years 2013, 2012 and 2011:

	Fiscal 2013	Fiscal 2012	Fiscal 2011
Average expected life	6 years	6 years	6 years
Average volatility	81%	69%	52%
Dividend yield	—	—	—
Risk-free interest rate	1.02%	1.31%	2.37%
Weighted average fair value	$ 31.23	$ 30.10	$ 29.34

Restricted Stock Units and Other Awards

The Company awards restricted stock units ("RSUs"), restricted stock awards ("RSAs"), and performance stock units ("PSUs") to eligible employees ("Grantee") which entitle the Grantee to receive shares of the Company's common stock. RSUs and PSUs are awards denominated in units that are settled in shares of the Company's common stock upon vesting. RSAs are awards of common stock that are restricted until the shares vest. In general, RSUs and RSAs vest based on a Grantee's continuing employment. The fair value of RSUs, RSAs and PSUs is based on the closing price of the Company's common stock on the grant date. Compensation expense for RSUs and RSAs is recognized ratably over a Grantee's service period. Compensation expense for PSUs is also recognized over a Grantee's service period, but only if and when the Company concludes that it is probable (more than likely) the performance condition(s) will be achieved. The assessment of probability of achievement is performed each period based on the relevant facts and circumstances at that time, and if the estimated grant-date fair value changes as a result of that assessment, the cumulative effect of the change on current and prior periods is recognized in the period of change. In addition, the Company awards deferred cash awards ("DCAs"), to Grantees which entitle a Grantee to receive cash paid over time upon vesting. The vesting of DCAs is conditioned on a Grantee's continuing employment. All awards are reserved for issuance under the Company's 2006 Incentive Plan and vest over periods determined by the Board of Directors, generally in the range of three to four years for RSUs, RSAs and DCAs, and three years for PSUs.

NOTES TO CONSOLIDATED FINANCIAL STATEMENTS—(Continued)

The following table summarizes the number and weighted average grant-date fair value of nonvested RSUs (amounts in thousands except grant date fair value and weighted average remaining contractual life):

	Share Units	Weighted Average Grant-Date Fair Value	Weighted Average Remaining Contractual Life (in Years)	Intrinsic Value (in Thousands)
Nonvested, September 29, 2012	81,834	$ 39.62	3.52	$ 1,943
Granted	175,789	$ 45.19		
Vested	(34,761)	$ 47.22		
Forfeited	(1,360)	$ 54.12		
Nonvested, September 28, 2013	221,502	$ 42.74	1.71	$ 16,586

As of September 28, 2013, total RSUs expected to vest totaled 218,459 shares with an intrinsic value of $16.4 million. The weighted average grant-date fair value of RSUs granted was $45.19 and $39.73 for fiscal 2013 and fiscal 2012, respectively. There were no RSUs granted prior to fiscal 2012.

The total intrinsic value of RSUs converted to shares of common stock during fiscal 2013 was $2.2 million. There were no RSUs converted to common stock prior to fiscal 2013.

The following table summarizes the number and weighted average grant-date fair value of nonvested PSUs based on the target award amounts in the PSU agreements as of September 28, 2013:

	Share Units	Weighted Average Grant-Date Fair Value
Outstanding on September 29, 2012	—	—
Granted	122,719	$ 41.28
Forfeited	(2,051)	$ 51.56
Outstanding on September 28, 2013(1)	120,668	$ 41.10

(1) The outstanding PSUs as of September 28, 2013, at the threshold award and maximum award levels were 96,534 and 144,802, respectively.

The weighted average grant-date fair value of PSUs granted was $41.28 in fiscal 2013. The Company did not issue grants for PSUs prior to fiscal 2013. There were no PSUs converted to shares of common stock during fiscal 2013.

In addition, in fiscal 2012, the Company issued a grant for 55,432 RSAs with an intrinsic value of $1.3 million as of September 29, 2012, which vested in fiscal 2013. The total intrinsic value of RSAs vested during fiscal 2013 was $2.7 million.

Employee Stock Purchase Plan

On October 5, 1998, the Company registered on Form S-8 the 1998 Employee Stock Purchase Plan. On March 13, 2008, the plan was amended and renamed the Amended and Restated Employee Stock Purchase Plan ("ESPP"). Under this plan, eligible employees may purchase shares of the Company's common stock, subject to certain limitations, at the lesser of 85 percent of the beginning or ending withholding period fair market value as defined in the plan. There are two six-month withholding periods in each fiscal year. At September 28, 2013, and September 29, 2012, options for 1,216,051 and 1,559,728 shares of common stock were available for purchase under the plan, respectively.

GREEN MOUNTAIN COFFEE ROASTERS, INC.

NOTES TO CONSOLIDATED FINANCIAL STATEMENTS—(Continued)

The grant-date fair value of employees' purchase rights granted during fiscal years 2013, 2012 and 2011 under the Company's ESPP is estimated using the Black-Scholes option-pricing model with the following assumptions:

	Fiscal 2013	Fiscal 2012	Fiscal 2011
Average expected life	6 months	6 months	6 months
Average volatility	86%	70%	57%
Dividend yield	—	—	—
Risk-free interest rate	0.13%	0.09%	0.19%
Weighted average fair value	$ 14.38	$ 11.61	$ 15.97

Stock-Based Compensation Expense

Stock-based compensation expense recognized in the Consolidated Statements of Operations in fiscal years 2013, 2012, and 2011 (in thousands):

	Fiscal 2013	Fiscal 2012	Fiscal 2011
Options	$ 14,151	$ 12,595	$ 8,206
RSUs/PSUs/RSAs	7,529	1,861	—
ESPP	4,401	3,412	2,155
Total stock-based compensation expense recognized in the Consolidated Statements of Operations	$ 26,081	$ 17,868	$ 10,361
Total related tax benefit	$ 9,936	$ 6,004	$ 3,147

As of September 28, 2013, total unrecognized compensation cost related to all nonvested stock-based compensation arrangements was approximately $30.5 million net of estimated forfeitures. This unrecognized cost is expected to be recognized over a weighted-average period of approximately 1.28 years at September 28, 2013.

16. Employee Retirement Plans

Defined Contribution Plans

The Company has a defined contribution plan which meets the requirements of section 401(k) of the Internal Revenue Code. All regular full-time U.S. employees of the Company who are at least eighteen years of age and work a minimum of 36 hours per week are eligible to participate in the plan. The plan allows employees to defer a portion of their salary on a pre-tax basis and the Company contributes 50% of amounts contributed by employees up to 6% of their salary. Company contributions to the plan were $5.2 million, $4.4 million, and $2.7 million, for fiscal years 2013, 2012, and 2011, respectively.

In conjunction with the Van Houtte acquisition, the Company also has several Canadian Group Registered Retirement Savings Plans ("GRRSP") and a Deferred Profit Sharing Plan ("DPSP"). Under these plans, employees can contribute a certain percentage of their salary and the Company can also make annual contributions to the plans. Company contributions to the Canadian plans were $1.4 million, $1.0 million and $0.8 million for fiscal years 2013, 2012, and 2011, respectively.

Defined Benefit Plans

The Company has a supplementary defined benefit retirement plan and a supplementary employee retirement plan (collectively the "Plans") for certain management employees in the Canada segment. The cost of the Plans is calculated according to actuarial methods that encompass management's best estimate regarding the future evolution of salary levels, the age of retirement of salaried employees and other actuarial factors. These Plans are not funded and there are no plan assets. Future benefits will be paid from the funds of the Company.

The projected benefit obligation was $1.4 million and $1.1 million as of September 28, 2013 and September 29, 2012, which is classified in *other long-term liabilities*. Net periodic pension expense (income) was $0.3 million, $(0.1) million and $0.5 million for fiscal years 2013, 2012, and 2011, respectively.

17. Deferred Compensation Plan

The 2002 Deferred Compensation Plan, amended in December 2007, permits certain highly compensated officers and employees of the Company and non-employee directors to defer eligible compensation payable for services rendered to the Company. On March 8, 2013, the Company registered on Form S-8 the 2002 Deferred Compensation Plan. Participants may elect to receive deferred compensation in the form of cash payments or shares of Company Common Stock on the date or dates selected by the participant or on such other date or dates specified in the Deferred Compensation Plan. The Deferred Compensation Plan is in effect for compensation earned on or after September 29, 2002. As of September 28, 2013, and September 29, 2012, 353,434 shares and 357,759 shares of Common Stock were available for future issuance under this Plan, respectively. During fiscal 2013, no rights to shares of Common Stock were exercised under this plan. As of September 28, 2013 and September 29, 2012, rights to acquire 59,561 shares and 55,236 shares of Common Stock were outstanding under this Plan, respectively. As of September 28, 2013, rights to acquire 37,005 shares of Common Stock were committed under this plan. As of September 29, 2012, there were no rights to acquire shares of Common Stock committed under this plan.

18. Accrued Expenses

Accrued expenses consisted of the following (in thousands) as of:

	September 28, 2013	September 29, 2012
Accrued compensation costs	$ 91,418	$ 38,458
Accrued customer incentives and promotions	53,689	28,374
Accrued freight, fulfillment and transportation costs	21,941	18,455
Accrued sustainability expenses	9,275	11,046
Accrued legal and professional services	8,278	5,010
Warranty reserve	7,804	20,218
Other	50,022	49,889
	$ 242,427	$ 171,450

19. Commitments and Contingencies

Lease Commitments

The Company leases office and retail space, production, distribution and service facilities, and certain equipment under various non-cancellable operating leases, with terms ranging from one to twenty years. Property leases normally require payment of a minimum annual rental plus a pro-rata share of certain landlord operating expenses. Total rent expense, under all operating leases approximated $23.1 million, $25.1 million, and $18.1 million in fiscal years 2013, 2012, and 2011, respectively. The Company has subleases relating to certain of its operating leases. Sublease income approximated $1.1 million, $0.3 million and $0.3 million for fiscal years 2013, 2012 and 2010, respectively.

In addition, the Company leases a manufacturing facility which is accounted for as a capital lease. The initial term of the lease is 15 years with six additional renewal terms of five years each at the Company's option. The lease requires payment of a minimum annual rental and the Company is responsible for property taxes, insurance and operating expenses.

In June 2012, the Company entered into an arrangement to lease approximately 425,000 square feet located in Burlington, Massachusetts to be constructed. The Burlington facilities will be used by the Domestic segment and will consolidate the three existing Massachusetts facilities that are currently in Reading, Wakefield and Woburn. As of September 28, 2013, approximately 150,000 square feet had been completed and is being used for research and development. The remaining 275,000 square feet is currently under construction and is anticipated to be completed during the summer of 2014.

Due to the Company's involvement in the construction project, including its obligations to fund certain costs of construction exceeding amounts incurred by the lessor, the Company is deemed to be the owner of the project, which includes a pre-existing structure on the site, even though the Company is not the legal owner. Accordingly, total project costs incurred during construction are capitalized as construction-in-progress along with a corresponding financing obligation for the project costs that are incurred by the lessor. In addition, the Company capitalized the estimated fair value of the pre-existing structure of $4.1 million at the date construction commenced as construction-in-progress with

GREEN MOUNTAIN COFFEE ROASTERS, INC.

NOTES TO CONSOLIDATED FINANCIAL STATEMENTS—(Continued)

a corresponding financing obligation. Upon completion of the project, the Company is expecting to have continuing involvement beyond a normal leaseback, and therefore will not be able to record a sale and derecognize the assets when construction is complete. As a result, the lease will be accounted for as a financing transaction and the recorded asset and related financing obligation will remain on the Balance Sheet.

As of September 28, 2013, future minimum lease payments under financing obligations, capital lease obligations and non-cancellable operating leases as well as minimum payments to be received under non-cancellable subleases are as follows (in thousands):

Fiscal Year	Capital Leases	Operating Leases	Subleases	Financing Obligations
2014	$ 3,518	$ 16,602	$ (1,021)	$ 2,029
2015	3,838	15,534	(1,012)	8,661
2016	3,837	11,797	(848)	9,580
2017	3,837	8,631	(690)	9,580
2018	3,837	5,280	(634)	9,665
Thereafter	31,980	20,140	(2,156)	113,722
Total	$ 50,847	$ 77,984	$ (6,361)	$ 153,237
Less: amount representing interest	(17,075)			
Present value of future minimum lease payments	$ 33,772			

The above table for financing obligations represents the portion of the future minimum lease payments which have been allocated to the facility under construction in Burlington, Massachusetts and will be recognized as reductions to the financing obligation and as interest expense upon completion of construction.

Legal Proceedings

On October 1, 2010, Keurig, Incorporated, a wholly-owned subsidiary of the Company ("Keurig"), filed suit against Sturm Foods, Inc. ("Sturm") in the United States District Court for the District of Delaware (Civil Action No. 1:10-CV-00841-SLR) for patent and trademark infringement, false advertising, and other claims, related to Sturm's sale of "Grove Square" beverage cartridges that claim to be compatible with Keurig brewers. On September 13, 2012, the District Court rendered a summary judgment decision in favor of Sturm on the patent claims in the suit. On October 17, 2013, the United States Federal Circuit Court of Appeals upheld the District Court's summary judgment decision. Separately, on February 19, 2013, Keurig and Sturm entered into a settlement agreement with respect to the trademark infringement, false advertising, and other claims at issue in the suit, all of which have now been dismissed. The settlement agreement did not materially impact the Company's consolidated financial results of operations.

On November 2, 2011, Keurig filed suit against JBR, INC., d/b/a Rogers Family Company ("Rogers") in the United States District Court for the District of Massachusetts (Civil Action No. 1:11-cv-11941-MBB) for patent infringement related to Rogers' sale of "San Francisco Bay" beverage cartridges for use with Keurig brewers. The suit alleges that the "San Francisco Bay" cartridges infringe certain Keurig patents (U.S. Patent Nos. D502,362, 7,165,488 and 7,347,138). Keurig sought an injunction prohibiting Rogers from selling these cartridges, as well as money damages. In late 2012, Rogers moved for summary judgment of no infringement as to all three asserted patents. On May 24, 2013, the District of Massachusetts granted Rogers' summary judgment motions. Keurig has since appealed the Court's ruling to the Federal Circuit, and that appeal is currently pending.

On May 9, 2011, an organization named Council for Education and Research on Toxics ("CERT"), purporting to act in the public interest, filed suit in Los Angeles Superior Court (*Council for Education and Research on Toxics v. Brad Barry LLC, et al.*, Case No. BC461182.) against several companies, including the Company, that roast, package, or sell coffee in California. The *Brad Barry* complaint alleges that coffee contains the chemical acrylamide and that the Company and the other defendants are required to provide warnings under section 25249.6 of the California Safe Drinking Water and Toxics Enforcement Act, better known as Proposition 65. The Brad Barry action has been consolidated for all purposes with another Proposition 65 case filed by CERT on April 13, 2010 over allegations of acrylamide in "ready to drink" coffee sold in restaurants, convenience stores, and do-nut shops. (*Council for Education and Research on Toxics v. Starbucks Corp., et al.*, Case No. BC 415759). The Company was not named in the *Starbucks* complaint. The Company has joined a joint defense group ("JDG") organized to address CERT's allegations, and the

GREEN MOUNTAIN COFFEE ROASTERS, INC.

NOTES TO CONSOLIDATED FINANCIAL STATEMENTS—(Continued)

Company intends to vigorously defend against these allegations. The Court has ordered the case phased for discovery and trial. The first phase of the case, which has been set for trial on September 8, 2014, is limited to three affirmative defenses shared by all defendants in both cases, with other affirmative defenses, plaintiff's prima facie case, and remedies deferred for subsequent phases. Discovery on the first phase of the case is underway. Because this lawsuit is only in a preliminary stage, the Company is unable to predict its outcome, the potential loss or range of loss, if any, associated with its resolution or any potential effect it may have on the Company or its operations.

On January 24, 2012, Teashot, LLC ("Teashot") filed suit against the Company, Keurig and Starbucks Corp. ("Starbucks") in the United States District Court for the District of Colorado (Civil Action No. 12-c v-00189-WJM-KMT) for patent infringement related to the making, using, importing, selling and/or offering for sale of K-Cup packs containing tea. The suit alleges that the Company, Keurig and Starbucks infringe a Teashot patent (U.S. Patent No. 5,895,672). Teashot seeks an injunction prohibiting the Company, Keurig and Starbucks from continued infringement, as well as money damages. Pursuant to the Company's Manufacturing, Sales and Distribution Agreement with Starbucks, the Company is defending and indemnifying Starbucks in connection with the suit. On March 13, 2012, the Company and Keurig, for themselves and Starbucks, filed an answer with the court, generally denying all of Teashot's allegations. The Company and Keurig, for themselves and Starbucks, are vigorously defending this lawsuit. On May 24, 2013, the Company and Keurig, for themselves and Starbucks, filed a motion for summary judgment of non-infringement. On July 19, 2013, Teashot filed a motion for partial summary judgment on certain other, unrelated issues. No hearing on the summary judgment motions has been scheduled. At this time, the Company is unable to predict the outcome of this lawsuit, the potential loss or range of loss, if any, associated with the resolution of this lawsuit or any potential effect it may have on the Company or its operations.

Securities and Exchange Commission ("SEC") Inquiry

As first disclosed on September 28, 2010, the staff of the SEC's Division of Enforcement continues to conduct an inquiry into matters at the Company. The Company is cooperating fully with the SEC staff's inquiry.

Stockholder Litigation

Two putative securities fraud class actions are presently pending against the Company and certain of its officers and directors, along with two putative stockholder derivative actions. The first pending putative securities fraud class action was filed on November 29, 2011, and the third putative securities fraud class action was filed on May 7, 2012. A consolidated putative stockholder derivative action pending in the United States District Court for the District of Vermont consists of five separate putative stockholder derivative complaints, the first two were filed after the Company's disclosure of the SEC inquiry on September 28, 2010, while the others were filed on February 10, 2012, March 2, 2012, and July 23, 2012, respectively. In addition, a putative stockholder derivative action is pending in the Superior Court of the State of Vermont for Washington County that was commenced following the Company's disclosure of the SEC inquiry on September 28, 2010.

The first pending putative securities fraud class action, captioned Louisiana Municipal Police Employees' Retirement System ("LAMPERS") v. Green Mountain Coffee Roasters, Inc., et al., Civ. No. 2:11-cv-00289, is pending in the United States District Court for the District of Vermont before the Honorable William K. Sessions, III. Plaintiffs' amended complaint alleges violations of the federal securities laws in connection with the Company's disclosures relating to its revenues and its inventory accounting practices. The amended complaint seeks class certification, compensatory damages, attorneys' fees, costs, and such other relief as the court should deem just and proper. Plaintiffs seek to represent all purchasers of the Company's securities between February 2, 2011 and November 9, 2011. The initial complaint filed in the action on November 29, 2011 included counts for alleged violations of (1) Sections 11, 12(a)(2) and 15 of the Securities Act of 1933 (the "Securities Act") against the Company, certain of its officers and directors, and the Company's underwriters in connection with a May 2011 secondary common stock offering; and (2) Section 10(b) of the Exchange Act and Rule 10b-5 against the Company and the officer defendants, and for violation of Section 20(a) of the Exchange Act against the officer defendants. Pursuant to the Private Securities Litigation Reform Act of 1995, 15 U.S.C. § 78u-4(a)(3), plaintiffs had until January 30, 2012 to move the court to serve as lead plaintiff of the putative class. Competing applications were filed and the Court appointed Louisiana Municipal Police Employees' Retirement System, Sjunde AP-Fonden, Board of Trustees of the City of Fort Lauderdale General Employees' Retirements System, Employees' Retirements System of the Government of the Virgin Islands, and Public Employees' Retirement System of Mississippi as lead plaintiffs' counsel on April 27, 2012. Pursuant to a schedule approved by the court, plaintiffs filed their amended complaint on October 22, 2012, and plaintiffs filed a corrected amended complaint on November 5, 2012. Plaintiffs' amended complaint does not allege any claims under the Securities Act against the Company, its officers and directors, or the Company's underwriters in connection with the May 2011 secondary common stock

GREEN MOUNTAIN COFFEE ROASTERS, INC.

NOTES TO CONSOLIDATED FINANCIAL STATEMENTS—(Continued)

offering. Defendants moved to dismiss the amended complaint on March 1, 2013 and the briefing of their motions was completed on June 26, 2013. An oral argument on the defendants' motions to dismiss was set for August 27, 2013 and has been rescheduled to December 12, 2013. The underwriters previously named as defendants notified the Company of their intent to seek indemnification from the Company pursuant to their underwriting agreement dated May 5, 2011 in regard to the claims asserted in this action.

The second pending consolidated putative securities fraud class action, captioned Fifield v. Green Mountain Coffee Roasters, Inc., Civ. No. 2:12-cv-00091, is also pending in the United States District Court for the District of Vermont before the Honorable William K. Sessions, III. Plaintiffs' amended complaint alleges violations of the federal securities laws in connection with the Company's disclosures relating to its forward guidance. The amended complaint includes counts for alleged violations of Section 10(b) of the Exchange Act and Rule 10b-5 against all defendants, and for alleged violation of Section 20(a) of the Exchange Act against the officer defendants. The amended complaint seeks class certification, compensatory damages, equitable and/or injunctive relief, attorneys' fees, costs, and such other relief as the court should deem just and proper. Plaintiffs seek to represent all purchasers of the Company's securities between February 2, 2012 and May 2, 2012. Pursuant to the Private Securities Litigation Reform Act of 1995, 15 U.S.C. § 78u-4(a)(3), plaintiffs had until July 6, 2012 to move the court to serve as lead plaintiff of the putative class. On July 31, 2012, the court appointed Kambiz Golesorkhi as lead plaintiff and approved his selection of Kahn Swick & Foti LLC as lead counsel. On August 14, 2012, the court granted the parties' stipulated motion for filing of an amended complaint and to set a briefing schedule for defendants' motions to dismiss. Pursuant to a schedule approved by the court, plaintiffs filed their amended complaint on October 23, 2012, adding William C. Daley as an additional lead plaintiff. Defendants moved to dismiss the amended complaint on January 17, 2013 and the briefing of their motions was completed on May 17, 2013. On September 26, 2013, the court issued an order granting defendants' motions and dismissing the amended complaint without prejudice and allowing plaintiffs a 30-day period within which to amend their complaint. On October 18, 2013, plaintiffs filed a notice of intent to appeal the court's September 26, 2013 order to the United States Court of Appeals for the Second Circuit. On November 1, 2013, following the expiration of the 30-day period to amend the complaint, defendants filed a motion for final judgment in District Court. Pursuant to an order issued by the Second Circuit, plaintiff-appellants' brief in the appeal of the District Court's decision is due no later than December 10, 2013 and defendant-appellees' brief is due no later than January 14, 2014.

The first putative stockholder derivative action, a consolidated action captioned In re Green Mountain Coffee Roasters, Inc. Derivative Litigation, Civ. No. 2:10-cv-00233, premised on the same allegations asserted in now-dismissed Horowitz v. Green Mountain Coffee Roasters, Inc., Civ. No. 2:10-cv-00227 securities class action complaint and the other pending putative securities class action complaints described above, is pending in the United States District Court for the District of Vermont before the Honorable William K. Sessions, III. On November 29, 2010, the federal court entered an order consolidating two actions and appointing the firms of Robbins Umeda LLP and Shuman Law Firm as co-lead plaintiffs' counsel. On February 23, 2011, the federal court approved a stipulation filed by the parties providing for a temporary stay of that action until the court rules on defendants' motions to dismiss the consolidated complaint in the Horowitz putative securities fraud class action. On March 7, 2012, the federal court approved a further joint stipulation continuing the temporary stay until the court either denies a motion to dismiss the Horowitz putative securities fraud class action or the Horowitz putative securities fraud class action is dismissed with prejudice. On April 27, 2012, the federal court entered an order consolidating the stockholder derivative action captioned Himmel v. Robert P. Stiller, et al., with two additional putative derivative actions, Musa Family Revocable Trust v. Robert P. Stiller, et al., Civ. No. 2:12-cv-00029, and Laborers Local 235 Benefit Funds v. Robert P. Stiller, et al., Civ. No. 2:12-cv- 00042. On November 14, 2012, the federal court entered an order consolidating an additional stockholder derivative action, captioned as Henry Cargo v. Robert P. Stiller, et al., Civ. No. 2:12-cv-00161, and granting plaintiffs leave to lift the stay for the limited purpose of filing a consolidated complaint. The consolidated complaint is asserted nominally on behalf of the Company against certain of its officers and directors. The consolidated complaint asserts claims for breach of fiduciary duty, waste of corporate assets, unjust enrichment, contribution, and indemnification and seeks compensatory damages, injunctive relief, restitution, disgorgement, attorney's fees, costs, and such other relief as the court should deem just and proper. On May 14, 2013, the court approved a joint stipulation filed by the parties providing for a temporary stay of the proceedings until the conclusion of the appeal in the Horowitz putative securities fraud class action. On August 1, 2013, the parties filed a further joint stipulation continuing the temporary stay until the court either denies a motion to dismiss the LAMPERS putative securities fraud class action or the LAMPERS putative securities fraud class action is dismissed with prejudice, which the court approved on August 2, 2013.

GREEN MOUNTAIN COFFEE ROASTERS, INC.

NOTES TO CONSOLIDATED FINANCIAL STATEMENTS—(Continued)

The second putative stockholder derivative action, M. Elizabeth Dickinson v. Robert P. Stiller, et al., Civ. No. 818-11-10, is pending in the Superior Court of the State of Vermont for Washington County. On February 28, 2011, the court approved a stipulation filed by the parties similarly providing for a temporary stay of that action until the federal court rules on defendants' motions to dismiss the consolidated complaint in the Horowitz putative securities fraud class action. As a result of the federal court's ruling in the Horowitz putative securities fraud class action, the temporary stay was lifted. On June 25, 2013, plaintiff filed an amended complaint in the action, which is asserted nominally on behalf of the Company against certain current and former directors and officers. The amended complaint is premised on the same allegations alleged in the Horowitz, LAMPERS, and Fifield putative securities fraud class actions. The amended complaint asserts claims for breach of fiduciary duty, unjust enrichment, waste of corporate assets, and alleged insider selling by certain of the named defendants. The amended complaint seeks compensatory damages, injunctive relief, restitution, disgorgement, attorneys' fees, costs, and such other relief as the court should deem just and proper. On August 7, 2013, the parties filed a further joint stipulation continuing the temporary stay until the court either denies a motion to dismiss the LAMPERS putative securities fraud class action or the LAMPERS putative securities fraud class action is dismissed with prejudice, which the court approved on August 21, 2013.

The Company and the other defendants intend to vigorously defend all the pending lawsuits. Additional lawsuits may be filed and, at this time, the Company is unable to predict the outcome of these lawsuits, the possible loss or range of loss, if any, associated with the resolution of these lawsuits or any potential effect they may have on the Company or its operations.

20. Related Party Transactions

The Company, from time to time, used travel services provided by Heritage Flight, a charter air services company acquired in September 2002 by Robert P. Stiller, who previously served on the Company's Board of Directors and who is a security holder of more than 5% of the Company's Common Stock. For fiscal years 2013, 2012, and 2011, the Company incurred expenses of $0.2 million, $0.7 million, and $0.7 million, respectively, for Heritage Flight travel services.

21. Earnings Per Share

The following table illustrates the reconciliation of the numerator and denominator of basic and diluted earnings per share computations (dollars in thousands, except share and per share data):

	Fiscal 2013	Fiscal 2012	Fiscal 2011
Numerator for basic and diluted earnings per share:			
Net income attributable to GMCR	$ 483,232	$ 362,628	$ 199,501
Denominator:			
Basic weighted average shares outstanding	149,638,636	154,933,948	146,214,860
Effect of dilutive securities—stock options	3,162,857	4,141,698	5,927,574
Diluted weighted average shares outstanding	152,801,493	159,075,646	152,142,434
Basic net income per common share	$ 3.23	$ 2.34	$ 1.36
Diluted net income per common share	$ 3.16	$ 2.28	$ 1.31

For the fiscal years 2013, 2012, and 2011, 822,000, 763,000, and 199,000 equity-based awards for shares of common stock, respectively, have been excluded in the calculation of diluted earnings per share because they were antidilutive.

GREEN MOUNTAIN COFFEE ROASTERS, INC.

NOTES TO CONSOLIDATED FINANCIAL STATEMENTS—(Continued)

22. Unaudited Quarterly Financial Data

The following table presents the quarterly information for fiscal 2013 (dollars in thousands, except per share data). Each fiscal quarter comprises 13 weeks.

Fiscal 2013	December 29, 2012	March 30, 2013	June 29, 2013	September 28, 2013
Net sales	$ 1,339,059	$ 1,004,792	$ 967,072	$ 1,047,177
Gross profit	$ 419,163	$ 415,146	$ 407,618	$ 377,459
Net income attributable to GMCR	$ 107,583	$ 132,421	$ 116,272	$ 126,956
Earnings per share:				
Basic	$ 0.72	$ 0.89	$ 0.78	$ 0.84
Diluted	$ 0.70	$ 0.87	$ 0.76	$ 0.83

The following table presents the quarterly information for fiscal 2012 (dollars in thousands, except per share data). Each fiscal quarter comprises 13 weeks, except the fiscal quarter ended September 29, 2012 which is comprised of 14 weeks.

Fiscal 2012	December 24, 2011	March 24, 2012	June 23, 2012	September 29, 2012
Net sales	$ 1,158,216	$ 885,052	$ 869,194	$ 946,736
Gross profit	$ 336,604	$ 313,038	$ 303,311	$ 316,446
Net income attributable to GMCR	$ 104,414	$ 93,031	$ 73,296	$ 91,887
Earnings per share:				
Basic	$ 0.67	$ 0.60	$ 0.47	$ 0.59
Diluted	$ 0.66	$ 0.58	$ 0.46	$ 0.58

The following table presents the quarterly information for fiscal 2011 (dollars in thousands, except per share data). Each fiscal quarter comprises 13 weeks.

Fiscal 2011	December 25, 2010	March 26, 2011	June 25, 2011	September 24, 2011
Net sales	$ 574,148	$ 647,658	$ 717,210	$ 711,883
Gross profit	$ 143,600	$ 242,855	$ 264,080	$ 254,090
Net income attributable to GMCR	$ 2,412	$ 65,372	$ 56,348	$ 75,369
Earnings per share:				
Basic	$ 0.02	$ 0.46	$ 0.38	$ 0.49
Diluted	$ 0.02	$ 0.44	$ 0.37	$ 0.47

23. Subsequent Event

On November 19, 2013, the Board of Directors declared the Company's first cash dividend of $0.25 per common share, payable on February 14, 2014 to shareholders of record at the close of business on January 17, 2014; and announced an indicated annual dividend of $1.00 per share (payable in $0.25 per quarter).

SCHEDULE II—VALUATION AND QUALIFYING ACCOUNTS

For the Fiscal Years Ended September 28, 2013,
September 29, 2012, and September 24, 2011
(Dollars in thousands)

Description	Balance at Beginning of Period	Acquisitions (Dispositions)	Charged to Costs and Expenses	Deductions	Balance at End of Period
Allowance for doubtful accounts:					
Fiscal 2013	$ 2,750	$ —	$ 689	$ 553	$ 2,886
Fiscal 2012	$ 3,404	$ (299)	$ 3,197	$ 3,552	$ 2,750
Fiscal 2011	$ 1,314	$ 1,115	$ 2,584	$ 1,609	$ 3,404

Description	Balance at Beginning of Period	Acquisitions (Dispositions)	Charged to Costs and Expenses	Deductions	Balance at End of Period
Sales returns reserve:					
Fiscal 2013	$ 31,767	$ —	$ 79,747	$ 80,760	$ 30,754
Fiscal 2012	$ 18,302	$ —	$ 107,436	$ 93,971	$ 31,767
Fiscal 2011	$ 12,742	$ —	$ 64,457	$ 58,897	$ 18,302

Description	Balance at Beginning of Period	Acquisitions (Dispositions)	Charged to Costs and Expenses	Deductions	Balance at End of Period
Warranty reserve(1):					
Fiscal 2013	$ 20,218	$ —	$ 6,948	$ 19,362	$ 7,804
Fiscal 2012	$ 14,728	$ —	$ 37,390	$ 31,900	$ 20,218
Fiscal 2011	$ 6,694	$ —	$ 35,450	$ 27,416	$ 14,728

(1) Includes warranty recoveries from suppliers of $0.8 million and $8.3 for fiscal 2013 and 2012, respectively. There were no recoveries during fiscal 2011.

Item 9. Changes in and Disagreements with Accountants on Accounting and Financial Disclosure

None.

Item 9A. Controls and Procedures

Evaluation of Disclosure Controls and Procedures

During the fourth quarter of fiscal 2013, under the supervision of and with the participation of management, including our Chief Executive Officer and Chief Financial Officer, we conducted an evaluation of the effectiveness of the design and operation of our disclosure controls and procedures, as defined in Rules 13a-15(e) and 15d-15(e) of the Securities and Exchange Act of 1934, as amended (the "Exchange Act"). Based on this evaluation, our Chief Executive Officer and Chief Financial Officer have concluded that, as of September 28, 2013, our disclosure controls and procedures were effective to ensure that information required to be disclosed in the reports we file or submit under the Exchange Act was recorded, processed, summarized and reported within the time periods specified in the SEC's rules and forms, and were effective.

Management's Report on Internal Control over Financial Reporting

Management is responsible for establishing and maintaining adequate internal control over financial reporting, as defined in Rules 13a-15(f) and 15d-15(f) of the Exchange Act. Internal control over financial reporting is a process designed by, or under the supervision of, the issuer's principal executive and principal financial officers, or persons performing similar functions, and effected by issuer's board of directors, management and other personnel, to provide reasonable assurance regarding the reliability of its financial reporting and the preparation of its financial statements for external purposes in accordance with generally accepted accounting principles and includes those policies and procedures that:

- pertain to the maintenance of records that, in reasonable detail, accurately and fairly reflect the transactions and dispositions of the assets of the Company;
- provide reasonable assurance that transactions are recorded as necessary to permit preparation of financial statements in accordance with generally accepted accounting principles,
- provide reasonable assurance that receipts and expenditures of the Company are being made only in accordance with authorizations of management and directors of the Company; and
- provide reasonable assurance regarding prevention or timely detection of unauthorized acquisition, use, or disposition of the Company's assets that could have a material effect on the financial statements.

Because of its inherent limitations, internal control over financial reporting may not prevent or detect misstatements. Also, projections of any evaluation of effectiveness to future periods are subject to the risk that controls may become inadequate because of changes in conditions or that the degree of compliance with the policies or procedures may deteriorate.

Under the supervision of and with the participation of management, including the Chief Executive Officer and Chief Financial Officer, the Company conducted an evaluation of the effectiveness of its internal control over financial reporting based on the criteria in *Internal Control—Integrated Framework* (1992) issued by the Committee of Sponsoring Organizations of the Treadway Commission ("COSO"). Based upon that evaluation, management concluded we maintained effective internal controls over financial reporting as of September 28, 2013 based on the criteria established in *Internal Control— Integrated Framework* (1992) issued by the COSO.

The effectiveness of the Company's internal control over financial reporting as of September 28, 2013 has been audited by PricewaterhouseCoopers LLP, an independent registered public accounting firm, as stated in their report which appears herein.

Changes in Internal Control over Financial Reporting

There have been no changes in our internal control over financial reporting during the fiscal quarter ended September 28, 2013 that have materially affected, or are reasonably likely to materially affect, our internal control over financial reporting.

Item 9B. Other Information

None.

Present Value Tables

Present Value

Periods	1%	2%	3%	4%	5%	6%	7%	8%	9%	10%	12%	14%	15%	16%	18%	20%
1	0.990	0.980	0.971	0.962	0.952	0.943	0.935	0.926	0.917	0.909	0.893	0.877	0.870	0.862	0.847	0.833
2	0.980	0.961	0.943	0.925	0.907	0.890	0.873	0.857	0.842	0.826	0.797	0.769	0.756	0.743	0.718	0.694
3	0.971	0.942	0.915	0.889	0.864	0.840	0.816	0.794	0.772	0.751	0.712	0.675	0.658	0.641	0.609	0.579
4	0.961	0.924	0.888	0.855	0.823	0.792	0.763	0.735	0.708	0.683	0.636	0.592	0.572	0.552	0.516	0.482
5	0.951	0.906	0.863	0.822	0.784	0.747	0.713	0.681	0.650	0.621	0.567	0.519	0.497	0.476	0.437	0.402
6	0.942	0.888	0.837	0.790	0.746	0.705	0.666	0.630	0.596	0.564	0.507	0.456	0.432	0.410	0.370	0.335
7	0.933	0.871	0.813	0.760	0.711	0.665	0.623	0.583	0.547	0.513	0.452	0.400	0.376	0.354	0.314	0.279
8	0.923	0.853	0.789	0.731	0.677	0.627	0.582	0.540	0.502	0.467	0.404	0.351	0.327	0.305	0.266	0.233
9	0.914	0.837	0.766	0.703	0.645	0.592	0.544	0.500	0.460	0.424	0.361	0.308	0.284	0.263	0.225	0.194
10	0.905	0.820	0.744	0.676	0.614	0.558	0.508	0.463	0.422	0.386	0.322	0.270	0.247	0.227	0.191	0.162
11	0.896	0.804	0.722	0.650	0.585	0.527	0.475	0.429	0.388	0.350	0.287	0.237	0.215	0.195	0.162	0.135
12	0.887	0.788	0.701	0.625	0.557	0.497	0.444	0.397	0.356	0.319	0.257	0.208	0.187	0.168	0.137	0.112
13	0.879	0.773	0.681	0.601	0.530	0.469	0.415	0.368	0.326	0.290	0.229	0.182	0.163	0.145	0.116	0.093
14	0.870	0.758	0.661	0.577	0.505	0.442	0.388	0.340	0.299	0.263	0.205	0.160	0.141	0.125	0.099	0.078
15	0.861	0.743	0.642	0.555	0.481	0.417	0.362	0.315	0.275	0.239	0.183	0.140	0.123	0.108	0.084	0.065
16	0.853	0.728	0.623	0.534	0.458	0.394	0.339	0.292	0.252	0.218	0.163	0.123	0.107	0.093	0.071	0.054
17	0.844	0.714	0.605	0.513	0.436	0.371	0.317	0.270	0.231	0.198	0.146	0.108	0.093	0.080	0.060	0.045
18	0.836	0.700	0.587	0.494	0.416	0.350	0.296	0.250	0.212	0.180	0.130	0.095	0.081	0.069	0.051	0.038
19	0.828	0.686	0.570	0.475	0.396	0.331	0.277	0.232	0.194	0.164	0.116	0.083	0.070	0.060	0.043	0.031
20	0.820	0.673	0.554	0.456	0.377	0.312	0.258	0.215	0.178	0.149	0.104	0.073	0.061	0.051	0.037	0.026
21	0.811	0.660	0.538	0.439	0.359	0.294	0.242	0.199	0.164	0.135	0.093	0.064	0.053	0.044	0.031	0.022
22	0.803	0.647	0.522	0.422	0.342	0.278	0.226	0.184	0.150	0.123	0.083	0.056	0.046	0.038	0.026	0.018
23	0.795	0.634	0.507	0.406	0.326	0.262	0.211	0.170	0.138	0.112	0.074	0.049	0.040	0.033	0.022	0.015
24	0.788	0.622	0.492	0.390	0.310	0.247	0.197	0.158	0.126	0.102	0.066	0.043	0.035	0.028	0.019	0.013
25	0.780	0.610	0.478	0.375	0.295	0.233	0.184	0.146	0.116	0.092	0.059	0.038	0.030	0.024	0.016	0.010
26	0.772	0.598	0.464	0.361	0.281	0.220	0.172	0.135	0.106	0.084	0.053	0.033	0.026	0.021	0.014	0.009
27	0.764	0.586	0.450	0.347	0.268	0.207	0.161	0.125	0.098	0.076	0.047	0.029	0.023	0.018	0.011	0.007
28	0.757	0.574	0.437	0.333	0.255	0.196	0.150	0.116	0.090	0.069	0.042	0.026	0.020	0.016	0.010	0.006
29	0.749	0.563	0.424	0.321	0.243	0.185	0.141	0.107	0.082	0.063	0.037	0.022	0.017	0.014	0.008	0.005
30	0.742	0.552	0.412	0.308	0.231	0.174	0.131	0.099	0.075	0.057	0.033	0.020	0.015	0.012	0.007	0.004
40	0.672	0.453	0.307	0.208	0.142	0.097	0.067	0.046	0.032	0.022	0.011	0.005	0.004	0.003	0.001	0.001
50	0.608	0.372	0.228	0.141	0.087	0.054	0.034	0.021	0.013	0.009	0.003	0.001	0.001	0.001		

Table B-2 | **Present Value of Ordinary Annuity of $1**

Present Value

Periods	1%	2%	3%	4%	5%	6%	7%	8%	9%	10%	12%	14%	15%	16%	18%	20%
1	0.990	0.980	0.971	0.962	0.952	0.943	0.935	0.926	0.917	0.909	0.893	0.877	0.870	0.862	0.847	0.833
2	1.970	1.942	1.913	1.886	1.859	1.833	1.808	1.783	1.759	1.736	1.690	1.647	1.626	1.605	1.566	1.528
3	2.941	2.884	2.829	2.775	2.723	2.673	2.624	2.577	2.531	2.487	2.402	2.322	2.283	2.246	2.174	2.106
4	3.902	3.808	3.717	3.630	3.546	3.465	3.387	3.312	3.240	3.170	3.037	2.914	2.855	2.798	2.690	2.589
5	4.853	4.713	4.580	4.452	4.329	4.212	4.100	3.993	3.890	3.791	3.605	3.433	3.352	3.274	3.127	2.991
6	5.795	5.601	5.417	5.242	5.076	4.917	4.767	4.623	4.486	4.355	4.111	3.889	3.784	3.685	3.498	3.326
7	6.728	6.472	6.230	6.002	5.786	5.582	5.389	5.206	5.033	4.868	4.564	4.288	4.160	4.039	3.812	3.605
8	7.652	7.325	7.020	6.733	6.463	6.210	5.971	5.747	5.535	5.335	4.968	4.639	4.487	4.344	4.078	3.837
9	8.566	8.162	7.786	7.435	7.108	6.802	6.515	6.247	5.995	5.759	5.328	4.946	4.772	4.607	4.303	4.031
10	9.471	8.983	8.530	8.111	7.722	7.360	7.024	6.710	6.418	6.145	5.650	5.216	5.019	4.833	4.494	4.192
11	10.368	9.787	9.253	8.760	8.306	7.887	7.499	7.139	6.805	6.495	5.938	5.453	5.234	5.029	4.656	4.327
12	11.255	10.575	9.954	9.385	8.863	8.384	7.943	7.536	7.161	6.814	6.194	5.660	5.421	5.197	4.793	4.439
13	12.134	11.348	10.635	9.986	9.394	8.853	8.358	7.904	7.487	7.103	6.424	5.842	5.583	5.342	4.910	4.533
14	13.004	12.106	11.296	10.563	9.899	9.295	8.745	8.244	7.786	7.367	6.628	6.002	5.724	5.468	5.008	4.611
15	13.865	12.849	11.938	11.118	10.380	9.712	9.108	8.559	8.061	7.606	6.811	6.142	5.847	5.575	5.092	4.675
16	14.718	13.578	12.561	11.652	10.838	10.106	9.447	8.851	8.313	7.824	6.974	6.265	5.954	5.668	5.162	4.730
17	15.562	14.292	13.166	12.166	11.274	10.477	9.763	9.122	8.544	8.022	7.120	6.373	6.047	5.749	5.222	4.775
18	16.398	14.992	13.754	12.659	11.690	10.828	10.059	9.372	8.756	8.201	7.250	6.467	6.128	5.818	5.273	4.812
19	17.226	15.678	14.324	13.134	12.085	11.158	10.336	9.604	8.950	8.365	7.366	6.550	6.198	5.877	5.316	4.843
20	18.046	16.351	14.877	13.590	12.462	11.470	10.594	9.818	9.129	8.514	7.469	6.623	6.259	5.929	5.353	4.870
21	18.857	17.011	15.415	14.029	12.821	11.764	10.836	10.017	9.292	8.649	7.562	6.687	6.312	5.973	5.384	4.891
22	19.660	17.658	15.937	14.451	13.163	12.042	11.061	10.201	9.442	8.772	7.645	6.743	6.359	6.011	5.410	4.909
23	20.456	18.292	16.444	14.857	13.489	12.303	11.272	10.371	9.580	8.883	7.718	6.792	6.399	6.044	5.432	4.925
24	21.243	18.914	16.936	15.247	13.799	12.550	11.469	10.529	9.707	8.985	7.784	6.835	6.434	6.073	5.451	4.937
25	22.023	19.523	17.413	15.622	14.094	12.783	11.654	10.675	9.823	9.077	7.843	6.873	6.464	6.097	5.467	4.948
26	22.795	20.121	17.877	15.983	14.375	13.003	11.826	10.810	9.929	9.161	7.896	6.906	6.491	6.118	5.480	4.956
27	23.560	20.707	18.327	16.330	14.643	13.211	11.987	10.935	10.027	9.237	7.943	6.935	6.514	6.136	5.492	4.964
28	24.316	21.281	18.764	16.663	14.898	13.406	12.137	11.051	10.116	9.307	7.984	6.961	6.534	6.152	5.502	4.970
29	25.066	21.844	19.188	16.984	15.141	13.591	12.278	11.158	10.198	9.370	8.022	6.983	6.551	6.166	5.510	4.975
30	25.808	22.396	19.600	17.292	15.372	13.765	12.409	11.258	10.274	9.427	8.055	7.003	6.566	6.177	5.517	4.979
40	32.835	27.355	23.115	19.793	17.159	15.046	13.332	11.925	10.757	9.779	8.244	7.105	6.642	6.233	5.548	4.997
50	39.196	31.424	25.730	21.482	18.256	15.762	13.801	12.233	10.962	9.915	8.304	7.133	6.661	6.246	5.554	4.999

Appendix C
The Statement of Cash Flows

Why Doesn't the Business Have Any Cash?

David National reviewed his company's income statement with a confused look on his face. The statement reported a net profit of $20,000 for the past quarter. David knew that sales had been increasing in his small sporting equipment retail shop, and he expected this trend to continue through the end of the year. But David didn't understand why the income statement showed a profit. The company's payroll clerk had called him earlier in the day and told him that there wasn't enough cash in the bank to pay the company's monthly salaries.

It didn't make sense to David that the company could report a $20,000 profit on the income statement but not have enough cash to pay the payroll. He figured that the newly hired accountant, Mark Maloney, must have made a mistake.

David picked up the phone to call Mark. He had several questions to ask him. Why didn't the company have any cash in the bank? How was the company using its cash? How could the company report a $20,000 profit but not have that much cash in the bank? Where did the cash received from customers go?

After speaking with his accountant, David learned that the profit reported on the income statement didn't represent cash and that it was important that he review the company's statement of cash flows. The statement of cash flows, Mark told him, reports the cash receipts and cash payments of the business. It shows the sources and uses of cash and helps answer the question "Where did the cash go?"

Why Is Cash So Important?

You can probably answer that question from your own experience. It takes cash to pay bills and to generate future income for a business. Businesses, such as Target Corporation, a retail corporation that sells everything from sporting equipment to food, closely monitor cash. Target is interested in where its cash came from (receipts) and how its cash is spent (payments). One way for Target to monitor its cash receipts and payments is by preparing a statement of cash flows. For example, on Target's 2013 statement of cash flows, the corporation reported that it paid $3.5 billion purchasing property and equipment and that it received $86 million cash receipts from disposing of property and equipment. It also reported that from 2012 to 2013 the corporation had a decrease in cash of $89 million, even though net income was $1.97 billion. In this appendix, you learn what a statement of cash flows is and why it is useful to a business. In addition, you learn how to prepare the statement and understand why companies and investors carefully monitor the statement of cash flows.

Appendix C Learning Objectives

1 Identify the purposes of the statement of cash flows and distinguish among operating, investing, and financing cash flows

2 Prepare the statement of cash flows by the indirect method

3 Use free cash flow to evaluate business performance

4 Prepare the statement of cash flows by the direct method (Appendix CA)

5 Prepare the statement of cash flows by the indirect method using a spreadsheet (Appendix CB)

WHAT IS THE STATEMENT OF CASH FLOWS?

Learning Objective 1

Identify the purposes of the statement of cash flows and distinguish among operating, investing, and financing cash flows

Up to this point, you have learned about three financial statements—the income statement, the statement of retained earnings, and the balance sheet. Each of these financial statements reports specific items about a company. The income statement reports net income or net loss for the time period. The statement of retained earnings reports the changes in retained earnings during the time period, and the balance sheet reports a company's financial position. None of these statements reports specifically on the changes in cash.

When a comparative balance sheet for two periods is presented, it shows whether cash increased or decreased. But the balance sheet does not show *why* cash increased or decreased. We need the statement of cash flows for that. The **statement of cash flows** reports on a business's cash receipts and cash payments for a specific period. This statement does the following:

Statement of Cash Flows

Reports on a business's cash receipts and cash payments for a specific period.

Cash Flows

Cash receipts and cash payments of a business.

- Reports on the **cash flows** of a business—where cash came from (receipts) and how cash was spent (payments).
- Reports why cash increased or decreased during the period.
- Covers a span of time and is dated the same as the income statement—"Year Ended December 31, 2016," for example.

Purpose of the Statement of Cash Flows

The statement of cash flows explains why net income as reported on the income statement does not equal the change in the cash balance. In essence, the statement of cash flows is the link between the accrual-based income statement and the cash reported on the balance sheet.

How do people use cash flow information? The statement of cash flows helps do the following:

- **Predict future cash flows.** Past cash receipts and payments help predict future cash flows.
- **Evaluate management.** Wise investment decisions help the business prosper, while unwise decisions cause the business to have problems. Investors and creditors use cash flow information to evaluate managers' decisions.
- **Predict ability to pay debts and dividends.** Lenders want to know whether they will collect on their loans. Stockholders want dividends on their investments. The statement of cash flows helps make these predictions.

Classification of Cash Flows

There are three basic types of cash flow activities, and the statement of cash flows has a section for each:

- Operating activities
- Investing activities
- Financing activities

Each section reports cash inflows (cash receipts coming into the company) and cash outflows (cash going out of the company) based on these three divisions.

Operating Activities

Operating activities is the first section on the statement of cash flows and is often the most important category. The **operating activities** section reports on activities that create revenue or expense in the entity's business. It reflects the day-to-day operations of the business such as cash receipts (cash inflows) from customers for the sales of merchandise inventory and services and the cash outflows for purchases of merchandise inventory or payment of operating expenses. The operating activities section also includes cash receipts (cash inflows) for interest and dividend income and cash payments (cash outflows) for interest expense and income tax expense.

Operating Activities
Activities that create revenue or expense in the entity's business; a section of the statement of cash flows.

Investing Activities

Investing activities is the second category listed on the statement of cash flows. This section reports cash receipts and cash payments that increase or decrease long-term assets such as property, plant, equipment, notes receivable, and investments. It includes the cash inflow from selling and the cash outflow for the purchase of these long-term assets. In addition, it includes the loaning (cash outflow) and collecting (cash inflow) of long-term notes receivable.

Investing Activities
Activities that increase or decrease long-term assets; a section of the statement of cash flows.

Financing Activities

The last category on the statement of cash flows is **financing activities**. Financing activities include cash inflows and outflows involved in long-term liabilities and equity. This includes issuing stock, paying dividends, and buying and selling treasury stock. It also includes borrowing money and paying off long-term liabilities such as notes payable, bonds payable, and mortgages payable.

Each section of the statement of cash flows affects a different part of the balance sheet. The operating activities section reports on how cash flows affect the current accounts—current assets and current liabilities. Investing activities affect the long-term assets. And the financing activities affect long-term liabilities and equity. Exhibit C-1 shows the relationship between operating, investing, and financing cash flows and the various parts of the balance sheet.

Financing Activities
Activities that increase or decrease long-term liabilities and equity; a section of the statement of cash flows.

Exhibit C-1 | **Operating, Investing, and Financing Cash Flows and the Balance Sheet Accounts**

| Operating Cash Flows → | Current Assets | Current Liabilities | ← Operating Cash Flows |
| Investing Cash Flows → | Long-Term Assets | Long-Term Liabilities / Equity | ← Financing Cash Flows |

Non-cash Investing and Financing Activities

The three sections of the statement of cash flows report only activities that involve cash. Companies do make investments that do not require cash. They also obtain financing other than cash. Such transactions are called **non-cash investing and financing activities**. Examples of these activities include the purchase of equipment financed by a long-term note payable or the contribution of equipment by a stockholder in exchange for common stock. These activities are not included in the statement of cash flows. Instead, they appear either as a separate schedule at the bottom of the statement or in the notes to the financial statements.

Exhibit C-2 summarizes the different sections on the statement of cash flows.

Non-cash Investing and Financing Activities
Investing and financing activities that do not involve cash.

Under IFRS, interest and dividend income may be reported either as an operating activity or as an investing activity. Interest and dividends paid may be reported either as an operating activity or as a financing activity.

Exhibit C-2 | **Sections of the Statement of Cash Flows**

Operating Activities	Cash Inflows: • From customers for the sales of merchandise inventory and services • For interest and dividend income Cash Outflows: • For the purchase of merchandise inventory and payment of operating expenses • For interest expense and income tax expense
Investing Activities	Cash Inflows: • From the sale of property, plant, equipment, and investments • From the collection of long-term notes receivable Cash Outflows: • To purchase property, plant, equipment, and investments • For loans made to borrowers
Financing Activities	Cash Inflows: • From issuance of stock and selling treasury stock • From receipt of borrowing money Cash Outflows: • For payment of dividends and buying treasury stock • For repayments of loans
Non-cash Investing and Financing Activities	A separate schedule that includes investing and financing activities that *do not* include cash

The statement of cash flows reports only activities that involve either the receipt of cash or the payment of cash. If a transaction does not involve cash, it will not be included in the operating, investing, or financing sections of the statement of cash flows.

Two Formats for Operating Activities

There are two ways to format the operating activities section of the statement of cash flows:

- The **indirect method** starts with net income and adjusts it to net cash provided by operating activities.
- The **direct method** restates the income statement in terms of cash. The direct method shows all the cash receipts and all the cash payments from operating activities.

The indirect and direct methods use different computations but produce the same amount of net cash flow from operating activities. Both methods present investing activities and financing activities in exactly the same format. Only the *operating activities* section is presented differently between the two methods.

We begin with the indirect method because most companies use it. To focus on the direct method, review Appendix CA, located at the end of this appendix.

Indirect Method
A format of the operating activities section of the statement of cash flows; starts with net income and reconciles to net cash provided by operating activities.

Direct Method
A format of the operating activities section of the statement of cash flows; lists the operating cash receipts and cash payments.

IFRS permits the use of either the direct or indirect method.

Identify each item as operating (O), investing (I), financing (F), or non-cash (N).

1. Cash receipt from the sale of equipment
2. Cash payment for salaries
3. Cash receipt from the collection of long-term notes receivable
4. Purchase of equipment in exchange for notes payable
5. Cash receipt from the issuance of common stock

Check your answers online in MyAccountingLab or at http://www.pearsonhighered.com/Horngren.

For more practice, see Short Exercises SC-1 and SC-2. MyAccountingLab

HOW IS THE STATEMENT OF CASH FLOWS PREPARED USING THE INDIRECT METHOD?

To prepare the statement of cash flows, you need the income statement for the current year, as well as the balance sheets from the current and prior year. In addition, you need to review the transactions for some additional information. For illustrative purposes, we will use ShopMart, Inc., a fictitious retail store that sells electronics, home furnishings, home supplies, and more. ShopMart's comparative balance sheet is shown in Exhibit C-3 (on the next page), and its

Learning Objective 2
Prepare the statement of cash flows by the indirect method

Exhibit C-3 | **Comparative Balance Sheet**

SHOPMART, INC.
Comparative Balance Sheet
December 31, 2016 and 2015

	2016	2015	Increase (Decrease)
Assets			
Current Assets:			
Cash	$ 22,000	$ 42,000	$ (20,000)
Accounts Receivable	90,000	73,000	17,000
Merchandise Inventory	143,000	145,000	(2,000)
Long-term Assets:			
Plants Assets	507,000	252,000	255,000
Accumulated Depreciation—Plant Assets	(47,000)	(42,000)	(5,000)
Total Assets	$ 715,000	$ 470,000	$ 245,000
Liabilities			
Current Liabilities:			
Accounts Payable	$ 90,000	$ 50,000	$ 40,000
Accrued Liabilities	5,000	10,000	(5,000)
Long-term Liabilities:			
Notes Payable	160,000	80,000	80,000
Total Liabilities	255,000	140,000	115,000
Stockholders' Equity			
Common Stock, no par	370,000	250,000	120,000
Retained Earnings	110,000	80,000	30,000
Treasury Stock	(20,000)	0	(20,000)
Total Stockholders' Equity	460,000	330,000	130,000
Total Liabilities and Stockholders' Equity	$ 715,000	$ 470,000	$ 245,000

income statement is shown in Exhibit C-4. Additional information provided by ShopMart includes the following:

- Purchased $310,000 in plant assets by paying cash.
- Sold plant assets with a cost of $55,000 and accumulated depreciation of $15,000, yielding a gain of $10,000.
- Received $90,000 cash from issuance of notes payable.
- Paid $10,000 cash to retire notes payable.
- Received $120,000 cash from issuing shares of common stock.
- Paid $20,000 cash for purchase of shares of treasury stock.

Exhibit C-4 | Income Statement

SHOPMART, INC. Income Statement Year Ended December 31, 2016		
Sales Revenue		$ 286,000
Cost of Goods Sold		156,000
Gross Profit		130,000
Operating Expenses:		
Salaries and Wages Expense	$ 56,000	
Depreciation Expense—Plant Assets	20,000	
Other Operating Expense	16,000	
Total Operating Expenses		92,000
Operating Income		38,000
Other Revenue and (Expenses):		
Interest Revenue	12,000	
Dividend Revenue	9,000	
Gain on Disposal of Plant Assets	10,000	
Interest Expense	(15,000)	
Total Other Revenues and (Expenses)		16,000
Income Before Income Taxes		54,000
Income Tax Expense		14,000
Net Income		$ 40,000

To prepare the statement of cash flows by the indirect method, we follow Steps 1–5:

Step 1: Complete the cash flows from operating activities section using net income and adjusting for increases or decreases in current assets (other than cash) and current liabilities. Also adjust for gains or losses from long-term assets and non-cash expenses such as depreciation expense.

Step 2: Complete the cash flows from investing activities section by reviewing the long-term assets section of the balance sheet.

Step 3: Complete the cash flows from financing activities section by reviewing the long-term liabilities and equity sections of the balance sheet.

Step 4: Compute the net increase or decrease in cash during the year. The change in cash is the key reconciling figure for the statement of cash flows and must match the change in cash reported on the comparative balance sheet.

Step 5: Prepare a separate schedule reporting any non-cash investing and financing activities.

Let's apply these steps to show the operating activities of ShopMart. Exhibit C-5 depicts the completed statement of cash flows.

Exhibit C-5 | Statement of Cash Flows—Indirect Method

SHOPMART, INC. Statement of Cash Flows Year Ended December 31, 2016		
Cash Flows from Operating Activities:		
Net Income		$ 40,000
Adjustments to Reconcile Net Income to Net Cash Provided by Operating Activities:		
Depreciation Expense—Plant Assets	$ 20,000	
Gain on Disposal of Plant Assets	(10,000)	
Increase in Accounts Receivable	(17,000)	
Decrease in Merchandise Inventory	2,000	
Increase in Accounts Payable	40,000	
Decrease in Accrued Liabilities	(5,000)	30,000
Net Cash Provided by Operating Activities		70,000
Cash Flows from Investing Activities:		
Cash Payment for Acquisition of Plant Assets	(310,000)	
Cash Receipt from Disposal of Plant Assets	50,000	
Net Cash Used for Investing Activities		(260,000)
Cash Flows from Financing Activities:		
Cash Receipt from Issuance of Notes Payable	90,000	
Cash Payment of Notes Payable	(10,000)	
Cash Receipt from Issuance of Common Stock	120,000	
Cash Payment for Purchase of Treasury Stock	(20,000)	
Cash Payment of Dividends	(10,000)	
Net Cash Provided by Financing Activities		170,000
Net Increase (Decrease) in Cash		(20,000)
Cash Balance, December 31, 2015		42,000
Cash Balance, December 31, 2016		$ 22,000

Step 1: Operating Activities

Step 2: Investing Activities

Step 3: Financing Activities

Step 4: Net Increase (Decrease) in Cash

Cash Flows from Operating Activities

When using the indirect method, the statement of cash flows operating activities section begins with net income (or net loss) because revenues and expenses, which affect net income, produce cash receipts and cash payments. Revenues bring in cash receipts, and expenses must be paid. But net income as shown on the income statement is accrual-based, and the cash flows (cash basis net income) do not always equal the accrual basis revenues and expenses. For example, sales *on account* generate revenues that increase net income, but the company has not yet collected cash from those sales. Accrued expenses decrease net income, but the company has not paid cash *if the expenses are accrued.*

To go from net income to cash flow from operating activities, we must make some adjustments to net income on the statement of cash flows. These additions and subtractions follow net income and are labeled *Adjustments to Reconcile Net Income to Net Cash Provided by Operating Activities.*

Depreciation, Depletion, and Amortization Expenses

These adjustments include adding back non-cash expenses such as depreciation, depletion, and amortization expenses. These expenses are added back to net income to reconcile net income to net cash flow from operating activities. Let's see why this occurs. Depreciation is recorded as follows:

Date	Accounts and Explanation	Debit	Credit
	Depreciation Expense—Plant Assets	20,000	
	Accumulated Depreciation—Plant Assets		20,000

$$\underset{\substack{\text{Accumulated}\\\text{Depreciation}\uparrow}}{\underline{\text{A}\downarrow}} = \underline{\text{L}} + \underset{\substack{\text{Depreciation}\\\text{Expense}\uparrow}}{\underline{\text{E}\downarrow}}$$

You can see that depreciation does not affect cash as there is no Cash account in the journal entry. Depreciation is a non-cash expense. The cash outflow related to depreciation occurred when the asset was purchased, not as it is depreciated. However, depreciation, like all the other expenses, decreases net income. Therefore, to go from net income to cash flows, we must remove depreciation by adding it back to net income.

SHOPMART, INC.
Statement of Cash Flows (Partial)
Year Ended December 31, 2016

Cash Flows from Operating Activities:	
Net Income	$ 40,000
Adjustments to Reconcile Net Income to Net Cash Provided by Operating Activities:	
Depreciation Expense—Plant Assets	$ 20,000

Suppose you had only two transactions during the period:

- Cash sale of $60,000
- Depreciation expense of $20,000

Accrual basis net income is $40,000 ($60,000 − $20,000), but cash flow from operations is $60,000. To reconcile from net income, depreciation of $20,000 must be added to net income, $40,000, to determine net cash flow from operations, $60,000. We would also add back any depletion and amortization expenses because they are non-cash expenses, similar to depreciation.

Gains and Losses on the Disposal of Long-Term Assets

Disposals of long-term assets such as land and buildings are investing activities, and these disposals usually create a gain or a loss. The gain or loss is included in net income, which is already in the operating activities section of the statement of cash flows. The gain or loss must be removed from net income on the statement of cash flows so the total cash receipts from the sale of the asset can be shown in the investing section.

Exhibit C-4, ShopMart's income statement, includes a gain on disposal of plant assets. During 2016, ShopMart sold equipment, and there was a gain of $10,000 on the sale. The gain was included in the calculation of net income on the income statement, so the gain must be removed from operating cash flows. The gain increased net income, so it is subtracted in the operating activities section.

SHOPMART, INC. Statement of Cash Flows (Partial) Year Ended December 31, 2016		
Cash Flows from Operating Activities:		
Net Income		$ 40,000
Adjustments to Reconcile Net Income to Net Cash Provided by Operating Activities:		
Depreciation Expense—Plant Assets	$ 20,000	
Gain on Disposal of Plant Assets	(10,000)	

What if there is a loss on disposal of plant assets?

On the other hand, a loss on the disposal of plant assets would decrease net income on the income statement, so the amount of the loss would be reversed to determine the net cash provided by operating activities on the statement of cash flows. For example, a $5,000 loss on disposal of plant assets would be a $5,000 addition to net income on the statement of cash flows to determine net cash provided by operating activities.

Changes in Current Assets and Current Liabilities

Most current assets and current liabilities result from operating activities. For example:

- Accounts receivable result from sales.
- Merchandise inventory relates to cost of goods sold, and so on.

Changes in the current asset and current liability accounts create adjustments to net income on the statement of cash flows, as follows:

- **An increase in a current asset other than cash causes a decrease in cash.** If Accounts Receivable, Merchandise Inventory, or Prepaid Expenses increases, then cash decreases. Therefore, we subtract the increase in the current asset from net income to get net cash flow from operating activities. For example, in Exhibit C-3, ShopMart's Accounts Receivable increased by $17,000. This increase in the current asset shows that there were more sales on account than cash collections from customers and is reported as a decrease in cash on the statement of cash flows.

- **A decrease in a current asset other than cash causes an increase in cash.** ShopMart's Merchandise Inventory decreased by $2,000. What caused the decrease? ShopMart must have sold some merchandise inventory and collected cash. Therefore, we add the decrease in Merchandise Inventory of $2,000 in the statement of cash flows.

- **An increase in a current liability causes an increase in cash.** ShopMart's Accounts Payable increased by $40,000. This means that cash was not spent at the time the expense was incurred, but rather it will be paid at a later time—resulting in a liability. Accordingly, even though net income was reduced by the expense, cash was not reduced. However, cash will be reduced later when ShopMart pays off its liability. Therefore, an increase in a current liability is added to net income in the statement of cash flows.

- **A decrease in a current liability causes a decrease in cash.** The payment of a current liability decreases cash. Therefore, we subtract decreases in current liabilities from net income to get net cash flow from operating activities. ShopMart's Accrued Liabilities decreased by $5,000. That change shows up as a $5,000 decrease in cash flows.

SHOPMART, INC. Statement of Cash Flows (Partial) Year Ended December 31, 2016		
Cash Flows from Operating Activities:		
Net Income		$ 40,000
Adjustments to Reconcile Net Income to Net Cash Provided by Operating Activities:		
Depreciation Expense—Plant Assets	$ 20,000	
Gain on Disposal of Plant Assets	(10,000)	
Increase in Accounts Receivable	(17,000)	
Decrease in Merchandise Inventory	2,000	
Increase in Accounts Payable	40,000	
Decrease in Accrued Liabilities	(5,000)	30,000

DECISIONS

What can be done to create a positive cash flow?

Meggie Mohamed, CEO, knew that the bank would carefully review her company's most recent statement of cash flows before determining if it would approve the loan needed for expansion. The bank loan officer had told her that it is important that the business show strong operating cash flows. Meggie knows that her company's operating cash flow for this past quarter will most likely be negative. Although the company recorded significant revenue, most of the revenue was recorded as receivables. Meggie expects that the cash will come in soon, but not in time to report a positive operating cash flow. What should Meggie do? What would you do?

Solution

Meggie could explain to the bank officer that her company is expecting to collect a significant amount of cash in the near future on outstanding receivables. She could provide detailed collection information including the estimated time frame of collection and the amount expected. Meggie also has another option. She could look into selling the receivables to another business, often called a factor. By selling the receivables, the company will be able to decrease its accounts receivable balance, increase its cash balance, and report a positive change in operating cash flows.

Evaluating Cash Flows from Operating Activities

During 2016, ShopMart's operating activities provided a net cash inflow of $70,000 ($40,000 + $30,000), so the amount is labeled Net Cash *Provided by* Operating Activities. If this amount were a net cash outflow, ShopMart would report Net Cash *Used for* Operating Activities.

SHOPMART, INC. Statement of Cash Flows (Partial) Year Ended December 31, 2016		
Cash Flows from Operating Activities:		
Net Income		$ 40,000
Adjustments to Reconcile Net Income to Net Cash Provided by Operating Activities:		
Depreciation Expense—Plant Assets	$ 20,000	
Gain on Disposal of Plant Assets	(10,000)	
Increase in Accounts Receivable	(17,000)	
Decrease in Merchandise Inventory	2,000	
Increase in Accounts Payable	40,000	
Decrease in Accrued Liabilities	(5,000)	30,000
Net Cash Provided by Operating Activities		70,000

The operating activities section (indirect method) always starts with accrual basis net income. Adjustments are then made to determine the cash basis net income. Exhibit C-6 summarizes the adjustments made to reconcile net income to net cash provided by operating activities.

Exhibit C-6 | **Adjustments Made to Reconcile Net Income to Net Cash Provided by Operating Activities**

Item	Adjustment on Statement of Cash Flows
Depreciation, Depletion, and Amortization Expense	+
Gains on Disposal of Long-term Assets	−
Losses on Disposal of Long-term Assets	+
Increases in Current Assets other than Cash	−
Decreases in Current Assets other than Cash	+
Increases in Current Liabilities	+
Decreases in Current Liabilities	−

Cash Flows from Investing Activities

Investing activities affect long-term assets, such as Plant Assets, Investments, and Notes Receivable. These are shown on ShopMart's balance sheet (Exhibit C-3). Now, let's see how to compute the investing cash flows.

When computing investing cash flows, it is helpful to evaluate the T-accounts for each long-term asset. The T-account will show if there was an acquisition or disposal that happened during the year. Let's look at the Plant Assets and Accumulated Depreciation accounts for ShopMart.

Plant Assets

12/31/2015	252,000		
Acquisitions	310,000	55,000	Disposals
12/31/2016	507,000		

Accumulated Depreciation—Plant Assets

		42,000	12/31/2015
Disposals	15,000	20,000	Depr. Exp.
		47,000	12/31/2016

> Depreciation Expense is from the income statement.

The beginning and ending balances for each account are taken directly from the comparative balance sheet. Depreciation expense has been included in the Accumulated Depreciation account, and this was taken from the income statement. The acquisition and disposal information came from the additional information provided when we introduced the example:

- Purchased $310,000 in plant assets by paying cash.
- Sold plant assets with a cost of $55,000 and accumulated depreciation of $15,000, yielding a gain of $10,000.

We now know that ShopMart paid $310,000 cash to purchase plant assets. This item is listed first in the investing activities section and shown as an outflow of cash, as indicated by the parentheses.

Next we need to determine the amount of cash received for the disposal of plant assets. Using the information provided, we can recreate the journal entry for the disposal and solve for the missing cash amount.

Date	Accounts and Explanation	Debit	Credit
	Cash	?	
	Accumulated Depreciation—Plant Assets	15,000	
	Gain on Disposal of Plant Assets		10,000
	Plant Assets		55,000

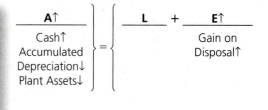

We compute the cash receipt from the disposal as follows:

$$\text{Cash received} = \text{Cost} - \text{Accumulated Depreciation} + \text{Gain} - \text{Loss}$$
$$= \$55,000 - \$15,000 + \$10,000$$
$$= \$50,000$$

The cash receipt from the sale of plant assets of $50,000 is shown next in the investing activities section. As there are no other changes to long-term assets, the net cash from investing activities is determined. Notice that this is a net cash outflow, as indicated by the parentheses, and is reported as Net Cash *Used for* Investing Activities.

> In this partial statement, we are showing only the investing activities section of the statement of cash flows. Remember that the investing activities section is reported after the operating activities section.

SHOPMART, INC.
Statement of Cash Flows (Partial)
Year Ended December 31, 2016

Cash Flows from Investing Activities:		
Cash Payment for Acquisition of Plant Assets	(310,000)	
Cash Receipt from Disposal of Plant Assets	50,000	
Net Cash Used for Investing Activities		(260,000)

Cash Flows from Financing Activities

Financing activities affect the long-term liability and equity accounts, such as Long-Term Notes Payable, Bonds Payable, Common Stock, and Retained Earnings. To determine the cash flows from financing activities, we need to review each of these account types.

Long-Term Liabilities

The T-account for ShopMart's Notes Payable is shown below. Additional information concerning notes payable is also provided by the company as follows:

- Received $90,000 cash from issuance of notes payable.
- Paid $10,000 cash to retire notes payable.

Notes Payable

		80,000	12/31/2015
Payment	10,000	90,000	Issuance
		160,000	12/31/2016

The beginning and ending balances of Notes Payable are taken from the comparative balance sheet. For ShopMart, a new issuance of notes payable is known to be a $90,000 cash receipt and is shown by the following journal entry:

$$\frac{A\uparrow}{Cash\uparrow} \Big\} = \Big\{ \frac{L\uparrow}{\substack{Notes \\ Payable\uparrow}} + \underline{\quad E \quad}$$

Date	Accounts and Explanation	Debit	Credit
	Cash	90,000	
	Notes Payable		90,000

In addition, ShopMart paid $10,000 cash to retire notes payable.

$$\frac{A\downarrow}{Cash\downarrow} \Big\} = \Big\{ \frac{L\downarrow}{\substack{Notes \\ Payable\downarrow}} + \underline{\quad E \quad}$$

Date	Accounts and Explanation	Debit	Credit
	Notes Payable	10,000	
	Cash		10,000

The cash inflow and cash outflow associated with these notes payable are listed first in the cash flows from financing activities section.

SHOPMART, INC. Statement of Cash Flows (Partial) Year Ended December 31, 2016	
Cash Flows from Financing Activities:	
Cash Receipt from Issuance of Notes Payable	90,000
Cash Payment of Notes Payable	(10,000)

ETHICS

Should the notes payable be reclassified?

Michael Reinstein had just left the office of his supervisor, Scott Medley. The supervisor had mentioned that Michael should reclassify a cash receipt from issuance of long-term notes payable as a short-term notes payable. Scott had shared with Michael that the chairman of the Board of Directors was placing intense pressure on him to report a positive cash flow from operating activities. Michael knew that if the company reclassified the notes payable, the business would no longer report the receipt in the financing activities section of the statement of cash flows. Instead, it would be shown as an increase in current liabilities resulting in a positive cash flow from operating activities. What should Michael do?

Solution

Michael should not reclassify the notes payable. By reclassifying the note, the company is misleading investors and reporting a positive operating cash flow when it does not have one. This misclassification is a violation of GAAP. If a notes payable is long-term, it should be reported in the financing activities section of the statement of cash flows.

Common Stock and Treasury Stock

Cash flows for financing activities are also determined by analyzing the stock accounts. For example, the amount of new issuances of stock is determined by analyzing the stock accounts and reviewing the additional information provided:

- Received $120,000 cash from issuing shares of common stock.
- Paid $20,000 cash for purchase of shares of treasury stock.

ShopMart's stock T-accounts are as follows:

Common Stock

		250,000	12/31/2015
Retirement	0	120,000	Issuance
		370,000	12/31/2016

Treasury Stock

12/31/2015	0		
Purchase	20,000	0	Disposal
12/31/2016	20,000		

The common stock account shows a new stock issuance of $120,000 and would be recorded by the following journal entry:

$$\left.\begin{array}{c} \underline{A\uparrow} \\ \text{Cash}\uparrow \end{array}\right\} = \left\{\begin{array}{ccc} \underline{L} & + & \underline{E\uparrow} \\ & & \text{Common} \\ & & \text{Stock}\uparrow \end{array}\right.$$

Date	Accounts and Explanation	Debit	Credit
	Cash	120,000	
	Common Stock		120,000

This is shown as $120,000 cash inflow in the financing activities section of the statement.

Treasury stock also changed on ShopMart's balance sheet. The T-account is showing an acquisition of treasury stock that would be recorded as follows:

$$\left.\begin{array}{c} \underline{A\downarrow} \\ \text{Cash}\downarrow \end{array}\right\} = \left\{\begin{array}{ccc} \underline{L} & + & \underline{E\downarrow} \\ & & \text{Treasury} \\ & & \text{Stock}\uparrow \end{array}\right.$$

Date	Accounts and Explanation	Debit	Credit
	Treasury Stock	20,000	
	Cash		20,000

The $20,000 is shown as a cash outflow in the financing section of the statement of cash flows for the purchase of treasury stock.

SHOPMART, INC.
Statement of Cash Flows (Partial)
Year Ended December 31, 2016

Cash Flows from Financing Activities:	
Cash Receipt from Issuance of Notes Payable	90,000
Cash Payment of Notes Payable	(10,000)
Cash Receipt from Issuance of Common Stock	120,000
Cash Payment for Purchase of Treasury Stock	(20,000)

Computing Dividend Payments

The amount of dividend payments can be computed by analyzing the Retained Earnings account. First, we input the balances from the balance sheet:

Retained Earnings			
		80,000	12/31/2015
Net Loss	?	?	Net Income
Dividends	?		
		110,000	12/31/2016

Retained Earnings increases when companies earn net income. Retained Earnings decreases when companies have a net loss and when they declare dividends. We know that ShopMart earned net income of $40,000 from the income statement in Exhibit C-4.

Retained Earnings

		80,000	12/31/2015
Net Loss	?	40,000	Net Income
Dividends	?		
		110,000	12/31/2016

> Net Income is from the income statement.

ShopMart can't have both net income and net loss for the same period; therefore, the missing value must be the amount of dividends ShopMart declared. Solving for the dividends follows:

Ending Retained Earnings = Beginning Retained Earnings + Net income − Net loss − Dividends
$110,000 = $80,000 + $40,000 − $0 − Dividends
Dividends = $80,000 + $40,000 − $0 − $110,000
Dividends = $10,000

So our final Retained Earnings T-account shows the following:

Retained Earnings

		80,000	12/31/2015
		40,000	Net Income
Dividends	10,000		
		110,000	12/31/2016

A stock dividend has *no* effect on Cash and is *not* reported in the financing activities section of the statement of cash flows. ShopMart had no stock dividends, only cash dividends, which will be shown as an outflow in the financing activities section of the statement of cash flows.

SHOPMART, INC.
Statement of Cash Flows (Partial)
Year Ended December 31, 2016

Cash Flows from Financing Activities:		
Cash Receipt from Issuance of Notes Payable	$ 90,000	
Cash Payment of Notes Payable	(10,000)	
Cash Receipt from Issuance of Common Stock	120,000	
Cash Payment for Purchase of Treasury Stock	(20,000)	
Cash Payment of Dividends	(10,000)	
Net Cash Provided by Financing Activities		170,000

Net Change in Cash and Cash Balances

To complete the statement of cash flows, the net change in cash and its effect on the beginning cash balance must be shown. This represents the total change in cash for the period and reconciles the statement of cash flows. First, the net increase or decrease in cash is computed by combining the cash provided by or used for operating, investing, and financing activities. In the case of ShopMart, there is a net decrease in the cash balance of $20,000 for the year and is calculated as follows:

$$
\begin{aligned}
\text{Net Increase (Decrease) in Cash} &= \text{Net Cash Provided by Operating Activities} - \text{Net Cash Used for} \\
&\quad \text{Investing Activities} + \text{Net Cash Provided by Financing Activities} \\
&= \$70,000 - \$260,000 + \$170,000 \\
&= \$(20,000)
\end{aligned}
$$

Next, the beginning cash from December 31, 2015, is listed at $42,000, as shown on the comparative balance sheet. The net decrease of $20,000 is subtracted from beginning cash of $42,000, which equals the ending cash balance on December 31, 2016, of $22,000. This is the key to the statement of cash flows—it explains why the cash balance for ShopMart decreased by $20,000, even though the company reported net income for the year.

SHOPMART, INC. Statement of Cash Flows (Partial) Year Ended December 31, 2016	
Net Cash Provided by Operating Activities	$ 70,000
Net Cash Used for Investing Activities	(260,000)
Net Cash Provided by Financing Activities	170,000
Net Increase (Decrease) in Cash	(20,000)
Cash Balance, December 31, 2015	42,000
Cash Balance, December 31, 2016	$ 22,000

Before moving on, take a moment to review the completed Statement of Cash Flows shown earlier in Exhibit C-5.

Non-cash Investing and Financing Activities

The last step in preparing the statement of cash flows is to prepare the non-cash investing and financing activities section. This section appears as a separate schedule of the statement of cash flows or in the notes to the financial statements. Our ShopMart example did not include transactions of this type because the company did not have any non-cash transactions during the year. So, to illustrate them, let's consider three non-cash transactions for another fictitious company, The Outdoors, Inc. How would they be reported? First, we gather the non-cash activities for the company:

1. Acquired $300,000 building by issuing common stock.
2. Acquired $70,000 land by issuing notes payable.
3. Retired $100,000 notes payable by issuing common stock.

Now, we consider each transaction individually.

1. The Outdoors issued common stock of $300,000 to acquire a building. The journal entry to record the purchase would be as follows:

Date	Accounts and Explanation	Debit	Credit
	Building	300,000	
	Common Stock		300,000

$$\underset{\text{Building}\uparrow}{A\uparrow} \Big\} = \Big\{ \underset{}{L} + \underset{\substack{\text{Common}\\\text{Stock}\uparrow}}{E\uparrow}$$

This transaction would not be reported on the statement of cash flows because no cash was paid or received. But the building and the common stock are important. The purchase of the building is an investing activity. The issuance of common stock is a financing activity. Taken together, this transaction is a *non-cash investing and financing activity.*

2. The second transaction listed indicates that The Outdoors acquired $70,000 of land by issuing a note. The journal entry to record the purchase would be as follows:

Date	Accounts and Explanation	Debit	Credit
	Land	70,000	
	Notes Payable		70,000

$$\underset{\text{Land}\uparrow}{A\uparrow} \Big\} = \Big\{ \underset{\substack{\text{Notes}\\\text{Payable}\uparrow}}{L\uparrow} + \underset{}{E}$$

This transaction would not be reported on the statement of cash flows because no cash was paid or received. But the land and the notes payable are important. The purchase of the land is an investing activity. The issuance of the note is a financing activity. Taken together, this transaction is a *non-cash investing and financing activity.*

3. The third transaction listed indicates that The Outdoors exchanged $100,000 of debt by issuing common stock. The journal entry to record the transaction would be as follows:

Date	Accounts and Explanation	Debit	Credit
	Notes Payable	100,000	
	Common Stock		100,000

$$\underset{}{A} \Big\} = \Big\{ \underset{\substack{\text{Notes}\\\text{Payable}\downarrow}}{L\downarrow} + \underset{\substack{\text{Common}\\\text{Stock}\uparrow}}{E\uparrow}$$

This transaction would not be reported on the statement of cash flows because no cash was paid or received. But the notes payable and the stock issuance are important. The payment on the note and the issuance of the common stock are both financing activities. Taken together, this transaction, even though it is two financing transactions, is reported in the *non-cash investing and financing activities.*

Non-cash investing and financing activities are reported in a separate part of the statement of cash flows. Exhibit C-7 (on the next page) illustrates non-cash investing and financing activities for The Outdoors. This information is either reported as a separate schedule following the statement of cash flows or can be disclosed in a note.

Exhibit C-7 | **Non-cash Investing and Financing Activities**

THE OUTDOORS, INC. Statement of Cash Flows (Partial) Year Ended December 31, 2016	
Non-cash Investing and Financing Activities:	
Acquisition of building by issuing common stock	$ 300,000
Acquisition of land by issuing notes payable	70,000
Retirement of notes payable by issuing common stock	100,000
Total Non-cash Investing and Financing Activities	**$ 470,000**

Try It!

6. Owl, Inc.'s accountants have assembled the following data for the year ended December 31, 2016:

Cash receipt from sale of equipment	$ 20,000
Depreciation expense	12,000
Cash payment of dividends	4,000
Cash receipt from issuance of common stock	12,000
Net income	30,000
Cash purchase of land	25,000
Increase in current liabilities	10,000
Decrease in current assets other than cash	8,000

Prepare Owl's statement of cash flows using the indirect method for the year ended December 31, 2016. Assume beginning and ending Cash are $12,000 and $75,000 respectively.

Check your answer online in MyAccountingLab or at http://www.pearsonhighered.com/Horngren.

For more practice, see Short Exercises SC-3 through SC-9. MyAccountingLab

---

Learning Objective 3

Use free cash flow to evaluate business performance

Free Cash Flow

The amount of cash available from operating activities after paying for planned investments in long-term assets and after paying dividends to shareholders. Net cash provided by operating activities – Cash payments planned for investments in long-term assets – Cash dividends.

HOW DO WE USE FREE CASH FLOW TO EVALUATE BUSINESS PERFORMANCE?

Throughout this appendix, we have focused on cash flows from operating, investing, and financing activities. Some investors want to know how much cash a company can "free up" for new opportunities. **Free cash flow** is the amount of cash available from operating activities after paying for planned investments in long-term assets and after paying cash dividends to shareholders. Free cash flow can be computed as follows:

Free cash flow = Net cash provided by operating activities − Cash payments planned for investments in long-term assets − Cash dividends

Many companies use free cash flow to estimate the amount of cash that would be available for unexpected opportunities. Suppose ShopMart expects net cash provided by operations of $200,000. Assume the company plans to spend $160,000 to modernize its retail facilities and pays $15,000 in cash dividends. In this case, ShopMart's free cash flow would be $25,000 ($200,000 – $160,000 – $15,000). If a good investment opportunity comes along, the company should have $25,000 cash available to invest.

7. Kalapono Company expects the following for 2016:
   - Net cash provided by operating activities of $100,000.
   - Net cash provided by financing activities of $10,000.
   - Net cash used for investing activities of $20,000 (no sales of long-term assets).
   - Cash dividends paid to stockholders was $2,000.

How much free cash flow does Kalapono expect for 2016?

Check your answer online in MyAccountingLab or at http://www.pearsonhighered.com/Horngren.

For more practice, see Short Exercise SC-10. MyAccountingLab

APPENDIX CA: Preparing the Statement of Cash Flows by the Direct Method

HOW IS THE STATEMENT OF CASH FLOWS PREPARED USING THE DIRECT METHOD?

The Financial Accounting Standards Board (FASB) prefers the direct method of reporting cash flows from operating activities. The direct method provides clearer information about the sources and uses of cash than does the indirect method. However, very few non-public companies use the direct method because it takes more computations than the indirect method. Investing and financing cash flows are exactly the same presentation under both direct and indirect methods. Because only the preparation of the operating activities section differs, it is all we discuss in this appendix.

To illustrate how the operating activities section of the statement of cash flows differs for the direct method, we use the ShopMart data we used within the main appendix.

Learning Objective 4

Prepare the statement of cash flows by the direct method

Cash Flows from Operating Activities

In the indirect method, we start with accrual basis net income and then adjust it to cash basis through a series of adjusting items. When using the direct method, we take each line item of the income statement and convert it from accrual to cash basis. So, in essence, the operating activities section of the direct-method cash flows statement is really just a cash-basis income statement. Now let's apply this information to ShopMart.

Cash Collections from Customers

The first item on the income statement is Sales Revenue. Sales Revenue represents the total of all sales, whether for cash or on account. The balance sheet account related to Sales

Revenue is Accounts Receivable. Accounts Receivable went from $73,000 at December 31, 2015, to $90,000 at December 31, 2016, an increase of $17,000. Sales Revenue can be converted to cash receipts from customers as follows:

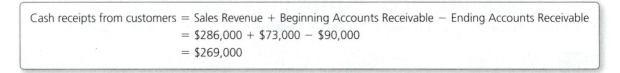

Cash receipts from customers = Sales Revenue + Beginning Accounts Receivable − Ending Accounts Receivable
= $286,000 + $73,000 − $90,000
= $269,000

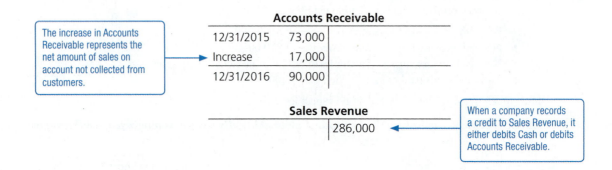

The increase in Accounts Receivable represents the net amount of sales on account not collected from customers.

Accounts Receivable

12/31/2015	73,000	
Increase	17,000	
12/31/2016	90,000	

Sales Revenue

	286,000

When a company records a credit to Sales Revenue, it either debits Cash or debits Accounts Receivable.

So, the cash ShopMart received from customers is $269,000. This is the first item in the operating activities section of the direct-method statement of cash flows.

SHOPMART, INC.
Statement of Cash Flows (Partial)
Year Ended December 31, 2016

Cash Flows from Operating Activities:	
Receipts:	
Collections from Customers	$ 269,000

Had ShopMart had a decrease in Accounts Receivable, the amount of cash collections from customers would be higher than Sales Revenue.

Cash Receipts of Interest

The income statement reports interest revenue of $12,000. The balance sheet account related to Interest Revenue is Interest Receivable. Because there is no Interest Receivable account on the balance sheet, the interest revenue must have all been received in cash. So, the statement of cash flows shows interest received of $12,000.

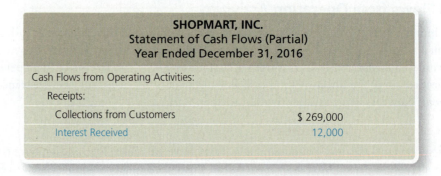

SHOPMART, INC.
Statement of Cash Flows (Partial)
Year Ended December 31, 2016

Cash Flows from Operating Activities:	
Receipts:	
Collections from Customers	$ 269,000
Interest Received	12,000

Cash Receipts of Dividends

The income statement reports dividend revenue of $9,000. The balance sheet account related to Dividend Revenue is Dividends Receivable. As with the interest, there is no Dividends Receivable account on the balance sheet. Therefore, the dividend revenue must have all been received in cash. So, the statement of cash flows shows cash received from dividends of $9,000.

SHOPMART, INC.
Statement of Cash Flows (Partial)
Year Ended December 31, 2016

Cash Flows from Operating Activities:		
Receipts:		
Collections from Customers	$ 269,000	
Interest Received	12,000	
Dividends Received on Investments	9,000	
Total Cash Receipts		$ 290,000

Payments to Suppliers

Payments to suppliers include all payments for the following:

- Merchandise inventory
- Operating expenses except employee compensation, interest, and income taxes

Suppliers, also called vendors, are those entities that provide the business with its merchandise inventory and essential services. The accounts related to supplier payments for merchandise inventory are Cost of Goods Sold, Merchandise Inventory, and Accounts Payable. Cost of Goods Sold on the income statement was $156,000. Merchandise Inventory decreased from $145,000 at December 31, 2015, to $143,000 at December 31, 2016. Accounts Payable increased from $50,000 at December 31, 2015, to $90,000 at December 31, 2016. We can calculate the cash paid for inventory as follows:

Cash paid for merchandise inventory = Cost of Goods Sold − Beginning Merchandise Inventory
+ Ending Merchandise Inventory + Beginning
Accounts Payable − Ending Accounts Payable
= $156,000 − $145,000 + $143,000 + $50,000 − $90,000
= $114,000

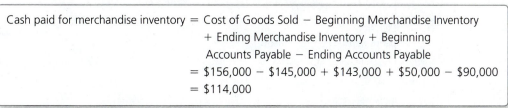

Merchandise Inventory

When a company records a debit to Merchandise Inventory, it either credits Cash or credits Accounts Payable.

12/31/2015	145,000		
Purchased	154,000	156,000	Sold
12/31/2016	143,000		

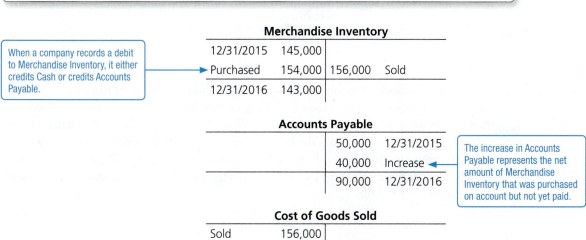

Accounts Payable

	50,000	12/31/2015
	40,000	Increase
	90,000	12/31/2016

The increase in Accounts Payable represents the net amount of Merchandise Inventory that was purchased on account but not yet paid.

Cost of Goods Sold

Sold	156,000

The accounts related to supplier payments for operating expenses are Other Operating Expense and Accrued Liabilities. Other operating expenses on the income statement were $16,000. Accrued Liabilities decreased from $10,000 at December 31, 2015, to $5,000 at December 31, 2016. Cash paid for operating expenses can be calculated as follows:

Cash paid for operating expenses = Other Operating Expense + Beginning Accrued Liabilities − Ending Accrued Liabilities
= $16,000 + $10,000 − $5,000
= $21,000

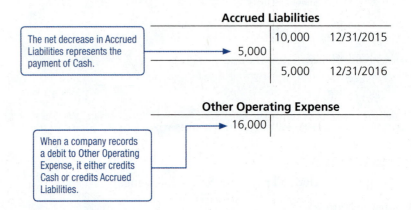

Adding them together, we get total cash paid to suppliers of $135,000 ($114,000 + $21,000).

SHOPMART, INC.
Statement of Cash Flows (Partial)
Year Ended December 31, 2016

Cash Flows from Operating Activities:		
Receipts:		
Collections from Customers	$ 269,000	
Interest Received	12,000	
Dividends Received on Investments	9,000	
Total Cash Receipts		$ 290,000
Payments:		
To Suppliers	(135,000)	

Payments to Employees

This category includes payments for salaries, wages, and other forms of employee compensation. Accrued amounts are not cash flows because they have not yet been paid. The accounts related to employee payments are Salaries and Wages Expense from the income statement and Salaries and Wages Payable from the balance sheet. Because there is not a Salaries and Wages Payable account on the balance sheet, the Salaries and Wages Expense account must represent all amounts paid in cash to employees. So, the statement of cash flows shows cash payments to employees of $56,000.

SHOPMART, INC.
Statement of Cash Flows (Partial)
Year Ended December 31, 2016

Cash Flows from Operating Activities:		
Receipts:		
Collections from Customers	$ 269,000	
Interest Received	12,000	
Dividends Received on Investments	9,000	
Total Cash Receipts		$ 290,000
Payments:		
To Suppliers	(135,000)	
To Employees	(56,000)	

Payments for Interest Expense and Income Tax Expense

These cash payments are reported separately from the other expenses. The accounts related to interest payments are Interest Expense from the income statement and Interest Payable from the balance sheet. Because there is no Interest Payable account on the balance sheet, the Interest Expense account from the income statement must represent all amounts paid in cash for interest. So, the statement of cash flows shows cash payments for interest of $15,000.

The accounts related to income tax payments are Income Tax Expense from the income statement and Income Tax Payable from the balance sheet. Because there is no Income Tax Payable account on the balance sheet, the Income Tax Expense account from the income statement must represent all amounts paid in cash for income tax. So, the statement of cash flows shows cash payments for income tax of $14,000.

SHOPMART, INC.
Statement of Cash Flows (Partial)
Year Ended December 31, 2016

Cash Flows from Operating Activities:		
Receipts:		
Collections from Customers	$ 269,000	
Interest Received	12,000	
Dividends Received on Investments	9,000	
Total Cash Receipts		$ 290,000
Payments:		
To Suppliers	(135,000)	
To Employees	(56,000)	
For Interest	(15,000)	
For Income Tax	(14,000)	
Total Cash Payments		(220,000)

Non-cash Expenses and Gains or Losses on Disposal of Long-Term Assets

Non-cash expenses and gains or losses on disposal of long-term assets are reported on the income statement but are not included in the operating activities when using the direct method. Non-cash expenses are not reported because these items do not affect cash.

Are depreciation expense and gain or loss on disposal of plant assets included in the operating activities section when using the direct method?

The cash received from the disposal of long-term assets is reported in the investing activities section, not the operating activities section.

Net Cash Provided by Operating Activities

To calculate net cash provided by operating activities using the direct method, we add all the cash receipts and cash payments described previously and find the difference. For ShopMart, total cash receipts were $290,000. Total cash payments were $220,000. So, net cash provided by operating activities is $70,000. If you refer back to the indirect method statement of cash flows shown in Exhibit C-5, you will find that it showed the same $70,000 for net cash provided by operating activities—only the method by which it was calculated was different.

The remainder of ShopMart's statement of cash flows is exactly the same as what we calculated using the indirect method. Exhibit CA-1 shows the completed statement of cash flows using the direct method for operating activities.

Exhibit CA-1 | **Statement of Cash Flows—Direct Method**

SHOPMART, INC. Statement of Cash Flows Year Ended December 31, 2016		
Cash Flows from Operating Activities:		
Receipts:		
Collections from Customers	$ 269,000	
Interest Received	12,000	
Dividends Received on Investments	9,000	
Total Cash Receipts		$ 290,000
Payments:		
To Suppliers	(135,000)	
To Employees	(56,000)	
For Interest	(15,000)	
For Income Tax	(14,000)	
Total Cash Payments		(220,000)
Net Cash Provided by Operating Activities		70,000
Cash Flows from Investing Activities:		
Cash Payment for Acquisition of Plant Assets	(310,000)	
Cash Receipt from Disposal of Plant Assets	50,000	
Net Cash Used for Investing Activities		(260,000)
Cash Flows from Financing Activities:		
Cash Receipt from Issuance of Notes Payable	90,000	
Cash Payment of Notes Payable	(10,000)	
Cash Receipt from Issuance of Common Stock	120,000	
Cash Payment for Purchase of Treasury Stock	(20,000)	
Cash Payment of Dividends	(10,000)	
Net Cash Provided by Financing Activities		170,000
Net Increase (Decrease) in Cash		(20,000)
Cash Balance, December 31, 2015		42,000
Cash Balance, December 31, 2016		$ 22,000

Try It!

8A. Big Island, Inc. began 2016 with cash of $40,000. During the year, Big Island earned revenue of $200,000 and collected $120,000 from customers. Expenses for the year totaled $160,000, of which Big Island paid $65,000 in cash to suppliers and $80,000 in cash to employees. The company received $2,000 cash for interest revenue and paid $10,000 for income taxes. Big Island also paid $35,000 to purchase equipment and a cash dividend of $15,000 to its stockholders during 2016. Prepare the company's operating activities section of the statement of cash flows for the year ended December 31, 2016. Use the direct method.

Check your answer online in MyAccountingLab or at http://www.pearsonhighered.com/Horngren.

For more practice, see Short Exercises SCA-11 through SCA-14. **My**AccountingLab

APPENDIX CB: Preparing the Indirect Statement of Cash Flows Using a Spreadsheet

HOW IS THE STATEMENT OF CASH FLOWS PREPARED USING THE INDIRECT METHOD AND A SPREADSHEET?

This appendix discussed the uses of the statement of cash flows in decision making and showed how to prepare the statement using T-accounts. The T-account approach works well as a learning device. In practice, however, most companies face complex situations. In these cases, a spreadsheet can help in preparing the statement of cash flows.

The spreadsheet starts with the beginning balance sheet and concludes with the ending balance sheet. Two middle columns—one for debit amounts and the other for credit amounts—complete the spreadsheet. These columns, labeled "Transaction Analysis," hold the data for the statement of cash flows. Accountants can prepare the statement directly from the lower part of the spreadsheet. This appendix is based on the ShopMart data used in this appendix. We illustrate this approach only with the indirect method for operating activities. This method could be used for the direct method as well.

The *indirect* method reconciles accrual basis net income to net cash provided by operating activities. Exhibit CB-1 (on the next page) is the spreadsheet for preparing the statement of cash flows by the *indirect* method. Panel A shows the transaction analysis, and Panel B gives the information to prepare the statement of cash flows.

Learning Objective 5

Prepare the statement of cash flows by the indirect method using a spreadsheet

Exhibit CB-1 | Spreadsheet for Statement of Cash Flows—Indirect Method

A	B	C	D	E	F	G
			SHOPMART, INC.			
			Spreadsheet for Statement of Cash Flows			
			Year Ended December 31, 2016			
Panel A—Balance Sheet:	**Balance 12/31/2015**		**Transaction Analysis**			**Balance 12/31/2016**
			DEBIT	**CREDIT**		
7 Cash	$ 42,000			20,000	(n)	$ 22,000
8 Accounts Receivable	73,000	(d)	17,000			90,000
9 Merchandise Inventory	145,000			2,000	(e)	143,000
10 Plant Assets	252,000	(h)	310,000	55,000	(c)	507,000
11 Accumulated Depreciation—Plant Assets	(42,000)	(c)	15,000	20,000	(b)	(47,000)
12 Total Assets	$ 470,000					$ 715,000
13						
14 Accounts Payable	50,000			40,000	(f)	90,000
15 Accured Liabilities	10,000	(g)	5,000			5,000
16 Notes Payable	80,000	(j)	10,000	90,000	(i)	160,000
17 Total Liabilities	140,000					255,000
18						
19 Common Stock, no par	250,000			120,000	(k)	370,000
20 Retained Earnings	80,000	(m)	10,000	40,000	(a)	110,000
21 Treasury Stock	0	(l)	20,000			(20,000)
22 Total Liabilities and Stockholders' Equity	$ 470,000		$ 387,000	$ 387,000		$ 715,000
23						
24 **Panel B—Statement of Cash Flows:**						
25 Cash Flows from Operating Activities:						
26 Net Income		(a)	40,000			
27 Adjustments to Reconcile Net Income to Net Cash Provided by Operating Activities:						
28 Depreciation Expense—Plant Assets		(b)	20,000			
29 Gain on Disposal of Plant Assets				10,000	(c)	
30 Increase in Accounts Receivable				17,000	(d)	
31 Decrease in Merchandise Inventory		(e)	2,000			
32 Increase in Accounts Payable		(f)	40,000			
33 Decrease in Accrued Liabilities				5,000	(g)	
34 Net Cash Provided by Operating Activities						
35 Cash Flows from Investing Activities:						
36 Cash Payment for Acquisition of Plant Assets				310,000	(h)	
37 Cash Receipt from Disposal of Plant Assets		(c)	50,000			
38 Net Cash Used for Investing Activities						
39 Cash Flows from Financing Activities:						
40 Cash Receipt from Issuance of Notes Payable		(i)	90,000			
41 Cash Payment of Notes Payable				10,000	(j)	
42 Cash Receipt from Issuance of Common Stock		(k)	120,000			
43 Cash Payment for Purchase of Treasury Stock				20,000	(l)	
44 Cash Payment of Dividends				10,000	(m)	
45 Net Cash Provided by Financing Activities						
46 Net Increase (Decrease) in Cash		(n)	20,000			
47 **Total**			$ 382,000	$ 382,000		
48						

The following is a listing of the transaction analysis provided on the spreadsheet using the indirect method:

a. Net income of $40,000 is the first operating cash inflow. Net income is entered on the spreadsheet (Panel B) as a debit to Net Income under Cash Flows from Operating Activities and as a credit to Retained Earnings on the balance sheet (Panel A).

b. Next come the adjustments to net income, starting with depreciation of $20,000— transaction (b)—which is debited to Depreciation Expense—Plant Assets and credited to Accumulated Depreciation—Plant Assets.

c. This transaction is the sale of plant assets. The $10,000 gain on the sale is entered as a credit to Gain on Disposal of Plant Assets—a subtraction from net income—under operating cash flows. This credit removes the $10,000 gain from operating activities because the cash proceeds from the sale were $50,000, not $10,000. The $50,000 sale amount is then entered on the spreadsheet under investing activities. Entry (c) is completed by crediting the plant assets' cost of $55,000 to the Plant Assets account and debiting Accumulated Depreciation—Plant Assets for $15,000.

d. Entry (d) debits Accounts Receivable for its $17,000 increase during the year. This amount is credited to Increase in Accounts Receivable under operating cash flows.

e. This entry credits Merchandise Inventory for its $2,000 decrease during the year. This amount is debited to Decrease in Merchandise Inventory under operating cash flows.

f. This entry credits Accounts Payable for its $40,000 increase during the year. Then it is debited to show as Increase in Accounts Payable under operating cash flows.

g. This entry debits Accrued Liabilities for its $5,000 decrease during the year. Then it is credited to show as Decrease in Accrued Liabilities under operating cash flows.

h. This entry debits Plant Assets for the purchase of $310,000 and credits Cash Payment for Acquisition of Plant Assets under investing cash flows.

i. This entry is represented by a credit to Notes Payable and a debit under cash flows from financing activities of $90,000 (Cash Receipt from Issuance of Notes Payable).

j. This entry is the opposite of (i). It is represented by a debit (reduction) of $10,000 to Notes Payable and a credit under Cash Flows from Financing Activities for Cash Payment of Notes Payable.

k. This entry debits Cash Receipts from Issuance of Common Stock of $120,000 under financing cash flows. The offsetting credit is to Common Stock.

l. The purchase of treasury stock debited the Treasury Stock account on the balance sheet $20,000. The corresponding cash flow entry Cash Payment for Purchase of Treasury Stock credits $20,000 to reduce cash flow.

m. The $10,000 reduction (debit) to the Retained Earnings account is the result of dividends declared and paid by the company. So, we show Cash Payment of Dividends as a credit in the financing section.

n. The final item in Exhibit CB-1 is the Net Increase (Decrease) in Cash. It is shown as a credit to Cash and a debit to Net Increase (Decrease) in Cash of $20,000.

In Panel B of Exhibit CB-1, the debits represent increases (or inflows) of cash and the credits represent decreases (or outflows). This is because debits increase Cash and credits decrease Cash.

9B. Muench, Inc.'s accountant has partially completed the spreadsheet for the statement of cash flows. Fill in the remaining missing information.

	A	B	C	D	E	F	G
1	MUENCH, INC.						
2	Spreadsheet for Statement of Cash Flows						
3	Year Ended December 31, 2016						
4							
5	**Panel A—Balance Sheet:**	Balance 12/31/2015		Transaction Analysis			Balance 12/31/2016
6				DEBIT	CREDIT		
7	Cash	$ 16,000					$ 20,000
8	Accounts Receivable	3,250					5,000
9	Plant Assets	14,000		1,000			15,000
10	Accumulated Depreciation	(100)			100		(200)
11	Total Assets	$ 33,150					$ 39,800
12							
13	Accounts Payable	5,000					3,500
14							
15	Common Stock, no par	24,150			5,850		30,000
16	Retained Earnings	4,000		5,700			6,300
17	Total Liabilities and Stockholders' Equity	$ 33,150					$ 39,800
18							
19	**Panel B—Statement of Cash Flows:**						
20	Cash Flows from Operating Activities:						
21	Net Income						
22	Adjustments to Reconcile Net Income to Net Cash Provided by Operating Activities:						
23	Depreciation Expense—Plant Assets			100			
24	Increase in Accounts Receivable						
25	Decrease in Accounts Payable						
26	Net Cash Provided by Operating Activities						
27	Cash Flows from Investing Activities:						
28	Cash Payment for Acquisition of Plant Assets				1,000		
29	Net Cash Used for Investing Activities						
30	Cash Flows from Financing Activities:						
31	Cash Receipt from Issuance of Common Stock			5,850			
32	Cash Payment of Dividends				5,700		
33	Net Cash Provided by Financing Activities						
34	Net Increase (Decrease) in Cash						
35							

Check your answer online in MyAccountingLab or at http://www.pearsonhighered.com/Horngren.

For more practice, see Short Exercise SCB-15.   MyAccountingLab

REVIEW

> ## Things You Should Know

1. What is the statement of cash flows?

- The statement of cash flows reports on a business's cash receipts and cash payments for a specific period.
- There are three basic types of cash flow activities:
  - Operating activities—Reports on activities that create revenue or expense in the entity's business
  - Investing activities—Reports cash receipts and cash payments that increase or decrease long-term assets
  - Financing activities—Includes cash receipts and cash payments involved in long-term liabilities and equity
- Non-cash investing and financing activities are not included in the statement of cash flows but appear either as a separate schedule at the bottom of the statement or in the notes to the financial statements.
- There are two ways to format operating activities on the statement of cash flows:
  - Indirect method—Starts with net income and adjusts it to net cash provided by operating activities
  - Direct method—Restates the income statement in terms of cash

2. How is the statement of cash flows prepared using the indirect method?

- **Step 1:** Complete the cash flows from operating activities section using net income and adjusting for increases or decreases in current assets (other than cash) and current liabilities. Also adjust for gains or losses on long-term assets and non-cash expenses.
- **Step 2:** Complete the cash flows from investing activities section by reviewing the long-term assets section of the balance sheet.
- **Step 3:** Complete the cash flows from financing activities section by reviewing the long-term liabilities and equity sections of the balance sheet.
- **Step 4:** Compute the net increase or decrease in cash during the year.
- **Step 5:** Prepare a separate schedule reporting any non-cash investing and financing activities.

3. How do we use free cash flow to evaluate business performance?

- Free cash flow is the amount of cash available from operating activities after paying for planned investments in long-term assets and after paying cash dividends to shareholders.
- Free cash flow = Net cash provided by operating activities − Cash payments planned for investments in long-term assets − Cash dividends.

4. How is the statement of cash flows prepared using the direct method? (Appendix CA)

- The operating activities section is the only section that differs between the direct and indirect methods.
- When using the direct method, each line item on the income statement is converted from accrual basis to cash basis.

5. **How is the statement of cash flows prepared using the indirect method and a spreadsheet? (Appendix CB)**

   • A spreadsheet can be used to help in preparing the statement of cash flows.

   • The spreadsheet helps accountants analyze the changes in balance sheet accounts.

> Summary Problem C-1

The Adams Corporation reported the following income statement for 2016 and comparative balance sheet for 2016 and 2015, along with transaction data for 2016:

ADAMS CORPORATION
Comparative Balance Sheet
December 31, 2016 and 2015

	2016	2015	Increase (Decrease)
Assets			
Current Assets:			
Cash	$ 22,000	$ 3,000	$ 19,000
Accounts Receivable	22,000	23,000	(1,000)
Merchandise Inventory	35,000	34,000	1,000
Long-term Assets:			
Plants Assets	153,200	97,200	56,000
Accumulated Depreciation—Plant Assets	(27,200)	(25,200)	(2,000)
Total Assets	$ 205,000	$ 132,000	$ 73,000
Liabilities			
Current Liabilities:			
Accounts Payable	$ 35,000	$ 26,000	$ 9,000
Accrued Liabilities	7,000	9,000	(2,000)
Income Tax Payable	10,000	10,000	0
Long-term Liabilities:			
Bonds Payable	84,000	53,000	31,000
Total Liabilities	136,000	98,000	38,000
Stockholders' Equity			
Common Stock, no par	52,000	20,000	32,000
Retained Earnings	27,000	19,000	8,000
Treasury Stock	(10,000)	(5,000)	(5,000)
Total Stockholders' Equity	69,000	34,000	35,000
Total Liabilities and Stockholders' Equity	$ 205,000	$ 132,000	$ 73,000

ADAMS CORPORATION
Income Statement
Year Ended December 31, 2016

Sales Revenue		$ 662,000
Cost of Goods Sold		560,000
Gross Profit		102,000
Operating Expenses:		
Salaries and Wages Expense	$ 46,000	
Depreciation Expense—Plant Assets	10,000	
Rent Expense	2,000	
Total Operating Expenses		58,000
Operating Income		44,000
Other Revenue and (Expenses):		
Loss on Disposal of Plant Assets	(2,000)	
Total Other Revenues and (Expenses)		(2,000)
Net Income Before Income Taxes		42,000
Income Tax Expense		16,000
Net Income		$ 26,000

Transaction data for 2016

Cash paid for purchase of equipment	$ 140,000
Cash payment of dividends	18,000
Issuance of common stock to retire bonds payable	13,000
Issuance of bonds payable to borrow cash	44,000
Cash receipt from issuance of common stock	19,000
Cash receipt from sale of equipment (Cost, $84,000; Accumulated Depreciation, $8,000)	74,000
Cash paid for purchase of treasury stock	5,000

Prepare Adams Corporation's statement of cash flows for the year ended December 31, 2016. Format cash flows from operating activities by the indirect method.

> Solution

ADAMS CORPORATION Statement of Cash Flows Year Ended December 31, 2016		
Cash Flows from Operating Activities:		
Net Income		$ 26,000
Adjustments to Reconcile Net Income to Net Cash Provided by Operating Activities:		
Depreciation Expense—Plant Assets	$ 10,000	
Loss on Disposal of Plant Assets	2,000	
Decrease in Accounts Receivable	1,000	
Increase in Merchandise Inventory	(1,000)	
Increase in Accounts Payable	9,000	
Decrease in Accrued Liabilities	(2,000)	19,000
Net Cash Provided by Operating Activities		45,000
Cash Flows from Investing Activities:		
Cash Payment for Acquisition of Plant Assets	(140,000)	
Cash Receipt from Disposal of Plant Assets	74,000	
Net Cash Used for Investing Activities		(66,000)
Cash Flows from Financing Activities:		
Cash Receipt from Issuance of Bonds Payable	44,000	
Cash Receipt from Issuance of Common Stock	19,000	
Cash Payment for Purchase of Treasury Stock	(5,000)	
Cash Payment of Dividends	(18,000)	
Net Cash Provided by Financing Activities		40,000
Net Increase (Decrease) in Cash		19,000
Cash Balance, December 31, 2015		3,000
Cash Balance, December 31, 2016		**$ 22,000**
Non-cash Investing and Financing Activities:		
Issuance of Common Stock to Retire Bonds Payable		$ 13,000
Total Non-cash Investing and Financing Activities		**$ 13,000**

Relevant T-accounts:

Plant Assets

12/31/2015	97,200		
Acquisitions	140,000	84,000	Disposals
12/31/2016	153,200		

Accumulated Depreciation—Plant Assets

		25,200	12/31/2015
Disposals	8,000	10,000	Depr. Exp.
		27,200	12/31/2016

Bonds Payable

		53,000	12/31/2015
Retirement	13,000	44,000	Issuance
		84,000	12/31/2016

Common Stock

		20,000	12/31/2015
Retirement	0	13,000	Issuance
		19,000	Issuance
		52,000	12/31/2016

Treasury Stock

12/31/2015	5,000		
Purchase	5,000	0	Disposal
12/31/2016	10,000		

Retained Earnings

		19,000	12/31/2015
		26,000	Net Income
Dividends	18,000		
		27,000	12/31/2016

> Key Terms

Cash Flows (p. C-2)

Direct Method (p. C-5)

Financing Activities (p. C-3)

Free Cash Flow (p. C-20)

Indirect Method (p. C-5)

Investing Activities (p. C-3)

Non-cash Investing and Financing Activities (p. C-4)

Operating Activities (p. C-3)

Statement of Cash Flows (p. C-2)

> Quick Check

Learning Objective 1

1. The purposes of the statement of cash flows are to
   a. evaluate management decisions.
   b. determine ability to pay debts and dividends.
   c. predict future cash flows.
   d. All of the above

Learning Objective 1

2. The main categories of cash flow activities are
   a. direct and indirect.
   b. current and long-term.
   c. non-cash investing and financing.
   d. operating, investing, and financing.

Learning Objective 1

3. Operating activities are most closely related to
   a. long-term assets.
   b. current assets and current liabilities.
   c. long-term liabilities and stockholders' equity.
   d. dividends and treasury stock.

Learning Objective 2

4. Which item does *not* appear on a statement of cash flows prepared by the indirect method?
   a. Collections from customers
   b. Depreciation expense
   c. Net income
   d. Gain on sale of land

Learning Objective 2

5. Leather Shop earned net income of $57,000 after deducting depreciation of $5,000 and all other expenses. Current assets decreased by $4,000, and current liabilities increased by $8,000. How much was Leather Shop's cash provided by operating activities (indirect method)?
   a. $40,000
   b. $66,000
   c. $48,000
   d. $74,000

Learning Objective 2

6. The Plant Assets account and Accumulated Depreciation—Plant Assets account of Star Media show the following:

Plant Assets

Beg.	100,000		
Acquisitions	428,000	52,500	Disposals
End.	475,500		

Accumulated Depreciation—Plant Assets

		20,000	12/31/2015
Disposals	10,500	34,000	Depr. Exp.
		43,500	12/31/2016

Star Media sold plant assets at an $11,000 loss. Where on the statement of cash flows should Star Media report the sale of plant assets? How much should the business report for the sale?
   a. Financing cash flows—cash receipt of $42,000
   b. Investing cash flows—cash receipt of $53,000
   c. Investing cash flows—cash receipt of $31,000
   d. Investing cash flows—cash receipt of $42,000

7. Mountain Water Corp. issued common stock of $28,000 to pay off long-term notes payable of $28,000. In what section(s) would these transactions be recorded?

Learning Objective 2

    a. Financing activities payment of note, $(28,000)

    b. Financing activities cash receipt, $28,000

    c. Non-cash investing and financing activities, $28,000

    d. Both a and b are correct.

8. Holmes, Inc. expects net cash flow from operating activities to be $160,000, and the company plans purchases of equipment of $83,000 and repurchases of stock of $24,000. What is Holmes's free cash flow?

Learning Objective 3

    a. $53,000   b. $160,000   c. $77,000   d. $83,000

9A. Maxwell Furniture Center had accounts receivable of $20,000 at the beginning of the year and $54,000 at year-end. Revenue for the year totaled $116,000. How much cash did the business collect from customers?

Learning Objective 4
Appendix CA

    a. $150,000   b. $62,000   c. $116,000   d. $82,000

10B. If accrued liabilities increased during the year, which of the following is correct when using a spreadsheet to complete the statement of cash flows (indirect method)?

Learning Objective 5
Appendix CB

    a. Increase in Accrued Liabilities would be debited

    b. Increase in Accrued Liabilities would be credited

    c. Accrued Liabilities would be debited

    d. None of the above is correct.

Check your answers at the end of the appendix.

ASSESS YOUR PROGRESS

> Review Questions

1. What does the statement of cash flows report?

2. How does the statement of cash flows help users of financial statements?

3. Describe the three basic types of cash flow activities.

4. What types of transactions are reported in the non-cash investing and financing activities section of the statement of cash flows?

5. Describe the two formats for reporting operating activities on the statement of cash flows.

6. Describe the five steps used to prepare the statement of cash flows by the indirect method.

7. Explain why depreciation expense, depletion expense, and amortization expense are added to net income in the operating activities section of the statement of cash flows when using the indirect method.

8. If a company experienced a loss on disposal of long-term assets, how would this be reported in the operating activities section of the statement of cash flows when using the indirect method? Why?

9. If current assets other than cash increase, what is the effect on cash? What about a decrease in current assets other than cash?

10. If current liabilities increase, what is the effect on cash? What about a decrease in current liabilities?

11. What accounts on the balance sheet must be evaluated when completing the investing activities section of the statement of cash flows?

12. What accounts on the balance sheet must be evaluated when completing the financing activities section of the statement of cash flows?

13. What should the net change in cash section of the statement of cash flows always reconcile with?

14. What is free cash flow, and how is it calculated?

15A. How does the direct method differ from the indirect method when preparing the operating activities section of the statement of cash flows?

16B. Why might a spreadsheet be helpful when completing the statement of cash flows?

> Short Exercises

Learning Objective 1

SC-1 Describing the purposes of the statement of cash flows

Financial statements all have a goal. The statement of cash flows does as well. Describe how the statement of cash flows helps investors and creditors perform each of the following functions:

a. Predict future cash flows.

b. Evaluate management decisions.

c. Predict the ability to make debt payments to lenders and pay dividends to stockholders.

Learning Objective 1

SC-2 Classifying items on the statement of cash flows

Cash flow items must be categorized into one of four categories. Identify each item as operating (O), investing (I), financing (F), or non-cash (N).

a. Cash purchase of merchandise inventory

b. Cash payment of dividends

c. Cash receipt from the collection of long-term notes receivable

d. Cash payment for income taxes

e. Purchase of equipment in exchange for notes payable

f. Cash receipt from the sale of land

g. Cash received from borrowing money

h. Cash receipt for interest income

i. Cash receipt from the issuance of common stock

j. Cash payment of salaries

SC-3 Classifying items on the indirect statement of cash flows

Learning Objective 2

Destiny Corporation is preparing its statement of cash flows by the *indirect* method. Destiny has the following items for you to consider in preparing the statement:

a. Increase in accounts payable

b. Payment of dividends

c. Decrease in accrued liabilities

d. Issuance of common stock

e. Gain on sale of building

f. Loss on sale of land

g. Depreciation expense

h. Increase in merchandise inventory

i. Decrease in accounts receivable

j. Purchase of equipment

Identify each item as a(n):

- Operating activity—addition to net income (O+) or subtraction from net income (O−)

- Investing activity—cash inflow (I+) or cash outflow (I−)

- Financing activity—cash inflow (F+) or cash outflow (F−)

- Activity that is not used to prepare the indirect statement of cash flows (N)

SC-4 Computing cash flows from operating activities—indirect method

Learning Objective 2

GDM Equipment, Inc. reported the following data for 2016:

Income Statement:	
Net Income	$ 44,000
Depreciation Expense	9,000
Balance Sheet:	
Increase in Accounts Receivable	9,000
Decrease in Accounts Payable	4,000

Compute GDM's net cash provided by operating activities—indirect method.

SC-5 Computing cash flows from operating activities—indirect method

Learning Objective 2

Smart Cellular accountants have assembled the following data for the year ended April 30, 2016:

Cash receipt from sale of land	$ 26,000	Net income	$ 62,000
Depreciation expense	4,000	Cash purchase of equipment	36,000
Cash payment of dividends	5,600	Decrease in current liabilities	18,000
Cash receipt from issuance of common stock	25,000	Increase in current assets other than cash	26,000

Prepare the *operating* activities section using the indirect method for Smart Cellular's statement of cash flows for the year ended April 30, 2016.

Note: Short Exercise SC-5 must be completed before attempting Short Exercise SC-6.

SC-6 Computing cash flows from investing and financing activities

Learning Objective 2

Use the data in Short Exercise SC-5 to complete this exercise. Prepare Smart Cellular's statement of cash flows using the indirect method for the year ended April 30, 2016. Assume beginning and ending Cash are $23,300 and $54,700, respectively.

Learning Objective 2

SC-7 Computing investing and financing cash flows

Stenback Media Corporation had the following income statement and balance sheet for 2016:

STENBACK MEDIA CORPORATION Income Statement Year Ended December 31, 2016	
Sales Revenue	$ 77,000
Depreciation Expense—Plant Assets	26,900
Other Expenses	48,500
Net Income	$ 1,600

STENBACK MEDIA CORPORATION Comparative Balance Sheet December 31, 2016 and 2015	2016	2015
Assets		
Current Assets:		
Cash	$ 4,900	$ 4,100
Accounts Receivable	9,100	8,100
Long-term Assets:		
Plants Assets	108,250	80,350
Accumulated Depreciation—Plant Assets	(33,250)	(6,350)
Total Assets	$ 89,000	$ 86,200
Liabilities		
Current Liabilities:		
Accounts Payable	$ 6,500	$ 4,000
Long-term Liabilities:		
Notes Payable	10,000	11,000
Total Liabilities	16,500	15,000
Stockholders' Equity		
Common Stock, no par	24,000	19,000
Retained Earnings	48,500	52,200
Total Stockholders' Equity	72,500	71,200
Total Liabilities and Stockholders' Equity	$ 89,000	$ 86,200

Requirements

1. Compute the acquisition of plant assets for Stenback Media Corporation during 2016. The business sold no plant assets during the year. Assume the company paid cash for the acquisition of plant assets.

2. Compute the payment of a long-term note payable. During the year, the business issued a $4,600 note payable.

Note: Short Exercise SC-7 must be completed before attempting Short Exercise SC-8.

SC-8 Preparing the statement of cash flows—indirect method

Learning Objective 2

Use the Stenback Media Corporation data in Short Exercise SC-7 and the results you calculated from the requirements. Prepare Stenbeck Media's statement of cash flows—indirect method—for the year ended December 31, 2016.

SC-9 Computing the change in cash; identifying non-cash transactions

Learning Objective 2

Brianna's Wedding Shops earned net income of $25,000, which included depreciation of $16,000. Brianna's acquired a $116,000 building by borrowing $116,000 on a long-term note payable.

Requirements

1. How much did Brianna's cash balance increase or decrease during the year?
2. Were there any non-cash transactions for the company? If so, show how they would be reported in the statement of cash flows.

SC-10 Computing free cash flow

Learning Objective 3

Shauna Lopez Company expects the following for 2016:

- Net cash provided by operating activities of $144,000.
- Net cash provided by financing activities of $60,000.
- Net cash used for investing activities of $84,000 (no sales of long-term assets).
- Cash dividends paid to stockholders of $10,000.

How much free cash flow does Lopez expect for 2016?

SCA-11 Preparing a statement of cash flows using the direct method

Learning Objective 4
Appendix CA

Green Bean, Inc. began 2016 with cash of $57,000. During the year, Green Bean earned revenue of $596,000 and collected $618,000 from customers. Expenses for the year totaled $433,000, of which Green Bean paid $214,000 in cash to suppliers and $209,000 in cash to employees. Green Bean also paid $146,000 to purchase equipment and a cash dividend of $56,000 to its stockholders during 2016. Prepare the company's statement of cash flows for the year ended December 31, 2016. Format operating activities by the direct method.

SCA-12 Preparing operating activities using the direct method

Learning Objective 4
Appendix CA

Miss Ella's Learning Center has assembled the following data for the year ended June 30, 2016:

Payments to suppliers	$ 118,000
Cash payment for purchase of equipment	38,000
Payments to employees	67,000
Payment of notes payable	26,000
Payment of dividends	6,500
Cash receipt from issuance of stock	15,000
Collections from customers	184,000
Cash receipt from sale of land	60,000
Cash balance, June 30, 2015	39,000

Prepare the *operating* activities section of the business's statement of cash flows for the year ended June 30, 2016, using the direct method.

Note: Short Exercise SCA-12 must be completed before attempting Short Exercise SCA-13.

Learning Objective 4
Appendix CA

SCA-13 Preparing the direct method statement of cash flows

Use the data in Short Exercise SCA-12 and your results. Prepare the business's complete statement of cash flows for the year ended June 30, 2016, using the *direct* method for operating activities.

Learning Objective 4
Appendix CA

SCA-14 Preparing the direct method statement of cash flows

White Toy Company reported the following comparative balance sheet:

WHITE TOY COMPANY Comparative Balance Sheet December 31, 2016 and 2015		
	2016	2015
Assets		
Current Assets:		
Cash	$ 17,000	$ 15,000
Accounts Receivable	58,000	47,000
Merchandise Inventory	75,000	87,000
Prepaid Expenses	2,500	1,500
Long-term Assets:		
Plants Assets, Net	228,000	183,000
Investments	79,000	90,000
Total Assets	$ 459,500	$ 423,500
Liabilities		
Current Liabilities:		
Accounts Payable	$ 45,000	$ 41,000
Salaries Payable	21,500	19,000
Accrued Liabilities	5,000	15,000
Long-term Liabilities:		
Notes Payable	66,000	70,000
Total Liabilities	137,500	145,000
Stockholders' Equity		
Common Stock, no par	41,000	37,000
Retained Earnings	281,000	241,500
Total Stockholders' Equity	322,000	278,500
Total Liabilities and Stockholders' Equity	$ 459,500	$ 423,500

Requirements

1. Compute the collections from customers during 2016 for White Toy Company. Sales Revenue totaled $136,000.

2. Compute the payments for inventory during 2016. Cost of Goods Sold was $80,000.

SCB-15 Using a spreadsheet to complete the statement of cash flows—indirect method

Learning Objective 5
Appendix CB

Companies can use a spreadsheet to complete the statement of cash flows. Each item that follows is recorded in the transaction analysis columns of the spreadsheet.

a. Net income

b. Increases in current assets (other than Cash)

c. Decreases in current liabilities

d. Cash payment for acquisition of plant assets

e. Cash receipt from issuance of common stock

f. Depreciation expense

Identify each as being recorded by a Debit or Credit in the *statement of cash flows section* of the spreadsheet.

> Exercises

EC-16 Classifying cash flow items

Learning Objective 1

Consider the following transactions:

a. Purchased equipment for $130,000 cash.

b. Issued $14 par preferred stock for cash.

c. Cash received from sales to customers of $35,000.

d. Cash paid to vendors, $17,000.

e. Sold building for $19,000 gain for cash.

f. Purchased treasury stock for $28,000.

g. Retired a notes payable with 1,250 shares of the company's common stock.

Identify the category of the statement of cash flows in which each transaction would be reported.

Learning Objective 1

EC-17 Classifying transactions on the statement of cash flows—indirect method

Consider the following transactions:

Date	Accounts and Explanation	Debit	Credit
a.	Cash	72,000	
	Common Stock		72,000
b.	Treasury Stock	16,500	
	Cash		16,500
c.	Cash	88,000	
	Sales Revenue		88,000
d.	Land	103,000	
	Cash		103,000
e.	Depreciation Expense—Equipment	6,800	
	Accumulated Depreciation—Equipment		6,800
f.	Dividends Payable	19,500	
	Cash		19,500
g.	Land	22,000	
	Notes Payable		22,000
h.	Cash	9,600	
	Equipment		9,600
i.	Bonds Payable	51,000	
	Cash		51,000
j.	Building	137,000	
	Notes Payable		137,000
k.	Loss on Disposal of Equipment	1,800	
	Accumulated Depreciation—Equipment	200	
	Equipment		2,000

Identify the category of the statement of cash flows in which each transaction would be reported.

Learning Objectives 1, 2

EC-18 Classifying items on the indirect statement of cash flows

The statement of cash flows categorizes like transactions for optimal reporting.

Identify each item as a(n):

- Operating activity—addition to net income (O+) or subtraction from net income (O−)
- Investing activity—cash inflow (I+) or cash outflow (I−)
- Financing activity—cash inflow (F+) or cash outflow (F−)
- Non-cash investing and financing activity (NIF)
- Activity that is not used to prepare the indirect statement of cash flows (N)

The *indirect* method is used to report cash flows from operating activities.

a. Loss on sale of land.

b. Acquisition of equipment by issuance of note payable.

c. Payment of long-term debt.

d. Acquisition of building by issuance of common stock.

e. Increase in Salaries Payable.

f. Decrease in Merchandise Inventory.

g. Increase in Prepaid Expenses.

h. Decrease in Accrued Liabilities.

i. Cash sale of land.

j. Issuance of long-term note payable to borrow cash.

k. Depreciation Expense.

l. Purchase of treasury stock.

m. Issuance of common stock.

n. Increase in Accounts Payable.

o. Net income.

p. Payment of cash dividend.

EC-19 Computing operating activities cash flow—indirect method

Learning Objective 2

Net Cash Prov. by Op. Act. $17,000

The records of Paramount Color Engraving reveal the following:

Net income	$ 40,000	Depreciation expense	$ 11,000
Sales revenue	47,000	Decrease in current liabilities	24,000
Loss on sale of land	5,000	Increase in current assets other than cash	15,000
Acquisition of land	39,000		

Compute cash flows from operating activities by the indirect method for year ended December 31, 2016.

EC-20 Computing operating activities cash flow—indirect method

Learning Objective 2

Net Cash Prov. by Op. Act. $71,500

The accounting records of XYZ Sales, Inc. include the following accounts:

Account	Beginning Balance	Ending Balance
Cash	$ 6,500	$ 4,000
Accounts Receivable	20,000	15,500
Merchandise Inventory	18,000	30,000
Accounts Payable	14,000	19,000

Accumulated Depreciation—Equipment				Retained Earnings			
		55,000	Jul. 1			62,000	Jul. 1
		4,000	Depr. Exp.	Dividends	19,000	70,000	Net Inc.
		59,000	Jul. 31			113,000	Jul. 31

Compute XYZ's net cash provided by (used for) operating activities during July 2016. Use the indirect method.

Learning Objective 2

Net Cash Prov. by Op. Act. $99,000

EC-21 Preparing the statement of cash flows—indirect method

The income statement of Supplements Plus, Inc. follows:

SUPPLEMENTS PLUS, INC. Income Statement Year Ended September 30, 2016		
Sales Revenue		$ 234,000
Cost of Goods Sold		91,000
Gross Profit		143,000
Operating Expenses:		
Salaries Expense	$ 55,000	
Depreciation Expense—Plant Assets	25,000	
Total Operating Expenses		80,000
Net Income Before Income Taxes		63,000
Income Tax Expense		10,000
Net Income		$ 53,000

Additional data follow:

a. Acquisition of plant assets is $121,000. Of this amount, $104,000 is paid in cash and $17,000 by signing a note payable.

b. Cash receipt from sale of land totals $26,000. There was no gain or loss.

c. Cash receipts from issuance of common stock total $30,000.

d. Payment of notes payable is $16,000.

e. Payment of dividends is $9,000.

f. From the balance sheet:

	September 30	
	2016	**2015**
Cash	$ 38,000	$ 12,000
Accounts Receivable	44,000	60,000
Merchandise Inventory	91,000	86,000
Plant Assets	201,000	80,000
Accumulated Depreciation	(35,000)	(10,000)
Land	75,000	101,000
Accounts Payable	31,000	15,000
Accrued Liabilities	20,000	26,000
Notes Payable (long-term)	17,000	16,000
Common Stock, no par	37,000	7,000
Retained Earnings	309,000	265,000

Prepare Supplements Plus's statement of cash flows for the year ended September 30, 2016, using the indirect method. Include a separate section for non-cash investing and financing activities.

EC-22 Computing cash flows for investing and financing activities

Consider the following facts for Vanilla Valley:

a. Beginning and ending Retained Earnings are $43,000 and $69,000, respectively. Net income for the period is $58,000.

b. Beginning and ending Plant Assets are $120,600 and $126,600, respectively.

c. Beginning and ending Accumulated Depreciation—Plant Assets are $18,600 and $20,600, respectively.

d. Depreciation Expense for the period is $13,000, and acquisitions of new plant assets total $27,000. Plant assets were sold at a $4,000 gain.

Requirements

1. How much are cash dividends?

2. What was the amount of the cash receipt from the sale of plant assets?

Learning Objective 2

2. Book Value on Plant Assets Sold $10,000

EC-23 Computing the cash effect

Stenback Exercise Equipment, Inc. reported the following financial statements for 2016:

Learning Objective 2

2. Payment: $6,000
4. Dividends $32,000

STENBACK EXERCISE EQUIPMENT, INC. Income Statement Year Ended December 31, 2016		
Sales Revenue		$ 711,000
Cost of Goods Sold		343,000
Gross Profit		368,000
Operating Expenses:		
Depreciation Expense	$ 51,000	
Other Operating Expenses	215,000	
Total Operating Expenses		266,000
Net Income		$ 102,000

STENBACK EXERCISE EQUIPMENT, INC.
Comparative Balance Sheet
December 31, 2016 and 2015

	2016	2015
Assets		
Current Assets:		
Cash	$ 21,000	$ 15,000
Accounts Receivable	56,000	50,000
Merchandise Inventory	84,000	88,000
Long-term Assets:		
Plants Assets	268,700	217,200
Accumulated Depreciation—Plant Assets	(41,700)	(34,200)
Investments	93,000	75,000
Total Assets	$ 481,000	$ 411,000
Liabilities		
Current Liabilities:		
Accounts Payable	$ 75,000	$ 74,000
Salaries Payable	2,000	4,000
Long-term Liabilities:		
Notes Payable	59,000	65,000
Total Liabilities	136,000	143,000
Stockholders' Equity		
Common Stock, no par	42,000	35,000
Retained Earnings	303,000	233,000
Total Stockholders' Equity	345,000	268,000
Total Liabilities and Stockholders' Equity	$ 481,000	$ 411,000

Requirements

1. Compute the amount of Stenback Exercise's acquisition of plant assets. Assume the acquisition was for cash. Stenback Exercise disposed of plant assets at book value. The cost and accumulated depreciation of the disposed asset was $43,500. No cash was received upon disposal.

2. Compute new borrowing or payment of long-term notes payable, with Stenback Exercise having only one long-term notes payable transaction during the year.

3. Compute the issuance of common stock with Stenback Exercise having only one common stock transaction during the year.

4. Compute the payment of cash dividends.

Note: Exercise EC-23 must be completed before attempting Exercise EC-24.

Learning Objective 2

EC-24 Preparing the statement of cash flows—indirect method

Net Cash Prov. by Op. Act.
$150,000

Use the Stenback Exercise Equipment data in Exercise EC-23. Prepare the company's statement of cash flows—indirect method—for the year ended December 31, 2016. Assume investments are purchased with cash.

EC-25 Identifying and reporting non-cash transactions

Learning Objective 2

Total Non-cash Inv. and
Fin. Act. $161,000

Motorcross, Inc. identified the following selected transactions that occurred during 2016:

a. Issued 850 shares of $5 par common stock for cash of $21,000.

b. Issued 5,600 shares of $5 par common stock for a building with a fair market value of $99,000.

c. Purchased new truck with a fair market value of $36,000. Financed it 100% with a long-term note.

d. Retired short-term notes of $26,000 by issuing 2,500 shares of $5 par common stock.

e. Paid long-term note of $8,500 to Bank of Tallahassee. Issued new long-term note of $17,000 to Bank of Trust.

Identify any non-cash transactions that occurred during the year, and show how they would be reported in the non-cash investing and financing activities section of the statement of cash flows.

EC-26 Analyzing free cash flow

Learning Objective 3

Use the Stenback Exercise Equipment data in Exercises EC-23 and EC-24. Stenback plans to purchase a truck for $31,000 and a forklift for $120,000 next year. In addition, it plans to pay cash dividends of $1,000. Assuming Stenback plans similar activity for 2017, what would be the amount of free cash flow?

ECA-27 Preparing operating activities cash flow—direct method

Learning Objective 4
Appendix CA

Net Cash Prov. by Op. Act. $1,000

The accounting records of Grand Auto Parts reveal the following:

Payment of salaries and wages	$ 33,000	Net income	$ 24,000
Depreciation expense	13,000	Payment of income tax	15,000
Payment of interest	14,000	Collection of dividend revenue	7,000
Payment of dividends	7,000	Payment to suppliers	57,000
Collections from customers	113,000		

Compute cash flows from operating activities using the *direct* method for the year ended December 31, 2016.

APPENDIX C

Learning Objective 4
Appendix CA

Net Cash Prov. by Op. Act. $77,000

ECA-28 Preparing the statement of cash flows—direct method

The income statement and additional data of Rolling Hills Corporation follow:

ROLLING HILLS CORPORATION Income Statement Year Ended June 30, 2016		
Sales Revenue		$ 229,000
Cost of Goods Sold		107,000
Gross Profit		122,000
Operating Expenses:		
Salaries Expense	$ 46,000	
Depreciation Expense—Plant Assets	28,000	
Advertising Expense	11,000	
Total Operating Expenses		85,000
Operating Income		37,000
Other Revenues and (Expenses):		
Dividend Revenue	10,500	
Interest Expense	(3,000)	
Total Other Revenues and (Expenses)		7,500
Net Income Before Income Taxes		44,500
Income Tax Expense		8,000
Net Income		$ 36,500

a. Collections from customers are $14,000 more than sales.

b. Dividend revenue, interest expense, and income tax expense equal their cash amounts.

c. Payments to suppliers are the sum of cost of goods sold plus advertising expense.

d. Payments to employees are $1,500 more than salaries expense.

e. Cash payment for the acquisition of plant assets is $108,000.

f. Cash receipts from sale of land total $25,000.

g. Cash receipts from issuance of common stock total $31,000.

h. Payment of long-term notes payable is $17,000.

i. Payment of dividends is $12,000.

j. Cash balance at June 30, 2015, was $28,000; at June 30, 2016, it was $24,000.

Prepare Rolling Hills Corporation's statement of cash flows for the year ended June 30, 2016. Use the *direct* method.

Learning Objective 4
Appendix CA

1. Cash Receipts from Cust.
$66,000

ECA-29 Computing cash flow items—direct method

Consider the following facts:

a. Beginning and ending Accounts Receivable are $25,000 and $27,000, respectively. Credit sales for the period total $68,000.

b. Cost of goods sold is $81,000.

c. Beginning Merchandise Inventory balance is $25,000, and ending Merchandise Inventory balance is $26,000.

d. Beginning and ending Accounts Payable are $13,000 and $10,000, respectively.

Requirements

1. Compute cash collections from customers.

2. Compute cash payments for merchandise inventory.

ECA-30 Computing cash flow items—direct method

Elite Mobile Homes reported the following in its financial statements for the year ended December 31, 2016:

<table>
<tr><th></th><th>2016</th><th>2015</th></tr>
<tr><td>Income Statement</td><td></td><td></td></tr>
<tr><td>Net Sales</td><td>$ 24,691</td><td>$ 21,555</td></tr>
<tr><td>Cost of Goods Sold</td><td>18,015</td><td>15,458</td></tr>
<tr><td>Depreciation Expense</td><td>273</td><td>229</td></tr>
<tr><td>Other Operating Expenses</td><td>4,427</td><td>4,221</td></tr>
<tr><td>Income Tax Expense</td><td>533</td><td>489</td></tr>
<tr><td>Net Income</td><td>$ 1,443</td><td>$ 1,158</td></tr>
<tr><td>Balance Sheet</td><td></td><td></td></tr>
<tr><td>Cash</td><td>$ 15</td><td>$ 11</td></tr>
<tr><td>Accounts Receivable</td><td>795</td><td>612</td></tr>
<tr><td>Merchandise Inventory</td><td>3,485</td><td>2,833</td></tr>
<tr><td>Property and Equipment, net</td><td>4,367</td><td>3,457</td></tr>
<tr><td>Accounts Payable</td><td>1,543</td><td>1,358</td></tr>
<tr><td>Accrued Liabilities</td><td>936</td><td>847</td></tr>
<tr><td>Long-term Liabilities</td><td>478</td><td>463</td></tr>
<tr><td>Common Stock, no par</td><td>675</td><td>445</td></tr>
<tr><td>Retained Earnings</td><td>5,030</td><td>3,800</td></tr>
</table>

Learning Objective 4
Appendix CA

2. Cash Paid for Merchandise Inventory $18,482
7. Dividends $213

Requirements

1. Compute the collections from customers.

2. Compute payments for merchandise inventory.

3. Compute payments of operating expenses.

4. Compute the acquisitions of property and equipment (no sales of property during 2016).

5. Compute the amount of borrowing, with Elite paying no long-term liabilities.

6. Compute the cash receipt from issuance of common stock.

7. Compute the payment of cash dividends.

ECB-31 Using a spreadsheet to prepare the statement of cash flows—indirect method

Use the Supplements Plus, Inc. data in Exercise EC-21 to prepare the spreadsheet for the 2016 statement of cash flows. Format cash flows from operating activities by the indirect method.

Learning Objective 5
Appendix CB

> Problems Group A

Learning Objectives 1, 2

2. Net Income $67,700
4. Net Cash Used by Op. Act.
$(61,250)

PC-32A Identifying the purpose and preparing the statement of cash flows—indirect method

Official Reserve Rare Coins (ORRC) was formed on January 1, 2016. Additional data for the year follow:

a. On January 1, 2016, ORRC issued no par common stock for $500,000.

b. Early in January, ORRC made the following cash payments:
1. For store fixtures, $54,000
2. For merchandise inventory, $270,000
3. For rent expense on a store building, $11,000

c. Later in the year, ORRC purchased merchandise inventory on account for $244,000. Before year-end, ORRC paid $144,000 of this accounts payable.

d. During 2016, ORRC sold 2,300 units of merchandise inventory for $225 each. Before year-end, the company collected 90% of this amount. Cost of goods sold for the year was $320,000, and ending merchandise inventory totaled $194,000.

e. The store employs three people. The combined annual payroll is $88,000, of which ORRC still owes $6,000 at year-end.

f. At the end of the year, ORRC paid income tax of $20,000. There are no income taxes payable.

g. Late in 2016, ORRC paid cash dividends of $35,000.

h. For store fixtures, ORRC uses the straight-line depreciation method, over five years, with zero residual value.

Requirements

1. What is the purpose of the statement of cash flows?

2. Prepare ORRC's income statement for the year ended December 31, 2016. Use the single-step format, with all revenues listed together and all expenses listed together.

3. Prepare ORRC's balance sheet at December 31, 2016.

4. Prepare ORRC's statement of cash flows using the indirect method for the year ended December 31, 2016.

Learning Objective 2

Net Cash Used for Inv. Act.
$(16,000)

PC-33A Preparing the statement of cash flows—indirect method

Accountants for Smithson, Inc. have assembled the following data for the year ended December 31, 2016:

	2016	2015
Current Assets:		
Cash	$ 102,700	$ 20,000
Accounts Receivable	63,500	69,500
Merchandise Inventory	85,000	80,000
Current Liabilities:		
Accounts Payable	$ 57,900	$ 56,000
Income Tax Payable	14,400	17,000

Transaction Data for 2016:

Issuance of common stock for cash	$ 42,000	Payment of notes payable	$ 42,100
Depreciation expense	25,000	Payment of cash dividends	52,000
Purchase of equipment with cash	73,000	Issuance of notes payable to borrow cash	60,000
Acquisition of land by issuing long-term notes payable	118,000		
		Gain on sale of building	4,000
Book value of building sold	53,000	Net income	69,500

Prepare Smithson's statement of cash flows using the indirect method. Include an accompanying schedule of non-cash investing and financing activities.

PC-34A Preparing the statement of cash flows—indirect method with non-cash transactions

The 2016 income statement and comparative balance sheet of McKnight, Inc. follow:

Learning Objective 2

1. Net Cash Prov. by Op. Act. $132,700

MCKNIGHT, INC.
Income Statement
Year Ended December 31, 2016

Sales Revenue		$ 441,000
Cost of Goods Sold		202,200
Gross Profit		238,800
Operating Expenses:		
Salaries Expense	$ 76,400	
Depreciation Expense—Plant Assets	14,200	
Other Operating Expenses	10,500	
Total Operating Expenses		101,100
Operating Income		137,700
Other Revenues and (Expenses):		
Interest Revenue	8,800	
Interest Expense	(21,600)	
Total Other Revenues and (Expenses)		(12,800)
Net Income Before Income Taxes		124,900
Income Tax Expense		19,500
Net Income		$ 105,400

MCKNIGHT, INC.
Comparative Balance Sheet
December 31, 2016 and 2015

	2016	2015
Assets		
Current Assets:		
Cash	$ 26,400	$ 15,100
Accounts Receivable	26,700	25,200
Merchandise Inventory	79,700	91,600
Long-term Assets:		
Plant Assets	118,510	110,310
Accumulated Depreciation—Plant Assets	(19,610)	(15,610)
Land	34,800	7,000
Total Assets	$ 266,500	$ 233,600
Liabilities		
Current Liabilities:		
Accounts Payable	$ 35,100	$ 30,500
Accrued Liabilities	28,200	30,100
Long-term Liabilities:		
Notes Payable	73,000	106,000
Total Liabilities	136,300	166,600
Stockholders' Equity		
Common Stock, no par	88,100	64,700
Retained Earnings	42,100	2,300
Total Stockholders' Equity	130,200	67,000
Total Liabilities and Stockholders' Equity	$ 266,500	$ 233,600

Additionally, McKnight purchased land of $27,800 by financing it 100% with long-term notes payable during 2016. During the year, there were no sales of land, no retirements of stock, and no treasury stock transactions. A plant asset was disposed of for $0. The cost and the accumulated depreciation of the disposed asset was $10,200. The plant acquisition was for cash.

Requirements

1. Prepare the 2016 statement of cash flows, formatting operating activities by the *indirect* method.

2. How will what you learned in this problem help you evaluate an investment?

PC-35A Preparing the statement of cash flows—indirect method, evaluating cash flows, and measuring free cash flows

Learning Objectives 2, 3

1. Net Cash Used for Inv. Act.
$(157,100)

The comparative balance sheet of Morston Educational Supply at December 31, 2016, reported the following:

	2016	2015
Current Assets:		
Cash	$ 85,400	$ 21,500
Accounts Receivable	14,800	21,500
Merchandise Inventory	63,000	59,400
Current Liabilities:		
Accounts Payable	$ 27,100	$ 26,100
Accrued Liabilities	10,400	10,900

Morston's transactions during 2016 included the following:

Payment of cash dividends	$ 20,200	Depreciation expense	$ 17,000
Purchase of equipment with cash	55,100	Purchase of building with cash	102,000
Issuance of long-term notes payable to borrow cash	47,000	Net income	59,600
Issuance of common stock for cash	114,000		

Requirements

1. Prepare the statement of cash flows of Morston Educational Supply for the year ended December 31, 2016. Use the indirect method to report cash flows from operating activities.

2. Evaluate Morston's cash flows for the year. Mention all three categories of cash flows, and give the reason for your evaluation.

3. If Morston plans similar activity for 2017, what is its expected free cash flow?

PCA-36A Preparing the statement of cash flows—direct method

**Learning Objective 4
Appendix CA**

2. Total Assets $1,177,800
3. Net Cash Prov. by Op. Act.
$356,500

Frontier Rare Coins (FRC) was formed on January 1, 2016. Additional data for the year follow:

a. On January 1, 2016, FRC issued no par common stock for $500,000.

b. Early in January, FRC made the following cash payments:
   1. For store fixtures, $51,000
   2. For merchandise inventory, $300,000
   3. For rent expense on the store building, $16,000

c. Later in the year, FRC purchased merchandise inventory on account for $239,000. Before year-end, FRC paid $139,000 of this accounts payable.

d. During 2016, FRC sold 2,900 units of merchandise inventory for $350 each. Before year-end, the company collected 90% of this amount. Cost of goods sold for the year was $270,000, and ending merchandise inventory totaled $269,000.

e. The store employs three people. The combined annual payroll is $84,000, of which FRC still owes $2,000 at year-end.

f. At the end of the year, FRC paid income tax of $20,000. There are no income taxes payable.

g. Late in 2016, FRC paid cash dividends of $39,000.

h. For store fixtures, FRC uses the straight-line depreciation method, over five years, with zero residual value.

Requirements

1. Prepare FRC's income statement for the year ended December 31, 2016. Use the single-step format, with all revenues listed together and all expenses listed together.

2. Prepare FRC's balance sheet at December 31, 2016.

3. Prepare FRC's statement of cash flows for the year ended December 31, 2016. Format cash flows from operating activities by the direct method.

Learning Objective 4
Appendix CA

1. Net Cash Prov. by Op. Act. $132,700
Collections from Cust. $439,500

PCA-37A Preparing the statement of cash flows—direct method

Use the McKnight, Inc. data from Problem PC-34A.

Requirements

1. Prepare the 2016 statement of cash flows by the direct method.

2. How will what you learned in this problem help you evaluate an investment?

Learning Objective 5
Appendix CB

Cash Pmt. of Div. $28,400
Cash Pmt. for Acq. of Land $25,600

PCB-38A Using a spreadsheet to prepare the statement of cash flows—indirect method

The 2016 comparative balance sheet and income statement of Allentown Group, Inc. follow. Allentown disposed of a plant asset at book value during 2016.

ALLENTOWN GROUP, INC. Income Statement Year Ended December 31, 2016		
Sales Revenue		$ 439,000
Cost of Goods Sold		205,300
Gross Profit		233,700
Operating Expenses:		
Salaries Expense	$ 76,600	
Depreciation Expense—Plant Assets	15,600	
Other Operating Expenses	49,800	
Total Operating Expenses		142,000
Operating Income		91,700
Other Revenues and (Expenses):		
Interest Revenue	11,700	
Interest Expense	(24,500)	
Total Other Revenues and (Expenses)		(12,800)
Net Income Before Income Taxes		78,900
Income Tax Expense		16,400
Net Income		$ 62,500

ALLENTOWN GROUP, INC.
Comparative Balance Sheet
December 31, 2016 and 2015

	2016	2015
Assets		
Current Assets:		
Cash	$ 9,000	$ 15,100
Accounts Receivable	42,300	43,300
Merchandise Inventory	97,200	93,400
Long-term Assets:		
Plant Assets	121,540	111,140
Accumulated Depreciation—Plant Assets	(20,240)	(16,840)
Land	37,600	12,000
Total Assets	$ 287,400	$ 258,100
Liabilities		
Current Liabilities:		
Accounts Payable	$ 24,800	$ 26,400
Accrued Liabilities	23,300	22,100
Long-term Liabilities:		
Notes Payable	54,000	67,000
Total Liabilities	102,100	115,500
Stockholders' Equity		
Common Stock, no par	131,300	122,700
Retained Earnings	54,000	19,900
Total Stockholders' Equity	185,300	142,600
Total Liabilities and Stockholders' Equity	$ 287,400	$ 258,100

Prepare the spreadsheet for the 2016 statement of cash flows. Format cash flows from operating activities by the indirect method. A plant asset was disposed of for $0. The cost and accumulated depreciation of the disposed asset was $12,200. There were no sales of land, no retirement of common stock, and no treasury stock transactions. Assume plant asset and land acquisitions were for cash.

> Problems Group B

PC-39B Identifying the purpose and preparing the statement of cash flows—indirect method

Learning Objectives 1, 2

Frank Rare Coins (FRC) was formed on January 1, 2016. Additional data for the year follow:

2. Net Income $521,400
3. Total Assets $1,038,400
4. Net Cash Prov. by Op. Act. $376,000

a. On January 1, 2016, FRC issued no par common stock for $450,000.

b. Early in January, FRC made the following cash payments:
   1. For store fixtures, $48,000
   2. For merchandise inventory, $260,000
   3. For rent expense on a store building, $14,000

c. Later in the year, FRC purchased merchandise inventory on account for $237,000. Before year-end, FRC paid $137,000 of this accounts payable.

d. During 2016, FRC sold 2,500 units of merchandise inventory for $400 each. Before year-end, the company collected 90% of this amount. Cost of goods sold for the year was $340,000, and ending merchandise inventory totaled $157,000.

e. The store employs three people. The combined annual payroll is $92,000, of which FRC still owes $2,000 at year-end.

f. At the end of the year, FRC paid income tax of $23,000. There was no income taxes payable.

g. Late in 2016, FRC paid cash dividends of $35,000.

h. For store fixtures, FRC uses the straight-line depreciation method, over five years, with zero residual value.

Requirements

1. What is the purpose of the statement of cash flows?

2. Prepare FRC's income statement for the year ended December 31, 2016. Use the single-step format, with all revenues listed together and all expenses listed together.

3. Prepare FRC's balance sheet at December 31, 2016.

4. Prepare FRC's statement of cash flows using the indirect method for the year ended December 31, 2016.

Learning Objective 2

PC-40B Preparing the statement of cash flows—indirect method

Accountants for Carlson, Inc. have assembled the following data for the year ended December 31, 2016:

Net Cash Prov. by Op. Act. $85,300

	2016	2015
Current Assets:		
Cash	$ 89,200	$ 18,000
Accounts Receivable	64,600	68,800
Merchandise Inventory	85,000	77,000
Current Liabilities:		
Accounts Payable	$ 57,500	$ 55,400
Income Tax Payable	14,700	16,200

Transaction Data for 2016:

Issuance of common stock for cash	$ 38,000	Payment of notes payable	$ 51,100
Depreciation expense	21,000	Payment of cash dividends	46,000
Purchase of equipment with cash	73,000	Issuance of notes payable to borrow cash	61,000
Acquisition of land by issuing long-term notes payable	122,000	Gain on sale of building	2,000
Book value of building sold	55,000	Net income	69,500

Prepare Carlson's statement of cash flows using the indirect method. Include an accompanying schedule of non-cash investing and financing activities.

PC-41B Preparing the statement of cash flows—indirect method with non-cash transactions

Learning Objective 2

1. Net Cash Prov.
by Op. Act. $132,000

The 2016 income statement and comparative balance sheet of McDonald, Inc. follow:

MCDONALD, INC. Income Statement Year Ended December 31, 2016		
Sales Revenue		$ 443,000
Cost of Goods Sold		203,200
Gross Profit		239,800
Operating Expenses:		
Salaries Expense	$ 78,400	
Depreciation Expense—Plant Assets	14,800	
Other Operating Expenses	10,300	
Total Operating Expenses		103,500
Operating Income		136,300
Other Revenues and (Expenses):		
Interest Revenue	8,300	
Interest Expense	(21,800)	
Total Other Revenues and (Expenses)		(13,500)
Net Income Before Income Taxes		122,800
Income Tax Expense		19,200
Net Income		$ 103,600

MCDONALD, INC. Comparative Balance Sheet December 31, 2016 and 2015		
	2016	2015
Assets		
Current Assets:		
Cash	$ 26,200	$ 15,100
Accounts Receivable	26,500	25,700
Merchandise Inventory	79,800	91,800
Long-term Assets:		
Plant Assets	117,240	109,480
Accumulated Depreciation—Plant Assets	(21,340)	(19,780)
Land	34,500	14,000
Total Assets	$ 262,900	$ 236,300
Liabilities		
Current Liabilities:		
Accounts Payable	$ 35,000	$ 30,000
Accrued Liabilities	28,300	30,900
Long-term Liabilities:		
Notes Payable	75,000	105,000
Total Liabilities	138,300	165,900
Stockholders' Equity		
Common Stock, no par	88,800	64,300
Retained Earnings	35,800	6,100
Total Stockholders' Equity	124,600	70,400
Total Liabilities and Stockholders' Equity	$ 262,900	$ 236,300

Additionally, McDonald purchased land of $20,500 by financing it 100% with long-term notes payable during 2016. During the year, there were no sales of land, no retirements of stock, and no treasury stock transactions. A plant asset was disposed of for $0. The cost and the accumulated depreciation of the disposed asset was $13,240. Plant asset was acquired for cash.

Requirements

1. Prepare the 2016 statement of cash flows, formatting operating activities by the *indirect* method.

2. How will what you learned in this problem help you evaluate an investment?

Learning Objectives 2, 3

1. Net Cash Used for Inv. Act.
$(156,000)

PC-42B Preparing the statement of cash flows—indirect method, evaluating cash flows, and measuring free cash flows

The comparative balance sheet of Morris Educational Supply at December 31, 2016, reported the following:

	2016	2015
Current Assets:		
Cash	$ 90,600	$ 22,500
Accounts Receivable	15,100	21,600
Merchandise Inventory	63,800	58,600
Current Liabilities:		
Accounts Payable	$ 30,600	$ 29,100
Accrued Liabilities	10,500	11,800

Morris's transactions during 2016 included the following:

Payment of cash dividends	$ 17,200	Depreciation expense	$ 17,200
Purchase of equipment with cash	55,000	Purchase of building with cash	101,000
Issuance of long-term notes payable to borrow cash	50,000	Net income	64,600
Issuance of common stock for cash	108,000		

Requirements

1. Prepare the statement of cash flows of Morris Educational Supply for the year ended December 31, 2016. Use the indirect method to report cash flows from operating activities.

2. Evaluate Morris's cash flows for the year. Mention all three categories of cash flows, and give the reason for your evaluation.

3. If Morris plans similar activity for 2017, what is its expected free cash flow?

Learning Objective 4
Appendix CA

1. Net Income $115,200
2. Total Assets $612,200
3. Collections from Cust. $464,000

PCA-43B Preparing the statement of cash flows—direct method

Official Reserve Rare Coins (ORRC) was formed on January 1, 2016. Additional data for the year follow:

a. On January 1, 2016, ORRC issued no par common stock for $450,000.

b. Early in January, ORRC made the following cash payments:
   1. For store fixtures, $49,000
   2. For merchandise inventory, $280,000
   3. For rent expense on a store building, $10,000

c. Later in the year, ORRC purchased merchandise inventory on account for $238,000. Before year-end, ORRC paid $158,000 of this accounts payable.

d. During 2016, ORRC sold 2,900 units of merchandise inventory for $200 each. Before year-end, the company collected 80% of this amount. Cost of goods sold for the year was $340,000, and ending merchandise inventory totaled $178,000.

e. The store employs three people. The combined annual payroll is $88,000, of which ORRC still owes $5,000 at year-end.

f. At the end of the year, ORRC paid income tax of $17,000. There was no income taxes payable.

g. Late in 2016, ORRC paid cash dividends of $38,000.

h. For store fixtures, ORRC uses the straight-line depreciation method, over five years, with zero residual value.

Requirements

1. Prepare ORRC's income statement for the year ended December 31, 2016. Use the single-step format, with all revenues listed together and all expenses listed together.

2. Prepare ORRC's balance sheet at December 31, 2016.

3. Prepare ORRC's statement of cash flows for the year ended December 31, 2016. Format cash flows from operating activities by the direct method.

PCA-44B Preparing the statement of cash flows—direct method

Use the McDonald data from Problem PC-41B.

Requirements

1. Prepare the 2016 statement of cash flows by the direct method.

2. How will what you learned in this problem help you evaluate an investment?

PCB-45B Using a spreadsheet to prepare the statement of cash flows—indirect method

The 2016 comparative balance sheet and income statement of Abilene Group, Inc. follow. Abilene disposed of a plant asset at book value in 2016.

Learning Objective 4
Appendix CA

1. Net Cash Prov. by Op. Act.
$132,000
Collections from Cust. $442,200

Learning Objective 5
Appendix CB

Cash Pmt. of Div. $28,900
Cash Pmt. of N/P $17,000

ABILENE GROUP, INC.
Income Statement
Year Ended December 31, 2016

Sales Revenue		$ 442,000
Cost of Goods Sold		205,200
Gross Profit		236,800
Operating Expenses:		
Salaries Expense	$ 76,800	
Depreciation Expense	15,900	
Other Operating Expenses	49,600	
Total Operating Expenses		142,300
Operating Income		94,500
Other Revenues and (Expenses):		
Interest Revenue	11,300	
Interest Expense	(24,200)	
Total Other Revenues and (Expenses)		(12,900)
Net Income Before Income Taxes		81,600
Income Tax Expense		16,600
Net Income		$ 65,000

ABILENE GROUP, INC.
Comparative Balance Sheet
December 31, 2016 and 2015

	2016	2015
Assets		
Current Assets:		
Cash	$ 10,600	$ 15,700
Accounts Receivable	41,900	43,500
Merchandise Inventory	96,300	93,100
Long-term Assets:		
Plant Assets	121,860	112,060
Accumulated Depreciation—Plant Assets	(21,060)	(17,560)
Land	39,600	14,000
Total Assets	$ 289,200	$ 260,800
Liabilities		
Current Liabilities:		
Accounts Payable	$ 25,100	$ 26,300
Accrued Liabilities	24,100	22,400
Long-term Liabilities:		
Notes Payable	44,000	61,000
Total Liabilities	93,200	109,700
Stockholders' Equity		
Common Stock, no par	140,400	131,600
Retained Earnings	55,600	19,500
Total Stockholders' Equity	196,000	151,100
Total Liabilities and Stockholders' Equity	$ 289,200	$ 260,800

Prepare the spreadsheet for the 2016 statement of cash flows. Format cash flows from operating activities by the indirect method. A plant asset was disposed of for $0. The cost and accumulated depreciation of the disposed asset was $12,400. There were no sales of land, no retirement of common stock, and no treasury stock transactions. Assume plant asset and land acquisitions were for cash.

> Continuing Problem

PC-46 Preparing the statement of cash flows—indirect method

Daniels Consulting's comparative balance sheet is shown on the next page.

DANIELS CONSULTING
Comparative Balance Sheet
December 31, 2017 and 2016

	2017	2016
Assets		
Current Assets:		
Cash	$ 1,457,524	$ 31,700
Accounts Receivable	25,700	700
Office Supplies	2,150	50
Long-term Assets:		
Plants Assets	84,800	4,800
Accumulated Depreciation—Plant Assets	(1,696)	(80)
Total Assets	$ 1,568,478	$ 37,170
Liabilities		
Current Liabilities:		
Accounts Payable	$ 7,300	$ 4,100
Salaries Payable	1,800	467
Unearned Revenue	0	1,600
Interest Payable	25,000	0
Long-term Liabilities:		
Notes Payable	500,000	0
Bonds Payable	900,000	0
Discount on Bonds Payable	(100,862)	0
Total Liabilities	1,333,238	6,167
Stockholders' Equity		
Common Stock, no par	115,240	240
Retained Earnings	120,000	30,763
Total Stockholders' Equity	235,240	31,003
Total Liabilities and Stockholders' Equity	$ 1,568,478	$ 37,170

Additional data follow:

a. Depreciation expense for the year, $1,616.

b. Daniels Consulting had no disposal of plant assets during the year. Plant assets were acquired for cash.

c. Amortization of the discount on bonds payable for the year, $11,206.

d. Daniels Consulting issued a bonds payable with a face value of $900,000, receiving cash of $787,932.

e. Net income for the year was $190,537.

f. Cash receipts from issuance of common stock totaled $115,000.

Prepare the statement of cash flows using the indirect method.

CRITICAL THINKING

> Decision Case C-1

Theater by Design and Show Cinemas are asking you to recommend their stock to your clients. Because Theater by Design and Show Cinemas earn about the same net income and have similar financial positions, your decision depends on their statement of cash flows, summarized as follows:

	Theater by Design		Show Cinemas	
Net Cash Provided by Operating Activities		$ 30,000		$ 70,000
Cash Provided by (Used for) Investing Activities:				
Purchase of Plant Assets	$ (20,000)		$ (100,000)	
Sale of Plant Assets	40,000	20,000	10,000	(90,000)
Cash Provided by (Used for) Financing Activities:				
Issuance of common stock		0		30,000
Payment of long-term debt		(40,000)		0
Net Increase (Decrease) in Cash		$ 10,000		$ 10,000

Based on their cash flows, which company looks better? Give your reasons.

> Ethical Issue C-1

Moss Exports is having a bad year. Net income is only $60,000. Also, two important overseas customers are falling behind in their payments to Moss, and Moss's accounts receivable are ballooning. The company desperately needs a loan. The Moss Exports Board of Directors is considering ways to put the best face on the company's financial statements. Moss's bank closely examines cash flow from operating activities. Daniel Peavey, Moss's controller, suggests reclassifying the receivables from the slow-paying clients as long-term. He explains to the board that removing the $80,000 increase in accounts receivable from current assets will increase net cash provided by operations. This approach may help Moss get the loan.

Requirements

1. Using only the amounts given, compute net cash provided by operations, both without and with the reclassification of the receivables. Which reporting makes Moss look better?

2. Under what condition would the reclassification of the receivables be ethical? Unethical?

> Financial Statement Case C-1

Details about a company's cash flows appear in a number of places in the annual report. Use **Starbucks Corporation's** Fiscal 2013 Annual Report to answer the following questions. Visit **http://www.pearsonhighered.com/Horngren** to view a link to Starbucks Corporation's Fiscal 2013 Annual Report.

Requirements

1. Which method does Starbucks use to report net cash flows from *operating* activities? How can you tell?

2. Starbucks earned net income during 2013. Did operations *provide* cash or *use* cash during 2013? Give the amount. How did operating cash during 2013 compare with 2012?

3. For the year ended September 29, 2013, did Starbucks pay cash dividends? If so, how much?

4. For the year ended September 29, 2013, did Starbucks use cash to purchase property, plant, and equipment? If so, how much?

MyAccountingLab   For a wealth of online resources, including exercises, problems, media, and immediate tutorial help, please visit http://www.myaccountinglab.com.

> Quick Check Answers

1. d   **2.** d   **3.** b   **4.** a   **5.** d   **6.** c   **7.** c   **8.** c   **9A.** d   **10B.** a

Appendix D
Financial Statement Analysis

What Companies Should I Invest In?

Clara Salerno misses her mom, Sylvia, a lot these days. Her mom always knew just the right words to say when Clara came to visit after a long hard day at work, and her mom's chocolate cookies always worked magic in making her feel better. Since her mom passed away six months ago, Clara has had to make a lot of decisions on her own. As executor of her mom's estate, she was responsible for helping the accountant and attorney finalize the financial details and the estate paperwork. Clara knew that once the estate was settled, she would be receiving a large amount of cash. She knew that deciding what to do with the cash would be a very important decision.

When Clara met with her financial planner, she shared her goals of paying off her student loans and other personal debt and then saving toward her retirement. She wanted to take the cash remaining after paying off her debts and invest it in the stock market. Clara was worried, though. She tried to stay current on the financial markets by reading the business section of the newspaper and listening to the financial news, but she wasn't sure how to decide which companies would be the best investment choices. Clara's financial planner advised her that there are a number of tools that she could use to evaluate companies and determine which company is more profitable. Other tools will be helpful in helping her determine trends across a period of time. Clara knew that with help from her financial planner and these tools she could make sense out of companies' financial statements and invest with a confidence that would make her mom proud.

What Are the Tools That Help Users Analyze a Business?

In this appendix, you learn about tools that allow users to see beyond the pure numbers on the financial statements and translate them into meaningful analysis. So far you have learned some of what it takes to prepare financial statements; now you will learn how to use financial statements to help manage a company effectively, make wise investments, and compare one company to another. Certified financial planners who work for companies, such as Raymond James Financial, Inc., a financial services holding company that operates a full-service brokerage and investment firm headquartered in Florida, analyze financial statements to compare a company's performance across several periods of time. This comparison helps investors determine how a company is performing over time. In addition, financial planners use another tool, called ratio analysis, to measure one company against other companies in the same industry. Whether you will be an investor, an employee, or a manager of a company, knowing how to evaluate a company's performance accurately will help you make smart business decisions.

Appendix D Learning Objectives

1. Explain how financial statements are used to analyze a business

2. Perform a horizontal analysis of financial statements

3. Perform a vertical analysis of financial statements

4. Compute and evaluate the standard financial ratios

5. Complete a corporate income statement including earnings per share (Appendix DA)

HOW ARE FINANCIAL STATEMENTS USED TO ANALYZE A BUSINESS?

In this appendix, we use what you have learned about financial statements to analyze Smart Touch Learning. We will determine if it was profitable, as well as its overall financial health.

Learning Objective 1
Explain how financial statements are used to analyze a business

Purpose of Analysis

Investors and creditors cannot evaluate a company by examining only one year's data. That is why most financial statements cover at least two periods. In fact, most financial analyses cover trends over three to five years. This appendix shows you how to use some of the analytical tools for charting a company's progress through time. These tools can be used by small business owners to measure performance, by financial analysts to analyze stock investments, by auditors to obtain an overall sense of a company's financial health, by creditors to determine credit risk, or by any other person wanting to compare financial data in relevant terms.

To accurately determine the financial performance of a company, such as Smart Touch Learning, we need to compare its performance in the following ways:

- from year to year
- with a competing company
- with the same industry as a whole

After this comparison, we will have a better idea of how to judge the company's present situation and predict what might happen in the near future.

Tools of Analysis

There are three main ways to analyze financial statements:

- Horizontal analysis provides a year-to-year comparison of a company's performance in different periods.
- Vertical analysis provides a way to compare different companies.
- Ratio analysis can be used to provide information about a company's performance. It is used most effectively to measure a company against other companies in the same industry and to denote trends within the company.

Corporate Financial Reports

Before we discuss the different tools available for financial statement analysis, let's review corporate financial reports.

Annual Reports

Publicly traded corporations have their stock listed on public stock exchanges, such as the New York Stock Exchange or the NASDAQ. They are required by the Securities and Exchange Commission (SEC) to file annual and quarterly reports (also called a *Form 10-K* and *Form 10-Q*). An **annual report** provides information about a company's financial condition. These reports help investors make informed investment decisions. A typical annual report begins with an overview of the business—including the industry the company is in, its growth strategy, and an overview of the company's brands. It also often discusses the company's competitors and the risks related to the company's business.

Annual Report

Provides information about a company's financial condition.

Management's Discussion and Analysis of Financial Condition and Results of Operations

Another part of the annual report is **management's discussion and analysis of financial condition and results of operations (MD&A)**. This section of the annual report is intended to help investors understand the results of operations and the financial condition of the company. It is important to realize that this section is written by the company and could present a biased view of the company's financial condition and results. This section of the report is the company's attempt to explain its financial statements and to discuss its performance.

The MD&A section is of interest to investors, though, because it often contains information that is not found in the financial data. Such information might include how a company is planning to spend its cash during the next year for property, plant, and equipment or whether significant changes are expected to occur that would cause revenue or expenses to increase or decrease in the future. This section often provides forward-looking information that can be useful to investors who are trying to estimate what future earnings will be for the company.

Management's Discussion and Analysis of Financial Condition and Results of Operations (MD&A)

The section of the annual report that is intended to help investors understand the results of operations and the financial condition of the company.

Report of Independent Registered Public Accounting Firm

A report of the independent registered public accounting firm (often referred to as the *auditor's report*) is included in an annual report. The audit report attests to the fairness of the presentation of the financial statements and states whether the financial statements are presented in accordance with Generally Accepted Accounting Principles (GAAP). This report is prepared by an independent external auditor who has performed an audit on the financial statements. In addition, the external auditor is responsible for assessing the effectiveness of the company's internal controls.

Most audit reports have *unqualified opinions*, which means that the financial statements are presented fairly, in all material respects. A *qualified opinion* might be issued if the financial statements include a departure from GAAP. If the auditor finds that the financial statements are not represented fairly, an *adverse opinion* would be given.

DECISIONS

Should an unqualified opinion be issued?

Patty Schneider was performing the independent audit for Drake Storage, Inc. Patty was reviewing the work that her staff auditors had completed, and she had several concerns about the company's financial statements. Patty's staff had determined that Drake had underreported its cost of goods sold in order to overstate net income. Patty had spoken to Drake Storage's audit committee and discussed her concerns. The audit committee disagreed with the accounting firm's findings. What should Patty do?

Solution

Patty's accounting firm should issue either a qualified opinion or an adverse opinion. To issue an unqualified opinion stating that the financial statements are presented fairly in all material respects would be misleading to investors and creditors. As an independent auditor, Patty's primary responsibility is to report on the fairness of the financial statements and assure the public that the financial statements are presented in accordance with GAAP. If they are not, her firm has a responsibility to issue either a qualified or adverse opinion.

Financial Statements

An annual report contains the four basic financial statements you have learned in this textbook: the balance sheet (sometimes referred to as *statement of financial position*), the income statement (or *statement of operations*), the statement of stockholders' equity, and the statement of cash flows. Corporations are required to report multiple-period information for all financial statements. For example, the **Green Mountain Coffee Roasters, Inc.** 2013 Annual Report presents financial data for the past three fiscal periods (2013, 2012, and 2011).

Notes to Financial Statements

Immediately following the financial statements are the notes to the financial statements. These notes include a summary of significant accounting policies and explanations of specific items on the financial statements. These notes are an important part of the financial statements and are often referred to by investors to understand the information included in the financial statements.

Match the different parts of the annual report with the appropriate description.

1. Includes the income statement, balance sheet, statement of stockholders' equity, and statement of cash flows.

2. Attests to the fairness of the presentation of the financial statements.

3. Includes a summary of significant accounting policies and explanations of specific items on the financial statements.

4. Is written by the company to help investors understand the results of operations and the financial condition of the company.

a. Notes to financial statements

b. Report of independent registered public accounting firm

c. Management's discussion and analysis of financial condition and results of operations (MD&A)

d. Financial statements

Check your answers online in MyAccountingLab or at http://www.pearsonhighered.com/Horngren.

For more practice, see Short Exercise SD-1. **MyAccountingLab**

HOW DO WE USE HORIZONTAL ANALYSIS TO ANALYZE A BUSINESS?

Many decisions hinge on whether the numbers—sales, expenses, and net income, for example—are increasing or decreasing. For example, have sales and other revenues risen from last year? By how much?

Sales may have increased, but considered in isolation, this fact is not very helpful. The *percentage change* in sales over time is more relative and, therefore, more helpful. For example, if a company had sales of $100,000 one year and sales increased by $50,000 the next year, that would be a significant increase. However, if the company had sales of $1 billion and sales increased by $50,000, that would not be significant. Therefore, it is often more relevant to know the percentage increase than the dollar increase.

Learning Objective 2

Perform a horizontal analysis of financial statements

Horizontal Analysis
The study of percentage changes in comparative financial statements. (Dollar amount of change / Base period amount) × 100.

The study of percentage changes in comparative financial statements is called **horizontal analysis**. Horizontal analysis compares one year to the next. Computing a percentage change in comparative statements requires two steps:

1. Compute the dollar amount of the change from the earlier period to the later period.
2. Divide the dollar amount of change by the earlier period amount. We call the earlier period the base period.

Horizontal analysis is illustrated for Smart Touch Learning as:

			Increase (Decrease)	
	2018	2017	Amount	Percentage
Net Sales	$858,000	$803,000	$55,000	6.8%

Smart Touch Learning's net sales increased by 6.8% during 2018, computed as follows:

Step 1: Compute the dollar amount of change in sales from 2017 to 2018:

$$\text{Dollar amount of change} = \text{Later period amount} - \text{Earlier period amount}$$
$$= \$858,000 - \$803,000$$
$$= \$55,000$$

Step 2: Divide the dollar amount of change by the base period amount and multiply by 100. This computes the percentage change for the period:

$$\text{Horizontal analysis \%} = (\text{Dollar amount of change} / \text{Base period amount}) \times 100$$
$$= (\$55,000 / \$803,000) \times 100$$
$$= 6.8*$$

*All percentage calculations are rounded to the nearest tenth for the rest of this appendix.

Horizontal Analysis of the Income Statement

The horizontal analysis of Smart Touch Learning's income statement is shown in Exhibit D-1. This comparative income statement reveals a significant amount of growth during 2018. Although gross profit only increased by 17.3%, Smart Touch Learning was able to trim its expenses, creating an 84.6% growth in net income.

Two items on Smart Touch Learning's income statement with the slowest growth rates are Cost of Goods Sold and Administrative Expenses. Cost of Goods Sold increased by only 0.8%, and administrative expenses decreased by 4.1%. On the bottom line, net income grew by an incredible 84.6%. That is real progress!

Exhibit D-1 | **Comparative Income Statement—Horizontal Analysis**

SMART TOUCH LEARNING Income Statement Years Ended December 31, 2018 and 2017				
			Increase (Decrease)	
	2018	**2017**	**Amount**	**Percentage**
Net Sales	$ 858,000	$ 803,000	$ 55,000	6.8%
Cost of Goods Sold	513,000	509,000	4,000	0.8
Gross Profit	345,000	294,000	51,000	17.3
Operating Expenses:				
Selling Expenses	126,000	114,000	12,000	10.5
Administrative Expenses	118,000	123,000	(5,000)	(4.1)
Total Operating Expenses	244,000	237,000	7,000	3.0
Operating Income	101,000	57,000	44,000	77.2
Other Revenues and (Expenses):				
Interest Revenue	4,000	0	4,000	—
Interest Expense	(24,000)	(14,000)	10,000	71.4
Total Other Revenues and (Expenses)	(20,000)	(14,000)	6,000	42.9
Income Before Income Taxes	81,000	43,000	38,000	88.4
Income Tax Expense	33,000	17,000	16,000	94.1
Net Income	$ 48,000	$ 26,000	$ 22,000	84.6%

Horizontal Analysis of the Balance Sheet

Horizontal analysis of Smart Touch Learning's comparative balance sheet is shown in Exhibit D-2 (on the next page). This analysis also shows growth in assets, with total assets increasing by 22.2%. Notice that both Cash and Prepaid Expenses decreased during the year, but this decrease was offset by increases in other assets.

Smart Touch Learning's liabilities also grew. Total liabilities increased by 33.0%, and Accrued Liabilities actually decreased, as indicated by the liability figure in parentheses. This is another indicator of positive growth for Smart Touch Learning.

Exhibit D-2 | **Comparative Balance Sheet—Horizontal Analysis**

SMART TOUCH LEARNING Balance Sheet December 31, 2018 and 2017				
			Increase (Decrease)	
	2018	**2017**	**Amount**	**Percentage**
Assets				
Current Assets:				
Cash and Cash Equivalents	$ 29,000	$ 32,000	$ (3,000)	(9.4)%
Accounts Receivable, Net	114,000	85,000	29,000	34.1
Merchandise Inventory	113,000	111,000	2,000	1.8
Prepaid Expenses	6,000	8,000	(2,000)	(25.0)
Total Current Assets	262,000	236,000	26,000	11.0
Long-term Investments	18,000	9,000	9,000	100.0
Property, Plant, and Equipment, Net	507,000	399,000	108,000	27.1
Total Assets	**$ 787,000**	**$ 644,000**	**$ 143,000**	**22.2%**
Liabilities				
Current Liabilities:				
Accounts Payable	$ 73,000	$ 68,000	$ 5,000	7.4
Accrued Liabilities	27,000	31,000	(4,000)	(12.9)
Notes Payable	42,000	27,000	15,000	55.6
Total Current Liabilities	142,000	126,000	16,000	12.7
Long-term Liabilities	289,000	198,000	91,000	46.0
Total Liabilities	431,000	324,000	107,000	33.0%
Stockholders' Equity				
Common Stock, no par	186,000	186,000	0	0.0%
Retained Earnings	170,000	134,000	36,000	26.9%
Total Stockholders' Equity	356,000	320,000	36,000	11.3%
Total Liabilities and Stockholders' Equity	**$ 787,000**	**$ 644,000**	**$ 143,000**	**22.2%**

Trend Analysis

Trend Analysis
A form of horizontal analysis in which percentages are computed by selecting a base period as 100% and expressing amounts for following periods as a percentage of the base period amount. (Any period amount / Base period amount) × 100.

Trend analysis is a form of horizontal analysis. Trend percentages indicate the direction a business is taking. For example, how have sales changed over a five-year period? What trend does net income show? These questions can be answered by trend analysis over a period, such as three to five years.

Trend analysis percentages are computed by selecting a base period (for example, the earliest year). The base period amounts are set equal to 100%. The amounts for each subsequent year are expressed as a percentage of the base amount. To compute trend analysis percentages, we divide each item for the following years by the base period amount and multiply by 100.

Trend % = (Any period amount / Base period amount) × 100

Assume Smart Touch Learning's Net Sales were $750,000 in 2014 and rose to $858,000 in 2018. To illustrate trend analysis, review the trend of net sales during 2014–2018. The base year is 2014, so that year's percentage is set equal to 100.

	2018	2017	2016	2015	2014
Net Sales	$ 858,000	$ 803,000	$ 780,000	$ 748,000	$ 750,000
Trend Percentages	114%	107%	104%	99.7%	100%

We want percentages for the five-year period 2014–2018. We compute these by dividing each year's net sales amount by the 2014 net sales amount and multiply by 100. For example, the trend percentage for 2015 is calculated as follows:

$$\text{Trend \%} = (\text{Any period amount} / \text{Base period amount}) \times 100$$
$$= (\$748,000 / \$750,000) \times 100$$
$$= 99.7\%$$

Notice that net sales decreased slightly in 2015, and then the rate of growth increased from 2016–2018. You can perform a trend analysis on any one or multiple item(s) you consider important. Trend analysis is widely used to predict the future health of a company.

Trend analysis and horizontal analysis are very similar, but they can be used to indicate different things for a company. **Horizontal analysis allows a company to see the percentage change from one year to the next. Trend analysis shows the percentage change from a base year forward to determine whether the trend in net sales, for example, is positive or negative over a longer period of time.**

What is the difference between horizontal analysis and trend analysis?

5. Freedom Corp. reported the following on its comparative income statement:

(In millions)	2017	2016
Revenue	$ 10,000	$ 8,000
Cost of Goods Sold	4,500	3,000

Prepare a horizontal analysis of revenues, cost of goods sold, and gross profit—both in dollar amounts and in percentages.

Check your answers online in MyAccountingLab or at http://www.pearsonhighered.com/Horngren.

For more practice, see Short Exercises SD-2 and SD-3. MyAccountingLab

HOW DO WE USE VERTICAL ANALYSIS TO ANALYZE A BUSINESS?

As you have seen, horizontal analysis and trend analysis percentages highlight changes in an item from year to year, or over *time*. But no single technique gives a complete picture of a business, so we also need vertical analysis.

Learning Objective 3
Perform a vertical analysis of financial statements

Vertical Analysis
An analysis of a financial statement that reveals the relationship of each statement item to its base amount, which is the 100% figure. (Specific item / Base amount) × 100.

Vertical analysis of a financial statement shows the relationship of each item to its base amount, which is the 100% figure. Every other item on the statement is then reported as a percentage of that base. For the income statement, net sales the base. For the balance sheet, total assets the base.

$$\text{Vertical analysis \%} = (\text{Specific item / Base amount}) \times 100$$

Vertical Analysis of the Income Statement

Exhibit D-3 shows the completed vertical analysis of Smart Touch Learning's 2018 and 2017 comparative income statement.

Exhibit D-3 | **Comparative Income Statement — Vertical Analysis**

SMART TOUCH LEARNING Income Statement Years Ended December 31, 2018 and 2017				
	2018	**Percent of Total**	**2017**	**Percent of Total**
Net Sales	$ 858,000	100.0%	$ 803,000	100.0%
Cost of Goods Sold	513,000	59.8	509,000	63.4
Gross Profit	345,000	40.2	294,000	36.6
Operating Expenses:				
Selling Expenses	126,000	14.7	114,000	14.2
Administrative Expenses	118,000	13.8	123,000	15.3
Total Operating Expenses	244,000	28.4	237,000	29.5
Operating Income	101,000	11.8	57,000	7.1
Other Revenues and (Expenses):				
Interest Revenue	4,000	0.5	0	0.0
Interest Expense	(24,000)	(2.8)	(14,000)	(1.7)
Total Other Revenues and (Expenses)	(20,000)	(2.3)	(14,000)	(1.7)
Income Before Income Taxes	81,000	9.4	43,000	5.4
Income Tax Expense	33,000	3.8	17,000	2.1
Net Income	$ 48,000	5.6%	$ 26,000	3.2%

The vertical analysis percentage for Smart Touch Learning's cost of goods sold is 59.8% of net sales (($513,000 / $858,000) × 100 = 59.8%) in 2018 and 63.4% (($509,000 / $803,000) × 100 = 63.4%) in 2017. This means that for every $1 in net sales, almost $0.60 in 2018 and approximately $0.63 in 2017 is spent on cost of goods sold.

Smart Touch Learning's net income is 5.6% of net sales in 2018 and 3.2% of net sales in 2017. That improvement from 2017 to 2018 is extremely good. Suppose under normal conditions a company's net income is 10% of revenues. A drop to 4% may cause the investors to be alarmed and sell their stock.

Vertical Analysis of the Balance Sheet

Exhibit D-4 depicts the vertical analysis of Smart Touch Learning's balance sheet. The base amount (100%) is total assets. The base amount is also total liabilities and stockholders' equity because they are exactly the same number (remember the accounting equation); in 2018, that's $787,000.

Exhibit D-4 | **Comparative Balance Sheet—Vertical Analysis**

	2018	Percent of Total	2017	Percent of Total
SMART TOUCH LEARNING Balance Sheet December 31, 2018 and 2017				
Assets				
Current Assets:				
Cash and Cash Equivalents	$ 29,000	3.7%	$ 32,000	5.0%
Accounts Receivable, Net	114,000	14.5	85,000	13.2
Merchandise Inventory	113,000	14.4	111,000	17.2
Prepaid Expenses	6,000	0.8	8,000	1.2
Total Current Assets	262,000	33.3	236,000	36.6
Long-term Investments	18,000	2.3	9,000	1.4
Property, Plant, and Equipment, Net	507,000	64.4	399,000	62.0
Total Assets	$ 787,000	100.0%	$ 644,000	100.0%
Liabilities				
Current Liabilities:				
Accounts Payable	$ 73,000	9.3%	$ 68,000	10.6%
Accrued Liabilities	27,000	3.4	31,000	4.8
Notes Payable	42,000	5.3	27,000	4.2
Total Current Liabilities	142,000	18.0	126,000	19.6
Long-term Liabilities	289,000	36.7	198,000	30.7
Total Liabilities	431,000	54.8	324,000	50.3
Stockholders' Equity				
Common Stock, no par	186,000	23.6	186,000	28.9
Retained Earnings	170,000	21.6	134,000	20.8
Total Stockholders' Equity	356,000	45.2	320,000	49.7
Total Liabilities and Stockholders' Equity	$ 787,000	100.0%	$ 644,000	100.0%

The vertical analysis of Smart Touch Learning's balance sheet reveals several interesting things:

- Current assets make up 33.3% of total assets in 2018 and 36.6% of total assets in 2017. This is typical for most companies with current assets representing close to 30% of total assets.
- Total liabilities are 54.8% of total assets in 2018, increasing slightly from 2017, 50.3%.
- Stockholders' equity makes up 45.2% of total assets in 2018 and 49.7% of total assets in 2017. The percentage share of total assets was nearly equally distributed between total liabilities and total equity for both years.

Common-Size Statements

Horizontal analysis and vertical analysis provide much useful data about a company. As we have seen, Smart Touch Learning's percentages depict a very successful company. But the data apply only to one business.

Common-Size Statement
A financial statement that reports only percentages (no dollar amounts).

Dollar Value Bias
The bias one sees from comparing numbers in absolute (dollars) rather than relative (percentage) terms.

To compare Smart Touch Learning to another company, we can use a common-size statement. A **common-size statement** reports only percentages—the same percentages that appear in a vertical analysis. By only reporting percentages, it removes dollar value bias when comparing one company to another company. **Dollar value bias** is the bias one sees from comparing numbers in absolute (dollars) rather than relative (percentage) terms. For us, $1 million seems like a large number. For some large companies, it is immaterial.

We could prepare common-size statements for Smart Touch Learning from year to year; however, we will start by preparing common-size income statements for Smart Touch Learning and Learning School, another fictitious company, both of which compete in the same industry. Which company earns a higher percentage of revenues as profits for its shareholders? Exhibit D-5 gives both companies' common-size income statements for 2018 so that we can compare them on a relative, not absolute, basis.

Exhibit D-5 | **Common-Size Income Statement—Smart Touch Learning Versus Learning School**

SMART TOUCH LEARNING Versus LEARNING SCHOOL Common-Size Income Statement Year Ended December 31, 2018		
	Smart Touch Learning	**Learning School**
Net Sales	100.0%	100.0%
Cost of Goods Sold	59.8	36.3
Gross Profit	40.2	63.7
Operating Expenses:		
Selling Expenses	14.7	21.8
Administrative Expenses	13.8	7.3
Total Operating Expenses	28.4	29.1
Operating Income	11.8	34.6
Other Revenues and (Expenses):		
Interest Revenue	0.5	11.5
Interest Expense	(2.8)	(10.3)
Total Other Revenues and (Expenses)	(2.3)	1.2
Income Before Income Taxes	9.4	35.8
Income Tax Expense	3.8	12.3
Net Income	**5.6%**	**23.5%**

Exhibit D-5 shows that Learning School was more profitable than Smart Touch Learning in 2018. Learning School's gross profit percentage is 63.7%, compared with Smart Touch Learning's 40.2%. This means that Learning School is earning more gross profit from every dollar of revenue than Smart Touch Learning is earning. And, most importantly, Learning School's percentage of net income to revenues is 23.5%. That means almost one-fourth of Learning School's revenues result in profits for the company's stockholders. Smart Touch Learning's percentage of net income to revenues, on the other hand, is 5.6%, significantly lower than Learning School's. Smart Touch Learning's lower net income is directly attributable to its larger percentage of cost of goods sold to net sales. Smart Touch Learning's cost of goods sold represents 59.8% of net sales, whereas Learning School's cost of goods sold is only 36.3%.

Benchmarking

Benchmarking is the practice of comparing a company with other leading companies. It often uses the common-size percentages in a graphical manner to highlight differences. There are two main types of benchmarks in financial statement analysis: benchmarking against a key competitor and benchmarking against the industry average.

Benchmarking
The practice of comparing a company with other leading companies.

Benchmarking Against a Key Competitor

Exhibit D-5 uses a key competitor, Learning School, to compare Smart Touch Learning's profitability. The two companies compete in the same industry, so Learning School serves as an ideal benchmark for Smart Touch Learning. The charts in Exhibit D-6 highlight the profitability difference between the companies. Focus on the segments of the graphs showing net income. Learning School is clearly more profitable than Smart Touch Learning.

Exhibit D-6 | Graphical Analysis of Common-Size Income Statement—Smart Touch Learning Versus Learning School

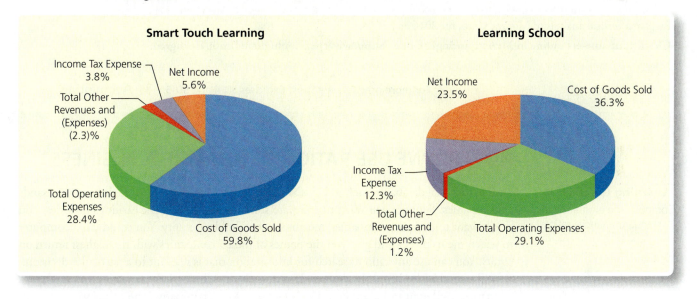

Benchmarking Against the Industry Average

The industry average can also serve as a very useful benchmark for evaluating a company. An industry comparison would show how Smart Touch Learning is performing alongside the average for the e-learning industry. *Annual Statement Studies*, published by the Risk Management Association, provides common-size statements for most industries. To compare Smart Touch Learning to the industry average, we would simply insert the industry-average common-size income statement in place of Learning School in Exhibit D-5.

As you are taking classes toward your degree, how do you know how quickly you can complete your studies? If you knew the average credit hours taken each semester was 12 credit hours, then 12 credit hours would be your benchmark. Comparing the number of classes you take to the average of 12 credit hours a semester is the same concept as benchmarking. Maybe you are taking 15 credit hours a semester. Then you'd be completing your degree faster than the average student. Maybe you take only 3 credit hours in the spring so you can work a part-time job. Then you'd be completing classes at a slower pace than average.

Try It!

6. Monroe Corp. reported the following amounts on its balance sheet at December 31, 2016 and 2015:

	2016	2015
Cash and Receivables	$ 35,000	$ 40,000
Merchandise Inventory	20,000	15,000
Property, Plant, and Equipment, Net	80,000	60,000
Total Assets	$ 135,000	$ 115,000

Prepare a vertical analysis of Monroe Corp. for 2016 and 2015.

Check your answers online in MyAccountingLab or at http://www.pearsonhighered.com/Horngren.

For more practice, see Short Exercises SD-4 and SD-5.   MyAccountingLab

HOW DO WE USE RATIOS TO ANALYZE A BUSINESS?

Learning Objective 4

Compute and evaluate the standard financial ratios

Online financial databases, such as LexisNexis and the Dow Jones, provide data on thousands of companies. Suppose you want to compare some companies' recent earnings histories. You might want to compare companies' returns on stockholders' equity. You could use a computer to search the databases and give you the names of the 20 companies with the highest return on equity. You can use any ratio to search for information that is relevant to a particular decision.

Remember, however, that no single ratio tells the whole picture of any company's performance. Different ratios explain different aspects of a company. The ratios we discuss in this appendix may be classified and used for the following purposes:

- Evaluating the ability to pay current liabilities
- Evaluating the ability to sell merchandise inventory and collect receivables
- Evaluating the ability to pay long-term debt
- Evaluating profitability
- Evaluating stock as an investment

We will use the comparative income statement and balance sheet of Smart Touch Learning, shown in Exhibit D-7, to discuss the ratios that can be used to evaluate a company. Let's begin by discussing ratios that can be used to evaluate a company's ability to pay its current liabilities.

Exhibit D-7 | **Comparative Financial Statements**

SMART TOUCH LEARNING Balance Sheet December 31, 2018 and 2017	2018	2017
Assets		
Current Assets:		
Cash and Cash Equivalents	$ 29,000	$ 32,000
Accounts Receivable, Net	114,000	85,000
Merchandise Inventory	113,000	111,000
Prepaid Expenses	6,000	8,000
Total Current Assets	262,000	236,000
Long-term Investments	18,000	9,000
Property, Plant, and Equipment, Net	507,000	399,000
Total Assets	$ 787,000	$ 644,000
Liabilities		
Current Liabilities:		
Accounts Payable	$ 73,000	$ 68,000
Accrued Liabilities	27,000	31,000
Notes Payable	42,000	27,000
Total Current Liabilities	142,000	126,000
Long-term Liabilities	289,000	198,000
Total Liabilities	431,000	324,000
Stockholders' Equity		
Common Stock, no par	186,000	186,000
Retained Earnings	170,000	134,000
Total Stockholders' Equity	356,000	320,000
Total Liabilities and Stockholders' Equity	$ 787,000	$ 644,000

SMART TOUCH LEARNING Income Statement Years Ended December 31, 2018 and 2017	2018	2017
Net Sales	$ 858,000	$ 803,000
Cost of Goods Sold	513,000	509,000
Gross Profit	345,000	294,000
Operating Expenses:		
Selling Expenses	126,000	114,000
Administrative Expenses	118,000	123,000
Total Operating Expenses	244,000	237,000
Operating Income	101,000	57,000
Other Revenues and (Expenses):		
Interest Revenue	4,000	0
Interest Expense	(24,000)	(14,000)
Total Other Revenues and (Expenses)	(20,000)	(14,000)
Income Before Income Taxes	81,000	43,000
Income Tax Expense	33,000	17,000
Net Income	$ 48,000	$ 26,000

Evaluating the Ability to Pay Current Liabilities

Determining a company's working capital is a good starting place to evaluate a company's ability to pay its current liabilities. **Working capital** measures the ability to meet short-term obligations with current assets. Working capital is defined as follows:

Working Capital
A measure of a business's ability to meet its short-term obligations with its current assets. Current assets – Current liabilities.

> Working capital = Current assets – Current liabilities

Smart Touch Learning's working capital at December 31, 2018 and 2017, is calculated as follows:

> Working capital = Current assets – Current liabilities
> 2018: $262,000 – $142,000 = $120,000
> 2017: $236,000 – $126,000 = $110,000

Smart Touch Learning's working capital is positive, indicating that the company has more current assets than current liabilities, but additional information would be helpful. Three additional decision tools based on working capital are the current ratio, cash ratio, and acid-test ratio.

Current Ratio

Current Ratio

Measures the company's ability to pay current liabilities from current assets. Total current assets / Total current liabilities.

The most widely used ratio is the **current ratio**, which is calculated as the total current assets divided by total current liabilities. The current ratio measures a company's ability to pay its current liabilities with its current assets.

The current ratios of Smart Touch Learning, at December 31, 2018 and 2017, along with the average for the industry, are as follows:

$$\text{Current ratio} = \frac{\text{Total current assets}}{\text{Total current liabilities}}$$

$$2018: \frac{\$262,000}{\$142,000} = 1.85$$

$$2017: \frac{\$236,000}{\$126,000} = 1.87$$

$$\text{Industry average} = 0.60$$

A high current ratio indicates that the business has sufficient current assets to maintain normal business operations. Compare Smart Touch Learning's current ratio of 1.85 for 2018 with the industry average of 0.60.

What is an acceptable current ratio? The answer depends on the industry. The norm for companies in most industries is around 1.50, as reported by the Risk Management Association. Smart Touch Learning's current ratio of 1.85 is strong. Keep in mind that we would not want to see a current ratio that is too high, say 2.5. This would indicate that the company is too liquid and, therefore, is not using its assets effectively. For example, the company may need to reduce merchandise inventory levels so as not to tie up available resources.

ETHICS

Should the debt be reclassified?

Victor Brannon, senior accountant for Moose Corporation, was preparing the latest financial ratios. He knew that the ratios were watched carefully by Moose Corporation's lenders due to strict loan agreements that required the corporation to maintain a minimum current ratio of 1.5. Victor knew that the past quarter's financial ratios would not meet the lenders' requirements. His boss, Cara Romano, suggested that Victor classify a note payable due in 11 months as a long-term liability. What should Victor do? What would you do?

Solution

Assets and liabilities are classified as current if they will be used or settled within one year or the operating cycle, whichever is longer. The classification between current and long-term is clear. Victor should not classify the note payable as a long-term liability. It should be classified as current even though the corporation will not meet the lenders' requirements.

Cash Ratio

Cash Ratio

A measure of a company's ability to pay current liabilities from cash and cash equivalents: (Cash + Cash equivalents) / Total current liabilities.

Cash is an important part of every business. Without an adequate supply of available cash, businesses cannot continue to operate. Businesses, therefore, monitor cash very carefully. One measure that can be used to calculate a company's liquidity is the cash ratio. The **cash ratio** helps to determine a company's ability to meet its short-term obligations and is calculated as cash plus cash equivalents divided by total current liabilities.

Notice that the cash ratio includes cash and cash equivalents. As a reminder, cash equivalents are highly liquid investments that can be converted into cash in three months or less. Examples of cash equivalents are money-market accounts and investments in U.S. government securities.

The cash ratios of Smart Touch Learning, at December 31, 2018 and 2017, along with the average for the industry are as follows:

$$\text{Cash ratio} = \frac{\text{Cash} + \text{Cash equivalents}}{\text{Total current liabilities}}$$

$$2018: \frac{\$29,000}{\$142,000} = 0.20$$

$$2017: \frac{\$32,000}{\$126,000} = 0.25$$

$$\text{Industry average} = 0.40$$

The cash ratio has decreased slightly from 2017 to 2018 due to a decrease in available cash and cash equivalents and an increase in total current liabilities. This ratio is the most conservative valuation of liquidity because it looks at only cash and cash equivalents, leaving out other current assets such as merchandise inventory and accounts receivable. Notice that for both years, the cash ratio was below 1.0. Having a cash ratio below 1.0 is a good thing. A cash ratio above 1.0 might signify that the company has an unnecessarily large amount of cash supply. This cash could be used to generate higher profits or be distributed as dividends to stockholders. However, a very low ratio doesn't send a strong message to investors and creditors that the company has the ability to repay its short-term debt.

Acid-Test (or Quick) Ratio

The **acid-test ratio** (sometimes called the *quick ratio*) tells us whether a company can pay all its current liabilities if they came due immediately. That is, could the company pass the acid test? The acid-test ratio is a more stringent measure than the current ratio, but it is not as stringent as the cash ratio.

To compute the acid-test ratio, we add cash and cash equivalents, short-term investments (those that may be sold in the next 12 months or the business operating cycle, whichever is longer), and net current receivables (accounts and notes receivable, net of allowances) and divide this sum by total current liabilities. Merchandise inventory and prepaid expenses are *not* included in the acid-test ratio because they are the least-liquid current assets. Smart Touch Learning's acid-test ratios for 2018 and 2017 follow:

Acid-Test Ratio
The ratio of the sum of cash, cash equivalents, short-term investments, and net current receivables to total current liabilities. The ratio tells whether the entity can pay all its current liabilities if they came due immediately. (Cash including cash equivalents + Short-term investments + Net current receivables) / Total current liabilities.

$$\text{Acid-test ratio} = \frac{\text{Cash including cash equivalents} + \text{Short-term investments} + \text{Net current receivables}}{\text{Total current liabilities}}$$

$$2018: \frac{\$29,000 + \$0 + \$114,000}{\$142,000} = 1.01$$

$$2017: \frac{\$32,000 + \$0 + \$85,000}{\$126,000} = 0.93$$

$$\text{Industry average} = 0.46$$

The company's acid-test ratio improved during 2018 and is significantly better than the industry average. The norm for the acid-test ratio ranges from 0.20 for shoe retailers to 1.20 for manufacturers of equipment, as reported by the Risk Management Association. An acid-test ratio of 0.90 to 1.00 is acceptable in most industries.

Evaluating the Ability to Sell Merchandise Inventory and Collect Receivables

In this section, we discuss five ratios that measure a company's ability to sell merchandise inventory and collect receivables.

Inventory Turnover

Inventory Turnover
Measures the number of times a company sells its average level of merchandise inventory during a period. Cost of goods sold / Average merchandise inventory.

The **inventory turnover** ratio measures the number of times a company sells its average level of merchandise inventory during a year. A high rate of turnover indicates ease in selling merchandise inventory; a low rate indicates difficulty. A value of 4 means that the company sold its average level of merchandise inventory four times—once every three months—during the year.

To compute inventory turnover, we divide cost of goods sold by the average merchandise inventory for the period. We use the cost of goods sold—not sales—because both cost of goods sold and inventory are stated *at cost*. Sales at *retail* are not comparable with merchandise inventory at *cost*.

Smart Touch Learning's inventory turnover for 2018 is as follows:

$$\text{Inventory turnover} = \frac{\text{Cost of goods sold}}{\text{Average merchandise inventory}}$$

$$2018: \frac{\$513,000}{[(\$111,000 + \$113,000)/2]} = 4.58$$

$$\text{Industry average} = 27.70$$

Cost of goods sold comes from the income statement (Exhibit D-7). Average merchandise inventory is figured by adding the beginning merchandise inventory of $111,000 to the ending inventory of $113,000 and dividing by 2. (See the balance sheet, Exhibit D-7. Remember that 2017's ending balances become 2018's beginning balances.)

Inventory turnover varies widely with the nature of the business. For example, most manufacturers of farm machinery have an inventory turnover close to three times a year. In contrast, companies that remove natural gas from the ground hold their merchandise inventory for a very short period of time and have an average turnover of 30. Smart Touch Learning's turnover of 4.58 times a year means, on average, the company has enough inventory to handle sales for almost 80 days (365 / 4.58 times). This is very low for its industry, which has an average turnover of 27.70 times per year. This ratio has identified an area in which Smart Touch Learning needs to improve.

Days' Sales in Inventory

Days' Sales in Inventory
Measures the average number of days that inventory is held by a company. 365 days / Inventory turnover.

Another key measure is the **days' sales in inventory** ratio. This measures the average number of days merchandise inventory is held by the company. Smart Touch Learning's days' sales in inventory for 2018 is as follows:

$$\text{Days' sales in inventory} = \frac{365 \text{ days}}{\text{Inventory turnover}}$$

$$2018: \frac{365 \text{ days}}{4.58} = 79.7 \text{ days}$$

$$\text{Industry average} = 13 \text{ days}$$

Days' sales in inventory varies widely, depending on the business. Smart Touch Learning's days' sales in inventory is 79.7 days—too high for its industry, which has an average days' sales in inventory ratio of only 13 days. This ratio has identified an area in which Smart Touch Learning needs to improve. Smart Touch Learning should focus on reducing average merchandise inventory held. By decreasing average merchandise inventory, the company can increase inventory turnover and lower the average days' sales in merchandise inventory. Smart Touch Learning will also be able to reduce its merchandise inventory storage and insurance costs as well as reduce the risk of holding obsolete merchandise inventory.

Gross Profit Percentage

Gross profit (sometimes called *gross margin*) is net sales minus the cost of goods sold. Merchandisers strive to increase the **gross profit percentage** (also called the *gross margin percentage*). This ratio measures the profitability of each net sales dollar above the cost of goods sold and is computed as gross profit divided by net sales revenue.

> **Gross Profit Percentage**
> Measures the profitability of each sales dollar above the cost of goods sold. Gross profit / Net sales revenue.

The gross profit percentage is one of the most carefully watched measures of profitability. It reflects a business's ability to earn a profit on the merchandise inventory. The gross profit earned on merchandise inventory must be high enough to cover the remaining operating expenses and to earn net income. A small increase in the gross profit percentage from last year to this year may signal an important rise in income. Conversely, a small decrease from last year to this year may signal trouble.

Smart Touch Learning's gross profit percentage for 2018 is as follows:

$$\text{Gross profit percentage} = \frac{\text{Gross profit}}{\text{Net sales revenue}}$$

$$2018: \frac{\$345,000}{\$858,000} = 0.402 = 40.2\%$$

$$\text{Industry average} = 43\%$$

Gross profit percentage varies widely, depending on the business. Smart Touch Learning's gross profit percentage is 40.2%, which is slightly lower than the industry average of 43%. This ratio has identified an area in which Smart Touch Learning needs to improve. To increase gross profit percentage, Smart Touch Learning needs to decrease the cost of the merchandise inventory and/or increase revenue (selling price). Additionally, addressing Smart Touch Learning's inventory turnover issues will probably help Smart Touch Learning to increase its gross profit percentage.

Accounts Receivable Turnover Ratio

The **accounts receivable turnover ratio** measures the number of times the company collects the average receivables balance in a year. The higher the ratio, the faster the cash collections. However, a receivable turnover that is too high may indicate that credit is too tight, causing the loss of sales to good customers. To compute accounts receivable turnover, we divide net credit sales (assuming all Smart Touch Learning's sales from Exhibit D-7 are on account) by average net accounts receivable.

> **Accounts Receivable Turnover Ratio**
> A ratio that measures the number of times the company collects the average accounts receivable balance in a year. Net credit sales / Average net accounts receivable.

Smart Touch Learning's accounts receivable turnover ratio for 2018 is computed as follows:

$$\text{Accounts receivable turnover ratio} = \frac{\text{Net credit sales}}{\text{Average net accounts receivable}}$$

$$2018: \frac{\$858,000}{[(\$85,000 + \$114,000)/2]} = 8.6$$

$$\text{Industry average} = 29.1$$

Net credit sales, assumed to equal net sales, comes from the income statement (Exhibit D-7). Average net accounts receivable is figured by adding the beginning Accounts

Receivable of $85,000 to the ending Accounts Receivable of $114,000 and dividing by 2. (See the balance sheet, Exhibit D-7.)

Smart Touch Learning's accounts receivable turnover ratio of 8.6 times per year is much slower than the industry average of 29.1. Why the difference? Smart Touch Learning is a fairly new business that sells to established people who pay their accounts over time. Further, this turnover coincides with the lower-than-average inventory turnover. So, Smart Touch Learning may achieve a higher accounts receivable turnover by increasing its inventory turnover ratio.

Days' Sales in Receivables

Days' Sales in Receivables
The ratio of average net accounts receivable to one day's sales. The ratio tells how many days it takes to collect the average level of accounts receivable. 365 days / Accounts receivable turnover ratio.

Days' sales in receivables, also called the *collection period*, indicates how many days it takes to collect the average level of receivables and is computed as 365 days divided by the accounts receivable turnover ratio. The number of days in average accounts receivable should be close to the number of days customers are allowed to make payment. The shorter the collection period, the more quickly the organization can use its cash. The longer the collection period, the less cash is available for operations.

To compute this ratio for Smart Touch Learning for 2018, we divide 365 days by the accounts receivable turnover ratio we previously calculated:

$$\text{Days' Sales in Receivables} = \frac{365 \text{ days}}{\text{Accounts receivable turnover ratio}}$$

$$2018: \frac{365 \text{ days}}{8.6} = 42.4 \text{ days}$$

$$\text{Industry average} = 25 \text{ days}$$

Smart Touch Learning's ratio tells us that 42.4 average days' sales remain in Accounts Receivable and need to be collected. The company's days' sales in receivables ratio is much higher (worse) than the industry average of 25 days. Smart Touch Learning might give its customers a longer time to pay, such as 45 days versus 30 days. Alternatively, Smart Touch Learning's credit department may need to review the criteria it uses to evaluate individual customers' credit. Without the customers' good paying habits, the company's cash flow would suffer.

Evaluating the Ability to Pay Long-Term Debt

The ratios discussed so far yield insight into current assets and current liabilities. They help us measure ability to sell merchandise inventory, collect receivables, and pay current liabilities. Most businesses also have long-term debt. Three key indicators of a business's ability to pay long-term liabilities are the debt ratio, the debt to equity ratio, and the times-interest-earned ratio.

Debt Ratio

Debt Ratio
Shows the proportion of assets financed with debt. Total liabilities / Total assets.

The relationship between total liabilities and total assets—called the **debt ratio**—shows the proportion of assets financed with debt and is calculated by dividing total liabilities by total assets. If the debt ratio is 100%, then all the assets are financed with debt. A debt ratio of 50% means that half the assets are financed with debt, and the other half are financed by the owners of the business. The higher the debt ratio, the higher the company's financial risk. The debt ratio can be used to evaluate a business's ability to pay its debts.

The debt ratios for Smart Touch Learning at the end of 2018 and 2017 follow:

$$\text{Debt ratio} = \frac{\text{Total liabilities}}{\text{Total assets}}$$

$$2018: \frac{\$431,000}{\$787,000} = 0.548 = 54.8\%$$

$$2017: \frac{\$324,000}{\$644,000} = 0.503 = 50.3\%$$

$$\text{Industry average} = 69\%$$

Both total liabilities and total asset amounts are from the balance sheet, presented in Exhibit D-7. Smart Touch Learning's debt ratio in 2018 of 54.8% is not very high. The Risk Management Association reports that the average debt ratio for most companies ranges from 57% to 67%, with relatively little variation from company to company. Smart Touch Learning's debt ratio indicates a fairly low-risk position compared with the industry average debt ratio of 69%.

Debt to Equity Ratio

The relationship between total liabilities and total equity—called the **debt to equity ratio**—shows the proportion of total liabilities relative to total equity. Thus, this ratio measures financial leverage. If the debt to equity ratio is greater than 1, then the company is financing more assets with debt than with equity. If the ratio is less than 1, then the company is financing more assets with equity than with debt. The higher the debt to equity ratio, the greater the company's financial risk.

The debt to equity ratios for Smart Touch Learning at the end of 2018 and 2017 follow:

$$\text{Debt to equity ratio} = \frac{\text{Total liabilities}}{\text{Total equity}}$$

$$2018: \frac{\$431,000}{\$356,000} = 1.21$$

$$2017: \frac{\$324,000}{\$320,000} = 1.01$$

$$\text{Industry average} = 2.23$$

Smart Touch Learning's debt to equity ratio in 2018 of 1.21 is not very high. Smart Touch Learning's debt to equity ratio indicates a fairly low-risk position compared with the industry average debt to equity ratio of 2.23.

Times-Interest-Earned Ratio

The debt ratio and debt to equity ratio say nothing about the ability to pay interest expense. Analysts and investors use the **times-interest-earned ratio** to evaluate a business's ability to pay interest expense. This ratio measures the number of times earnings before interest and taxes (EBIT) can cover (pay) interest expense. This ratio is also called the *interest-coverage ratio*. A high times-interest-earned ratio indicates a business's ease in paying interest expense; a low ratio suggests difficulty. The times-interest-earned ratio is calculated as EBIT (Net income + Income tax expense + Interest expense) divided by interest expense.

Debt to Equity Ratio
A ratio that measures the proportion of total liabilities relative to total equity. Total liabilities / Total equity.

Times-Interest-Earned Ratio
Evaluates a business's ability to pay interest expense. (Net income + Income tax expense + Interest expense) / Interest expense.

Calculation of Smart Touch Learning's times-interest-earned ratio follows:

$$\text{Times-interest-earned ratio} = \frac{\text{Net income} + \text{Income tax expense} + \text{Interest expense}}{\text{Interest expense}}$$

$$2018: \frac{\$48,000 + \$33,000 + \$24,000}{\$24,000} = 4.38$$

$$2017: \frac{\$26,000 + \$17,000 + \$14,000}{\$14,000} = 4.07$$

$$\text{Industry average} = 7.80$$

The company's times-interest-earned ratios of 4.38 for 2018 and 4.07 for 2017 are significantly lower than the industry average of 7.80 times, but it is slightly better than the ratio for the average U.S. business. The norm for U.S. business, as reported by the Risk Management Association, falls in the range of 2.0 to 3.0. When you consider Smart Touch Learning's debt ratio and its times-interest-earned ratio, Smart Touch Learning appears to have little difficulty paying its liabilities.

Evaluating Profitability

The fundamental goal of business is to earn a profit. Ratios that measure profitability often are reported in the business press. Let's examine five profitability measures.

Profit Margin Ratio

Profit Margin Ratio
A profitability measure that shows how much net income is earned on every dollar of net sales. Net income / Net sales.

The **profit margin ratio** shows the percentage of each net sales dollar earned as net income. In other words, the profit margin ratio shows how much net income a business earns on every $1.00 of sales. This ratio focuses on the profitability of a business and is calculated as net income divided by net sales.

Smart Touch Learning's profit margin ratio follows:

$$\text{Profit margin ratio} = \frac{\text{Net income}}{\text{Net sales}}$$

$$2018: \frac{\$48,000}{\$858,000} = 0.056 = 5.6\%$$

$$2017: \frac{\$26,000}{\$803,000} = 0.032 = 3.2\%$$

$$\text{Industry average} = 1.7\%$$

Both net income and net sales amounts are from the income statement presented in Exhibit D-7. Companies strive for a high profit margin. The higher the profit margin, the more sales dollars end up as profit. The increase in Smart Touch Learning's profit margin ratio from 2017 to 2018 is significant and identifies the company as more successful than the average e-learning providers, whose profit margin ratio is 1.7%.

Rate of Return on Total Assets

Rate of Return on Total Assets
A ratio that measures the success a company has in using its assets to earn income. (Net income + Interest expense) / Average total assets.

The **rate of return on total assets** measures a company's success in using assets to earn a profit. There are two ways that a company can finance its assets:

• Debt—A company can borrow cash from creditors to purchase assets. Creditors earn interest on the money that is loaned.

• Equity—A company receives cash or other assets from stockholders. Stockholders invest in the company and hope to receive a return on their investment.

Rate of return on total assets is calculated by adding interest expense to net income and dividing by average total assets. Interest expense is added back to net income to determine the real return on the assets regardless of the corporation's financing choices (debt or equity).

Computation of the rate of return on total assets ratio for Smart Touch Learning follows:

$$\text{Rate of return on total assets} = \frac{\text{Net income} + \text{Interest expense}}{\text{Average total assets}}$$

$$2018: \frac{\$48,000 + \$24,000}{[(\$644,000 + \$787,000) / 2]} = 0.101 = 10.1\%$$

$$\text{Industry average} = 6.0\%$$

Net income and interest expense come from the income statement (Exhibit D-7). Average total assets is figured by adding the beginning total assets of $644,000 to the ending total assets of $787,000 and dividing by 2. (See the balance sheet, Exhibit D-7.) Smart Touch Learning's rate of return on total assets ratio of 10.1% is much better than the industry average of 6.0%.

Asset Turnover Ratio

The **asset turnover ratio** measures the amount of net sales generated for each average dollar of total assets invested. This ratio measures how well a company is using its assets to generate sales revenues. To compute this ratio, we divide net sales by average total assets.

Smart Touch Learning's 2018 asset turnover ratio is as follows:

$$\text{Asset turnover ratio} = \frac{\text{Net sales}}{\text{Average total assets}}$$

$$2018: \frac{\$858,000}{[(\$644,000 + \$787,000) / 2]} = 1.20 \text{ times}$$

$$\text{Industry average} = 3.52 \text{ times}$$

Asset Turnover Ratio
Measures how efficiently a business uses its average total assets to generate sales. Net sales / Average total assets.

Smart Touch Learning's asset turnover ratio of 1.20 is much lower than the industry average of 3.52 times, indicating that Smart Touch Learning is generating less net sales for each average dollar of total assets invested. Recall that Smart Touch Learning's gross profit percentage was lower than the industry's also. Normally, companies with high gross profit percentages will have low asset turnover. Companies with low gross profit percentages will have high asset turnover ratios. This is another area in which Smart Touch Learning's management must consider options to increase sales and decrease its average total assets to improve this ratio.

Rate of Return on Common Stockholders' Equity

A popular measure of profitability is **rate of return on common stockholders' equity**, often shortened to *return on equity*. This ratio shows the relationship between net income available to common stockholders and their average common equity invested in the company. The rate of return on common stockholders' equity shows how much income is earned for each $1 invested by the common shareholders.

To compute this ratio, we first subtract preferred dividends from net income to get net income available to the common stockholders. (Smart Touch Learning does not have any preferred stock issued, so preferred dividends are zero.) Then we divide net income available to common stockholders by average common stockholders' equity during the year. Common equity is total stockholders' equity minus preferred equity. Average

Rate of Return on Common Stockholders' Equity
Shows the relationship between net income available to common stockholders and their average common equity invested in the company. (Net income – Preferred dividends) / Average common stockholders' equity.

common stockholders' equity is the average of the beginning and ending common stock-holders' equity balances.

The 2018 rate of return on common stockholders' equity for Smart Touch Learning follows:

$$\text{Rate of return on common stockholders' equity} = \frac{\text{Net income} - \text{Preferred dividends}}{\text{Average common stockholders' equity}}$$

$$2018: \frac{\$48,000 - \$0}{[(\$320,000 + \$356,000)/2]} = 0.142 = 14.2\%$$

Industry average = 10.5%

Smart Touch Learning's rate of return on common stockholders' equity of 14.2% is higher than its rate of return on total assets of 10.1%. This difference results from borrowing at one rate—say, 8%—and investing the money to earn a higher rate, such as the firm's 14.2% return on equity. This practice is called **trading on the equity**, or using *leverage*. It is directly related to the debt ratio. The higher the debt ratio, the higher the leverage. Companies that finance operations with debt are said to *leverage* their positions.

During good times, leverage increases profitability. But leverage can have a negative impact on profitability as well. Therefore, leverage is a double-edged sword, increasing profits during good times but compounding losses during bad times. Compare Smart Touch Learning's rate of return on common stockholders' equity with the industry average of 10.5%. Once again, Smart Touch Learning is performing much better than the average company in its industry. A rate of return on common stockholders' equity of 15% to 20% year after year is considered good in most industries. At 14.2%, Smart Touch Learning is doing well.

Earnings per Share (EPS)

Earnings per share (EPS) is perhaps the most widely quoted of all financial statistics. EPS is the only ratio that must appear on the financial statements. Earnings per share reports the amount of net income (loss) for each share of the company's *outstanding common stock*. Earnings per share is calculated as net income minus preferred dividends divided by the weighted average number of common shares outstanding. Preferred dividends are subtracted from net income because the preferred stockholders have the first claim to dividends. The computation for the weighted average number of common shares outstanding is covered in advanced accounting courses. For simplicity, we will determine earnings per share on the average number of shares outstanding, calculated as the beginning balance plus ending balance divided by two.

FASB requires that earnings per share appear on the income statement. Corporations report a separate EPS figure for each element of income, which is shown in more detail in Appendix DA at the end of this appendix.

Smart Touch Learning's EPS for 2018 and 2017 follow. (Note that Smart Touch Learning had 10,000 shares of common stock outstanding throughout both years.)

Trading on the Equity
Earning more income on borrowed money than the related interest expense, thereby increasing the earnings for the owners of the business.

Earnings per Share (EPS)
Amount of a company's net income (loss) for each share of its outstanding common stock. (Net income − Preferred dividends) / Weighted average number of common shares outstanding.

$$\text{Earnings per share} = \frac{\text{Net income} - \text{Preferred dividends}}{\text{Weighted average number of common shares outstanding}}$$

$$2018: \frac{\$48,000 - \$0}{10,000 \text{ shares}} = \$4.80 \text{ / share}$$

$$2017: \frac{\$26,000 - \$0}{10,000 \text{ shares}} = \$2.60 \text{ / share}$$

Industry average = $9.76 / share

Smart Touch Learning's EPS increased significantly in 2018 (by almost 85%). Its stockholders should not expect this big a boost in EPS every year. Most companies strive to increase EPS by 10% to 15% annually, and leading companies do so. But even the most successful companies have an occasional bad year. EPS for the industry at $9.76 is a little more than twice Smart Touch Learning's 2018 EPS. Therefore, Smart Touch Learning needs to work on continuing to increase EPS by increasing its net income so that it is more competitive with other companies in its industry.

Evaluating Stock as an Investment

Investors purchase stock to earn a return on their investment. This return consists of two parts: (1) gains (or losses) from selling the stock at a price above (or below) purchase price and (2) dividends. The ratios we examine in this section help analysts evaluate stock investments.

Price/Earnings Ratio

The **price/earnings ratio** is the ratio of the market price of a share of common stock to the company's earnings per share. The price/earnings ratio shows the market price of $1 of earnings. This ratio, abbreviated P/E, appears in many print or online stock listings and measures the value that the stock market places on a company's earnings.

Calculations for the P/E ratios of Smart Touch Learning follow. These market prices of common stock for real companies can be obtained from a financial Web site, a stockbroker, or the company's Web site. The market price for Smart Touch Learning's common stock was $60 at the end of 2018 and $35 at the end of 2017. The earnings per share values were calculated immediately before the P/E ratio.

$$\text{Price/earnings ratio} = \frac{\text{Market price per share of common stock}}{\text{Earnings per share}}$$

$$2018: \frac{\$60 \text{ per share}}{\$4.80 \text{ per share}} = 12.50$$

$$2017: \frac{\$35 \text{ per share}}{\$2.60 \text{ per share}} = 13.46$$

$$\text{Industry average} = 17.79$$

Smart Touch Learning's P/E ratio for 2018 of 12.50 means that the company's stock is selling at 12.5 times one year's earnings. Smart Touch Learning would like to see this ratio increase in future years in order to be more in line with the industry average P/E of 17.79.

Dividend Yield

Dividend yield is the ratio of annual dividends per share to the stock's market price per share. This ratio measures the percentage of a stock's market value that is returned annually as dividends to shareholders. *Preferred* stockholders, who invest primarily to receive dividends, pay special attention to dividend yield.

Price/Earnings Ratio
The ratio of the market price of a share of common stock to the company's earnings per share. Measures the value that the stock market places on $1 of a company's earnings. Market price per share of common stock / Earnings per share.

Dividend Yield
Ratio of annual dividends per share of stock to the stock's market price per share. Measures the percentage of a stock's market value that is returned annually as dividends to stockholders. Annual dividend per share / Market price per share.

Assume Smart Touch Learning paid annual cash dividends of $1.20 per share of common stock in 2018 and $1.00 in 2017. As noted previously, market prices of the company's common stock were $60 in 2018 and $35 in 2017. The firm's dividend yields on common stock follow:

$$\text{Dividend yield} = \frac{\text{Annual dividend per share}}{\text{Market price per share}}$$

$$2018: \frac{\$1.20 \text{ per share}}{\$60 \text{ per share}} = 0.020 = 2.0\%$$

$$2017: \frac{\$1.00 \text{ per share}}{\$35 \text{ per share}} = 0.029 = 2.9\%$$

Industry average = 3.6%

> In this calculation, we are determining the dividend yield for common stock. Dividend yield can also be calculated for preferred stock.

An investor who buys Smart Touch Learning's common stock for $60 can expect to receive 2.0% of the investment annually in the form of cash dividends. The industry, however, is paying out 3.6% annually. An investor might be willing to accept lower dividends (cash now) if the stock's market price is growing (cash later when the stock is sold).

Dividend Payout

Dividend Payout
The ratio of dividends declared per common share relative to the earnings per share of the company. Annual dividend per share / Earnings per share.

Dividend payout is the ratio of annual dividends declared per common share relative to the earnings per share of the company. This ratio measures the percentage of earnings paid annually to common shareholders as cash dividends.

Recall that Smart Touch Learning paid annual cash dividends of $1.20 per share of common stock in 2018 and $1.00 in 2017. Earnings per share were calculated as $4.80 per share for 2018 and $2.60 for 2017. So, Smart Touch Learning's dividend payout yields are as follows:

$$\text{Dividend payout} = \frac{\text{Annual dividend per share}}{\text{Earnings per share}}$$

$$2018: \frac{\$1.20 \text{ per share}}{\$4.80 \text{ per share}} = 0.25 = 25\%$$

$$2017: \frac{\$1.00 \text{ per share}}{\$2.60 \text{ per share}} = 0.38 = 38\%$$

Industry average = 63%

Smart Touch Learning's dividend payout ratios of 25% in 2018 and 38% in 2017 are less than the industry average of 63%. Smart Touch Learning, being a fairly new company, might be retaining more of its earnings for growth and expansion. An investor who buys

Smart Touch Learning's common stock may predict annual cash dividends to be about 25% of earnings, based on the 2018 dividend payout ratio. This investor would want to see higher market prices and higher asset turnover for Smart Touch Learning in the future for Smart Touch Learning to stay competitive.

Red Flags in Financial Statement Analyses

Analysts look for *red flags* in financial statements that may signal financial trouble. Recent accounting scandals highlight the importance of these red flags. The following conditions may reveal that the company is too risky.

- **Movement of sales, merchandise inventory, and receivables.** Sales, merchandise inventory, and receivables generally move together. Increased sales lead to higher receivables and may require more merchandise inventory (or higher inventory turnover) to meet demand. Unexpected or inconsistent movements among sales, merchandise inventory, and receivables make the financial statements look suspect.

- **Earnings problems.** Has net income decreased significantly for several years in a row? Did the company report net income in previous years but now is reporting net loss? Most companies cannot survive losses year after year.

- **Decreased cash flow.** Cash flow validates net income. Is net cash flow from operating activities consistently lower than net income? If so, the company is in trouble. Are the sales of plant assets a major source of cash? If so, the company may face a cash shortage.

- **Too much debt.** How does the company's debt ratio compare to that of major competitors? If the debt ratio is too high, the company may be unable to pay its debts.

- **Inability to collect receivables.** Are days' sales in receivables growing faster than for competitors? If so, a cash shortage may be looming.

- **Buildup of merchandise inventories.** Is inventory turnover too slow? If so, the company may be unable to sell goods, or it may be overstating merchandise inventory.

Do any of these red flags apply to Smart Touch Learning from the analyses we did in the appendix? Although the financial statements depict a strong and growing company, the analysis pointed out several areas of weakness for Smart Touch Learning that include low inventory turnover, low accounts receivable turnover, low gross profit margin, low times interest earned, low asset turnover, and low earnings per share. Smart Touch Learning should continue to carefully monitor its financial statements as it continues to grow. Exhibit D-8 (on the next page) summarizes the financial ratios that you have learned in this appendix.

Exhibit D-8 | **Using Ratios in Financial Statement Analysis**

Ratio	Computation	Information Provided
Evaluating the ability to pay current liabilities:		
Working capital	Current assets − Current liabilities	A business's ability to meet its short-term obligations with its current assets.
Current ratio	$\dfrac{\text{Total current assets}}{\text{Total current liabilities}}$	The company's ability to pay current liabilities from current assets.
Cash ratio	$\dfrac{\text{Cash + Cash equivalents}}{\text{Total current liabilities}}$	The company's ability to pay current liabilities from cash and cash equivalents.
Acid-test ratio	$\dfrac{\text{Cash including cash equivalents + Short-term investments + Net current receivables}}{\text{Total current liabilities}}$	The company's ability to pay all its current liabilities if they came due immediately.
Evaluating the ability to sell merchandise inventory and collect receivables:		
Inventory turnover	$\dfrac{\text{Cost of goods sold}}{\text{Average merchandise inventory}}$	The number of times a company sells its average level of merchandise inventory during a period.
Days' sales in inventory	$\dfrac{\text{365 days}}{\text{Inventory turnover}}$	The average number of days that inventory is held by a company.
Gross profit percentage	$\dfrac{\text{Gross profit}}{\text{Net sales revenue}}$	The profitability of each sales dollar above the cost of goods sold.
Accounts receivable turnover ratio	$\dfrac{\text{Net credit sales}}{\text{Average net accounts receivable}}$	The number of times the company collects the average receivables balance in a year.
Days' sales in receivables	$\dfrac{\text{365 days}}{\text{Accounts receivable turnover ratio}}$	The number of days' sales it takes to collect the average level of receivables.

Exhibit D-8 | Continued

Ratio	Computation	Information Provided
Evaluating the ability to pay long-term debt:		
Debt ratio	$\dfrac{\text{Total liabilities}}{\text{Total assets}}$	The proportion of assets financed with debt.
Debt to equity ratio	$\dfrac{\text{Total liabilities}}{\text{Total equity}}$	The proportion of total liabilities relative to total equity.
Times-interest-earned ratio	$\dfrac{\text{Net income} + \text{Income tax expense} + \text{Interest expense}}{\text{Interest expense}}$	A business's ability to pay interest expense.
Evaluating profitability:		
Profit margin ratio	$\dfrac{\text{Net income}}{\text{Net sales}}$	How much net income is earned on every dollar of net sales.
Rate of return on total assets	$\dfrac{\text{Net income} + \text{Interest expense}}{\text{Average total assets}}$	The success a company has in using its assets to earn income.
Asset turnover ratio	$\dfrac{\text{Net sales}}{\text{Average total assets}}$	How efficiently a business uses its average total assets to generate sales.
Rate of return on common stockholders' equity	$\dfrac{\text{Net income} - \text{Preferred dividends}}{\text{Average common stockholders' equity}}$	The relationship between net income available to common stockholders and their average common equity invested in the company.
Earnings per share	$\dfrac{\text{Net income} - \text{Preferred dividends}}{\text{Weighted average number of common shares outstanding}}$	Amount of a company's net income (loss) for each share of its outstanding common stock.
Evaluating stock as an investment:		
Price/earnings ratio	$\dfrac{\text{Market price per share of common stock}}{\text{Earnings per share}}$	The value the stock market places on $1 of a company's earnings.
Dividend yield	$\dfrac{\text{Annual dividend per share}}{\text{Market price per share}}$	The percentage of a stock's market value that is returned annually as dividends to stockholders.
Dividend payout	$\dfrac{\text{Annual dividend per share}}{\text{Earnings per share}}$	Ratio of dividends declared per common share relative to the earnings per share of the company.

The financial statements of Ion Corporation include the following items:

	Current Year	Preceding Year
Balance Sheet:		
Cash	$ 6,000	$ 8,000
Short-term Investments	4,400	10,700
Net Accounts Receivable	21,600	29,200
Merchandise Inventory	30,800	27,600
Prepaid Expenses	6,000	3,600
Total Current Assets	68,800	79,100
Total Current Liabilities	53,200	37,200
Income Statement:		
Net Sales Revenue	$ 184,800	
Cost of Goods Sold	126,000	

Compute the following ratios for the current year:

7. Current ratio
8. Acid-test ratio
9. Inventory turnover
10. Gross profit percentage

Check your answers online in MyAccountingLab or at http://www.pearsonhighered.com/Horngren.

For more practice, see Short Exercises SD-6 through SD-12. MyAccountingLab

APPENDIX DA: The Corporate Income Statement

HOW IS THE COMPLETE CORPORATE INCOME STATEMENT PREPARED?

Learning Objective 5

Complete a corporate income statement including earnings per share

A corporation's income statement includes some unique items that do not often apply to smaller businesses. These unique items are listed after determining the corporation's income from continuing operations. We will review the fictitious company Kevin's Vintage Guitars, Inc.'s income statement for year ended December 31, 2016, shown in Exhibit DA-1, to illustrate these items.

Exhibit DA-1 | **Kevin's Vintage Guitars, Inc.—Income Statement**

KEVIN'S VINTAGE GUITARS, INC.
Income Statement
Year Ended December 31, 2016

Net Sales	$ 500,000	Continuing Operations
Cost of Goods Sold	240,000	
Gross Profit	260,000	
Operating Expenses	181,000	
Operating Income	79,000	
Other Revenues and (Expenses):		
Gain on Sale of Equipment	11,000	
Income Before Income Taxes	90,000	
Income Tax Expense	36,000	
Income from Continuing Operations	54,000	
Discontinued Operations (less applicable tax of $14,000)	21,000	Special Items
Income Before Extraordinary Items	75,000	
Extraordinary Loss (less applicable tax saving of $8,000)	(12,000)	
Net Income	**$ 63,000**	
Earnings per Share of Common Stock (20,000 shares outstanding):		
Income from Continuing Operations	$ 2.70	
Income from Discontinued Operations	1.05	
Income Before Extraordinary Items	3.75	Earnings per Share
Extraordinary Loss	(0.60)	
Net Income	**$ 3.15**	

Continuing Operations

In Exhibit DA-1, the first section reports continuing operations. This part of the business should continue from period to period. Income from continuing operations, therefore, helps investors make predictions about future earnings. We may use this information to predict that Kevin's Vintage Guitars, Inc. may earn approximately $54,000 next year.

The continuing operations of Kevin's Vintage Guitars, Inc. include two items that warrant explanation:

- Kevin's Vintage Guitars had a gain on the sale of equipment, which is outside the company's core business of selling vintage guitars. This is why the gain is reported in the "other" category—separately from Kevin's Vintage Guitars's operating income.

- Income tax expense of $36,000 is subtracted to arrive at income from continuing operations. Kevin's Vintage Guitars's income tax rate is 40% ($90,000 × 0.40 = $36,000).

After continuing operations, an income statement may include two distinctly different gains and losses: discontinued operations and extraordinary items.

Discontinued Operations

Most corporations engage in several lines of business. For example, General Motors Company is best known for its automobiles, but it also has a financing company and leasing subsidiary called General Motors Financial Company, Inc.

Each identifiable division of a company is called a segment of the business. A company may sell a segment of its business. For example, General Motors Company sold its financing company (GMAC) but continued its automobile segment. The disposal of the financing segment would be reported as discontinued operations for General Motors Company.

Financial analysts are always keeping tabs on companies they follow and predict companies' net income. Most analysts do not include the results of discontinued operations in financial analysis because the discontinued segments will not be around in the future. The income statement reports information on the segments that have been sold under the heading Discontinued Operations. In our example, income from discontinued operations of $35,000 is taxed at 40% and is reported as shown in Exhibit DA-1. A loss on discontinued operations is reported similarly, but with a subtraction for the income tax *savings* on the loss (the tax savings reduces the loss).

Gains and losses on the normal sale of plant assets are *not* reported as discontinued operations. Instead, they are reported as "Other Revenues and (Expenses)" among continuing operations because companies dispose of old plant assets and equipment more frequently than business segments.

Extraordinary Items

Extraordinary gains and losses, also called *extraordinary items*, are both unusual and infrequent. GAAP defines *infrequent* as an event that is not expected to recur in the foreseeable future, considering the environment in which the company operates. Losses from natural disasters (floods, earthquakes, and tornadoes) and the taking of company assets by a foreign government (expropriation) could be considered to be extraordinary items. They are reported separately from continuing operations because of their infrequent and unusual nature.

Extraordinary items are reported along with their income tax effect. During 2016, Kevin's Vintage Guitars lost $20,000 of inventory in a flood. This flood loss reduced both Kevin's Vintage Guitars's income and its income tax. The tax effect decreases the net amount of Kevin's Vintage Guitars's loss the same way income tax reduces net income. An extraordinary loss can be reported along with its tax effect, as follows:

Extraordinary Flood Loss	$ (20,000)
Less: Income Tax Savings ($20,000 × 40%)	8,000
Extraordinary Flood Loss, Net of Tax	$ (12,000)

Trace this item to the income statement in Exhibit DA-1. An extraordinary gain is reported the same as a loss—net of the income tax effect. The following items do *not* qualify as extraordinary:

- Gains and losses on the sale of plant assets
- Losses due to lawsuits
- Losses due to employee labor strikes
- Natural disasters that occur frequently in the area (such as hurricanes in Florida)

These gains and losses fall outside the business's central operations, so they are reported on the income statement as other gains and losses, but they aren't extraordinary. One example for Kevin's Vintage Guitars is the gain on sale of equipment reported in the Other Revenues and (Expenses) section, as part of income from continuing operations in Exhibit DA-1.

Earnings per Share

The final segment of a corporate income statement reports the company's earnings per share, abbreviated as EPS. A company that reports a discontinued operation or an extraordinary item must report earnings per share for each of these line items either on the face of the income statement (as shown in Exhibit DA-1) or in the notes to the financial statements.

11A. Rocky Corporation's accounting records include the following items, listed in no particular order, at December 31, 2016:

Other Revenues and (Expenses)	$ (6,000)	Extraordinary Loss	$ 2,800
Net Sales	70,800	Cost of Goods Sold	29,200
Gain on Discontinued Operations	4,800	Operating Expenses	22,000

The income tax rate for Rocky Corporation is 30%. Prepare Rocky's income statement for the year ended December 31, 2016. Omit earnings per share. Use a multi-step format.

Check your answers online in MyAccountingLab or at http://www.pearsonhighered.com/Horngren.

For more practice, see Short Exercises SDA-13 and SDA-14. **My**AccountingLab

REVIEW

> Things You Should Know

1. How are financial statements used to analyze a business?

- There are three main ways to analyze financial statements:
  - Horizontal analysis
  - Vertical analysis
  - Ratio analysis
- Annual reports provide information about a company's financial condition and include the following:
  - Management's discussion and analysis of financial condition and results of operations (MD&A)
  - Report of independent registered public accounting firm
  - Financial statements
  - Notes to the financial statements

2. **How do we use horizontal analysis to analyze a business?**

   - Horizontal analysis is the study of percentage changes in comparative financial statements. It compares one year to the next. (Dollar amount of change / Base period amount) $\times$ 100.

   - Trend analysis is a form of horizontal analysis in which percentages are computed by selecting a base year as 100% and expressing the amounts for following periods as a percentage of the base period amount. (Any period amount / Base period amount) $\times$ 100.

3. **How do we use vertical analysis to analyze a business?**

   - Vertical analysis reveals the relationship of each statement item to its base amount, which is the 100% figure. (Specific item / Base amount) $\times$ 100.

     - For the income statement, net sales is the base.

     - For the balance sheet, total assets is the base.

   - Common-size statements are financial statements that report only percentages—the same percentages that appear in vertical analysis.

   - Benchmarking is the practice of comparing a company with other leading companies.

4. **How do we use ratios to analyze a business?**

   - Ratios can be used to evaluate a company's:

     - ability to pay current liabilities

     - ability to sell merchandise inventory and collect receivables

     - ability to pay long-term debt

     - profitability

     - stock as an investment

   - Exhibit D-8 summarizes common ratios that can be used to analyze a business.

5. **How is the complete corporate income statement prepared? (Appendix DA)**

   - A corporation's income statement includes the following unique items listed after determining the calculation for income for continuing operations:

     - Discontinued operations—a segment of a business that has been discontinued

     - Extraordinary items—items that are both unusual and infrequent

   - Earnings per share must be reported either on the face of the income statement or in the notes to the financial statements.

> Summary Problem D-1

Kimball Corporation makes iPod covers and has the following comparative income statement for years ended December 31, 2017 and 2016:

KIMBALL CORPORATION Income Statement Years Ended December 31, 2017 and 2016		
	2017	2016
Revenues:		
Net Sales	$ 300,000	$ 250,000
Other Revenues	0	1,000
Total Revenues	300,000	251,000
Expenses:		
Cost of Goods Sold	214,200	170,000
Engineering, Selling, and Administrative Expenses	54,000	48,000
Interest Expense	6,000	5,000
Income Tax Expense	9,000	3,000
Other Expenses	2,700	0
Total Expenses	285,900	226,000
Net Income	$ 14,100	$ 25,000

Requirements

Perform a horizontal analysis and a vertical analysis of Kimball Corporation. State whether 2017 was a good year or a bad year, and give your reasons.

> Solution

KIMBALL CORPORATION Income Statement Years Ended December 31, 2017 and 2016				
			Increase (Decrease)	
	2017	2016	Amount	Percentage
Revenues:				
Net Sales	$ 300,000	$ 250,000	$ 50,000	20.0%
Other Revenues	0	1,000	(1,000)	—
Total Revenues	300,000	251,000	49,000	19.5
Expenses:				
Cost of Goods Sold	214,200	170,000	44,200	26.0
Engineering, Selling, and Administrative Expenses	54,000	48,000	6,000	12.5
Interest Expense	6,000	5,000	1,000	20.0
Income Tax Expense	9,000	3,000	6,000	200.0
Other Expenses	2,700	0	2,700	—
Total Expenses	285,900	226,000	59,900	26.5
Net Income	$ 14,100	$ 25,000	$ (10,900)	(43.6)%

The horizontal analysis shows that net sales increased 20.0%. Total expenses increased by 26.5%, and net income decreased 43.6%. So, even though Kimball's net sales increased, the company's expenses increased by a larger percentage, netting an overall 43.6% reduction in net income between the years. That indicates that 2017 was a bad year in comparison to 2016. This analysis identifies areas in which management should review more data. For example, cost of goods sold increased 26.0%. Managers would want to know why this increase occurred to determine whether the company can implement cost-saving strategies (such as purchasing from other, lower-cost vendors).

KIMBALL CORPORATION Income Statement Years Ended December 31, 2017 and 2016				
	2017	**Percent**	**2016**	**Percent**
Revenues:				
Net Sales	$ 300,000	100.0%	$ 250,000	100.0%
Other Revenues	0	0.0	1,000	0.4
Total Revenues	300,000	100.0	251,000	100.4
Expenses:				
Cost of Goods Sold	214,200	71.4	170,000	68.0
Engineering, Selling, and Administrative Expenses	54,000	18.0	48,000	19.2
Interest Expense	6,000	2.0	5,000	2.0
Income Tax Expense	9,000	3.0	3,000	1.2
Other Expenses	2,700	0.9	0	0
Total Expenses	285,900	95.3	226,000	90.4
Net Income	$ 14,100	4.7%	$ 25,000	10.0%

The vertical analysis shows changes in the line items as percentages of net sales. A few notable items are:

- Cost of Goods Sold increased from 68.0% to 71.4%;
- Engineering, Selling, and Administrative Expenses decreased from 19.2% to 18.0%.

These two items are Kimball's largest dollar expenses, so their percentage changes are important. This indicates that cost controls need to be improved, especially for COGS.

The 2017 net income declined to 4.7% of sales, compared with 10.0% the preceding year. Kimball's increase in cost of goods sold is the biggest factor in the overall decrease in net income as a percentage of sales. The horizontal analysis showed that although net sales increased 20% from 2016 to 2017, the amount of each of those sales dollars resulting in net income decreased.

> Summary Problem D-2

JAVA, INC.
Four-Year Selected Financial Data
Years Ended January 31, 2017–2014

Operating Results:	2017	2016	2015	2014
Net Sales	$ 13,848	$ 13,673	$ 11,635	$ 9,054
Cost of Goods Sold	9,704	8,599	6,775	5,318
Interest Expense	109	75	45	46
Income from Operations	338	1,455	1,817	1,333
Income Tax Expense	100	263	338	247
Net Income (Net Loss)	(8)	877	1,127	824
Cash Dividends	76	75	76	77
Financial Position:				
Merchandise Inventory	1,677	1,904	1,462	1,056
Total Assets	7,591	7,012	5,189	3,963
Current Ratio	1.48:1	0.95:1	1.25:1	1.20:1
Stockholders' Equity	3,010	2,928	2,630	1,574
Average Number of Shares of Common Stock Outstanding	860	879	895	576

Requirements

Using the financial data presented above, compute the following ratios and evaluate Java's results for 2017–2015:

1. Profit margin ratio
2. Earnings per share
3. Inventory turnover
4. Times-interest-earned ratio
5. Rate of return on common stockholders' equity
6. Gross profit percentage

> Solution

	2017	2016	2015
1. Profit margin ratio	$\dfrac{\$(8)}{\$13,848} = (0.06\%)$	$\dfrac{\$877}{\$13,673} = 6.4\%$	$\dfrac{\$1,127}{\$11,635} = 9.7\%$
2. Earnings per share	$\dfrac{\$(8)}{860 \text{ shares}} = \$(0.01) \text{ per share}$	$\dfrac{\$877}{879 \text{ shares}} = \$1.00 \text{ per share}$	$\dfrac{\$1,127}{895 \text{ shares}} = \$1.26 \text{ per share}$
3. Inventory turnover	$\dfrac{\$9,704}{(\$1,904 + \$1,677)/2} = 5.4 \text{ times}$	$\dfrac{\$8,599}{(\$1,462 + \$1,904)/2} = 5.1 \text{ times}$	$\dfrac{\$6,775}{(\$1,056 + \$1,462)/2} = 5.4 \text{ times}$
4. Times-interest-earned ratio	$\dfrac{[\$(8) + \$100 + \$109]}{\$109} = 1.8 \text{ times}$	$\dfrac{(\$877 + \$263 + \$75)}{\$75} = 16.2 \text{ times}$	$\dfrac{(\$1,127 + \$338 + \$45)}{\$45} = 33.6 \text{ times}$
5. Rate of return on common stockholders' equity	$\dfrac{\$(8)}{(\$2,928 + \$3,010)/2} = (0.3\%)$	$\dfrac{\$877}{(\$2,630 + \$2,928)/2} = 31.6\%$	$\dfrac{\$1,127}{(\$1,574 + \$2,630)/2} = 53.6\%$
6. Gross profit percentage	$\dfrac{(\$13,848 - \$9,704)}{\$13,848} = 29.9\%$	$\dfrac{(\$13,673 - \$8,599)}{\$13,673} = 37.1\%$	$\dfrac{(\$11,635 - \$6,775)}{\$11,635} = 41.8\%$

Evaluation: During this period, Java's operating results deteriorated on all these measures except inventory turnover. The times-interest-earned ratio and rate of return on common stockholders' equity percentages are down sharply. From these data, it is clear that Java could sell its coffee, but not at the markups the company enjoyed in the past. The final result, in 2017, was a net loss for the year.

> Key Terms

Accounts Receivable Turnover Ratio (p. D-19)

Acid-Test Ratio (p. D-17)

Annual Report (p. D-4)

Asset Turnover Ratio (p. D-23)

Benchmarking (p. D-13)

Cash Ratio (p. D-16)

Common-Size Statement (p. D-12)

Current Ratio (p. D-16)

Days' Sales in Inventory (p. D-18)

Days' Sales in Receivables (p. D-20)

Debt Ratio (p. D-20)

Debt to Equity Ratio (p. D-21)

Dividend Payout (p. D-26)

Dividend Yield (p. D-25)

Dollar Value Bias (p. D-12)

Earnings per Share (EPS) (p. D-24)

Gross Profit Percentage (p. D-19)

Horizontal Analysis (p. D-6)

Inventory Turnover (p. D-18)

Management's Discussion and Analysis of Financial Condition and Results of Operations (MD&A) (p. D-4)

Price/Earnings Ratio (p. D-25)

Profit Margin Ratio (p. D-22)

Rate of Return on Common Stockholders' Equity (p. D-23)

Rate of Return on Total Assets (p. D-22)

Times-Interest-Earned Ratio (p. D-21)

Trading on the Equity (p. D-24)

Trend Analysis (p. D-8)

Vertical Analysis (p. D-10)

Working Capital (p. D-15)

> Quick Check

Liberty Corporation reported the following financial statements:

LIBERTY CORPORATION Comparative Balance Sheet December 31, 2017 and 2016		
	2017	**2016**
Assets		
Current Assets:		
Cash and Cash Equivalents	$ 2,450	$ 2,094
Accounts Receivable	1,813	1,611
Merchandise Inventory	1,324	1,060
Prepaid Expenses	1,709	2,120
Total Current Assets	7,296	6,885
Other Assets	18,500	15,737
Total Assets	**$ 25,796**	**$ 22,622**
Liabilities		
Current Liabilities	$ 7,230	$ 8,467
Long-term Liabilities	4,798	3,792
Total Liabilities	12,028	12,259
Stockholders' Equity		
Common Stock, no par	6,568	4,363
Retained Earnings	7,200	6,000
Total Stockholders' Equity	13,768	10,363
Total Liabilities and Stockholders' Equity	**$ 25,796**	**$ 22,622**

LIBERTY CORPORATION Income Statement Year Ended December 31, 2017	
Net Sales	$ 20,941
Cost of Goods Sold	7,055
Gross Profit	13,886
Operating Expenses	7,065
Operating Income	6,821
Interest Expense	210
Income Before Income Taxes	6,611
Income Tax Expense	2,563
Net Income	**$ 4,048**

Learning Objective 1

1. What part of the Liberty's annual report is written by the company and could present a biased view of financial conditions and results?

   a. Balance Sheet

   b. Management's Discussion and Analysis of Financial Condition and Results of Operations (MD&A)

   c. Auditor's Report

   d. Income Statement

Learning Objective 2

2. Horizontal analysis of Liberty's balance sheet for 2017 would report

   a. Cash as 9.50% of total assets.

   b. a 17% increase in Cash and Cash Equivalents.

   c. a current ratio of 1.01.

   d. inventory turnover of 6 times.

Learning Objective 3

3. Vertical analysis of Liberty's balance sheet for 2017 would report

   a. Cash as 9.50% of total assets.   c. a current ratio of 1.01.

   b. inventory turnover of 6 times.   d. a 17% increase in Cash.

Learning Objective 4

4. Which statement best describes Liberty's acid-test ratio for 2017?

   a. Greater than 1   c. Less than 1

   b. Equal to 1   d. None of the above

Learning Objective 4

5. Liberty's inventory turnover during 2017 was (amounts rounded)

   a. 6 times.   c. 8 times.

   b. 7 times.   d. not determinable from the data given.

Learning Objective 4

6. Assume all sales are on credit. During 2017, Liberty's days' sales in receivables ratio was (amounts rounded)

   a. 34 days.   b. 30 days.   c. 32 days.   d. 28 days.

Learning Objective 4

7. Which measure expresses Liberty's times-interest-earned ratio? (amounts rounded)

   a. 54.7%   b. 19 times   c. 34.5%   d. 32 times

Learning Objective 4

8. Liberty's rate of return on common stockholders' equity can be described as

   a. weak.   b. normal.   c. strong.   d. average.

Learning Objective 4

9. The company has 2,500 shares of common stock outstanding. What is Liberty's earnings per share?

   a. $1.62   b. $1.75   c. $2.73   d. 2.63 times

Learning Objective 5
Appendix DA

10A. In order for an item to be reported in the extraordinary items section of the income statement, it must be

   a. unusual.   c. unusual or infrequent.

   b. infrequent.   d. unusual and infrequent.

Check your answers at the end of the appendix.

ASSESS YOUR PROGRESS

> Review Questions

1. What are the three main ways to analyze financial statements?

2. What is an annual report? Briefly describe the key parts of the annual report.

3. What is horizontal analysis, and how is a percentage change computed?

4. What is trend analysis, and how does it differ from horizontal analysis?

5. What is vertical analysis? What item is used as the base for the income statement? What item is used as the base for the balance sheet?

6. Describe a common-size statement and how it might be helpful in evaluating a company.

7. What is benchmarking, and what are the two main types of benchmarks in financial statement analysis?

8. Briefly describe the ratios that can be used to evaluate a company's ability to pay current liabilities.

9. Briefly describe the ratios that can be used to evaluate a company's ability to sell merchandise inventory and collect receivables.

10. Briefly describe the ratios that can be used to evaluate a company's ability to pay long-term debt.

11. Briefly describe the ratios that can be used to evaluate a company's profitability.

12. Briefly describe the ratios that can be used to evaluate a company's stock as an investment.

13. What are some common red flags in financial statement analysis?

14A. What is reported in the discontinued operations section of the income statement?

15A. Describe the types of items that would be reported in the extraordinary items section of the income statement.

> Short Exercises

SD-1 Explaining financial statements

Learning Objective 1

Caleb King is interested in investing in Orange Corporation. What types of tools should Caleb use to evaluate the company?

SD-2 Performing horizontal analysis

Learning Objective 2

McDonald Corp. reported the following on its comparative income statement:

(In millions)	2017	2016	2015
Revenue	$ 9,910	$ 9,700	$ 9,210
Cost of Goods Sold	7,210	6,900	6,125

Prepare a horizontal analysis of revenues and gross profit—both in dollar amounts and in percentages—for 2017 and 2016.

Learning Objective 2

SD-3 Calculating trend analysis

Variline Corp. reported the following revenues and net income amounts:

(In millions)	2017	2016	2015	2014
Revenue	$ 9,990	$ 9,890	$ 9,290	$ 9,090
Net Income	7,750	7,570	5,670	4,990

Requirements

1. Calculate Variline's trend analysis for revenues and net income. Use 2014 as the base year, and round to the nearest percent.

2. Which measure increased at a higher rate during 2015–2017?

Learning Objective 3

SD-4 Performing vertical analysis

Hoosier Optical Company reported the following amounts on its balance sheet at December 31, 2016 and 2015:

	2016	2015
Cash and Receivables	$ 77,825	$ 70,200
Merchandise Inventory	55,825	52,780
Property, Plant, and Equipment, Net	141,350	137,020
Total Assets	$ 275,000	$ 260,000

Prepare a vertical analysis of Hoosier assets for 2016 and 2015.

Learning Objective 3

SD-5 Preparing common-size income statement

Data for Martinez, Inc. and Rosario Corp. follow:

	Martinez	Rosario
Net Sales	$ 10,000	$ 17,000
Cost of Goods Sold	6,210	12,359
Other Expenses	3,180	3,825
Net Income	$ 610	$ 816

Requirements

1. Prepare common-size income statements.

2. Which company earns more net income?

3. Which company's net income is a higher percentage of its net sales?

Use the following information for Short Exercises SD-6 through SD-10.

Shine's Companies, a home improvement store chain, reported the following summarized figures:

SHINE'S COMPANIES Income Statement Years Ended May 31, 2016 and 2015		
	2016	**2015**
Net Sales	$ 57,200,000	$ 41,100,000
Cost of Goods Sold	20,600,000	29,300,000
Interest Expense	700,000	630,000
All Other Expenses	6,900,000	8,400,000
Net Income	**$ 29,000,000**	**$ 2,770,000**

SHINE'S COMPANIES Balance Sheet May 31, 2016 and 2015						
Assets				**Liabilities**		
	2016	**2015**			**2016**	**2015**
Cash	$ 2,200,000	$ 1,800,000		Total Current Liabilities	$ 24,000,000	$ 12,900,000
Short-term Investments	26,000,000	10,000,000		Long-term Liabilities	13,400,000	10,800,000
Accounts Receivable	7,200,000	5,400,000		Total Liabilities	37,400,000	23,700,000
Merchandise Inventory	7,100,000	8,200,000		**Stockholders' Equity**		
Other Current Assets	9,000,000	1,800,000		Common Stock	13,000,000	13,000,000
Total Current Assets	51,500,000	27,200,000		Retained Earnings	33,100,000	18,500,000
All Other Assets	32,000,000	28,000,000		Total Equity	46,100,000	31,500,000
Total Assets	**$ 83,500,000**	**$ 55,200,000**		Total Liabilities and Equity	**$ 83,500,000**	**$ 55,200,000**

Shine's has 100,000 common shares outstanding during 2016.

SD-6 Evaluating current ratio

Learning Objective 4

Requirements

1. Compute Shine's Companies' current ratio at May 31, 2016 and 2015.

2. Did Shine's Companies' current ratio improve, deteriorate, or hold steady during 2016?

Learning Objective 4

SD-7 Computing inventory, gross profit, and receivables ratios

Requirements

1. Compute the inventory turnover, days' sales in inventory, and gross profit percentage for Shine's Companies for 2016.

2. Compute days' sales in receivables during 2016. Round dollar amounts to three decimal places. Assume all sales were on account.

3. What do these ratios say about Shine's Companies' ability to sell inventory and collect receivables?

Learning Objective 4

SD-8 Measuring ability to pay liabilities

Requirements

1. Compute the debt ratio and the debt to equity ratio at May 31, 2016, for Shine's Companies.

2. Is Shine's ability to pay its liabilities strong or weak? Explain your reasoning.

Learning Objective 4

SD-9 Measuring profitability

Requirements

1. Compute the profit margin ratio for Shine's Companies for 2016.

2. Compute the rate of return on total assets for 2016.

3. Compute the asset turnover ratio for 2016.

4. Compute the rate of return on common stockholders' equity for 2016.

5. Are these rates of return strong or weak? Explain your reasoning.

Learning Objective 4

SD-10 Computing EPS and P/E ratio

Requirements

1. Compute earnings per share (EPS) for 2016 for Shine's. Round to the nearest cent.

2. Compute Shine's Companies' price/earnings ratio for 2016. The market price per share of Shine's stock is $65.50.

3. What do these results mean when evaluating Shine's Companies' profitability?

Learning Objective 4

SD-11 Using ratios to reconstruct an income statement

Vintage Mills's income statement appears as follows (amounts in thousands):

VINTAGE MILLS Income Statement Year Ended December 31, 2016	
Net Sales	$ 7,300
Cost of Goods Sold	(a)
Selling and Administrative Expenses	1,700
Interest Expense	(b)
Other Expenses	135
Income Before Income Taxes	1,325
Income Tax Expense	(c)
Net Income	(d)

Use the following ratio data to complete Vintage Mills's income statement.

1. Inventory turnover is 4.70 (beginning Merchandise Inventory was $750; ending Merchandise Inventory was $710).

2. Profit margin ratio is 0.16.

SD-12 Using ratios to reconstruct a balance sheet

Learning Objective 4

Walsham Mills's balance sheet appears as follows (amounts in thousands):

WALSHAM MILLS
Balance Sheet
December 31, 2016

Assets			Liabilities		
Cash	$	60	Total Current Liabilities		$ 1,800
Accounts Receivables		(a)	Long-term Note Payable		(e)
Merchandise Inventory		725	Other Long-term Liabilities		770
Prepaid Expenses		(b)	Total Liabilities		(f)
Total Current Assets		(c)			
Plant Assets, Net		(d)	**Stockholders' Equity**		
Other Assets		2,000	Stockholders' Equity		2,675
Total Assets		$ 6,500	Total Liabilities and Stockholders' Equity	$	(g)

Use the following ratio data to complete Walsham Mills's balance sheet.

a. Current ratio is 0.86.

b. Acid-test ratio is 0.40.

SDA-13 Preparing a corporate income statement

Learning Objective 5
Appendix DA

TST Corporation's accounting records include the following items, listed in no particular order, at December 31, 2016:

Other Revenues and (Expenses)	$ (10,000)	Extraordinary Loss	$ 16,600
Net Sales	266,000	Cost of Goods Sold	79,000
Gain on Discontinued Operations	34,500	Operating Expenses	65,000

The income tax rate for TST Corporation is 50%.

Prepare TST's income statement for the year ended December 31, 2016. Omit earnings per share. Use the multi-step format.

SDA-14 Reporting earnings per share

Learning Objective 5
Appendix DA

Return to the TST data in Short Exercise SDA-13. TST had 8,000 shares of common stock outstanding during 2016. TST declared and paid preferred dividends of $4,000 during 2016.

Show how TST reports EPS data on its 2016 income statement.

APPENDIX D

> Exercises

Learning Objective 2

1. Net Income 35.7%

ED-15 Performing horizontal analysis—income statement

Data for McCormick Designs, Inc. follow:

MCCORMICK DESIGNS, INC. Comparative Income Statement Years Ended December 31, 2016 and 2015		
	2016	**2015**
Net Sales Revenue	$ 431,250	$ 373,000
Expenses:		
Cost of Goods Sold	202,000	189,000
Selling and Administrative Expenses	100,050	92,550
Other Expenses	8,000	2,150
Total Expenses	310,050	283,700
Net Income	**$ 121,200**	**$ 89,300**

Requirements

1. Prepare a horizontal analysis of the comparative income statement of McCormick Designs, Inc. Round percentage changes to one decimal place.

2. Why did 2016 net income increase by a higher percentage than net sales revenue?

Learning Objective 2

1. 2017 Net Income 166%

ED-16 Computing trend analysis

Grand Oaks Realty's net revenue and net income for the following five-year period, using 2013 as the base year, follow:

	2017	2016	2015	2014	2013
Net Revenue	$ 1,315,000	$ 1,188,000	$ 1,160,000	$ 1,011,000	$ 1,038,000
Net Income	126,000	115,000	82,000	77,000	76,000

Requirements

1. Compute a trend analysis for net revenue and net income. Round to the nearest full percent.

2. Which grew faster during the period, net revenue or net income?

ED-17 Performing vertical analysis of a balance sheet

Tri Designs, Inc. has the following data:

Learning Objective 3

2016 Current Assets: 15.7%

TRI DESIGNS, INC. Comparative Balance Sheet December 31, 2016 and 2015		
	2016	**2015**
Assets		
Total Current Assets	$ 54,950	$ 72,250
Property, Plant, and Equipment, Net	250,250	158,950
Other Assets	44,800	57,800
Total Assets	**$ 350,000**	**$ 289,000**
Liabilities		
Total Current Liabilities	$ 49,700	$ 47,685
Long-term Debt	118,300	196,520
Total Liabilities	168,000	244,205
Stockholders' Equity		
Total Stockholders' Equity	182,000	44,795
Total Liabilities and Stockholders' Equity	**$ 350,000**	**$ 289,000**

Perform a vertical analysis of Tri Designs's balance sheet for each year.

ED-18 Preparing common-size income statements

Refer to the data presented for McCormick Designs, Inc. in Exercise ED-15.

Learning Objective 3

1. 2016 Net Income 28.1%

Requirements

1. Prepare a comparative common-size income statement for McCormick Designs, Inc. using the 2016 and 2015 data. Round percentages to one-tenth percent (three decimal places).

2. To an investor, how does 2016 compare with 2015? Explain your reasoning.

ED-19 Computing working capital changes

Data for Outreach Enterprises follows:

Learning Objective 4

2017 Working Capital $200,000

	2017	2016	2015
Total Current Assets	$ 380,000	$ 330,000	$ 290,000
Total Current Liabilities	180,000	165,000	145,000

Compute the dollar amount of change and the percentage of change in Outreach Enterprises's working capital each year during 2017 and 2016. What do the calculated changes indicate?

Learning Objective 4

e. 78 days

ED-20 Computing key ratios

The financial statements of Victory's Natural Foods include the following items:

	Current Year	Preceding Year
Balance Sheet:		
Cash	$ 20,000	$ 24,000
Short-term Investments	18,000	26,000
Net Accounts Receivable	50,000	78,000
Merchandise Inventory	70,000	66,000
Prepaid Expenses	12,000	10,000
Total Current Assets	170,000	204,000
Total Current Liabilities	129,000	92,000
Income Statement:		
Net Credit Sales	$ 478,000	
Cost of Goods Sold	318,000	

Compute the following ratios for the current year:

a. Current ratio

b. Cash ratio

c. Acid-test ratio

d. Inventory turnover

e. Days' sales in inventory

f. Days' sales in receivables

g. Gross profit percentage (assume all sales are on credit)

Learning Objective 4

d. 2016 0.61

ED-21 Analyzing the ability to pay liabilities

Big Bend Photo Shop has asked you to determine whether the company's ability to pay current liabilities and total liabilities improved or deteriorated during 2016. To answer this question, you gather the following data:

	2016	2015
Cash	$ 56,000	$ 51,000
Short-term Investments	31,000	0
Net Accounts Receivable	134,000	136,000
Merchandise Inventory	257,000	297,000
Total Assets	540,000	550,000
Total Current Liabilities	285,000	202,000
Long-term Notes Payable	46,000	58,000
Income from Operations	170,000	178,000
Interest Expense	54,000	45,000

Compute the following ratios for 2016 and 2015, and evaluate the company's ability to pay its current liabilities and total liabilities:

a. Current ratio

b. Cash ratio

c. Acid-test ratio

d. Debt ratio

e. Debt to equity ratio

ED-22 Analyzing profitability

Varsity, Inc.'s comparative income statement follows. The 2015 data are given as needed.

1. 2017 11.6%

VARSITY, INC. Comparative Income Statement Years Ended December 31, 2017 and 2016			
Dollars in thousands	**2017**	**2016**	**2015**
Net Sales	$ 185,000	$ 153,000	
Cost of Goods Sold	96,000	87,000	
Selling and Administrative Expenses	46,500	39,500	
Interest Expense	9,500	10,500	
Income Tax Expense	11,500	9,000	
Net Income	$ 21,500	$ 7,000	
Additional data:			
Total Assets	$ 200,000	$ 188,000	$ 169,000
Common Stockholders' Equity	92,000	87,500	80,000
Preferred Dividends	2,000	2,000	0
Common Shares Outstanding During the Year	20,000	20,000	10,000

Requirements

1. Calculate the profit margin ratio for 2017 and 2016.
2. Calculate the rate of return on total assets for 2017 and 2016.
3. Calculate the asset turnover ratio for 2017 and 2016.
4. Calculate the rate of return on common stockholders' equity for 2017 and 2016.
5. Calculate the earnings per share for 2017 and 2016.
6. Calculate the 2017 dividend payout on common stock. Assume dividends per share for common stock are equal to $0.75 per share.
7. Did the company's operating performance improve or deteriorate during 2017?

ED-23 Evaluating a stock as an investment

Data for Regal State Bank follow:

Dividend Yield 2016 1.2%

	2016	2015
Net Income	$ 56,000	$ 47,200
Dividends—Common	16,000	16,000
Dividends—Preferred	16,000	16,000
Total Stockholders' Equity at Year-End (includes 80,000 shares of common stock)	770,000	580,000
Preferred Stock	220,000	220,000
Market Price per Share of Common Stock	$ 16.50	$ 11.00

Evaluate the common stock of Regal State Bank as an investment. Specifically, use the three stock ratios to determine whether the common stock has increased or decreased in attractiveness during the past year.

Learning Objective 4

Total Assets $2,000,000

ED-24 Using ratios to reconstruct a balance sheet

The following data are adapted from the financial statements of Jim's Shops, Inc.:

Total Current Assets	$ 1,054,000
Accumulated Depreciation	1,600,000
Total Liabilities	1,480,000
Preferred Stock	0
Debt Ratio	74%
Current Ratio	1.55

Prepare Jim's condensed balance sheet as of December 31, 2016.

Learning Objective 5
Appendix DA

Net Income $155,400

EDA-25 Preparing a multi-step income statement

Cloud Photographic Supplies, Inc.'s accounting records include the following for 2016:

Income Tax Saving—Extraordinary Loss	$ 10,400	Sales	$ 575,000
Income Tax Saving—Loss on Discontinued Operations	6,000	Operating Expenses (Including Income Tax)	140,000
Extraordinary Loss	26,000	Cost of Goods Sold	255,000
Loss on Discontinued Operations	15,000		

Prepare Cloud's multi-step income statement for 2016. Omit earnings per share.

Learning Objective 5
Appendix DA

Net Income $14.25

EDA-26 Computing earnings per share

Falconi Academy Surplus had 55,000 shares of common stock and 5,000 shares of 1%, $10 par value preferred stock outstanding through December 31, 2016. Income from continuing operations for 2016 was $679,750, and loss on discontinued operations (net of income tax saving) was $66,000. Falconi also had an extraordinary gain (net of tax) of $170,500.

Compute Falconi's earnings per share for 2016, starting with income from continuing operations.

> Problems Group A

Learning Objectives 2, 4

2. 2017 15.9%

PD-27A Computing trend analysis and return on common equity

Net sales revenue, net income, and common stockholders' equity for Shawnee Mission Corporation, a manufacturer of contact lenses, follow for a four-year period.

	2017	2016	2015	2014
Net Sales Revenue	$ 764,000	$ 702,000	$ 642,000	$ 665,000
Net Income	57,000	45,000	38,000	47,000
Ending Common Stockholders' Equity	362,000	356,000	328,000	294,000

Requirements

1. Compute trend analyses for each item for 2015–2017. Use 2014 as the base year, and round to the nearest whole percent.

2. Compute the rate of return on common stockholders' equity for 2015–2017, rounding to three decimal places.

PD-28A Performing vertical analysis

The Roost Department Stores, Inc. chief executive officer (CEO) has asked you to compare the company's profit performance and financial position with the averages for the industry. The CEO has given you the company's income statement and balance sheet as well as the industry average data for retailers.

ROOST DEPARTMENT STORES, INC. Income Statement Compared with Industry Average Year Ended December 31, 2016		
	Roost	Industry Average
Net Sales	$ 779,000	100.0%
Cost of Goods Sold	526,604	65.8
Gross Profit	252,396	34.2
Operating Expenses	163,590	19.7
Operating Income	88,806	14.5
Other Expenses	5,453	0.4
Net Income	$ 83,353	14.1%

ROOST DEPARTMENT STORES, INC. Balance Sheet Compared with Industry Average December 31, 2016		
	Roost	Industry Average
Current Assets	$ 316,780	70.9%
Fixed Assets, Net	120,320	23.6
Intangible Assets, Net	7,990	0.8
Other Assets	24,910	4.7
Total Assets	$ 470,000	100.0%
Current Liabilities	$ 217,140	48.1%
Long-term Liabilities	104,340	16.6
Total Liabilities	321,480	64.7
Stockholders' Equity	148,520	35.3
Total Liabilities and Stockholders' Equity	$ 470,000	100.0%

Requirements

1. Prepare a vertical analysis for Roost for both its income statement and balance sheet.

2. Compare the company's profit performance and financial position with the average for the industry.

Note: Problem PD-28A must be completed before attempting Problem PD-29A.

PD-29A Preparing common-size statements, analysis of profitability and financial position, comparison with the industry, and using ratios to evaluate a company

Consider the data for Roost Department Stores presented in Problem PD-28A.

Requirements

1. Prepare a common-size income statement and balance sheet for Roost. The first column of each statement should present Roost's common-size statement, and the second column, the industry averages.

2. For the profitability analysis, compute Roost's (a) gross profit percentage and (b) profit margin ratio. Compare these figures with the industry averages. Is Roost's profit performance better or worse than the industry average?

3. For the analysis of financial position, compute Roost's (a) current ratio and (b) debt to equity ratio. Compare these ratios with the industry averages. Assume the current ratio industry average is 1.47, and the debt to equity industry average is 1.83. Is Roost's financial position better or worse than the industry averages?

Learning Objective 4

1. Current Ratio 1.49

PD-30A Determining the effects of business transactions on selected ratios

Financial statement data of *Off Road Traveler Magazine* include the following items:

Cash	$ 23,000
Accounts Receivable, Net	80,000
Merchandise Inventory	184,000
Total Assets	637,000
Accounts Payable	103,000
Accrued Liabilities	38,000
Short-term Notes Payable	51,000
Long-term Liabilities	224,000
Net Income	74,000
Common Shares Outstanding	50,000

Requirements

1. Compute *Off Road Traveler*'s current ratio, debt ratio, and earnings per share. Round all ratios to two decimal places, and use the following format for your answer:

Current Ratio	Debt Ratio	Earnings per Share

2. Compute the three ratios after evaluating the effect of each transaction that follows. Consider each transaction *separately*.
   a. Purchased merchandise inventory of $48,000 on account.
   b. Borrowed $127,000 on a long-term note payable.
   c. Issued 56,000 shares of common stock, receiving cash of $106,000.
   d. Received cash on account, $5,000.

Learning Objective 4

1. 2016 e. 49%

PD-31A Using ratios to evaluate a stock investment

Comparative financial statement data of Dangerfield, Inc. follow:

DANGERFIELD, INC. Comparative Income Statement Years Ended December 31, 2016 and 2015		
	2016	2015
Net Sales	$ 465,000	$ 428,000
Cost of Goods Sold	237,000	214,000
Gross Profit	228,000	214,000
Operating Expenses	138,000	136,000
Income from Operations	90,000	78,000
Interest Expense	10,000	16,000
Income Before Income Tax	80,000	62,000
Income Tax Expense	23,000	25,000
Net Income	$ 57,000	$ 37,000

DANGERFIELD, INC. Comparative Balance Sheet December 31, 2016 and 2015			
	2016	**2015**	**2014***
Assets			
Current Assets:			
Cash	$ 94,000	$ 93,000	
Accounts Receivable, Net	107,000	116,000	$ 102,000
Merchandise Inventory	145,000	160,000	210,000
Prepaid Expenses	19,000	8,000	
Total Current Assets	365,000	377,000	
Property, Plant, and Equipment, Net	217,000	178,000	
Total Assets	**$ 582,000**	**$ 555,000**	596,000
Liabilities			
Total Current Liabilities	$ 228,000	$ 242,000	
Long-term Liabilities	114,000	98,000	
Total Liabilities	342,000	340,000	
Stockholders' Equity			
Preferred Stock, 3%	96,000	96,000	
Common Stockholders' Equity, no par	144,000	119,000	91,000
Total Liabilities and Stockholders' Equity	**$ 582,000**	**$ 555,000**	

* Selected 2014 amounts

1. Market price of Dangerfield's common stock: $76.67 at December 31, 2016, and $37.20 at December 31, 2015.

2. Common shares outstanding: 13,000 during 2016 and 11,000 during 2015 and 2014.

3. All sales are on credit.

Requirements

1. Compute the following ratios for 2016 and 2015:
   a. Current ratio
   b. Cash ratio
   c. Times-interest-earned ratio
   d. Inventory turnover
   e. Gross profit percentage
   f. Debt to equity ratio
   g. Rate of return on common stockholders' equity
   h. Earnings per share of common stock
   i. Price/earnings ratio

2. Decide (a) whether Dangerfield's ability to pay debts and to sell inventory improved or deteriorated during 2016 and (b) whether the investment attractiveness of its common stock appears to have increased or decreased.

Learning Objective 4

1. Best Digital e. $4.67

PD-32A Using ratios to decide between two stock investments

Assume that you are purchasing an investment and have decided to invest in a company in the digital phone business. You have narrowed the choice to Best Digital Corp. and Very Zone, Inc. and have assembled the following data.

Selected income statement data for the current year:

	Best Digital	Very Zone
Net Sales (all on credit)	$ 417,925	$ 493,845
Cost of Goods Sold	207,000	259,000
Interest Expense	0	14,000
Net Income	56,000	72,000

Selected balance sheet and market price data at the *end* of the current year:

	Best Digital	Very Zone
Current Assets:		
Cash	$ 23,000	$ 21,000
Short-term Investments	38,000	15,000
Accounts Receivable, Net	37,000	47,000
Merchandise Inventory	65,000	97,000
Prepaid Expenses	22,000	18,000
Total Current Assets	$ 185,000	$ 198,000
Total Assets	$ 261,000	$ 325,000
Total Current Liabilities	100,000	99,000
Total Liabilities	100,000	131,000
Common Stock, $1 par (12,000 shares)	12,000	
$1 par (17,000 shares)		17,000
Total Stockholders' Equity	161,000	194,000
Market Price per Share of Common Stock	$ 70.05	$ 97.52
Dividends Paid per Common Share	$ 0.60	$ 0.40

Selected balance sheet data at the *beginning* of the current year:

	Best Digital	Very Zone
Balance Sheet:		
Accounts Receivable, net	$ 42,000	$ 49,000
Merchandise Inventory	81,000	90,000
Total Assets	258,000	275,000
Common Stock, $1 par (12,000 shares)	12,000	
$1 par (17,000 shares)		17,000

Your strategy is to invest in companies that have low price/earnings ratios but appear to be in good shape financially. Assume that you have analyzed all other factors and that your decision depends on the results of ratio analysis.

Requirements

1. Compute the following ratios for both companies for the current year:
   a. Acid-test ratio
   b. Inventory turnover
   c. Days' sales in receivables
   d. Debt ratio
   e. Earnings per share of common stock
   f. Price/earnings ratio
   g. Dividend payout

2. Decide which company's stock better fits your investment strategy.

PDA-33A Preparing an income statement

The following information was taken from the records of Grey Motorsports, Inc. at November 30, 2016:

Learning Objective 5
Appendix DA

Net Income $108,600

Selling Expenses	$ 125,000	Common Stock, $5 Par Value,	
Administrative Expenses	95,000	30,500 shares authorized and issued	$ 152,500
Income from Discontinued Operations	11,000	Preferred Stock, $3 No-Par Value,	
Cost of Goods Sold	440,000	5,000 shares issued	250,000
Treasury Stock—Common (500 shares)	4,000	Income Tax Expense: Continuing Operations	35,000
Net Sales Revenue	797,000	Income Tax Expense: Income from Discontinued Operations	4,400

Prepare a multi-step income statement for Grey Motorsports for the fiscal year ended November 30, 2016. Include earnings per share.

> Problems **Group B**

PD-34B Computing trend analysis and return on common equity

Net sales revenue, net income, and common stockholders' equity for Atkinson Mission Corporation, a manufacturer of contact lenses, follow for a four-year period.

Learning Objectives 2, 4

2. 2016 10.2%

	2017	2016	2015	2014
Net Sales Revenue	$ 763,000	$ 704,000	$ 641,000	$ 661,000
Net Income	57,000	35,000	33,000	43,000
Ending Common Stockholders' Equity	370,000	358,000	330,000	298,000

Requirements

1. Compute trend analyses for each item for 2015–2017. Use 2014 as the base year, and round to the nearest whole percent.

2. Compute the rate of return on common stockholders' equity for 2015–2017, rounding to three decimal places.

Learning Objective 2

1. Net Income 10.9%

PD-35B Performing vertical analysis

The Russell Department Stores, Inc. chief executive officer (CEO) has asked you to compare the company's profit performance and financial position with the averages for the industry. The CEO has given you the company's income statement and balance sheet as well as the industry average data for retailers.

RUSSELL DEPARTMENT STORES, INC. Income Statement Compared with Industry Average Year Ended December 31, 2016		
	Russell	Industry Average
Net Sales	$ 780,000	100.0%
Cost of Goods Sold	528,060	65.8
Gross Profit	251,940	34.2
Operating Expenses	159,900	19.7
Operating Income	92,040	14.5
Other Expenses	7,020	0.4
Net Income	$ 85,020	14.1%

RUSSELL DEPARTMENT STORES, INC. Balance Sheet Compared with Industry Average December 31, 2016		
	Russell	Industry Average
Current Assets	$ 323,520	70.9%
Fixed Assets, Net	124,800	23.6
Intangible Assets, Net	8,160	0.8
Other Assets	23,520	4.7
Total Assets	$ 480,000	100.0%
Current Liabilities	$ 221,760	48.1%
Long-term Liabilities	108,480	16.6
Total Liabilities	330,240	64.7
Stockholders' Equity	149,760	35.3
Total Liabilities and Stockholders' Equity	$ 480,000	100.0%

Requirements

1. Prepare a vertical analysis for Russell for both its income statement and balance sheet.
2. Compare the company's profit performance and financial position with the average for the industry.

Note: Problem PD-35B must be completed before attempting Problem PD-36B.

Learning Objectives 3, 4

1. Current Assets 67.4%

PD-36B Preparing common-size statements, analysis of profitability and financial position, comparison with the industry, and using ratios to evaluate a company

Consider the data for Russell Department Stores presented in Problem PD-35B.

Requirements

1. Prepare a common-size income statement and balance sheet for Russell. The first column of each statement should present Russell's common-size statement, and the second column, the industry averages.
2. For the profitability analysis, compute Russell's (a) gross profit percentage and (b) profit margin ratio. Compare these figures with the industry averages. Is Russell's profit performance better or worse than the industry average?
3. For the analysis of financial position, compute Russell's (a) current ratio and (b) debt to equity ratio. Compare these ratios with the industry averages. Assume the current ratio industry average is 1.47, and the debt to equity industry average is 1.83. Is Russell's financial position better or worse than the industry averages?

PD-37B Determining the effects of business transactions on selected ratios

Financial statement data of *Yankee Traveler's Magazine* include the following items:

Learning Objective 4

1. Earnings per Share $1.83

Cash	$ 21,000
Accounts Receivable, Net	82,000
Merchandise Inventory	183,000
Total Assets	634,000
Accounts Payable	102,000
Accrued Liabilities	38,000
Short-term Notes Payable	46,000
Long-term Liabilities	222,000
Net Income	73,000
Common Shares Outstanding	40,000

Requirements

1. Compute *Yankee Traveler's* current ratio, debt ratio, and earnings per share. Round all ratios to two decimal places, and use the following format for your answer:

Current Ratio	Debt Ratio	Earnings per Share

2. Compute the three ratios after evaluating the effect of each transaction that follows. Consider each transaction *separately*.
   a. Purchased merchandise inventory of $42,000 on account.
   b. Borrowed $123,000 on a long-term note payable.
   c. Issued 4,000 shares of common stock, receiving cash of $106,000.
   d. Received cash on account, $7,000.

PD-38B Using ratios to evaluate a stock investment

Comparative financial statement data of Canfield, Inc. follow:

Learning Objective 4

1. 2015 d. 1.15

CANFIELD, INC. Comparative Income Statement Years Ended December 31, 2016 and 2015		
	2016	2015
Net Sales	$ 459,000	$ 424,000
Cost of Goods Sold	237,000	215,000
Gross Profit	222,000	209,000
Operating Expenses	137,000	135,000
Income from Operations	85,000	74,000
Interest Expense	12,000	14,000
Income Before Income Tax	73,000	60,000
Income Tax Expense	19,000	25,000
Net Income	$ 54,000	$ 35,000

CANFIELD, INC.
Comparative Balance Sheet
December 31, 2016 and 2015

	2016	2015	2014*
Assets			
Current Assets:			
Cash	$ 99,000	$ 96,000	
Accounts Receivable, Net	110,000	116,000	$ 101,000
Merchandise Inventory	145,000	163,000	210,000
Prepaid Expenses	12,000	7,000	
Total Current Assets	366,000	382,000	
Property, Plant, and Equipment, Net	219,000	180,000	
Total Assets	$ 585,000	$ 562,000	598,000
Liabilities			
Total Current Liabilities	$ 223,000	$ 246,000	
Long-term Liabilities	120,000	95,000	
Total Liabilities	343,000	341,000	
Stockholders' Equity			
Preferred Stock, 3%	98,000	98,000	
Common Stockholders' Equity, no par	144,000	123,000	85,000
Total Liabilities and Stockholders' Equity	$ 585,000	$ 562,000	

* Selected 2014 amounts

1. Market price of Canfield's common stock: $84.32 at December 31, 2016, and $51.75 at December 31, 2015.

2. Common shares outstanding: 10,000 during 2016 and 9,000 during 2015 and 2014.

3. All sales are on credit.

Requirements

1. Compute the following ratios for 2016 and 2015:
    a. Current ratio
    b. Cash ratio
    c. Times-interest-earned ratio
    d. Inventory turnover
    e. Gross profit percentage
    f. Debt to equity ratio
    g. Rate of return on common stockholders' equity
    h. Earnings per share of common stock
    i. Price/earnings ratio

2. Decide (a) whether Canfield's ability to pay debts and to sell inventory improved or deteriorated during 2016 and (b) whether the investment attractiveness of its common stock appears to have increased or decreased.

PD-39B Using ratios to decide between two stock investments

Assume that you are purchasing an investment and have decided to invest in a company in the digital phone business. You have narrowed the choice to Digital Plus Corp. and Red Zone, Inc. and have assembled the following data.

Selected income statement data for the current year:

	Digital Plus	Red Zone
Net Sales (all on credit)	$ 416,830	$ 497,130
Cost of Goods Sold	207,000	259,000
Interest Expense	0	17,000
Net Income	54,000	76,000

Selected balance sheet and market price data at the *end* of the current year:

	Digital Plus	Red Zone
Current Assets:		
Cash	$ 24,000	$ 15,000
Short-term Investments	37,000	14,000
Accounts Receivable, Net	38,000	46,000
Merchandise Inventory	65,000	99,000
Prepaid Expenses	17,000	14,000
Total Current Assets	$ 181,000	$ 188,000
Total Assets	$ 263,000	$ 324,000
Total Current Liabilities	102,000	95,000
Total Liabilities	102,000	132,000
Common Stock, $1 par (10,000 shares)	10,000	
$2 par (16,000 shares)		32,000
Total Stockholders' Equity	161,000	192,000
Market Price per Share of Common Stock	$ 86.40	$ 104.50
Dividends Paid per Common Share	$ 1.20	$ 1.00

Selected balance sheet data at the *beginning* of the current year:

	Digital Plus	Red Zone
Balance Sheet:		
Accounts Receivable, Net	$ 42,000	$ 51,000
Merchandise Inventory	81,000	89,000
Total Assets	259,000	275,000
Common Stock, $1 par (10,000 shares)	10,000	
$2 par (16,000 shares)		32,000

Your strategy is to invest in companies that have low price/earnings ratios but appear to be in good shape financially. Assume that you have analyzed all other factors and that your decision depends on the results of ratio analysis.

Learning Objective 4

1c. Red Zone 36 days

APPENDIX D

Requirements

1. Compute the following ratios for both companies for the current year:
   a. Acid-test ratio
   b. Inventory turnover
   c. Days' sales in receivables
   d. Debt ratio
   e. Earnings per share of common stock
   f. Price/earnings ratio
   g. Dividend payout

2. Decide which company's stock better fits your investment strategy.

Learning Objective 5
Appendix DA

Net Income $149,800

PDA-40B Preparing an income statement

The following information was taken from the records of Shepard Motorsports, Inc. at November 30, 2016:

Selling Expenses	$ 150,000	Common Stock, $8 Par Value,	
		29,500 shares authorized and issued	$ 236,000
Administrative Expenses	95,000	Preferred Stock, $7 No-Par Value,	
Income from Discontinued Operations	7,000	9,000 shares issued	630,000
Cost of Goods Sold	425,000	Income Tax Expense: Continuing Operations	45,000
Treasury Stock—Common (1,500 shares)	16,500	Income Tax Expense: Income from	
Net Sales Revenue	860,600	Discontinued Operations	2,800

Prepare a multi-step income statement for Shepard Motorsports for the fiscal year ended November 30, 2016. Include earnings per share.

> Continuing Problem

PD-41 Using ratios to evaluate a stock investment

This problem continues the Daniels Consulting situation from Problem PC-46 of Appendix C. Assuming Daniels Consulting's net income for the year was $90,537 and knowing that the current market price of Daniels's stock is $200 per share, calculate the following ratios for 2017 for the company:

a. Current ratio

b. Cash ratio

c. Debt ratio

d. Debt to equity ratio

e. Earnings per share

f. Price/earnings ratio

g. Rate of return on common stockholders' equity

DANIELS CONSULTING
Comparative Balance Sheet
December 31, 2017 and 2016

	2017	2016
Assets		
Current Assets:		
Cash	$ 1,457,524	$ 31,700
Accounts Receivable	25,700	700
Office Supplies	2,150	50
Long-term Assets:		
Plants Assets	84,800	4,800
Accumulated Depreciation—Plant Assets	(1,696)	(80)
Total Assets	$ 1,568,478	$ 37,170
Liabilities		
Current Liabilities:		
Accounts Payable	$ 7,300	$ 4,100
Salaries Payable	1,800	467
Unearned Revenue	0	1,600
Interest Payable	25,000	0
Long-term Liabilities:		
Notes Payable	500,000	0
Bonds Payable	900,000	0
Discount on Bonds Payable	(100,862)	0
Total Liabilities	1,333,238	6,167
Stockholders' Equity		
Common Stock, $1 par	115,240	240
Retained Earnings	120,000	30,763
Total Stockholders' Equity	235,240	31,003
Total Liabilities and Stockholders' Equity	$ 1,568,478	$ 37,170

APPENDIX D

COMPREHENSIVE PROBLEM

> Comprehensive Problem for Appendix D

Analyzing a company for its investment potential

In its annual report, WRM Athletic Supply, Inc. includes the following five-year financial summary:

WRM ATHLETIC SUPPLY, INC.
Five-Year Financial Summary (Partial; adapted)

(Dollar amounts in thousands except per share data)	2020	2019	2018	2017	2016	2015
Net Sales	$ 290,000	$ 215,000	$ 194,000	$ 165,000	$ 139,000	
Net Sales Increase	35%	11%	18%	19%	17%	
Domestic Comparative Store Sales Increase	5%	7%	5%	8%	10%	
Other Income—Net	2,050	1,810	1,790	1,660	1,300	
Cost of Goods Sold	218,660	163,400	150,350	129,360	110,227	
Selling and Administrative Expenses	41,236	36,356	31,679	27,408	22,516	
Interest:						
Interest Expense	(1,010)	(1,360)	(1,370)	(1,060)	(870)	
Interest Income	120	160	165	225	155	
Income Tax Expense	4,430	3,830	3,690	3,380	2,760	
Net Income	26,834	12,024	8,866	5,677	4,082	
Per Share of Common Stock:						
Net Income	1.80	1.50	1.40	1.20	0.98	
Dividends	0.40	0.38	0.34	0.30	0.26	
Financial Position						
Current Assets, Excluding Merchandise Inventory	$ 30,400	$ 27,500	$ 26,200	$ 24,900	$ 21,700	
Merchandise Inventory at LIFO Cost	24,200	22,500	21,400	19,900	17,100	$ 16,400
Property, Plant, and Equipment, Net	51,100	45,600	40,700	35,200	25,900	
Total Assets	105,700	95,600	88,300	80,000	64,700	
Current Liabilities	32,200	27,100	28,700	25,800	16,700	
Long-term Debt	22,600	21,700	17,100	18,300	12,600	
Stockholders' Equity	50,900	46,800	42,500	35,900	35,400	
Financial Ratios						
Acid-Test Ratio	0.9	1.0	0.9	1.0	1.3	
Rate of Return on Total Assets	27.7%	14.6%	12.2%	9.3%	8.3%	
Rate of Return on Common Stockholders' Equity	54.9%	26.9%	22.6%	15.9%	15.4%	

APPENDIX D

Requirements

1. Analyze the company's financial summary for the fiscal years 2016–2020 to decide whether to invest in the common stock of WRM. Include the following sections in your analysis, and fully explain your final decision.
   a. Trend analysis for net sales and net income (use 2016 as the base year).
   b. Profitability analysis.
   c. Evaluation of the ability to sell merchandise inventory (WRM uses the LIFO method).
   d. Evaluation of the ability to pay debts.
   e. Evaluation of dividends.

CRITICAL THINKING

> Decision Case D-1

Lance Berkman is the controller of Saturn, a dance club whose year-end is December 31. Berkman prepares checks for suppliers in December, makes the proper journal entries, and posts them to the appropriate accounts in that month. However, he holds on to the checks and mails them to the suppliers in January.

Requirements

1. What financial ratio(s) is(are) most affected by the action?
2. What is Berkman's purpose in undertaking this activity?

> Ethical Issue D-1

Ross's Lipstick Company's long-term debt agreements make certain demands on the business. For example, Ross may not purchase treasury stock in excess of the balance of retained earnings. Also, long-term debt may not exceed stockholders' equity, and the current ratio may not fall below 1.50. If Ross fails to meet any of these requirements, the company's lenders have the authority to take over management of the company.

  Changes in consumer demand have made it hard for Ross to attract customers. Current liabilities have mounted faster than current assets, causing the current ratio to fall to 1.47. Before releasing financial statements, Ross's management is scrambling to improve the current ratio. The controller points out that an investment can be classified as either long-term or short-term, depending on management's intention. By deciding to convert an investment to cash within one year, Ross can classify the investment as short-term—a current asset. On the controller's recommendation, Ross's board of directors votes to reclassify long-term investments as short-term.

Requirements

1. What effect will reclassifying the investments have on the current ratio? Is Ross's true financial position stronger as a result of reclassifying the investments?
2. Shortly after the financial statements are released, sales improve; so, too, does the current ratio. As a result, Ross's management decides not to sell the investments it had reclassified as short-term. Accordingly, the company reclassifies the investments as long-term. Has management behaved unethically? Give the reasoning underlying your answer.

> Financial Statement Case D-1

Use **Starbucks Corporation**'s Fiscal 2013 Annual Report to answer the following questions. Visit **http://www.pearsonhighered.com/Horngren** to view a link to the Starbucks Corporation Annual Report.

Requirements

1. Compute trend analyses for total net revenues and net earnings. Use October 2, 2011, as the base year. What is the most notable aspect of these data?

2. Perform a vertical analysis for Starbucks Corporation's asset section of the balance sheet as of September 29, 2013, and September 30, 2012.

> Team Projects

Team Project D-1

Select an industry you are interested in, and pick any company in that industry to use as the benchmark. Then select two other companies in the same industry. For each category of ratios, compute all the ratios for the three companies. Write a two-page report that compares the two companies with the benchmark company.

Team Project D-2

Select a company and obtain its financial statements. Convert the income statement and the balance sheet to common size, and compare the company you selected to the industry average. The Risk Management Association's *Annual Statement Studies* and Dun & Bradstreet's *Industry Norms & Key Business Ratios* publish common-size statements for most industries.

MyAccountingLab   For a wealth of online resources, including exercises, problems, media, and immediate tutorial help, please visit **http://www.myaccountinglab.com**.

> Quick Check Answers

1. b   **2.** b   **3.** a   **4.** c   **5.** a   **6.** b   **7.** d   **8.** c   **9.** a   **10A.** d

Glossary

Absorption Costing. The product costing method that assigns direct materials, direct labor, variable manufacturing overhead, and fixed manufacturing overhead to products. Required by GAAP for external reporting. (p. 1123)

Accelerated Depreciation Method. A depreciation method that expenses more of the asset's cost near the start of its useful life and less at the end of its useful life. (p. 540)

Account. A detailed record of all increases and decreases that have occurred in an individual asset, liability, or equity during a specific period. (p. 54)

Accounting. The information system that measures business activities, processes the information into reports, and communicates the results to decision makers. (p. 2)

Accounting Cycle. The process by which companies produce their financial statements for a specific period. (p. 197)

Accounting Equation. The basic tool of accounting, measuring the resources of the business (what the business owns or has control of) and the claims to those resources (what the business owes to creditors and to the owners). Assets = Liabilities + Equity. (p. 9)

Accounting Information System (AIS). A system that collects, records, stores, and processes accounting data to produce information that is useful for decision makers. (p. 373)

Accounting Rate of Return (ARR). A capital investment analysis method that measures the profitability of an investment. Average annual operating income / Average amount invested. (p. 1439)

Account Number. On a check, the number that identifies the account upon which the payment is drawn. (p. 444)

Accounts Payable. A short-term liability that will be paid in the future. (p. 13)

Accounts Payable Subsidiary Ledger. A subsidiary ledger that includes an accounts payable account for each vendor that contains detailed information such as the amount purchased, paid, and owed. (p. 378)

Accounts Receivable. The right to receive cash in the future from customers for goods sold or for services performed. (pp. 13, 480)

Accounts Receivable Subsidiary Ledger. A subsidiary ledger that includes an accounts receivable account for each customer that contains detailed information such as the amount sold, received, and owed. (p. 377)

Accounts Receivable Turnover Ratio. A ratio that measures the number of times the company collects the average accounts receivable balance in a year. Net credit sales / Average net accounts receivable. (pp. 502, 891)

Accrual Basis Accounting. Accounting method that records revenues when earned and expenses when incurred. (p. 116)

Accrued Expense. An expense that the business has incurred but has not yet paid. (p. 128)

Accrued Liability. A liability for which the business knows the amount owed but the bill has not been paid. (p. 55)

Accrued Revenue. A revenue that has been earned but for which the cash has not yet been collected. (p. 131)

Accumulated Depreciation. The sum of all the depreciation expense recorded to date for a depreciable asset. (p. 125)

Acid-Test Ratio. The ratio of the sum of cash, cash equivalents, short-term investments, and net current receivables to total current liabilities. The ratio tells whether the entity could pay all its current liabilities if they came due immediately. (Cash including cash equivalents + Short-term investments + Net current receivables) / Total current liabilities. (pp. 502, 889)

Activity-Based Costing (ABC). Focuses on the costs of activities as the building blocks for allocating indirect costs to products and services. (p. 1317)

Activity-Based Management (ABM). Using activity-based cost information to make decisions that improve customer satisfaction while also increasing profits. (p. 1317)

Adjunct Account. An account that is directly related to another account. Adjunct accounts have the same normal balance as the related account and are added to the related account on the balance sheet. (p. 741)

Adjusted Trial Balance. A list of all the accounts with their adjusted balances. (p. 136)

Adjusting Entry. An entry made at the end of the accounting period that is used to record revenues to the period in which they are earned and expenses to the period in which they occur. (p. 121)

Administrative Expenses. Expenses incurred that are not related to marketing the company's goods and services. (p. 265)

Aging-of-Receivables Method. A method of estimating uncollectible receivables by determining the balance of the Allowance for Bad Debts account based on the age of individual accounts receivable. (p. 493)

Allocation Base. A denominator that links indirect costs to cost objects. Ideally, the allocation base is the primary cost driver of the indirect costs. (p. 992)

Allowance for Bad Debts. A contra account, related to accounts receivable, that holds the estimated amount of uncollectible accounts. (p. 487)

Allowance Method. A method of accounting for uncollectible receivables in which the company estimates bad debts expense instead of waiting to see which customers the company will not collect from. (p. 487)

Amortization. The process by which businesses spread the allocation of an intangible asset's cost over its useful life. (p. 553)

Amortization Schedule. A schedule that details each loan payment's allocation between principal and interest and the beginning and ending loan balances. (p. 729)

Annual Report. Provides information about a company's financial condition. (p. 876)

Annuity. A stream of equal cash payments made at equal time intervals. (pp. 749 Appendix 14A, 1443)

Appropriation of Retained Earnings. Restriction of a portion of retained earnings that is recorded by a journal entry. (p. 697)

Assets. Economic resources that are expected to benefit the business in the future. Something the business owns or has control of. (p. 10)

Asset Turnover Ratio. Measures how efficiently a business uses its average total assets to generate sales. Net sales / Average total assets. (pp. 557, 895, 1338)

Audit. An examination of a company's financial statements and records. (p. 8)

Authorized Stock. The maximum number of shares of stock that the corporate charter allows the corporation to issue. (p. 675)

Available-for-Sale (AFS) Investment. A debt security or an equity security in which the investor holds less than 20% of the voting stock and that isn't a trading investment or a held-to-maturity investment. (p. 779)

Bad Debts Expense. The cost to the seller of extending credit. It arises from the failure to collect from some credit customers. (p. 485)

Balanced Scorecard. The performance evaluation system that requires management to consider both financial performance measures and operational performance measures when judging the performance of a company and its subunits. (p. 1328)

Balance Sheet. Reports on the assets, liabilities, and owner's equity of the business as of a specific date. (p. 19)

Bank Reconciliation. A document explaining the reasons for the difference between a depositor's cash records and the depositor's cash balance in its bank account. (p. 446)

Bank Statement. A document from the bank that reports the activity in the customer's account. It shows the bank account's beginning and ending balances and lists the month's cash transactions conducted through the bank account. (p. 445)

Benchmarking. The practice of comparing a company with other leading companies. (p. 885)

Bond Payable. A long-term debt issued to multiple lenders called bondholders, usually in increments of $1,000 per bond. (p. 732)

Book Value. A depreciable asset's cost minus accumulated depreciation. (pp. 126, 538)

Breakeven Point. The sales level at which operating income is zero. Total revenues equal total costs. (p. 1112)

Budget. A financial plan that managers use to coordinate a business's activities. (pp. 939, 1169)

Budgetary Slack. Occurs when managers intentionally understate expected revenues or overstate expected expenses to increase the chances of receiving favorable performance evaluations. (p. 1172)

Callable Bonds. Bonds that the issuer may call and pay off at a specified price whenever the issuer wants. (p. 744)

Canceled Checks. Physical or scanned copies of the maker's cashed (paid) checks. (p. 445)

Capital Asset. An operational asset used for a long period of time. (p. 1432)

Capital Budgeting. The process of planning to invest in long-term assets in a way that returns the most profitability to the company. (p. 1432)

Capital Deficiency. A partnership's claim against a partner. Occurs when a partner's capital account has a debit balance. (p. 644)

Capital Expenditure. An expenditure that increases the capacity or efficiency of a plant asset or extends its useful life. Capital expenditures are debited to an asset account. (p. 535)

Capital Expenditures Budget. The budget that presents the company's plan for purchasing property, plant, equipment, and other long-term assets. (p. 1175)

Capital Investment. The acquisition of a capital asset. (p. 1432)

Capital Rationing. The process of ranking and choosing among alternative capital investments based on the availability of funds. (p. 1434)

Capital Stock. Represents the individual's ownership of the corporation's capital. (p. 675)

Capitalize. Recording the acquisition of land, building, or other assets by debiting (increasing) an asset account. (p. 533)

Carrying Amount of Bonds. A bond payable *minus* the discount account current balance or *plus* the premium account current balance. (p. 739)

Cash Basis Accounting. Accounting method that records revenues only when cash is received and expenses only when cash is paid. (p. 116)

Cash Budget. The budget that details how the business expects to go from the beginning cash balance to the desired ending cash balance. (p. 1175)

Cash Equivalent. A highly liquid investment that can be converted into cash in three months or less. (p. 451)

Cash Flows. Cash receipts and cash payments of a business. (p. 810)

Cash Payments Journal. Special journal used to record cash payments by check and currency. (p. 387)

Cash Ratio. A measure of a company's ability to pay current liabilities from cash and cash equivalents: (Cash + Cash equivalents) / Total current liabilities. (pp. 451, 888)

Cash Receipts Journal. Special journal used to record cash receipts. (p. 381)

Centralized Company. A company in which major planning and controlling decisions are made by top management. (p. 1322)

Certified Management Accountants (CMAs). Certified professionals who specialize in accounting and financial management knowledge. They typically work for a single company. (p. 4)

Certified Public Accountants (CPAs). Licensed professional accountants who serve the general public. (p. 4)

Chart of Accounts. A list of all of a company's accounts with their account numbers. (p. 56)

Check. A document that instructs a bank to pay the designated person or business a specified amount of money. (p. 444)

Classified Balance Sheet. A balance sheet that places each asset and each liability into a specific category. (p. 184)

Closing Entries. Entries that transfer the revenues, expenses, and Owner, Withdrawals balances to the Owner, Capital account to prepare the company's books for the next period. (p. 189)

Closing Process. A step in the accounting cycle that occurs at the end of the period. The closing process consists of journalizing and posting the closing entries to set the balances of the revenues, expenses, Income Summary, and Owner, Withdrawals accounts to zero for the next period. (p. 189)

Cloud Computing. Software and data are stored on a third-party server instead of by the business and can be accessed by employees via the Internet. (p. 392)

Collusion. Two or more people working together to circumvent internal controls and defraud a company. (p. 435)

Commercial Substance. A characteristic of a transaction that causes a change in future cash flows. (p. 558 Appendix 10A)

Common-Size Statement. A financial statement that reports only percentages (no dollar amounts). (p. 884)

Common Stock. Represents the basic ownership of a corporation. (pp. 12, 676)

Compound Interest. Interest calculated on the principal and on all previously earned interest. (pp. 749 Appendix 14A, 1443)

Compound Journal Entry. A journal entry that is characterized by having multiple debits and/or multiple credits. (p. 67)

Comprehensive Income. A company's change in total stockholders' equity from all sources other than owners' investments and dividends. (p. 789)

Conservatism. A business should report the least favorable figures in the financial statements when two or more possible options are presented. (p. 324)

Consistency Principle. A business should use the same accounting methods and procedures from period to period. (p. 323)

Consolidated Statements. Financial statements that combine the balance sheets, income statements, and statements of cash flow of the parent company with those of its controlling interest affiliates. (p. 786)

Consolidation Accounting. The way to combine the financial statements of two or more companies that have the same owners. (p. 786)

Constraint. A factor that restricts production or sale of a product. (p. 1393)

Contingent Liability. A potential liability that depends on some future event. (p. 595)

Contra Account. An account that is paired with, and is listed immediately after, its related account in the chart of accounts and associated financial statement and whose normal balance is the opposite of the normal balance of the related account. (p. 125)

Contributed Capital. Owner contributions to a corporation. (p. 12)

Contribution Margin. The amount that contributes to covering the fixed costs and then to providing operating income. Net sales revenue – Variable costs. (p. 1107)

Contribution Margin Income Statement. The income statement that groups cost by behavior—variable or fixed—and highlights the contribution margin. (p. 1108)

Contribution Margin Ratio. The ratio of contribution margin to net sales revenue. Contribution margin / Net sales revenue. (p. 1108)

Control Account. An account whose balance equals the sum of the balances in a group of related accounts in a subsidiary ledger. (p. 378)

Controllable Cost. A cost that a manager has the power to influence by his or her decisions. (p. 1331)

Controlling. Implementing plans and evaluating the results of business operations by comparing the actual results to the budget. (p. 939)

Controlling Interest Investment. An equity security in which the investor owns more than 50% of the investee's voting stock. (p. 780)

Conversion Costs. The cost to convert raw materials into finished goods: Direct labor plus manufacturing overhead. (pp. 947, 1038)

Copyright. Exclusive right to reproduce and sell a book, musical composition, film, other work of art, or intellectual property. (p. 554)

Corporation. A business organized under state law that is a separate legal entity. (pp. 6, 674)

Cost-Based Transfer Price. A transfer price based on the cost of producing the goods. (p. 1345)

Cost/Benefit Analysis. Weighing costs against benefits to help make decisions. (p. 940)

Cost Center. A responsibility center whose manager is only responsible for controlling costs. (p. 1324)

Cost Driver. The primary factor that causes a cost to increase or decrease. (p. 992)

Cost Object. Anything for which managers want a separate measurement of cost. (p. 946)

Cost of Goods Available for Sale. The total cost spent on inventory that was available to be sold during a period. (p. 328)

Cost of Goods Manufactured. The manufacturing costs of the goods that finished the production process in a given accounting period. (p. 949)

Cost of Goods Sold (COGS). The cost of the merchandise inventory that the business has sold to customers. (p. 246)

Cost-Plus Pricing. A method to manage costs and profits by determining the price. Full product cost + Desired profit = Cost-plus price. (p. 1384)

Cost Principle. A principle that states that acquired assets and services should be recorded at their actual cost. (pp. 7, 532)

Cost Structure. The proportion of fixed costs to variable costs. (p. 1118)

Cost Variance. Measures how well the business keeps unit costs of material and labor inputs within standards. (p. 1263)

Cost-Volume-Profit (CVP) Analysis. A planning tool that expresses the relationships among costs, volume, and prices and their effects on profits and losses. (p. 1109)

Credit. The right side of a T-account. (p. 58)

Credit Memorandum. An increase in a bank account. (p. 447)

Creditor. Any person or business to whom a business owes money. (p. 4)

Credit Terms. The payment terms of purchase or sale as stated on the invoice. (p. 250)

Cumulative Preferred Stock. Preferred stock whose owners must receive all dividends in arrears plus the current year dividend before the corporation pays dividends to the common stockholders. (p. 689)

Current Asset. An asset that is expected to be converted to cash, sold, or used up during the next 12 months or within the business's normal operating cycle if the cycle is longer than a year. (p. 185)

Current Liability. A liability that must be paid with cash or with goods and services within one year or within the entity's operating cycle if the cycle is longer than a year. (pp. 185, 580)

Current Portion of Notes Payable. The amount of the principal that is payable within one year. (p. 583)

Current Ratio. Measures the company's ability to pay current liabilities from current assets. Total current assets / Total current liabilities. (pp. 198, 888)

Days' Sales in Inventory. Measures the average number of days that inventory is held by a company. 365 days / Inventory turnover. (pp. 342, 890)

Days' Sales in Receivables. The ratio of average net accounts receivable to one day's sales. The ratio tells how many days it takes to collect the average level of accounts receivable. 365 days / Accounts receivable turnover ratio. (pp. 503, 892)

Debentures. Unsecured bonds backed only by the credit worthiness of the bond issuer. (p. 734)

Debit. The left side of a T-account. (p. 58)

Debit Memorandum. A decrease in a bank account. (p. 447)

Debtor. The party to a credit transaction who takes on an obligation/payable. (p. 480)

Debt Ratio. Shows the proportion of assets financed with debt. Total liabilities / Total assets. (pp. 79, 892)

Debt to Equity Ratio. A ratio that measures the proportion of total liabilities relative to total equity. Total liabilities / Total equity. (pp. 747, 893)

Debt Security. Represents a credit relationship with another company or governmental entity that typically pays interest for a fixed period. (p. 778)

Decentralized Company. A company that is divided into business segments, with segment managers making planning and controlling decisions for their segments. (p. 1322)

Deferred Expense. An asset created when a business makes advance payments of future expenses. (p. 121)

Deferred Revenue. A liability created when a business collects cash from customers in advance of completing a service or delivering a product. (p. 127)

Deficit. Debit balance in the Retained Earnings account. (p. 697)

Degree of Operating Leverage. The ratio that measures the effects that fixed costs have on changes in operating income when sales volume changes. Contribution margin / Operating income. (p. 1119)

Depletion. The process by which businesses spread the allocation of a natural resource's cost over its usage. (p. 552)

Deposit in Transit. A deposit recorded by the company but not yet by its bank. (p. 446)

Deposit Ticket. A bank form that is completed by the customer and shows the amount of each deposit. (p. 444)

Depreciable Cost. The cost of a plant asset minus its estimated residual value. (p. 537)

Depreciation. The process by which businesses spread the allocation of a plant asset's cost over its useful life. (pp. 124, 531)

Differential Analysis. A method that looks at how operating income would differ under each decision alternative; leaves out irrelevant information. (p. 1379)

Direct Cost. Cost that can be easily and cost-effectively traced to a cost object. (p. 946)

Direct Labor (DL). The labor cost of employees who convert raw materials into finished products. (p. 947)

Direct Materials (DM). Materials that become a physical part of a finished product and whose costs are easily traced to the finished product. (p. 947)

Direct Method. A format of the operating activities section of the statement of cash flows; lists the operating cash receipts and cash payments. (p. 813)

Direct Write-off Method. A method of accounting for uncollectible receivables in which the company records bad debts expense when a customer's account receivable is uncollectible. (p. 485)

Disclosure Principle. A business's financial statements must report enough information for outsiders to make knowledgeable decisions about the company. (p. 323)

Discount on Bonds Payable. Occurs when a bond's issue price is less than face value. (p. 734)

Discount Rate. Management's minimum desired rate of return on a capital investment. (p. 1449)

Dishonor a Note. Failure of a note's maker to pay a note receivable at maturity. (p. 500)

Dissolution. Ending of a partnership. (p. 622)

Dividend. A distribution of a corporation's earnings to stockholders. (p. 676)

Dividend in Arrears. A preferred stock dividend is in arrears if the dividend has not been paid for the year and the preferred stock is cumulative. (p. 689)

Dividend Payout. The ratio of dividends declared per common share relative to the earnings per share of the company. Annual dividend per share / Earnings per share. (p. 898)

Dividend Yield. Ratio of annual dividends per share of stock to the stock's market price per share. Measures the percentage of a stock's market value that is returned annually as dividends to stockholders. Annual dividend per share / Market price per share. (p. 897)

Dollar Value Bias. The bias one sees from comparing numbers in absolute (dollars) rather than relative (percentage) terms. (p. 884)

Double-Declining-Balance Method. An accelerated depreciation method that computes annual depreciation by multiplying the depreciable asset's decreasing book value by a constant percent that is two times the straight-line depreciation rate. (p. 540)

Double-Entry System. A system of accounting in which every transaction affects at least two accounts. (p. 58)

Earnings per Share (EPS). Amount of a company's net income (loss) for each share of its outstanding common stock. (Net income – Preferred dividends) / Weighted average number of common shares outstanding. (pp. 699, 896)

Economic Entity Assumption. An organization that stands apart as a separate economic unit. (p. 6)

Effective-Interest Amortization Method. An amortization model that calculates interest expense based on the current carrying amount of the bond

and the market interest rate at issuance, then amortizes the difference between the cash interest payment and calculated interest expense as a decrease to the discount or premium. (p. 754 Appendix 14B)

Efficiency Variance. Measures how well the business uses its materials or human resources. (p. 1263)

Electronic Data Interchange (EDI). A streamlined process that bypasses paper documents altogether. Computers of customers communicate directly with the computers of suppliers to automate routine business transactions. (p. 440)

Electronic Funds Transfer (EFT). A system that transfers cash by electronic communication rather than by paper documents. (p. 445)

Encryption. Rearranging plain-text messages by a mathematical process—the primary method of achieving security in e-commerce. (p. 434)

Enterprise Resource Planning (ERP). Software system that can integrate all of a company's functions, departments, and data into a single system. (pp. 392, 941)

Equity. The owners' claims to the assets of the business. (p. 10)

Equity Security. Represents stock ownership in another company that sometimes pays dividends. (p. 778)

Equivalent Units of Production (EUP). Used to measure the amount of materials added to or work done on partially completed units and expressed in terms of fully completed units. (p. 1038)

Evaluated Receipts Settlement (ERS). A procedure that compresses the payment approval process into a single step by comparing the receiving report to the purchase order. (p. 440)

Expenses. The cost of selling goods or services. (p. 10)

External Auditor. An outside accountant, completely independent of the business, who evaluates the controls to ensure that the financial statements are presented fairly in accordance with GAAP. (p. 433)

Extraordinary Repair. Repair work that generates a capital expenditure because it extends the asset's life past the normal expected life. (p. 535)

Face Value. The amount a borrower must pay back to the bondholders on the maturity date. (p. 733)

Fair Value. The price that would be used if the investments were sold on the market. (p. 786)

Federal Insurance Contributions Act (FICA). The federal act that created the Social Security tax that provides retirement, disability, and medical benefits. (p. 586)

Financial Accounting. The field of accounting that focuses on providing information for external decision makers. (p. 3)

Financial Accounting Standards Board (FASB). The private organization that oversees the creation and governance of accounting standards in the United States. (p. 6)

Financial Budget. The budget that includes he cash budget and the budgeted financial statements. (p. 1175)

Financial Leverage. Occurs when a company earns more income on borrowed money than the related interest expense. (p. 737)

Financial Statements. Business documents that are used to communicate information needed to make business decisions. (p. 17)

Financing Activities. Activities that increase or decrease long-term liabilities and equity; a section of the statement of cash flows. (p. 811)

Finished Goods Inventory (FG). Completed goods that have not yet been sold. (p. 945)

Firewall. A device that enables members of a local network to access the network, while keeping nonmembers out of the network. (p. 434)

First-In, First-Out (FIFO) Method. An inventory costing method in which the first costs into inventory are the first costs out to cost of goods sold. Ending inventory is based on the costs of the most recent purchases. (p. 328)

First-In, First-Out (FIFO) Method (for Process Costing). Determines the cost of equivalent units of production by accounting for beginning inventory costs separately from current period costs. It assumes the first units started in the production process are the first units completed and sold. (p. 1060 Appendix 20A)

Fiscal Year. An accounting year of any 12 consecutive months that may or may not coincide with the calendar year. (p. 118)

Fixed Cost. A cost that remains the same *in total*, regardless of changes over wide ranges of volume of activity. (p. 1101)

Flexible Budget. A budget prepared for various levels of sales volume. (pp. 1173, 1256)

Flexible Budget Variance. The difference between actual results and the expected results in the flexible budget for the *actual* units sold. (p. 1257)

FOB Destination. Situation in which the buyer takes ownership (title) to the goods at the delivery destination point and the seller typically pays the freight. (p. 253)

FOB Shipping Point. Situation in which the buyer takes ownership (title) to the goods after the goods leave the seller's place of business (shipping point) and the buyer typically pays the freight. (p. 253)

Franchise. Privilege granted by a business to sell a product or service under specified conditions. (p. 555)

Free Cash Flow. The amount of cash available from operating activities after paying for planned investments in long-term assets and after paying dividends to shareholders. Net cash provided by operating activities – Cash payments planned for investments in long-term assets – Cash dividends. (p. 828)

Freight In. The transportation cost to ship goods into the purchaser's warehouse; therefore, it is freight on purchased goods. (p. 253)

Freight Out. The transportation cost to ship goods out of the seller's warehouse; therefore, it is freight on goods sold to a customer. (p. 253)

General Partner. A partner who has unlimited personal liability in the partnership. (p. 624)

General Partnership. A form of partnership in which each partner is a co-owner of the business, with all the privileges and risks of ownership. (p. 623)

Generally Accepted Accounting Principles (GAAP). Accounting guidelines, currently formulated by the *Financial Accounting Standards Board (FASB)*; the main U.S. accounting rule book. (p. 6)

Goal Congruence. Aligning the goals of business segment managers and other subordinates with the goals of top management. (p. 1323)

Going Concern Assumption. Assumes that the entity will remain in operation for the foreseeable future. (p. 7)

Goodwill. Excess of the cost of an acquired company over the sum of the market values of its net assets (assets minus liabilities). (p. 555)

Gross Pay. The total amount of salary, wages, commissions, and any other employee compensation before taxes and other deductions. (p. 585)

Gross Profit. Excess of net Sales Revenue over Cost of Goods Sold. (p. 247)

Gross Profit Percentage. Measures the profitability of each sales dollar above the cost of goods sold. Gross profit / Net sales revenue. (pp. 267, 891)

Hardware. Electronic equipment that includes computers, monitors, printers, and the network that connects them. (p. 392)

Held-to-Maturity (HTM) Investment. A debt security the investor intends to hold until it matures. (p. 779)

High-Low Method. A method used to separate mixed costs into their variable and fixed components, using the highest and lowest activity levels. (p. 1104)

Horizontal Analysis. The study of percentage changes in comparative financial statements. (Dollar amount of change / Base period amount) × 100. (p. 878)

Impairment. A permanent decline in asset value. (p. 553)

Imprest System. A way to account for petty cash by maintaining a constant balance in the petty cash account. At any time, cash plus petty cash tickets must total the amount allocated to the petty cash fund. (p. 441)

Income Statement. Reports the *net income* or *net loss* of the business for a specific period. (p. 17)

Income Summary. A temporary account into which revenues and expenses are transferred prior to their final transfer into the Owner, Capital account. Summarizes net income (or net loss) for the period. (p. 190)

Income Tax Expense. Expense incurred by a corporation related to federal and state income taxes. (p. 695)

Income Tax Withholding. Income tax deducted from an employee's gross pay. (p. 585)

Indirect Cost. Cost that cannot be easily or cost-effectively traced to a cost object. (p. 946)

Indirect Labor. Labor costs for activities that support the production process but either cannot be conveniently traced directly to specific finished products or are not large enough to justify tracing to the specific product. (p. 947)

Indirect Materials. Materials used in making a product but whose costs either cannot be conveniently traced directly to specific finished products or are not large enough to justify tracing to the specific product. (p. 947)

Indirect Method. A format of the operating activities section of the statement of cash flows; starts with net income and reconciles to net cash provided by operating activities. (p. 813)

Intangible Asset. An asset with no physical form that is valuable because of the special rights it carries. (pp. 185, 553)

Interest. The revenue to the payee for loaning money—the expense to the debtor. (p. 496)

Interest Period. The period of time during which interest is computed. It extends from the original date of the note to the maturity date. (p. 496)

Interest Rate. The percentage rate of interest specified by the note. (p. 496)

Internal Auditor. An employee of the business who ensures the company's employees are following company policies, that the company meets all legal requirements, and that operations are running efficiently. (p. 433)

Internal Control. The organizational plan and all the related measures adopted by an entity to safeguard assets, encourage employees to follow company policies, promote operational efficiency, and ensure accurate and reliable accounting records. (p. 431)

Internal Control Report. A report by management describing its responsibility for and the adequacy of internal controls over financial reporting. (p. 432)

Internal Rate of Return (IRR). The rate of return, based on discounted cash flows, of a capital investment. The interest rate that makes the NPV of the investment equal to zero. (p. 1454)

International Accounting Standards Board (IASB). The private organization that oversees the creation and governance of *International Financial Reporting Standards (IFRS)*. (p. 8)

International Financial Reporting Standards (IFRS). A set of global accounting guidelines, formulated by the *International Accounting Standards Board (IASB)*. (p. 8)

Inventory Costing Method. A method of approximating the flow of inventory costs in a business that is used to determine the amount of cost of goods sold and ending merchandise inventory. (p. 327)

Inventory Shrinkage. The loss of inventory that occurs because of theft, damage, and errors. (p. 261)

Inventory Turnover. Measures the number of times a company sells its average level of merchandise inventory during a period. Cost of goods sold / Average merchandise inventory. (pp. 342, 890)

Investee. The corporation that issued the bond or stock to the investor. (p. 778)

Investment Center. A responsibility center whose manager is responsible for generating profits and efficiently managing the center's invested capital. (p. 1324)

Investing Activities. Activities that increase or decrease long-term assets; a section of the statement of cash flows. (p. 811)

Investor. The owner of a bond or stock of a corporation. (p. 778)

Invoice. A seller's request for payment from the purchaser. (p. 248)

Irrelevant Cost. A cost that does not affect the decision because it is not in the future or does not differ among alternatives. (p. 1379)

Issue Price. The price the stock initially sells for the first time it is sold. (p. 678)

Issued Stock. Stock that has been issued but may or may not be held by stockholders. (p. 675)

Job. The production of a unique product or specialized service. May be one unit or a batch of units. (p. 983)

Job Cost Record. A document that shows the direct materials, direct labor, and manufacturing overhead costs for an individual job. (p. 983)

Job Order Costing System. An accounting system that accumulates costs by job. Used by companies that manufacture unique products or provide specialized services. (pp. 983, 1034)

Joint Cost. A cost of a production process that yields multiple products. (p. 1402)

Journal. A record of transactions in date order. (p. 62)

Just-In-Time (JIT) Management. A cost management system in which a company produces products just in time to satisfy needs. Suppliers deliver materials just in time to begin production, and finished units are completed just in time for delivery to the customer. (p. 941)

Key Performance Indicator (KPI). A summary performance measure that helps managers assess whether the company is achieving its goals. (p. 1328)

Labor Time Record. A record used to assign direct labor cost to specific jobs. (p. 988)

Lag Indicator. A performance measure that indicates past performance. (p. 1327)

Land Improvement. A depreciable improvement to land, such as fencing, sprinklers, paving, signs, and lighting. (p. 532)

Large Stock Dividend. A stock dividend greater than 20% to 25% of the issued and outstanding stock. (p. 691)

Last-In, First-Out (LIFO) Method. An inventory costing method in which the last costs into inventory are the first costs out to cost of goods sold. The method leaves the oldest costs—those of beginning inventory and the earliest purchases of the period—in ending inventory. (p. 329)

Lead Indicator. A performance measure that forecasts future performance. (p. 1327)

Ledger. The record holding all the accounts of a business, the changes in those accounts, and their balances. (p. 57)

Legal Capital. The portion of stockholders' equity that cannot be used for dividends. (p. 687)

Liabilities. Debts that are owed to creditors. (pp. 10, 580)

Limited-Liability Company (LLC). A company in which each member is only liable for his or her own actions. (pp. 6, 624)

Limited Liability Partnership (LLP). A form of partnership in which each partner is protected from the malpractice or negligence of the other partners. (p. 624)

Limited Partner. A partner who has limited personal liability in the partnership. (p. 624)

Limited Partnership (LP). A partnership with at least two classes of partners; one or more general partners and one or more limited partners. (p. 624)

Liquidation. The process of going out of business by selling the entity's assets, paying its liabilities, and distributing any remaining cash to the owners based on their equity balances. (p. 640)

Liquidity. A measure of how quickly an item can be converted to cash. (p. 184)

License. Privilege granted by a government to use public property in performing services. (p. 555)

Lock-Box System. A system in which customers send their checks to a post office box that belongs to a bank. A bank employee empties the box daily and records the deposits into the company's bank account. (p. 437)

Long-Term Asset. An asset that will not be converted to cash or used up within the business's operating cycle or one year, whichever is greater. (p. 185)

Long-Term Investment. Investments in bonds (debt securities) or stocks (equity securities) in which the company intends to hold the investment for longer than one year. (pp. 185, 779)

Long-Term Liability. A liability that does not need to be paid within one year or within the entity's operating cycle, whichever is longer. (pp. 185, 580)

Lower-of-Cost-or-Market (LCM) Rule. Rule that merchandise inventory should be reported in the financial statements at whichever is lower—its historical cost or its market value. (p. 337)

Maker. The party who issues the check. (p. 444)

Management Accountability. The manager's responsibility to wisely manage the resources of an organization. (p. 940)

Management by Exception. When managers concentrate on results that are outside the accepted parameters. (p. 1278)

Management's Discussion and Analysis of Financial Condition and Results of Operations (MD&A). The section of the annual report that is intended to help investors understand the results of operations and the financial condition of the company. (p. 876)

Managerial Accounting. The field of accounting that focuses on providing information for internal decision makers. (p. 3)

Manufacturing Company. A company that uses labor, equipment, supplies, and facilities to convert raw materials into finished products. (p. 945)

Manufacturing Overhead (MOH). Manufacturing costs that cannot be easily and cost-effectively traced to a cost object. Includes all manufacturing costs except direct materials and direct labor. (p. 947)

Margin of Safety. The excess of expected sales over breakeven sales. The amount sales can decrease before the company incurs an operating loss. (p. 1117)

Market-Based Transfer Price. A transfer price based on the current market value of the goods. (p. 1344)

Market Interest Rate. The interest rate that investors demand in order to loan their money. (p. 736)

Master Budget. The set of budgeted financial statements and supporting schedules for the entire organization; includes the operating budget, capital expenditures budget, and financial budget. (p. 1174)

Matching Principle. Guides accounting for expenses, ensures that all expenses are recorded when they are incurred during the period, and matches those expenses against the revenues of the period. (p. 119)

Materiality Concept. A company must perform strictly proper accounting only for items that are significant to the business's financial situation. (p. 324)

Materials Requisition. Request for the transfer of raw materials to the production floor. (p. 986)

Maturity Date. The date when a note is due. (p. 480)

Maturity Value. The sum of the principal plus interest due at maturity. (p. 496)

Memorandum Entry. An entry in the journal that notes a significant event but has no debit or credit amount. (p. 694)

Merchandise Inventory. The merchandise that a business sells to customers. (p. 245)

Merchandiser. A business that sells merchandise, or goods, to customers. (p. 245)

Merchandising Company. A company that resells products previously bought from suppliers. (p. 944)

Mixed Cost. A cost that has both fixed and variable components. (p. 1103)

Modified Accelerated Cost Recovery System (MACRS). A depreciation method that is used for tax purposes. (p. 543)

Monetary Unit Assumption. The assumption that requires the items on the financial statements to be measured in terms of a monetary unit. (p. 8)

Mortgages Payable. Long-term debts that are backed with a security interest in specific property. (p. 730)

Multi-Step Income Statement. Income statement format that contains subtotals to highlight significant relationships. In addition to net income, it reports gross profit and operating income. (p. 265)

Mutual Agency. Every partner can bind the business to a contract within the scope of the partnership's regular business operations. (p. 622)

Natural Resource. An asset that comes from the earth and is consumed. (p. 552)

Net Income. The result of operations that occurs when total revenues are greater than total expenses. (p. 10)

Net Loss. The result of operations that occurs when total expenses are greater than total revenues. (p. 10)

Net Pay. Gross pay minus all deductions. The amount of compensation that the employee actually takes home. (p. 585)

Net Present Value (NPV). A capital investment analysis method that measures the net difference between the present value of the investment's net cash inflows and the investment's cost. (p. 1449)

Net Purchases. Purchases less purchase returns and allowances less purchase discounts. (p. 270 Appendix 5A)

Net Realizable Value. The net value a company expects to collect from its accounts receivable. Accounts Receivable less Allowance for Bad Debts. (p. 487)

Net Sales Revenue. The amount a company has earned on sales of merchandise inventory after returns, allowances, and discounts have been taken out. Sales Revenue less Sales Returns and Allowances and Sales Discounts. (p. 259)

Network. The system of electronic linkages that allows different computers to share the same information. (p. 392)

Non-cash Investing and Financing Activities. Investing and financing activities that do not involve cash. (p. 812)

Noncumulative Preferred Stock. Preferred stock whose owners do not receive passed dividends. (p. 689)

Nonsufficient Funds (NSF) Check. A check for which the maker's bank account has insufficient money to pay the check. (p. 447)

No-Par Stock. Stock that has no amount (par) assigned to it. (p. 677)

Normal Balance. The balance that appears on the increase side of an account. (p. 59)

Notes Payable. A written promise made by the business to pay a debt, usually involving interest, in the future. (p. 55)

Notes Receivable. A written promise that a customer will pay a fixed amount of principal plus interest by a certain date in the future. (pp. 55, 480)

Obsolete. An asset is considered obsolete when a newer asset can perform the job more efficiently than the old. (p. 536)

Operating Activities. Activities that create revenue or expense in the entity's business; a section of the statement of cash flows. (p. 811)

Operating Budget. The set of budgets that projects sales revenue, cost of goods sold, and selling and administrative expenses, all of which feed into the cash budget and then the budgeted financial statements. (p. 1174)

Operating Cycle. The time span during which cash is paid for goods and services, which are then sold to customers from whom the business collects cash. (p. 185)

Operating Expenses. Expenses, other than Cost of Goods Sold, that are incurred in the entity's major ongoing operations. (p. 247)

Operating Income. Measures the results of the entity's major ongoing activities. Gross profit minus operating expenses. (p. 265)

Operating Leverage. Effects that fixed costs have on changes in operating income when sales volume changes. (p. 1119)

Operational Budget. A short-term financial plan used to coordinate the activities needed to achieve the short-term goals of the company. (p. 1173)

Opportunity Cost. The benefit given up by choosing an alternative course of action. (pp. 1345, 1400)

Other Revenues and Expenses. Revenues or expenses that are outside the normal, day-to-day operations of a business, such as a gain or loss on the sale of plant assets or interest expense. (p. 266)

Outstanding Check. A check issued by a company and recorded on its books but not yet paid by its bank. (p. 446)

Outstanding Stock. Issued stock in the hands of stockholders. (p. 676)

Overallocated Overhead. Occurs when the actual manufacturing overhead costs are less than allocated manufacturing overhead costs. (p. 997)

Owner's Capital. Owner contributions to business. (p. 10)

Owner's Withdrawals. Payments of equity to the owner. (p. 10)

Paid-In Capital. Represents amounts received from the stockholders of a corporation in exchange for stock. (p. 677)

Paid-In Capital in Excess of Par. Represents amounts received from stockholders in excess of par value. (p. 679)

Parent Company. A company that owns a controlling interest in another company. (p. 786)

Partnership. A business with two or more owners that is not organized as a corporation. (p. 6, 621)

Partnership Agreement. The contract between partners that specifies such items as the name, location, and nature of the business; the name, capital contribution, and duties of each partner; and the method of sharing profits and losses among the partners. (p. 621)

Par Value. An amount assigned by a company to a share of its stock. (p. 677)

Patent. An intangible asset that is a federal government grant conveying an exclusive 20-year right to produce and sell a process, product, or formula. (p. 554)

Payback. A capital investment analysis method that measures the length of time it takes to recover, in net cash inflows, the cost of the initial investment. (p. 1436)

Payee. The individual or business to whom the check is paid. (p. 444)

Payroll Register. A schedule that summarizes the earnings, withholdings, and net pay for each employee. (pp. 444, 588)

Performance Evaluation System. A system that provides top management with a framework for maintaining control over the entire organization. (p. 1326)

Pension Plan. A plan that provides benefits to retired employees. (p. 593)

Percent-of-Receivables Method. A method of estimating uncollectible receivables by determining the balance of the Allowance for Bad Debts account based on a percentage of accounts receivable. (p. 491)

Percent-of-Sales Method. A method of estimating uncollectible receivables that calculates bad debts expense based on a percentage of net credit sales. (p. 489)

Period Cost. Operating cost that is expensed in the accounting period in which it is incurred. (p. 943)

Periodic Inventory System. An inventory system that requires businesses to obtain a physical count of inventory to determine quantities on hand. (p. 247)

Permanent Account. An account that is *not* closed at the end of the period—the asset, liability, and Owner, Capital accounts. (p. 190)

Perpetual Inventory System. An inventory system that keeps a running computerized record of merchandise inventory. (p. 247)

Petty Cash. A fund containing a small amount of cash that is used to pay for minor expenditures. (p. 440)

Planning. Choosing goals and deciding how to achieve them. (p. 939)

Plant Asset. Long-lived, tangible asset, such as land, buildings, and equipment, used in the operation of a business. (pp. 123, 185, 531)

Post-Audit. The comparison of the actual results of capital investments to the projected results. (p. 1434)

Post-Closing Trial Balance. A list of the accounts and their balances at the end of the period after journalizing and posting the closing entries. It should include only permanent accounts. (p. 195)

Posting. Transferring data from the journal to the ledger. (p. 62)

Predetermined Overhead Allocation Rate. Estimated overhead cost per unit of the allocation base, calculated at the beginning of the accounting period. Total estimated overhead costs / Total estimated quantity of the overhead allocation base. (pp. 881, 1313)

Preemptive Right. Stockholder's right to maintain his or her proportionate ownership in the corporation. (p. 676)

Preferred Stock. Stock that gives its owners certain advantages over common stockholders, such as the right to receive dividends before the common stockholders and the right to receive assets before the common stockholders if the corporation liquidates. (p. 677)

Premium. The amount above par at which a stock is issued. (p. 678)

Premium on Bonds Payable. Occurs when a bond's issue price is more than face value. (p. 734)

Prepaid Expense. A payment of an expense in advance. (p. 55)

Present Value. The amount a person would invest now to receive a greater amount in the future. (p. 735)

Prevention Costs. Costs incurred to avoid poor-quality goods or services. (p. 1013)

Price/Earnings Ratio. The ratio of the market price of a share of common stock to the company's earnings per share. Measures the value that the stock market places on $1 of a company's earnings. Market price per share of common stock / Earnings per share. (pp. 700, 897)

Price-Setter. A company that has control over the prices of its products and services because its products and services are unique and there is little competition. (p. 1381)

Price-Taker. A company that has little control over the prices of its products and services because its products and services are not unique or competition is intense. (p. 1381)

Prime Costs. Direct materials plus direct labor. (p. 947)

Principal. The amount loaned out by the payee and borrowed by the maker of the note. (p. 496)

Prior-Period Adjustment. A correction to Retained Earnings for an error of an earlier period. (p. 697)

Process. One of a series of steps in manufacturing production; usually associated with making large quantities of similar items. (p. 1034)

Process Costing System. An accounting system that accumulates costs by process. Used by companies that manufacture identical units through a series of uniform production steps or processes. (pp. 983, 1034)

Product Cost. The cost of purchasing or making a product. The cost is recorded as an asset and then expensed when the product is sold. (p. 944)

Production Cost Report. A report prepared by a processing department for equivalent units of production, production costs, and the assignment of those costs to the completed and in process units. (p. 1040)

Profitability Index. Computes the number of dollars returned for every dollar invested, with all calculations performed in present value dollars. Present value of net cash inflows / Initial investment. (p. 1453)

Profit Center. A responsibility center whose manager is responsible for generating revenue and controlling costs and, therefore, profits. (p. 1324)

Profit Margin Ratio. A profitability measure that shows how much operating income is earned on every dollar of net sales. Operating income / Net sales. (pp. 894, 1338)

Public Company. A company that sells its stock to the general public. (p. 431)

Purchase Allowance. An amount granted to the purchaser as an incentive to keep goods that are not "as ordered." (p. 251)

Purchase Discount. A discount that businesses offer to purchasers as an incentive for early payment. (p. 250)

Purchase Return. A situation in which sellers allow purchasers to return merchandise that is defective, damaged, or otherwise unsuitable. (p. 251)

Purchases Journal. Special journal used to record all purchases of merchandise inventory, office supplies, and other assets on account. (p. 385)

Rate of Return on Common Stockholders' Equity. Shows the relationship between net income available to common stockholders and their average common equity invested in thecompany. (Net income − Preferred dividends) / Average common stockholders' equity. (pp. 700, 895)

Rate of Return on Total Assets. A ratio that measures the success a company has in using its assets to earn income. (Net income + Interest expense) / Average total assets. (pp. 791, 894)

Raw Materials Inventory (RM). Materials used to manufacture a product. (p. 945)

Receivable. A monetary claim against a business or an individual. (p. 480)

Relative-Market-Value Method. A method of allocating the total cost (100%) of multiple assets purchased at one time. Total cost is divided among the assets according to their relative market values. (p. 534)

Relevant Cost. A cost that is relevant to a particular decision because it is a future cost and differs among alternatives. (p. 1378)

Relevant Information. Expected future data that differ among alternatives. (p. 1378)

Relevant Range. The range of volume where total fixed costs and variable cost per unit remain constant. (p. 1106)

Remittance Advice. An optional attachment to a check that tells the business the reason for the payment. (p. 437)

Residual Income (RI). A measure of profitability and efficiency computed as actual operating income less a specified minimum acceptable operating income. (p. 1340)

Residual Value. The expected value of a depreciable asset at the end of its useful life. (pp. 124, 537)

Responsibility Accounting System. A system for evaluating the performance of each responsibility center and its manager. (p. 1324)

Responsibility Center. A part of the organization for which a manager has decision-making authority and accountability for the results of those decisions. (p. 1323)

Retailer. A type of merchandiser that buys merchandise either from a manufacturer or a wholesaler and then sells those goods to consumers. (p. 245)

Retained Earnings. Equity earned by profitable operations of a corporation that is not distributed to stockholders. (pp. 12, 677)

Return on Assets (ROA). Measures how profitably a company uses its assets. Net income / Average total assets. (p. 22)

Return on Investment (ROI). A measure of profitability and efficiency. Operating income / Average total assets. (p. 1337)

Revenue Center. A responsibility center whose manager is only responsible for generating revenue. (p. 1324)

Revenue Expenditure. An expenditure that does not increase the capacity or efficiency of an asset or extend its useful life. Revenue expenditures are debited to an expense account. (p. 535)

Revenue Recognition Principle. Requires companies to record revenue when it has been earned and determines the amount of revenue to record. (p. 118)

Revenues. Amounts earned from delivering goods or services to customers. (p. 10)

Reversing Entry. A special journal entry that eases the burden of accounting for transactions in the next period. Such entries are the exact opposite of a prior adjusting entry. (p. 202 Appendix 4A)

Routing Number. On a check, the 9-digit number that identifies the bank upon which the payment is drawn. (p. 444)

S Corporation. A corporation with 100 or fewer stockholders that can elect to be taxed in the same way as a partnership. (p. 624)

Sales Discounts. Reduction in the amount of cash received from a customer for early payment. (p. 257)

Sales Journal. Special journal used to record credit sales. (p. 378)

Sales Mix. The combination of products that make up total sales. (p. 1120)

Sales Returns and Allowances. Decreases in the seller's receivable from a customer's return of merchandise or from granting the customer an allowance from the amount owed to the seller. (p. 257)

Sales Revenue. The amount that a merchandiser earns from selling its inventory. (p. 256)

Sales Volume Variance. The difference between the expected results in the flexible budget for the *actual* units sold and the static budget. (p. 1258)

Sarbanes-Oxley Act (SOX). Requires companies to review internal control and take responsibility for the accuracy and completeness of their financial reports. (pp. 8, 431)

Secured Bonds. Bonds that give bondholders the right to take specified assets of the issuer if the issuer fails to pay principal or interest. (p. 734)

Securities and Exchange Commission (SEC). U.S. governmental agency that oversees the U.S. financial markets. (p. 6)

Security. A share or interest representing financial value. (p. 778)

Selling Expenses. Expenses related to marketing and selling the company's goods and services. (p. 265)

Sensitivity Analysis. A "what if" technique that estimates profit or loss results if sales price, costs, volume, or underlying assumptions change. (p. 1115)

Separation of Duties. Dividing responsibilities between two or more people to limit fraud and promote accuracy of accounting records. (p. 434)

Serial Bonds. Bonds that mature in installments at regular intervals. (p. 734)

Server. The main computer where data are stored, which can be accessed from many different computers. (p. 375)

Service Company. A company that sells services—time, skills, and/or knowledge—instead of products. (p. 943)

Short-Term Investments. Investments in debt and equity securities that are highly liquid and that the investor intends to sell in one year or less. (p. 779)

Short-Term Note Payable. A written promise made by the business to pay a debt, usually involving interest, within one year or less. (p. 582)

Signature Card. A card that shows each authorized person's signature for a bank account. (p. 444)

Significant Interest Investment. An equity security in which the investor owns from 20% to 50% of the investee's voting stock. (p. 780)

Simple Interest. Interest calculated only on the principal amount. (pp. 749 Appendix 14A, 1443)

Single-Step Income Statement. Income statement format that groups all revenues together and then lists and deducts all expenses together without calculating any subtotals. (p. 264)

Small Stock Dividend. A stock dividend of less than 20% to 25% of the issued and outstanding stock. (p. 691)

Social Security (FICA) Tax. Federal Insurance Contributions Act (FICA) tax, which is withheld from employees' pay and matched by the employer. (p. 586)

Software. Set of programs or instructions that drives the computer to perform the work desired. (p. 392)

Sole Proprietorship. A business with a single owner. (p. 6)

Source Document. Provides the evidence and data for accounting transactions. (pp. 61, 374)

Special Journal. An accounting journal designed to record one specific type of transaction. (p. 376)

Specific Identification Method. An inventory costing method based on the specific cost of particular units of inventory. (p. 327)

Stakeholder. An individual or group that has an interest in a business, including customers, creditors, suppliers, and investors. (p. 940)

Standard. A price, cost, or quantity that is expected under normal conditions. (p. 1260)

Standard Cost System. An accounting system that uses standards for product costs—direct materials, direct labor, and manufacturing overhead. (p. 1260)

Stated Interest Rate. The interest rate that determines the amount of cash interest the borrower pays and the investor receives each year. (p. 734)

Stated Value Stock. No-par stock that has been assigned an amount similar to par value. (p. 677)

Statement of Cash Flows. Reports on a business's cash receipts and cash payments for a specific period. (pp. 20, 810)

Statement of Owner's Equity. Shows the changes in the owner's capital account for a specific period. (p. 18)

Statement of Partners' Equity. Summary of the changes in each partner's capital account for a specific period of time. (p. 626)

Statement of Retained Earnings. Reports how the company's retained earnings balance changed from the beginning to the end of the period. (p. 20)

Static Budget. A budget prepared for only one level of sales volume. (pp. 1173, 1255)

Static Budget Variance. The difference between actual results and the expected results in the static budget. (p. 1255)

Stock Certificate. Paper evidence of ownership in a corporation. (p. 675)

Stock Dividend. A distribution by a corporation of its own stock to its stockholders. (p. 690)

Stockholder. A person who owns stock in a corporation. (p. 7)

Stockholders' Equity. A corporation's equity that includes paid-in capital and retained earnings. (p. 677)

Stock Split. An increase in the number of issued and outstanding shares of stock coupled with a proportionate reduction in the par value of the stock. (p. 694)

Straight-Line Method. A depreciation method that allocates an equal amount of depreciation each year. (Cost − Residual value) / Useful life. (pp. 124, 538)

Straight-Line Amortization Method. An amortization method that allocates an equal amount of bond discount or premium to each interest period over the life of the bond. (p. 739)

Strategic Budget. A long-term financial plan used to coordinate the activities needed to achieve the long-term goals of the company. (p. 1173)

Subsidiary Company. A company that is controlled by another corporation. (p. 786)

Subsidiary Ledger. Record of accounts that provides supporting details on individual balances, the total of which appears in a general ledger account. (p. 377)

Sunk Cost. A cost that was incurred in the past and cannot be changed regardless of which future action is taken. (p. 1379)

T-Account. A summary device that is shaped like a capital *T* with debits posted on the left side of the vertical line and credits on the right side of the vertical line. (p. 58)

Target Full Product Cost. The full cost to develop, produce, and deliver the product or service. (p. 1382)

Target Pricing. A method to manage costs and profits by determining the target full product cost. Revenue at market price − Desired profit = Target full product cost. (p. 1382)

Target Profit. The operating income that results when sales revenue minus variable and fixed costs equals management's profit goal. (p. 1110)

Temporary Account. An account that relates to a particular accounting period and is closed at the end of that period—the revenues, expenses, Income Summary, and Owner, Withdrawals accounts. (p. 189)

Term Bonds. Bonds that all mature at the same time. (p. 734)

Time Period Concept. Assumes that a business's activities can be sliced into small time segments and that financial statements can be prepared for specific periods, such as a month, quarter, or year. (p. 118)

Times-Interest-Earned Ratio. Evaluates a business's ability to pay interest expense. (Net income + Income tax expense + Interest expense) / Interest expense. (pp. 597, 893)

Time Value of Money. Recognition that money earns interest over time. (p. 735)

Timing Difference. Difference that arises between the balance on the bank statement and the balance on the company's books because of a time lag in recording transactions. (p. 446)

Total Quality Management (TQM). A philosophy designed to integrate all organizational areas in order to provide customers with superior products and services, while meeting organizational goals throughout the value chain. (p. 941)

Trademark. An asset that represents distinctive identifications of a product or service. (p. 555)

Trading Investment. A debt security or an equity security in which the investor holds less than 20% of the voting stock and that the investor plans to sell in the very near future. (p. 779)

Trading on the Equity. Earning more income on borrowed money than the related interest expense, thereby increasing the earnings for the owners of the business. (p. 896)

Transaction. An event that affects the financial position of the business and can be measured with faithful representation. (p. 11)

Transfer Price. The transaction amount of one unit of goods when the transaction occurs between divisions within the same company. (p. 1343)

Transferred In Costs. Costs that were incurred in a previous process and brought into a later process as part of the product's cost. (p. 1046)

Treasury Stock. A corporation's own stock that it has previously issued and later reacquired. (p. 683)

Trend Analysis. A form of horizontal analysis in which percentages are computed by selecting a base period as 100% and expressing amounts for following periods as a percentage of the base period amount. (Any period amount / Base period amount) × 100. (p. 880)

Trial Balance. A list of all ledger accounts with their balances at a point in time. (p. 77)

Triple Bottom Line. Evaluating a company's performance by its economic (profits), social (people), and environmental (planet) impact. (p. 941)

Underallocated Overhead. Occurs when the actual manufacturing overhead costs are more than allocated manufacturing overhead costs. (p. 997)

Underwriter. A firm that handles the issuance of a company's stock to the public, usually assuming some of the risk by agreeing to buy the stock if the firm cannot sell all of the stock to its clients. (p. 678)

Unearned Revenue. A liability created when a business collects cash from customers in advance of providing services or delivering goods. (p. 55)

Unemployment Compensation Tax. Payroll tax paid by employers to the government, which uses the cash to pay unemployment benefits to people who are out of work. (p. 590)

Units-of-Production Method. A depreciation method that allocates a varying amount of depreciation each year based on an asset's usage. (p. 539)

Unlimited Personal Liability. When a partnership (or a sole proprietorship) cannot pay its debts with business assets, the partners (or the proprietor) must use personal assets to meet the debt. (p. 622)

Useful Life. Length of the service period expected from an asset. May be expressed in time, such as months or years, or usage, such as units produced, hours used (for machinery), or miles driven (for a truck). (p. 537)

Value Chain. Includes all activities that add value to a company's products and services. (p. 941)

Variable Cost. A cost that increases or decreases *in total* in direct proportion to increases or decreases in the volume of activity. (p. 1100)

Variable Costing. The product costing method that assigns only variable manufacturing costs to products: direct materials, direct labor, and variable manufacturing overhead. Used for internal reporting. (p. 1123)

Variance. The difference between an actual amount and the budgeted amount; labeled as favorable if it increases operating income and unfavorable if it decreases operating income. (p. 1255)

Vendor. The individual or business from whom a company purchases goods. (p. 246)

Vertical Analysis. An analysis of a financial statement that reveals the relationship of each statement item to its base amount, which is the 100% figure. (Specific item / Base amount) × 100. (p. 882)

Warranty. An agreement that guarantees a company's product against defects. (p. 593)

Weighted-Average Method. An inventory costing method based on the weighted-average cost per unit of inventory that is calculated after each purchase. Weighted-average cost per unit is determined by dividing the cost of goods available for sale by the number of units available. (p. 331)

Weighted-Average Method (for Process Costing). Determines the average cost of equivalent units of production by combining beginning inventory costs with current period costs. (p. 1047)

Wholesaler. A type of merchandiser that buys goods from manufacturers and then sells them to retailers. (p. 245)

Working Capital. A measure of a business's ability to meet its short-term obligations with its current assets. Current assets − Current liabilities. (p. 887)

Work-in-Process Inventory (WIP). Goods that have been started in the manufacturing process but are not yet complete. (p. 945)

Worksheet. An internal document that helps summarize data for the preparation of financial statements. (p. 139)

Subject Index

Company Index

Photo Credits

Photo Credits

Front Matter

Page iii: (top) Bill Woodhull; (middle) Richard Smith; (bottom) Kam-Wah Tsui

Chapter 18

Page 937: (top) Jiri Hera/Shutterstock; (middle right) Mihai Simonia/Shutterstock; (bottom left) Chris Ryan/Alamy; page 938 (top right) Africa Studio/Shutterstock

Chapter 19

Page 981: Elena Elisseeva/Alamy; (middle right) Maxx-Studio/Shutterstock; (bottom left) EdBockStock/Alamy; page 982: (top right) M.Brodie/Alamy; page 985: Rido/Shutterstock; page 997: Mike Flippo/Shutterstock

Chapter 20

Page 1033: (top) Jakub Krechowicz/Shutterstock; (middle right) Tetra Images/Alamy; (bottom left) Kadmy/Fotolia; page 1034: (top right) Seaskylab/Shutterstock; page 1048: Lithian/Shutterstock; page 1069: Monkey Business Images/Shutterstock

Chapter 21

Page 1099: (top) Jmiks/Shutterstock; (middle right) Timmary/Shutterstock; (bottom left) Martin Barraud/Alamy; page 1100: (top right) Scanrail/Fotolia; page 1103: Shutterstock; page 1105: Lisa F. Young/Shutterstock; page 1133: Rido/Shutterstock

Chapter 22

Page 1168: Ali Ender Birer/Shutterstock; (middle left) Peredniankina/Shutterstock; (bottom right) OJO Images Ltd./ Alamy; page 1169: (middle right) Ilolab/Shutterstock; page 1181: Mike Flippo/Shutterstock; page 1202: Lithian/Shutterstock

Chapter 23

Page 1253: (top) Fotonic/Shutterstock; (middle right) Dorling Kindersley; (bottom left) Fancy/Alamy; page 1254: (top right) Worker/Shutterstock; page 1266: Monkey Business Images/Shutterstock

Chapter 24

Page 1311: (top) kzww/Shutterstock; (middle right) Maks Narodenko/Shutterstock; (bottom left) bikeriderlondon/ Shutterstock; page 1312: (top right) imageBROKER/Alamy; page 1321: Iodrakon/Shutterstock; page 1338: Shutterstock

Chapter 25

Page 1377: (top) Vereshchagin Dmitry/Shutterstock; (middle right) WojciechBeczynski/Shutterstock; (bottom left) EchoCultural/Getty Images; Julia Ivantsova/Shutterstock; page 1378: (top left) elnavegante/Shutterstock; (middle right) bizoo_n/Fotolia; page 1379: Lisa F. Young/Shutterstock; page 1383: Rido/Shutterstock

Chapter 26

Page 1431: (top) Olga Nayashkova/Shutterstock; (middle right) Crepesoles/Shutterstock; (bottom left) Wavebreakmedia/ Shutterstock; page 1432: (top left) Krapivin/Shutterstock; (middle right) Mats/Shutterstock; page 1435: Mike Flippo/ Shutterstock; page 1439: Lithian/Shutterstock

Appendix C

Page C-1: (top) Nielskliim/Shutterstock; (middle left) Kongsky/Shutterstock; (bottom right) HomeArt/Shutterstock; page C-2: (top right) Aaron Amat/Shutterstock; (middle right) Sean Gladwell/Shutterstock; page C-10: Iodrakon/ Shutterstock; page C-25: Shutterstock

Appendix D

Page D-2: (top) Get4net/Fotolia; (middle left) Rangizzz/Fotolia; (bottom right) Imagemore Co. Ltd./Alamy; page D-3: (middle right) Pokomeda/Shutterstock; page D-9: Lisa F. Young/Shutterstock